# Eighth Edition / ALL NEW

## The No. 1 Price Guide to
# M.I. HUMMEL®
## Figurines, Plates, More . . .

P9-CES-348

- accurate prices
- easy-to-use
- pocket size

by renowned expert
## ROBERT L. MILLER

special consultant
DEAN A. GENTH
appraiser - collector-specialist of
Goebel "M.I. Hummel" Figurines

**PORTFOLIO PRESS**
**Huntington, New York 11743**

*This book is dedicated to my wife Ruth,
the "Original" M.I. HUMMEL Figurine Collector.*

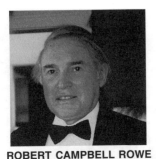

**ROBERT CAMPBELL ROWE**

This 8th Edition Price Guide is dedicated to
our very close Friend and Publisher of all our
Hummel Books since we started in 1975.

Robert Campbell Rowe

President of PORTFOLIO PRESS
Huntington, New York

*Special Tribute*

"We have worked together for a quarter of a
century of Hummel books and have never had
a formal contract nor a dispute!"

With our sincere thanks!

**The No. 1 Price Guide to**
# M.I. HUMMEL
**Eighth Edition Second Printing**

# Introduction

This price guide is designed to meet the growing needs of dealers and insurance underwriters, as well as the collector-enthusiast. It is primarily intended as an aid in identifying, dating and pricing both current and older "M.I. Hummel" figurines, along with plates, bells, lamps, and other related "M.I. Hummel" items produced through the years by W. Goebel Porzellanfabrik of Rödental, Germany.

The publication of this book has been approved by W. Goebel Porzellanfabrik, the sole manufacturers of the "M.I. Hummel" figurines, plates, and bells.

The format of this guide provides a flexible bracket or price range, rather than one arbitrary price for each item. It is extremely difficult to assign an exact value for each figurine since many factors can affect this valuation. Prices do vary from one section of the country to another—and even sales within a given area may be at different figures. General economic conditions prevailing at the time of sale can affect valuations too. Exact values on older specimens of Hummel figurines are impossible to ascertain, because so many factors must be taken into consideration. In such instances, the rarity of the piece, its general condition (whether mint, restored, damaged), its color, its authenticity, and finally, its appeal to the collector, must be considered.

The price ranges quoted in this book reflect the current retail prices as opposed to wholesale or dealer prices. Thus a person selling a certain item cannot expect to receive the top bracket price in most instances. Some dealers use the price ranges in this guide as a "bench mark," and offer the seller a percentage of either the high or the low figure. Again the rarity of the piece enters into the actual value determination. After reading the above, you may question the worth of any price guide in the first place. However, the author firmly believes the growth in Hummel collecting over many years dictates the necessity for such a yardstick of value. More and more collectors, novices and veterans alike, have been asking, "What should I expect to pay for this or that figurine?" "What should I sell my figurines for?" "What should I insure my collection for?" These questions are answered intelligently in this up-to-date list of values. The easy-to-read format provides simple and understandable information which reflects prices on today's market.

The author, having years of experience in buying and selling "M.I. Hummel" figurines and related items, would be the first to admit that there are wide fluctuations or variations in market prices today. It would be foolhardy and misleading to think that this or any other price guide could assign exact values for each and every Hummel piece. What has been provided in this guide is an accurate and reasonable range or "norm" so that the collector, dealer, or insurance agent can intelligently place a true valuation on each item. When it comes to a matter of worth, you must remember: it is "what the buyer is willing to pay, and the seller is willing to accept" that really sets the price. It takes *two* to strike a bargain!

*Robert L. Miller*

—Robert L. Miller

We solicit your questions, suggestions, opinions and criticisms. If we can be of help in making your collecting more complete and enjoyable, or if you just want to say "hello"— call or write:

Robert L. Miller
112 Woodland Drive
P.O. Box 210
Eaton, Ohio 45320-0210
1-937-456-3735 or 1-937-456-4152

# The Remarkable Story of Sister M.I. Hummel

**C**hildren are children the world over, impish or shy, saucy or quiet, mischievous or thoughtful . . . language differences don't matter, nor do variances in national custom. The innocence of childhood produces a universality that is loved and understood everywhere.This is perhaps the key to the remarkable and enduring popularity of the wonderful creations of Sister Maria Innocentia Hummel.

Berta Hummel was born in the town of Massing in Lower Bavaria, Germany, on May 21, 1909, one of six children of Adolph and Viktoria Hummel. Although a closely knit family, the children were not carbon copies of one another. While her older sisters were industriously helping their mother with household chores, Berta was busy drawing, making costumes for her dolls, and putting on theatricals for family and friends.

War broke out when she was only six. Her father was drafted into the army and the family was left without his guiding influence. Berta, whose artistic talents he had always encouraged, began to show signs of willfulness and lack of discipline, often taxing the patience of her teachers. Fortunately, her creativity was to be recognized early; due to the efforts of one of her teachers, she was enrolled at a fine religious boarding school at Simbach, near Massing, the Institute of English Sisters.

It was here that she first received artistic direction. Her flair for scenic and costume design fostered just for fun in the family's backyard, now began to emerge as a genuine talent. Soon she was designing for school productions. In four years, she progressed from only sketching the friends of her childhood and illustrating folk tales to painting landscapes in watercolor.

The religious training at the school proved to be good discipline, and her development into a young lady and a promising artist was a delight to behold.

In 1927, when she was 18, Berta's proud father went with her to Munich where she was enrolled in the Academy of Fine Arts, to be on some familiar ground in otherwise strange territory, she took up residence outside the Academy in a dormitory run by a religious order.

The Academy, a prestigious center of design and applied arts, provided her with still more extensive training. Soon she began to paint in oils, and her experience with costumes was now expanded to include weaving of fabrics and designing clothing.

She was soon under the wing of a leading artist and teacher, who hoped she would remain at the Academy after graduation as his assistant. But a conflict was developing within Berta. Although she was gaining a great knowledge of art, its history, its scope and an exciting awareness of what travel and study in other cities, perhaps even other lands, might offer a young student, she was still the simple Bavarian girl from a warm, loving family, and her ties to her background were strong. Her feelings of religion were profound, and through a warm friendship at the dormitory with two Franciscan nuns who were also studying at the Academy, became even more important.

Her wonderful sense of fun never left her, and to the delight of her fellow students (and often the chagrin of the Mother Superior) she would play pranks at the residence. But more than anything, she was a gentle, emotional person, deeply affected by people and events.

In 1929, Hitler's National Socialist Party was on the rise in Munich, making specific promises of employment within the party. It offered an economic stability in depression years for sympathizers among the students of the Academy. But the militarism and politics of the Nazis were counter to Berta's sensitivities, and she turned with even greater need to the quiet, withdrawn life of her two religious friends.

With graduation drawing near, the pressures were becoming stronger for her to make a decision. On the one hand were her professors, eager for her to remain with them and continue her promising development. But on the other hand, with the frightening political atmosphere growing, there was the draw of fulfillment to be found behind the cloistered walls of a convent where she could continue her art while serving humanity through her devotion to God.

By the time of graduation in March 1931, she had made her decision. On April 22, she entered the convent of Siessen at Saulgau, and two years later was ordained Sister Maria Innocentia of the Sisters of the Third Order of St. Francis.

While a novice, she had taught art to children in kindergarten, and by late 1933 had so developed that she exhibited her work in a nearby town. In March 1933, the convent at Siessen sent a letter with proof sheets of sketches of the artist Berta Hummel to the publishing company in Munich named "Ars Sacra Josef Mueller Verlag," who specialized in the printing of religious art and books. Ars Sacra was very appreciative of the first pictures and asked for more sketches. Thus started a prosperous relationship between Sister Maria Innocentia Hummel and the publishing house "Ars Sacra Josef Mueller." The

artwork of Sister Maria Innocentia was first known to the public in the two-dimensional form. The postcards with the Hummel motifs became very popular and found their way into the United States shortly before World War II. Franz Goebel, fourth-generation head of W. Goebel, first became aware of her in 1934, and sought permission from her and the convent to translate her sketches of sparkling children and serene religious figures into three-dimensional form. This marked the beginning of a relationship between Sister Maria Innocentia, the convent and W. Goebel that continues to endure, long years after her death.

But dark clouds were hovering everywhere, and soon the sisters began to live in dread, for the Nazi government was determined to close the convent. In late 1940, the convent became a repatriation center for German nationals from other countries, and a small group of nuns, Sister Maria Innocentia included, remained to care for them.

It was a time of great deprivation. No longer able to remain in her spacious studio because of the terribly overcrowded conditions, Sister Maria Innocentia lived in a small, damp, basement room. Food and fuel were scarce, and she became terribly weakened by a lung infection. True to her dominant spirit, however, she tried to continue to work.

By November 1944 she was so ill that she was admitted to a sanitarium for treatment where her illness was finally diagnosed as chronic tuberculosis. In April 1945, the war ended and, feeling somewhat strengthened, Sister Maria Innocentia returned to the convent to help with the enormous task of rebuilding. Her spirit as ever was strong, but her physical condition had deteriorated so that she was forced to enter another sanitarium the following September, leaving it in late September 1946 to return to her beloved convent.

On November 6, 1946, at the hour of noon, the chapel bells rang out in solemn proclamation of the death of Sister Maria Innocentia at the age of 37.

A young life, full of spirit and love, came to a tragic end. But the youthful, loving spirit lives on in the pert faces of the Hummel children and the gentle bearing of the madonnas that are with us in ceramic. If we look at them a certain way, we can almost hear them breathe!

# You Won't Believe This, But. . . .

Some very early "M.I. Hummel" figurines were not marked "Hum" in their original form! It has recently been discovered that the figurines we know today as Hum 1, Hum 2 and Hum 3 were once marked "FF 15, FF 16 and FF 17", respectively!

According to factory records, when "Puppy Love, Little Fiddler and Book Worm" were originally sculpted the series designation had not yet been determined. They were assigned these markings on an interim basis and were provisionally registered on 2 January 1935. When the licensing agreement with the Convent of Siessen was signed at the end of January 1935, the system was changed. Sister Maria Innocentia Hummel was now an acknowledged Goebel artist, and her artwork was designated its own series' reference. As was customary, it became the first three letters of her last name. Therefore, any figurines based on her art done before that date had to be remarked. Since these three were the first to be sculpted, they became "Hum 1, Hum 2 and Hum 3". The figurine FF 17, according to factory records, must be one of the first samples from the mother mold. Probably no more than six samples were made.

# "Double Crown" Trademark

**Incised Crown    1935-1949    Stamped Crown**

This term is used to describe the Goebel Company trademark found on some "M.I. Hummel" figurines. On "double crown" pieces the "crown" trademark is usually found both incised and stamped.

According to recent information from the Goebel Factory, they state: "We have not yet been able to locate "undoubted" records. With some certainty it can be assumed that the incised crown mark was used until 1945. Afterwards, supposedly, the crown mark was *stamped* on all figurines. However, it could happen that figurines with the incised crown mark from stock on hand were additionally provided with the *stamped* crown mark. It is quite unascertainable today which figurines and how many were marked in this way, i.e., with both incised and stamped crown mark. The years from 1945 to 1948 can be regarded as the transition period."

---
**PRICES IN THIS GUIDE**

We are in a period of DISCOUNTING of many items in our society. "M.I. Hummel" figurines are no exception. The prices in this guide give the relative values in relationship to new or current prices of (TM 8) trademark items. If the new figurines are discounted, the older models will likely be discounted, too, but possibly in a lesser degree. This guide reduces all items to one common denominator.

---

# History and Explanation of Marks and Symbols

**Incised Crown**  **1935-1949**  **Stamped Crown**

**M.J. Hummel** © ☙

**1935-1955**

Made in U.S. Zone
Germany.

MADE IN
U.S.
ZONE

Made in
U.S.-Zone
Germany.

U.S. Zone

Germany.

U.S.-Zone
Germany.

U.S.-Zone
Germany

U.S. Zone
Germany.

Made in
U.S. Zone

MADE IN GERMANY

Made in U.S. Zone

Germany.

U.S. Zone

**1946-1948**

**Incised**  **Stamped**  **(R)**

© W. Goebel
**Full Bee**  © **W. GOEBEL**

**1950-1955**

The "wide-crown-WG" trademark was used on the first "M.I. Hummel" figurines produced in 1935. On the earliest figurines it was incised on the bottom of the base along with the "M.I. Hummel" signature on the top or side of the base. Between 1935 and 1955, the company occasionally used a © ☙ mark on the side or top of the base of some models. It is seen occasionally to the right of the "M.I. Hummel" signature. The "crown" appears either incised or stamped. When both are used on the same piece it is known as a "double crown" mark.

From 1946 through 1948 it was necessary to add the stamped words "Made in the U.S. Zone Germany." This mark was used within various types of frames or without a frame, underglazed or stamped over the glaze in black ink.

In 1950, four years after Sister M.I. Hummel's death, Goebel wished in some way to pay tribute to her fine artistry. They radically changed the trademark, instituting the use of a bee flying high with a "V." (Hummel means "bumble bee" in German, and the "V" stands for "Verkaufsgesellschaft" or distribution company.) This mark, known as the full bee trademark, was used until 1955 and appeared — sometimes both incised and underglazed—in black or blue and occasionally in green or magenta. In addition, the stamp "Germany" and later "West Germany" appeared. An (R) appearing beside the trademark stands for "Registered."

Sometimes the molds were produced with a lightly incised circle on the bottom of the base in which the trademark was centered. It has no significance other than as a target for the location of the decal. Some current production figurines still have this incised circle even though it is no longer used for that purpose.

Always searching for a mark that would blend esthetics with professionalism, the company continued to modify the trademark. In 1956, the company—still using the bee inside the "V"—made the bee smaller, with its wing tips parallel with the top of the "V". In 1957, the bee remained, although once again rising slightly above the "V". In 1958, the bee was smaller still and it flew deep within the "V", reflecting the changing trends of modern design. The year 1959 saw the beginning of stylization and the wings of the bee became sharply angular.

In 1960, the completely stylized bee with "V" mark came into use, appearing with "W. Germany." It was used in one form or another until 1979. In addition to its appearance with "W. Germany" to the right (1960–1963), it appeared above the "West Germany" (1960–1972), and to the left of the "three line mark" (mid-1960's to 1972). The three line mark was used intermittently and sometimes concurrently with the small, stylized 1960–1972 mark. It was the most prominent trademark in use prior to the "Goebel bee" trademark.

It became apparent that the public was equating the "V and Bee" mark only with "M.I. Hummel" items, not realizing that the mark included the full scope of Goebel products. It was decided to experiment further with marks. In 1972, satisfied that it now had a mark designating a quality Goebel product, the company began using a printed "Goebel" with the stylized bee poised between the letters "b" and "e."

Since 1976, the Goebel trademark on Hummel figurines has been affixed by a decal on top of the glaze. It is possible for two figurines on the primary market to have differing decals.

In 1979, the stylized bee was dropped and only the name Goebel appears. The year of production will be on the base next to the initials of the chief decorator.

In 1991, the W. (West) was deleted, with only the word Germany remaining, since Germany is once again a united country. The original "crown" has been added to the (TM7) trademark.

In the Year 2000, the beginning of a new Millennium, the trademark was once again changed. The "bumblebee" symbol, to honor the memory of Sister Maria Innocentia Hummel was reinstated to the (TM 8) current trademark.

The above information is a concise documentation of all W. Goebel trademarks authorized for use on "M.I. Hummel" figurines. In searching for accurate documentation on all W. Goebel trademarks used in conjunction with "M.I. Hummel" figurines, the author made a thorough investigation of the W. Goebel archives and queried the world's leading collectors. But it is always possible that a few rare and undocumented variations may exist.

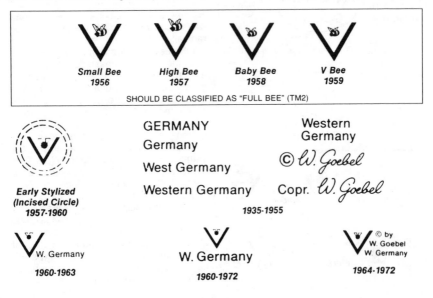

**Small Bee**
1956

**High Bee**
1957

**Baby Bee**
1958

**V Bee**
1959

SHOULD BE CLASSIFIED AS "FULL BEE" (TM2)

**Early Stylized (Incised Circle)**
1957-1960

GERMANY

Germany

West Germany

Western Germany

1935-1955

Western Germany

© W. Goebel

Copr. W. Goebel

W. Germany

1960-1963

W. Germany

1960-1972

© by W. Goebel W. Germany

1964-1972

Evolution of Goebel Bee Trademark in use since 1972
(The copyright symbols © ® are found in various sizes and locations)

Goebel trademark
(since 1979)

Goebel trademark
(since 1991)

Current trademark
(since 2000)

---

### M. J. Hummel © ✍

Between 1935 and 1955, the company occasionally used a © ✍ mark on the side or top of the base of some models, before or after the "M.I. Hummel" signature. This is *NOT* considered a (TM 1) or "crown" trademark! It only means "copyright by W. Goebel".

---

# DOUBLE TRADEMARK FIGURINES

Occasionally an older "M.I. Hummel" figurine will be found with an incised "crown" trademark as well as a stamped "full bee" trademark on the same figurine. It is neither a crown nor a full bee; it is a *combination*. A figurine with this double mark would have been sold in the very early 1950's. The incised crown was in the mold, and the figurine itself was quite possibly produced in the late 1940's, but then actually painted and sold in the early 1950's during the change over from one trademark to the other.

When using the *No. 1 Price Guide* to determine the value of a figurine with both the crown and the full bee trademark, we recommend using the high side of the full bee price bracket and the low side of the crown bracket. For example, HUM 1 "Puppy Love" with full bee (TM 2) is listed at $550 to $600, and the same with a crown (TM 1) is valued at $750 to $1000. The new bracket value would be $600 to $750.

This double marking makes it a distinctive piece and puts it in a class by itself. It is better (or earlier) than a double full bee or a plain full bee, but not quite as good (or as early) as the crown or double crown marking. This combination of two different trademarks normally occurred only during this brief change over period and has not happened since, to my knowledge. Not all models can be found with this combination marking, and it is good to have an example of this in your collection.

**EXAMPLE:** ❶ $750–1000 ❷ $550–600 } 600–750

A "double crown" trademark—a term used to describe the Goebel Company trademark found on *some* M.I. Hummel figurines, both incised as well as stamped, are usually very nice examples, but will not usually add greatly to their value. This is compensated for in the high side of the price bracket.

# The Collection

**H**ere is the revised and fully-authorized documentation of the complete collection of "M.I. Hummel" figurines, plates, plaques and all other art objects. This is the most definitive listing and photographic collection ever assembled. This list, compiled from the W. Goebel production journal in Rödental, West Germany, constitutes a record of all "M.I. Hummel" figurines identification numbers run in ascending order from 1 to 2111. English names of the figurines, as well as their sizes, notes, and most models, will be found in the special annotated listing.

All sizes are approximate and depend upon exact method of measurement. Minor variations occur frequently and therefore should not be considered significant.

"M.I. Hummel" figurine identification numbers and their corresponding figurines are divided into eight distinct categories:

**Open Edition (OE):** Pieces currently in W. Goebel's production program.

**Closed Edition (CE):** Pieces formerly in W. Goebel production program but no longer produced. Also, <u>models</u> that are still being produced, but have a <u>trademark</u> that is no longer used, are shown as (CE) Closed Editions.

**Open Number (ON):** An identification number, which in W. Goebel's numerical identification system has not yet been used, but which may be used to identify new "M.I. Hummel" figurines as they are released in the future.

**Closed Number (CN):** An identification number in W. Goebel's numerical identification system that was used to identify a design or sample models for possible production, but then for various reasons never authorized for release.

**Possible Future Edition (PFE):** Pieces that have been designed and approved for production and possible release in future years.

**Temporarily Withdrawn (TW):** Pieces that have been suspended or withdrawn from Goebel's current production program, but may be reinstated and produced at some future date.

**Exclusive Edition (EE):** Pieces that are originally sold only to members of the M.I. Hummel Club.

**PREVIEW EDITION (PE):** Figurines with an M.I. Hummel Club backstamp offered exclusively to members for a special preview period. After its first two years of production, it may become an open edition (OE) available to the general public, bearing a regular Goebel backstamp only.

Many collectors are interested in the trademarks that were used on "M.I. HUMMEL" figurines; therefore, we have used the numbering system shown below:

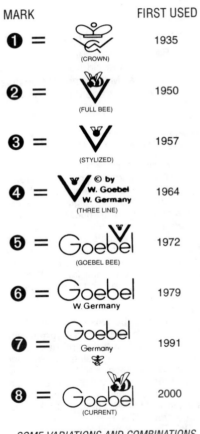

| MARK | | FIRST USED |
|---|---|---|
| ❶ = | (CROWN) | 1935 |
| ❷ = | (FULL BEE) | 1950 |
| ❸ = | (STYLIZED) | 1957 |
| ❹ = | © by W. Goebel W. Germany (THREE LINE) | 1964 |
| ❺ = | Goebel (GOEBEL BEE) | 1972 |
| ❻ = | Goebel W Germany | 1979 |
| ❼ = | Goebel Germany | 1991 |
| ❽ = | Goebel (CURRENT) | 2000 |

*SOME VARIATIONS AND COMBINATIONS USED IN BETWEEN ABOVE DATES*

This numbering system is used to identify each mark that can be found on a particular figurine. There will be some exceptions to this rule. Some early figurines will be found with no trademark or model numbers at all. This fact does not lessen their value to any great extent, but does make it more difficult to determine their age. When figurines vary greatly in size, we will use the "bracket" system, showing the smallest to the largest size, i.e. 5½" to 6". Your measurement may vary depending on what means you use to measure. To properly measure a figurine, you should place it on a flat surface, then stand a ruler beside it.

Place another ruler or straight object horizontally touching the highest point of the figurine and the perpendicular ruler. You will then have an accurate measurement.

### Decoration-designations for "M.I. Hummel" figurines

All "M.I. Hummel" figurines are hand-painted according to "M.I. Hummel's" original design. The decoration techniques had to be numbered because the factory uses so many.

The "M.I. Hummel" decor is done in painting method number eleven. A stroke-eleven (/11) is added to the model number following the size indicator in the factory's literature and price lists. *It does not*, however, appear incised on the base. In this book we only refer to incised numbers.

| Decor. No. | Marked | Description |
|---|---|---|
| 11 | /11 | all matte-finish colors in rich variety of pastels inspired by rural surroundings |
| 11 blue | /11 blue | madonna with dark blue cloak; rest of figurine in pastels |
| 13 | /13 | ivory decoration in pastels |
| 6 blue | /6 blue | madonna with pastel blue cloak; rest of figurine in matching pastels |
| 6 red | /6 red | madonna with light red cloak; rest of figurine in matching pastels |
| 83 | /83 | matte-finish shading on bisque body |
| H | /H | brown matte decor, very rare—not made after 1955 |
| W | /W | white overglaze |

**SPECIAL NOTE:** In previous price guides we listed trademark 1, 2, 3, 4, 5 and 6 items as Open Editions (OE), which was not quite accurate. We wanted to indicate that a certain *model* was still being produced, even though the trademark had changed.

With this edition, we show each former trademark as a Closed Edition (CE).The only Open Editions (OE) will be items with trademark eight (TM 8) that are currently in W. Goebel's production program.

# Alphabetical Listing

| NAME | HUM No. | NAME | HUM No. |
|------|---------|------|---------|

## PLAQUES

# Permanently Retired
# M.I. Hummel Figurines
# Final Issue

| | | |
|---|---|---|
| 1988 | Puppy Love | HUM 1 |
| 1989 | Strolling Along | HUM 5 |
| 1990 | Signs of Spring | HUM 203 2/0 203/1 |
| 1991 | Globe Trotter | HUM 79 (Final Issue decal) |
| 1992 | Lost Sheep | HUM 68 2/0 & 68/0 (Final Issue decal) |
| 1993 | Farewell | HUM 65 (Final Issue decal) |
| 1994 | Accordion Boy | HUM 185 (Final Issue decal) |
| 1995 | Duet | HUM 130 (Final Issue decal) |
| 1996 | Happy Pastime | HUM 69 (Final Issue decal) |
| 1997 | Mother's Darling | HUM 175 (Final Issue decal) |
| 1998 | Boots | HUM 143/0–143/I (Final Issue decal) |
| 1999 | Congratulations | HUM 17/0I (Final Issue decal) |
| 2000 | Auf Wiedersehen | HUM 153/0–153/I (Final Issue decal) |

Beginning in 1990 the factory initiated the practice of applying a "FINAL ISSUE" (plus the year) backstamp on all permanently retired figurines. The final issue figurines usually have a small gold commemorative medallion attached by string to each figurine being retired.

Beginning in 1991 the factory initiated the practice of applying a "FIRST ISSUE" (plus the year) backstamp on all newly released figurines during the first year of production.

Hundreds and hundreds of hours have gone into this 8th edition of the "No. 1 Price Guide to M.I. Hummel Figurines". We have checked, rechecked and even double checked all information, prices etc. We sincerely want this to be the most accurate, complete and up to date guide to "M.I. Hummel" figurine collecting on the market today. We want it to be *your* "bible"! — as some of you have said. We apologize if we have omitted any pertinent information, missed any typographical errors, or "goofed" in any way. We have tried our best! If you have any questions, suggestions, opinions or criticisms — please call or write. Our address and phone number is in the front of this book.

Sincerely,

Robert L. Miller

*While working on this new 8th Edition of the No. 1 Price Guide to M.I. Hummel Figurines, I was given the following history of HUM 78 "Blessed Child", formerly called "Infant of Krumbad." I decided to share it with all of you M.I. Hummel figurine collectors. Cheryl Gorski, of Goebel North America, researched the entire history of this figurine through both the Factory and the Convent of Siessen, including a personal interview with Sister Antje. The results of her study was provided for publication in this 8th edition of the Price Guide. Cheryl states that this is the true and complete history of this special figurine.*

*Hope you enjoy! Thank you, Cheryl.*

## Blessed Child (Hum 78) (nee *Infant of Krumbad*)

W. Goebel Porzellanfabrik in Roedental, Germany has been creating figurines inspired by the artwork of Fransiscan Sister Maria Innocentia Hummel for more than 60 years. During her lifetime, Sister Maria Innocentia reviewed each figurine inspired by her creative vision. Tody, figurines are sculpted by a Master Sculptor and then approved by the Artistic Board of the Convent of Siessen (to which Sister Hummel belonged). Each authentic *M.I. Hummel* figurine created by W. Goebel Porzellanfabrik is given a Hum or mold number for identification and cataloguing purposes. The Hum number is consistent throughout the world and is incised on the underside of the base of each figurine. Figurines are also given names; however, these names may differ between markets—such as Europe and North America.

The *M.I. Hummel* figurine Hum 78, depicting the infant Jesus, was named *Christkind* in the European market and has never had any other name. Literally translated from German, *Christkind* means *Christ Child*. However, in the North American market, the figurine was first named *Infant of Krumbad*. This name was changed to *Blessed Child* in 1985 and remains so today.

In order to understand the significance of the *Infant of Krumbad* name, it is important to become familiar with the relationship between two charitable institutions: the Sanatorium of Krumbad and the Convent of Siessen. A Sanatorium is a convalescent or rehabilitation facility.

The Sanatorium of Krumbad is a center for convalescence and recuperation following long bouts with illness or disease. Located in Krumbach some 60 miles north and east of Siessen, the Sanatorium has been in existence for more than 500 years. (The town was originally called Krumbad but was eventually changed—the facility retains this original name.)

Beginning in 1937, Sister Maria Innocentia had several periods of convalescence at the facility to offset the influence of tuberculosis. She enjoyed the company of the patients, the visitors and the staff at the facility. As she would regain her strength, she would return to the Convent of Siessen. In gratitude for the many kindnesses bestowed upon her during her visits to Krumbad, Sister Maria Innocentia decided to send a gift to the Mother Superior there.

One of the works in production at W. Goebel Porzellanfabrik at the time was the *Christkind* (Hum 78). Sister Maria Innocentia requested a number of these figurines for her use as personal gifts. Since the factory could not produce as many as she required in a timely manner, plaster figurines were created for her instead. The sometimes still-wet figurines were given to the Sister who then hand-painted the pieces and sent them to friends and institutions as gifts.

One such piece was Sister Maria Innocentia's thank you to the Sanatorium of Krumbad. Being so moved, the sisters of Krumbad treated the very special gift of Sister Maria Innocentia with great reverence. This moving legacy gave birth the the name, *Infant of Krumbad,* used in North America for many years. Since this story was not well-known to casual *M.I. Hummel* collectors, the name was changed to *Blessed Child* as it is more descriptive of the figurine.

# UNDERSTANDING THE "M.I. HUMMEL" NUMBERING SYSTEM

An *M.I. Hummel* figurine with a plain or whole number, (no size designator) indicates that this model was made in one size only. Any figurine that is made in a larger size will have a Roman numeral from /I to /X. The larger the Roman numeral, the greater the size of the figurine.

Figurines smaller than the standard size are designated by Arabic numbers, followed by a slash "/" zero. The general rule is, the larger the Arabic number, the smaller the figurine size. The presence of this zero to the right of the designator indicates that the figurine is smaller than the standard size.

Here are a couple of examples of incised model numbers:

| | | |
|---|---|---|
| 195 2/0 | HUM 195 "Barnyard Hero" | 4 inches |
| 195/I | HUM 195 "Barnyard Hero" | 5½ inches |

The size designation system can be best demonstrated by this key:

|  |  |  |
|---|---|---|
| | / IV | |
| | / III | The larger the Roman |
| | / II | numeral, the larger |
| | /I | the size. |
| **figurine no. /** _____ | /0 | **standard size** |
| | 1/0 | |
| | 2/0 | The larger the Arabic |
| | 3/0 | number, the smaller |
| | 4/0 | the size. |

There are exceptions to all rules! This does *not* guarantee that two figurines of the same model number will be the same height. This variation can be the results of "mold growth" of the old plaster working molds used prior to 1954. It is also possible that a figurine has been restyled slightly and will still have the same model number and size designator. An example would be HUM 10/III "Flower Madonna" which was restyled in 1956 and reduced in size by approximately 1½ inches, but still retained the same model number. Sometimes in the early years, an Arabic 10/3 was used instead of 10/III or 136/5 instead of 136/V. In some cases an Arabic or Roman numeral will appear to the left of the model number, such as on old lamp bases (II/112) or (2/112) or on candy boxes (III/53). Another example: HUM 153 "Auf Wiedersehen" was made originally in one size only. In the early 1950's a smaller size was created and numbered 153/0 or "standard" size for this model, while the original size became 153/I indicating it was larger than the new "standard" size 153/0.

In understanding the size designation system of "*M.I. Hummel*" figurines, it is important to remember that the designations apply differently to each specific figurine model, but that generally the larger and smaller sizes of the same model will follow this system.

**HUM 1**      *Rare old style (TM 1)*         *New style (TM 3)*
**Puppy Love (CE)**

First modeled by master sculptor Arthur Moeller in 1935. A very few early models were made with the head tilted at a different angle and without the tie. This old style is considered extremely rare and would command a premium of $4,000 to $5,000. Always featured with a black hat. In old catalog listed as the "Little Violinist." "Puppy Love" was permanently retired by Goebel in the fall of 1988 and will not be produced again. The original issue price was 35¢ in 1935! Old 1955 price list shows a price of $6.50 while 1988 price list shows a price of $125, the last year it was sold on the primary market. A rare terra cotta "Puppy Love" was recently found in Florida. It has an incised (TM 1) crown trademark and an incised number "T-1." Value would be $4,000 to 5,000 in terra cotta finish. According to old Goebel product book, a sample was produced by Arthur Moeller in 1935 of "Puppy Love" with an attached "pot," similar to HUM 16/I "Little Hiker" with attached "pot." Value $5,000 to 10,000 if found. For more information, see: Rare/Unique Sample Variations of "M. I. Hummel" Figurines in back of this book.

☐ FF 15 . . . . (Original Number) . . . . . . . . . . . $5000–10,000 (Early Sample)
☐ II/1 . . . . . . (With Attached "Pot") . . . . . . . . $5000–10,000 (Early Sample)
☐ T-1 . . . . . . (Terra Cotta Material). . . . . . . . $4000–5000 (Early Sample)
☐ 1 . . . . . . . (No Tie–Head tilted right) . . . . . $4000–5000 (Early Sample)
☐ 1 . . . . . . . 5 to 5¼″ . . . . . . (CE). . . ❶ . . . $750–1000
☐ 1 . . . . . . . 5 to 5¼″ . . . . . . (CE). . . ❷ . . . $550–600
☐ 1 . . . . . . . 5 to 5¼″ . . . . . . (CE). . . ❸ . . . $500–550
☐ 1 . . . . . . . 5 to 5¼″ . . . . . . (CE). . . ❹ . . . $400–500
☐ 1 . . . . . . . 5 to 5¼″ . . . . . . (CE). . . ❺ . . . $350–400
☐ 1 . . . . . . . 5 to 5¼″ . . . . . . (CE). . . ❻ . . . $300–350

**FINAL ISSUE**
1988

1

## HUM 2
## Little Fiddler

Also modeled by master sculptor Arthur Moeller in 1935, this figurine differs from the boy in "Puppy Love" in the fact that it always has a brown hat with an orange hat band. There are many size variations and all sizes have now been restyled with the new textured finish. Old name: "Violinist" or "The Wandering Fiddler." Same as HUM 4 except for the color of hat. Sometimes incised 2/3 instead of 2/III. A new miniature size figurine was issued in the fall of 1984 with a suggested retail price of $39 to match a new miniature plate series called the "Little Music Makers"—one each year for four years. This is the first in the series. This miniature size figurine has an incised 1984 copyright date. The large sizes (2/II and 2/III) were "temporarily withdrawn" from production on 31 December 1989, but may be reinstated at some future date. A few sample pieces have been found decorated with bright colors and glossy finish of the "Faience" technique—value would be $5,000 to 6,000 depending on size and condition. In 1985 Goebel produced a limited edition of 50 pieces of Hum 2/1 (7½") with a gold painted base for a Goebel sponsored contest in Europe celebrating 5 years of M. I. Hummel figurines. It has a special round backstamp: "50 Jahre M. I. Hummel-Figuren 1935–1985"—value would be $1,500 to 2,000. The miniature size (2 4/0) was (TW) "Temporarily Withdrawn" from the North American market on 31 December 1997, but may be reinstated at some future date.

☐ FF 16 . . . . (Original Number) . . . . . . . . . . . $5000–10,000 (Early Sample)
☐ 2 4/0. . . . . 3" . . . . . . . . . . . . (CE). . . ❻ . . . $125–140
☐ 2 4/0. . . . . 3" . . . . . . . . . . . . (TW) . . ❼ . . . $115–120
☐ 2/0 . . . . . 5¾ to 6½" . . . . . (CE). . . ❶ . . . $700–850
☐ 2/0 . . . . . 5¾ to 6½" . . . . . (CE). . . ❷ . . . $425–500
☐ 2/0 . . . . . 5¾ to 6½" . . . . . (CE). . . ❸ . . . $350–400
☐ 2/0 . . . . . 5¾ to 6½" . . . . . (CE). . . ❹ . . . $325–350
☐ 2/0 . . . . . 5¾ to 6½" . . . . . (CE). . . ❺ . . . $270–300
☐ 2/0 . . . . . 5¾ to 6½" . . . . . (CE). . . ❻ . . . $260–270
☐ 2/0 . . . . . 5¾ to 6½" . . . . . (CE). . . ❼ . . . $255–260
☐ 2/0 . . . . . 5¾ to 6½" . . . . . (**OE**). . . ❽ . . . $255
☐ 2/I . . . . . 7½" . . . . . . . . . (CE). . . ❶ . . . $1100–1500
☐ 2/I . . . . . 7½ to 8" . . . . . . (CE). . . ❷ . . . $650–925
☐ 2/I . . . . . 7½ to 8" . . . . . . (CE). . . ❸ . . . $560–650
☐ 2/I . . . . . 7½ to 8" . . . . . . (CE). . . ❹ . . . $460–550
☐ 2/I . . . . . 7½ to 8" . . . . . . (CE). . . ❺ . . . $420–430
☐ 2/I . . . . . 7½ to 8" . . . . . . (CE). . . ❻ . . . $410–420
☐ 2/I . . . . . 7½ to 8" . . . . . . (TW) . . ❼ . . . $400–410
☐ 2/II . . . . . 10¾" . . . . . . . . . (CE). . . ❶ . . . $2500–3500
☐ 2/II . . . . . 10¾" . . . . . . . . . (CE). . . ❷ . . . $1800–2300
☐ 2/II . . . . . 10¾" . . . . . . . . . (CE). . . ❸ . . . $1500–1600
☐ 2/II . . . . . 10¾" . . . . . . . . . (CE). . . ❹ . . . $1300–1500
☐ 2/II . . . . . 10¾" . . . . . . . . . (CE). . . ❺ . . . $1200–1300

*(prices continued on next page)*

| | | | | | |
|---|---|---|---|---|---|
| ☐ 2/II | 10¾" | (TW) | ❻ | $1100–1200 |
| ☐ 2/III | 12¼" | (CE) | ❶ | $3500–4000 |
| ☐ 2/III | 12¼" | (CE) | ❷ | $2300–2800 |
| ☐ 2/III | 12¼" | (CE) | ❸ | $1600–1800 |
| ☐ 2/III | 12¼" | (CE) | ❹ | $1400–1600 |
| ☐ 2/III | 12¼" | (CE) | ❺ | $1300–1400 |
| ☐ 2/III | 12¼" | (TW) | ❻ | $1200–1300 |

*3/I*

## HUM 3
### Book Worm

This figurine was modeled by master sculptor Arthur Moeller in 1935. Old name: "Little Book Worm." Size 3/I has only one flower on page, while sizes 3/II and 3/III have two flowers on page. Sometimes incised 3/2 instead of 3/II and 3/3 instead of 3/III but does not affect the value as Arabic or Roman size indicators were used interchangeably for no basic reason. Same design was used for HUM 8. "Book Worm" was restyled by master sculptor Gerhard Skrobek in 1972 with the new textured finish. Size 3/II has an incised 1972 copyright date. Size 3/III has no incised copyright date at all. The large sizes (3/II and 3/III) were "temporarily withdrawn" (TW) from production on 31 December 1989, but may be reinstated at some future date. A few sample pieces have been found decorated with bright colors and glossy finish of the "Faience" technique—value would be $3,000–5000 depending on size and condition. See "Faience" article in back of Price Guide.

| | | | | |
|---|---|---|---|---|
| ☐ FF 17 | (Original Number) | | | $5000–10,000 (Early Sample) |
| ☐ 3/I | 5½" | (CE) | ❶ | $900–1100 |
| ☐ 3/I | 5½" | (CE) | ❷ | $600–700 |
| ☐ 3/I | 5½" | (CE) | ❸ | $475–500 |
| ☐ 3/I | 5½" | (CE) | ❹ | $400–475 |
| ☐ 3/I | 5½" | (CE) | ❺ | $370–400 |
| ☐ 3/I | 5½" | (CE) | ❻ | $360–370 |
| ☐ 3/I | 5½" | (CE) | ❼ | $355–360 |
| ☐ 3/I | 5½" | (OE) | ❽ | $355 |
| ☐ 3/II | 8" | (CE) | ❶ | $2500–3500 |
| ☐ 3/II | 8" | (CE) | ❷ | $1800–2300 |
| ☐ 3/II | 8" | (CE) | ❸ | $1500–1600 |
| ☐ 3/II | 8" | (CE) | ❹ | $1300–1500 |
| ☐ 3/II | 8 to 9" | (CE) | ❺ | $1200–1300 |
| ☐ 3/II | 8 to 9" | (TW) | ❻ | $1100–1200 |
| ☐ 3/III | 9 to 9½" | (CE) | ❶ | $3500–4000 |
| ☐ 3/III | 9 to 9½" | (CE) | ❷ | $2300–2800 |
| ☐ 3/III | 9 to 9½" | (CE) | ❸ | $1600–1800 |
| ☐ 3/III | 9 to 9½" | (CE) | ❹ | $1450–1600 |
| ☐ 3/III | 9 to 10" | (CE) | ❺ | $1350–1450 |
| ☐ 3/III | 9 to 10" | (TW) | ❻ | $1250–1350 |

*Notice great variations in sizes*

## HUM 4
### Little Fiddler

Same as HUM 2 except it has a charcoal black hat. Many size variations. Old name: "Violinist" or "The Wandering Fiddler." First modeled by master sculptor Arthur Moeller in 1935 but current production models have been restyled with the new textured finish. One of several figurines that make up the Hummel orchestra. A very few early models were made with the head tilted at a different angle and without tie. This old style is considered extremely rare and would command a premium of $3000–4000. See old style "Puppy Love" HUM 1. A few sample pieces have been found made of hard porcelain material—value $2000–3000. The original issue price was 40¢ in 1935! According to old Goebel product book, a sample was produced by Arthur Moeller in 1935 of "Little Fiddler" with an attached "pot," similar to HUM 16/I "Little Hiker" with attached "pot." Value $5,000 to 10,000 if found. "Faience" finish—value $4,000 to 5,000.

| | | | | | |
|---|---|---|---|---|---|
| ☐ 4 | 4¾ to 5¾" | (CE) | ❶ | $650–800 |
| ☐ 4 | 4¾ to 5¾" | (CE) | ❷ | $400–500 |
| ☐ 4 | 4¾ to 5¾" | (CE) | ❸ | $325–375 |
| ☐ 4 | 4¾ to 5¾" | (CE) | ❹ | $300–325 |
| ☐ 4 | 4¾ to 5¾" | (CE) | ❺ | $270–300 |
| ☐ 4 | 4¾ to 5¾" | (CE) | ❻ | $250–270 |
| ☐ 4 | 4¾ to 5¾" | (CE) | ❼ | $235–240 |
| ☐ 4 | 4¾ to 5¾" | (OE) | ❽ | $235 |

*Old style (TM 1)*    *"Faience" (TM 1)*    *New style (TM 6)*    *Hard Porcelain (TM 1)*

New style                              Old style

**HUM 5**
**Strolling Along (CE)**
Originally modeled by master sculptor Arthur Moeller in 1935. Older models have
eyes that glance off to one side. Restyled by Gerhard Skrobek in 1962 with eyes looking straight ahead. Color of dog will vary. "Strolling along" was permanently retired by
Goebel in the fall of 1989 and will not be produced again. Old 1955 price list shows a
price of $6.00 while 1989 price list shows a price of $120, the last year it was sold on
the primary market. Original issue price was 50¢ in 1935! According to old Goebel
product book, a sample was produced by Arthur Moeller in 1935 of "Strolling Along"
with an attached "pot," similar to HUM 16/I "Little Hiker" with attached "pot." Value
$5,000 to 10,000 if found.

| | | | | | |
|---|---|---|---|---|---|
| ☐ 5 | 4¾ to 5¾" | (CE) | ❶ | $700–950 | |
| ☐ 5 | 4¾ to 5¾" | (CE) | ❷ | $500–600 | |
| ☐ 5 | 4¾ to 5¾" | (CE) | ❸ | $450–500 | |
| ☐ 5 | 4¾ to 5¾" | (CE) | ❹ | $350–450 | |
| ☐ 5 | 4¾ to 5¾" | (CE) | ❺ | $300–350 | |
| ☐ 5 | 4¾ to 5¾" | (CE) | ❻ | $275–300 | |

FINAL ISSUE
1989

---

**HUM TERM**

**DOUBLE CROWN:** This term is used to
describe the Goebel Company trademark
found on some "M. I. Hummel" figurines. On
"double crown" pieces the crown trademark
is found both incised and stamped.

---

*TM 1*    *TM 3*    *TM 6*

## HUM 6
### Sensitive Hunter

Modeled by master sculptor Arthur Moeller in 1935. Was originally called "The Timid Hunter." The lederhosen straps on older models of size 6 or 6/0 are parallel in back. Newer models have crossed-strap suspenders. Model 6/0 in TM 3 straps are found both ways. All other sizes have crossed straps in all time periods. Sometimes incised 6/2 instead of 6/II. All sizes were restyled in 1981 and now have a more natural-looking *brown* rabbit instead of the original *orange*-colored rabbit. Some variations in the position of the ears of the rabbit in older models. A new small size "Sensitive Hunter" was issued in 1985 at a suggested retail price of $60. It has an incised 1984 copyright date. This small size (6 2/0) was listed as "Temporarily Withdrawn" (TW) from production in January 1999. The large size (6/II) was listed as "Temporarily Withdrawn" (TW) from production on 31 December 1984 but could possibly be reinstated at some future date. The small size (6/0) "Sensitive Hunter" sold for $6.00 in 1955.

*TM 1*    *TM 3*    *TM 6*

**TM 1**          **TM 3**          **TM 6**

Size (6/I) was listed as (TW) "Temporarily Withdrawn" in January 1999.
Note: Red ring on base indicates this was a painter's sample and should not have left the factory.

☐ 6 2/0. . . . . 4" . . . . . . . . . . . (CE). . . ❻ . . . $175–180
☐ 6 2/0. . . . . 4" . . . . . . . . . . . (TW) . . ❼ . . . $170–175
☐ 6/0 . . . . . . 4¾" . . . . . . . . . . (CE). . . ❶ . . . $650–800
☐ 6/0 . . . . . . 4¾" . . . . . . . . . . (CE). . . ❷ . . . $400–500
☐ 6/0 . . . . . . 4¾" . . . . . . . . . . (CE). . . ❸ . . . $325–350
☐ 6/0 . . . . . . 4¾" . . . . . . . . . . (CE). . . ❹ . . . $300–325
☐ 6/0 . . . . . . 4¾" . . . . . . . . . . (CE). . . ❺ . . . $275–300
☐ 6/0 . . . . . . 4¾" . . . . . . . . . . (CE). . . ❻ . . . $250–275
☐ 6/0 . . . . . . 4¾" . . . . . . . . . . (CE). . . ❼ . . . $235–240
☐ 6/0 . . . . . . 4¾" . . . . . . . . . . (OE). . . ❽ . . . $235
☐ 6/I . . . . . . 5½ to 6" . . . . . . (CE). . . ❶ . . . $850–1000
☐ 6/I . . . . . . 5½ to 6" . . . . . . (CE). . . ❷ . . . $500–600
☐ 6/I . . . . . . 5½ to 6" . . . . . . (CE). . . ❸ . . . $375–425
☐ 6/I . . . . . . 5½" . . . . . . . . . . . (CE). . . ❹ . . . $350–375
☐ 6/I . . . . . . 5½" . . . . . . . . . . . (CE). . . ❺ . . . $325–350
☐ 6/I . . . . . . 5½" . . . . . . . . . . . (CE). . . ❻ . . . $300–325
☐ 6/I . . . . . . 5½" . . . . . . . . . . . (TW) . . ❼ . . . $280–285
☐ 6/II . . . . . 7 to 7½" . . . . . . (CE). . . ❶ . . . $1500–2000
☐ 6/II . . . . . 7 to 7½" . . . . . . (CE). . . ❷ . . . $950–1250
☐ 6/II . . . . . 7 to 7½" . . . . . . (CE). . . ❸ . . . $550–650
☐ 6/II . . . . . 7 to 7½" . . . . . . (CE). . . ❹ . . . $475–550
☐ 6/II . . . . . 7 to 7½" . . . . . . (CE). . . ❺ . . . $425–475
☐ 6/II . . . . . 7 to 7½" . . . . . . (TW) . . ❻ . . . $350–425
☐ 6 . . . . . . . 5" . . . . . . . . . . . . (CE). . . ❶ . . . $850–1000

---

**HUM TERM**

**SCARCE:** (Webster) Infrequently seen or found. Not plentiful or abundant.

*Just a few of the many size variations*

## HUM 7
## Merry Wanderer

Can be found in more size variations than any other figurine. A six–foot model was placed in front of the Goebel factory in Roedental in 1971 to commemorate Goebel's 100th anniversary and in 1987 an eight-foot model was unveiled in front of the former headquarters of the Goebel Collectors' Club (now The M. I. Hummel Club) in Tarrytown, New York. First modeled by master sculptor Arthur Moeller in 1935. Was restyled by master sculptor Gerhard Skrobek in size 7/II with the new textured finish in 1972, with an incised copyright date. Size 7/III was restyled in 1978 but without an incised copyright date. Older models of size 7/I have what collectors call a "double base" or "stair step" base. This accounts for the wide price variation of 7/I in trademark 3 since it was produced with either normal or "double base." All sizes and all time periods of HUM 7 usually have only five buttons on vest. Sometimes incised 7/2 instead of 7/II. The 32 inch model (HUM 7/X) was first sold in the U.S. market in 1976 and "temporarily withdrawn" (TW) from production as of 1 January 1991, but was reinstated on the May 15, 1995 price list. The large sizes (7/II and 7/III) were "temporarily withdrawn" (TW) from production on 31 December 1989, but may be reinstated at some future date. The small size "Merry Wanderer" (7/0) sold for $6.00 in 1955. A few sample pieces have been found decorated with bright colors and glossy finish of the "Faience" technique—value would be $4000–7000 depending on size and condition. See "Faience" article in back of Price Guide. In 1996 a promotional figurine with a bright *red* satchel was produced for a chain of gift shops in the Caribbean Islands. Bears a special backstamp "Exclusively for Little Switzerland" in size 7/0. Original retail price was $249 plus shipping charges.

| | | | | | |
|---|---|---|---|---|---|
| ☐ 7/0 | 6 to 6¼" | (CE) | **❶** | $750–1000 |
| ☐ 7/0 | 6 to 6¼" | (CE) | **❷** | $475–650 |
| ☐ 7/0 | 6 to 6¼" | (CE) | **❸** | $425–450 |
| ☐ 7/0 | 6 to 6¼" | (CE) | **❹** | $375–400 |
| ☐ 7/0 | 6 to 6¼" | (CE) | **❺** | $350–370 |
| ☐ 7/0 | 6 to 6¼" | (CE) | **❻** | $335–340 |
| ☐ 7/0 | 6 to 6¼" | (CE) | **❼** | $330–335 |
| ☐ 7/0 | 6 to 6¼" | (**OE**) | **❽** | $330 |

*(prices continued on next page)*

☐ 7/I . . . . . . 7 to 8" . . . . . . . . (CE) . . . **①** . . . $1500–1750 (Double base)
☐ 7/I . . . . . . 7 to 8" . . . . . . . . (CE) . . . **②** . . . $1300–1500 (Double base)
☐ 7/I . . . . . . 7 to 8" . . . . . . . . (CE) . . . **③** . . . $1200–1300 (Double base)
☐ 7/I . . . . . . 7 to 8" . . . . . . . . (CE) . . . **③** . . . $600–750 (Plain base)
☐ 7/I . . . . . . 7 to 8" . . . . . . . . (CE) . . . **④** . . . $500–600
☐ 7/I . . . . . . 7 to 8" . . . . . . . . (CE) . . . **⑤** . . . $475–500
☐ 7/I . . . . . . 7 to 8" . . . . . . . . (CE) . . . **⑥** . . . $450–475
☐ 7/I . . . . . . 7 to 8" . . . . . . . . (TW) . . **⑦** . . . $425–450
☐ 7/II . . . . . 9½ to 10¼" . . . . (CE) . . . **①** . . . $3000–3500
☐ 7/II . . . . . 9½ to 10¼" . . . . (CE) . . . **②** . . . $1900-2750
☐ 7/II . . . . . 9½ to 10¼" . . . . (CE) . . . **③** . . . $1700–1800
☐ 7/II . . . . . 9½ to 10¼" . . . . (CE) . . . **④** . . . $1500–1700
☐ 7/II . . . . . 9½ to 10¼" . . . . (CE) . . . **⑤** . . . $1250–1275
☐ 7/II . . . . . 9½ to 10¼" . . . . (CE) . . . **⑥** . . . $1225–1250
☐ 7/II . . . . . 9½ to 10¼" . . . . (TW) . . **⑦** . . . $1200–1225
☐ 7/III. . . . . 11 to 12" . . . . . . (CE) . . . **①** . . . $3300–4000
☐ 7/III. . . . . 11 to 12" . . . . . . (CE) . . . **②** . . . $2500–3000
☐ 7/III. . . . . 11 to 12" . . . . . . (CE) . . . **③** . . . $1700–2000
☐ 7/III. . . . . 11 to 12" . . . . . . (CE) . . . **④** . . . $1400–1500
☐ 7/III. . . . . 11 to 12" . . . . . . (CE) . . . **⑤** . . . $1300–1350
☐ 7/III. . . . . 11 to 12" . . . . . . (TW) . . **⑥** . . . $1250–1300
☐ 7/X . . . . . . 32" . . . . . . . . . . . (CE) . . . **⑤** . . . $15,000–25,000
☐ 7/X . . . . . . 32" . . . . . . . . . . . (CE) . . . **⑥** . . . $15,000–25,000
☐ 7/X . . . . . . 32 to 33" . . . . . . (CE) . . . **⑦** . . . $15,000–25,000
☐ 7/X . . . . . . 32 to 33" . . . . . . (**OE**) . . **⑧** . . . $25,000

*Little Switzerland*

*Faience style painting
7/I "double base" variation*

9

### HUM 8
### Book Worm
Same as HUM 3 except smaller in size. Has only one flower on page. Old name: "Little Book Worm." Factory records indicate that this figurine was modeled by master sculptor Reinhold Unger in 1935. This figurine sold for $8.00 in 1955.

| | | | | |
|---|---|---|---|---|
| ☐ 8 | 4 to 4½″ | (CE) | ❶ | $700–850 |
| ☐ 8 | 4 to 4½″ | (CE) | ❷ | $425–500 |
| ☐ 8 | 4 to 4½″ | (CE) | ❸ | $350–400 |
| ☐ 8 | 4 to 4½″ | (CE) | ❹ | $325–350 |
| ☐ 8 | 4 to 4½″ | (CE) | ❺ | $290–300 |
| ☐ 8 | 4 to 4½″ | (CE) | ❻ | $270–290 |
| ☐ 8 | 4 to 4½″ | (CE) | ❼ | $255–260 |
| ☐ 8 | 4 to 4½″ | (OE) | ❽ | $255 |

*New*       *Very old*

### HUM 9
### Begging His Share
There is much size variation in this figurine. Originally modeled by master sculptor Arthur Moeller in 1935 as a candleholder. Restyled in 1964, reduced slightly in size and made with a solid cake rather than with a hole for a candle. Can be found in trademark 3 with or without hole for candle. Called "Congratulatory Visit" in some old catalogues. Very early models have brightly colored striped socks. Has also been found in "crown" trademark without hole for candle. Listed as (TW) "Temporarily Withdrawn" in Jan 99.

*(prices continued on next page)*

*New style*       *Old style*

| | | | | | |
|---|---|---|---|---|---|
| ☐ 9 | . . . . . . 5¼ to 6″ | . . . . . . (CE) | . . . ❶ | . . . $750–900 |
| ☐ 9 | . . . . . . 5¼ to 6″ | . . . . . . (CE) | . . . ❷ | . . . $450–600 |
| ☐ 9 | . . . . . . 5¼ to 6″ | . . . . . . (CE) | . . . ❸ | . . . $350–400 |
| ☐ 9 | . . . . . . 5¼ to 6″ | . . . . . . (CE) | . . . ❹ | . . . $325–350 |
| ☐ 9 | . . . . . . 5¼ to 6″ | . . . . . . (CE) | . . . ❺ | . . . $300–325 |
| ☐ 9 | . . . . . . 5¼ to 6″ | . . . . . . (CE) | . . . ❻ | . . . $285–290 |
| ☐ 9 | . . . . . . 5¼ to 6″ | . . . . . . (TW) | . . ❼ | . . . $280–285 |

*This very rare example of "Begging His Share" without the normal base was recently found in Europe—value $7000–8000. Has also been found with "Faience" technique of painting.*

*Old 10/3*   *New 10/III*   *Old 10/I*   *New 10/I*

## HUM 10
### Flower Madonna

First created in 1935 by master sculptor Reinhold Unger. In 1956 the mold was renewed (restyled) by Theo R. Menzenbach and made approximately 2 inches smaller. The halo was changed at that time from the open style to the flat style. It has been produced in white overglaze, pastel blue cloak, brown cloak, ivory cloak and pastel yellow. Also has been found in reddish brown terra cotta finish, signed "M. I. Hummel" with the "crown" trademark in both 10/I and 10/3 size. The older color variations will usually range from $2,500 to $3,500 depending on color, condition and other variations. Old catalogues list it as large as 14 inches. Some earlier models appear with only the number 10 (no size designator). Also called "Sitting Madonna with Child" or "Virgin With Flowers" in old catalogues. Sometimes incised 10/3 instead of 10/III. (See page 26.) Both 10/I and 10/III are (TW) "Temporarily Withdrawn."

*(prices continued on next page)*

*Old 10/3*       *New 10/III*       *Old 10/I*       *New 10/I*

*Note variation in halo*

| | | | | Color | White |
|---|---|---|---|---|---|---|
| 10/I | 7½ to 9½" | (CE) | ❶ | ☐ $800–950 | ☐ $500–600 |
| 10/I | 7¾ to 9½" | (CE) | ❷ | ☐ $700–800 | ☐ $300–475 |
| 10/III | 12 to 13" | (CE) | ❶ | ☐ $900–1300 | ☐ $450–750 |
| 10/III | 12 to 13" | (CE) | ❷ | ☐ $800–900 | ☐ $450–650 |
| 10/I | 7¾ to 8¼" | (CE) | ❸ | ☐ $575–675 | ☐ $275–300 |
| 10/I | 7¾ to 8¼" | (CE) | ❹ | ☐ $525–575 | ☐ $250–275 |
| 10/I | 7¾ to 8¼" | (CE) | ❺ | ☐ $500–525 | ☐ $225–250 |
| 10/I | 7¾ to 8¼" | (CE) | ❻ | ☐ $475–500 | ☐ $200–225 |
| 10/I | 7¾ to 8¼" | (TW) | ❼ | ☐ $470–480 | ☐ $175–200 |
| 10/III | 11 to 11½" | (CE) | ❷ | ☐ $650–900 | ☐ $425–500 |
| 10/III | 11 to 11½" | (CE) | ❸ | ☐ $600–650 | ☐ $400–450 |
| 10/III | 11 to 11½" | (CE) | ❹ | ☐ $550–600 | ☐ $375–400 |
| 10/III | 11 to 11½" | (CE) | ❺ | ☐ $525–550 | ☐ $325–350 |
| 10/III | 11 to 11½" | (TW) | ❻ | ☐ $500–525 | ☐ $300–325 |

### HUM 11
### Merry Wanderer

Same style as Hum 7. Also modeled by master sculptor Arthur Moeller in 1935. Most models of "Merry Wanderer" have five buttons on vest. Some models in size 11 2/0 have six or seven buttons, and usually command a slight premium of 10%–15%. According to old Goebel product book, a sample was produced by Arthur Moeller in 1935 of HUM 11/0 "Merry Wanderer" with an attached "pot," similar to HUM 16/I "Little Hiker" with attached "pot." Value $5,000 to 10,000 if found.

*(prices continued on next page)*

| ☐ 11 | 4¾" | (CE) | ❶ | $600–750 |
|---|---|---|---|---|
| ☐ 11 2/0 | 4¼ to 4½" | (CE) | ❶ | $450–550 |
| ☐ 11 2/0 | 4¼ to 4½" | (CE) | ❷ | $250–325 |
| ☐ 11 2/0 | 4¼ to 4½" | (CE) | ❸ | $225–250 |
| ☐ 11 2/0 | 4¼ to 4½" | (CE) | ❹ | $190–225 |
| ☐ 11 2/0 | 4¼ to 4½" | (CE) | ❺ | $175–190 |
| ☐ 11 2/0 | 4¼ to 4½" | (CE) | ❻ | $160–175 |
| ☐ 11 2/0 | 4¼ to 4½" | (CE) | ❼ | $160–165 |
| ☐ 11 2/0 | 4¼ to 4½" | (**OE**) | ❽ | $170 |
| ☐ 11/0 | 4¾ to 5" | (CE) | ❶ | $550–700 |
| ☐ 11/0 | 4¾ to 5" | (CE) | ❷ | $400–500 |
| ☐ 11/0 | 4¾ to 5" | (CE) | ❸ | $325–375 |
| ☐ 11/0 | 4¾ to 5" | (CE) | ❹ | $300–325 (Difficult to find in TM 4) |
| ☐ 11/0 | 4¾ to 5" | (CE) | ❺ | $275–300 |
| ☐ 11/0 | 4¾ to 5" | (CE) | ❻ | $250–275 |
| ☐ 11/0 | 4¾ to 5" | (TW) | ❼ | $225–230 |

*12 (TM 1)*　　　*12/1 (TM 2)*　　　*12 2/0 (TM 2)*　　　*12 2/0 (TM 5)*

**HUM 12**
**Chimney Sweep**
Originally modeled by master sculptor Arthur Moeller in 1935, but has been restyled several times through the years. There is much size variation in both sizes. Many old crown (TM 1) trademark pieces have a high gloss finish. A 1992 Sampler kit contained a special ceramic chimney and roof top display base for use with the small size 12 2/0 Chimney Sweep. Called "SMOKY" in old catalogue.

| ☐ 12 2/0 | 4 to 4¼" | (CE) | ❷ | $250–325 |
|---|---|---|---|---|
| ☐ 12 2/0 | 4 to 4¼" | (CE) | ❸ | $175–200 |
| ☐ 12 2/0 | 4 to 4¼" | (CE) | ❹ | $160–175 |
| ☐ 12 2/0 | 4 to 4¼" | (CE) | ❺ | $150–160 |
| ☐ 12 2/0 | 4 to 4¼" | (CE) | ❻ | $145–150 |
| ☐ 12 2/0 | 4 to 4¼" | (CE) | ❼ | $140–145 |
| ☐ 12 2/0 | 4 to 4¼" | (**OE**) | ❽ | $140 |
| ☐ 12/I | 5½ to 6½" | (CE) | ❶ | $700–850 |
| ☐ 12/I | 5½ to 6½" | (CE) | ❷ | $425–500 |
| ☐ 12/I | 5½ to 6½" | (CE) | ❸ | $350–400 |
| ☐ 12/I | 5½ to 6½" | (CE) | ❹ | $325–350 |

*(prices continued on next page)*

| | | | | | |
|---|---|---|---|---|---|
| ☐ 12/I | 5½ to 6½" | (CE) | **❺** | $270–300 |
| ☐ 12/I | 5½ to 6½" | (CE) | **❻** | $260–270 |
| ☐ 12/I | 5½ to 6½" | (CE) | **❼** | $255–260 |
| ☐ 12/I | 5½ to 6½" | (OE) | **❽** | $255 |
| ☐ 12 | 6 to 6¼" | (CE) | **❶** | $750–900 |
| ☐ 12 | 6 to 6¼" | (CE) | **❷** | $450–525 |

13/V         13/2         *Old 13/2*         13/II New

**HUM 13**
**Meditation**

First modeled by master sculptor Reinhold Unger in 1935 in two sizes: 13/0 and 13/2. Size 13/2 was originally styled with flowers in the back half of basket, but in 1978 was restyled by master sculptor Gerhard Skrobek with no flowers in basket. Large size (13/V) was modeled by Theo R. Menzenbach in 1957 with full basket of flowers. The small size (13/2/0) was modeled by master sculptor Gerhard Skrobek in 1962. Three variations in hair ribbons were used through the years in 13/0 size: the early crown mark figurines usually had a very short pigtail with only a red painted band for the ribbon; the early full bee trademark examples were made with a longer pigtail but no ribbon or bows at all; the later models were made with the longer pigtails and a little red bow or ribbon on each pigtail. All "Meditations" made since the early 1950's would be of this last style. A 1962 copyright date appears on newer models of size 13/2/0. Also called "The Little Messenger." Sometimes 13/2 instead of 13/II and 13/5 instead of 13/V. The larger size (13/II) was listed as "temporarily withdrawn" (TW) from production on 31 December 1984 and (13/V) was listed as "temporarily withdrawn" (TW) on 31 December 1989, but may be reinstated at some future date. An unusual "Meditation" was recently found in Europe marked "13/I" and another here in the U.S. Our example measures 5¼", has a "crown" (TM 1) trademark, but I can*not* find a signature on it.

*(prices continued on next page)*

Recent information located in an old Goebel product book indicates that master sculptor Reinhold Unger in 1935 produced samples of "Meditation" in the 13/0 size with a round attached "pot" and another with an oblong attached "bowl." The "pot" has no markings other than a "crown" (TM 1) trademark and the "M. I. Hummel" signature on the figurine. The piece with the "bowl" is marked "KZ 27/I," a "double crown" (TM 1 +1) trademark and a signature on the figurine. The "KZ 27/I" indicates that he used a bowl that had been designed for *Goebel* figurine KZ 27. For more information, see: Rare/Unique Sample Variations of "M. I. Hummel" Figurines in the back of this book. Both sizes (13 2/0) and (13/0) were listed as (TW) "Temporarily Withdrawn" in January 1999.

| | | | | | |
|---|---|---|---|---|---|
| ☐ 13 2/0 | 4¼" | (CE) | ❷ | $250–350 |
| ☐ 13 2/0 | 4¼" | (CE) | ❸ | $225–250 |
| ☐ 13 2/0 | 4¼" | (CE) | ❹ | $190–225 |
| ☐ 13 2/0 | 4¼" | (CE) | ❺ | $175–190 |
| ☐ 13 2/0 | 4¼" | (CE) | ❻ | $160–175 |
| ☐ 13 2/0 | 4¼" | (TW) | ❼ | $160–165 |
| ☐ 13/0 | 5 to 6" | (CE) | ❶ | $700–850 |
| ☐ 13/0 | 5 to 6" | (CE) | ❷ | $425–500 |
| ☐ 13/0 | 5 to 6" | (CE) | ❸ | $350–400 |
| ☐ 13/0 | 5 to 6" | (CE) | ❹ | $325–350 |
| ☐ 13/0 | 5 to 6" | (CE) | ❺ | $270–300 |
| ☐ 13/0 | 5 to 6" | (CE) | ❻ | $260–270 |
| ☐ 13/0 | 5 to 6" | (TW) | ❼ | $245–250 |
| ☐ 13 | 7 to 7¼" | (CE) | ❶ | $4000–5000 |
| ☐ 13/I. | 5¼" | (CE) | ❶ | $1500–2000 |
| ☐ 13/II | 7 to 7¼" | (CE) | ❶ | $4000–5000 |
| ☐ 13/II | 7 to 7¼" | (CE) | ❷ | $3500–4000 |
| ☐ 13/II | 7 to 7¼" | (CE) | ❸ | $3000–3500 |
| ☐ 13/II | 7 to 7¼" | (CE) | ❺ | $400–450 |
| ☐ 13/II | 7 to 7¼" | (TW) | ❻ | $350–400 |
| ☐ 13/V | 13¼ to 14" | (CE) | ❶ | $4000–5000 |
| ☐ 13/V | 13¼ to 14" | (CE) | ❷ | $3000–3500 |
| ☐ 13/V | 13¼ to 14" | (CE) | ❸ | $1700–2200 |
| ☐ 13/V | 13¼ to 14" | (CE) | ❹ | $1350–1500 |

**13/0 with "Pot" (TM 1)**          **13/0 with "Bowl" (TM 1+1)**

14/B                                    14/A

## HUM 14
### Book Worm, Bookends, Boy and Girl
These figurines are weighted with sand through a hole on the bottom and closed with a cork or plastic plug. Sometimes sealed with a paper sticker and inscription "75 Years Goebel." The girl is the same as HUM 3 and HUM 8 except that the pictures on book are black and white rather than in color. Modeled by master sculptor Reinhold Unger in 1935. The boy was made only as part of bookend set and not normally sold separately. This policy, however, was changed and the boy could be purchased alone and unweighted. This was done mainly to satisfy collectors who desired a figurine to match the 1980 Annual Bell that had a motif similar to the bookend boy. Then in 1981 HUM 415 "Thoughtful" was released in the U.S. market to match the annual bell. "Bookworm" bookends were "temporarily withdrawn" (TW) from production on 31 December 1989. Listed at $315.00 a pair on the 1989 price list, the last year sold on the primary market. "Bookworm" bookends were listed at $15.00 a pair on 1955 price list. In 1993 "Bookworm" bookends could be purchased from Danbury Mint, Norwalk, Connecticut by mail order only, but they are no longer available from them. Bookworm boy has been found with number "14" only (NO "A") incised on the bottom. Boy was called "Learned Man" in very old catalogues.

☐ 14 . . . . . . 5½" . . . . . . . . . . (CE) . . . ❶ . . . $600–800
☐ 14 A&B . . . 5½" . . . . . . . . . . . (CE) . . . ❶ . . . $1200–1600
☐ 14 A&B . . . 5½" . . . . . . . . . . . (CE) . . . ❷ . . . $650–750
☐ 14 A&B . . . 5½" . . . . . . . . . . . (CE) . . . ❸ . . . $600–650
☐ 14 A&B . . . 5½" . . . . . . . . . . . (CE) . . . ❹ . . . $550–600
☐ 14 A&B . . . 5½" . . . . . . . . . . . (CE) . . . ❺ . . . $500–550
☐ 14 A&B . . . 5½" . . . . . . . . . . . (CE) . . . ❻ . . . $450–500
☐ 14 A&B . . . 5½" . . . . . . . . . . . (TW) . . . ❼ . . . $400–450
☐ 14 A . . . . . 5½" . . . . . . . . . . . (CE) . . . ❺ . . . $250–275
☐ 14 A . . . . . 5½" . . . . . . . . . . . (CE) . . . ❻ . . . $225–250

16

*15/0 (TM 2) 6"*        *15/0 (TM 2) 5¼"*        *15 2/0 (TM 6)*
*(Note size variation)*

**HUM 15**
**Hear Ye, Hear Ye**
Old name: "Night Watchman." There are some variations in color of mittens. Right hand facing photo (left hand of figurine) shows fingers on older models. Originally modeled by master sculptor Arthur Moeller in 1935. Older models usually incised 15/2 instead of 15/II. A new small size (15 2/0) "Hear Ye, Hear Ye" was first issued in 1985 with a suggested retail price of $60. It has an incised 1984 copyright date.The 6 inch size 15/I sold for $7.50 on 1955 price list. A few sample pieces have been found decorated with bright colors and glossy finish of the "Faience" technique—valued $3000–5000. Size (15/I) was listed as "Temporarily Withdrawn" (TW) from production in January 1999.

| | | | | |
|---|---|---|---|---|
| ☐ 15 2/0 | 4" | (CE) | ➏ | $185–190 |
| ☐ 15 2/0 | 4" | (CE) | ➐ | $180–185 |
| ☐ 15 2/0 | 4" | (**OE**) | ➑ | $180 |
| ☐ 15/0 | 5 to 5½" | (CE) | ➊ | $600–750 |
| ☐ 15/0 | 5¼ to 6" | (CE) | ➋ | $350–450 |
| ☐ 15/0 | 5 to 5¼" | (CE) | ➌ | $300–325 |
| ☐ 15/0 | 5 to 5¼" | (CE) | ➍ | $275–300 |
| ☐ 15/0 | 5 to 5¼" | (CE) | ➎ | $250–270 |
| ☐ 15/0 | 5 to 5¼" | (CE) | ➏ | $240–250 |
| ☐ 15/0 | 5 to 5¼" | (CE) | ➐ | $235–240 |
| ☐ 15/0 | 5 to 5¼" | (**OE**) | ➑ | $235 |
| ☐ 15/I | 6 to 6½" | (CE) | ➊ | $700–900 |
| ☐ 15/I | 6 to 6¾" | (CE) | ➋ | $450–600 |
| ☐ 15/I | 6 to 6¼" | (CE) | ➌ | $375–400 |
| ☐ 15/I | 6 to 6¼" | (CE) | ➍ | $350–375 |
| ☐ 15/I | 6 to 6¼" | (CE) | ➎ | $310–340 |
| ☐ 15/I | 6 to 6¼" | (CE) | ➏ | $290–310 |
| ☐ 15/I | 6 to 6¼" | (TW) | ➐ | $280–285 |
| ☐ 15/II | 7 to 7½" | (CE) | ➊ | $1200–1500 |
| ☐ 15/II | 7 to 7½" | (CE) | ➋ | $750–1000 |
| ☐ 15/II | 7 to 7½" | (CE) | ➌ | $650–750 |
| ☐ 15/II | 7 to 7½" | (CE) | ➍ | $550–650 |

*(prices continued on next page)*

```
☐ 15/II . . . . . 7 to 7½" . . . . . . (CE). . . ❺ . . . $500–525
☐ 15/II . . . . . 7 to 7½" . . . . . . (CE). . . ❻ . . . $475–500
☐ 15/II . . . . . 7 to 7½" . . . . . . (TW) . . ❼ . . . $450–475
☐ 15 . . . . . . 7¼" . . . . . . . . . . (CE). . . ❶ . . . $1400–1700
```

*16/I (TM 2)*          *16/I with "Pot" (TM 1)*

## HUM 16
### Little Hiker

This figurine was originally modeled by master sculptor Arthur Moeller in 1935. The old name of "Happy-Go-Lucky" was used in early catalogues. Slight changes can be noticed when comparing older models with new. Many old crown trademark pieces have a high gloss finish. An early sample painting variation is found with green jacket and blue hat—value $1500–2000. The large size (16/I) "Little Hiker" was (TW) "Temporarily Withdrawn" from the U.S. market at the end of 1997. According to old Goebel product book, a sample was produced by Arthur Moeller in 1935 of "Little Hiker" with an attached "pot." Value $5,000 to 10,000 when found. For more information, see: Rare/ Unique Sample Variations of "M. I. Hummel" Figurines in back of this book.

```
☐ 16 2/0. . . . 3¾ to 4¼" . . . . . (CE). . . ❶ . . . $350–450
☐ 16 2/0. . . . 3¾ to 4¼" . . . . . (CE). . . ❷ . . . $250–300
☐ 16 2/0. . . . 3¾ to 4¼" . . . . . (CE). . . ❸ . . . $175–200
☐ 16 2/0. . . . 3¾ to 4¼" . . . . . (CE). . . ❹ . . . $160–175
☐ 16 2/0. . . . 3¾ to 4¼" . . . . . (CE). . . ❺ . . . $150–160
☐ 16 2/0. . . . 3¾ to 4¼" . . . . . (CE). . . ❻ . . . $145–150
☐ 16 2/0. . . . 3¾ to 4¼" . . . . . (CE). . . ❼ . . . $140–145
☐ 16 2/0. . . . 3¾ to 4¼" . . . . . (OE). . . ❽ . . . $140
☐ 16 . . . . . . 5½ to 5¾" . . . . . (CE). . . ❶ . . . $650–750
☐ 16 . . . . . . 5½ to 5¾" . . . . . (CE). . . ❷ . . . $450–550
☐ 16/I. . . . . . 5½ to 6" . . . . . . (CE). . . ❶ . . . $600–700
☐ 16/I. . . . . . 5½ to 6" . . . . . . (CE). . . ❷ . . . $400–500
☐ 16/I. . . . . . 5½ to 6" . . . . . . (CE). . . ❸ . . . $350–400
☐ 16/I. . . . . . 5½ to 6" . . . . . . (CE). . . ❹ . . . $300–350
☐ 16/I. . . . . . 5½ to 6" . . . . . . (CE). . . ❺ . . . $275–300
☐ 16/I. . . . . . 5½ to 6" . . . . . . (CE). . . ❻ . . . $260–275
☐ 16/I. . . . . . 5½ to 6" . . . . . . (TW) . . ❼ . . . $245–250
```

*Current production on left*

*Rare sample (TM 1)*

## HUM 17
### Congratulations

First modeled by master sculptor Reinhold Unger in 1935. Called "I Congratulate" in old catalogues. Older models do not have socks. Restyled in 1971 by master sculptor Gerhard Skrobek, who added socks, new hair and textured finish. Larger size (17/2) is no longer produced and considered rare. Early crown mark pieces are marked 17 with either a zero or a 2 directly underneath. Old catalogue dated 1955 lists size of 3C\v which is believed to be in error. Crown and some full bee pieces have the handle of the horn pointing to the back. Since the larger size is closed edition (CE) and will not be produced again in the future, the size designator on the remaining size will eventually be eliminated, according to factory information, and will be incised 17 only. (This has not happened.) "Congratulations" (17/0) was permanently retired in the fall of 1999 and will not be produced again. According to old Goebel product book, a sample was produced by Reinhold Unger in 1935 of "Congratulations" with an attached "pot," but was not approved for production by Siessen Convent. Value $5,000 to 10,000 when found. For more information, see: Rare/Unique Sample Variations of "M. I. Hummel" Figurines in back of this book.

| | | | | |
|---|---|---|---|---|
| ☐ 17/0 | 5½ to 6″ | (CE) | ❶ | $600–750 |
| ☐ 17/0 | 5½ to 6″ | (CE) | ❷ | $350–450 |
| ☐ 17/0 | 5½ to 6″ | (CE) | ❸ | $300–325 |
| ☐ 17/0 | 5½ to 6″ | (CE) | ❹ | $275–300 |
| ☐ 17/0 | 6″ | (CE) | ❺ | $250–275 |
| ☐ 17/0 | 6″ | (CE) | ❻ | $240–250 |
| ☐ 17/0 | 6″ | (CE) | ❼ | $230–235 |
| ☐ 17/2 | 7¾ to 8¼″ | (CE) | ❶ | $6500–8000 |
| ☐ 17/2 | 7¾ to 8¼″ | (CE) | ❷ | $5500–6500 |
| ☐ 17/2 | 7¾ to 8¼″ | (CE) | ❸ | $4500–5500 |

**FINAL ISSUE**
1999

---
### HUM TERM

**HUM NO.:** Mold number or model number incised on the bottom of each "M.I. Hummel" figurine at the factory. This number is used for identification purposes.

---

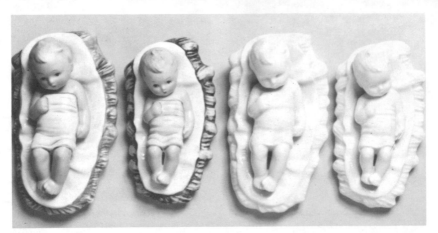

*Early models larger than newer models*

## HUM 18
### Christ Child

Early models measure 3¾" x 6½". Old name: "Christmas Night." At one time this piece was sold in Belgium in the white overglaze finish and would now be considered extremely rare. These white pieces usually bring about double the price of a colored piece. Originally modeled by master sculptor Reinhold Unger in 1935. Christ Child in white overglaze finish listed at $4.00 on 1955 price list. Christ Child was "Temporarily Withdrawn" (TW) from production on 31 December 1990, but was reinstated on 1997 price list, but is once again listed as (TW) "Temporarily Withdrawn" in January 1999.

| | | | | |
|---|---|---|---|---|
| ☐ 18 | 3¾ × 6½" | (CE) | ❶ | $400–550 |
| ☐ 18 | 3¾ × 6½" | (CE) | ❷ | $250–300 |
| ☐ 18 | 3¾ × 6½" | (CE) | ❸ | $225–250 |
| ☐ 18 | 3¼ × 6" | (CE) | ❹ | $200–225 |
| ☐ 18 | 3¼ × 6" | (CE) | ❺ | $175–200 |
| ☐ 18 | 3¼ × 6" | (CE) | ❻ | $170–175 |
| ☐ 18 | 3¼ × 6" | (TW) | ❼ | $165–170 |

## HUM 19
### Prayer Before Battle, Ashtray (CN)

Factory book of models indicates: "Big round tray with praying child (with flag and trumpet) standing at wooden (toy) horse. Prayer Before Battle, modeled by A. Moeller—June 20, 1935." An additional note states that this item was not accepted by the Convent at Siessen. An example of this rare piece was recently located on the East Coast of the U.S. This is the best photograph we could obtain. The piece is actually an ashtray and does have the "M. I. Hummel" signature, scratched in by hand. It is different material than the normal "M. I. Hummel" figurines. The owner washed it in an automatic dishwasher and

*(continued on next page)*

much of the paint washed off. It is likely that this piece had not been fired after the painting process, thus the paint washed off. The final firing locks on the paint in a normally completed figurine, thus enabling the collector to wash them without fear of damage.

☐ 19 . . . . . . 5½" . . . . . . . . . . (CN) . . . ❶ . . . $5,000–10,000

*TM 1 Normal*        *TM 1 Reversed horn*

## HUM 20
### Prayer Before Battle
Created in 1935 by master sculptor Arthur Moeller. Only slight variations between old and new models. Some color variations, but most noticeable difference is in size. Newer models are smaller. Some older pieces of HUM 20 will have a little paint or highlight inside the handle of the horn; most newer ones do not have. Also, another interesting variation appears on the front of the horn. Sometimes this area is recessed on older examples; most newer figurines will be almost flat and will have a little paint for highlight in this area. These are interesting variations, but they will not affect the value. Prayer Before Battle listed for $7.50 on old 1955 price list. Recently found with handle of horn reversed or upside down. Painting of little flag will also vary—either with light color or dark color on top of flag. Has been found with horn missing completely. Also found decorated with bright colors and glossy finish of the "faience" technique style of painting—value $3,000 to 4,000.

☐ 20 . . . . . . 4 to 4½" . . . . . . (CE) . . . ❶ . . . $500–650
☐ 20 . . . . . . 4 to 4½" . . . . . . (CE) . . . ❷ . . . $350–400
☐ 20 . . . . . . 4 to 4½" . . . . . . (CE) . . . ❸ . . . $250–275
☐ 20 . . . . . . 4 to 4½" . . . . . . (CE) . . . ❹ . . . $225–250
☐ 20 . . . . . . 4 to 4½" . . . . . . (CE) . . . ❺ . . . $210–225
☐ 20 . . . . . . 4 to 4½" . . . . . . (CE) . . . ❻ . . . $200–210
☐ 20 . . . . . . 4 to 4½" . . . . . . (CE) . . . ❼ . . . $195–200
☐ 20 . . . . . . 4 to 4½" . . . . . . (OE) . . . ❽ . . . $195

**HUM 21**
**Heavenly Angel**
First figurine to have "½" size designator. Much variation in size. Old name: "Little Guardian" or "Celestial Messenger." First modeled by master sculptor Reinhold Unger in 1935. Sometimes incised 21/2 instead of 21/II. According to factory information, this figurine was also sold in white overglaze at one time. "Heavenly Angel" motif was used for the first annual plate in 1971 (HUM 264), and as a "tree topper" in 1994 (HUM 755). The only other "M. I. Hummel" figurine with "½" size designator is "Blessed Child" HUM 78/II½ sold only at the Siessen convent. The large size 21/II was listed as (TW) "Temporarily Withdrawn" on the 1993 price list, while the 1992 price list shows a price of $390, the last year it was sold on the primary market. Size (21/I) was listed as (TW) "Temporarily Withdrawn" in January 1999.

| | | | | | |
|---|---|---|---|---|---|
| ☐ 21/0 | 4 to 4¾" | (CE) | ❶ | $400–500 |
| ☐ 21/0 | 4 to 4¾" | (CE) | ❷ | $225–275 |
| ☐ 21/0 | 4 to 4¾" | (CE) | ❸ | $190–210 |
| ☐ 21/0 | 4 to 4¾" | (CE) | ❹ | $170–180 |
| ☐ 21/0 | 4 to 4¾" | (CE) | ❺ | $160–170 |
| ☐ 21/0 | 4 to 4¾" | (CE) | ❻ | $155–160 |
| ☐ 21/0 | 4 to 4¾" | (CE) | ❼ | $150–155 |
| ☐ 21/0 | 4 to 4¾" | (OE) | ❽ | $150 |
| ☐ 21/0½ | 5¾ to 6½" | (CE) | ❶ | $700–850 |
| ☐ 21/0½ | 5¾ to 6½" | (CE) | ❷ | $425–500 |
| ☐ 21/0½ | 5¾ to 6½" | (CE) | ❸ | $350–400 |
| ☐ 21/0½ | 5¾ to 6½" | (CE) | ❹ | $325–350 |
| ☐ 21/0½ | 5¾ to 6½" | (CE) | ❺ | $270–300 |
| ☐ 21/0½ | 5¾ to 6½" | (CE) | ❻ | $260–270 |
| ☐ 21/0½ | 5¾ to 6½" | (CE) | ❼ | $255–260 |
| ☐ 21/0½ | 5¾ to 6½" | (OE) | ❽ | $255 |
| ☐ 21/I | 6¾ to 7¼" | (CE) | ❶ | $750–1000 |
| ☐ 21/I | 6¾ to 7¼" | (CE) | ❷ | $450–550 |
| ☐ 21/I | 6¾ to 7¼" | (CE) | ❸ | $400–450 |
| ☐ 21/I | 6¾ to 7¼" | (CE) | ❹ | $325–375 |
| ☐ 21/I | 6¾ to 7¼" | (CE) | ❺ | $315–325 |
| ☐ 21/I | 6¾ to 7¼" | (CE) | ❻ | $310–315 |
| ☐ 21/I | 6¾ to 7¼" | (TW) | ❼ | $300–310 |
| ☐ 21/II | 8½ to 8¾" | (CE) | ❶ | $1200–1600 |
| ☐ 21/II | 8½ to 8¾" | (CE) | ❷ | $700–1000 |
| ☐ 21/II | 8½ to 8¾" | (CE) | ❸ | $600–700 |
| ☐ 21/II | 8½ to 8¾" | (CE) | ❹ | $500–600 |
| ☐ 21/II | 8½ to 8¾" | (CE) | ❺ | $450–475 |
| ☐ 21/II | 8½ to 8¾" | (CE) | ❻ | $435–450 |
| ☐ 21/II | 8½ to 8¾" | (TW) | ❼ | $425–435 |

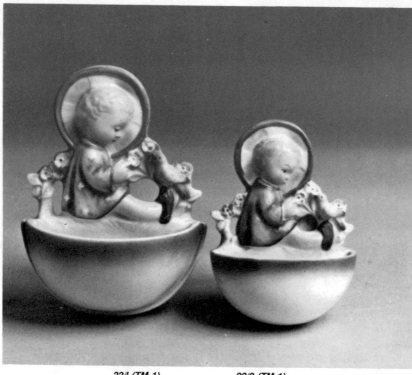

*22/I (TM 1)*          *22/0 (TM 1)*

## HUM 22
### Holy Water Font, Angel With Bird (Angel Sitting)
First modeled by master sculptor Reinhold Unger in 1935. Old name: "Sitting Angel."
Variations in size, color and design of bowl are found on other models. This small size
font sold for $1.35 on 1955 price list. Current 2000 price list name: "*Angel Sitting.*"

| | | | | | |
|---|---|---|---|---|---|
| ☐ 22 | 3⅛ to 4½" | (CE) | ❶ | $300–325 |
| ☐ 22/0 | 3 × 4" | (CE) | ❶ | $250–300 |
| ☐ 22/0 | 3 × 4" | (CE) | ❷ | $125–150 |
| ☐ 22/0 | 3 × 4" | (CE) | ❸ | $70–80 |
| ☐ 22/0 | 3 × 4" | (CE) | ❹ | $65–70 |
| ☐ 22/0 | 3 × 4" | (CE) | ❺ | $60–65 |
| ☐ 22/0 | 3 × 4" | (CE) | ❻ | $55–60 |
| ☐ 22/0 | 3 × 4" | (CE) | ❼ | $52–55 |
| ☐ 22/0 | 3 × 4" | (OE) | ❽ | $52 |
| ☐ 22/I | 3½ to 4⅞" | (CE) | ❶ | $500–600 |
| ☐ 22/I | 3½ to 4⅞" | (CE) | ❷ | $400–500 |
| ☐ 22/I | 3½ to 4⅞" | (CE) | ❸ | $300–400 |

---
**HUM TERM**

**SCARCE:** (Webster) Infrequently seen or
found. Not Plentiful or abundant.

---

*23/3 (TM 1)*  *23/I (TM 1+1)*  *23/I (TM 3)*

## HUM 23
### Adoration
This ever popular design was modeled by master sculptor Reinhold Unger in 1935. Size 23/I was restyled in 1978, with new textured finish, by master modeler Gerhard Skrobek. Older models can be found with either Arabic (23/3) or Roman (23/III) three. Both sizes were sold in white overglaze at one time in Belgium and would be considered rare today—value would be $1,500 to 2,000 for the small size and $3,000 to 4,000 for the large, depending on trademark and condition. Old name: "Ave Maria." Most older models have rounded corners on the base of the large size while newer models are more square. Early double crown-marked, large size found without size designator—23 only. Early crown-marked, small size usually found without flowers on base. The small size adoration (23/I) sold for $12.00 on 1955 price list. Large size (23/III) was listed as (TW) "Temporarily Withdrawn" in January 1999.

| | | | | |
|---|---|---|---|---|
| ☐ 23/I | 6¼ to 7″ | (CE) | ❶ | $1100–1300 |
| ☐ 23/I | 6¼ to 7″ | (CE) | ❷ | $600–800 |
| ☐ 23/I | 6¼ to 7″ | (CE) | ❸ | $500–575 |
| ☐ 23/I | 6¼ to 7″ | (CE) | ❹ | $450–500 |
| ☐ 23/I | 6¼ to 7″ | (CE) | ❺ | $425–450 |
| ☐ 23/I | 6¼ to 7″ | (CE) | ❻ | $410–420 |
| ☐ 23/I | 6¼ to 7″ | (CE) | ❼ | $400–410 |
| ☐ 23/I | 6¼ to 7″ | (OE) | ❽ | $400 |
| ☐ 23 | 8¾ to 9″ | (CE) | ❶ | $1600–2100 |
| ☐ 23/III | 8¾ to 9″ | (CE) | ❶ | $1500–2000 |
| ☐ 23/III | 8¾ to 9″ | (CE) | ❷ | $900–1250 |
| ☐ 23/III | 8¾ to 9″ | (CE) | ❸ | $800–900 |
| ☐ 23/III | 8¾ to 9″ | (CE) | ❹ | $675–775 |
| ☐ 23/III | 8¾ to 9″ | (CE) | ❺ | $625–675 |
| ☐ 23/III | 8¾ to 9″ | (CE) | ❻ | $600–625 |
| ☐ 23/III | 8¾ to 9″ | (TW) | ❼ | $595–600 |

**24/III (TM 1+1)**                                    **24/I (TM 2)**

## HUM 24
### Lullaby, Candleholder

Records show that this figurine was first modeled in 1935. Both Arthur Moeller and Reinhold Unger are given credit—possibly one created the small size while the other the larger size. Variations are found in size and construction of socket for candle on size 24/I. Old name: "Cradle Song." Also made without hole for candle—see HUM 262. Sometimes incised 24/3 instead of 24/III. In the spring of 1982 the large size (24/III) was listed by Goebel as "Temporarily Withdrawn," to be possibly reinstated at a future date. The small size (24/I) also was "Temporarily Withdrawn" from production on 31 December 1989, but was once again listed on the 1997 price list for $210. Both the large size (24/3) and the small (24/I) have been found in Belgium in white overglaze in the (TM2) "full bee" trademark. Value $2,000 to 4,000 each. The small size (24/I) was again listed as (TW) in January 1999.

| | | | | | |
|---|---|---|---|---|---|
| ☐ 24/I | 3½ × 5 to 5½" | (CE) | ❶ | $550–700 |
| ☐ 24/I | 3½ × 5 to 5½" | (CE) | ❷ | $350–425 |
| ☐ 24/I | 3½ × 5 to 5½" | (CE) | ❸ | $275–300 |
| ☐ 24/I | 3½ × 5 to 5½" | (CE) | ❹ | $250–275 |
| ☐ 24/I | 3½ × 5 to 5½" | (CE) | ❺ | $230–250 |
| ☐ 24/I | 3½ × 5 to 5½" | (CE) | ❻ | $220–230 |
| ☐ 24/I | 3½ × 5" | (TW) | ❼ | $210–215 |
| ☐ 24/III | 6¼ × 8¾" | (CE) | ❶ | $1500–1900 |
| ☐ 24/III | 6¼ × 8¾" | (CE) | ❷ | $950–1250 |
| ☐ 24/III | 6¼ × 8¾" | (CE) | ❸ | $600–700 |
| ☐ 24/III | 6¼ × 8¾" | (CE) | ❹ | $525–600 |
| ☐ 24/III | 6¼ × 8¾" | (CE) | ❺ | $500–525 |
| ☐ 24/III | 6¼ × 8¾" | (TW) | ❻ | $475–500 |

*Crown (TM 1)*       *Full bee (TM 2)*

## HUM 25
### Angelic Sleep, Candleholder

Records indicate that this figurine was first modeled in 1935 and that both Arthur Moeller and Reinhold Unger were involved with the design. At one time this figurine was sold in Belgium in the white overglaze finish and would now be considered rare. Listed as "Angel's Joy" in some old catalogues. In some old, as well as new catalogues and price lists, shown as 25/I in error. Made only one size and incised 25 only. (Candleholder figures are not always photographed with candles with this guide.) This figurine was "Temporarily Withdrawn" (TW) from production on 31 December 1989, but may be reinstated at some future date.

☐ 25 . . . . . . 3½ × 5 to 5½" . . (CE). . . ❶ . . . $550–700
☐ 25 . . . . . . 3½ × 5 to 5½" . . (CE). . . ❷ . . . $350–425
☐ 25 . . . . . . 3½ × 5 to 5½" . . (CE). . . ❷ . . . $1500–2000 (White Overglaze)
☐ 25 . . . . . . 3½ × 5 to 5½" . . (CE). . . ❸ . . . $260–280
☐ 25 . . . . . . 3½ × 5 to 5½" . . (CE). . . ❹ . . . $220–260
☐ 25 . . . . . . 3½ × 5 to 5½" . . (CE). . . ❺ . . . $210–220
☐ 25 . . . . . . 3½ × 5 to 5½" . . (TW) . . ❻ . . . $200–210

---
### A MEMORIAL TRIBUTE
1909 ∗ 1946
Sr. Maria Innocentia Hummel

---

This special Memorial Tribute HUM 10/I in pure white overglaze was released in the fall of 1996. It comes with a handcrafted wooden display base with a commemorative brass plaque, and a special commemorative backstamp which reads: "A Memorial Tribute 1909 ∗ 1946 Sr. Maria Innocentia Hummel" in addition to the (TM 7) trademark. The official issue price was $225 in 1996.

**26/0 (TM 2)**          **26/1 (TM 2)**

## HUM 26
### Holy Water Font, Child Jesus

Originally modeled by master sculptor Reinhold Unger in 1935. The normal color for the gown is a dark red but is occasionally found in a light blue color or green color. All that I have ever seen with the blue gown were in the small (26/0) size and with the small stylized (TM 3) trademark. Old crown mark and full bee pieces in both sizes usually have scalloped edge on bowl of font. This "Christ Child" font listed for $1.35 on 1955 price list. Listed as (TW) "Temporarily Withdrawn" from production in January 1999.

☐ 26/0 . . . . . 2¾ × 5¼" . . . . . (CE). . . **❶** . . . $225–275
☐ 26/0 . . . . . 2¾ × 5¼" . . . . . (CE). . . **❷** . . . $125–150
☐ 26/0 . . . . . 2¾ × 5¼" . . . . . (CE). . . **❸** . . . $70–80
☐ 26/0 . . . . . 2¾ × 5¼" . . . . . (CE). . . **❹** . . . $60–70
☐ 26/0 . . . . . 2¾ × 5¼" . . . . . (CE). . . **❺** . . . $55–60
☐ 26/0 . . . . . 2¾ × 5¼" . . . . . (CE). . . **❻** . . . $50–55
☐ 26/0 . . . . . 2¾ × 5¼" . . . . . (TW) . . **❼** . . . $50–52
☐ 26 . . . . . . 3 × 5¾" . . . . . . (CE). . . **❶** . . . $350–550
☐ 26/I . . . . . 3¼ × 6" . . . . . . (CE). . . **❶** . . . $300–500
☐ 26/I . . . . . 3¼ × 6" . . . . . . (CE). . . **❷** . . . $250–300
☐ 26/I . . . . . 3¼ × 6" . . . . . . (CE). . . **❸** . . . $200–250

27/I (TM 1)                27/3 (TM 1)

## HUM 27
### Joyous News
This figurine was made in two sizes. The small size is a candleholder while the larger size is a figurine. Both were modeled by master sculptor Reinhold Unger in 1935. 27/I is so similar to III/40/I that it is extremely difficult to tell the difference unless they are clearly marked. The small size "Joyous News" candleholder (27/I) is no longer produced and is considered rare. Usually found only in crown trademark. Can be found with the candleholder on the front side or on the back side. 27/I is also sometimes found with light purple shoes. Some models designed to hold .6 cm size candles while others designed to hold 1 cm size candles. The small size also found with incised number III/27/1 which indicates made for larger 1 cm size candles. The larger size "Joyous News" is rare in the older trademarks: TM 1, TM 2 and TM 3 but was reinstated in 1978 using the original molds, and the original number 27/3 (Arabic 3). In 1979 when it was restyled with the new textured finish the number was changed to 27/III (Roman III). Both 27/3 (old mold) and 27/III (new mold) can be found in TM 5. Large size (27/III) was listed as (TW) "Temporarily Withdrawn" in January 1999.

| | | | | | |
|---|---|---|---|---|---|
| ☐ 27/I | 2¾" | (CE) | ❶ | $300–500 |
| ☐ 27/I | 2¾" | (CE) | ❷ | $250–400 |
| ☐ 27/3 | 4¼ × 4¾" | (CE) | ❶ | $1500–2000 |
| ☐ 27/3 | 4¼ × 4¾" | (CE) | ❷ | $1000–1500 |
| ☐ 27/3 | 4¼ × 4¾" | (CE) | ❸ | $750–1000 |
| ☐ 27/3 | 4¼ × 4¾" | (CE) | ❺ | $260–280 |
| ☐ 27/III | 4¼ × 4¾" | (CE) | ❻ | $250–260 |
| ☐ 27/III | 4¼ × 4¾" | (TW) | ❼ | $245–250 |

---

**HUM TERM**

**PAINT FLAKE:** The term used to designate a flaw in a ceramic figurine whereby the paint has been chipped. This type flaw does not go beyond the glazed surface.

*28/III (TM 3)*                    *28/II (Double crown)*

## HUM 28
### Wayside Devotion
First modeled by master sculptor Reinhold Unger in 1935. Old name: "The Little Shepherd" or "Evensong." According to factory information, this figurine was also sold in white overglaze finish at one time. Sometimes incised 28/2 instead of 28/II or 28/3 instead of 28/III. Also found without a size designator on the large size—incised 28 only. The small size 28/II was restyled by Gerhard Skrobek in the early 1970's. Made without the shrine (see HUM 99) and was named "Eventide." The small size "Wayside Devotion" listed for $16.50 on 1955 price list. The large size (28/III) was listed as (TW) "Temporarily Withdrawn" in January 1999.

| | | | | |
|---|---|---|---|---|
| ☐ 28/II | 7 to 7½″ | (CE) | ❶ | $1200–1500 |
| ☐ 28/II | 7 to 7½″ | (CE) | ❷ | $750–900 |
| ☐ 28/II | 7 to 7½″ | (CE) | ❸ | $600–700 |
| ☐ 28/II | 7 to 7½″ | (CE) | ❹ | $550–600 |
| ☐ 28/II | 7 to 7½″ | (CE) | ❺ | $500–550 |
| ☐ 28/II | 7 to 7½″ | (CE) | ❻ | $485–500 |
| ☐ 28/II | 7 to 7½″ | (CE) | ❼ | $475–485 |
| ☐ 28/II | 7 to 7½″ | (OE) | ❽ | $475 |
| ☐ 28 | 8¾″ | (CE) | ❶ | $1700–1900 |
| ☐ 28/III | 8¾″ | (CE) | ❶ | $1400–1700 |
| ☐ 28/III | 8¾″ | (CE) | ❷ | $1000–1200 |
| ☐ 28/III | 8¾″ | (CE) | ❸ | $800–900 |
| ☐ 28/III | 8¾″ | (CE) | ❹ | $700–800 |
| ☐ 28/III | 8¾″ | (CE) | ❺ | $650–700 |
| ☐ 28/III | 8¾″ | (CE) | ❻ | $625–650 |
| ☐ 28/III | 8¾″ | (TW) | ❼ | $600–615 |

29 Crown (TM 1)          29/0 Full bee (TM 2)          248/0 (TM 4)

## HUM 29
### Holy Water Font, Guardian Angel
(CE) Closed Edition. Modeled by master sculptor Reinhold Unger in 1935 in two sizes. Because of the fragile wing design, it was discontinued in 1958 and replaced with a new design by Gerhard Skrobek and given the new model number HUM 248.

| | | | | |
|---|---|---|---|---|
| ☐ 29 | 2½ × 5¾" | (CE) | ❶ | $1300–1500 |
| ☐ 29/0 | 2⅞ × 6" | (CE) | ❶ | $1300–1500 |
| ☐ 29/0 | 2⅞ × 6" | (CE) | ❷ | $1000–1250 |
| ☐ 29/0 | 2⅞ × 6" | (CE) | ❸ | $950–1000 |
| ☐ 29/I | 3 × 6⅜" | (CE) | ❶ | $1750–2000 |
| ☐ 29/I | 3 × 6⅜" | (CE) | ❷ | $1500–1750 |

---

**HUM TERM**

**DECIMAL POINT:** This incised "period" or dot was used in a somewhat random fashion by the W. Goebel Porzellanfabrik over the years. The decimal point is and was primarily used to reduce confusion in reading the incised numbers on the underside of the figurines. Example: 66. helps one realize that the designation is sixty-six and not ninety-nine.

---

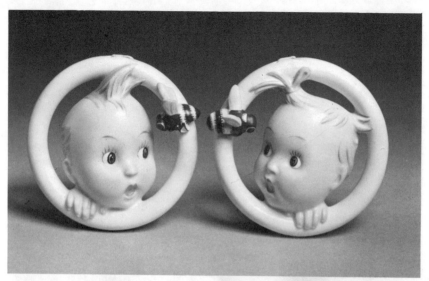

*30/0 A*         *30/0 B*

*30/0 A*     *30/I A*

*30/0 B*     *30/I B*

## HUM 30
### Ba-Bee-Ring

Old name: "Hummel Rings." Originally modeled in 1935 by master sculptor Reinhold Unger. There is some size variation between old and new pieces. Early red color rings are extremely rare. Now produced in tan color only. The girl, 30 B always has orange color hair ribbon, except on red color rings, then it is blue. Although now made in only one size, current production models still have incised "O" size designator. Factory representatives state that this "will possibly disappear sometime in the future." Priced by the set of two. Also found unpainted in white overglaze finish. "Ba-Bee-Rings" sold for $4.00 a pair on 1955 price list.

☐ 30/0 A&B . 4¾ × 5″ . . . . . . (CE). . . **❶** . . . $550–700
☐ 30/0 A&B . 4¾ × 5″ . . . . . . (CE). . . **❷** . . . $350–450
☐ 30/0 A&B . 4¾ × 5″ . . . . . . (CE). . . **❸** . . . $290–310
☐ 30/0 A&B . 4¾ × 5″ . . . . . . (CE). . . **❹** . . . $260–280
☐ 30/0 A&B . 4¾ × 5″ . . . . . . (CE). . . **❺** . . . $250–260
☐ 30/0 A&B . 4¾ × 5″ . . . . . . (CE). . . **❻** . . . $240–250
☐ 30/0 A&B . 4¾ × 5″ . . . . . . (CE). . . **❼** . . . $236–240
☐ 30/0 A&B . 4¾ × 5″ . . . . . . (**OE**). . . **❽** . . . $236
☐ 30/I A&B . . 5¼ × 6″ . . . . . . (CE). . . **❶** . . . $2000–3500
☐ 30/0 A&B. . Red Rings . . . . . (CE). . . **❶** . . . $6000–7000
☐ 30/I A&B . . Red Rings . . . . . (CE). . . **❶** . . . $8000–9000

*Note black child on left*

*(TM 1+1) Double crown*          *Stamped with "Hummel" family crest*

## HUM 31
### Silent Night with Black Child/Advent Group with Candle (CE)
Similar to HUM 54 except embossed earring and bare feet of black child. Modeled in 1935 by master sculptor Arthur Moeller but not produced in quantity. HUM 31 was also produced and sold with all white children and also considered extremely rare. HUM 31 was still listed in old German price lists as late as 1956. That does not necessarily mean that it was produced and sold at that time. It could possibly have been listed in error since so very, very few have been located. According to factory representatives, a few HUM 54 were produced with a black child, but wearing shoes instead of bare feet or without shoes with white marks to indicate toes. The figurine photographed here is particularly unique since it was originally purchased from Mrs. Victoria Hummel, the mother of Sister Hummel. Her mother died on 24 October 1983 at the age of 98. This figurine is part of the Robert L. Miller collection.

☐ 31 . . . . . . 3½ × 5″ . . . . . . (CE). . . ❶ . . . $10,000–15,000 (White children)
☐ 31 . . . . . . 3½ × 5″ . . . . . . (CE). . . ❶ . . . $20,000–25,000 (Black child)

---

**— HUM TERM —**

**DOUBLE CROWN:** This term is used to describe the Goebel Company trademark found on some "M. I. Hummel" figurines. On "double crown" pieces the crown trademark is found both incised and stamped.

| 32/0 (TM 1+1) | 32/0 (TM 2) | 32/I (TM 1) |

## HUM 32
### Little Gabriel

There are many size variations in this figurine that was first modeled by master sculptor Reinhold Unger in 1935. Called "Joyous News" in some old catalogues. Newer models have no size designator since it is now produced in only the small size. The large size is found incised 32/I or 32 only and is considered rare. "Little Gabriel" was restyled in 1982 with several changes—arms are now apart, angle of the wings is longer and the incised "M. I. Hummel" signature is on the top of the base rather than on the side, as in the past. Listed as (TW) "Temporarily Withdrawn" in January 1999.

| | | | | | |
|---|---|---|---|---|---|
| ☐ 32/0 | 5 to 5½" | (CE) | ❶ | $450–550 |
| ☐ 32/0 | 5 to 5½" | (CE) | ❷ | $300–375 |
| ☐ 32/0 | 5 to 5½" | (CE) | ❸ | $225–250 |
| ☐ 32/0 | 5 to 5½" | (CE) | ❹ | $200–225 |
| ☐ 32/0 | 5" | (CE) | ❺ | $180–200 |
| ☐ 32 | 5" | (CE) | ❺ | $180–200 |
| ☐ 32 | 5" | (CE) | ❻ | $170–180 |
| ☐ 32 | 5" | (TW) | ❼ | $165–170 |
| ☐ 32/I | 5¾ to 6" | (CE) | ❶ | $2000–2500 |
| ☐ 32/I | 5¾ to 6" | (CE) | ❷ | $1500–2000 |
| ☐ 32/I | 5¾ to 6" | (CE) | ❸ | $1200–1500 |
| ☐ 32 | 5¾ to 6" | (CE) | ❶ | $2000–2500 |
| ☐ 32 | 5¾ to 6" | (CE) | ❷ | $1500–2000 |

| New (TM 6) | Old (TM 5) |

## HUM 33
### Ashtray, Joyful

First modeled by master sculptor Reinhold Unger in 1935. Older models have slightly different construction of ashtray and are usually slightly larger. HUM 33 "Joyful Ashtray" was listed as "Temporarily Withdrawn" (TW) from production on 31 December 1984, but may be reinstated at some future date. It is very unlikely, in our opinion, that this item will ever be made again. Also found decorated in the "Faience" technique with bright colors and glossy finish—value would be $3,000 to 5,000. An unusual example was recently found with orange dress and blue shoes, which is the reverse of the normal colors—value $2000 to 3000.

| | | | | | |
|---|---|---|---|---|---|
| ☐ 33 | 3¾ × 6″ | (CE) | ❶ | $400–650 |
| ☐ 33 | 3¾ × 6″ | (CE) | ❷ | $300–350 |
| ☐ 33 | 3½ × 6″ | (CE) | ❸ | $220–250 |
| ☐ 33 | 3½ × 6″ | (CE) | ❹ | $200–220 |
| ☐ 33 | 3½ × 6″ | (CE) | ❺ | $190–200 |
| ☐ 33 | 3½ × 6″ | (TW) | ❻ | $175–190 |

---

**HUM TERM**

**PAINT RUB**: A general wearing away of the paint surface of a figurine in a particular spot. This condition is usually caused by excessive handling of a figurine, thin paint in a given area of the figurine, or the excessive use of abrasive cleaners.

*(TM 2)*

**HUM 34**
**Ashtray, Singing Lesson**
First modeled by master sculptor Arthur Moeller in 1935. Slight variation in colors of older models. Several variations in construction on bottom of ashtray. The "M.I. Hummel" signature is usually found under the lip of the ashtray on most older models, and on top of rim on newer models. "Singing Lesson" ashtray was (TW) "Temporarily Withdrawn" from production on 31 December 1989, but may be reinstated at some future date.

☐ 34 . . . . . . 3½ to 6¼″ . . . . . (CE). . . ❶ . . . $450–650
☐ 34 . . . . . . 3½ to 6¼″ . . . . . (CE). . . ❷ . . . $300–350
☐ 34 . . . . . . 3½ to 6¼″ . . . . . (CE). . . ❸ . . . $220–250
☐ 34 . . . . . . 3½ to 6¼″ . . . . . (CE). . . ❹ . . . $200–220
☐ 34 . . . . . . 3½ to 6¼″ . . . . . (CE). . . ❺ . . . $190–200
☐ 34 . . . . . . 3½ to 6¼″ . . . . . (TW) . . ❻ . . . $175–190

---

**HUM-INFO**

An authentic Goebel "M.I. Hummel" Figurine will always have a plain incised model number. It will *never* have an alphabetical prefix in front of the number (such as: HM, FE, HX etc.) *If* it *has* an alphabetical pre-fix—it is a *Goebel* item and not "M.I. Hummel." Alphabetical letters may appear after a HUM number (such as: A, B, C etc.)—this indicates that it part of a set. Example: HUM 239 A, 239 B, or 239 C. This is a good "rule of thumb" guide to remember when looking at a figurine with a *Goebel* trademark.

*35/I (TM 1)*          *35/0 (TM 1)*

## HUM 35
### Holy Water Font, Good Shepherd
First modeled by master sculptor Reinhold Unger in 1935. There are slight variations in size as well as variations in the construction of the bowl of font. Also found in the large size without a size designator—incised 35 only. Recently found with yellow lambs and green grass by angel's feet. Both sizes have been found made in porcelain rather than the normal ceramics.

☐ 35/0 . . . . . 2½ × 4¾" . . . . . (CE). . . **❶** . . . $225–275
☐ 35/0 . . . . . 2½ × 4¾" . . . . . (CE). . . **❷** . . . $125–150
☐ 35/0 . . . . . 2½ × 4¾" . . . . . (CE). . . **❸** . . . $70–80
☐ 35/0 . . . . . 2½ × 4¾" . . . . . (CE). . . **❹** . . . $65–70
☐ 35/0 . . . . . 2½ × 4¾" . . . . . (CE). . . **❺** . . . $60–65
☐ 35/0 . . . . . 2½ × 4¾" . . . . . (CE). . . **❻** . . . $55–60
☐ 35/0 . . . . . 2½ × 4¾" . . . . . (CE). . . **❼** . . . $52–55
☐ 35/0 . . . . . 2½ × 4¾" . . . . . (**OE**). . . **❽** . . . $52
☐ 35 . . . . . . 2¾ × 5¾" . . . . . (CE). . . **❶** . . . $400–450
☐ 35/I . . . . . 2¾ × 5¾" . . . . . (CE). . . **❶** . . . $375–425
☐ 35/I . . . . . 2¾ × 5¾" . . . . . (CE). . . **❷** . . . $275–375
☐ 35/I . . . . . 2¾ × 5¾" . . . . . (CE). . . **❸** . . . $175–225

*36/I (TM 1)*        *36/0 (TM 1)*

## HUM 36
### Holy Water Font, Child with Flowers

First modeled by master sculptor Reinhold Unger in 1935. There are slight variations in size, color and in the construction of the bowl of the font. Also called "Flower Angel" or "Angel with Flowers."

| | | | | |
|---|---|---|---|---|
| ☐ 36/0 | 3¼ × 4¼" | (CE) | ❶ | $225–275 |
| ☐ 36/0 | 3¼ × 4¼" | (CE) | ❷ | $125–150 |
| ☐ 36/0 | 3¼ × 4¼" | (CE) | ❸ | $70–80 |
| ☐ 36/0 | 3¼ × 4¼" | (CE) | ❹ | $65–70 |
| ☐ 36/0 | 3¼ × 4¼" | (CE) | ❺ | $60–65 |
| ☐ 36/0 | 3¼ × 4¼" | (CE) | ❻ | $55–60 |
| ☐ 36/0 | 3¼ × 4¼" | (CE) | ❼ | $52–55 |
| ☐ 36/0 | 3¼ × 4¼" | (OE) | ❽ | $52 |
| ☐ 36 | 3½ × 4½" | (CE) | ❶ | $400–450 |
| ☐ 36/I | 3½ × 4½" | (CE) | ❶ | $375–425 |
| ☐ 36/I | 3½ × 4½" | (CE) | ❷ | $275–375 |
| ☐ 36/I | 3½ × 5" | (CE) | ❸ | $175–225 |

---

**HUM TERM**

**GOEBEL BEE**: A name used to describe the trademark used by the Goebel Company from 1972 until 1979. This trademark incorporates the GOEBEL name with the V and bee. Also known as (TM 5).

**New model (TM 5)**                    **Old model (TM 1)**

## HUM 37
### Herald Angels, Candleholder
Many variations through the years. On older models the candleholder is much taller than on the newer ones. The order of placement of the angels may vary on the older models. Current production pieces have a half-inch wider base. Originally modeled in 1935 by master sculptor Reinhold Unger. Early "crown" mark examples are sometimes found with light purple shoes rather than the dark brown shoes found on newer models. "Herald Angels" candleholder was (TW) "Temporarily Withdrawn" from production on 31 December 1989, but may be reinstated at some future date. A few sample pieces have been found decorated with bright colors and glossy finish of the "Faience" technique—value would be $3000 to 5000.

| ☐ 37 | 2¾ × 4″ | (CE) | ❶ | $600–800 |
|------|---------|------|---|----------|
| ☐ 37 | 2¾ × 4″ | (CE) | ❷ | $400–450 |
| ☐ 37 | 2¾ × 4 to 4½″ | (CE) | ❸ | $250–275 |
| ☐ 37 | 2¾ × 4 to 4½″ | (CE) | ❹ | $225–250 |
| ☐ 37 | 2¾ × 4 to 4½″ | (CE) | ❺ | $200–225 |
| ☐ 37 | 2¾ × 4 to 4½″ | (TW) | ❻ | $180–200 |

───── **HUM TERM** ─────

**OUT OF PRODUCTION**: A term used by the Goebel Company to designate items that are not currently in production, yet have not been given an official classification as to their eventual fate. Some items listed as out of production may become closed editions, remain temporarily withdrawn, or ultimately return to current production status.

38/0 (TM 3)          39/0 (TM 3)          40/0 (TM 3)

**HUM 38**
**Angel, Joyous News with Lute,**
**Candleholder**

**HUM 39**
**Angel, Joyous News with Accordion,**
**Candleholder**

**HUM 40**
**Angel, Joyous News with Trumpet,**
**Candleholder**
Roman numerals to the left of the HUM
number indicate the size of the candle
that fits into the figurine. Size I is .6 cm,
size III is 1 cm. (Note: Not all figurines

which hold candles are photographed
with candles in this book, but they are
usually sold with candles.) Also called
"Little Heavenly Angel" in old catalogues.
Also known as "Angel Trio" candleholders. Candleholders are always on right
side of angel. These three figurines were
originally modeled in 1935 by master
sculptor Reinhold Unger. Very early
pieces do not have a size designator—
incised 38. 39. 40. only. Since these figurines are relatively small in size, the
signature may be only "Hum" on the back
or on the leg of the angel. HUM 38/0
sometimes found with green shoes.

☐ 1/38/0 . . . . 2 to 2½″ . . . . . . (CE) . . . ❶ . . . $150–200
☐ 1/38/0 . . . . 2 to 2½″ . . . . . . (CE) . . . ❷ . . . $100–125
☐ 1/38/0 . . . . 2 to 2½″ . . . . . . (CE) . . . ❸ . . . $90–100
☐ 1/38/0 . . . . 2 to 2½″ . . . . . . (CE) . . . ❹ . . . $80–90
☐ 1/38/0 . . . . 2 to 2½″ . . . . . . (CE) . . . ❺ . . . $75–80
☐ 1/38/0 . . . . 2 to 2½″ . . . . . . (CE) . . . ❻ . . . $70–75
☐ 1/38/0 . . . . 2 to 2½″ . . . . . . (CE) . . . ❼ . . . $68–70
☐ 1/38/0 . . . . 2 to 2½″ . . . . . . (OE) . . . ❽ . . . $68
☐ III/38/0 . . . 2 to 2½″ . . . . . . (CE) . . . ❶ . . . $150–200
☐ III/38/0 . . . 2 to 2½″ . . . . . . (CE) . . . ❷ . . . $100–125
☐ III/38/0 . . . 2 to 2½″ . . . . . . (CE) . . . ❸ . . . $90–100
☐ III/38/0 . . . 2 to 2½″ . . . . . . (CE) . . . ❹ . . . $80–90
☐ III/38/0 . . . 2 to 2½″ . . . . . . (CE) . . . ❺ . . . $70–80
☐ III/38/0 . . . 2 to 2½″ . . . . . . (TW) . . . ❻ . . . $60–70
☐ III/38/I . . . . 2½ to 2¾″ . . . . . (CE) . . . ❶ . . . $300–350
☐ III/38/I . . . . 2½ to 2¾″ . . . . . (CE) . . . ❷ . . . $250–300
☐ III/38/I . . . . 2½ to 2¾″ . . . . . (CE) . . . ❸ . . . $200–250

*(prices continued on next page)*

| | | | | |
|---|---|---|---|---|
| ☐ 1/39/0 . . . . 2 to 2½″ . . . . . . (CE) . . . **❶** . . . $150–200 |
| ☐ 1/39/0 . . . . 2 to 2½″ . . . . . . (CE) . . . **❷** . . . $100–125 |
| ☐ 1/39/0 . . . . 2 to 2½″ . . . . . . (CE) . . . **❸** . . . $90–100 |
| ☐ 1/39/0 . . . . 2 to 2½″ . . . . . . (CE) . . . **❹** . . . $80–90 |
| ☐ 1/39/0 . . . . 2 to 2½″ . . . . . . (CE) . . . **❺** . . . $75–80 |
| ☐ 1/39/0 . . . 2 to 2½″ . . . . . . (CE) . . . **❻** . . . $70–75 |
| ☐ 1/39/0 . . . 2 to 2½″ . . . . . . (CE) . . . **❼** . . . $68–70 |
| ☐ 1/39/0 . . . . 2 to 2½″ . . . . . . (**OE**) . . . **❽** . . . $68 |
| ☐ III/39/0 . . . 2 to 2½″ . . . . . . (CE) . . . **❶** . . . $150–200 |
| ☐ III/39/0 . . . 2 to 2½″ . . . . . . (CE) . . . **❷** . . . $100–125 |
| ☐ III/39/0 . . . 2 to 2½″ . . . . . . (CE) . . . **❸** . . . $90–100 |
| ☐ III/39/0 . . . 2 to 2½″ . . . . . . (CE) . . . **❹** . . . $80–90 |
| ☐ III/39/0 . . . 2 to 2½″ . . . . . . (CE) . . . **❺** . . . $70–80 |
| ☐ III/39/0 . . . 2 to 2½″ . . . . . . (TW) . . . **❻** . . . $60–70 |
| ☐ III/39/I . . . 2½ to 2¾″ . . . . . (CE) . . . **❶** . . . $300–350 |
| ☐ III/39/I . . . 2½ to 2¾″ . . . . . (CE) . . . **❷** . . . $250–300 |
| ☐ III/39/I . . . 2½ to 2¾″ . . . . . (CE) . . . **❸** . . . $200–250 |
| | | | | |
| ☐ 1/40/0 . . . . 2 to 2½″ . . . . . . (CE) . . . **❶** . . . $150–200 |
| ☐ 1/40/0 . . . . 2 to 2½″ . . . . . . (CE) . . . **❷** . . . $100–125 |
| ☐ 1/40/0 . . . . 2 to 2½″ . . . . . . (CE) . . . **❸** . . . $90–100 |
| ☐ 1/40/0 . . . . 2 to 2½″ . . . . . . (CE) . . . **❹** . . . $80–90 |
| ☐ 1/40/0 . . . . 2 to 2½″ . . . . . . (CE) . . . **❺** . . . $75–80 |
| ☐ 1/40/0 . . . . 2 to 2½″ . . . . . . (CE) . . . **❻** . . . $70–75 |
| ☐ 1/40/0 . . . . 2 to 2½″ . . . . . . (CE) . . . **❼** . . . $68–70 |
| ☐ 1/40/0 . . . . 2 to 2½″ . . . . . . (**OE**) . . . **❽** . . . $68 |
| ☐ III/40/0 . . . 2 to 2½″ . . . . . . (CE) . . . **❶** . . . $150–200 |
| ☐ III/40/0 . . . 2 to 2½″ . . . . . . (CE) . . . **❷** . . . $100–125 |
| ☐ III/40/0 . . . 2 to 2½″ . . . . . . (CE) . . . **❸** . . . $90–100 |
| ☐ III/40/0 . . . 2 to 2½″ . . . . . . (CE) . . . **❹** . . . $80–90 |
| ☐ III/40/0 . . . 2 to 2½″ . . . . . . (CE) . . . **❺** . . . $70–80 |
| ☐ III/40/0 . . . 2 to 2½″ . . . . . . (TW) . . . **❻** . . . $60–70 |
| ☐ III/40/I . . . 2½ to 2¾″ . . . . . (CE) . . . **❶** . . . $300–350 |
| ☐ III/40/I . . . 2½ to 2¾″ . . . . . (CE) . . . **❷** . . . $250–300 |
| ☐ III/40/I . . . 2½ to 2¾″ . . . . . (CE) . . . **❸** . . . $200–250 |

**HUM 41**

**Singing Lesson (without base) (CN)**

Factory book of models indicates this piece is similar to HUM 34 (Singing Lesson, Ashtray). Closed 31 October 1935. No known examples.

☐ 41 . . . . . . . . . . . . . . . . . (CN) . . . . . . . $5,000–10,000

---

— **HUM TERM** —

**CURRENT PRODUCTION:** The term used to describe those items currently being produced by the W. Goebel Porzellanfabrik of Roedental, West Germany.

---

*42/0 (TM 1)*                    *42/I (TM 1)*

## HUM 42
### Good Shepherd

First modeled by master sculptor Reinhold Unger in 1935. Normally has a rust-colored gown. Factory sample of small size 42/0 has light blue gown. Several examples are now in private collections, including the Robert L. Miller collection, value $2,000–3,000. Size 42/I is considered rare and no longer produced in large size. Factory information states that (0) size designator will eventually be dropped from number. Current production still incised 42/0. Small size (42/0) was listed as (TW) "Temporarily Withdrawn" in January 1999.

| | | | | | |
|---|---|---|---|---|---|
| ☐ 42/0 | 5¾ to 6¼″ | (CE) | **❶** | $750–900 |
| ☐ 42/0 | 6¼ to 6½″ | (CE) | **❷** | $425–600 |
| ☐ 42/0 | 6¼ to 6½″ | (CE) | **❸** | $375–425 |
| ☐ 42/0 | 6¼ to 6½″ | (CE) | **❹** | $325–375 |
| ☐ 42/0 | 6¼″ | (CE) | **❺** | $300–325 |
| ☐ 42/0 | 6¼″ | (CE) | **❻** | $290–300 |
| ☐ 42/0 | 6¼″ | (TW) | **❼** | $280–290 |
| ☐ 42/I | 7¼ to 7¾″ | (CE) | **❶** | $7000–8000 |
| ☐ 42/I | 7¼ to 8″ | (CE) | **❷** | $6000–7000 |
| ☐ 42/I | 7¼ to 8″ | (CE) | **❸** | $5000–6000 |

(TM 2)　　　　　　　(TM 1)　　　　　　　(TM 3)

## HUM 43
### March Winds
Many size variations with older pieces slightly larger. First modeled by master sculptor Reinhold Unger in 1935. Called "Urchin" in some old catalogues. There is some variation in the front "flap" of boy's trousers; sometimes this is in the mold, other times made with white paint—not attributed to any certain time period. In 1996 a 2¾" size (3¼" with base) with incised model number 43 5/0 was produced as part of the "Pen Pals" series of personalized name card table decorations. The original issue price was $55.

☐ 43 5/0. . . . 2¾" . . . . . . . . . . (OE). . . ❼ . . . $55
☐ 43 . . . . . . 4¾ to 5½" . . . . . (CE). . . ❶ . . . $450–600
☐ 43 . . . . . . 4¾ to 5½" . . . . . (CE). . . ❷ . . . $275–375
☐ 43 . . . . . . 4¾ to 5½" . . . . . (CE). . . ❸ . . . $250–275
☐ 43 . . . . . . 4¾ to 5½" . . . . . (CE). . . ❹ . . . $200–250
☐ 43 . . . . . . 4¾ to 5½" . . . . . (CE). . . ❺ . . . $190–200
☐ 43 . . . . . . 4¾ to 5½" . . . . . (CE). . . ❻ . . . $185–190
☐ 43 . . . . . . 4¾ to 5½" . . . . . (CE). . . ❼ . . . $180–185
☐ 43 . . . . . . 4¾ to 5½" . . . . . (OE). . . ❽ . . . $180

---
**HUM TERM**

**HOLLOW MOLD:** The term used by "M. I. Hummel" collectors to describe a figurine that is open on the underside of the base. With these particular bases the collector can visually see into the cavity of the figurine.

---

*44 A*          *44 B*

## HUM 44 A
### Culprits, Table Lamp
Originally modeled by master sculptor Arthur Moeller in 1935. Older models have a half-inch larger base, and hole for electrical switch on top of base. They usually have a 1935 copyright date incised. "Culprits" table lamp was (TW) "Temporarily Withdrawn" from production on 31 December 1989, but may be reinstated at some future date.

| | | | | |
|---|---|---|---|---|
| ☐ 44 | 8½ to 9½″ | (CE) | **❶** | $650–750 |
| ☐ 44A | 8½ to 9½″ | (CE) | **❶** | $500–650 |
| ☐ 44A | 8½ to 9½″ | (CE) | **❷** | $425–475 |
| ☐ 44A | 8½ to 9½″ | (CE) | **❸** | $400–425 |
| ☐ 44A | 8½″ | (CE) | **❹** | $375–400 |
| ☐ 44A | 8½″ | (CE) | **❺** | $350–375 |
| ☐ 44A | 8½″ | (TW) | **❻** | $325–350 |

## Hum 44 B
### Out of Danger, Table Lamp
Originally modeled by master sculptor Arthur Moeller in 1935. Older models have a half-inch larger base, and hole for electrical switch on top of base. They usually have a 1936 copyright date incised. Variation in color of the girl's dress. Old "crown" trademark (TM 1) examples are found with girl in black dress while the normal blue dress is found on all others. "Out of Danger" table lamp was (TW) "Temporarily Withdrawn" from production on 31 December 1989, but may be reinstated at some future date.

| | | | | |
|---|---|---|---|---|
| ☐ 44B | 8½ to 9½″ | (CE) | **❶** | $500–650 |
| ☐ 44B | 8½ to 9½″ | (CE) | **❷** | $425–475 |
| ☐ 44B | 8½ to 9½″ | (CE) | **❸** | $400–425 |
| ☐ 44B | 8½″ | (CE) | **❹** | $375–400 |
| ☐ 44B | 8½″ | (CE) | **❺** | $350–375 |
| ☐ 44B | 8½″ | (TW) | **❻** | $325–350 |

*Many size and color variations*

**HUM 45**
**Madonna With Halo**

**HUM 46**
**Madonna Without Halo**

These beautiful Madonnas were first modeled by master sculptor Reinhold Unger in 1935. Sometimes called "The Holy Virgin" in old catalogues. There are many size variations as well as color variations. Produced in white overglaze, pastel blue, pastel pink, heavy blue and ivory finish. Also has been found in reddish brown terra cotta finish signed "M. I. Hummel" but without incised number—height 11 inches. Value $2,000 to 3,000. Some pieces have been mismarked 45 instead of 46, etc. Some pieces have been found with both 45 and 46 on the same piece. In the spring of 1982 the large sizes (45/III and 46/III) (both white overglaze finish as well as color) were listed by Goebel as "temporarily withdrawn," to be possibly reinstated at a future date. Sometimes an Arabic size designator is used on older models. The small sizes (45/0 and 46/0), both in white overglaze finish as well as color, were "temporarily withdrawn" (TW) from production on 31 December 1984, but may be reinstated at some future date. The medium size (46/I), both in white overglaze finish and in color, were "temporarily withdrawn" (TW) from production on 31 December 1989, but may be reinstated at some future date. This leaves only the 45/I "Madonna With Halo" as an "open edition" in this series at this time. Some "crown" (TM 1) trademark pieces have been found with*out* the usual "M. I. Hummel" signature, but do have the normal 45 or 46 model number.

*(prices continued on next page)*

|  |  |  | | Color | White |
|---|---|---|---|---|---|
| 45/0 | 10½" | (CE) | ❶ | $200–275 | $125–175 |
| 45/0 | 10½ to 11¾" | (CE) | ❷ | $95–175 | $85–125 |
| 45/0 | 10½" | (CE) | ❸ | $85–95 | $55–70 |
| 45/0 | 10½" | (CE) | ❹ | $70–85 | $50–55 |
| 45/0 | 10½" | (CE) | ❺ | $65–70 | $45–50 |
| 45/0 | 10½" | (TW) | ❻ | $60–65 | $40–45 |

|  |  |  | | Color | White |
|---|---|---|---|---|---|
| 45/I | 11½ to 13¼" | (CE) | ❶ | $300–400 | $150–200 |
| 45/I | 11½ to 13¼" | (CE) | ❷ | $175–225 | $100–150 |
| 45/I | 11½ to 13¼" | (CE) | ❸ | $170–175 | $90–100 |
| 45/I | 11½ to 13¼" | (CE) | ❹ | $165–170 | $85–95 |
| 45/I | 11½ to 13¼" | (CE) | ❺ | $160–165 | $80–85 |
| 45/I | 11½ to 13¼" | (CE) | ❻ | $155–160 | $75–80 |
| 45/I | 11½ to 13¼" | (CE) | ❼ | $150–155 | $75–80 |
| 45/I | 11½ to 13¼" | (OE) | ❽ | $150 |  |
| 45/III | 15½ to 16¾" | (CE) | ❶ | $400–600 | $250–350 |
| 45/III | 15½ to 16¾" | (CE) | ❷ | $275–375 | $175–225 |
| 45/III | 15½ to 16¾" | (CE) | ❸ | $175–220 | $140–165 |
| 45/III | 15½ to 16¾" | (CE) | ❹ | $165–175 | $115–140 |
| 45/III | 15½ to 16¾" | (CE) | ❺ | $155–165 | $110–115 |
| 45/III | 15½ to 16¾" | (TW) | ❻ | $150–155 | $105–110 |

|  |  |  | | Color | White |
|---|---|---|---|---|---|
| 46/0 | 10¼" | (CE) | ❶ | $200–275 | $125–175 |
| 46/0 | 10¼" | (CE) | ❷ | $95–175 | $85–125 |
| 46/0 | 10¼" | (CE) | ❸ | $85–95 | $55–70 |
| 46/0 | 10¼" | (CE) | ❹ | $70–85 | $50–55 |
| 46/0 | 10¼" | (CE) | ❺ | $65–70 | $45–50 |
| 46/0 | 10¼" | (TW) | ❻ | $60–65 | $40–45 |
| 46/I | 11¼ to 13" | (CE) | ❶ | $300–400 | $300–400 |
| 46/I | 11¼ to 13" | (CE) | ❷ | $170–225 | $170–225 |
| 46/I | 11¼ to 13" | (CE) | ❸ | $160–170 | $160–170 |
| 46/I | 11¼ to 13" | (CE) | ❹ | $155–160 | $155–160 |
| 46/I | 11¼ to 13" | (CE) | ❺ | $145–150 | $145–150 |
| 46/I | 11¼ to 13" | (TW) | ❻ | $140–145 | $140–145 |
| 46/III | 15¼ to 16¼" | (CE) | ❶ | $400–600 | $250–350 |
| 46/III | 15¼ to 16¼" | (CE) | ❷ | $275–375 | $175–225 |
| 46/III | 15¼ to 16¼" | (CE) | ❸ | $175–220 | $140–165 |
| 46/III | 15¼ to 16¼" | (CE) | ❹ | $165–175 | $115–140 |
| 46/III | 15¼ to 16¼" | (CE) | ❺ | $155–165 | $110–115 |
| 46/III | 15¼ to 16¼" | (TW) | ❻ | $150–155 | $105–110 |

NOTE: HUM 1 through HUM 46 were all put
on the market in 1935.

---

**HUM TERM**

**WHITE OVERGLAZE**: The term used to
designate an item that has not been
painted, but has been glazed and fired.
These pieces are completely white. All "M. I.
Hummel" items are produced in this finish
before being individually hand painted.

*47/II (TM 5)          47/0 (TM 2)          47/0 (TM 5)          47 3/0 (TM 1)*

## HUM 47
### Goose Girl

First modeled by master sculptor Arthur Moeller in 1936. There are many size variations between the older and newer models. Sometimes called "Little Gooseherd" in old catalogues. Older models have a blade of grass between the geese. This has been eliminated completely or reduced in size on newer models. The large size 47/II was restyled with the new textured finish in the early 1970's. Sometimes incised 47/2 or 47.2. instead of 47/II. Large size (47/II) was listed as (TW) "temporarily withdrawn" on 1993 price list. Recent information located in an old Goebel product book indicates that master sculptor Arthur Moeller in 1935 produced samples of "Goose Girl" in the 47/0 size with a round attached "pot" and another with an oblong attached "bowl." The sample with the "bowl" is now in the collection of a collector in the Midwest. An example with the attached round "pot" was recently found in Europe. For more information, see: Rare/Unique Sample Variations of "M. I. Hummel" Figurines in back of this book.

| ☐ 47 3/0. . . . 4 to 4¼″ . . . . . . (CE). . . ❶ . . . $500–650 |
| ☐ 47 3/0. . . . 4 to 4¼″ . . . . . . (CE). . . ❷ . . . $300–400 |
| ☐ 47 3/0. . . . 4 to 4¼″ . . . . . . (CE). . . ❸ . . . $250–300 |
| ☐ 47 3/0. . . . 4 to 4¼″ . . . . . . (CE). . . ❹ . . . $225–250 |
| ☐ 47 3/0. . . . 4 to 4¼″ . . . . . . (CE). . . ❺ . . . $210–225 |
| ☐ 47 3/0. . . . 4 to 4¼″ . . . . . . (CE). . . ❻ . . . $200–210 |
| ☐ 47 3/0. . . . 4 to 4¼″ . . . . . . (CE). . . ❼ . . . $195–200 |
| ☐ 47 3/0. . . . 4 to 4¼″ . . . . . . (OE). . . ❽ . . . $195 |
| ☐ 47/0 . . . . . 4¾ to 5¼″ . . . . . (CE). . . ❶ . . . $650–800 |
| ☐ 47/0 . . . . . 4¾ to 5¼″ . . . . . (CE). . . ❷ . . . $400–650 |
| ☐ 47/0 . . . . . 4¾ to 5¼″ . . . . . (CE). . . ❸ . . . $350–400 |
| ☐ 47/0 . . . . . 4¾ to 5¼″ . . . . . (CE). . . ❹ . . . $300–350 |
| ☐ 47/0 . . . . . 4¾ to 5¼″ . . . . . (CE). . . ❺ . . . $280–300 |
| ☐ 47/0 . . . . . 4¾ to 5¼″ . . . . . (CE). . . ❻ . . . $275–280 |
| ☐ 47/0 . . . . . 4¾ to 5¼″ . . . . . (CE). . . ❼ . . . $270–275 |
| ☐ 47/0 . . . . . 4¾ to 5¼″ . . . . . (OE). . . ❽ . . . $270 |
| ☐ 47/II . . . . . 7 to 8″. . . . . . . (CE). . . ❶ . . . $1000–1300 |
| ☐ 47/II . . . . . 7 to 8″. . . . . . . (CE). . . ❷ . . . $700–900 |
| ☐ 47/II . . . . . 7 to 7½″ . . . . . . (CE). . . ❸ . . . $600–700 |
| ☐ 47/II . . . . . 7 to 7½″ . . . . . . (CE). . . ❹ . . . $500–600 |
| ☐ 47/II . . . . . 7 to 7½″ . . . . . . (CE). . . ❺ . . . $420–440 |
| ☐ 47/II . . . . . 7 to 7½″ . . . . . . (CE). . . ❻ . . . $410–420 |
| ☐ 47/II . . . . . 7 to 7½″ . . . . . . (TW) . . ❼ . . . $400–410 |
| ☐ 47 . . . . . . 5″ . . . . . . . . . . . (CE). . . ❶ . . . $800–900 |

## HUM 48
## Madonna Plaque

This bas-relief plaque was first modeled by master sculptor Reinhold Unger in 1936. Old crown mark pieces are slightly smaller in size. Newer models have hole on back for hanging while older models have two small holes to use for hanging on wall with cord. Sometimes incised 48/2 instead of 48/II and 48/5 instead of 48/V. Also sold in white overglaze finish at one time in Belgium but are now considered rare. Very early models have a flat back while all others have a recessed back. Large size 48/II was listed as "temporarily withdrawn" (TW) from production on 31 December 1984, and the small size 48/0 was "temporarily withdrawn" (TW) from production on 31 December 1989, but may be reinstated at some future date.

*Current Model*

| | | | | | |
|---|---|---|---|---|---|
| ☐ 48/0 | 3¼ × 4¼″ | (CE) | ❶ | $325–375 |
| ☐ 48/0 | 3¼ × 4¼″ | (CE) | ❷ | $175–225 |
| ☐ 48/0 | 3¼ × 4¼″ | (CE) | ❸ | $110–135 |
| ☐ 48/0 | 3¼ × 4¼″ | (CE) | ❹ | $95–110 |
| ☐ 48/0 | 3⅓ × 4¼″ | (CE) | ❺ | $90–95 |
| ☐ 48/0 | 3¼ × 4¼″ | (TW) | ❻ | $85–90 |
| ☐ 48 | 4¾ × 5¾″ | (CE) | ❶ | $650–850 |
| ☐ 48/II | 4¾ × 5¾″ | (CE) | ❶ | $550–800 |
| ☐ 48/II | 4¾ × 5¾″ | (CE) | ❷ | $375–525 |
| ☐ 48/II | 4¾ × 5¾″ | (CE) | ❸ | $190–250 |
| ☐ 48/II | 4¾ × 5¾″ | (CE) | ❹ | $160–190 |
| ☐ 48/II | 4¾ × 5¾″ | (CE) | ❺ | $135–145 |
| ☐ 48/II | 4¾ × 5¾″ | (TW) | ❻ | $130–135 |
| ☐ 48/V | 8¾ × 10¾″ | (CE) | ❶ | $1500–2000 |
| ☐ 48/V | 8¾ × 10¾″ | (CE) | ❷ | $1250–1500 |
| ☐ 48/V | 8¾ × 10¾″ | (CE) | ❸ | $1000–1250 |
| ☐ 48/II | 4¾ × 5¾″ | (CE) | ❸ | $500–600 (white overglaze) |

*Early sample with bowl*

*White variation of 48/0*

47

*49/I (TM 1+1)*       *49/0 (TM 1+1)*       *49 3/0 (TM 1)*

**HUM 49**
**To Market**

First modeled by master sculptor Arthur Moeller in 1936. Sometimes called "Brother and Sister" in old catalogues. Small size 49 3/0 never has bottle in basket. Some newly produced figurines in 6¼ size have appeared without a size designator. Only the number 49 is incised on the bottom along with the 5 trademark. This was corrected on later production. Girl is same as HUM 98 "Sister." The large size (49/I) was listed as "Temporarily Withdrawn" (TW) on 31 December 1984, but may be reinstated at some future date. The suggested retail price on the large size (49/I) on the 1984 price list was $240. Recent information located in an old Goebel product book indicates that master sculptor Arthur Moeller in 1935 produced a sample of "To Market" in the 5 inch size with an attached "bowl" similar to HUM 13/0 "Meditation" with attached "bowl." An example of this rare piece has NOT been found, as of this writing. For more information, see: Rare/Unique Sample Variations of "M. I. Hummel" Figurines in back of this book. Size (49/0) was listed as (TW) "Temporarily Withdrawn" in January 1999.

| | | | | | |
|---|---|---|---|---|---|
| ☐ 49 3/0 | 4" | (CE) | ❶ | $500–650 |
| ☐ 49 3/0 | 4" | (CE) | ❷ | $300–375 |
| ☐ 49 3/0 | 4" | (CE) | ❸ | $250–275 |
| ☐ 49 3/0 | 4" | (CE) | ❹ | $210–230 |
| ☐ 49 3/0 | 4" | (CE) | ❺ | $200–210 |
| ☐ 49 3/0 | 4" | (CE) | ❻ | $190–200 |
| ☐ 49 3/0 | 4" | (CE) | ❼ | $185–190 |
| ☐ 49 3/0 | 4" | (**OE**) | ❽ | $185 |
| ☐ 49/0 | 5 to 5½" | (CE) | ❶ | $750–1000 |
| ☐ 49/0 | 5 to 5½" | (CE) | ❷ | $450–625 |
| ☐ 49/0 | 5 to 5½" | (CE) | ❸ | $425–450 |
| ☐ 49/0 | 5 to 5½" | (CE) | ❹ | $375–425 |
| ☐ 49/0 | 5 to 5½" | (CE) | ❺ | $350–375 |
| ☐ 49/0 | 5 to 5½" | (CE) | ❻ | $335–350 |
| ☐ 49/0 | 5 to 5½" | (TW) | ❼ | $325–335 |
| ☐ 49/I | 6¼ to 6½" | (CE) | ❶ | $1400–1700 |
| ☐ 49/I | 6¼ to 6½" | (CE) | ❷ | $1200–1400 |
| ☐ 49/I | 6¼ to 6½" | (CE) | ❸ | $550–700 |
| ☐ 49/I | 6¼ to 6¼" | (CE) | ❹ | $500–550 |
| ☐ 49/I | 6¼ to 6¼" | (CE) | ❺ | $450–475 |
| ☐ 49/I | 6¼ to 6¼" | (TW) | ❻ | $425–450 |

*(prices continued on next page)*

| | | | | |
|---|---|---|---|---|
| ☐ 49 | 6¼ to 6½" | (CE) | ❶ | $1400–1700 |
| ☐ 49 | 6¼ to 6½" | (CE) | ❷ | $1200–1400 |
| ☐ 49 | 6¼ to 6½" | (CE) | ❺ | $600–700 |

*50/I (TM 5)*          *50/0 (TM 5)*          *50 2/0 (TM 3)*

## HUM 50
### Volunteers

Originally modeled by master sculptor Reinhold Unger in 1936. Listed as "Playing Soldiers" in old catalogues. Sizes 50/0 and 50/I are difficult to find in older trademarks but were reinstated in 1979 with (TM 5) trademark. The original drawing for this figurine was used by Ars Sacra Herbert Dubler on small note paper bearing a 1943 copyright date. The large size (50/I) was listed as "temporarily withdrawn" (TW) from production on 31 December 1984, but may be reinstated at some future date. The small size (50 2/0) was produced with special commemorative backstamp in limited quantity and was available only through U.S. Military Exchanges; retail price was $150–175. The suggested retail price on the large size (50/I) on the 1984 price list was $240.

| | | | | |
|---|---|---|---|---|
| ☐ 50 2/0 | 4¾ to 5" | (CE) | ❷ | $425–500 |
| ☐ 50 2/0 | 4¾ to 5" | (CE) | ❸ | $350–400 |
| ☐ 50 2/0 | 4¾ to 5" | (CE) | ❹ | $325–350 |
| ☐ 50 2/0 | 4¾ to 5" | (CE) | ❺ | $270–300 |
| ☐ 50 2/0 | 4¾ to 5" | (CE) | ❻ | $260–270 |
| ☐ 50 2/0 | 4¾ to 5" | (CE) | ❼ | $255–260 |
| ☐ 50 2/0 | 4¾ to 5" | (OE) | ❽ | $255 |
| ☐ 50/0 | 5½ to 6" | (CE) | ❶ | $850–1100 |
| ☐ 50/0 | 5½ to 6" | (CE) | ❷ | $500–650 |
| ☐ 50/0 | 5½ to 6" | (CE) | ❸ | $450–475 |
| ☐ 50/0 | 5½ to 6" | (CE) | ❹ | $400–450 |
| ☐ 50/0 | 5½ to 6" | (CE) | ❺ | $360–390 |
| ☐ 50/0 | 5½ to 6" | (CE) | ❻ | $355–360 |
| ☐ 50/0 | 5½ to 6" | (CE) | ❼ | $350–355 |
| ☐ 50/0 | 4¾ to 6" | (OE) | ❽ | $350 |
| ☐ 50/I | 6½ to 7" | (CE) | ❶ | $1200–1500 |
| ☐ 50/I | 6½ to 7" | (CE) | ❷ | $750–950 |
| ☐ 50/I | 6½ to 7" | (CE) | ❸ | $600–750 |

*HUM 50 2/0 (TM 7)*
*Commemorative*

*(prices continued on next page)*

49

| 50/I | 6½ to 7" | (CE) | ❹ | $550–600 |
|---|---|---|---|---|
| 50/I | 6½ to 7" | (CE) | ❺ | $475–500 |
| 50/I | 6½ to 7" | (TW) | ❻ | $450–475 |
| 50 | 7" | (CE) | ❶ | $1250–1550 |

*51/I (TM1)*　　　*51/0 (TM 1)*　　　*51 2/0 (TM 5)*　　　*50 3/0 (TM 1)*

**HUM 51**
**Village Boy**
First modeled by master sculptor Arthur Moeller in 1936. Has been slightly restyled several times through the years. Size 51/0 was restyled by Theo R. Menzenbach in 1960. Some newer models have a 1961 incised copyright date. Called "Country Boy" in old catalogues. Many size variations in the older pieces. Occasionally found in the small size 51 3/0 in crown trademark with yellow tie and blue jacket—value: $1500–2000. The large size (51/I) was listed as "temporarily withdrawn" (TW) from production on 31 December 1984, but could possibly be reinstated at some future date. The small size 51 3/0 are also found with orange socks in (TM 1) & (TM 2) trademarks. In 1996 a new 2¾" size (3¼" with base) with incised model number 51 5/0 was produced as part of the six piece set of "Pen Pals" series of personalized name card table decorations. The original issue price was $55 in 1996.

| 51 5/0 | 3" | (OE) | ❼ | $55 |
|---|---|---|---|---|
| 51 3/0 | 4" | (CE) | ❶ | $350–450 |
| 51 3/0 | 4" | (CE) | ❷ | $225–300 |
| 51 3/0 | 4" | (CE) | ❸ | $175–200 |
| 51 3/0 | 4" | (CE) | ❹ | $155–175 |
| 51 3/0 | 4" | (CE) | ❺ | $150–155 |
| 51 3/0 | 4" | (CE) | ❻ | $145–150 |
| 51 3/0 | 4" | (CE) | ❼ | $140–145 |
| 51 3/0 | 4" | (OE) | ❽ | $140 |
| 51 2/0 | 5" | (CE) | ❶ | $400–525 |
| 51 2/0 | 5" | (CE) | ❷ | $250–350 |
| 51 2/0 | 5" | (CE) | ❸ | $225–250 |
| 51 2/0 | 5" | (CE) | ❹ | $200–225 |
| 51 2/0 | 5" | (CE) | ❺ | $185–200 |
| 51 2/0 | 5" | (CE) | ❻ | $180–185 |
| 51 2/0 | 5" | (CE) | ❼ | $175–180 |
| 51 2/0 | 5" | (OE) | ❽ | $175 |
| 51/0 | 6 to 6¾" | (CE) | ❶ | $700–900 |
| 51/0 | 6 to 6¾" | (CE) | ❷ | $450–550 |

*(prices continued on next page)*

| | | | | | |
|---|---|---|---|---|---|
| ☐ 51/0 . . . . . 6 to 6¾" . . . . . . (CE). . . **❸** . . . $375–400 |
| ☐ 51/0 . . . . . 6 to 6¾" . . . . . . (CE). . . **❹** . . . $325–375 |
| ☐ 51/0 . . . . . 6 to 6¾" . . . . . . (CE). . . **❺** . . . $300–325 |
| ☐ 51/0 . . . . . 6 to 6¾" . . . . . . (CE). . . **❻** . . . $290–300 |
| ☐ 51/0 . . . . . 6 to 6¾" . . . . . . (TW) . . **❼** . . . $280–285 |
| ☐ 51/I . . . . . 7¼ to 8" . . . . . . (CE). . . **❶** . . . $800–1100 |
| ☐ 51/I . . . . . 7¼ to 8" . . . . . . (CE). . . **❷** . . . $500–600 |
| ☐ 51/I . . . . . 7¼ to 8" . . . . . . (CE). . . **❸** . . . $400–475 |
| ☐ 51/I . . . . . 7¼ to 8" . . . . . . (CE). . . **❹** . . . $350–400 |
| ☐ 51/I . . . . . 7¼ to 8" . . . . . . (CE). . . **❺** . . . $320–350 |
| ☐ 51/I . . . . . 7¼ to 8" . . . . . . (TW) . . **❻** . . . $300–320 |
| ☐ 51 . . . . . . 8" . . . . . . . . . . . (CE). . . **❶** . . . $900–1150 |

Old    52/I    New            Old    52/0    New

## HUM 52
### Going to Grandma's
Originally modeled in 1936 by master sculptor Reinhold Unger. Called "Little Mothers of the Family" in old catalogues. All large size and older small size figurines were produced with rectangular base. Small size was restyled in the early 1960's and changed to an oval base. The objects protruding from the cone represent candy and sweets rather than flowers. The cone appears empty on the large size models. In 1979 size 52/I was restyled with a new textured finish, an oval base and sweets in the cone. Both the old and new styles are found with (TM 5) trademark. The large size (52/I) was listed as "Temporarily Withdrawn" (TW) from production on 31 December 1984, but could possibly be reinstated at some future date. The suggested retail price on the large size 52/I on the 1984 price list was $240. On most older figurines, the girl with the basket has a pink colored petticoat painted under her dress. The other girl has only a blue hemline showing. Newer models in trademarks 4, 5, 6 and 7 do *not* have this area painted.

| | | | | | |
|---|---|---|---|---|---|
| ☐ 52/0 . . . . . 4½ to 5" . . . . . . (CE). . . **❶** . . . $750–1000 |
| ☐ 52/0 . . . . . 4½ to 5" . . . . . . (CE). . . **❷** . . . $450–600 |
| ☐ 52/0 . . . . . 4½ to 5" . . . . . . (CE). . . **❸** . . . $400–450 |
| ☐ 52/0 . . . . . 4½ to 5" . . . . . . (CE). . . **❹** . . . $325–375 |
| ☐ 52/0 . . . . . 4½ to 5" . . . . . . (CE). . . **❺** . . . $300–325 |

*(prices continued on next page)*

| | | | | | |
|---|---|---|---|---|---|
| ☐ 52/0 | 4½ to 5" | (CE) | ❻ | $290–300 |
| ☐ 52/0 | 4½ to 5" | (CE) | ❼ | $285–290 |
| ☐ 52/0 | 4½ to 5" | **(OE)** | ❽ | $285 |
| ☐ 52/I | 6 to 6¼" | (CE) | ❶ | $1250–1500 |
| ☐ 52/I | 6 to 6¼" | (CE) | ❷ | $800–950 |
| ☐ 52/I | 6 to 6¼" | (CE) | ❸ | $650–800 |
| ☐ 52/I | 6 to 6¼" | (CE) | ❺ | $550–800 old style (rectangular) |
| ☐ 52/I | 6 to 6½" | (CE) | ❺ | $425–525 new style (oval) |
| ☐ 52/I | 6 to 6¼" | (TW) | ❻ | $400–425 |
| ☐ 52 | 6¼" | (CE) | ❶ | $1300–1600 |
| ☐ 52 | 6¼" | (CE) | ❷ | $850–1000 |

**HUM 53**
**Joyful**

First modeled by master sculptor Reinhold Unger in 1936. Many size variations—older pieces usually much larger. Listed as "Singing Lesson" in old catalogues, but also called "Banjo Betty" in an old 1950 catalogue. Some early crown (TM 1) trademark examples have orange dress and blue, purple or brown shoes. Value: $2,000 to 3,000. Newer models have a brown banjo. A sample was produced by Reinhold Unger in 1936 of "Joyful" with an attached "pot" but was not approved by the Siessen Convent for production. Value: $5,000 to $10,000. For more information, see: Rare/Unique Sample Variations of "M. I. Hummel" figurines in back of this book. Listed as (TW) "Temporarily Withdrawn" in January 1999.

| | | | | | |
|---|---|---|---|---|---|
| ☐ 53 | 3½ to 4¼" | (CE) | ❶ | $350–450 |
| ☐ 53 | 3½ to 4¼" | (CE) | ❷ | $225–300 |
| ☐ 53 | 3½ to 4¼" | (CE) | ❸ | $190–220 |
| ☐ 53 | 3½" | (CE) | ❹ | $170–190 |
| ☐ 53 | 3½" | (CE) | ❺ | $150–170 |
| ☐ 53 | 3½" | (CE) | ❻ | $145–150 |
| ☐ 53 | 3½" | (TW) | ❼ | $140–145 |

---

**PRICES IN THIS GUIDE**

We are in a period of DISCOUNTING of many items in our society. "M.I. Hummel" figurines are no exception. The prices in this guide give the relative values in relationship to new or current prices of (TM 8) trademark items. If the new figurines are discounted, the older models will likely be discounted, too, but possibly in a lesser degree. This guide reduces all items to one common denominator.

| Old bowl style | New jar style | New music box |

## HUM III/53
### Joyful, Box

Bowl style box first produced in 1936. Jar style first produced and sold in 1964. Model number is found on underside of lid. "M. I. Hummel" signature is found on topside of lid directly behind figure. "Joyful" candy box was "Temporarily Withdrawn" (TW) from production on 31 December 1989, but may be reinstated at some future date. In 1996 a new music box was produced with model number IV/53 applied by decal on the bottom. This is one of four in a series of music boxes produced for the European market only at this time. May be sold in the U.S. market at some future date. Newer models have a brown banjo.

☐ III/53 . . . . 6½″ . . . . . . . . . . (CE). . . ❶ . . . $750–850
☐ III/53 . . . . 6½″ . . . . . . . . . . (CE). . . ❷ . . . $575–650
☐ III/53 . . . . 6½″ . . . . . . . . . . (CE). . . ❸ . . . $475–550 (Old Style)
☐ III/53 . . . . 5¾″ . . . . . . . . . . (CE). . . ❸ . . . $300–350 (New Style)
☐ III/53 . . . . 5¾″ . . . . . . . . . . (CE). . . ❹ . . . $250–275
☐ III/53 . . . . 5¾″ . . . . . . . . . . (CE). . . ❺ . . . $225–250
☐ III/53 . . . . 5¾″ . . . . . . . . . . (TW) . . ❻ . . . $200–225
☐ IV/53 . . . . 5¾″ . . . . . . . . . . (CE). . . ❼ . . . $175 (approximate) (Europe only)

---

### HUM TERM

**OUT OF PRODUCTION:** A term used by the Goebel Company to designate items that are not currently in production, yet have not been given an official classification as to their eventual fate. Some items listed as out of production may become closed editions, remain temporarily withdrawn, or ultimately return to current production status.

## HUM 54
### Silent Night, Candleholder

This candleholder was first modeled by master sculptor Reinhold Unger in 1936. There are some color variations in the wings of angel. Early crown mark figurines are usually very light in color. Older pieces have smaller socket for candle. Almost identical to the model used for HUM 31 with the exception of the embossed earring and bare feet. Factory representatives state that a small quantity of HUM 54 were painted with a black child in the standing position—usually wearing shoes, but also found with bare feet and painted toes, and a painted rather than an embossed earring. An unusual painting variation recently found painted with *two* black children. Listed as (TW) "Temporarily Withdrawn" in January 1999.

| | | | | |
|---|---|---|---|---|
| ☐ 54 | 3½ × 4¾" | (CE) | ❶ | $850–1100 |
| ☐ 54 | 3½ × 4¾" | (CE) | ❷ | $550–700 |
| ☐ 54 | 3½ × 4¾" | (CE) | ❸ | $475–500 |
| ☐ 54 | 3½ × 4¾" | (CE) | ❹ | $425–475 |
| ☐ 54 | 3½ × 4¾" | (CE) | ❺ | $400–425 |
| ☐ 54 | 3½ × 4¾" | (CE) | ❻ | $375–395 |
| ☐ 54 | 3½ × 4¾" | (CE) | ❶ | $10,000–12,000 (with Black Child) |
| ☐ 54 | 3½ × 4¾" | (CE) | ❷ | $7,500–10,000 (with Black Child) |
| ☐ 54 | 3½ × 4¾" | (CE) | ❷ | $10,000–15,000 (*two* Black Children) |
| ☐ 54 | 3½ × 4¾" | (TW) | ❼ | $360–370 |

---

**HUM TERM**

**UNDERGLAZE:** The term used to describe especially the number 5 trademark that appears actually underneath the glaze as opposed to the later version of the number 5 trademark that appears on the top of the glaze.

*Old style*          *New style*

*Old style*          *New style*

## HUM 55
### Saint George

First modeled by master sculptor Reinhold Unger in 1936. Early crown mark models are sometimes found with bright orange-red saddle on horse. Old name: "Knight St. George" or "St. George and Dragon." The original drawing by Sister Hummel for this figurine was reproduced in the 1934 German edition of "Das Hummel Buch," published by Emil Fink of Stuttgart, Germany. Restyled in 1986. Variations in the wings of the dragon and minor changes in the tail of horse. It appears that the factory was probably experiencing excessive breakage in this figurine. Was listed as (TW) "Temporarily Withdrawn" from production in January 1999, but could possibly be reinstated at some future date.

| | | | | |
|---|---|---|---|---|
| ☐ 55 | 6¾" | (CE) | ❶ | $2500–3000 (with Red saddle) |
| ☐ 55 | 6¾" | (CE) | ❶ | $1000–1300 |
| ☐ 55 | 6¾" | (CE) | ❷ | $600–750 |
| ☐ 55 | 6¾" | (CE) | ❸ | $450–525 |
| ☐ 55 | 6¾" | (CE) | ❹ | $400–450 |
| ☐ 55 | 6¾" | (CE) | ❺ | $375–400 |
| ☐ 55 | 6¾" | (CE) | ❻ | $360–375 |
| ☐ 55 | 6¾" | (TW) | ❼ | $350–360 |

56A       56B

## HUM 56 A
**Culprits**
Originally modeled in 1936 by master sculptor Arthur Moeller but has been restyled in later years. Restyled figurines have an extra branch by boy's feet. Variations in height and size of base. Old name "Apple Thief." Crown mark and early full bee trademarked pieces incised 56 only. Older models have the boy's eyes open while newer version eyes are looking down at dog.

| | | | | | |
|---|---|---|---|---|---|
| ☐ 56 | 6¼ to 6¾″ | (CE) | ❶ | $850–1100 |
| ☐ 56/A | 6¼ to 6¾″ | (CE) | ❷ | $500–650 |
| ☐ 56/A | 6¼ to 6¾″ | (CE) | ❸ | $450–500 |
| ☐ 56/A | 6¼ to 6¾″ | (CE) | ❹ | $375–450 |
| ☐ 56/A | 6¼ to 6¾″ | (CE) | ❺ | $360–375 |
| ☐ 56/A | 6¼ to 6¾″ | (CE) | ❻ | $350–360 |
| ☐ 56/A | 6¼ to 6¾″ | (CE) | ❼ | $345–350 |
| ☐ 56/A | 6¼ to 6¾″ | (OE) | ❽ | $345 |

## HUM 56 B
**Out of Danger**
This companion figurine was first modeled by master sculptor Arthur Moeller in March of 1952, therefore will not be found with the crown trademark. Variation in height, and size of base. On older models the girl's eyes are open; on the newer version her eyes are looking down at dog. Full bee models have an extra flower on base.

| | | | | | |
|---|---|---|---|---|---|
| ☐ 56/B | 6¼ to 6¾″ | (CE) | ❷ | $500–650 |
| ☐ 56/B | 6¼ to 6¾″ | (CE) | ❸ | $450–500 |
| ☐ 56/B | 6¼ to 6¾″ | (CE) | ❹ | $375–450 |
| ☐ 56/B | 6¼ to 6¾″ | (CE) | ❺ | $360–375 |
| ☐ 56/B | 6¼ to 6¾″ | (CE) | ❻ | $350–360 |
| ☐ 56/B | 6¼ to 6¾″ | (CE) | ❼ | $345–350 |
| ☐ 56/B | 6¼ to 6¾″ | (OE) | ❽ | $345 |

**57/1**        **57/0**

## HUM 57
## Chick Girl

First modeled by master sculptor Reinhold Unger in 1936 and later remodeled by master sculptor Gerhard Skrobek in 1964. Small size has two chicks in basket while large size has three chicks. Old name: "Little Chicken Mother" or "The Little Chick Girl." There are three different styles of construction that have been used on bottom of base: quartered, doughnut and plain. A new small size (57 2/0) was issued in 1985 with a suggested retail price of $60. Has an incised 1984 copyright date. According to old Goebel product book, a sample was produced by Arthur Moeller in 1936 of "Chick Girl" with an attached "pot," similar to HUM 16/I "Little Hiker" with attached "pot." Value: $5,000 to 7,000 if found. For more information, see: Rare/Unique Sample Variations of "M. I. Hummel" figurines in back of this book.

| | | | | |
|---|---|---|---|---|
| ☐ 57 2/0 | . . . 3″ | (CE) | ❻ | . . . . $180–190 |
| ☐ 57 2/0 | . . . 3″ | (CE) | ❼ | . . . . $175–180 |
| ☐ 57 2/0 | . . . 3″ | **(OE)** | ❽ | . . . . $175 |
| ☐ 57/0 | . . . . 3½″ | (CE) | ❶ | . . . . $500–650 |
| ☐ 57/0 | . . . . 3½″ | (CE) | ❷ | . . . . $300–375 |
| ☐ 57/0 | . . . . 3½″ | (CE) | ❸ | . . . . $250–290 |
| ☐ 57/0 | . . . . 3½″ | (CE) | ❹ | . . . . $225–250 |
| ☐ 57/0 | . . . . 3½″ | (CE) | ❺ | . . . . $210–220 |
| ☐ 57/0 | . . . . 3½″ | (CE) | ❻ | . . . . $200–210 |
| ☐ 57/0 | . . . . 3½″ | (CE) | ❼ | . . . . $195–200 |
| ☐ 57/0 | . . . . 3½″ | **(OE)** | ❽ | . . . . $195 |
| ☐ 57/I | . . . . 4¼″ | (CE) | ❶ | . . . . $750–1000 |
| ☐ 57/I | . . . . 4¼″ | (CE) | ❷ | . . . . $450–600 |
| ☐ 57/I | . . . . 4¼″ | (CE) | ❸ | . . . . $400–450 |
| ☐ 57/I | . . . . 4¼″ | (CE) | ❹ | . . . . $350–400 |
| ☐ 57/I | . . . . 4¼″ | (CE) | ❺ | . . . . $340–350 |
| ☐ 57/I | . . . . 4¼″ | (CE) | ❻ | . . . . $320–340 |
| ☐ 57/I | . . . . 4¼″ | (TW) Jan '99 | ❼ | . . . . $310–320 |
| ☐ 57 | . . . . . 4 to 4⅜″ | (CE) | ❶ | . . . . $800–1050 |
| ☐ 57 | . . . . . 3¾ to 4⅜″ | (CE) | ❷ | . . . . $500–650 |

*Old bowl style*     *New jar style*     *New music box*

### HUM III/57 Chick Girl, Box

Bowl style first produced in 1936. Jar style first produced and sold in 1964. Sometimes found with the incised number III 57/0 on the bowl style pieces. Model number is found on underside of lid. "M. I. Hummel" signature is found on topside of lid directly behind figure. "Chick Girl" candy box was (TW) "Temporarily Withdrawn" from production on 31 December 1989, but may be reinstated at some future date. In 1996 a new music box was produced with model number IV/57 applied by decal on the bottom. This is one of four in a series of music boxes produced for the European market only at this time. May be sold in the U.S. market at some future date.

| | | | | | | |
|---|---|---|---|---|---|---|
| ☐ III/57 | . . . . | 6 to 6¼″ | . . . . . . | (CE) | . . . ❶ | . . . $750–850 |
| ☐ III/57 | . . . . | 6 to 6¼″ | . . . . . . | (CE) | . . . ❷ | . . . $575–650 |
| ☐ III/57 | . . . . | 6 to 6¼″ | . . . . . . | (CE) | . . . ❸ | . . . $475–550 (Old Style) |
| ☐ III/57 | . . . . | 5″ | . . . . . . . . | (CE) | . . . ❸ | . . . $300–350 (New Style) |
| ☐ III/57 | . . . . | 5″ | . . . . . . . . | (CE) | . . . ❹ | . . . $250–275 |
| ☐ III/57 | . . . . | 5″ | . . . . . . . . | (CE) | . . . ❺ | . . . $225–250 |
| ☐ III/57 | . . . . | 5″ | . . . . . . . . | (TW) | . . . ❻ | . . . $200–225 |
| ☐ IV/57 | . . . . | 6″ | . . . . . . . . | (CE) | . . . ❼ | . . . $175 (approximate) (Europe only) |

*58/I*　　　*58/0*

### HUM 58
### Playmates

Originally modeled by master sculptor Reinhold Unger in 1936 and later restyled by master sculptor Gerhard Skrobek in 1964. Some size and color variations between old and new figurines. Both ears of rabbit pointing up on large size 58/I. Ears are separated on small size 58/0. Old name: "Just Friends." Three different styles of construction on bottom of base: quartered, doughnut and plain. A new small size (58 2/0) "Playmates" was issued in 1986 with a suggested retail price of $68. Has an incised 1984 copyright date. According to old Goebel product book, a sample was produced by Reinhold Unger in 1936 of "Playmates" with an attached "pot," similar to HUM 16/I "Little Hiker" with attached "pot." Value: $5,000 to 7,000 if found. No known examples. For more information, see: Rare/Unique Sample Variations of "M. I. Hummel" figurines in back of this book.

| | | | | | |
|---|---|---|---|---|---|
| ☐ 58 2/0 | . . . 3½″ | . . . . . . . . . | (CE) | . . . . . . ❻ | . . . $180–185 |
| ☐ 58 2/0 | . . . 3½″ | . . . . . . . . . | (CE) | . . . . . . ❼ | . . . $175–180 |
| ☐ 58 2/0 | . . . 3½″ | . . . . . . . . . | (**OE**) | . . . . . . ❽ | . . . $175 |
| ☐ 58/0 | . . . . . 4″ | . . . . . . . . . | (CE) | . . . . . . ❶ | . . . $500–650 |
| ☐ 58/0 | . . . . . 4″ | . . . . . . . . . | (CE) | . . . . . . ❷ | . . . $300–375 |
| ☐ 58/0 | . . . . . 4″ | . . . . . . . . . | (CE) | . . . . . . ❸ | . . . $250–290 |
| ☐ 58/0 | . . . . . 4″ | . . . . . . . . . | (CE) | . . . . . . ❹ | . . . $225–250 |
| ☐ 58/0 | . . . . . 4″ | . . . . . . . . . | (CE) | . . . . . . ❺ | . . . $210–220 |
| ☐ 58/0 | . . . . . 4″ | . . . . . . . . . | (CE) | . . . . . . ❻ | . . . $200–210 |
| ☐ 58/0 | . . . . . 4″ | . . . . . . . . . | (CE) | . . . . . . ❼ | . . . $195–200 |
| ☐ 58/0 | . . . . . 4″ | . . . . . . . . . | (**OE**) | . . . . . . ❽ | . . . $195 |
| ☐ 58/I | . . . . 4¼″ | . . . . . . . . . | (CE) | . . . . . . ❶ | . . . $750–1000 |
| ☐ 58/I | . . . . 4¼″ | . . . . . . . . . | (CE) | . . . . . . ❷ | . . . $450–600 |
| ☐ 58/I | . . . . 4¼″ | . . . . . . . . . | (CE) | . . . . . . ❸ | . . . $400–450 |
| ☐ 58/I | . . . . 4¼″ | . . . . . . . . . | (CE) | . . . . . . ❹ | . . . $350–400 |
| ☐ 58/I | . . . . 4¼″ | . . . . . . . . . | (CE) | . . . . . . ❺ | . . . $340–350 |
| ☐ 58/I | . . . . 4¼″ | . . . . . . . . . | (CE) | . . . . . . ❻ | . . . $320–340 |
| ☐ 58/I | . . . . 4¼″ | . . . . . . . . . | (TW) Jan '99 | . . . ❼ | . . . $310–320 |
| ☐ 58 | . . . . . . 4 to 4½″ | . . . . . . | (CE) | . . . . . . ❶ | . . . $800–1050 |
| ☐ 58 | . . . . . . 4 to 4½″ | . . . . . . | (CE) | . . . . . . ❷ | . . . $500–650 |

Old bowl style    New jar style    New    New

## HUM III/58   Playmates, Box

Bowl style first produced in 1936. Jar style first produced and sold in 1964. Sometimes found with the incised number III 58/0 on the old bowl style pieces. Model number is found on underside of lid. "M. I. Hummel" signature is found on topside of lid directly behind figure. "Playmates" candy box was (TW) "Temporarily Withdrawn" from production on 31 December 1989. In 1996 a new music box was produced with model number IV/58 applied by decal on the bottom. This is one of four in a series of music boxes produced for the European market only at this time. In 1996 a new "M. I. Hummel" collector box was issued through The Danbury Mint, Norwalk, CT and sold by mail order only. It is the same as the "jar" style box. The only difference is that color graphics have been added.

☐ III/58 . . . . 6¾" . . . . . . . . . (CE). . . ❶ . . . $750–850
☐ III/58 . . . . 6¾" . . . . . . . . . (CE). . . ❷ . . . $575–650
☐ III/58 . . . . 6¾" . . . . . . . . . (CE). . . ❸ . . . $475–550 (Old Style)
☐ III/58 . . . . 5½" . . . . . . . . . (CE). . . ❸ . . . $300–350 (New Style)
☐ III/58 . . . . 5½" . . . . . . . . . (CE). . . ❹ . . . $250–275
☐ III/58 . . . . 5½" . . . . . . . . . (CE). . . ❺ . . . $225–250
☐ III/58 . . . . 5½" . . . . . . . . . (CE). . . ❻ . . . $200–225
☐ III/58 . . . . 5½" . . . . . . . . . (CE). . . ❼ . . . $200 (plus shipping) (Danbury)
☐ IV/58 . . . . 6½" . . . . . . . . . (CE). . . ❼ . . . $175 (approximate) (Europe only)

Wooden poles      Plastic poles      Metal poles

## HUM 59
### Skier

First modeled by master sculptor Reinhold Unger in 1936. Older models were sold with wooden poles and fiber disks; newer models with plastic poles for a short period of time. The metal poles have been used since 1970. Many size variations; the full bee pieces usually the largest. Original wooden poles are reflected in the prices of the older models. Original plastic poles are the most difficult to locate and some avid collectors would probably pay a premium for them.

*(prices continued on next page)*

| ☐ 59 | . . . . . . 5 to 6". . . . . . . . | (CE). . . ❶ . . . | $700–850 |
| ☐ 59 | . . . . . . 5 to 6". . . . . . . . | (CE). . . ❷ . . . | $400–525 |
| ☐ 59 | . . . . . . 5 to 6". . . . . . . . | (CE). . . ❸ . . . | $325–350 |
| ☐ 59 | . . . . . . 5 to 6". . . . . . . . | (CE). . . ❹ . . . | $270–300 |
| ☐ 59 | . . . . . . 5 to 6". . . . . . . . | (CE). . . ❺ . . . | $245–270 |
| ☐ 59 | . . . . . . 5 to 6". . . . . . . . | (CE). . . ❻ . . . | $240–245 |
| ☐ 59 | . . . . . . 5 to 6". . . . . . . . | (CE). . . ❼ . . . | $235–240 |
| ☐ 59 | . . . . . . 5 to 6". . . . . . . . | (OE). . . ❽ . . . | $235 |

60B          60/A

### HUM 60 A Farm Boy
### HUM 60 B Goose Girl, Bookends

First produced in September 1936. Trademarks usually stamped on wood base rather than on figurine. The number 60 A is found incised on bottom of feet of "Farm Boy" in crown and full bee trademarks. Have been unable to find a similar number on any "Goose Girls" that have been separated from wooden base. See HUM 148 and HUM 149 for additional information. This pair of bookends was listed as "temporarily withdrawn" (TW) from production on 31 December 1984, but may be reinstated at some future date. Note: 60/A and 60/B have "Hummel" incised on back of slippers on some TM 1 and TM 2 examples.

| ☐ 60 A&B | . . 4¾". . . . . . . . . . | (CE). . . ❶ . . . | $950–1250 |
| ☐ 60 A&B | . . 4¾". . . . . . . . . . | (CE). . . ❷ . . . | $650–950 |
| ☐ 60 A&B | . . 4¾". . . . . . . . . . | (CE). . . ❸ . . . | $425–500 |
| ☐ 60 A&B | . . 4¾". . . . . . . . . . | (CE). . . ❹ . . . | $425–500 |
| ☐ 60 A&B | . . 4¾". . . . . . . . . . | (CE). . . ❺ . . . | $400–425 |
| ☐ 60 A&B | . . 4¾". . . . . . . . . . | (TW) . . ❻ . . . | $400–425 |

**HUM 61 A Playmates**
**HUM 61 B Chick Girl, Bookends**
First produced in November 1936. Trademarks stamped on wood base rather than on figurine. This pair of bookends was listed as "temporarily withdrawn" (TW) on 31 December 1984, but may be reinstated at some future date.

☐ 61 A&B . . 4" . . . . . . . . . . . . (CE). . . ❶ . . . $950–1250
☐ 61 A&B . . 4" . . . . . . . . . . . . (CE). . . ❷ . . . $650–950
☐ 61 A&B . . 4" . . . . . . . . . . . . (CE). . . ❸ . . . $425–500
☐ 61 A&B . . 4" . . . . . . . . . . . . (CE). . . ❹ . . . $425–500
☐ 61 A&B . . 4" . . . . . . . . . . . . (CE). . . ❺ . . . $400–425
☐ 61 A&B . . 4" . . . . . . . . . . . . (TW) . . ❻ . . . $400–425

**HUM 62**
**Happy Pastime, Ashtray**
Slight difference in construction of ashtray on older models. Crown mark piece has "M. I. Hummel" signature on back of ashtray while newer models have signature on back of girl. First modeled by master sculptor Arthur Moeller in 1936. "Happy Pastime" ashtray was "temporarily withdrawn" (TW) from production on 31 December 1989, but may be reinstated at some future date.

☐ 62 . . . . . . 3½ × 6¼" . . . . . . (CE). . . ❶ . . . $450–650
☐ 62 . . . . . . 3½ × 6¼" . . . . . . (CE). . . ❷ . . . $300–350
☐ 62 . . . . . . 3½ × 6¼" . . . . . . (CE). . . ❸ . . . $225–250
☐ 62 . . . . . . 3½ × 6¼" . . . . . . (CE). . . ❹ . . . $200–225
☐ 62 . . . . . . 3½ × 6¼" . . . . . . (CE). . . ❺ . . . $175–200
☐ 62 . . . . . . 3½ × 6¼" . . . . . . (TW) . . ❻ . . . $150–175

## HUM 63
## Singing Lesson

First modeled by master sculptor Arthur Moeller in 1937. Some variations in size between old and new models. Sometimes a slight variation in tilt of boy's head and position of hand. Old name: "Duet" or "Critic." "Singing Lesson" is the motif used on the 1979 Annual Plate, HUM 272. Sometimes found with no "dots" on horn. Older models have a donut base while newer models have a plain base. Also found with either one, two or three flowers on hat.

| ☐ 63 | 2¾ to 3" | (CE) | ❶ | $400–500 |
| ☐ 63 | 2¾ to 3" | (CE) | ❷ | $250–350 |
| ☐ 63 | 2¾ to 3" | (CE) | ❸ | $180–200 |
| ☐ 63 | 2¾ to 3" | (CE) | ❹ | $160–180 |
| ☐ 63 | 2¾ to 3" | (CE) | ❺ | $155–160 |
| ☐ 63 | 2¾ to 3" | (CE) | ❻ | $150–155 |
| ☐ 63 | 2¾ to 3" | (CE) | ❼ | $145–150 |
| ☐ 63 | 2¾ to 3" | (OE) | ❽ | $145 |

*Old bowl style*          *New jar style*          *New music box*

## HUM III/63
## Singing Lesson, Box

Bowl style first produced in 1937. Jar style first produced and sold in 1964. Old name: "Duet" box. Model number is found on underside of lid. "M. I. Hummel" signature is found on topside of lid directly behind figure. "Singing Lesson" candy box was "temporarily withdrawn" (TW) from production on 31 December 1989, but may be reinstated at some future date. In 1996 a new music box was produced with model number IV/63 applied by decal on the bottom. This is one of four in a series of music boxes produced for the European market only at this time. May be sold in the U.S. market at some future date.

| ☐ III/63 | 5¾" | (CE) | ❶ | $750–850 |
| ☐ III/63 | 5¾" | (CE) | ❷ | $575–650 |
| ☐ III/63 | 5¾" | (CE) | ❸ | $475–550 (Old Style) |
| ☐ III/63 | 4¾" | (CE) | ❸ | $300–350 (New Style) |
| ☐ III/63 | 4¾" | (CE) | ❹ | $250–275 |
| ☐ III/63 | 4¾" | (CE) | ❺ | $225–250 |
| ☐ III/63 | 4¾" | (TW) | ❻ | $200–225 |
| ☐ IV/63 | 4¾" | (CE) | ❼ | $175 (approximate) (Europe only) |

*(TM 2)*          *Double crown (TM 1+1)*          *(TM 3)*

## HUM 64
### Shepherd's Boy
First modeled by master sculptor Arthur Moeller in 1937. Restyled with the new tex-tured finish in the late 1970's by master sculptor Gerhard Skrobek. Many size varia-tions—note photo. Old name: "The Good Shepherd." "Shepherd's Boy" sold for $9.00 on old 1955 price list. Older figurines have a donut base while newer models have a plain base.

☐ 64 . . . . . . 5½ to 6¼" . . . . . (CE). . . **❶** . . . $700–850
☐ 64 . . . . . . 5½ to 6¼" . . . . . (CE). . . **❷** . . . $400–550
☐ 64 . . . . . . 5½ to 6¼" . . . . . (CE). . . **❸** . . . $350–400
☐ 64 . . . . . . 5½" . . . . . . . . . . (CE). . . **❹** . . . $300–350
☐ 64 . . . . . . 5½" . . . . . . . . . . (CE). . . **❺** . . . $290–300
☐ 64 . . . . . . 5½" . . . . . . . . . . (CE). . . **❻** . . . $280–285
☐ 64 . . . . . . 5½" . . . . . . . . . . (CE). . . **❼** . . . $275–280
☐ 64 . . . . . . 5½" . . . . . . . . . . (OE). . . **❽** . . . $275

┌──────── **HUM TERM** ────────┐

**DOUGHNUT BASE**: A term used to describe the raised circular support on the underside of a figurine. Many figurine bases with a cir-cle inside the regular circular base gave rise to the term, but has now been used to describe many bases with the circular sup-port on the underside.

└────────────────────────┘

*65 (TM 2)*          *65/I (TM 3)*          *65/0 (TM 2)*

## HUM 65
### Farewell

First modeled by master sculptor Arthur Moeller in 1937. Restyled in 1964 by master sculptor Gerhard Skrobek. The small size (65/0) was modeled in 1955 by Gerhard Skrobek. 65/0 is extremely rare since only a few sample pieces were produced. Called "So Long" or "Good Bye" in some old catalogues. Many size variations. Currently produced in only one size with incised number 65 only. A new variation of "Farewell" was created by error in the early 1980's. During the assembly process, the basket was improperly placed, giving the appearance that part of the handle was missing. This "missing handle" variation now commands a premium of $50 to $100. "Farewell" was permanently retired at the end of 1993 and will not be produced again. The 1993 production bear a special "FINAL ISSUE" backstamp and a small gold "FINAL ISSUE" commemorative tag.

| | | | | | |
|---|---|---|---|---|---|
| ☐ 65 | 4¾" | (CE) | ❺ | $325–350 |
| ☐ 65 | 4¾" | (CE) | ❻ | $300–325 |
| ☐ 65 | 4¾" | (CE) | ❼ | $275–300 |
| ☐ 65/0 | 4" | (CE) | ❷ | $6000–8000 |
| ☐ 65/0 | 3¾" | (CE) | ❸ | $5000–6000 |
| ☐ 65/I | 4½ to 4⅞" | (CE) | ❶ | $750–1000 |
| ☐ 65/I | 4½ to 4⅞" | (CE) | ❷ | $450–575 |
| ☐ 65/I | 4½ to 4⅞" | (CE) | ❸ | $400–450 |
| ☐ 65/I | 4½ to 4⅞" | (CE) | ❹ | $350–400 |
| ☐ 65/I | 4½ to 4⅞" | (CE) | ❺ | $325–350 |
| ☐ 65 | 4¾ to 5" | (CE) | ❶ | $750–1000 |
| ☐ 65 | 4¾ to 5" | (CE) | ❷ | $450–575 |

> FINAL ISSUE
> 1993

---

**HUM TERM**

**OPEN EDITION**: Pieces currently in W. Goebel's production program.

*Double crown (TM 1+1)*          *Full bee (TM 2)*

## HUM 66
### Farm Boy

Many size variations. Old name: "Three Pals " or "Happy-Go-Lucky Fellow." Originally modeled in 1937 by master sculptor Arthur Moeller. Also called "Little Pig-Driver" in some old catalogues. "Farm Boy" sold for $9.00 on old 1955 price list.

| | | | | | |
|---|---|---|---|---|---|
| ☐ 66 | 5 to 5¾" | (CE) | ❶ | $700–900 |
| ☐ 66 | 5 to 5¾" | (CE) | ❷ | $400–550 |
| ☐ 66 | 5 to 5¾" | (CE) | ❸ | $350–400 |
| ☐ 66 | 5 to 5¾" | (CE) | ❹ | $310–350 |
| ☐ 66 | 5 to 5¾" | (CE) | ❺ | $285–310 |
| ☐ 66 | 5 to 5¾" | (CE) | ❻ | $275–285 |
| ☐ 66 | 5 to 5¾" | (CE) | ❼ | $270–275 |
| ☐ 66 | 5 to 5¾" | (OE) | ❽ | $270 |

---
**HUM TERM**

**DECIMAL POINT**: This incised "period" or dot was used in a somewhat random fashion by the W. Goebel Porzellanfabrik over the years. The decimal point is and was primarily used to reduce confusion in reading the incised numbers on the underside of the figurines. Example: 66. helps one realize that the designation is sixty-six and not ninety-nine.

---

*Full bee (TM 2)*                    *Crown (TM 1)*

**HUM 67**
**Doll Mother**

First modeled by master sculptor Arthur Moeller in 1937 but has been restyled in recent years. Slight difference in hair ribbon on girl. Old name: "Little Doll Mother" or "Little Mother of Dolls" in some catalogues. "Doll Mother" sold for $8.00 on old 1955 price list. An unusual painting variation has recently been found with a white blanket with red cross stripes instead of the normal *pink* color and red stripes, in (TM 1) trademark. Value: $750–1,000. A special "60th Anniversary" figurine of "Doll Mother" was issued in 1997 with a special backstamp and a round gold medallion with: "HUM 67 Doll Mother 1937–1997 (and) 60th" in a round circle. This figurine was first introduced at the Leipzig Trade Fair in 1937.

| | | | | |
|---|---|---|---|---|
| ☐ 67 | 4¼ to 4¾" | (CE) | ❶ | $650–850 |
| ☐ 67 | 4¼ to 4¾" | (CE) | ❷ | $400–500 |
| ☐ 67 | 4¼ to 4¾" | (CE) | ❸ | $325–350 |
| ☐ 67 | 4¼ to 4¾" | (CE) | ❹ | $275–325 |
| ☐ 67 | 4¼ to 4¾" | (CE) | ❺ | $250–275 |
| ☐ 67 | 4¼ to 4¾" | (CE) | ❻ | $245–250 |
| ☐ 67 | 4¼ to 4¾" | (CE) | ❼ | $240–245 |
| ☐ 67 | 4¼ to 4¾" | (OE) | ❽ | $240 |

───── **HUM TERM** ─────

**MOLD GROWTH**: In the earlier days of figurine production the working molds were made of plaster of paris. As these molds were used, the various molded parts became larger due to the repeated usage. With modern technology at the Goebel factory and the use of acrylic resin molds, this problem has been eliminated and today the collector finds very few size differences within a given size designation.

| 68 2/0 | 68/0 | 68 Crown | 68 Full bee | 68 Double crown |

## HUM 68
### Lost Sheep

Originally modeled by master sculptor Arthur Moeller in 1937 and later restyled by a combination of several modelers. Many size and color variations. Older models have dark brown or gray trousers. Similar to HUM 64 "Shepherd's Boy" except for single lamb and different colors. "Lost Sheep" sold for $7.50 on old 1955 price list. Both sizes of "Lost Sheep" were permanently retired by Goebel in the fall of 1992 and will not be produced again. The suggested retail prices for "Lost Sheep" on the 1992 price list were $125 and $180.

| | | | | |
|---|---|---|---|---|
| ☐ 68 2/0 | . . . 4¼ to 4½″ | . . . . . (CE) | . . . ❷ | . . . $250–350 |
| ☐ 68 2/0 | . . . 4¼ to 4½″ | . . . . . (CE) | . . . ❸ | . . . $225–250 |
| ☐ 68 2/0 | . . . 4¼ to 4½″ | . . . . . (CE) | . . . ❹ | . . . $190–225 |
| ☐ 68 2/0 | . . . 4¼ to 4½″ | . . . . . (CE) | . . . ❺ | . . . $180–190 |
| ☐ 68 2/0 | . . . 4¼ to 4½″ | . . . . . (CE) | . . . ❻ | . . . $170–180 |
| ☐ 68 2/0 | . . . 4¼ to 4½″ | . . . . . (CE) | . . . ❼ | . . . $160–170 |
| ☐ 68/0 | . . . . . 5½″ | . . . . . . . (CE) | . . . ❷ | . . . $350–450 |
| ☐ 68/0 | . . . . . 5½″ | . . . . . . . (CE) | . . . ❸ | . . . $300–350 |
| ☐ 68/0 | . . . . . 5½″ | . . . . . . . (CE) | . . . ❹ | . . . $275–300 |
| ☐ 68/0 | . . . . . 5½″ | . . . . . . . (CE) | . . . ❺ | . . . $250–275 |
| ☐ 68/0 | . . . . . 5½″ | . . . . . . . (CE) | . . . ❻ | . . . $225–250 |
| ☐ 68/0 | . . . . . 5½″ | . . . . . . . (CE) | . . . ❼ | . . . $200–225 |
| ☐ 68 | . . . . . . 5½ to 6½″ | . . . . . (CE) | . . . ❶ | . . . $600–750 |
| ☐ 68 | . . . . . . 5½ to 6½″ | . . . . . (CE) | . . . ❷ | . . . $400–500 |
| ☐ 68 | . . . . . . 5½ to 6½″ | . . . . . (CE) | . . . ❸ | . . . $350–400 |

FINAL ISSUE
1992

---

**HUM TERM**

**OVERSIZE**: This description refers to a piece that has experienced "mold growth" size expansion. A figurine that measures larger than the standard size is said to be "oversized."

## HUM 69
## Happy Pastime

First modeled by master sculptor Arthur Moeller in 1937. Very little difference between old and new models. Older models slightly larger and usually do *not* have dots or head scarf. Called "Knitter" in old catalogues. The "M.I. Hummel" signature is very faint or difficult to see on some old models. Occasionally found with a stamped "M. I. Hummel" signature on the bottom. "Happy Pastime" is the motif used on the 1978 Annual Plate, Hum 271. "Happy Pastime" was permanently retired by Goebel as of 31 December 1996 and will not be produced again. The 1996 production bears a special "Final Issue" backstamp and a small gold "Final Issue" commemorative tag. The suggested retail price on the 1996 price list was $175.

| | | | | | | |
|---|---|---|---|---|---|---|
| ☐ 69 | 3¼ to 3½″ | (CE) | ❶ | $500–650 |
| ☐ 69 | 3¼ to 3½″ | (CE) | ❷ | $300–400 |
| ☐ 69 | 3¼ to 3½″ | (CE) | ❸ | $250–275 |
| ☐ 69 | 3¼ to 3½″ | (CE) | ❹ | $225–250 |
| ☐ 69 | 3¼ to 3½″ | (CE) | ❺ | $210–225 |
| ☐ 69 | 3¼ to 3½″ | (CE) | ❻ | $200–210 |
| ☐ 69 | 3¼ to 3½″ | (CE) | ❼ | $190–200 |

FINAL ISSUE
1996

*Old bowl style*

*New jar style*

## HUM III/69
## Happy Pastime, Box

Bowl style first produced in 1937. Jar style first produced and sold in 1964. Model number is found on underside of lid. "M.I.Hummel" signature is found on topside of lid directly behind figure. "Happy Pastime" candy box was "temporarily withdrawn"(TW) from production on 31 December 1989, but may be reinstated at some future date.

| | | | | | | |
|---|---|---|---|---|---|---|
| ☐ III/69 | 6½″ | (CE) | ❶ | $750–850 | |
| ☐ III/69 | 6½″ | (CE) | ❷ | $575–650 | |
| ☐ III/69 | 6½″ | (CE) | ❸ | $475–550 | (Old Style) |
| ☐ III/69 | 5¼″ | (CE) | ❸ | $300–350 | (New Style) |
| ☐ III/69 | 5¼″ | (CE) | ❹ | $250–275 | |
| ☐ III/69 | 5¼″ | (CE) | ❺ | $225–250 | |
| ☐ III/69 | 5¼″ | (TW) | ❻ | $200–225 | |

**HUM 70**
**Holy Child**
Factory records indicate this was originally modeled in 1937 by a combination of modelers. Was sold in white overglaze (unpainted) finish at one time in Belgium and would be considered rare today. Has been restyled in later years with newer models having the textured finish on gown and robe. Many size variations. Also listed as "Child Jesus" in some old catalogues. "Holy Child" was "temporarily withdrawn" (TW) from production on 31 December 1990, but is once again back on current price lists in (TM 7) trademark. The suggested retail price for "Holy Child" on the 1990 price list was $130. Listed as (TW) "Temporarily Withdrawn" in January 1999.

| | | | | | |
|---|---|---|---|---|---|
| ☐ 70 | . . . . . | 6¾ to 7½" | . . . . . (CE) | . . . ❶ | . . . $750–850 |
| ☐ 70 | . . . . . | 6¾ to 7½" | . . . . . (CE) | . . . ❷ | . . . $375–500 |
| ☐ 70 | . . . . . | 6¾ to 7½" | . . . . . (CE) | . . . ❸ | . . . $350–375 |
| ☐ 70 | . . . . . | 6¾ to 7½" | . . . . . (CE) | . . . ❹ | . . . $325–350 |
| ☐ 70 | . . . . . | 6¾ to 7½" | . . . . . (CE) | . . . ❺ | . . . $300–325 |
| ☐ 70 | . . . . . | 6¾ to 7½" | . . . . . (CE) | . . . ❻ | . . . $290–300 |
| ☐ 70 | . . . . . | 6¾" | . . . . . . . . . . (TW) | . . ❼ | . . . $280–285 |

---

**HUM TERM**

**U.S. ZONE**: The words "U.S. ZONE—GERMANY" were used on figurines produced by the W. Goebel Porzellanfabrik after W.W. II when the country of Germany was yet undivided and the Goebel Factory was part of the U.S. Zone. The U.S. ZONE marking was used either alone or with the Crown trademark from 1946 until 1948. Once the country was divided into East and West, the W. Goebel Porzellanfabrik used the Western or West designation.

| 71 (TM 2) | 71/I (TM 6) | 71 2/0 (TM 6) |

## HUM 71
### Stormy Weather

Originally modeled by master sculptor Reinhold Unger in 1937. Has been restyled several times through the years. Many size variations. Full bee models are usually the largest size. Old name "Under One Roof." Slight difference between old and new models other than size. Several variations in structure of bottom of base design. This motif was used for the first Anniversary Plate, HUM 280 in 1975. A new small size (71 2/0) was issued in the spring of 1985 at a suggested retail price of $120. The large size has now been renumbered 71/1. There are two variations of the new small size. The first production appeared with the inside of the umbrella hand painted with obvious brush strokes while later production has the inside painted by air brush. These early pieces usually sell for $500–750. "Stormy Weather" sold for $16.50 on old 1955 price list. A special painting variation of the small size HUM 71 2/0 was produced in 1997 for QVC television program and sold by mail order. The price was $279.50 plus shipping and handling. It was painted with a yellow umbrella with tan colored highlights, a decal signature on back of umbrella and a special "60th Anniversary" backstamp. Now available at local retailers.

☐ 71 2/0 . . . 4½ to 5″ . . . . . . (CE) . . . ❻ . . . $350–360
☐ 71 2/0 . . . 4½ to 5″ . . . . . . (CE) . . . ❼ . . . $345–350
☐ 71 2/0 . . . 4½ to 5″ . . . . . . (OE) . . . ❽ . . . $345
☐ 71 . . . . . 6 to 7″ . . . . . . . . (CE) . . . ❶ . . . $1100–1350
☐ 71 . . . . . 6 to 7″ . . . . . . . . (CE) . . . ❷ . . . $800–950
☐ 71 . . . . . 6 to 7″ . . . . . . . . (CE) . . . ❸ . . . $650–675
☐ 71 . . . . . 6 to 6¼″ . . . . . . (CE) . . . ❹ . . . $600–650
☐ 71 . . . . . 6 to 6¼″ . . . . . . (CE) . . . ❺ . . . $540–590
☐ 71 . . . . . 6 to 6¼″ . . . . . . (CE) . . . ❻ . . . $525–540
☐ 71/I . . . . 6 to 6¼″ . . . . . . (CE) . . . ❻ . . . $515–525
☐ 71/I . . . . 6 to 6¼″ . . . . . . (CE) . . . ❼ . . . $510–515
☐ 71/I . . . . 6 to 6¼″ . . . . . . (OE) . . . ❽ . . . $510

NOTE: See page 487 RARE VARIATIONS in back of book for an unusual variation of this figurine.

| (TM 1) | (TM 3) | (TM 6) |

**HUM 72**
**Spring Cheer**
First modeled in 1937 by master sculptor Reinhold Unger. Older models have yellow dress and no flowers in right hand. Restyled in 1965 by master sculptor Gerhard Skrobek who added flowers to right hand and changed color of dress to dark green. Both mold variations can be found with (TM3) stylized trademark. Older style can also be found with dark green dress. This variation would be considered rare and would bring a premium usually anywhere from $1,500 to $2,000. Old name:"Spring Flowers". Crown mark pieces have a flower on reverse side. Later production pieces omitted this flower. "Spring Cheer" was listed as (TW) "Temporarily Withdrawn" from production on 31 December 1984, but may be reinstated at some future date. The suggested retail price for "Spring Cheer" on the 1984 price list was $55.

| | | | | | |
|---|---|---|---|---|---|
| ☐ 72 | 5 to 5½" | (CE) | ❶ | $500–650 |
| ☐ 72 | 5 to 5½" | (CE) | ❷ | $325–400 |
| ☐ 72 | 5 to 5½" | (CE) | ❸ | $300–325 |
| ☐ 72 | 5 to 5½" | (CE) | ❹ | $250–300 |
| ☐ 72 | 5 to 5½" | (CE) | ❺ | $225–250 |
| ☐ 72 | 5 to 5½" | (TW) | ❻ | $200–225 |

---

**HUM TERM**

**CURRENT PRODUCTION**: The term used to describe those items currently being produced by the W. Goebel Porzellanfabrik of Rödental, West Germany.

---

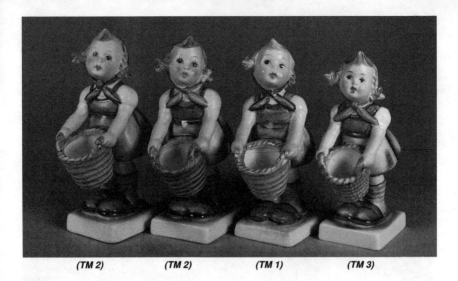

| (TM 2) | (TM 2) | (TM 1) | (TM 3) |

## HUM 73
### Little Helper

Originally modeled in 1937 by master sculptor Reinhold Unger. Very little variation between old and new pieces. Older figurines are usually slightly larger. Old name: "Diligent Betsy" or "The Little Sister" in some old catalogues. "Little Helper" sold for $4.00 on old 1955 price list.

☐ 73 . . . . . . 4¼ to 4½″ . . . . . (CE). . . ❶ . . . $400–500
☐ 73 . . . . . . 4¼ to 4½″ . . . . . (CE). . . ❷ . . . $250–325
☐ 73 . . . . . . 4¼ to 4½″ . . . . . (CE). . . ❸ . . . $190–200
☐ 73 . . . . . . 4¼ to 4½″ . . . . . (CE). . . ❹ . . . $155–190
☐ 73 . . . . . . 4¼ to 4½″ . . . . . (CE). . . ❺ . . . $150–155
☐ 73 . . . . . . 4¼ to 4½″ . . . . . (CE). . . ❻ . . . $145–150
☐ 73 . . . . . . 4¼ to 4½″ . . . . . (CE). . . ❼ . . . $140–145
☐ 73 . . . . . . 4¼ to 4½″ . . . . . (OE). . . ❽ . . . $140

---

### HUM TERM

**RARE**: (Webster) marked by unusual quality, merit, or appeal. Distinctive, superlative or extreme of its kind, seldom occurring or found, uncommon.

---

### HUM TERM

**REINSTATED**: The term used to indicate that a figurine has been placed back into production by the W. Goebel Porzellanfabrik after some prior classification of non-production.

| Crown (TM 1) | Crown (TM 1) | Full bee (TM 2) | Stylized (TM 3) |

## HUM 74
### Little Gardener

Originally modeled by master sculptor Reinhold Unger in 1937 but has undergone many changes through the years. Older models have an oval base. Restyled in the early 1960's and changed to a round base and smaller flower. Many color variations on girl's apron. "Little Gardener" sold for $4.00 on old 1955 price list. Used as a *demonstration promotion* piece for 1992 *with a special backstamp*–sold only at stores having a Goebel "M. I. Hummel" promotion in 1992. Not sold at other stores for two years. Now back in current production. "Little Gardener" has *not* been found with (TM 4) "three line" trademark at time of printing.

☐ 74 . . . . . . 4 to 4½" . . . . . . (CE). . . ❶ . . . $400–500
☐ 74 . . . . . . 4 to 4½" . . . . . . (CE). . . ❷ . . . $225–300
☐ 74 . . . . . . 4 to 4½" . . . . . . (CE). . . ❸ . . . $175–200
☐ 74 . . . . . . 4 to 4½" . . . . . . (CE). . . ❹ . . . $500–750
☐ 74 . . . . . . 4 to 4½" . . . . . . (CE). . . ❺ . . . $150–155
☐ 74 . . . . . . 4 to 4½" . . . . . . (CE). . . ❻ . . . $145–150
☐ 74 . . . . . . 4 to 4½" . . . . . . (CE). . . ❼ . . . $140–145
☐ 74 . . . . . . 4 to 4½" . . . . . . (OE). . . ❽ . . . $140

---

**HUM TERM**

**THREE LINE TRADEMARK**: The symbol used by the W. Goebel Porzellanfabrik from 1964 until 1972 as their factory trademark. The name for this trademark was adopted to recognize that the V and bee was accompanied by three lines of print to the right of the V. Also known as TM 4.

(TM 1)                          (TM 3)

## HUM 75
### Holy Water Font, White Angel
First modeled by master sculptor Reinhold Unger in 1937. Newer models have hole for
hanging font. Older models provide a hole only on back. Variation in construction of
bowl. Also called "Angelic Prayer" in some catalogues. Also found in terra cotta finish.
Value $1000–1500. Listed as (TW) "Temporarily Withdrawn" in January 1999.

☐ 75 . . . . . . 3¼ to 4½" . . . . . (CE). . . ❶ . . . $225–275
☐ 75 . . . . . . 3¼ to 4½" . . . . . (CE). . . ❷ . . . $125–150
☐ 75 . . . . . . 3¼ to 4½" . . . . . (CE). . . ❸ . . . $70–80
☐ 75 . . . . . . 3¼ to 4½" . . . . . (CE). . . ❹ . . . $60–70
☐ 75 . . . . . . 3¼ to 4½" . . . . . (CE). . . ❺ . . . $50–60
☐ 75 . . . . . . 3¼ to 4½" . . . . . (CE). . . ❻ . . . $45–50
☐ 75 . . . . . . 3¼ to 4½" . . . . . (TW) . . ❼ . . . $45–50

### HUM 76 A
### Doll Mother

### HUM 76 B
### Prayer Before Battle, Bookends
No known examples other than this half
of set which was located in Goebel factory. Originally modeled by master
sculptor Arthur Moeller. Factory note indicates: "Not produced after 28 February
1938."

☐ 76 . . . . . . A & B . . . . . . . . (CE). . . ❶ . . . $10,000–15,000

## HUM 77
**Holy Water Font, Cross With Doves**
First modeled by master sculptor Reinhold Unger in 1937 but according to factory information was made as samples only and never in production. Listed as a closed edition on 21 October 1937. As of this date, ten examples are known to exist. One is now in the Robert L. Miller Collection, thanks to a collector from California. Has also been found in white overglaze (unpainted) finish.

☐ 77 . . . . . . 1¾ x 6¼″. . . . . . (CN). . . . . . . . $5,000–10,000

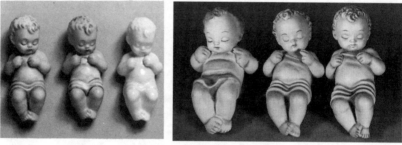

| Bisque | Color | White | Old style | New style | Current style |

## HUM 78
**Blessed Child (Infant of Krumbad)**
In 1985 the official name was changed from "Infant of Krumbad" to the "Blessed Child." It was also listed as "In the Crib" in an old 1950 catalogue. This figurine has been produced in three different finishes. Produced in brownish bisque finish (U.S. Market); full color and white overglaze (various other countries), sometimes found in Belgium. Note variations in older models. First modeled by master sculptor Erich Lautensack in 1937. (Lautensack died during the Second World War.) Restyled by master sculptor Gerhard Skrobek in 1965. The two small holes on the back are designed to hold a wire halo. Full color and white overglaze pieces command varied premiums. Also found with the incised number 78/6 (arabic) in (TM 1) "crown" and (TM 2) "full bee" trademarks only.

Factory records for Blessed Child indicate the following:

**Originally modeled by:**          **Restyled:**
78/0 . . . . . . . Lautensack . . . 1937 . . . Skrobek. . . . 1962 (discontinued 1983)
78/I. . . . . . . . Skrobek . . . . . 1964 . . . Skrobek. . . . 1965
78/II . . . . . . . Skrobek . . . . . 1964 . . . Skrobek. . . . 1965
78/III . . . . . . . Lautensack . . . 1937 . . . Skrobek. . . . 1965
78/V . . . . . . . Skrobek . . . . . 1963 . . . Skrobek. . . . 1965
78/VI or 78/6 . . Lautensack . . . 1937 . . . Skrobek. . . . 1965
78/VIII. . . . . . . Lautensack . . . 1937 . . . Skrobek. . . . 1965

*(prices continued on next page)*

**B.C.W** . . . . . . . . . . . . . . . . . . . . . . . . . . . . .

| | | | | | | |
|---|---|---|---|---|---|---|
| ☐☐☐ | 78/0 | 2¼". | (CE) | ❷ | | $200–300 |
| ☐☐☐ | 78/0 | 2¼". | (CE) | ❸ | | $150–200 |
| ☐☐☐ | 78/I | 2½". | (CE) | ❸ | | $40–50 |
| ☐☐☐ | 78/I | 2½". | (CE) | ❹ | | $35–40 |
| ☐☐☐ | 78/I | 2½". | (CE) | ❺ | | $30–35 |
| ☐☐☐ | 78/I | 2½". | (TW) | ❻ | | $30–35 |
| ☐☐☐ | 78/II | 3½". | (CE) | ❸ | | $50–60 |
| ☐☐☐ | 78/II | 3½". | (CE) | ❹ | | $45–50 |
| ☐☐☐ | 78/II | 3½". | (CE) | ❺ | | $40–45 |
| ☐☐☐ | 78/II | 3½". | (TW) | ❻ | | $35–40 |
| ☐☐☐ | 78/III | 4½ to 5¼" | (CE) | ❶ | | $350–400 |
| ☐☐☐ | 78/III | 4½ to 5¼" | (CE) | ❷ | | $250–350 |
| ☐☐☐ | 78/III | 4½ to 5¼" | (CE) | ❸ | | $60–70 |
| ☐☐☐ | 78/III | 4½ to 5¼" | (CE) | ❹ | | $55–60 |
| ☐☐☐ | 78/III | 4½ to 5¼" | (CE) | ❺ | | $50–55 |
| ☐☐☐ | 78/III | 4½ to 5¼" | (TW) | ❻ | | $45–50 |
| ☐☐☐ | 78/V | 7½ to 7¾" | (CE) | ❸ | | $125–150 |
| ☐☐☐ | 78/V | 7½ to 7¾" | (CE) | ❹ | | $100–125 |
| ☐☐☐ | 78/V | 7½ to 7¾" | (CE) | ❺ | | $90–100 |
| ☐☐☐ | 78/V | 7½ to 7¾" | (TW) | ❻ | | $80–90 |
| ☐☐☐ | 78/VI | 10 to 11¼" | (CE) | ❶ | | $600–850 |
| ☐☐☐ | 78/VI | 10 to 11¼" | (CE) | ❷ | | $400–600 |
| ☐☐☐ | 78/VI | 10 to 11¼" | (CE) | ❸ | | $200–250 |
| ☐☐☐ | 78/VI | 10 to 11¼" | (CE) | ❹ | | $200–250 |
| ☐☐☐ | 78/VI | 10 to 11¼" | (CE) | ❺ | | $150–175 |
| ☐☐☐ | 78/VI | 10 to 11¼" | (TW) | ❻ | | $150–175 |
| ☐☐☐ | 78/VIII | 13¼ to 14¼" | (CE) | ❶ | | $750–1000 |
| ☐☐☐ | 78/VIII | 13¼ to 15" | (CE) | ❷ | | $500–750 |
| ☐☐☐ | 78/VIII | 13¼ to 14¼" | (CE) | ❸ | | $350–400 |
| ☐☐☐ | 78/VIII | 13¼ to 14¼" | (CE) | ❹ | | $350–400 |
| ☐☐☐ | 78/VIII | 13¼ to 14¼" | (CE) | ❺ | | $300–325 |
| ☐☐☐ | 78/VIII | 13¼ to 14¼" | (TW) | ❻ | | $300–325 |
| ☐☐☐ | 78/II½ | 4¼". | (CE) | ❻ | | $100–150 |
| ☐☐☐ | 78/II½ | 4¼". | **(OE)** | ❼–❽ | | $75–100 |

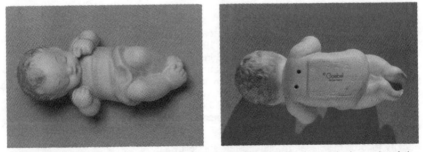

A new small size "Blessed Child" is now being produced for the exclusive sale of the Siessen Convent in Germany. It has an incised 78/II½ model number, incised 1987 copyright date and the current (TM 6) trademark. This is only the second time a "Hummel" figurine has been produced using the "1/2" size designator. (The other figurine is "Heavenly Angel" HUM 21/0½.) This new "Blessed Child" reverts back to the old original style modeled by Lautensack rather than the newer Skrobek design. The price at the Siessen Convent was DM 89 or approximately $53 in U.S. currency in 1999. The Siessen Convent sometimes have an old style 2¼" "Blessed Child" for sale with TM 7 for sale at DM 49 ($29).

*New (TM 3)*          *Old (TM 1)*

**HUM 79**
**Globe Trotter**

Originally modeled by master sculptor Arthur Moeller in 1937. Remodeled in 1955 at which time the basket weave was changed from a double weave to a single weave. Crown mark pieces usually have a tan-colored handle on umbrella while others are black. Some variation of color on the inside of basket. Some old catalogues list name as "Happy Traveller." Some older models have dark green hat. This motif is used on the 1973 Annual Plate, HUM 266. "Globe Trotter" was permanently retired by Goebel in the fall of 1991 and will not be produced again. The 1991 price list shows a price of $170, the last year it was sold on the primary market. Both TM 6 and TM 7 can be found with "Final Issue" decal, and "Final Issue" medallion.

| | | | | | |
|---|---|---|---|---|---|
| ☐ 79 | 5 to 5¼" | (CE) | ❶ | $500–750 |
| ☐ 79 | 5 to 5½" | (CE) | ❷ | $375–500 |
| ☐ 79 | 5 to 5¼" | (CE) | ❸ | $300–350 |
| ☐ 79 | 5 to 5¼" | (CE) | ❹ | $275–300 |
| ☐ 79 | 5 to 5¼" | (CE) | ❺ | $250–275 |
| ☐ 79 | 5 to 5¼" | (CE) | ❻ | $225–250 |
| ☐ 79 | 5 to 5¼" | (CE) | ❼ | $200–225 |

FINAL ISSUE
1991

*New*          *Old*

77

### HUM 80
### Little Scholar

Original model made by master sculptor Arthur Moeller in 1937. Some color variations. Old models have brown shoes. The cone in boy's right arm is called Schultute or Zuckertute, a paper cone containing school supplies and other goodies, which German parents traditionally give their children on the first day of school. "Little Scholar" sold for $7.00 on old 1955 price list. "Crown" and some early "full bee" pieces have a hole in the pretzel on the top of the cone. Later pieces are solid.

| | | | | |
|---|---|---|---|---|
| ☐ 80 | 5¼ to 5¾″ | (CE) | ❶ | $650–800 |
| ☐ 80 | 5¼ to 5¾″ | (CE) | ❷ | $375–500 |
| ☐ 80 | 5¼ to 5¾″ | (CE) | ❸ | $325–350 |
| ☐ 80 | 5¼ to 5¾″ | (CE) | ❹ | $280–325 |
| ☐ 80 | 5¼ to 5¾″ | (CE) | ❺ | $260–280 |
| ☐ 80 | 5¼ to 5¾″ | (CE) | ❻ | $255–260 |
| ☐ 80 | 5¼ to 5¾″ | (CE) | ❼ | $250–255 |
| ☐ 80 | 5¼ to 5¾″ | (OE) | ❽ | $250 |

---

#### HUM TERM

**SAMPLE MODEL**: Generally a figurine that was made as a sample only and not approved by the Siessen Convent for production. Sample models (in the true sense of the term) are extremely rare items and command a premium price on the secondary market.

| 81 (TM 1) | 81/0 (TM 2) | 81 2/0 (TM 2) | 81 2/0 (TM 3) |

## HUM 81
### School Girl

Old name: "Primer Girl" or "Little Scholar." Original model made by master sculptor Arthur Moeller in 1937. Many size variations as well as color variations. Size 81 2/0 basket filled; all others, baskets empty. Old catalogue listing of 7¾" is in error. This motif is used on the 1980 Annual Plate, HUM 273. Early "crown" trademark examples are sometimes found with orange color skirt and blouse rather than the normal dark colored blouse. Large size (81/0) was (TW) "Temporarily Withdrawn" in January 1999.

- [ ] 81 2/0 . . . 4¼ to 4¾" . . . . . (CE). . . ❶ . . . $450–600
- [ ] 81 2/0 . . . 4¼ to 4¾" . . . . . (CE). . . ❷ . . . $250–350
- [ ] 81 2/0 . . . 4¼ to 4¾" . . . . . (CE). . . ❸ . . . $225–250
- [ ] 81 2/0 . . . 4¼ to 4¾" . . . . . (CE). . . ❹ . . . $200–225
- [ ] 81 2/0 . . . 4¼ to 4¾" . . . . . (CE). . . ❺ . . . $180–200
- [ ] 81 2/0 . . . 4¼ to 4¾" . . . . . (CE). . . ❻ . . . $175–180
- [ ] 81 2/0 . . . 4¼ to 4¾" . . . . . (CE). . . ❼ . . . $170–175
- [ ] 81 2/0 . . . 4¼ to 4¾" . . . . . (OE). . . ❽ . . . $170
- [ ] 81/0 . . . . . 4¾ to 5¼" . . . . . (CE). . . ❶ . . . $550–700
- [ ] 81/0 . . . . . 4¾ to 5¼" . . . . . (CE). . . ❷ . . . $325–450
- [ ] 81/0 . . . . . 4¾ to 5¼" . . . . . (CE). . . ❸ . . . $300–325
- [ ] 81/0 . . . . . 4¾ to 5¼" . . . . . (CE). . . ❹ . . . $270–300
- [ ] 81/0 . . . . . 4¾ to 5¼" . . . . . (CE). . . ❺ . . . $245–270
- [ ] 81/0 . . . . . 4¾ to 5¼" . . . . . (CE). . . ❻ . . . $235–245
- [ ] 81/0 . . . . . 4¾ to 5¼" . . . . . (TW) . ❼ . . . $225–230 60th Anni Decal 1998
- [ ] 81 . . . . . . 5⅛ to 5½" . . . . . (CE). . . ❶ . . . $600–750
- [ ] 81 . . . . . . 5⅛ to 5½" . . . . . (CE). . . ❷ . . . $350–475

| 82/2 | 82/0 | 82/0 | 82 2/0 | 82 2/0 |

## HUM 82
### School Boy

First modeled by master sculptor Arthur Moeller in 1938. Many size variations. Old name: "Little Scholar," "School Days" or "Primer Boy." The larger size 82/II (82/2) has been considered rare but is once again back in current production. See HUM 329. To my knowledge, the large size (82/II) was not produced in (TM 4) "three line" trademark. Large size (82/II) was (TW) "Temporarily Withdrawn" in January 1999.

☐ 82 2/0 . . . 4 to 4½″ . . . . . . (CE). . . ❶ . . . $450–600
☐ 82 2/0 . . . 4 to 4½″ . . . . . . (CE). . . ❷ . . . $250–350
☐ 82 2/0 . . . 4 to 4½″ . . . . . . (CE). . . ❸ . . . $225–250
☐ 82 2/0 . . . 4 to 4½″ . . . . . . (CE). . . ❹ . . . $200–225
☐ 82 2/0 . . . 4 to 4½″ . . . . . . (CE). . . ❺ . . . $180–200
☐ 82 2/0 . . . 4 to 4½″ . . . . . . (CE). . . ❻ . . . $175–180
☐ 82 2/0 . . . 4 to 4½″ . . . . . . (CE). . . ❼ . . . $170–175
☐ 82 2/0 . . . 4 to 4½″ . . . . . . (OE). . . ❽ . . . $170
☐ 82 . . . . . . 5 . . . . . . . . . . (CE). . . ❶ . . . $625–775
☐ 82/0 . . . . . 4¾ to 6″ . . . . . . (CE). . . ❶ . . . $600–750
☐ 82/0 . . . . . 4¾ to 6″ . . . . . . (CE). . . ❷ . . . $350–500
☐ 82/0 . . . . . 4¾ to 6″ . . . . . . (CE). . . ❸ . . . $325–350
☐ 82/0 . . . . . 4¾ to 6″ . . . . . . (CE). . . ❹ . . . $275–325
☐ 82/0 . . . . . 4¾ to 6″ . . . . . . (CE). . . ❺ . . . $250–270
☐ 82/0 . . . . . 4¾ to 6″ . . . . . . (CE). . . ❻ . . . $240–250
☐ 82/0 . . . . . 4¾ to 6″ . . . . . . (CE). . . ❼ . . . $235–240
☐ 82/0 . . . . . 4¾ to 6″ . . . . . . (OE). . . ❽ . . . $235
☐ 82/II . . . . . 7½″ . . . . . . . . . (CE). . . ❶ . . . $1200–1600
☐ 82/II . . . . . 7½″ . . . . . . . . . (CE). . . ❷ . . . $900–1100
☐ 82/II . . . . . 7½″ . . . . . . . . . (CE). . . ❸ . . . $600–700
☐ 82/II . . . . . 7½″ . . . . . . . . . (CE). . . ❺ . . . $550–600
☐ 82/II . . . . . 7½″ . . . . . . . . . (CE). . . ❻ . . . $525–550
☐ 82/II . . . . . 7½″ . . . . . . . . . (TW) . . ❼ . . . $500–510

*Left to right,* Angel Serenade TM 1, TM 2, TM 3, and TM 5 from an angle looking down on the base of each figurine.

*Left to right,* Angel Serenade TM 1, TM 2, TM 3, and TM 5 from the front.

## HUM 83

### Angel Serenade (with Lamb)

Old name: "Psalmist" in some early Goebel catalogues. First modeled by master sculptor Reinhold Unger in 1938. In the 1950's and 1960's, "Angel Serenade" was considered rare or hard-to-find, but, according to Goebel terminology, it was not in their "current production program" for quite a few years. In the late 1970's "Angel Serenade" was put back into the Goebel current production program, and it probably was at this time that the change was made in the position of the figure on the base. The details of the angel and the lamb remained almost identical. The "Angel Serenade" name is also used for HUM 214/D (part of the small Nativity set) and HUM 260/E (part of the large Nativity set). To my knowledge, it has been produced in all eight trademark periods—although I do not have a TM 4 "three line" trademark example in our personal collection.

☐ 83 . . . . . . 5½ to 5¾″ . . . . . (CE). . . ❶ . . . $600–750
☐ 83 . . . . . . 5½ to 5¾″ . . . . . (CE). . . ❷ . . . $500–550
☐ 83 . . . . . . 5½ to 5¾″ . . . . . (CE). . . ❸ . . . $400–500
☐ 83 . . . . . . 5½ to 5¾″ . . . . . (CE). . . ❹ . . . $300–400
☐ 83 . . . . . . 5½ to 5¾″ . . . . . (CE). . . ❺ . . . $270–300
☐ 83 . . . . . . 5½ to 5¾″ . . . . . (CE). . . ❻ . . . $260–265
☐ 83 . . . . . . 5½ to 5¾″ . . . . . (CE). . . ❼ . . . $255–260    60th Anni Decal 1998
☐ 83 . . . . . . 5½ to 5¾″ . . . . . (OE). . . ❽ . . . $255

*(TM 2)*       *(TM 3)*

**HUM 84**
**Worship**

Originally modeled by master sculptor Reinhold Unger in 1938. Old name: "At The Wayside" or "Devotion" in some catalogues. The small size 84/0 was also sold in white overglaze at one time in Belgium and would be considered rare. Current models of the large size 84/V have "M.I. Hummel" signature on back of shrine while older models have signature on back of base. Sometimes incised 84/5 instead of 84/V. The large size (84/V) was "temporarily withdrawn" (TW) from production on 31 December 1989, but may be reinstated at some future date.

| | | | | | |
|---|---|---|---|---|---|
| ☐ 84 | White 5¼" | (CE) | ❶ | $1000–1500 | |
| ☐ 84 | 5¼" | (CE) | ❶ | $475–625 | |
| ☐ 84/0 | 5 to 5½" | (CE) | ❶ | $450–600 | |
| ☐ 84/0 | 5 to 5½" | (CE) | ❷ | $300–375 | |
| ☐ 84/0 | 5 to 5½" | (CE) | ❸ | $250–275 | |
| ☐ 84/0 | 5" | (CE) | ❹ | $215–250 | |
| ☐ 84/0 | 5" | (CE) | ❺ | $200–215 | |
| ☐ 84/0 | 5" | (CE) | ❻ | $195–200 | |
| ☐ 84/0 | 5" | (CE) | ❼ | $190–195 | 60th Anni Decal 1998 |
| ☐ 84/0 | 5" | (**OE**) | ❽ | $190 | |
| ☐ 84/V | 12½ to 13¼" | (CE) | ❶ | $2000–3000 | |
| ☐ 84/V | 12½ to 13¼" | (CE) | ❷ | $1500–2000 | |
| ☐ 84/V | 12½ to 13¼" | (CE) | ❸ | $1225–1450 | |
| ☐ 84/V | 12½ to 13¼" | (CE) | ❹ | $1175–1225 | |
| ☐ 84/V | 12½ to 13¼" | (CE) | ❺ | $1150–1175 | |
| ☐ 84/V | 12½ to 13¼" | (TW) | ❻ | $1125–1150 | |

*Note fingers*

## HUM 85
### Serenade

First modeled by master sculptor Arthur Moeller in 1938. Many size variations. Note variation of boy's fingers on flute—cannot be attributed to any one time period. Old model with 85/0 number has fingers up. Size 85/0 has recently been restyled with a new hair style and textured finish. Normal hat color is dark gray or black. Older models also found with light gray hat. Old large size figurine with crown trademark has 85 number. Also found with incised number 85.0. or 85. in crown trademark in the small size. Sometimes incised 85/2 instead of 85/II. One of several figurines that make up the Hummel orchestra. Old name: "The Flutist." A new miniature size figurine was issued in 1985 with a suggested retail price of $39 to match a new mini size plate series called the "Little Music Makers"—one each year for four years. This is the second in the series. 85 4/0 has an incised 1984 copyright date. 85 4/0 was "Temporarily Withdrawn" on 31 December 1997. A large 24 inch "Serenade" is currently on display at the factory showroom in Rödental.

| ☐ | 85 4/0 | . . . 3½" . . . . . . . . . . | (CE) | . . ❻ | . . . $125–130 |
|---|---|---|---|---|---|
| ☐ | 85 4/0 | . . . 3½" . . . . . . . . . . | (TW) | . . ❼ | . . . $120–125 |
| ☐ | 85/0 | . . . . 4¾ to 5¼" . . . . . . | (CE) | . . ❶ | . . . $400–500 |
| ☐ | 85/0 | . . . . 4¾ to 5¼" . . . . . | (CE) | . . ❷ | . . . $225–300 |
| ☐ | 85/0 | . . . . 4¾ to 5¼" . . . . . | (CE) | . . ❸ | . . . $200–225 |
| ☐ | 85/0 | . . . . 4¾ to 5¼" . . . . . | (CE) | . . ❹ | . . . $180–200 |
| ☐ | 85/0 | . . . . 4¾ to 5¼" . . . . . | (CE) | . . ❺ | . . . $170–180 |
| ☐ | 85/0 | . . . . 4¾ to 5¼" . . . . . | (CE) | . . ❻ | . . . $165–170 |
| ☐ | 85/0 | . . . . 4¾ to 5¼" . . . . . | (CE) | . . ❼ | . . . $160–165 |
| ☐ | 85/0 | . . . . 4¾ to 5¼" . . . . . | (OE) | . . ❽ | . . . $160 |
| ☐ | 85 | . . . . . . 7 to 7½" . . . . . . | (CE) | . . ❶ | . . . $1250–1550 |
| ☐ | 85 | . . . . . . 7 to 7½" . . . . . . | (CE) | . . ❷ | . . . $775–975 |
| ☐ | 85/II | . . . . 7 to 7½" . . . . . . | (CE) | . . ❶ | . . . $1200–1500 |
| ☐ | 85/II | . . . . 7 to 7½" . . . . . . | (CE) | . . ❷ | . . . $750–950 |
| ☐ | 85/II | . . . . 7 to 7½" . . . . . . | (CE) | . . ❸ | . . . $650–700 |
| ☐ | 85/II | . . . . 7 to 7½" . . . . . . | (CE) | . . ❹ | . . . $600–650 |
| ☐ | 85/II | . . . . 7 to 7½" . . . . . . | (CE) | . . ❺ | . . . $550–600 |
| ☐ | 85/II | . . . . 7 to 7½" . . . . . . | (CE) | . . ❻ | . . . $525–550 |
| ☐ | 85/II | . . . . 7 to 7½" . . . . . . | (TW) | . . ❼ | . . . $500–510 |

### HUM 86
### Happiness

First modeled by master sculptor Reinhold Unger in 1938. Many size variations. Made with either square or rectangular base. Old name: "Wandersong" or "Traveller's Song" in early Goebel catalogue. Occasionally found with both pig tails down on older models.

| ☐ 86 | 4½ to 5″ | (CE) | **❶** | $400–500 | |
| ☐ 86 | 4½ to 5″ | (CE) | **❷** | $250–350 | |
| ☐ 86 | 4½ to 5″ | (CE) | **❸** | $200–225 | |
| ☐ 86 | 4½ to 5″ | (CE) | **❹** | $175–200 | |
| ☐ 86 | 4½ to 5″ | (CE) | **❺** | $170–175 | |
| ☐ 86 | 4½ to 5″ | (CE) | **❻** | $165–170 | |
| ☐ 86 | 4½ to 5″ | (CE) | **❼** | $160–165 | 60th Anni Decal 1998 |
| ☐ 86 | 4½ to 5″ | **(OE)** | **❽** | $160 | |

### HUM 87
### For Father

First modeled in 1938 by master sculptor Arthur Moeller. Some size and color variations between old and new models. Boy is carrying white (with brownish-tan highlights) radishes and beer stein. Some models have orange-colored vegetables that would appear to be carrots—usually found only with "full bee" (TM 2) or early stylized (TM 3) trademarks. The orange carrot variation normally sells in the $2,500 to $4,000 price range. Old name: "Father's Joy." "For Father" is now part of new "Personal Touch" program and the stein can be personalized by a Goebel artist for a $20 fee.

| ☐ 87 | 5½″ | (CE) | **❶** | $650–800 | |
| ☐ 87 | 5½″ | (CE) | **❷** | $400–525 | |
| ☐ 87 | 5½″ | (CE) | **❸** | $325–375 | |
| ☐ 87 | 5½″ | (CE) | **❹** | $275–325 | |
| ☐ 87 | 5½″ | (CE) | **❺** | $265–275 | |
| ☐ 87 | 5½″ | (CE) | **❻** | $260–265 | |
| ☐ 87 | 5½″ | (CE) | **❼** | $255–260 | 60th Anni Decal 1998 |
| ☐ 87 | 5½″ | **(OE)** | **❽** | $255 | |

88 (TM 1)    88/II (TM 3)    88/I (TM 4)

## HUM 88
### Heavenly Protection

Originally modeled by master sculptor Reinhold Unger in 1938. Some size and color variations between old and new models. Small size 88/I first put on the market in early 1960's. Some pieces have an incised 1961 copyright date on bottom. Older pieces sometimes incised 88/2 instead of 88/II. Some variation in the location of the "M.I. Hummel" signature on the back side of this figurine. Sometimes on the base, some-times on the bottom of the robe or sometimes in a diagonal position on the robe. The large size 88/II was listed on the 1993 and 1994 price lists as (TW) Temporarily With-drawn, but is once again back on the 1995 and succeeding price lists. Has also been found in white overglaze (unpainted) finish. Large size (88/II) was (TW) "Temporarily Withdrawn" in January 1999.

| | | | | | |
|---|---|---|---|---|---|
| ☐ 88 | 9¼" | (CE) | ❶ | $1800–2400 | |
| ☐ 88 | 9¼" | (CE) | ❷ | $1300–1600 | |
| ☐ 88 | 8¾ to 9¼" | (CE) | ❸ | $1100–1200 | |
| ☐ 88/I | 6¼ to 6¾" | (CE) | ❸ | $650–750 | |
| ☐ 88/I | 6¼ to 6¾" | (CE) | ❹ | $575–650 | |
| ☐ 88/I | 6¼ to 6¾" | (CE) | ❺ | $540–575 | |
| ☐ 88/I | 6¼ to 6¾" | (CE) | ❻ | $520–530 | |
| ☐ 88/I | 6¼ to 6¾" | (CE) | ❼ | $510–520 | 60th Anni Decal 1998 |
| ☐ 88/I | 6¼ to 6¾" | (OE) | ❽ | $510 | |
| ☐ 88/II | 8¾ to 9" | (CE) | ❷ | $1100–1300 | |
| ☐ 88/II | 8¾ to 9" | (CE) | ❸ | $1000–1100 | |
| ☐ 88/II | 8¾ to 9" | (CE) | ❹ | $900–1000 | |
| ☐ 88/II | 8¾ to 9" | (CE) | ❺ | $850–900 | |
| ☐ 88/II | 8¾ to 9" | (CE) | ❻ | $825–850 | |
| ☐ 88/II | 8¾ to 9" | (TW) | ❼ | $800–825 | |

*89/I New (TM 3)*          *89/I Old (TM 1)*

## HUM 89
### Little Cellist

Modeled by master sculptor Arthur Moeller in 1938. Restyled in the early 1960's. Many size variations through the years. Older examples of size 89/I have eyes open and looking straight ahead. Newer pieces have eyes looking down. Older pieces have rectangular base while newer pieces have rectangular base with corners squared off. Found with either 89/2 or 89/II on older models. Name listed as "Musician" in some old catalogues. The large size 89/II was listed on the 1993 price list as (TW) "Temporarily Withdrawn" and is still *not* back on current price lists.

| | | | | | |
|---|---|---|---|---|---|
| ☐ 89/I | 5¼ to 6¼" | (CE) | ❶ | $650–850 | |
| ☐ 89/I | 5¼ to 6¼" | (CE) | ❷ | $400–525 | |
| ☐ 89/I | 5¼ to 6¼" | (CE) | ❸ | $325–375 | |
| ☐ 89/I | 5¼ to 6¼" | (CE) | ❹ | $280–325 | |
| ☐ 89/I | 5¼ to 6¼" | (CE) | ❺ | $265–280 | |
| ☐ 89/I | 5¼ to 6¼" | (CE) | ❻ | $260–265 | |
| ☐ 89/I | 5¼ to 6¼" | (CE) | ❼ | $255–260 | 60th Anni Dcal 1998 |
| ☐ 89/I | 5¼ to 6¼" | (OE) | ❽ | $255 | |
| ☐ 89/II | 7½ to 7¾" | (CE) | ❶ | $1200–1500 | |
| ☐ 89/II | 7½ to 7¾" | (CE) | ❷ | $800–1000 | |
| ☐ 89/II | 7½ to 7¾" | (CE) | ❸ | $650–750 | |
| ☐ 89/II | 7½ to 7¾" | (CE) | ❹ | $600–650 | |
| ☐ 89/II | 7½ to 7¾" | (CE) | ❺ | $500–550 | |
| ☐ 89/II | 7½ to 7¾" | (CE) | ❻ | $475–500 | |
| ☐ 89/II | 7½ to 7¾" | (TW) | ❼ | $450–475 | |
| ☐ 89 | 7½" | (CE) | ❶ | $1250–1600 | |

*Factory sample*

**HUM 90**
**Eventide**

**HUM 90**
**Adoration (Without Shrine), Bookends**

Records indicate that this set of bookends was made in 1938 by a team of artists, which possibly included Reinhold Unger. Factory sample only. Extremely rare. Not produced after 28 February 1938. Listed as a closed edition. One half of this rare bookend (minus the wood base) was recently located in Michigan. This piece does not have the "M.I. Hummel" signature nor any identifying numbers—only a little dried glue remaining, indicating it had originally been attached to another object. Keep looking! Maybe you can locate the other half! Note position of lambs in photo, then see HUM 99 "Eventide" for interesting comparison.

☐ 90 A & B . . . . . . . . . . . . . . (CE). . . . . . . $10,000–15,000
☐ 90 B . . . . . 4" . . . . . . . . . . . (CE). . . . . . . $5,000–7,500

*Found in Michigan*

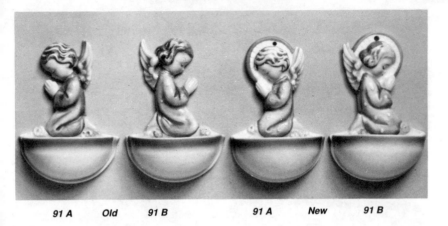

91 A     Old     91 B       91 A     New     91 B

## HUM 91 A & B
### Holy Water Font, Angels at Prayer

Angel facing left was apparently made first since early crown mark pieces are incised 91 only (not part of set). Angel facing right (91 B) was probably introduced slightly later. Now listed as a pair—91 A & B. First modeled by master sculptor Reinhold Unger in 1938. Older models (left) do not have halos while more recent designs have halos and a redesigned water bowl. Trademarks 1, 2 and 3 are without halos, 3, 4, 5 and 6 with halos. Note: trademark 3 can be found either way.

Priced for pair.

| | | | | |
|---|---|---|---|---|
| ☐ 91 . . . . . . 3¼ × 4½″ . . . . . | (CE). . . | ❶ | . . . | $400–500 |
| ☐ 91 A & B . 3⅜ × 5″ . . . . . . | (CE). . . | ❶ | . . . | $400–500 |
| ☐ 91 A & B . 3⅜ × 5″ . . . . . . | (CE). . . | ❷ | . . . | $200–250 |
| ☐ 91 A & B . 3⅜ × 5″ . . . . . . | (CE). . . | ❸ | . . . | $130–150 |
| ☐ 91 A & B . 3⅜ × 5″ . . . . . . | (CE). . . | ❹ | . . . | $115–125 |
| ☐ 91 A & B . 3⅜ × 5″ . . . . . . | (CE). . . | ❺ | . . . | $110–115 |
| ☐ 91 A & B . 3⅜ × 5″ . . . . . . | (CE). . . | ❻ | . . . | $105–110 |
| ☐ 91 A & B . 3⅜ × 5″ . . . . . . | (CE). . . | ❼ | . . . | $104–105 |
| ☐ 91 A & B . 3⅜ × 5″ . . . . . . | (OE). . . | ❽ | . . . | $104 |

---

**HUM TERM**

**UNDERGLAZE:** The term used to describe especially the number 5 trademark that appears actually underneath the glaze as opposed to the later version of the number 5 trademark that appears on the top of the glaze.

---

**HUM TERM**

**OVERSIZE:** This description refers to a piece that has experienced "mold growth" size expansion. A figurine that measures larger than the standard size is said to be "oversized."

Old (TM 2)                          New (TM 4)

## HUM 92
### Merry Wanderer, Plaque

Many size variations. Crown mark pieces can be found in both sizes. Some have incised 1938 copyright date, others do not. Some pieces have "M.I. Hummel" signature on both front and back, while others have signature on back only. Some TM 2 plaques have copyright (©WG) on front lower right, signature on back. Originally modeled by master sculptor Arthur Moeller in 1938 but restyled several times in later years. The "Merry Wanderer" plaque was (TW) "Temporarily Withdrawn" from production on 31 December 1989, but may be reinstated at some future date.

☐ 92 . . . . 4½ × 5 to 5 × 5½" . (CE). . . ❶ . . . $450–575
☐ 92 . . . . 4½ × 5 to 5 × 5½" . (CE). . . ❷ . . . $275–350
☐ 92 . . . 4½ × 5" . . . . . . . . . (CE). . . ❸ . . . $225–275
☐ 92 . . . 4½ × 5" . . . . . . . . . (CE). . . ❹ . . . $175–225
☐ 92 . . . . 4½ × 5" . . . . . . . . . (CE). . . ❺ . . . $160–170
☐ 92 . . . . 4½ × 5" . . . . . . . . . (TW) . . ❻ . . . $150–160

---

**PRICES IN THIS GUIDE**

We are in a period of DISCOUNTING of many items in our society. "M.I. Hummel" figurines are no exception. The prices in this guide give the relative values in relationship to new or current prices of (TM 8) trademark items. If the new figurines are discounted, the older models will likely be discounted, too, but possibly in a lesser degree. This guide reduces all items to one common denominator.

*Rare old style (TM 1+1)*     *New (TM 1)*

## HUM 93
### Little Fiddler, Plaque
Originally modeled by master sculptor Arthur Moeller in 1938. Many size variations. Two different backgrounds as noted in photograph. Older model (left) extremely rare. Some models have 1938 copyright date. Some pieces have "M.I. Hummel" signature on both front and back, while others have signature on back only, or front only. Also sold in white overglaze at one time. The background on the left is similar to HUM 107. The "Little Fiddler" plaque was (TW) "Temporarily Withdrawn" from production on 31 December 1989, but may be reinstated at some future date.

☐ 93 . . . . 4½ × 5 to 5 × 5½". (CE). . . ❶ . . . $450–575
☐ 93 . . . . 4½ × 5 to 5 × 5½". (CE). . . ❷ . . . $275–350
☐ 93 . . . . 4½ × 5" . . . . . . . . . (CE). . . ❸ . . . $225–275
☐ 93 . . . . 4½ × 5" . . . . . . . . . (CE). . . ❹ . . . $175–225
☐ 93 . . . . 4½ × 5" . . . . . . . . . (CE). . . ❺ . . . $160–170
☐ 93 . . . . 4½ × 5" . . . . . . . . . (TW) . . ❻ . . . $150–160
☐ 93 . . . . Rare old style   . . . . (CE). . . ❶ . . . $3,000–4,000

---

### HUM TERM

**RARE:** (Webster) marked by unusual quality, merit, or appeal. Distinctive, superlative or extreme of its kind, seldom occuring or found, uncommon.

---

*94/I (TM 2)*        *94/I (TM 3)*        *94 3/0 (TM 2)*

**HUM 94**
**Surprise**

Records indicate this model was produced by a team of sculptors in 1938. Old name: "The Duet" or "Hansel and Gretel." Also found listed with name of: "What's Up?" Older pieces marked "94" or "94/I" have rectangular base. All newer models have oval base. Slight variation in suspender straps on older models. Numbering errors occur occasionally—as an example, we have size 94/I that is marked 94/II in trademark 3. This trademark, however, has been "slashed" indicating that it was probably sold to a factory employee. The small size 94 3/0 does not have the detail that the larger sizes have. Large size (94/I) was (TW) "Temporarily Withdrawn" in January 1999.

| | | | | |
|---|---|---|---|---|
| ☐ 94 3/0 | . . . 4 to 4¼″ | . . . . . . | (CE). . . ❶ | . . . $450–550 |
| ☐ 94 3/0 | . . . 4 to 4¼″ | . . . . . . | (CE). . . ❷ | . . . $275–375 |
| ☐ 94 3/0 | . . . 4 to 4¼″ | . . . . . . | (CE). . . ❸ | . . . $225–250 |
| ☐ 94 3/0 | . . . 4 to 4¼″ | . . . . . . | (CE). . . ❹ | . . . $200–225 |
| ☐ 94 3/0 | . . . 4 to 4¼″ | . . . . . . | (CE). . . ❺ | . . . $190–200 |
| ☐ 94 3/0 | . . . 4 to 4¼″ | . . . . . . | (CE). . . ❻ | . . . $185–190 |
| ☐ 94 3/0 | . . . 4 to 4¼″ | . . . . . . | (CE). . . ❼ | . . . $180–185 |
| ☐ 94 3/0 | . . . 4 to 4¼″ | . . . . . . | (**OE**). . . ❽ | . . . $180 |
| ☐ 94/I | . . . . . 5¼ to 5½″ | . . . . | (CE). . . ❶ | . . . $750–950 |
| ☐ 94/I | . . . . . 5¼ to 5½″ | . . . . | (CE). . . ❷ | . . . $500–650 |
| ☐ 94/I | . . . . . 5¼ to 5½″ | . . . . | (CE). . . ❸ | . . . $425–475 |
| ☐ 94/I | . . . . . 5¼ to 5½″ | . . . . | (CE). . . ❹ | . . . $400–425 |
| ☐ 94/I | . . . . . 5¼ to 5½″ | . . . . | (CE). . . ❺ | . . . $350–390 |
| ☐ 94/I | . . . . . 5¼ to 5½″ | . . . . | (CE). . . ❻ | . . . $335–350 |
| ☐ 94/I | . . . . . 5¼ to 5½″ | . . . . | (TW) . . ❼ | . . . $325–335 |
| ☐ 94 | . . . . . . 5¾″ | . . . . . . . . . | (CE). . . ❶ | . . . $800–1000 |
| ☐ 94 | . . . . . . 5¾″ | . . . . . . . . . | (CE). . . ❷ | . . . $550–700 |

*(TM 1)*     *(TM 2)*     *(TM 6)*

**HUM 95**
**Brother**

Many size and color variations. Old name: "Our Hero" or "Hero of The Village." Same boy as used in HUM 94 "Surprise." Records indicate this figurine was first modeled in 1938 by a team of sculptors. "Brother" sold for $6.50 on old 1955 price list. A special 60th anniversary decal and metal tag was used on 1998 production.

| | | | | |
|---|---|---|---|---|
| ☐ 95 | 5¼ to 5¾" | (CE) | ❶ | $600–800 |
| ☐ 95 | 5¼ to 5¾" | (CE) | ❷ | $350–500 |
| ☐ 95 | 5¼ to 5¾" | (CE) | ❸ | $300–325 |
| ☐ 95 | 5¼ to 5¾" | (CE) | ❹ | $275–300 |
| ☐ 95 | 5¼ to 5¾" | (CE) | ❺ | $250–275 |
| ☐ 95 | 5¼ to 5¾" | (CE) | ❻ | $245–250 |
| ☐ 95 | 5¼ to 5¾" | (CE) | ❼ | $240–245   60th Anni Decal 1998 |
| ☐ 95 | 5¼ to 5¾" | **(OE)** | ❽ | $240 |

---
**HUM TERM**

**RÖDENTAL:** The town in Germany where the W. Goebel Porzellanfabrik is situated. Rödental is located near Coburg and lies only a few miles from the former East German border. In 1981 Rödental became the official Sister City of Eaton, Ohio due to the longtime "Hummel" relationship with Robert L. & Ruth Miller.

---

## HUM 96
### Little Shopper

Many size variations. Old name: "Errand Girl," "Gretel" or "Meg" in some older catalogues. Some catalogues and price lists indicate size as 5½". This is believed, by this author, to be in error. I have *never* seen it over 5 inches in over thirty years of collecting. Records indicate this figurine was first modeled in 1938 by a team of sculptors possibly including master sculptor Reinhold Unger. Same girl as used in HUM 94 "Surprise." "Little Shopper" sold for $5.50 on old 1955 price list.

☐ 96 . . . . . . 4½ to 5" . . . . . . (CE). . . ❶ . . . $425–550
☐ 96 . . . . . . 4½ to 5" . . . . . . (CE). . . ❷ . . . $275–350
☐ 96 . . . . . . 4½ to 5" . . . . . . (CE). . . ❸ . . . $210–240
☐ 96 . . . . . . 4½ to 5" . . . . . . (CE). . . ❹ . . . $190–210
☐ 96 . . . . . . 4½ to 5" . . . . . . (CE). . . ❺ . . . $180–190
☐ 96 . . . . . . 4½ to 5" . . . . . . (CE). . . ❻ . . . $175–180
☐ 96 . . . . . . 4½ to 5" . . . . . . (CE). . . ❼ . . . $170–175
☐ 96 . . . . . . 4½ to 5" . . . . . . (OE). . . ❽ . . . $170

---
## HUM TERM

**SECONDARY MARKET**: The buying and selling of items after the initial retail purchase has been transacted. Often times this post-retail trading is also referred to as the "after market." This very publication is intended to serve as a guide for the secondary market values of "M. I. Hummel" items.

---

**HUM 97**
**Trumpet Boy**
Originally modeled by master sculptor Arthur Moeller in 1938. Many size variations. Boy's coat is normally green. Old "U.S. Zone" specimen has blue coat shaded with green. Old name: "The Little Musician." There are a few rare pieces with the inscription "Design Patent No. 116,464" stamped on the bottom. This indicates that this piece was originally sold in England to comply with an English requirement that each figurine carry the respective design patent number. This variation valued from $1000–1500. "Trumpet Boy" sold for $5.50 on old 1955 price list. "Trumpet Boy" was (TW) "Temporarily Withdrawn" from the U.S. market 31 December 1997, but may be reinstated at some future date.

| | | | | |
|---|---|---|---|---|
| ☐ 97 | 4½ to 4¾" | (CE) | ❶ | $400–525 |
| ☐ 97 | 4½ to 5¼" | (CE) | ❷ | $250–300 |
| ☐ 97 | 4½ to 5¼" | (CE) | ❸ | $200–225 |
| ☐ 97 | 4½ to 4¾" | (CE) | ❹ | $180–200 |
| ☐ 97 | 4½ to 4¾" | (CE) | ❺ | $170–180 |
| ☐ 97 | 4½ to 4¾" | (CE) | ❻ | $165–170 |
| ☐ 97 | 4½ to 4¾" | (TW) | ❼ | $150–160 |

| 98/0 (TM 3) | 98 (TM 1) | 98 2/0 (TM 4) |

## HUM 98
### Sister

When first modeled in 1938 by master sculptor Arthur Moeller, this figurine was produced in one size only with the incised number 98. A smaller size was issued in the early 1960's with the incised number 98 2/0. At the same time, the large size was changed to 98/0. Many size variations; otherwise very little change between old and new models. Old name: "The Shopper" or "The First Shopping" in some old catalogues. Some small size pieces have an incised 1962 copyright date. In 1996 a 2⅞" size (3⅛" with base) with incised model number 98 5/0 was produced as part of the "Pen Pals" series of personalized name card table decorations. The original issue price was $55.

"Sister" is same girl as used on HUM 49 "To Market." "Sister" sold for $6.50 on old 1955 price list. Large size (98/0) was (TW) "Temporarily Withdrawn" in January 1999. Small size (98 2/0) had special 60th anniversary decal on 1998 production.

| | | | | | |
|---|---|---|---|---|---|
| ☐ 98 5/0 | . . . 2⅞" | . . . . . . . . . . | (OE) | . . . ❼ | . . . $55 |
| ☐ 98 | . . . . . 5¾" | . . . . . . . . . . | (CE) | . . . ❶ | . . . $550–700 |
| ☐ 98 | . . . . . 5¾" | . . . . . . . . . . | (CE) | . . . ❷ | . . . $350–450 |
| ☐ 98 | . . . . . 5¾" | . . . . . . . . . . | (CE) | . . . ❸ | . . . $325–350 |
| ☐ 98 2/0 | . . . 4½ to 4¾" | . . . . . . | (CE) | . . . ❸ | . . . $225–250 |
| ☐ 98 2/0 | . . . 4½ to 4¾" | . . . . . . | (CE) | . . . ❹ | . . . $190–225 |
| ☐ 98 2/0 | . . . 4½ to 4¾" | . . . . . | (CE) | . . . ❺ | . . . $180–190 |
| ☐ 98 2/0 | . . . 4½ to 4¾" | . . . . . | (CE) | . . . ❻ | . . . $175–180 |
| ☐ 98 2/0 | . . . 4½ to 4¾" | . . . . . | (CE) | . . . ❼ | . . . $170–175   60th Anni Decal 1998 |
| ☐ 98 2/0 | . . . 4½ to 4¾" | . . . . . | (OE) | . . . ❽ | . . . $170 |
| ☐ 98/0 | . . . . . 5¼ to 5½" | . . . . . | (CE) | . . . ❸ | . . . $300–325 |
| ☐ 98/0 | . . . . . 5¼ to 5½" | . . . . . | (CE) | . . . ❹ | . . . $275–300 |
| ☐ 98/0 | . . . . . 5¼ to 5½" | . . . . . | (CE) | . . . ❺ | . . . $250–275 |
| ☐ 98/0 | . . . . . 5¼ to 5½" | . . . . . | (CE) | . . . ❻ | . . . $240–250 |
| ☐ 98/0 | . . . . . 5¼ to 5½" | . . . . . | (TW) | . . ❼ | . . . $230–235 |

## HUM 99
### Eventide

Records indicate this model was produced in 1938 by a combination of modelers. Almost identical with "Wayside Devotion" HUM 28 but without the shrine. Many size variations. Note photo of rare crown mark piece with lambs in different position directly in front of children. At one time this figurine was sold in Belgium in the white overglaze finish and would now be considered rare. Eventide was listed as (TW) "Temporarily Withdrawn" in January 1999.

*Normal (TM 1)*                    *Rare version (TM 1)*

☐ 99 . . . . . . 4¼ × 5″ . . . . . . (CE). . . ❶ . . . $950–1250
☐ 99 . . . . . . 4¼ × 5″ . . . . . . (CE). . . ❷ . . . $600–750
☐ 99 . . . . . . 4¼ × 5″ . . . . . . (CE). . . ❸ . . . $500–550
☐ 99 . . . . . . 4¼ × 5″ . . . . . . (CE). . . ❹ . . . $425–500
☐ 99 . . . . . . 4¼ × 5″ . . . . . . (CE). . . ❺ . . . $390–425
☐ 99 . . . . . . 4¼ × 5″ . . . . . . (CE). . . ❻ . . . $370–390
☐ 99 . . . . . . 4¼ × 5″ . . . . . . (TW) . . ❼ . . . $360–370
☐ 99 . . . . . . Rare version . . . (CE). . . ❶ . . . $3000–3500

---

**HUM TERM**

**RARE:** (Webster) marked by unusual quality, merit, or appeal. Distinctive, superlative or extreme of its kind, seldom occurring or found, uncommon.

---

**HUM 100**
**Shrine,Table Lamp(CE)**
This extremely rare lamp is similar to the figurine "Adoration" HUM 23. First modeled
by Erich Lautensack in 1938 and produced in very limited quantities. Only a few examples known to exist. The example in our collection has a light beige-colored post, an
incised crown trademark plus the stamped "U.S. Zone". Another example had a dark
brown post, an incised crown trademark plus stamped "full bee." Also had 6/50 date.

☐ 100 . . . . . 7½" . . . . . . . . . . (CE). . . ❶ . . . $8,000–10,000

*Front view (TM 1)*

*Rare plain post (TM 1)*

**HUM 101**
**To Market, Table Lamp (CE)**

Originally modeled by master sculptor Arthur Moeller in 1937. Listed as a closed edition on factory records 20 April 1937. Redesigned and limited quantity produced in early 1950's with "tree trunk" post. Some incised with number II/101, III/101 and others with 101 only. Lamp was adapted from figurine "To Market" HUM 49. Master sculptor Arthur Moeller redesigned this lamp in 1952 into the 9½ inch size HUM 223.

☐ 101 . . . . . 6½" . . . . . . . . . (CE). . . ❶ . . . $8,000–10,000 Plain Post
☐ 101 . . . . . 6½" . . . . . . . . . (CE). . . ❷ . . . $6000–8000 Plain Post
☐ 101 . . . . . 7½" . . . . . . . . . (CE). . . ❶ . . . $1,500–2,000 Tree trunk post
☐ 101 . . . . . 7½" . . . . . . . . . (CE). . . ❷ . . . $750–1000
☐ 101 . . . . . 7½" . . . . . . . . . (CE). . . ❸ . . . $500–750

*Plain post      Tree trunk post*

**HUM 102**
**Volunteers, Table Lamp (CE)**
Originally modeled by Erich Lautensack in 1937. Listed as a closed edition in factory records 20 April 1937. In 1979 a rare specimen was found in Seattle, Washington, and is now in the Robert L. Miller collection. This piece has a double crown (incised and stamped) trademark. Since 1979 several other specimens have been found and the Goebel factory now has one in their archives.

☐ 102 . . . . . 7½" . . . . . . . . . (CE) . . . ❶ . . . $8,000–10,000

**HUM 103**
**Farewell, Table Lamp (CE)**
Originally modeled by Erich Lautensack in 1937. Listed as a closed edition on factory records 20 April 1937. Several examples of this extremely rare lamp have recently been found and one is now in the Robert L. Miller collection. A second specimen was recently presented to the Goebel factory for their archives in Rödental, Germany. Since 1983 several other specimens have been found, but is still considered extremely rare.

☐ 103 . . . . . 7½" . . . . . . . . . (CE) . . . ❶ . . . $8,000–10,000

## HUM 104
### Eventide, Table Lamp (CE)
Originally modeled by Reinhold Unger in 1938. Listed as a closed edition on factory records 3 March 1938. This lamp was originally called "Wayside Devotion" in our earlier books but is now correctly named "Eventide." The first known example of this extremely rare lamp base was purchased from its original owner in northern Indiana and is now in the Robert L. Miller collection. The lamp was located through the help of Ralph and Terry Kovel and their syndicated newspaper column on antiques. Notice the position of lambs in this photo and then compare with photo of "Eventide" HUM 99.

☐ 104 . . . . . 7½″ . . . . . . . . . . (CE) . . . ❶ . . . $8,000–10,000

*Double crown (TM 1+1)*    *Double crown (TM 1+1)*

## HUM 105
### Adoration With Bird (CE)
Very limited production. Listed as a closed edition on factory records 24 May 1938. All known examples have double crown (incised and stamped) trademark. Notice difference in pigtail of little girl in this comparative photograph. Unable to locate information on original sculptor or date of original model; probably master sculptor Reinhold Unger who created model for "Adoration" HUM 23 which is similar in design. This figurine is considered extremely rare.

☐ 105 . . . . . 4¾″ . . . . . . . . . . (CE) . . . ❶ . . . $7,000–8,000

*106 (TM 1)*          *107 (TM 1)*

**HUM 106**
**Merry Wanderer,**
**Plaque with wood frame (CE)**
Very limited production. Listed as a closed edition on factory records 1 August 1938. First modeled by master sculptor Arthur Moeller in 1938. Similar to all-ceramic plaque of "Merry Wanderer" HUM 92 except for wood frame. Some variation in frames. Considered extremely rare.

☐ 106 . . . . . 6 × 6″. . . . . . . . (CE). . . ❶ . . . $3,000-4,000

**HUM 107**
**Little Fiddler,**
**Plaque with wood frame (CE)**
Very limited production. Listed as a closed edition on factory records 1 August 1938. First modeled by master sculptor Arthur Moeller in 1938. Similar to the all-ceramic plaque of "Little Fiddler" HUM 93 (rare old style background) except for the wood frame. Some variation in frames. Considered extremely rare.

☐ 107 . . . . . 6 × 6″. . . . . . . . (CE). . . ❶ . . . $3,000–4,000

---

**HUM TERM**

**PREVIEW EDITION:** Figurines with an M.I. Hummel Club backstamp offered exclusively to members for a special preview period. After its first two years of production, it may become an open edition (OE) available to the general public, bearing a regular Goebel backstamp only.

*(TM 1+USZ)   HS 01 (Not 108)   (TM 1+2)*

## HUM 108
### Angel With Two Children At Feet (CN)

Originally modeled by master sculptor Reinhold Unger in 1938. No known examples. Listed on factory records of 14 October 1938 as a wall decoration. Pictured here is Goebel item HS 01 listed in 1950 Goebel catalogue. Factory representatives state that is possibly a Hummel design—probably rejected by Siessen Convent and then later marketed as a Goebel item. When and if found with the "M. I. Hummel" signature and incised 108 would have a value of $10,000–15,000. Note hair on boy: blonde on left while dark hair on right as we face photo. Several examples of Goebel HS 01 have been found and are now in private collections—including the Robert L. Miller collection.

☐ 108 . . . . . . . . . . . . . . . . . . (CN). . . . ❶ . . . . . . $10,000–15,000
☐ Goebel HS 01 . . . . 10¼″ . . (CE). . . . ❶ . . . . . . $3000–5000
☐ Goebel HS 01 . . . . 10¼″ . . (CE) . . ❶ + ❷ . . . . $2500–4500

---

**HUM TERM**

**SAMPLE MODEL**: Generally a figurine that was made as a sample only and not approved by the Siessen Convent for production. Sample models (in the true sense of the term) are extremely rare items and command a premium price on the secondary market.

---

*109/II (TM 3)*     *109 (TM 1 + 1)*     *109/0 (TM 2)*

## HUM 109
### Happy Traveller

First modeled by master sculptor Arthur Moeller in 1938 and has been produced in all trademark periods. The large size was permanently retired by Goebel in the spring of 1982. Early pieces were usually incised 109/2 instead of 109/II. Small size only is still in current production. Sometimes the small size is found without the size designator in trademarks 3,4 and 5. Listed as "Wanderer" in old catalogues. Small size was restyled in 1980 with the new textured finish. The small size normally has black handles on the umbrella while the large size has tan.

☐ 109/0 . . . . 4¾ to 5″ . . . . . . (CE). . . ❷ . . . $275–350
☐ 109/0 . . . . 4¾ to 5″ . . . . . . (CE). . . ❸ . . . $225–250
☐ 109 . . . . . 4¾ to 5″ . . . . . . (CE). . . ❸ . . . $225–250
☐ 109/0 . . . . 4¾ to 5″ . . . . . . (CE). . . ❹ . . . $200–225
☐ 109 . . . . . 4¾ to 5″ . . . . . . (CE). . . ❹ . . . $200–225
☐ 109/0 . . . . 4¾ to 5″ . . . . . . (CE). . . ❺ . . . $185–190
☐ 109 . . . . . 4¾ to 5″ . . . . . . (CE). . . ❺ . . . $185–190
☐ 109/0 . . . . 4¾ to 5″ . . . . . . (CE). . . ❻ . . . $180–185
☐ 109/0 . . . . 4¾ to 5″ . . . . . . (CE). . . ❼ . . . $175–180
☐ 109/0 . . . . 4¾ to 5″ . . . . . . (OE). . . ❽ . . . $175
☐ 109 . . . . . 7¾″. . . . . . . . . (CE). . . ❶ . . . $1200–1500
☐ 109 . . . . . 7½″. . . . . . . . . (CE). . . ❷ . . . $800–900
☐ 109/II . . . . 7½″. . . . . . . . . (CE). . . ❸ . . . $500–550
☐ 109/II . . . . 7½″. . . . . . . . . (CE). . . ❹ . . . $450–500
☐ 109/II . . . . 7½″. . . . . . . . . (CE). . . ❺ . . . $400–425
☐ 109/II . . . . 7½″. . . . . . . . . (CE). . . ❻ . . . $375–400

110 (TM 1)                    110/0 (TM 3)

## HUM 110
### Let's Sing

Originally modeled by master sculptor Reinhold Unger in 1938. There are many size variations. Some have an incised 1938 copyright date. Sometimes found with "©W. Goebel." Some incised model numbers are difficult to read because of the extremely small bases. "Let's Sing" sold for $6.00 on old 1955 price list. See: HUM 114 "Let's Sing" ashtray.

| | | | | |
|---|---|---|---|---|
| ☐ 110 | 4" | (CE) | ❶ | $475–600 |
| ☐ 110 | 4" | (CE) | ❷ | $325–400 |
| ☐ 110/0 | 3 to 3¼" | (CE) | ❶ | $350–500 |
| ☐ 110/0 | 3 to 3¼" | (CE) | ❷ | $225–300 |
| ☐ 110/0 | 3 to 3¼" | (CE) | ❸ | $195–225 |
| ☐ 110/0 | 3 to 3¼" | (CE) | ❹ | $165–195 |
| ☐ 110/0 | 3 to 3¼" | (CE) | ❺ | $160–165 |
| ☐ 110/0 | 3 to 3¼" | (CE) | ❻ | $155–160 |
| ☐ 110/0 | 3 to 3¼" | (CE) | ❼ | $150–155 |
| ☐ 110/0 | 3 to 3¼" | (OE) | ❽ | $150 |
| ☐ 110/I | 3½ to 4" | (CE) | ❷ | $300–375 |
| ☐ 110/I | 3½ to 4" | (CE) | ❸ | $250–300 |
| ☐ 110/I | 3½ to 4" | (CE) | ❹ | $225–250 |
| ☐ 110/I | 3½ to 4" | (CE) | ❺ | $205–225 |
| ☐ 110/I | 3½ to 4" | (CE) | ❻ | $200–205 |
| ☐ 110/I | 3½ to 4" | (CE) | ❼ | $195–200 |
| ☐ 110/I | 3½ to 4" | (OE) | ❽ | $195 |

> ### HUM TERM
>
> **OVERSIZE**: This description refers to a piece that has experienced "mold growth" size expansion. A figurine that measures larger than the standard size is said to be "oversized."

*Old bowl style*

*New jar style*

**HUM III/110**
**Let's Sing, Box**
Bowl style first produced in 1938. Jar style first produced and sold in 1964. Model number is found on underside of lid. The "M .I. Hummel" signature is found on topside of lid directly behind figure. "Let's Sing" candy box was (TW) "Temporarily Withdrawn" from production on 31 December 1989, but may be reinstated at some future date.

☐ III/110. . . . 6¼″ . . . . . . . . . . (CE). . . **❶** . . . $750–850
☐ III/110. . . . 6¼″ . . . . . . . . . . (CE). . . **❷** . . . $575–650
☐ III/110. . . . 6¼″ . . . . . . . . . . (CE). . . **❸** . . . $475–550 (Old Style)
☐ III/110. . . . 5¼″ . . . . . . . . . . (CE). . . **❸** . . . $300–350 (New Style)
☐ III/110. . . . 5¼″ . . . . . . . . . . (CE). . . **❹** . . . $250–275
☐ III/110. . . . 5¼″ . . . . . . . . . . (CE). . . **❺** . . . $225–250
☐ III/110. . . . 5¼″ . . . . . . . . . . (TW) . . **❻** . . . $200–225

---

**HUM TERM**

**PAINT RUB**: A general wearing away of the paint surface of a figurine in a particular spot. This condition is usually caused by excessive handling of a figurine, thin paint in a given area of the figurine, or the excessive use of abrasive cleaners.

---

**HUM TERM**

**FAIENCE:** (pronounced *fay-ontz* or fi-ons) is a term for earthenware decorated with opaque colored glazes. A few early samples were produced experimentally by Goebel on "M.I. Hummel" figurines using this technique.

*111/I (TM 1)*                    *111 3/0 (TM 4)*

**HUM 111**
**Wayside Harmony**
First modeled in 1938 by master sculptor Reinhold Unger. There are many size variations. Normally has green-colored socks, but some crown and full bee trademark pieces have yellow socks in the small (111 3/0) size. Old name: "Just Sittin-Boy." Some models have a 1938 incised copyright date. The small size "Wayside Harmony" listed for $5.00 while the large size listed for $10.00 on 1955 price list. Large size (111/I) was (TW) "Temporarily Withdrawn" in January 1999.

| | | | | | |
|---|---|---|---|---|---|
| ☐ 111 3/0 | . . 3¾ to 4" | . . . . . . | (CE). . . | ❶ . . . | $400–550 |
| ☐ 111 3/0 | . . 3¾ to 4" | . . . . . . | (CE). . . | ❷ . . . | $275–350 |
| ☐ 111 3/0 | . . 3¾ to 4" | . . . . . . | (CE). . . | ❸ . . . | $225–250 |
| ☐ 111 3/0 | . . 3¾ to 4" | . . . . . . | (CE). . . | ❹ . . . | $200–225 |
| ☐ 111 3/0 | . . 3¾ to 4" | . . . . . . | (CE). . . | ❺ . . . | $185–200 |
| ☐ 111 3/0 | . . 3¾ to 4" | . . . . . . | (CE). . . | ❻ . . . | $180–185 |
| ☐ 111 3/0 | . . 3¾ to 4" | . . . . . . | (CE). . . | ❼ . . . | $175–180 |
| ☐ 111 3/0 | . . 3¾ to 4" | . . . . . . | (**OE**). . . | ❽ . . . | $175 |
| ☐ 111/I | . . . . 5 to 5½" | . . . . . . | (CE). . . | ❶ . . . | $650–800 |
| ☐ 111/I | . . . . 5 to 5½" | . . . . . . | (CE). . . | ❷ . . . | $450–550 |
| ☐ 111/I | . . . . 5 to 5½" | . . . . . . | (CE). . . | ❸ . . . | $400–450 |
| ☐ 111/I | . . . . 5 to 5½" | . . . . . . | (CE). . . | ❹ . . . | $350–400 |
| ☐ 111/I | . . . . 5 to 5½" | . . . . . . | (CE). . . | ❺ . . . | $340–350 |
| ☐ 111/I | . . . . 5 to 5½" | . . . . . . | (CE). . . | ❻ . . . | $330–340 |
| ☐ 111/I | . . . . 5 to 5½" | . . . . . . | (TW) . . | ❼ . . . | $320–330 |
| ☐ 111 | . . . . . 5½" | . . . . . . . . . . . | (CE). . . | ❶ . . . | $700–850 |

*II/111 (TM 2)*           *224/I (TM 4)*

**HUM II/111**
**Wayside Harmony, Table Lamp (CE)**
This number was used briefly in the early 1950's. Later changed to 224/I. The only difference is that the boy is slightly larger. Some models have been found with number III/111/I.

☐ II/111 . . . . 7½" . . . . . . . . . . (CE). . . ❶ . . . $600–800
☐ II/111 . . . . 7½" . . . . . . . . . . (CE). . . ❷ . . . $450–550
☐ II/111 . . . . 7½" . . . . . . . . . . (CE). . . ❸ . . . $375–525

---
**HUM TERM**

**PAINT FLAKE**: The term used to designate a flaw in a ceramic figurine whereby the paint has been chipped. This type flaw does not go beyond the glazed surface.

---

107

*112/I (TM 2)*                    *112 3/0 (TM 4)*

**HUM 112**
**Just Resting**
First modeled in 1938 by master sculptor Reinhold Unger. Many size variations. Old
name: "Just Sittin-Girl." Some models have a 1938 incised copyright date. There is an
unusual example of size 112/I without a basket in front of the girl (not shown). The
direction of the basket handle varies on old "crown" trademark examples. Large size
(112/I) was (TW) "Temporarily Withdrawn" from production in January 1999.

| | | | | | |
|---|---|---|---|---|---|
| ☐ 112 3/0. . . | 3¾ to 4″ | . . . . . . | (CE). . . | ❶ | . . . $400–550 |
| ☐ 112 3/0. . . | 3¾ to 4″ | . . . . . . | (CE). . . | ❷ | . . . $275–350 |
| ☐ 112 3/0. . . | 3¾ to 4″ | . . . . . . | (CE). . . | ❸ | . . . $225–250 |
| ☐ 112 3/0. . . | 3¾ to 4″ | . . . . . . | (CE). . . | ❹ | . . . $200–225 |
| ☐ 112 3/0. . . | 3¾ to 4″ | . . . . . . | (CE). . . | ❺ | . . . $185–200 |
| ☐ 112 3/0. . . | 3¾ to 4″ | . . . . . . | (CE). . . | ❻ | . . . $180–185 |
| ☐ 112 3/0. . . | 3¾ to 4″ | . . . . . . | (CE). . . | ❼ | . . . $175–180 |
| ☐ 112 3/0. . . | 3¾ to 4″ | . . . . . . | (**OE**). . . | ❽ | . . . $175 |
| ☐ 112/I . . . . | 4¾ to 5½″ | . . . . . | (CE). . . | ❶ | . . . $650–800 |
| ☐ 112/I . . . . | 4¾ to 5½″ | . . . . . | (CE). . . | ❷ | . . . $450–550 |
| ☐ 112/I . . . . | 4¾ to 5½″ | . . . . . | (CE). . . | ❸ | . . . $400–450 |
| ☐ 112/I . . . . | 4¾ to 5½″ | . . . . . | (CE). . . | ❹ | . . . $350–400 |
| ☐ 112/I . . . . | 4¾ to 5½″ | . . . . . | (CE). . . | ❺ | . . . $340–350 |
| ☐ 112/I . . . . | 4¾ to 5½″ | . . . . . | (CE). . . | ❻ | . . . $330–340 |
| ☐ 112/I . . . . | 4¾ to 5½″ | . . . . . | (TW) | ❼ | . . . $320–330 |
| ☐ 112 . . . . . | 5½″ | . . . . . . . . . | (CE). . . | ❶ | . . . $700–850 |

| II/112 (TM 2) | 225/I (TM 5) | 112 (TM 1+1) |

## HUM II/112
### Just Resting, Table Lamp (CE)
This number was used briefly in the early 1950's. Later changed to 225/I. The only difference is that the girl is slightly larger. Some models have a 1938 incised copyright date. Some models have been found with numbers III/112/I and 2/112/I. Very hard to find with these numbers. An unusual variation was found in Sweden in 1991 with a "double crown" trademark, incised "M. I. Hummel" signature on back of tree trunk and incised number 112 only. It is now in the Robert L. Mlller collection. Possibly a "prototype" or at least a "mother mould sample." The base is too small to be used successfully as a lamp and was re-designed with a larger round base. The history of this lamp is still unknown and I have not been able to locate another sample like this one, nor any information on it at the factory. A similar variation of the companion lamp of "Wayside Harmony" HUM 111 is yet to be found.

☐ II/112 . . . . 7½" . . . . . . . . . (CE). . . ❶ . . . $600–800
☐ II/112 . . . . 7½" . . . . . . . . . (CE). . . ❷ . . . $450–550
☐ II/112 . . . . 7½" . . . . . . . . . (CE). . . ❸ . . . $375–525
☐ 112 . . . . . 7" . . . . . . . . . . (CE) . ❶ + ❶ . $5,000–6,000

---
**HUM TERM**

**DOUBLE CROWN:** This term is used to describe the Goebel Company trademark found on some "M. I. Hummel" figurines. On "double crown" pieces the crown trademark is found both incised and stamped.

---

### HUM 113
### Heavenly Song, Candleholder (CE)
Originally modeled by master sculptor Arthur Moeller in 1938 but was produced in very limited quantities. Sometimes mistaken for HUM 54 "Silent Night;" which is similar. Was scheduled for production again in 1978 and listed in some catalogues and price lists, but because of its similarity to HUM 54 "Silent Night" the factory decided it should not be produced again. In 1980 it was listed as a closed edition. At least one piece is known to exist with the 5 trademark. All specimens would now be considered extremely rare. Also found decorated in bright colors and glossy finish of the "Faience" technique. Usually sell for $3000–5000.

| | | | | | |
|---|---|---|---|---|---|
| ☐ 113 | 3½ × 4¾″ | (CE) | ❶ | $6,000–10,000 |
| ☐ 113 | 3½ × 4¾″ | (CE) | ❷ | $4,500–5,500 |
| ☐ 113 | 3½ × 4¾″ | (CE) | ❸ | $3,500–4,500 |
| ☐ 113 | 3½ × 4¾″ | (CE) | ❺ | $3,000–3,500 |

*Old style (TM 2)*             *New style (TM 2)*

### HUM 114
### Let's Sing, Ashtray
First modeled in 1938 by master sculptor Reinhold Unger with the ashtray on the left as we face the figurine (boy's right). Restyled in 1959 by master sculptor Theo R. Menzenbach with the ashtray on the right as we face the figurine (boy's left). Old style would be considered difficult to find today. Both styles can be found with the (TM 2) full bee trademark. This accounts for the wide price variation in TM 2 trademark prices.

| | | | | | |
|---|---|---|---|---|---|
| ☐ 114 | 3½ × 6¼″ | (CE) | ❶ | $850–1000 (Old Style) |
| ☐ 114 | 3½ × 6¼″ | (CE) | ❷ | $600–850 (Old Style) |
| ☐ 114 | 3½ × 6¼″ | (CE) | ❷ | $250–350 (New Style) |
| ☐ 114 | 3½ × 6¼″ | (CE) | ❸ | $225–250 |
| ☐ 114 | 3½ × 6¼″ | (CE) | ❹ | $170–225 |
| ☐ 114 | 3½ × 6¼″ | (CE) | ❺ | $160–170 |
| ☐ 114 | 3½ × 6¼″ | (TW) | ❻ | $150–160 |

*115 / Mel 1*          *116 / Mel 2*          *117 / Mel 3*

**HUM 115**
**Advent Candlestick, Girl With Nosegay**
**HUM 116**
**Advent Candlestick, Girl With Fir Tree**
**HUM 117**
**Advent Candlestick, Boy with Horse**
These three figurines were first modeled by master sculptor Reinhold Unger in 1939. They are similar to HUM 239 A, B & C (without candleholders). Very early models were incised with "Mel" instead of "M. I. Hummel." Reportedly sold only in Germany. Note: "Mel" is the last three letters of Hum**mel**. Some "Mel" pieces have been found with the early stylized trademark indicating that both "Hummel" and "Mel" pieces were being produced and marketed at the same time. Mel 1, Mel 2, and Mel 3 usually sell for $300 to $350 each depending on the condition.

| | | | | | |
|---|---|---|---|---|---|
| ☐ 115 | 3½" | (CE) | ❶ | $200–250 |
| ☐ 115 | 3½" | (CE) | ❷ | $110–135 |
| ☐ 115 | 3½" | (CE) | ❸ | $85–90 |
| ☐ 115 | 3½" | (CE) | ❹ | $80–85 |
| ☐ 115 | 3½" | (CE) | ❺ | $75–80 |
| ☐ 115 | 3½" | (CE) | ❻ | $70–75 |
| ☐ 115 | 3½" | (CE) | ❼ | $68–70 |
| ☐ 115 | 3½" | (OE) | ❽ | $68 |
| ☐ 116 | 3½" | (CE) | ❶ | $200–250 |
| ☐ 116 | 3½" | (CE) | ❷ | $110–135 |
| ☐ 116 | 3½" | (CE) | ❸ | $85–90 |
| ☐ 116 | 3½" | (CE) | ❹ | $80–85 |
| ☐ 116 | 3½" | (CE) | ❺ | $75–80 |
| ☐ 116 | 3½" | (CE) | ❻ | $70–75 |
| ☐ 116 | 3½" | (CE) | ❼ | $68–70 |
| ☐ 116 | 3½" | (OE) | ❽ | $68 |
| ☐ 117 | 3½" | (CE) | ❶ | $200–250 |
| ☐ 117 | 3½" | (CE) | ❷ | $110–135 |
| ☐ 117 | 3½" | (CE) | ❸ | $85–90 |
| ☐ 117 | 3½" | (CE) | ❹ | $80–85 |
| ☐ 117 | 3½" | (CE) | ❺ | $75–80 |
| ☐ 117 | 3½" | (CE) | ❻ | $70–75 |
| ☐ 117 | 3½" | (CE) | ❼ | $68–70 |
| ☐ 117 | 3½" | (OE) | ❽ | $68 |

*New style (TM 3)*          *Old style (TM 1+2)*

**HUM 118**
**Little Thrifty, Bank**
This figurine is actually a bank. Made with a metal lock & key on bottom. Originally modeled by master sculptor Arthur Moeller in 1939. Restyled by Rudolf Wittman in 1963. Older models have a slightly different base design as noted in photograph. The object into which "Little Thrifty" is putting her coin is a medieval form of a poor box, something which can still be found in old European churches. To my knowledge, not produced with TM 4. "Little Thrifty" sold for $6.00 on old 1955 price list. Found with either gold or silver coin.

☐ 118 . . . . . 5 to 5½" . . . . . . (CE). . . ❶ . . . $500–750
☐ 118 . . . . . 5 to 5½" . . . . . . (CE). . . ❷ . . . $400–450
☐ 118 . . . . . 5 to 5½" . . . . . . (CE). . . ❸ . . . $225–275
☐ 118 . . . . . 5 to 5½" . . . . . . (CE). . . ❺ . . . $195-200
☐ 118 . . . . . 5 to 5½" . . . . . . (CE). . . ❻ . . . $190–195
☐ 118 . . . . . 5 to 5½" . . . . . . (CE). . . ❼ . . . $185–190
☐ 118 . . . . . 5 to 5½" . . . . . . (**OE**). . . ❽ . . . $185

┌─────────── **HUM TERM** ───────────┐

**OVERSIZE**: This description refers to a piece that has experienced "mold growth" size expansion. A figurine that measures larger than the standard size is said to be "oversized."

└──────────────────────────────┘

119 (TM 2)      119 (TM 2)      119 2/0 (TM 6)

## HUM 119
### Postman

Many size variations although officially made in one size only. First modeled by master sculptor Arthur Moeller in 1939. Later restyled by master sculptor Gerhard Skrobek in 1970 giving it the new textured finish. Newer models have four letters in the mail bag while older models have five letters. A new small size "Postman" (119 2/0) was released in 1989 with a suggested retail price of $90. It was modeled by master sculptor Gerhard Skrobek in 1985. It has an incised 1985 copyright date. Note letters on (119 2/0). The large size has been renumbered 119/0 and the old 119 is now classified as a closed edition (CE) because of this change.

☐ 119 2/0. . . 4½″ . . . . . . . . . . (CE). . . ❻ . . . $175–180
☐ 119 2/0. . . 4½″ . . . . . . . . . . (CE). . . ❼ . . . $170–175
☐ 119 2/0. . . 4½″ . . . . . . . . . . (**OE**). . . ❽ . . . $170
☐ 119 . . . . . 5 to 5½″ . . . . . . . (CE). . . ❶ . . . $600–750
☐ 119 . . . . . 4¾ to 5½″ . . . . . (CE). . . ❷ . . . $350–450 (small hat)
☐ 119 . . . . . 4¾ to 5½″ . . . . . (CE). . . ❸ . . . $300–325 (small hat)
☐ 119 . . . . . 5 to 5½″ . . . . . . . (CE). . . ❹ . . . $270–300
☐ 119 . . . . . 5 to 5½″ . . . . . . . (CE). . . ❺ . . . $250–270
☐ 119 . . . . . 5 to 5½″ . . . . . . . (CE). . . ❻ . . . $245–250
☐ 119 . . . . . 5 to 5½″ . . . . . . . (CE). . . ❻ . . . $240–245
☐ 119/0 . . . . 5½″ . . . . . . . . . . (CE). . . ❼ . . . $235–240
☐ 119/0 . . . . 5½″ . . . . . . . . . . (**OE**). . . ❽ . . . $235

**HUM 120**
**Joyful and Let's Sing (on wooden base), Bookends (CE)**
No known examples. Listed as a closed edition on factory records 16 June 1939. Records indicate this was made in 1939 by a combination of sculptors. Probably similar in design to Hum 122.

☐ 120 . . . . . (CE) . . . . . . . . . ❶ . . . . . $10,000–20,000

**HUM 121**
**Wayside Harmony and Just Resting (on wooden base), Bookends (CE)**
Listed as a closed edition on factory records 16 June 1939. Records indicate this was made in 1939 by a combination of sculptors. This bookend (half only) was recently located in central Europe and is now part of the Robert L. Miller collection.

☐ 121 A . . . . (CE) . . . . . . . . . ❶ . . . . . $5,000–10,000
☐ 121 B . . . . (CE) . . . . . . . . . ❶ . . . . $5,000–10,000

*Factory prototypes*

**HUM 122**
**Puppy Love and Serenade With Dog (on wooden base), Bookends (CE)**
Factory sample only. Listed as a closed edition on factory records 16 June 1939. Records indicate this was made in 1939 by a combination of sculptors.

☐ 122 . . . . . (CE) . . . . . . . . . ❶ . . . . $10,000–20,000

**Old style (TM 2)**                    **New style (TM 5)**

**HUM 123**
**Max and Moritz**
First modeled by master sculptor Arthur Moeller in 1939. Color variations found in early "Crown" (TM I) pieces—"Max" with black hair and black shoes;—"Moritz" with brown shoes instead of black. Restyled in the early 1970's with the new textured finish. Color of boys' hair will vary. Old name: "Good Friends" in some catalogues. "Max and Moritz" sold for $8.00 on old 1955 price list. See: HUM 553 "Scamp" and HUM 554 "Cheeky Fellow"—how one old figurine has been made into two new ones!

☐ 123 . . . . . 5 to 5½" . . . . . . (CE). . . ❶ . . . $650–800
☐ 123 . . . . . 5 to 5½" . . . . . . (CE). . . ❷ . . . $400–500
☐ 123 . . . . . 5 to 5½" . . . . . . (CE). . . ❸ . . . $325–375
☐ 123 . . . . . 5 to 5½" . . . . . . (CE). . . ❹ . . . $290–325
☐ 123 . . . . . 5 to 5½" . . . . . . (CE). . . ❺ . . . $270–290
☐ 123 . . . . . 5 to 5½" . . . . . . (CE). . . ❻ . . . $260–265
☐ 123 . . . . . 5 to 5½" . . . . . . (CE). . . ❼ . . . $255–260
☐ 123 . . . . . 5 to 5½" . . . . . . (**OE**). . . ❽ . . . $255

---
**HUM TERM**

**STYLIZED TRADEMARK**: The symbol used by the Goebel Company from 1957 until 1964. It is recognized by the V with a bumblebee that has triangular or "stylized" wings.

---

124/0 (TM 7)          124/I (TM 2)          124 (TM 1)

## HUM 124
### Hello
Many size variations. Earliest models produced had grey coat, grey trousers and pink vest. Changed to brown coat, green trousers and pink vest in early 1950's. Changed to dark brown coat, light brown trousers and blue-white vest in mid-1960's. Originally modeled by master sculptor Arthur Moeller in 1939. Has been restyled several times through the years. Old name: "The Boss" or "Der Chef." The large size 124/I had been difficult to find but was put back on the market in 1978, then in the spring of 1982 was listed as "temporarily withdrawn" by Goebel, to be reinstated at a later date. The small size only is still in current production. Some models have been painted with open eyes while most models have eyes looking down.

| | | | | |
|---|---|---|---|---|
| ☐ 124 . . . . . 6½″ . . . . . . . . . . | (CE) . . . | ❶ | . . . | $800–1000 |
| ☐ 124 . . . . . 6½″ . . . . . . . . . . | (CE) . . . | ❷ | . . . | $450–600 |
| ☐ 124/0 . . . . 5¾ to 6¼″ . . . . . | (CE) . . . | ❷ | . . . | $400–450 |
| ☐ 124/0 . . . . 5¾ to 6¼″ . . . . . | (CE) . . . | ❸ | . . . | $350–400 |
| ☐ 124/0 . . . . 5¾ to 6¼″ . . . . . | (CE) . . . | ❹ | . . . | $290–350 |
| ☐ 124/0 . . . . 5¾ to 6¼″ . . . . . | (CE) . . . | ❺ | . . . | $265–290 |
| ☐ 124/0 . . . . 5¾ to 6¼″ . . . . . | (CE) . . . | ❻ | . . . | $260–265 |
| ☐ 124/0 . . . . 5¾ to 6¼″ . . . . . | (CE) . . . | ❼ | . . . | $255–260 |
| ☐ 124/0 . . . . 5¾ to 6¼″ . . . . . | (OE) . . . | ❽ | . . . | $255 |
| ☐ 124/I . . . . 6¾ to 7″ . . . . . . | (CE) . . . | ❶ | . . . | $800–1000 |
| ☐ 124/I . . . . 6¾ to 7″ . . . . . . | (CE) . . . | ❷ | . . . | $450–600 |
| ☐ 124/I . . . . 6¾ to 7″ . . . . . . | (CE) . . . | ❸ | . . . | $400–450 |
| ☐ 124/I . . . . 6¾ to 7″ . . . . . . | (CE) . . . | ❹ | . . . | $350–400 |
| ☐ 124/I . . . . 6¾ to 7″ . . . . . . | (CE) . . . | ❺ | . . . | $300–350 |
| ☐ 124/I . . . . 6¾ to 7″ . . . . . . | (TW) . . . | ❻ | . . . | $275–300 |

*New style (TM 3)*          *Old style (TM 1)*

**HUM 125**
**Vacation Time, Plaque**
First modeled in 1939 by master sculptor Arthur Moeller. Restyled in 1960 by master sculptor Theo R. Menzenbach. Slight color variations on older models. The newer model has five fence posts while the older one has six. Old name: "Happy Holidays" or "On Holiday." Newer models produced without string for hanging, only a hole on back for hanging. Both old style and new style can be found with the stylized (TM 3) trademark. "Vacation Time" plaque was (TW) "Temporarily Withdrawn" from production on 31 December 1989, but may be reinstated at some future date. Reissued with (TM 7) trademark in 1998 in a combination package with "Vacation Time" HummelScape (Mark # 1002-D). Retail price for both pieces $260.

☐ 125 ..... 4⅜ × 5¼" ..... (CE)... ❶ ... $600–750
☐ 125 ..... 4⅜ × 5¼" ..... (CE)... ❷ ... $450–550
☐ 125 ..... 4⅜ × 5¼" ..... (CE)... ❸ ... $375–450 (Old Style)
☐ 125 ..... 4 × 4¾" ...... (CE)... ❸ ... $275–350 (New Style)
☐ 125 ..... 4 × 4¾" ...... (CE)... ❹ ... $255–275
☐ 125 ..... 4 × 4¾" ...... (CE)... ❺ ... $245–255
☐ 125 ..... 4 × 4¾" ...... (CE)... ❻ ... $235–245
☐ 125 ..... 4 × 4¾" ...... (TW) .. ❼ ... $225–235

*With HummelScape*

117

**HUM 126**
**Retreat to Safety, Plaque**
First modeled by master sculptor Arthur Moeller in 1939. Older plaques are slightly larger. Slight color variations on older models. This same motif is also produced as a figurine by the same name although the colors are different. See "Retreat to Safety" HUM 201. "Retreat to Safety" plaque was (TW) "Temporarily Withdrawn" from production on 31 December 1989, but may be reinstated at some future date.

☐ 126 . . . 4¾ × 4¾″ to 5 × 5″ . . (CE) . . . ❶ . . . $550–700
☐ 126 . . . 4¾ × 4¾″ to 5 × 5″ . . (CE) . . . ❷ . . . $400–500
☐ 126 . . . 4¾ × 4¾″ . . . . . . . . . (CE) . . . ❸ . . . $275–350
☐ 126 . . . 4¾ × 4¾″ . . . . . . . . . (CE) . . . ❹ . . . $225–275
☐ 126 . . . 4¾ × 4¾″ . . . . . . . . . (CE) . . . ❺ . . . $190–200
☐ 126 . . . 4¾ × 4¾″ . . . . . . . . . (TW) . . ❻ . . . $185–190

---

**——— HUM TERM ———**

**OUT OF PRODUCTION:** A term used by the Goebel Company to designate items that are not currently in production, yet have not been given an official classification as to their eventual fate. Some items listed as out of production may become closed editions, remain temporarily withdrawn, or ultimately return to current production status.

(TM 2)          (U.S. Zone)          (TM 1+1)          (TM 3)

## HUM 127
### Doctor

Originally modeled by master sculptor Arthur Moeller in 1939. Has been restyled several times during the years. Many variations in size through the years with older examples slightly larger. Old name: "The Doll Doctor." Legs of doll sometimes protrude over edge of base. Newer models now have the "textured" finish.

| | | | | |
|---|---|---|---|---|
| ☐ 127 | 4¾ to 5¼″ | (CE) | ❶ | $450–650 |
| ☐ 127 | 4¾ to 5¼″ | (CE) | ❷ | $300–350 |
| ☐ 127 | 4¾ to 5¼″ | (CE) | ❸ | $225–275 |
| ☐ 127 | 4¾ to 5¼″ | (CE) | ❹ | $200–225 |
| ☐ 127 | 4¾ to 5¼″ | (CE) | ❺ | $190–200 |
| ☐ 127 | 4¾ to 5¼″ | (CE) | ❻ | $185–190 |
| ☐ 127 | 4¾ to 5¼″ | (CE) | ❼ | $180–185 |
| ☐ 127 | 4¾ to 5″ | (OE) | ❽ | $180 |

---

**HUM TERM**

**"SLASH" MARK:** At one time, an imperfect or flawed figurine produced by Goebel and found during final inspection was marked by grinding a small groove or "slash" through the trademark. These pieces were then sold to factory employees as "seconds." Some of these "slash" marked pieces eventually found their way on to the secondary market and sold to uninformed collectors. Goebel abandoned this practice many years ago.

---

## HUM 128
### Baker

This figurine was first modeled in 1939 by master sculptor Arthur Moeller. Has been restyled several times during the years—most recently in the mid-1970's with the new textured finish. Slight color variations can be noticed. Some older "crown" examples have eyes open. The little baker is holding a "Gugelhupf" round pound cake, a popular Bavarian treat.

| | | | | | |
|---|---|---|---|---|---|
| ☐ 128 | 4¾ to 5″ | (CE) | ❶ | $600–750 |
| ☐ 128 | 4¾ to 5″ | (CE) | ❷ | $350–425 |
| ☐ 128 | 4¾ to 5″ | (CE) | ❸ | $300–325 |
| ☐ 128 | 4¾ to 5″ | (CE) | ❹ | $270–300 |
| ☐ 128 | 4¾ to 5″ | (CE) | ❺ | $245–270 |
| ☐ 128 | 4¾ to 5″ | (CE) | ❻ | $240–245 |
| ☐ 128 | 4¾ to 5″ | (CE) | ❼ | $235–240 |
| ☐ 128 | 4¾ to 5″ | (OE) | ❽ | $235 |

---

**HUM TERM**

**FAIENCE:** (pronounced *fay-ontz* or fi-ons) is a term for earthenware decorated with opaque colored glazes. A few early samples were produced experimentally by Goebel on "M.I. Hummel" figurines using this technique.

---

(TM 2)　　　　(TM 1)　　　　(TM 6)　　　　(TM 3)

(TM 6)　　　(TM 6)

**HUM 129**
**Band Leader**

First modeled by master sculptor Arthur Moeller in 1939. Many size and color varia-tions. Old name: "Leader." One of several figurines that make up the Hummel orches-tra. A new miniature size was issued in 1987 with a suggested retail price of $50 to match a new mini plate series called the "Little Music Makers"—one each year for four years. This is the fourth and last in the series. This miniature figurine has an incised 1985 copyright date. The miniature "Band Leader" is made without a music stand. The miniature size (129 4/0) was (TW) "Temporarily Withdrawn" from production on 31 December 1997 and as a (CE) "Closed Edition" on 1 January 1999.

☐ 129 4/0. . . 3¼″. . . . . . . . . . . (CE). . . ❻ . . . $125–140
☐ 129 4/0. . . 3¼″. . . . . . . . . . . (CE). . . ❼ . . . $120–125
☐ 129 . . . . . 5 to 5⅞″ . . . . . . (CE). . . ❶ . . . $600–750
☐ 129 . . . . . 5 to 5⅞″ . . . . . . (CE). . . ❷ . . . $350–450
☐ 129 . . . . . 5 to 5⅞″ . . . . . . (CE). . . ❸ . . . $290–340
☐ 129 . . . . . 5 to 5⅞″ . . . . . . (CE). . . ❹ . . . $265–290
☐ 129 . . . . . 5 to 5⅞″ . . . . . . (CE). . . ❺ . . . $245–265
☐ 129/0 . . . . 5 to 5¼″ . . . . . . (CE). . . ❻ . . . $240–245
☐ 129/0 . . . . 5 to 5¼″ . . . . . . (CE). . . ❼ . . . $235–240
☐ 129/0 . . . . 5 to 5¼″ . . . . . . (**OE**). . . ❽ . . . $235
☐ 129/III. . . . (Special Edition) . . . . . . ❼ . . . . (Hong Kong only)

121

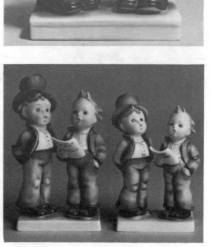

**Normal model**                    **(TM 2)**    **(Without ties)**    **(TM 3)**

## HUM 130
### Duet

Many size variations—from 5 to 5½". Originally modeled in 1939 by master sculptor Arthur Moeller. Early crown mark pieces have incised notes as well as painted notes on sheet music. Some early crown mark examples have a small "lip" on top edge of base. This variation should be valued from *$1,000 to $1,500.* Old name: "The Songsters." One of several figurines that make up the Hummel orchestra. "Duet" is similar to a combination of "Street Singer" HUM 131 and "Soloist" HUM 135. Occasionally found without tie on either boy. This variation would command a premium of over $3,000. "Duet" was permanently retired by Goebel in the fall of 1995 and will not be produced again.

| | | | | |
|---|---|---|---|---|
| ☐ 130 | 5 to 5½" | (CE) | ❶ | $800–1000 |
| ☐ 130 | 5 to 5½" | (CE) | ❷ | $550–650 |
| ☐ 130 | 5 to 5½" | (CE) | ❸ | $400–450 |
| ☐ 130 | 5 to 5½" | (CE) | ❹ | $335–400 |
| ☐ 130 | 5 to 5½" | (CE) | ❺ | $325–335 |
| ☐ 130 | 5 to 5½" | (CE) | ❻ | $310–325 |
| ☐ 130 | 5 to 5½" | (CE) | ❼ | $300–310 |
| ☐ 130 | (without ties) | (CE) | ❷ or ❸ | $2,000–3,500 |
| ☐ 130 | (with "lip" base) | (CE) | ❶ | $1,000–1,500 |

> **FINAL ISSUE**
> 1995

---

**HUM TERM**

> **UNDERGLAZE**: The term used to describe especially the number 5 trademark that appears actually underneath the glaze as opposed to the later version of the number 5 trademark that appears on the top of the glaze.

*(TM 2)*          *(TM 3)*          *(TM 1)*

## HUM 131
### Street Singer
Many size variations as well as some slight color variations of this popular figurine. Originally modeled by master sculptor Arthur Moeller in 1939. Old name: "Soloist." One of several figurines that make up the Hummel orchestra.

☐ 131 . . . . . 5 to 5½″ . . . . . . (CE). . . ❶ . . . $550–700
☐ 131 . . . . . 5 to 5½″ . . . . . . (CE). . . ❷ . . . $375–450
☐ 131 . . . . . 5 to 5½″ . . . . . . (CE). . . ❸ . . . $300–350
☐ 131 . . . . . 5 to 5½″ . . . . . . (CE). . . ❹ . . . $260–300
☐ 131 . . . . . 5 to 5½″ . . . . . . (CE). . . ❺ . . . $240–260
☐ 131 . . . . . 5 to 5½″ . . . . . . (CE). . . ❻ . . . $235–240
☐ 131 . . . . . 5 to 5½″ . . . . . . (CE). . . ❼ . . . $230–235
☐ 131 . . . . . 5 to 5½″ . . . . . . (OE). . . ❽ . . . $230

---
**HUM TERM**

**WAFFLE BASE**: Another term to describe the quartered or divided bases.

---

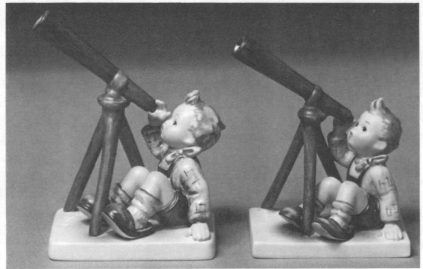

*New model (TM 6)*            *Old model (TM 2)*

## HUM 132
### Star Gazer

A very few older models have blue shirt. Most models in all trademark periods have purple shirts. Also some color variations on telescope. No cross-strap on boy's lederhosen on older models. "M. I. Hummel" signature is straight on early models; curved on later models. First modeled by master sculptor Arthur Moeller in 1939. Restyled by master sculptor Gerhard Skrobek in 1980 with the new textured finish and slightly rounded corners on the base. A special figurine was produced for sale to the U.S. military stationed in Bosnia in 1996. Inscribed on base: "Looking for a Peaceful World." Value $250–300.

| | | | | | |
|---|---|---|---|---|---|
| ☐ 132 | . . . . . 4¾" | . . . . . . . . . . | (CE) | . . . ❶ | . . . $600–800 |
| ☐ 132 | . . . . . 4¾" | . . . . . . . . . . | (CE) | . . . ❷ | . . . $400–500 |
| ☐ 132 | . . . . . 4¾" | . . . . . . . . . . | (CE) | . . . ❸ | . . . $325–375 |
| ☐ 132 | . . . . . 4¾" | . . . . . . . . . . | (CE) | . . . ❹ | . . . $275–325 |
| ☐ 132 | . . . . . 4¾" | . . . . . . . . . . | (CE) | . . . ❺ | . . . $255–275 |
| ☐ 132 | . . . . . 4¾" | . . . . . . . . . . | (CE) | . . . ❻ | . . . $250–255 |
| ☐ 132 | . . . . . 4¾" | . . . . . . . . . . | (CE) | . . . ❼ | . . . $245–250 |
| ☐ 132 | . . . . . 4¾ to 5" | . . . . . . . | (OE) | . . . ❽ | . . . $245 |

TM 1          TM 2          TM 6

## HUM 133
### Mother's Helper

This is the only figurine (in current production) produced with a cat. A similar figurine with a cat is named "Helping Mother" HUM 325 which is classified as a (PFE) possible future edition, and may be released at a later date. Older figurines are slightly larger in size. Originally modeled in 1939 by master sculptor Arthur Moeller. Note variations in photo. Some recently found examples have legs of stool reversed—value $750–1000.

☐ 133 . . . . . 4¾ to 5″ . . . . . . (CE). . . **①** . . . $550–700
☐ 133 . . . . . 4¾ to 5″ . . . . . . (CE). . . **②** . . . $375–450
☐ 133 . . . . . 4¾ to 5″ . . . . . . (CE). . . **③** . . . $300–325
☐ 133 . . . . . 4¾ to 5″ . . . . . . (CE). . . **④** . . . $270–300
☐ 133 . . . . . 4¾ to 5″ . . . . . . (CE). . . **⑤** . . . $250–270
☐ 133 . . . . . 4¾ to 5″ . . . . . . (CE). . . **⑥** . . . $245–250
☐ 133 . . . . . 4¾ to 5″ . . . . . . (CE). . . **⑦** . . . $240–245
☐ 133 . . . . . 4¾ to 5″ . . . . . . (**OE**). . . **⑧** . . . $240

*Reversed legs*

125

**HUM 134**
**Quartet, Plaque**
First modeled by master sculptor Arthur Moeller in 1939. Older models have "M.I. Hummel" signature on back while newer models have signature incised on front. Older models provided with two holes for cord to hang on wall while newer models have a centered hole on back for hanging. Quartet, Plaque was (TW) "Temporarily Withdrawn" from production on 31 December 1990, but may be reinstated at some future date.

☐ 134 . . . . . 5½ × 6¼" . . . . . (CE). . . **❶** . . . $800–1000
☐ 134 . . . . . 5½ × 6¼" . . . . . (CE). . . **❷** . . . $525–625
☐ 134 . . . . . 5½ × 6¼" . . . . . (CE). . . **❸** . . . $375–425
☐ 134 . . . . . 5½ × 6¼" . . . . . (CE). . . **❹** . . . $325–375
☐ 134 . . . . . 5½ × 6¼" . . . . . (CE). . . **❺** . . . $260–270
☐ 134 . . . . . 5½ × 6¼" . . . . . (TW) . . **❻** . . . $250–260

---

**HUM TERM**

**THREE LINE TRADEMARK**: The symbol used by the W. Goebel Porzellanfabrik from 1964 until 1972 as their factory trademark. The name for this trademark was adopted to recognize that the V and bee was accompanied by three lines of print to the right of the V. Also known as TM 4.

*135 (TM 1)*      *135 (TM 3)*      *135 4/0 (TM 6)*

**HUM 135**
**Soloist**

Many size variations between old and new figurines. Originally modeled in 1940 by master sculptor Arthur Moeller. Old name "High Tenor." Similar to singer in figurine "Duet" HUM 130. One of several figurines that can be used to make up the Hummel orchestra. A new miniature size figurine was issued in 1986 with the suggested retail price of $45. Designed to match a new mini plate series called the "Little Music Makers"—one each year for four years. This is the third in the series. This miniature figurine has an incised 1985 copyright date. The large size has been renumbered 135/0 and the old 135 is now classified as a (CE) "Closed Edition" because of this change. The miniature size (135 4/0) was (TW) "Temporarily Withdrawn" from production on 31 December 1997. In 1996 a 2¾" size (3¼" with base) with incised model number 135 5/0 was produced as part of the "Pen Pals" series of personalized name card table decorations. The original issue price was $55. In 1998 "Silent Night Chapel" HummelScape (Mark # 1007-D) was sold exclusively by Bronner's of Frankenmuth, MI with a "Special Event Figurine" with Bronner's Logo on the bottom.

| | | | | |
|---|---|---|---|---|
| ☐ 135 5/0 | 2¾" | (OE) | ❼ | $55 |
| ☐ 135 4/0 | 3" | (CE) | ❻ | $125–140 |
| ☐ 135 4/0 | 3" | (TW) | ❼ | $120–125 |
| ☐ 135 | 4½ to 5" | (CE) | ❶ | $400–500 |
| ☐ 135 | 4½ to 5" | (CE) | ❷ | $300–350 |
| ☐ 135 | 4½ to 5" | (CE) | ❸ | $200–225 |
| ☐ 135 | 4½ to 5" | (CE) | ❹ | $180–200 |
| ☐ 135 | 4½ to 5" | (CE) | ❺ | $175–180 |
| ☐ 135 | 4½ to 5" | (CE) | ❻ | $170–175 |
| ☐ 135/0 | 4¾" | (CE) | ❻ | $165–170 |
| ☐ 135/0 | 4¾" | (CE) | ❼ | $160–165 |
| ☐ 135/0 | 4¾" | (OE) | ❽ | $160 |

*136/I (TM 5)*

*136 Terra cotta (TM 1)*

## HUM 136
### Friends

Originally modeled by master sculptor Reinhold Unger in 1940. Spots on deer will vary slightly—sometimes three rows rather than two rows. Old name: "Good Friends" or "Friendship." The small size 136/I usually has an incised 1947 copyright date. Sold at one time in reddish-brown terra cotta finish in size 136 (10″) with incised crown trademark. Very limited production in this finish; would be considered extremely rare. Value: *$10,000–15,000.* Also old crown trademark example (large size) found in white overglaze finish, but probably not sold that way. Sometimes incised 136/5 instead of 136/V. Also found in a smaller 9¾″ size in a dark chocolate brown finish. The large size (136/V) was listed as (TW) "Temporarily Withdrawn" in January 1999.

| | | | | | |
|---|---|---|---|---|---|
| ☐ 136/I | . . . . 5 to 5⅜″ | . . . . . . | (CE). . . | ❶ . . . | $800–950 |
| ☐ 136/I | . . . . 5 to 5⅜″ | . . . . . . | (CE). . . | ❷ . . . | $400–500 |
| ☐ 136/I | . . . . 5 to 5⅜″ | . . . . . . | (CE). . . | ❸ . . . | $325–375 |
| ☐ 136/I | . . . . 5 to 5⅜″ | . . . . . . | (CE). . . | ❹ . . . | $275–325 |
| ☐ 136/I | . . . . 5 to 5⅜″ | . . . . . . | (CE). . . | ❺ . . . | $250–275 |
| ☐ 136/I | . . . . 5 to 5⅜″ | . . . . . . | (CE). . . | ❻ . . . | $245–250 |
| ☐ 136/I | . . . . 5 to 5⅜″ | . . . . . . | (CE). . . | ❼ . . . | $240–245 |
| ☐ 136/I | . . . . 5 to 5⅜″ | . . . . . . | (**OE**). . . | ❽ . . . | $240 |
| ☐ 136/V | . . . 10¾ to 11″ | . . . . . | (CE). . . | ❶ . . . | $3000–4000 |
| ☐ 136/V | . . . 10¾ to 11″ | . . . . . | (CE). . . | ❷ . . . | $1750–2500 |
| ☐ 136/V | . . . 10¾ to 11″ | . . . . . | (CE). . . | ❸ . . . | $1600–1750 |
| ☐ 136/V | . . . 10¾ to 11″ | . . . . . | (CE). . . | ❹ . . . | $1500–1600 |
| ☐ 136/V | . . . 10¾ to 11″ | . . . . . | (CE). . . | ❺ . . . | $1450–1500 |
| ☐ 136/V | . . . 10¾ to 11″ | . . . . . | (CE). . . | ❻ . . . | $1400–1450 |
| ☐ 136/V | . . . 10¾ to 11″ | . . . . . | (TW) . | ❼ . . . | $1350–1380 |
| ☐ 136 | . . . . 10½″ | . . . . . . . . . | (CE). . . | ❶ . . . | $3000–4000 |
| ☐ 136 | . . . . 10½″ | . . . . . . . . . | (CE). . . | ❷ . . . | $2000–3000 |
| ☐ 136 | . . . . 10″ | . . . . . . . . . . | (CE). . . | ❶ . . . | $10,000–15,000 (terra cotta) |
| ☐ 136 | . . . . 9¾″ | . . . . . . . . . . | (CE). . . | ❶ . . . | $10,000–15,000 (dark chocolate brown) |

137 A (TM 1)                    137 B (TM 2)

137A Rear view

**HUM 137**
**Child in Bed, Wall Plaque**
**HUM 137 A (Child looking left) (CE)**
**HUM 137 B (Child looking right) (CE)**
Originally modeled by master sculptor Arthur Moeller in 1940 as a set of two small wall plaques—one child looking left and one child looking right. Pictured here is the first known example of 137 A which was found hanging on a kitchen wall somewhere in Hungary in 1986. Since that time several other examples have been found in Europe. The child looking right (HUM 137 B) has been on the market for years and can be found in all trademark periods. Current production models are numbered 137 only, incised on the back along with the "M.I. Hummmel" signature. Also called "Baby Ring with Ladybug" or "Ladybug Plaque" in old catalogues. A rare "Mel 14" was recently found in Amsterdam, Holland. It is identical in size, color and construction to HUM 137 B "Child in Bed" wall plaque. This piece has *no* "M. I. Hummel" signature, but is clearly incised "Mel 14" along with a "double crown" trademark. Factory records indicate it was sculpted on 18 July 1940. HUM 137 was listed as (TW) "Temporarily Withdrawn" in January 1999.

☐ 137 A.... 3 × 3"........ (CE)... ❶ ... $5,000–7,000
☐ 137 B.... 3 × 3"........ (CE)... ❶ ... $350–550
☐ 137 B.... 3 × 3"........ (CE)... ❷ ... $200–225
☐ 137 B.... 3 × 3"........ (CE)... ❸ ... $110–135
☐ 137 B.... 3 × 3"........ (CE)... ❹ ... $85–110
☐ 137 B.... 3 × 3"........ (CE)... ❺ ... $80–85
☐ 137 ..... 3 × 3"........ (CE)... ❺ ... $75–80
☐ 137 ..... 3 × 3"........ (CE)... ❻ ... $70–75
☐ 137 ..... 3 × 3"........ (TW) . ❼ ... $70–75
☐ Mel 14 ... 3 × 3"........ (CN)... ❶ ... $2,000–2,500

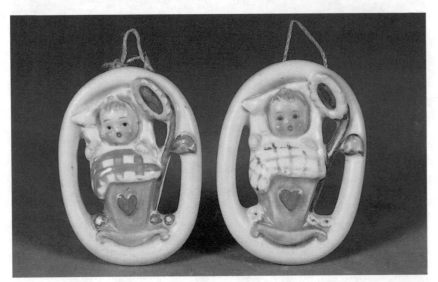

*(TM 1+1)*                    *(TM 3)*

## HUM 138 (CN)
### Tiny Baby In Crib, Wall Plaque

According to factory information this small plaque was never produced for sale. The original model was made by master sculptor Arthur Moeller in 1940. Now listed on factory records as a Closed Number (CN) meaning that this design was produced as a sample model, but then for various reasons never authorized for release. Apparently, a very few examples left the factory and have been found in Germany. This plaque would be considered extremely rare. Recently found factory records indicate this was originally produced as "Mel 15" in 1940. Color variations have been found in (TM 1) examples.

☐ 138 . . . . . 2¼ × 3″ . . . . . . (CN). . . ❶ . . . $4,000–5,000
☐ 138 . . . . . 2¼ × 3″ . . . . . . (CN). . . ❷ . . . $3,000–3,500
☐ Mel 15 . . . 2¼ × 3″ . . . . . . (CN). . . ❶ . . . $2,000–2,500

---

#### HUM TERM

**RÖDENTAL**: The town in Germany where the W. Goebel Porzellanfabrik is situated. Rödental is located near Coburg and lies only a few miles from the former East German border. In 1981 Rödental became the official Sister City of Eaton, Ohio due to the longtime "Hummel" relationship with Robert L. Miller.

Crown (TM 1)          Stylized (TM 3)          Full Bee (TM 2)

## HUM 139
### Flitting Butterfly, Wall Plaque

First modeled by master sculptor Arthur Moeller in 1940, this plaque is also known as "Butterfly Plaque." Early crown mark pieces have no dots on girl's dress. The "M.I. Hummel" signature has been on the back during all time periods. Redesigned in the 1960's with no air space behind girl's head. Some design and color variations have evolved through the years of production. To my knowledge, not produced in trademark 4. Recently found factory records indicate this was originally produced as "Mel 16" in 1940. Listed as (TW) "Temporarily Withdrawn" in January 1999.

| | | | | |
|---|---|---|---|---|
| ☐ 139 | 2½ × 2½″ | (CE) | ❶ | $350–550 |
| ☐ 139 | 2½ × 2½″ | (CE) | ❷ | $200–250 |
| ☐ 139 | 2½ × 2½″ | (CE) | ❸ | $100–150 |
| ☐ 139 | 2½ × 2½″ | (CE) | ❺ | $78–80 |
| ☐ 139 | 2½ × 2½″ | (CE) | ❻ | $75–78 |
| ☐ 139 | 2½ × 2½″ | (TW) | ❼ | $75–78 |
| ☐ Mel 16 | 2½ × 2½″ | (CN) | ❶ | $2,000–2,500 |

---

### HUM TERM

**PAINTER'S SAMPLE**: A figurine used by the painters at the Goebel factory which serves as a reference figurine for the painting of subsequent pieces. The painters of "M.I. Hummel" figurines attempt to paint their individual pieces to match the painter's sample as precisely as possible. Painter's Samples are sometimes marked with a red line around the side of the base.

*Both (TM 6) (Note horn, doors and windows)*

## HUM 140
### The Mail is Here, Plaque

Originally modeled by master sculptor Arthur Moeller in 1940, this plaque can be found in all trademark periods. At one time it was sold in Belgium in the white overglaze finish and would now be considered rare. Old name: "Post Carriage." Also known to collectors as "Mail Coach" plaque. In 1952 this same motif was made into a figurine by the same name (HUM226) by master sculptor Arthur Moeller. "The Mail is Here" plaque was (TW) "Temporarily Withdrawn" from production on 31 December 1989, but may be reinstated at some future date. Several variations can be found in the doors and windows of the coach as well as the handle of the horn—sometimes down instead of up. This cannot be attributed to any one time period.

☐ 140 . . . . . 4¼ × 6¾″ . . . . . (CE). . . ❶ . . . $1000–1500 (white overglaze)
☐ 140 . . . . . 4¼ × 6¾″ . . . . . (CE). . . ❶ . . . $650–950
☐ 140 . . . . . 4¼ × 6¾″ . . . . . (CE). . . ❷ . . . $450–550
☐ 140 . . . . . 4¼ × 6¾″ . . . . . (CE). . . ❸ . . . $325–350
☐ 140 . . . . . 4¼ × 6¾″ . . . . . (CE). . . ❹ . . . $300–325
☐ 140 . . . . . 4¼ × 6¾″ . . . . . (CE). . . ❺ . . . $275–300
☐ 140 . . . . . 4¼ × 6¾″ . . . . . (TW) . . ❻ . . . $250–275

141/V      Old    141/I    New      Old    141 3/0    New

**HUM 141**
**Apple Tree Girl**

First modeled by master sculptor Arthur Moeller in 1940 and has been restyled many times during the years that it has been produced. There are many size variations and early models have a tapered brown base. The smaller models have always been made without the bird in the tree. Size 141/V was first produced in the early 1970's and is found in 4, 5, 6 and 7 trademarks only. Size 141/X was first produced in 1975. Old name: "Spring" or "Springtime." This same motif is used on the 1976 Annual Plate, HUM 269; Table Lamp, HUM 229; and Bookends, HUM 252 A. Size 141/X was (TW) "Temporarily Withdrawn" from production on 31 December 1990, but may be reinstated at some future date.

☐ 141 3/0 . . . 4 to 4¼″ . . . . . . (CE) . . . ❶ . . . $400–500
☐ 141 3/0 . . . 4 to 4¼″ . . . . . . (CE) . . . ❷ . . . $300–350
☐ 141 3/0 . . . 4 to 4¼″ . . . . . . (CE) . . . ❸ . . . $225–250
☐ 141 3/0 . . . 4 to 4¼″ . . . . . . (CE) . . . ❹ . . . $200–225
☐ 141 3/0 . . . 4 to 4¼″ . . . . . . (CE) . . . ❺ . . . $180–190
☐ 141 3/0 . . . 4 to 4¼″ . . . . . . (CE) . . . ❻ . . . $175–180
☐ 141 3/0 . . . 4 to 4¼″ . . . . . . (CE) . . . ❼ . . . $170–175
☐ 141 3/0 . . . 4 to 4¼″ . . . . . . (**OE**) . . . ❽ . . . $170
☐ 141 . . . . . 6 to 6¾″ . . . . . . (CE) . . . ❶ . . . $800–900
☐ 141 . . . . . 6 to 6¾″ . . . . . . (CE) . . . ❷ . . . $600–700
☐ 141/I . . . . 6 to 6¾″ . . . . . . (CE) . . . ❶ . . . $700–800
☐ 141/I . . . . 6 to 6¾″ . . . . . . (CE) . . . ❷ . . . $525–625
☐ 141/I . . . . 6 to 6¾″ . . . . . . (CE) . . . ❸ . . . $425–450
☐ 141/I . . . . 6 to 6¾″ . . . . . . (CE) . . . ❹ . . . $360–425
☐ 141/I . . . . 6 to 6¾″ . . . . . . (CE) . . . ❺ . . . $350–360
☐ 141/I . . . . 6 to 6¾″ . . . . . . (CE) . . . ❻ . . . $340–350
☐ 141/I . . . . 6 to 6¾″ . . . . . . (CE) . . . ❼ . . . $330–340
☐ 141/I . . . . 6 to 6¾″ . . . . . . (**OE**) . . . ❽ . . . $330
☐ 141/V . . . 10¼″ . . . . . . . . . (CE) . . . ❹ . . . $1500–1700
☐ 141/V . . . 10¼″ . . . . . . . . . (CE) . . . ❺ . . . $1450–1500
☐ 141/V . . . 10¼″ . . . . . . . . . (CE) . . . ❻ . . . $1425–1450
☐ 141/V . . . 10¼″ . . . . . . . . . (CE) . . . ❼ . . . $1400–1425
☐ 141/V . . . 10¼″ . . . . . . . . . (**OE**) . . . ❽ . . . $1400
☐ 141/X . . . 32″ . . . . . . . . . . (CE) . . . ❺ . . . $15,000–25,000
☐ 141/X . . . 32″ . . . . . . . . . . (TW) . . . ❻ . . . $15,000–25,000

142/V       Old   142/I   New      Old   142 3/0   New

**HUM 142**
**Apple Tree Boy**

This companion figurine to "Apple Tree Girl" was also modeled by master sculptor Arthur Moeller in 1940, and has been restyled many times during the years. There are many size variations and early models have a tapered brown base. The small size 142 3/0 with trademark 2 usually has a red feather in the boy's hat. Size 142/V was first produced in the early 1970's and is found in 4, 5, 6 and 7 trademarks only. Old name: "Autumn" or "Fall." Smaller models have always been made without the bird in the tree. The same motif is used on the 1977 Annual Plate, HUM 270; Table Lamp, HUM 230; and Bookends, HUM 252 B. Recently found with (TM 3) small "stylized" (1960–1972) trademark.

*(continued on next page)*

| ☐ 142 3/0. . . 4 to 4¼″ . . . . . . (CE). . . ❶ . . . $400–500 |
| ☐ 142 3/0. . . 4 to 4¼″ . . . . . . (CE). . . ❷ . . . $300–350 |
| ☐ 142 3/0. . . 4 to 4¼″ . . . . . . (CE). . . ❸ . . . $225–250 |
| ☐ 142 3/0. . . 4 to 4¼″ . . . . . . (CE). . . ❹ . . . $200–225 |
| ☐ 142 3/0. . . 4 to 4¼″ . . . . . . (CE). . . ❺ . . . $180–190 |
| ☐ 142 3/0. . . 4 to 4¼″ . . . . . . (CE). . . ❻ . . . $175–180 |
| ☐ 142 3/0. . . 4 to 4¼″ . . . . . . (CE). . . ❼ . . . $170–175 |
| ☐ 142 3/0. . . 4 to 4¼″ . . . . . . (OE). . . ❽ . . . $170 |
| ☐ 142 . . . . . 6 to 6⅞″ . . . . . . (CE). . . ❶ . . . $800–900 |
| ☐ 142 . . . . . 6 to 6⅞″ . . . . . . (CE). . . ❷ . . . $600–700 |
| ☐ 142/I . . . . 6 to 6⅞″ . . . . . . (CE). . . ❶ . . . $700–800 |
| ☐ 142/I . . . . 6 to 6⅞″ . . . . . . (CE). . . ❷ . . . $525–625 |
| ☐ 142/I . . . . 6 to 6⅞″ . . . . . . (CE). . . ❸ . . . $425–450 |
| ☐ 142/I . . . . 6 to 6⅞″ . . . . . . (CE). . . ❹ . . . $360–425 |
| ☐ 142/I . . . . 6 to 6⅞″ . . . . . . (CE). . . ❺ . . . $350–360 |
| ☐ 142/I . . . . 6 to 6⅞″ . . . . . . (CE). . . ❻ . . . $340–350 |
| ☐ 142/I . . . . 6 to 6⅞″ . . . . . . (CE). . . ❼ . . . $330–340 |
| ☐ 142/I . . . . 6 to 6⅞″ . . . . . . (OE). . . ❽ . . . $330 |
| ☐ 142/V . . . . 10¼″. . . . . . . . (CE). . . ❸ . . . $1750–2000 |
| ☐ 142/V . . . . 10¼″. . . . . . . . (CE). . . ❹ . . . $1500–1700 |
| ☐ 142/V . . . . 10¼″. . . . . . . . (CE). . . ❺ . . . $1450–1500 |
| ☐ 142/V . . . . 10¼″. . . . . . . . (CE). . . ❻ . . . $1425–1450 |
| ☐ 142/V . . . . 10¼″. . . . . . . . (CE). . . ❼ . . . $1400–1425 |
| ☐ 142/V . . . . 10¼″. . . . . . . . (OE). . . ❽ . . . $1400 |

*Old style*

*New style*

## HUM 142
**Apple Tree Boy** *(continued from previous page)*
According to factory information, size 142/X (also known as "Jumbo" size) was first produced in the early 1960's with number 142/10 incised and the stylized trademark incised rather than stamped. A Canadian collector has a very early "Jumbo" Apple Tree Boy with the "full bee" (TM 2) trademark but no model number incised on it. The "Jumbo" size 142/X was restyled in the mid 1970's by master sculptor Gerhard Skrobek. Notice that the older model has two apples while the restyled version has four apples. The newer version is slightly larger because of the extended branch on the boy's right. Size 142/X was (TW) "Temporarily Withdrawn" from production on 31 December 1990, but may be reinstated at some future date.

- ☐ 142/X . . . . 30″ . . . . . . . . . . (CE). . . ❷ . . . $26,000–30,000
- ☐ 142/X . . . . 30″ . . . . . . . . . . (CE). . . ❸ . . . $17,000–26,000
- ☐ 142/X . . . . 30″ . . . . . . . . . . (CE). . . ❹ . . . $16,000–25,000
- ☐ 142/X . . . . 30 to 32″ . . . . . . (CE). . . ❺ . . . $15,000–25,000
- ☐ 142/X . . . . 30 to 32″ . . . . . . (CE). . . ❻ . . . $15,000–25,000
- ☐ 142/X . . . . 30 to 32″ . . . . . . (CE). . . ❼ . . . $15,000–25,000
- ☐ 142/X . . . . 30 to 32″ . . . . . . (**OE**). . . ❽ . . . $25,000

**143 (TM 1)**          **143/0 (TM 2)**          **143/0 (TM 5)**

## HUM 143
**Boots**

When first modeled by master sculptor Arthur Moeller in 1940 this figurine was produced in one size only with the incised model number 143. A smaller size was issued in the mid-1950's with the incised model number 143/0. At the same time, the large size was changed to 143/I. There have been many size variations—from 5 to 5½″ on the small; from 6 to 6¾″ on the large. Old name: "Shoemaker." Both sizes were restyled with the new "textured" finish by master modeler Gerhard Skrobek in the late 1970's. Both sizes of "Boots" were permanently retired by Goebel on 31 December 1998 and will not be produced again.

☐ 143/0 . . . . 5 to 5½″ . . . . . . (CE). . . ❶ . . . $550–700
☐ 143/0 . . . . 5 to 5½″ . . . . . . (CE). . . ❷ . . . $370–450
☐ 143/0 . . . . 5 to 5½″ . . . . . . (CE). . . ❸ . . . $300–325
☐ 143/0 . . . . 5 to 5½″ . . . . . . (CE). . . ❹ . . . $270–300
☐ 143/0 . . . . 5 to 5½″ . . . . . . (CE). . . ❺ . . . $245–270
☐ 143/0 . . . . 5 to 5½″ . . . . . . (CE). . . ❻ . . . $235–245
☐ 143/0 . . . . 5 to 5½″ . . . . . . (CE). . . ❼ . . . $225–235
☐ 143/I . . . . 6½ to 6¾″ . . . . . (CE). . . ❶ . . . $850–1000
☐ 143/I . . . . 6½ to 6¾″ . . . . . (CE). . . ❷ . . . $600–700
☐ 143/I . . . . 6½ to 6¾″ . . . . . (CE). . . ❸ . . . $450–525
☐ 143/I . . . . 6½ to 6¾″ . . . . . (CE). . . ❹ . . . $425–450
☐ 143/I . . . . 6½ to 6¾″ . . . . . (CE). . . ❺ . . . $390–425
☐ 143/I . . . . 6½ to 6¾″ . . . . . (CE). . . ❻ . . . $370–390
☐ 143/I . . . . 6½ to 6¾″ . . . . . (CE). . . ❼ . . . $360–370
☐ 143 . . . . . 6¾″. . . . . . . . . . (CE). . . ❶ . . . $900–1050
☐ 143 . . . . . 6¾″. . . . . . . . . . (CE). . . ❷ . . . $650–750

*FINAL ISSUE*
1998

### HUM 144
### Angelic Song
Originally modeled in 1941 by master sculptor Reinhold Unger. Little variation between old and new models. Old names: "Angels" or "Holy Communion."

☐ 144 . . . . . 4" . . . . . . . . . . . (CE). . . ❶ . . . $400–525
☐ 144 . . . . . 4" . . . . . . . . . . . (CE). . . ❷ . . . $275–325
☐ 144 . . . . . 4" . . . . . . . . . . . (CE). . . ❸ . . . $225–250
☐ 144 . . . . . 4" . . . . . . . . . . . (CE). . . ❹ . . . $200–225
☐ 144 . . . . . 4" . . . . . . . . . . . (CE). . . ❺ . . . $185–200
☐ 144 . . . . . 4" . . . . . . . . . . . (CE). . . ❻ . . . $180–185
☐ 144 . . . . . 4" . . . . . . . . . . . (CE). . . ❼ . . . $175–180
☐ 144 . . . . . 4" . . . . . . . . . . . (OE). . . ❽ . . . $175

### HUM 145
### Little Guardian
This figurine was first modeled by master sculptor Reinhold Unger in 1941. The only noticeable difference would be in size, with the older pieces slightly larger.

☐ 145 . . . . . 3¾ to 4" . . . . . . (CE). . . ❶ . . . $400–525
☐ 145 . . . . . 3¾ to 4" . . . . . . (CE). . . ❷ . . . $275–325
☐ 145 . . . . . 3¾ to 4" . . . . . . (CE). . . ❸ . . . $225–250
☐ 145 . . . . . 3¾ to 4" . . . . . . (CE). . . ❹ . . . $200–225
☐ 145 . . . . . 3¾ to 4" . . . . . . (CE). . . ❺ . . . $185–200
☐ 145 . . . . . 3¾ to 4" . . . . . . (CE). . . ❻ . . . $180–185
☐ 145 . . . . . 3¾ to 4" . . . . . . (CE). . . ❼ . . . $175–180
☐ 145 . . . . . 3¾ to 4" . . . . . . (OE). . . ❽ . . . $175

*Old (TM 2)*          *New (TM 3)*

**HUM 146**
**Holy Water Font, Angel Duet**
First modeled by master sculptor Reinhold Unger in 1941. This font has been restyled several times through the years with noticeable variations in the shape of angels' wings, construction of the back, holes between angels' heads and wings. Newer examples are completely solid and have the new textured finish. Listed as (TW) "Temporarily Withdrawn" in January 1999.

☐ 146 . . . . . 3½ × 4¾" . . . . . (CE). . . ❶ . . . $175–225
☐ 146 . . . . . 3½ × 4¾" . . . . . (CE). . . ❷ . . . $125–150
☐ 146 . . . . . 3½ × 4¾" . . . . . (CE). . . ❸ . . . $80–100
☐ 146 . . . . . 3½ × 4¾" . . . . . (CE). . . ❹ . . . $75–80
☐ 146 . . . . . 3½ × 4¾" . . . . . (CE). . . ❺ . . . $70–75
☐ 146 . . . . . 3½ × 4¾" . . . . . (CE). . . ❻ . . . $65–70
☐ 146 . . . . . 3½ × 4¾" . . . . . (TW) . . ❼ . . . $60–65

---

**PRICES IN THIS GUIDE**

We are in a period of DISCOUNTING of many items in our society. "M.I. Hummel" figurines are no exception. The prices in this guide give the relative values in relationship to new or current prices of (TM 8) trademark items. If the new figurines are discounted, the older models will likely be discounted, too, but possibly in a lesser degree. This guide reduces all items to one common denominator.

---

*Old (TM 1)*          *New (TM 3)*

**HUM 147**
**Holy Water Font, Angel Shrine**
Originally modeled in 1941 by master sculptor Reinhold Unger and has been produced in all trademark periods. Older models are usually larger. Some variation in construction of back of font and water bowl. Old name: "Angel Devotion."

☐ 147 . . . 3 × 5 to 3⅛ × 5¼" . (CE). . . ❶ . . . $225–275
☐ 147 . . . 3 × 5 to 3⅛ × 5¼" . (CE). . . ❷ . . . $125–175
☐ 147 . . . 3 × 5" . . . . . . . . . . (CE). . . ❸ . . . $80–100
☐ 147 . . . 3 × 5" . . . . . . . . . . (CE). . . ❹ . . . $75–80
☐ 147 . . . 3 × 5" . . . . . . . . . . (CE). . . ❺ . . . $70–75
☐ 147 . . . 3 × 5" . . . . . . . . . . (CE). . . ❻ . . . $65–70
☐ 147 . . . 3 × 5" . . . . . . . . . . (CE). . . ❼ . . . $62–65
☐ 147 . . . 3 × 5" . . . . . . . . . . (**OE**). . . ❽ . . . $62

**HUM 148 (CN)**
Factory records indicate this was the same as the boy from HUM 60/A (Farm Boy, Bookend). Modeled in 1941 by a combination of the modelers. Listed as a Closed Number on 28 February 1941. No known examples or photographs.

☐ 148 . . . . . . . . . . . . . . . . . . (CN). . . . . . . .

**HUM 149 (CN)**
Factory records indicate this was the same as the girl from HUM 60/B (Goose Girl, Bookend). Modeled in 1941 by a combination of modelers. Listed as a Closed Number on 28 February 1941. No known examples or photographs. A Closed Number (CN): an identification number in W. Goebel's numerical identification system, used to identify a design or sample model intended for possible production but then for various reasons never authorized for release.

☐ 149 . . . . . . . . . . . . . . . . . . (CN). . . . . . . .

*150 (TM 1)*          *150/0 (TM 2)*          *150 2/0 (TM 5)*

## HUM 150
### Happy Days

"Happy Days" was the very first "M.I. Hummel" figurine my wife, Ruth, acquired to start her collection. It reminded her of our daughter and son. We no longer have this first piece, as one of the children broke it; has since been replaced by an intact piece! "Happy Days" was first modeled in 1942 by a combination of modelers. All large size and older pieces have an extra flower on the base. The large size in the crown trademark usually does not have a size designator; incised 150 only. Sizes (150/0) and (150/I) had been in very limited production, but were both put back on the market in the 1970's. Both sizes (150/0) and (150/I) were listed as (TW) "Temporarily Withdrawn" in January 1999.

| | | | | |
|---|---|---|---|---|
| ☐ 150 2/0 | 4¼" | (CE) | ❷ | $325–400 |
| ☐ 150 2/0 | 4¼" | (CE) | ❸ | $250–275 |
| ☐ 150 2/0 | 4¼" | (CE) | ❹ | $225–250 |
| ☐ 150 2/0 | 4¼" | (CE) | ❺ | $210–225 |
| ☐ 150 2/0 | 4¼" | (CE) | ❻ | $205–210 |
| ☐ 150 2/0 | 4¼" | (CE) | ❼ | $200–205 |
| ☐ 150 2/0 | 4¼" | (OE) | ❽ | $200 |
| ☐ 150/0 | 5 to 5¼" | (CE) | ❷ | $525–625 |
| ☐ 150/0 | 5 to 5¼" | (CE) | ❸ | $425–475 |
| ☐ 150/0 | 5 to 5¼" | (CE) | ❹ | $390–425 |
| ☐ 150/0 | 5 to 5¼" | (CE) | ❺ | $360–390 |
| ☐ 150/0 | 5 to 5¼" | (CE) | ❻ | $340–360 |
| ☐ 150/0 | 5 to 5¼" | (TW) | ❼ | $330–340 |
| ☐ 150/I | 6¼ to 6½" | (CE) | ❶ | $1250–1550 |
| ☐ 150/I | 6¼ to 6½" | (CE) | ❷ | $850–950 |
| ☐ 150/I | 6¼ to 6½" | (CE) | ❸ | $675–775 |
| ☐ 150/I | 6¼ to 6½" | (CE) | ❹ | $600–675 |
| ☐ 150/I | 6¼ to 6½" | (CE) | ❺ | $550–600 |
| ☐ 150/I | 6¼ to 6½" | (CE) | ❻ | $525–550 |
| ☐ 150/I | 6¼ to 6½" | (TW) | ❼ | $500–510 |
| ☐ 150 | 6¼" | (CE) | ❶ | $1300–1600 |
| ☐ 150 | 6¼" | (CE) | ❷ | $900–1000 |

**HUM 151**
**Madonna Holding Child**
Known as the "Madonna with the Blue Cloak." Modeled by master sculptor Reinhold
Unger in 1942. Was produced in five color variations: white overglaze, pastel blue
cloak, dark blue cloak, brown cloak, and ivory finish. This figurine had not been produced for many years but was put back into production in 1977 and was produced in
white overglaze and pastel blue only. Can now be found in (TM 5) and (TM 6) trademarks. This figurine sold for $44.00 on old 1955 price list. "Madonna Holding Child" in
both color and white overglaze finish were (TW) "Temporarily Withdrawn" from production on 31 December 1989, but may be reinstated at some future date. I have never
seen this figurine with (TM 3) "stylized" or (TM 4) "three line" trademark.

☐ 151 . . . . . 12½" Blue . . . . . (CE). . . ❶ . . . $2000–3000
☐ 151 . . . . . 12½" Blue . . . . . (CE). . . ❷ . . . $2000–2500
☐ 151 . . . . . 12½" Blue . . . . . (CE). . . ❺ . . . $925–950
☐ 151 . . . . . 12½" Blue . . . . . (TW) . . ❻ . . . $900–925
☐ 151 . . . . . 12½" White . . . . (CE). . . ❶ . . . $1500–2500
☐ 151 . . . . . 12½" White . . . . (CE). . . ❷ . . . $1000–2000
☐ 151 . . . . . 12½" White . . . . (CE). . . ❺ . . . $425–450
☐ 151 . . . . . 12½" White . . . . (TW) . . ❻ . . . $400–425
☐ 151 . . . . . 12½" Brown . . . . (CE). . . ❶ . . . $9000–12,000
☐ 151 . . . . . 12½" Ivory . . . . . (CE). . . ❶ . . . $9000–12,000
☐ 151 . . . . . 12½" Dk. Blue . . (CE). . . ❶ . . . $9000–12,000

*152 (TM 1)*                    *152/0 A (TM 2)*

## HUM 152 A
### Umbrella Boy
Originally modeled by master sculptor Arthur Moeller in 1942. The crown mark piece in our collection is incised 152 only and is considered rare with that trademark. The large size was restyled in 1972 with a thin umbrella and new textured finish. Older models usually have the umbrella handle fastened on boy's right shoe while in newer models the handle is fastened to his left shoe. The small size was first produced in 1954 and can be found in all trademarks except the crown. Some small size examples have a *stamped* 1951 or 1956 copyright date while others have an *incised* 1957 date. Old name: "In Safety" or "Boy Under Umbrella."

| | | | | |
|---|---|---|---|---|
| ☐ 152/0 A | 4¾" | (CE) | ❷ | $1100–1600 |
| ☐ 152/0 A | 4¾" | (CE) | ❸ | $850–1000 |
| ☐ 152/0 A | 4¾" | (CE) | ❹ | $750–850 |
| ☐ 152/0 A | 4¾" | (CE) | ❺ | $725–750 |
| ☐ 152/0 A | 4¾" | (CE) | ❻ | $700–725 |
| ☐ 152/0 A | 4¾" | (CE) | ❼ | $675–700 |
| ☐ 152/0 A | 4¾" | (OE) | ❽ | $675 |
| ☐ 152 | 8" | (CE) | ❶ | $4000–7000 |
| ☐ 152 | 8" | (CE) | ❷ | $2400–2900 |
| ☐ 152 A | 8" | (CE) | ❷ | $2200–2700 |
| ☐ 152 A | 8" | (CE) | ❸ | $1800–2000 |
| ☐ 152 A | 8" | (CE) | ❹ | $1725–1800 |
| ☐ 152/II A | 8" | (CE) | ❹ | $1725–1800 |
| ☐ 152/II A | 8" | (CE) | ❺ | $1700–1725 |
| ☐ 152/II A | 8" | (CE) | ❻ | $1675–1700 |
| ☐ 152/II A | 8" | (CE) | ❼ | $1650–1675 |
| ☐ 152/II A | 8" | (OE) | ❽ | $1650 |

*152/II B (TM 4)*        *152/0 B (TM 3)*

**HUM 152 B**
**Umbrella Girl**
Originally modeled by master sculptor Arthur Moeller in 1949. We have never been able to locate "Umbrella Girl" with the crown trademark for our collection. It would be considered extremely rare, if it actually does exist. The large size was restyled in 1972 with a thin umbrella and new textured finish. The small size was first produced in 1954 and can be found in all trademarks except the crown. Some small size examples have an incised 1951 copyright date while others have an incised 1957 date. Old name: "In Safety" or "Girl Under Umbrella."

☐ 152/0 B . . 4¾″. . . . . . . . . . (CE). . . ❷ . . . $1100–1600
☐ 152/0 B . . 4¾″. . . . . . . . . . (CE). . . ❸ . . . $850–1000
☐ 152/0 B . . 4¾″. . . . . . . . . . (CE). . . ❹ . . . $750–850
☐ 152/0 B . . 4¾″. . . . . . . . . . (CE). . . ❺ . . . $725–750
☐ 152/0 B . . 4¾″. . . . . . . . . . (CE). . . ❻ . . . $700–725
☐ 152/0 B . . 4¾″. . . . . . . . . . (CE). . . ❼ . . . $675–700
☐ 152/0 B . . 4¾″. . . . . . . . . . (OE). . . ❽ . . . $675
☐ 152 B. . . . 8″ . . . . . . . . . . . (CE). . . ❶ . . . $4000–7000
☐ 152 B. . . . 8″ . . . . . . . . . . . (CE). . . ❷ . . . $2200–2700
☐ 152 B. . . . 8″ . . . . . . . . . . . (CE). . . ❸ . . . $1800–2000
☐ 152 B. . . . 8″ . . . . . . . . . . . (CE). . . ❹ . . . $1725–1800
☐ 152/II B . . 8″ . . . . . . . . . . . (CE). . . ❹ . . . $1725–1800
☐ 152/II B . . 8″ . . . . . . . . . . . (CE). . . ❺ . . . $1700–1725
☐ 152/II B . . 8″ . . . . . . . . . . . (CE). . . ❻ . . . $1675–1700
☐ 152/II B . . 8″ . . . . . . . . . . . (CE). . . ❼ . . . $1650–1675
☐ 152/II B . . 8″ . . . . . . . . . . . (OE). . . ❽ . . . $1650

| | | |
|---|---|---|
| *153/0* | *153/I* | *153/0 Boy with hat (CE)* |

## HUM 153
### Auf Wiedersehen

Originally modeled by master sculptor Arthur Moeller in 1943. First produced in the large size only with plain 153 incised number. The small size was introduced in the early 1950's with the boy wearing a hat and waving his hand—always with full bee trademark and "0" size designator directly under the number "153"—considered rare. This style was made in the small size only. Both sizes have been restyled in recent years. Both styles of the small size can be found in full bee trademark. Also called "Good Bye" in old catalogues. In 1993 the small size 153/0 was used as part of a special limited edition (25,000 sets worldwide) memorial to the Berlin Airlift. (See photo in back of this book.) Both sizes of "Auf Wiedersehen" will be permanently retired by Goebel on 31 December 2000 and will not be produced again. They both have a "Final Issue 2000" backstamp and small gold "Final Issue" medallion in addition to the new (TM 8) trademark. The large size (153/I) was retired exclusively on QVC with HUMMELSCAPE #1011-D in a Limited Edition of 6500 pieces, and is no longer available in the U.S., but available in other markets through 2000.

| | | | | | |
|---|---|---|---|---|---|
| ☐ 153/0 | 5½ to 6" | (CE) | ❷ | $425–525 | |
| ☐ 153/0 | 5½ to 6" | (CE) | ❸ | $350–400 | |
| ☐ 153/0 | 5½ to 6" | (CE) | ❹ | $320–350 | |
| ☐ 153/0 | 5½ to 6" | (CE) | ❺ | $300–320 | |
| ☐ 153/0 | 5½ to 6" | (CE) | ❻ | $280–300 | |
| ☐ 153/0 | 5½ to 6" | (CE) | ❼ | $285–290 | |
| ☐ 153/0 | 5½ to 6" | (OE) | ❽ | $285 | |
| ☐ 153/0 | 5¼" | (CE) | ❷ | $3000–4000 | (with hat) |
| ☐ 153 | 6¾ to 7" | (CE) | ❶ | $900–1200 | |
| ☐ 153 | 6¾ to 7" | (CE) | ❷ | $650–750 | |
| ☐ 153/I | 6¾ to 7" | (CE) | ❶ | $750–1050 | |
| ☐ 153/I | 6¾ to 7" | (CE) | ❷ | $600–700 | |
| ☐ 153/I | 6¾ to 7" | (CE) | ❸ | $475–525 | |
| ☐ 153/I | 6¾ to 7" | (CE) | ❹ | $425–475 | |
| ☐ 153/I | 6¾ to 7" | (CE) | ❺ | $360–390 | |
| ☐ 153/I | 6¾ to 7" | (CE) | ❻ | $340–360 | |
| ☐ 153/I | 6¾ to 7" | (CE) | ❼ | $330–340 | |
| ☐ 153/I | 6¾ to 7" | (OE) | ❽ | $340 | |

FINAL ISSUE
MILLENNIUM
2000

| 154/0 | 154/0 | 154/I | 154 (CE) |

## HUM 154
### Waiter

Originally modeled by master sculptor Arthur Moeller in 1943. Was first produced in the 6½" size and incised number 154 only, with gray coat and gray striped trousers. In the early 1950's the colors were changed to blue coat and tan striped trousers, and "Waiter" was produced in two sizes: 154/0 and 154/I. Has been produced with various names on bottle. "Rhein-wine" or "Rhein Wine" are the most common. "Whisky," "Hiher Mchie" and other illegible names have been used. Old name: "Chef of Service" or "Little Waiter" in some old catalogues. Both sizes have recently been restyled with the new "textured" finish. Large size (154/I) was listed as (TW) "Temporarily Withdrawn" in January 1999.

☐ 154/0 . . . . 6 to 6¼" . . . . . . (CE). . . **❶** . . . $600–800
☐ 154/0 . . . . 6 to 6¼" . . . . . . (CE). . . **❷** . . . $375–475
☐ 154/0 . . . . 6 to 6¼" . . . . . . (CE). . . **❸** . . . $325–350
☐ 154/0 . . . . 6 to 6¼" . . . . . . (CE). . . **❹** . . . $300–325
☐ 154/0 . . . . 6 to 6¼" . . . . . . (CE). . . **❺** . . . $260–280
☐ 154/0 . . . . 6 to 6¼" . . . . . . (CE). . . **❻** . . . $255–260
☐ 154/0 . . . . 6 to 6¼" . . . . . . (CE). . . **❼** . . . $250–255
☐ 154/0 . . . . 6 to 6¼" . . . . . . (**OE**). . **❽** . . . $250
☐ 154/I . . . . 6½ to 7" . . . . . . (CE). . . **❶** . . . $750–1000
☐ 154/I . . . . 6½ to 7" . . . . . . (CE). . . **❷** . . . $500–600
☐ 154/I . . . . 6½ to 7" . . . . . . (CE). . . **❸** . . . $450–500
☐ 154/I . . . . 6½ to 7" . . . . . . (CE). . . **❹** . . . $375–450
☐ 154/I . . . . 6½ to 7" . . . . . . (CE). . . **❺** . . . $350–375
☐ 154/I . . . . 6½ to 7" . . . . . . (CE). . . **❻** . . . $340–350
☐ 154/I . . . . 6½ to 7" . . . . . . (TW) . **❼** . . . $325–335
☐ 154 . . . . . 6½" . . . . . . . . . . (CE). . . **❶** . . . $850–1150
☐ 154 . . . . . 6½" . . . . . . . . . . (CE). . . **❷** . . . $550–700
☐ 154/0 . . . . 6¼" . . . . . . . . . . (CE). . . **❷** . . . $1600–2100 (with whisky)

**HUM 155 (CN)**
Factory records indicate: Madonna with cloak, sitting with child on her lap, Reinhold Unger in 1943. Listed as Closed Number on 18 May 1943. No known examples or photographs.

☐ 155 . . . . . . . . . . . . . . . . . (CN). . . . . . .


**HUM 156 (CN)**
Factory records indicate: Wall picture with sitting woman and child, Arthur Moeller in 1943. Listed as Closed Number on 18 May 1943. No known examples or photographs.

☐ 156 . . . . . . . . . . . . . . . . . (CN). . . . . . .

**HUM 157 (CN)**
Factory records indicate: Boy standing with flower basket. Sample model sculpted by Arthur Moeller in 1943. Considered for production but was never made. This factory sample does not have "M. I. Hummel" signature. Listed as Closed Number on 17 September 1943. No known examples in private collections—factory archive samples only.

☐ 157 . . . . . . . . . . . . . . . . . (CN). . . . . . . .

---

**HUM TERM**

**HUM NO.:** Mold number or model number incised on the bottom of each "M.I. Hummel" figurine at the factory. This number is used for identification purposes.

### HUM 158 (CN)
Factory records indicate: Girl standing with dog in her arms. Sample model sculpted by Arthur Moeller in 1943. Considered for production but was never made. This factory sample does not have "M. I. Hummel" signature. Listed as Closed Number on 17 September 1943. No known examples in private collections—factory archives samples only.

☐ 158 . . . . . . . . . . . . . . . . . (CN). . . . . . . .

### HUM 159 (CN)
Factory records indicate: Girl standing with flowers in her arms. Sample model sculpted by Arthur Moeller in 1943. Considered for production but was never made. This factory sample does not have "M.I. Hummel" signature. Listed as Closed Number on 17 September 1943. No known examples in private collections—factory archives samples only.

☐ 159 . . . . . . . . . . . . . . . . . (CN). . . . . . . .

**HUM 160 (CN)**
Factory records indicate: Girl standing in tiered dress and bouquet of flowers. Sample model sculpted by Reinhold Unger in 1943. Considered for production but was never made. This factory sample does not have "M. I. Hummel" signature. Listed as Closed Number on 17 September 1943. No known examples in private collections—factory archive samples only.

☐ 160 . . . . . . . . . . . . . . . . . (CN). . . . . . . .

**HUM 161 (CN)**
Factory records indicate: Girl standing with hands in her pockets. Sample model sculpted by Reinhold Unger in 1943. Considered for production but was never made. This factory sample does not have "M. I. Hummel" signature. Listed as Closed Number on 17 September 1943. No known examples in private collections—factory archive samples only.

☐ 161 . . . . . . . . . . . . . . . . . (CN). . . . . . . .

**HUM 162 (CN)**

Factory records indicate: Girl standing with pocket-book (handbag). Sample model sculpted by Reinhold Unger in 1943. Listed as Closed Number on 11 October 1943. No known examples or photographs.

☐ 162 . . . . . . . . . . . . . . . . . . (CN). . . . . . . .

*Old style (TM 1)*　　　　*New style (TM 3)*

**HUM 163**
**Whitsuntide**

Originally modeled by master sculptor Arthur Moeller in 1946. Can be found in all trademarks except TM 4. Older models are larger than newer models. Old name: "Christmas". Sometimes referred to as "Happy New Year". Angel on base holds red or yellow candle on older models. Unusual variation has small hole in angel's cupped hands where candle should be. Had been considered rare at one time, but was put back into current production in 1978 and can be found with TM 5, TM 6 and TM 7. Listed as (TW) "Temporarily Withdrawn" in January 1999.

☐ 163 . . . . . 6½ to 7″ . . . . . . (CE). . . ❶ . . . $1000–1200
☐ 163 . . . . . 6½ to 7″ . . . . . . (CE). . . ❷ . . . $850–1000
☐ 163 . . . . . 6½ to 7″ . . . . . . (CE). . . ❸ . . . $650–800
☐ 163 . . . . . 6½ to 7″ . . . . . . (CE). . . ❺ . . . $350–390
☐ 163 . . . . . 6½ to 7″ . . . . . . (CE). . . ❻ . . . $340–350
☐ 163 . . . . . 6½ to 7″ . . . . . . (TW) . . ❼ . . . $330–340

Old    New

## HUM 164
### Holy Water Font, Worship
First modeled by master sculptor Reinhold Unger in 1946. There are variations in construction of this font in that older models do not have a rim on back side of bowl while newer models do. Also color variations on lip of water bowl—older ones were handpainted; newer ones are shaded with airbrush.

| | | | | | |
|---|---|---|---|---|---|
| ☐ 164 | 3¼ × 5″ | (CE) | ❶ | $250–300 |
| ☐ 164 | 3¼ × 5″ | (CE) | ❷ | $150–200 |
| ☐ 164 | 3¼ × 5″ | (CE) | ❸ | $90–110 |
| ☐ 164 | 3¼ × 5″ | (CE) | ❹ | $75–90 |
| ☐ 164 | 3¼ × 5″ | (CE) | ❺ | $70–75 |
| ☐ 164 | 3¼ × 5″ | (CE) | ❻ | $65–70 |
| ☐ 164 | 3¼ × 5″ | (CE) | ❼ | $62–65 |
| ☐ 164 | 3¼ × 5″ | (OE) | ❽ | $62 |

## HUM 165
### Swaying Lullaby, Wall Plaque
Originally modeled by master sculptor Arthur Moeller in 1946. Not pictured in older catalogues; most collectors were not aware of the existence of this plaque until the early 1970's. Our first purchase came through an American soldier who had been stationed in Panama. Put back into current production in 1978 and was available in (TM 5) and (TM 6). Older models have the "M.I. Hummel" signature on the back while newer models have signature on front lower right corner. Old name: "Child in a Hammock." Inscription reads: "Dreaming of better times." Restyled in 1979. Current production models are slightly thicker in depth, with signature on back. Was (TW) "Temporarily Withdrawn" from production on 31 December 1989. Reissued in 1999 with (TM 7) trademark and a "Sweet Dreams" (Mark # 1012-D) HummelScape display combination package for $325.

*(TM 3) "Stylized" trademark*

| | | | | | |
|---|---|---|---|---|---|
| ☐ 165 | 4½ × 5¼″ | (CE) | ❶ | $800–1100 |
| ☐ 165 | 4½ × 5¼″ | (CE) | ❷ | $550–800 |
| ☐ 165 | 4½ × 5¼″ | (CE) | ❸ | $375–525 |
| ☐ 165 | 4½ × 5¼″ | (CE) | ❺ | $225–250 |
| ☐ 165 | 4½ × 5¼″ | (TW) | ❻ | $200–225 |
| ☐ 165 | 4½ × 5¼″ | (OE) | ❼ | $325 (with HummelScape) |

### HUM 166
### Boy With Bird, Ashtray
This ashtray was modeled by master sculptor Arthur Moeller in 1946. Only slight variations in color and construction through the years; no major differences between old and new models. "Boy with Bird" ashtray was (TW) "Temporarily Withdrawn" from production on 31 December 1989, but may be reinstated at some future date.

| | | | | | | |
|---|---|---|---|---|---|---|
| ☐ 166 | 3¼ × 6″ | (CE) | **❶** | $450–650 |
| ☐ 166 | 3¼ × 6″ | (CE) | **❷** | $275–325 |
| ☐ 166 | 3¼ × 6″ | (CE) | **❸** | $190–210 |
| ☐ 166 | 3¼ × 6″ | (CE) | **❹** | $160–190 |
| ☐ 166 | 3¼ × 6″ | (CE) | **❺** | $150–160 |
| ☐ 166 | 3¼ × 6″ | (TW) | **❻** | $140–150 |

**Old-crown (TM 1)**          **Old (TM 2)**          **New (TM 3)**

### HUM 167
### Holy Water Font, Angel with Bird
Also referred to as: "Angel-Bird" or "Angel Sitting" font. Newer models have a hole at top of font for hanging. Older models have hole on back of font for hanging. We recently found old crown (TM1) font that has both hole at top and on back, is smaller in size and has no rim on back edge of bowl. Variations in color on lip of water bowl—older ones were handpainted; newer ones are shaded with airbrush. First modeled by Reinhold Unger in 1945.

| | | | | | |
|---|---|---|---|---|---|
| ☐ 167 | 3¼ × 4⅛″ | (CE) | **❶** | $250–300 |
| ☐ 167 | 3¼ × 4⅛″ | (CE) | **❷** | $150–200 |
| ☐ 167 | 3¼ × 4⅛″ | (CE) | **❸** | $90–110 |
| ☐ 167 | 3¼ × 4⅛″ | (CE) | **❹** | $75–90 |
| ☐ 167 | 3¼ × 4⅛″ | (CE) | **❺** | $70–75 |
| ☐ 167 | 3¼ × 4⅛″ | (CE) | **❻** | $65–70 |
| ☐ 167 | 3¼ × 4⅛″ | (CE) | **❼** | $62–65 |
| ☐ 167 | 3¼ × 4⅛″ | (OE) | **❽** | $62 |

*Stylized trademark (TM 3)*

**HUM 168**
**Standing Boy, Wall Plaque**
Originally modeled by master sculptor Arthur Moeller in 1948. Not pictured in older catalogues; most collectors were not aware of the existence of this plaque until the early 1970's. Very limited early production, probably sold mostly in European market. Put back into current production in 1978 and was available in TM 5 and TM 6. Older models have only "Hummel" on front, lower left, along with "© WG" in lower right corner. Newer models have "M.I. Hummel" signature incised on back. This same motif was made into a figurine in 1979 by master sculptor Gerhard Skrobek; see HUM 399 "Valentine Joy." "Standing Boy" wall plaque was (TW) "Temporarily Withdrawn" from production on 31 December 1989, but may be reinstated at some future date. To my knowledge, not produced in (TM 4) "three line" trademark.

☐ 168 . . . . . 4⅛ × 5½″ . . . . . (CE). . . ❶ . . . $800–1100
☐ 168 . . . . . 4⅛ × 5½″ . . . . . (CE). . . ❷ . . . $550–800
☐ 168 . . . . . 4⅛ × 5½″ . . . . . (CE). . . ❸ . . . $375–525
☐ 168 . . . . . 4⅛ × 5½″ . . . . . (CE). . . ❺ . . . $225–250
☐ 168 . . . . . 4⅛ × 5½″ . . . . . (TW) . . ❻ . . . $200–225

---

**———— HUM TERM ————**

**BAS RELIEF:** Sculptural relief in which the projection from the surrounding surface is slight. This type of raised work is found on the annual and anniversary "M.I. Hummel" plates.

*Old style (TM 1)*                          *New style (TM 3)*

**HUM 169**
**Bird Duet**

Originally modeled in 1945 by master sculptor Arthur Moeller; later restyled in 1967 by current master sculptor Gerhard Skrobek. Many variations between old and new figurines. Variations are noted in angel's wings, gown and position of baton. Color variation in birds, angel's hair and gown, as well as music stand. "Bird Duet" is part of the "Personal Touch Personalization" program and can be personalized with a name or date by a Goebel artist for a $20 fee. Also sold with "Celestial Harmony" HummelScape (Mark # 1021-D) gift set at $205.

☐ 169 . . . . . 3¾ to 4″ . . . . . . (CE). . . ❶ . . . $425–550
☐ 169 . . . . . 3¾ to 4″ . . . . . . (CE). . . ❷ . . . $250–325
☐ 169 . . . . . 3¾ to 4″ . . . . . . (CE). . . ❸ . . . $210–230
☐ 169 . . . . . 3¾ to 4″ . . . . . . (CE). . . ❹ . . . $190–210
☐ 169 . . . . . 3¾ to 4″ . . . . . . (CE). . . ❺ . . . $185–190
☐ 169 . . . . . 3¾ to 4″ . . . . . . (CE). . . ❻ . . . $180–185
☐ 169 . . . . . 3¾ to 4″ . . . . . . (CE). . . ❼ . . . $175–180
☐ 169 . . . . . 3¾ to 4″ . . . . . . (OE). . . ❽ . . . $175

---

**HUM TERM**

**SECONDARY MARKET**: The buying and selling of items after the initial retail purchase has been transacted. Often times this post-retail trading is also referred to as the "after market." This very publication is intended to serve as a guide for the secondary market values of "M. I. Hummel" items.

*170/III (TM 5)*             *170/I (TM 4)*

## HUM 170
### School Boys

First modeled by master sculptor Reinhold Unger in 1943 and later remodeled by master sculptor Gerhard Skrobek in 1961. Originally produced in one size with incised number 170 only. Small size first produced in the early 1960's and has an incised 1961 copyright date. Old name: "Difficult Problems." Some color variations on older models —middle boy with green rather than maroon trousers. Large size was again restyled in the early 1970's with the new textured finish and 1972 copyright date. In the spring of 1982 the large size (170/III) was permanently retired by Goebel and will not be produced again. The small size 170/I is still in current production. HUM 460 "Authorized Retailer Plaque" was issued in 1986 utilizing the middle boy as part of the plaque motif. Issued in eight different languages. See: HUM 460.

| | | | | | |
|---|---|---|---|---|---|
| ☐ 170/I | . . . . 7¼ to 7½" | . . . . . | (CE) | . . . ❸ | . . . $1650–1750 |
| ☐ 170/I | . . . . 7¼ to 7½" | . . . . . | (CE) | . . . ❹ | . . . $1550–1600 |
| ☐ 170/I | . . . . 7¼ to 7½" | . . . . . | (CE) | . . . ❺ | . . . $1500–1550 |
| ☐ 170/I | . . . . 7¼ to 7½" | . . . . . | (CE) | . . . ❻ | . . . $1450–1500 |
| ☐ 170/I | . . . . 7¼ to 7½" | . . . . . | (CE) | . . . ❼ | . . . $1400–1450 |
| ☐ 170/I | . . . . 7¼ to 7½" | . . . . . | (**OE**) | . . . ❽ | . . . $1400 |
| ☐ 170 | . . . . . 10 to 10¼" | . . . . . | (CE) | . . . ❶ | . . . $4000–5000 |
| ☐ 170 | . . . . . 10 to 10¼" | . . . . . | (CE) | . . . ❷ | . . . $3000–4000 |
| ☐ 170 | . . . . . 10 to 10¼" | . . . . . | (CE) | . . . ❸ | . . . $2200–2300 |
| ☐ 170/III | . . . . 10 to 10¼" | . . . . . | (CE) | . . . ❸ | . . . $2200–2300 |
| ☐ 170/III | . . . . 10 to 10¼" | . . . . . | (CE) | . . . ❹ | . . . $2100–2200 |
| ☐ 170/III | . . . . 10 to 10¼" | . . . . . | (CE) | . . . ❺ | . . . $2000–2100 |
| ☐ 170/III | . . . . 10 to 10¼" | . . . . . | (CE) | . . . ❻ | . . . $1900–2000 |

*Old style (TM 1)*       *New style (TM 6)*

**HUM 171**
**Little Sweeper**
This figurine was first modeled by master sculptor Reinhold Unger in 1944. Very little change between older and newer models. Old name: "Mother's Helper." Restyled in 1981 by master sculptor Gerhard Skrobek. The current production now has the new textured finish and is slightly larger. A new miniature size figurine was issued in 1988 with a suggested retail price of $45 to match a new miniature plate series called the "Little Homemakers"—one each year for four years. This is the first in the series. The miniature size figurine has an incised 1986 copyright date. The normal size will be renumbered 171/0 and the old number 171 is now classified as a closed edition (CE) because of this change. The miniature size (171 4/0) was (TW) "Temporarily Withdrawn" from production on 31 December 1997.

☐ 171 4/0. . . 3" . . . . . . . . . . . (CE). . . ❻ . . . $125–140
☐ 171 4/0. . . 3" . . . . . . . . . . . (TW) . . ❼ . . . $115–120
☐ 171 . . . . . 4¼". . . . . . . . . . (CE). . . ❶ . . . $400–500
☐ 171 . . . . . 4¼". . . . . . . . . . (CE). . . ❷ . . . $250–300
☐ 171 . . . . . 4¼". . . . . . . . . . (CE). . . ❸ . . . $230–240
☐ 171 . . . . . 4¼". . . . . . . . . . (CE). . . ❹ . . . $195–230
☐ 171 . . . . . 4¼". . . . . . . . . . (CE). . . ❺ . . . $190–195
☐ 171 . . . . . 4¼". . . . . . . . . . (CE). . . ❻ . . . $185–190
☐ 171/0 . . . . 4¼". . . . . . . . . . (CE). . . ❻ . . . $180–185
☐ 171/0 . . . . 4¼ to 4½" . . . . . (CE). . . ❼ . . . $175–180
☐ 171/0 . . . . 4¼ to 4½" . . . . . **(OE)**. . . ❽ . . . $175

Crown (TM 1)          Full Bee (TM 2)          Stylized (TM 3)

## HUM 172
### Festival Harmony (Mandolin)
Originally modeled in 1947 by master sculptor Reinhold Unger in the large size only with incised number 172. Old crown mark and some full bee examples have the bird resting on flowers in front of angel (rare). Restyled in the early 1950's with bird resting on mandolin and one flower at hem of angel's gown. Restyled again in the late 1960's with the new textured finish and flowers placed at angel's feet. There are variations in color of gown and color of birds. The small size (172/0) was modeled by master sculptor Theo R. Menzenbach in 1961 and can be found in one style only. The large size (172/II) was (TW) "Temporarily Withdrawn" from production on 31 December 1984, but may be reinstated at some future date. A new miniature size figurine, 172 4/0 in a matte finish was put on the market in 1994 with a suggested retail price of $95. It has an incised 1991 copyright date and a "FIRST ISSUE 1994" Decal on the bottom. Both sizes (172 4/0) and (172/0) were listed as (TW) "Temporarily Withdrawn" in January 1999.

| | | | | | |
|---|---|---|---|---|---|
| ☐ 172 4/0 | 3⅛" | (TW) | ❼ | $120–125 | |
| ☐ 172/0 | 8" | (CE) | ❸ | $500–650 | |
| ☐ 172/0 | 8" | (CE) | ❹ | $400–475 | |
| ☐ 172/0 | 8" | (CE) | ❺ | $380–400 | |
| ☐ 172/0 | 8" | (CE) | ❻ | $360–380 | |
| ☐ 172/0 | 8" | (TW) | ❼ | $350–360 | |
| ☐ 172/II | 10¼ to 10¾" | (CE) | ❸ | $650–800 | |
| ☐ 172/II | 10¼ to 10¾" | (CE) | ❹ | $550–600 | |
| ☐ 172/II | 10¼ to 10¾" | (CE) | ❺ | $475–500 | |
| ☐ 172/II | 10¼ to 10¾" | (TW) | ❻ | $450–475 | |
| ☐ 172 | 10¾" | (CE) | ❶ | $3000–3500 (Bird in front) | |
| ☐ 172 | 10¾" | (CE) | ❷ | $2500–3000 (Bird in front) | |
| ☐ 172 | 10¾" | (CE) | ❷ | $1250–1500 (Flower at hem) | |
| ☐ 172 | 10¾" | (CE) | ❸ | $1000–1250 (Flower at hem) | |

*Crown (TM 1)*       **Full Bee (TM 2)**       *Stylized (TM 3)*

**HUM 173**
**Festival Harmony (Flute)**
Originally modeled in 1947 by master sculptor Reinhold Unger in the large size only with incised number 173. Old crown mark and some full bee examples have a much larger bird and flower in front of angel (rare). Restyled in the early 1950's with smaller bird and one flower at hem of angel's gown. Restyled again in the late 1960's with the new textured finish and flowers placed at angel's feet. There are variations in color of gown and color of birds. The small size (173/0) was modeled by master sculptor Theo R. Menzenbach in 1961 and can be found in one style only. The large size (173/II) was (TW) "Temporarily Withdrawn" from production on 31 December 1984, but may be reinstated at some future date. A new miniature size figurine, 173 4/0 in a matte finish was put on the market in 1995 with a suggested retail price of $95. It has an incised 1991 copyright date and a "FIRST ISSUE 1995" decal on the bottom. Both sizes (173 4/0) and (173/0) were listed as (TW) "Temporarily Withdrawn" in January 1999.

☐ 173 4/0 . . 3⅛″ . . . . . . . . (TW) . . ❼ . . . $120–125
☐ 173/0 . . . 8″ . . . . . . . . . (CE) . . . ❸ . . . $500–650
☐ 173/0 . . . 8″ . . . . . . . . . (CE) . . . ❹ . . . $400–475
☐ 173/0 . . . 8″ . . . . . . . . . (CE) . . . ❺ . . . $380–400
☐ 173/0 . . . 8″ . . . . . . . . . (CE) . . . ❻ . . . $360–380
☐ 173/0 . . . 8″ . . . . . . . . . (TW) . . ❼ . . . $350–360
☐ 173/II . . . 10¼ to 11″ . . . (CE) . . . ❸ . . . $650–800
☐ 173/II . . . 10¼ to 11″ . . . (CE) . . . ❹ . . . $550–600
☐ 173/II . . . 10¼ to 11″ . . . (CE) . . . ❺ . . . $475–500
☐ 173/II . . . 10¼ to 11″ . . . (TW) . . ❻ . . . $450–475
☐ 173 . . . . . 11″ . . . . . . . . (CE) . . . ❶ . . . $3000–3500 (Flowers up front of dress)
☐ 173 . . . . . 11″ . . . . . . . . (CE) . . . ❷ . . . $2500–3000 (Flowers up front of dress)
☐ 173 . . . . . 11″ . . . . . . . . (CE) . . . ❷ . . . $1250–1500 (Flower at hem)
☐ 173 . . . . . 11″ . . . . . . . . (CE) . . . ❸ . . . $1000–1250 (Flower at hem)

*TM 1*                    *TM 2*                    *TM 5*

## HUM 174
### She Loves Me, She Loves Me Not!

Originally modeled by master sculptor Arthur Moeller in 1945. Has been restyled several times. Early crown mark pieces have smaller feather in boy's hat, no flower on left fence post and eyes are open. The 2, 3 and 4 trademark period pieces have a flower on left fence post and eyes are open. Current production pieces have no flower on left fence post (same as crown mark piece) but with eyes looking down. Newer models have an incised 1955 copyright date. Some (TM 1) crown examples have the flower on the fence post, as well as TM 2, 3 & 4 trademark periods.

| | | | | | |
|---|---|---|---|---|---|
| ☐ 174 | 4¼" | (CE) | ❶ | $550–700 |
| ☐ 174 | 4¼" | (CE) | ❷ | $350–450 |
| ☐ 174 | 4¼" | (CE) | ❸ | $290–300 |
| ☐ 174 | 4¼" | (CE) | ❹ | $260–290 |
| ☐ 174 | 4¼" | (CE) | ❺ | $250–260 |
| ☐ 174 | 4¼" | (CE) | ❻ | $245–250 |
| ☐ 174 | 4¼" | (CE) | ❼ | $240–245 |
| ☐ 174 | 4¼" | (OE) | ❽ | $240 |

*TM 1*          *TM 2*

158

**Old style (TM 1)**                    **New style (TM 3)**

**HUM 175**
**Mother's Darling**
Older models have pink and green-colored kerchiefs (bags) while newer models have blue ones. Trademark (TM 3) can be found in both color variations. Older models do not have polka dots on head scarf. Old name: "Happy Harriet." First modeled by master sculptor Arthur Moeller in 1945, and has been restyled several times since then. "Mother's Darling" was permanently retired by Goebel on 31 December 1997 and will not be produced again. It has a "Final Issue 1997" backstamp and small gold "Final Issue" medallion.

☐ 175 . . . . . 5½" . . . . . . . . . . (CE) . . . ❶ . . . $600–800 (pink & green)
☐ 175 . . . . . 5½" . . . . . . . . . . (CE) . . . ❷ . . . $400–525 (pink & green)
☐ 175 . . . . . 5½" . . . . . . . . . . (CE) . . . ❸ . . . $325–375 (both ways)
☐ 175 . . . . . 5½" . . . . . . . . . . (CE) . . . ❹ . . . $285–325
☐ 175 . . . . . 5½" . . . . . . . . . . (CE) . . . ❺ . . . $260–285
☐ 175 . . . . . 5½" . . . . . . . . . . (CE) . . . ❻ . . . $250–260
☐ 175 . . . . . 5½" . . . . . . . . . . (CE) . . . ❼ . . . $240–250

FINAL ISSUE
1997

---

**HUM TERM**

**PAINTER'S SAMPLE**: A figurine used by the painters at the Goebel factory which serves as a reference figurine for the painting of subsequent pieces. The painters of "M. I. Hummel" figurines attempt to paint their individual pieces to match the painter's sample as precisely as possible. Painter's Samples are sometimes marked with a red line around the side of the base.

*176/I New (TM 6)*          *176 Old (TM 1)*

**HUM 176**
**Happy Birthday**
When first modeled in 1945 by master sculptor Arthur Moeller this figurine was produced in one size only with the incised number 176. A smaller size was issued in the
mid-1950's with the incised number 176/0 and an oval base. At the same time, the
large size was changed to 176/I. The large size figurine has always had a round base
until it was completely restyled in 1979 and now has an oval base, also. The large size
(176/I) was listed as (TW) "Temporarily Withdrawn" in January 1999, but may be reinstated at some future date.

| | | | | | |
|---|---|---|---|---|---|
| ☐ 176/0 | . . . . 5″ | . . . . . . . . . . . . | (CE). . . | ❷ . . . | $400–500 |
| ☐ 176/0 | . . . . 5″ | . . . . . . . . . . . . | (CE). . . | ❸ . . . | $325–375 |
| ☐ 176/0 | . . . . 5″ | . . . . . . . . . . . . | (CE). . . | ❹ . . . | $280–325 |
| ☐ 176/0 | . . . . 5″ | . . . . . . . . . . . . | (CE). . . | ❺ . . . | $270–280 |
| ☐ 176/0 | . . . . 5″ | . . . . . . . . . . . . | (CE). . . | ❻ . . . | $265–270 |
| ☐ 176/0 | . . . . 5″ | . . . . . . . . . . . . | (CE). . . | ❼ . . . | $260–265 |
| ☐ 176/0 | . . . . 5″ | . . . . . . . . . . . . | (**OE**). . . | ❽ . . . | $260 |
| ☐ 176/I | . . . . 5½″ | . . . . . . . . . . | (CE). . . | ❶ . . . | $800–1100 |
| ☐ 176/I | . . . . 5½″ | . . . . . . . . . . | (CE). . . | ❷ . . . | $550–700 |
| ☐ 176/I | . . . . 5½″ | . . . . . . . . . . | (CE). . . | ❸ . . . | $450–525 |
| ☐ 176/I | . . . . 5½″ | . . . . . . . . . . | (CE). . . | ❹ . . . | $390–450 |
| ☐ 176/I | . . . . 5½″ | . . . . . . . . . . | (CE). . . | ❺ . . . | $360–390 |
| ☐ 176/I | . . . . 5½″ | . . . . . . . . . . | (CE). . . | ❻ . . . | $340–360 |
| ☐ 176/I | . . . . 5½″ | . . . . . . . . . . | (TW) . . | ❼ . . . | $330–340 |
| ☐ 176 | . . . . . 5½″ | . . . . . . . . . . | (CE). . . | ❶ . . . | $850–1150 |
| ☐ 176 | . . . . . 5½″ | . . . . . . . . . . | (CE). . . | ❷ . . . | $600–750 |

*177 (TM 2)*　　　　　　　　　*177/I (TM 4)*

## HUM 177
### School Girls

First modeled by master sculptor Reinhold Unger in 1946 and later remodeled by master sculptor Theo R. Menzenbach in 1961. Originally produced in one size with incised number 177 only. Small size first produced in the early 1960's and has an incised 1961 copyright date. Old name: "Master Piece." Some slight color variations on older models, particularly the shoes. Large size again restyled in the early 1970's with the new textured finish and a 1972 incised copyright date. In the spring of 1982 the large size (177/III) was permanently retired by Goebel and will not be produced again. The small size (177/I) is still in current production. See HUM 255 "Stitch in Time" and HUM 256 "Knitting Lesson" for interesting comparison.

| | | | | | |
|---|---|---|---|---|---|
| ☐ 177/I | 7½" | (CE) | ❸ | $1650–1750 |
| ☐ 177/I | 7½" | (CE) | ❹ | $1550–1600 |
| ☐ 177/I | 7½" | (CE) | ❺ | $1500–1550 |
| ☐ 177/I | 7½" | (CE) | ❻ | $1450–1500 |
| ☐ 177/I | 7½" | (CE) | ❼ | $1400–1450 |
| ☐ 177/I | 7½" | (OE) | ❽ | $1400 |
| ☐ 177 | 9½" | (CE) | ❶ | $4000–5000 |
| ☐ 177 | 9½" | (CE) | ❷ | $3000–4000 |
| ☐ 177 | 9½" | (CE) | ❸ | $2200–2300 |
| ☐ 177/III | 9½" | (CE) | ❸ | $2200–2300 |
| ☐ 177/III | 9½" | (CE) | ❹ | $2100–2200 |
| ☐ 177/III | 9½" | (CE) | ❺ | $2000–2100 |
| ☐ 177/III | 9½" | (CE) | ❻ | $1900–2000 |

*Old style (TM 2)*              *New style (TM 4)*

**HUM 178**
**Photographer, The**
Originally modeled by master sculptor Reinhold Unger in 1948 and has been restyled several times through the years. There are many size variations with the older model being larger. Some color variations on dog and camera. Newer models have a 1948 copyright date.

☐ 178 . . . . . 4¾ to 5¼″ . . . . . (CE). . . ❶ . . . $750–1100
☐ 178 . . . . . 4¾ to 5¼″ . . . . . (CE). . . ❷ . . . $500–650
☐ 178 . . . . . 4¾ to 5¼″ . . . . . (CE). . . ❸ . . . $430–480
☐ 178 . . . . . 4¾ to 5¼″ . . . . . (CE). . . ❹ . . . $370–430
☐ 178 . . . . . 4¾ to 5¼″ . . . . . (CE). . . ❺ . . . $345–370
☐ 178 . . . . . 4¾ to 5¼″ . . . . . (CE). . . ❻ . . . $340–345
☐ 178 . . . . . 4¾ to 5¼″ . . . . . (CE). . . ❼ . . . $335–340
☐ 178 . . . . . 4¾ to 5¼″ . . . . . (OE). . . ❽ . . . $335

--- **HUM TERM** ---

**TERRA COTTA:** A reddish clay used in an experimental fashion by artisans at the W. Goebel Porzellanfabrik. There are a few sample pieces of "M.I. Hummel" figurines that were produced with the terra cotta material. These terra cotta pieces have the look of the reddish-brown clay and were not painted.

Old style (TM 1)                    New style (TM 3)

**HUM 179**
**Coquettes**
Modeled originally by master sculptor Arthur Moeller in 1948 and has been restyled in recent years. Older examples are usually slightly larger in size. Minor color variations can be found in older models. Listed as (TW) "Temporarily Withdrawn" in January 1999, but may be reinstated at some future date.

☐ 179 . . . . . 5 to 5½" . . . . . . (CE). . . ❶ . . . $800–1100
☐ 179 . . . . . 5 to 5¼" . . . . . . (CE). . . ❷ . . . $500–650
☐ 179 . . . . . 5 to 5¼" . . . . . . (CE). . . ❸ . . . $450–500
☐ 179 . . . . . 5 to 5¼" . . . . . . (CE). . . ❹ . . . $370–450
☐ 179 . . . . . 5 to 5¼" . . . . . . (CE). . . ❺ . . . $350–370
☐ 179 . . . . . 5 to 5¼" . . . . . . (CE). . . ❻ . . . $335–350
☐ 179 . . . . . 5 to 5¼" . . . . . . (TW) . . ❼ . . . $325–335

---

**HUM TERM**

**WHITE OVERGLAZE:** The term used to designate an item that has not been painted, but has been glazed and fired. These pieces are completely white. All "M.I. Hummel" items are produced in this finish before being individually hand painted.

163

*New style (TM 6)*                    *Old style (TM 6)*

## HUM 180
### Tuneful Goodnight, Wall Plaque

Modeled by master sculptor Arthur Moeller in 1946. Recently restyled in 1981 by master sculptor Rudolf Wittman, a twenty-five-year veteran of the Goebel factory. In the restyled version, the position of the girl's head and hairstyle have been changed, as well as the position of the horn which is no longer attached to the heart-shaped back. Old name: "Happy Bugler" plaque. Had been considered rare and was difficult to find, but is readily available with (TM 5) and (TM 6) trademarks. "Tuneful Goodnight" wall plaque was (TW) "Temporarily Withdrawn" from production on 31 December 1989, but may be reinstated at some future date. Early "crown" (TM 1) also found made of porcelain instead of normal ceramic material, usually smaller in size.

| ☐ 180 | 4½ x 4¼" | (CE) | ❶ | $900–1200 (Porcelain) |
|-------|----------|------|---|------------------------|
| ☐ 180 | 5 x 4¾" | (CE) | ❶ | $600–800 |
| ☐ 180 | 5 x 4¾" | (CE) | ❷ | $400–550 |
| ☐ 180 | 5 x 4¾" | (CE) | ❸ | $350–400 |
| ☐ 180 | 5 x 4¾" | (CE) | ❹ | $300–350 |
| ☐ 180 | 5 x 4¾" | (CE) | ❺ | $225–240 |
| ☐ 180 | 5 x 4¾" | (TW) | ❻ | $200–225 |

*(TM 3)*          *(TM 1)*

━━━━━LATE NEWS━━━━━

"Tuneful Goodnight" to be re-introduced in spring of 2000 with "Heart of Hearts" HummelScape Collectors Set.

**HUM 181**
**Old Man Reading Newspaper (CN)**
This unusual piece was made as a sample only in 1948 by master sculptor Arthur Moeller and was not approved by the Siessen Convent for production. It was not considered typical of Sister M.I. Hummel's work, although it is an exact reproduction of one of her early sketches. This early sample *does* have the familiar "M.I. Hummel" signature and is part of the Robert L. Miller collection. Listed as a Closed Number on 18 February 1948 and will not be produced again. Often referred to as one of the "Mamas" and the "Papas." Also produced as a lamp base; see HUM 202. Several other examples have been found in recent years.

☐ 181 . . . . . 6¾" . . . . . . . . . . (CN). . . . . . . $15,000–20,000

---

**HUM TERM**

**DECIMAL POINT:** This incised "period" or dot was used in a somewhat random fashion by the W. Goebel Porzellanfabrik over the years. The decimal point is and was primarily used to reduce confusion in reading the incised numbers on the underside of the figurines. Example: 66. helps one realize that the designation is sixty-six and not ninety-nine.

---

*New style (TM 5)*          *Old style (TM 1)*

**HUM 182**
**Good Friends**
Originally modeled by master sculptor Arthur Moeller in 1946 and later restyled by master sculptor Gerhard Skrobek in 1976. The current model is slightly larger and has the new textured finish. Called "Friends" in old catalogues.

☐ 182 . . . . . 4 to 4¼″ . . . . . . (CE). . . ❶ . . . $550–750
☐ 182 . . . . . 4 to 4¼″ . . . . . . (CE). . . ❷ . . . $350–475
☐ 182 . . . . . 4 to 4¼″ . . . . . . (CE). . . ❸ . . . $300–325
☐ 182 . . . . . 4 to 4¼″ . . . . . . (CE). . . ❹ . . . $265–300
☐ 182 . . . . . 4 to 4¼″ . . . . . . (CE). . . ❺ . . . $245–265
☐ 182 . . . . . 4 to 4¼″ . . . . . . (CE). . . ❻ . . . $240–245
☐ 182 . . . . . 4 to 4¼″ . . . . . . (CE). . . ❼ . . . $235–240
☐ 182 . . . . . 4 to 4¼″ . . . . . . **(OE)**. . . ❽ . . . $235

---

**HUM TERM**

**MOLD GROWTH:** In the earlier days of figurine production the working molds were made of plaster of paris. As these molds were used, the various molded parts became larger due to the repeated usage. With modern technology at the Goebel factory and the use of acrylic resin molds, this problem has been eliminated and today the collector finds very few size differences within a given size designation.

*Old style (TM 1)*                    *New style (TM 6)*

## HUM 183
### Forest Shrine

First modeled in 1946 by master sculptor Reinhold Unger and can be found with all trademarks except trademark 4. Had been considered rare but was put back into production in 1977 and can be found with 5, 6 and 7 trademarks. Older models have a shiny finish on the deer while newer models have a dull finish. Old name: "Doe at Shrine." This figurine has recently been restyled with a more lifelike finish on the deer. Listed as (TW) "Temporarily Withdrawn" in January 1999, but may be reinstated at some future date.

- [ ] 183. . . 9″ . . (CE). . ❶ . . $1500–1900
- [ ] 183. . . 9″ . . (CE). . ❷ . . $1000–1300
- [ ] 183. . . 9″ . . (CE). . ❸ . . $700–950
- [ ] 183. . . 9″ . . (CE). . ❺ . . $650–700
- [ ] 183. . . 9″ . . (CE). . ❻ . . $625–650
- [ ] 183. . . 9″ . . (TW) . ❼ . . $595–600

*Japanese Copy*

167

Old style (TM 1)          New style (TM 3)          New style (TM 6)

## HUM 184
### Latest News

First modeled by master sculptor Arthur Moeller in 1946. Older models were made with square base and boy's eyes open. Restyled in the mid-1960's and changed to round base and boy's eyes looking down at paper. At one time the newspaper was produced without any name so that visitors to the factory could have the name of their choice put on. An endless variety of names can be found. Most common names are: "Das Allerneueste," "Munchener Presse" and "Latest News." Some collectors specialize in collecting the different names on the newspaper and will pay from $500 to $1,000 for some names. Some catalogues list as 184/O.S. which means: Ohne Schrift (without lettering). Early "crown" (TM 1) also found made of porcelain instead of normal ceramic material, usually smaller in size. "Latest News" is now part of the "Personal Touch Personalization" program and can be personalized with a name and date by a Goebel artist for a $20.00 fee. In recent years countless special inscriptions have been produced for various dealers and various occasions, such as: "Cayman News," "Island News," "Bermuda News," "Stars & Stripes," "Milwaukee Journal-Sentinel," "The Chancellor's Visit," "The Hummel Museum," etc.

☐ 184 . . . . . 4¼ to 4½" . . . . . (CE). . . ❶ . . . $1500–2000 (Porcelain)
☐ 184 . . . . . 5 to 5¼" . . . . . . (CE). . . ❶ . . . $800–1100
☐ 184 . . . . . 5 to 5¼" . . . . . . (CE). . . ❷ . . . $550–700
☐ 184 . . . . . 5 to 5¼" . . . . . . (CE). . . ❸ . . . $425–500
☐ 184 . . . . . 5 to 5¼" . . . . . . (CE). . . ❹ . . . $380–425
☐ 184 . . . . . 5 to 5¼" . . . . . . (CE). . . ❺ . . . $360–380
☐ 184 . . . . . 5" . . . . . . . . . . (CE). . . ❻ . . . $350–360
☐ 184 . . . . . 5" . . . . . . . . . . (CE). . . ❼ . . . $340–350
☐ 184 . . . . . 5" . . . . . . . . . . (OE). . . ❽ . . . $340

*(TM 7) left*
*(TM 1) right*

168

New        Old

### HUM 185
### Accordion Boy

First modeled by master sculptor Reinhold Unger in 1947, this figurine has never had a major restyling although there are many size variations due mainly to "mold growth." In the early years, the molds were made of plaster of paris and had a tendency to "wash out" or erode with use, thereby producing figurines each being slightly larger than the last. Since 1954, the use of acrylic resin for modeling has led to greater uniformity in the figurines themselves. There are some slight color variations on the accordion. Old name: "On the Alpine Pasture." One of several figurines that make up the Hummel orchestra. "Accordian Boy" was permanently retired at the end of 1994 and will not be produced again. The 1994 production bear a special "Final Issue" backstamp and a small gold "Final Issue" commemorative tag.

| | | | | | |
|---|---|---|---|---|---|
| ☐ 185 | 5 to 6″ | (CE) | ❶ | $550–750 |
| ☐ 185 | 5 to 6″ | (CE) | ❷ | $375–450 |
| ☐ 185 | 5 to 6″ | (CE) | ❸ | $300–325 |
| ☐ 185 | 5″ | (CE) | ❹ | $270–300 |
| ☐ 185 | 5″ | (CE) | ❺ | $240–270 |
| ☐ 185 | 5″ | (CE) | ❻ | $225–240 |
| ☐ 185 | 5″ | (CE) | ❼ | $200–225 |

FINAL ISSUE
1994

New        Old

### HUM 186
### Sweet Music

Originally modeled in 1947 by master sculptor Reinhold Unger. Many size variations. Was restyled slightly in the mid-1960's. Some old crown mark pieces have white slippers with blue-green stripes instead of the normal brownish color. This variation will usually sell for $1,000 to $1,500. Old name: "Playing To The Dance." One of several figurines that make up the Hummel orchestra.

| | | | | | |
|---|---|---|---|---|---|
| ☐ 186 | 5 to 5½″ | (CE) | ❶ | $1,000–1,500 (with striped slippers) |
| ☐ 186 | 5 to 5½″ | (CE) | ❶ | $550–750 |
| ☐ 186 | 5 to 5½″ | (CE) | ❷ | $375–450 |
| ☐ 186 | 5 to 5½″ | (CE) | ❸ | $300–325 |
| ☐ 186 | 5″ | (CE) | ❹ | $270–300 |
| ☐ 186 | 5″ | (CE) | ❺ | $245–270 |
| ☐ 186 | 5″ | (CE) | ❻ | $240–245 |
| ☐ 186 | 5″ | (CE) | ❼ | $235–240 |
| ☐ 186 | 5″ | (OE) | ❽ | $235 |

□ *All Black Lettering*

□ *Dotted "i"s No Quotations*

□ *Note Quotation Marks*

□ *"Moon" Style*

□ *Factory sample*

□ *"Moon" Style*

□ *"Moon" Style*

□ *Rare factory sample*

## HUM 187
### M.I. Hummel Plaques (In English)
There seems to have been an endless variety of plaques throughout the years, some for dealers and some for collectors. Originally modeled by master sculptor Reinhold

□                                                □     *Australian Dealer*

□                                                □

□                                                □     *Current Model*

Unger in 1947 and later restyled by Gerhard Skrobek in 1962. Two incised copyright dates have been used, 1947 and 1976. Current display plaques for collectors are incised 187 A. At one time in recent years, dealers' names were printed on the plaques for Australian dealers only. Pictured here is only a small portion of the many variations issued. 187 (with 1947 copyright date) and 187 A (with 1976 copyright date) can both be found with TM 5. Retired from production in 1986 but put back into service in 1990 with new graphics.

□ 187 . . . . . 5½ x 4" . . . . . . . (CE). . . ❶ . . . $1250–1600
□ 187 . . . . . 5½ x 4" . . . . . . . (CE). . . ❷ . . . $750–900
□ 187 . . . . . 5½ x 4" . . . . . . . (CE). . . ❸ . . . $500–600
□ 187 . . . . . 5½ x 4" . . . . . . . (CE). . . ❹ . . . $450–500
□ 187 . . . . . 5½ x 4" . . . . . . . (CE). . . ❺ . . . $175–225
□ 187A . . . . 5½ x 4" . . . . . . . (CE). . . ❺ . . . $175–225
□ 187A . . . . 5½ x 4" . . . . . . . (CE). . . ❻ . . . $150–175
□ 187A . . . . 5½ x 4" . . . . . . . (CE). . . ❻ . . . $115–120
□ 187A . . . . 5½ x 4" . . . . . . . (CE). . . ❼ . . . $110–115

**HUM 187 (SPECIAL)**
**W.G.P. "Service" Plaque**
This service plaque was first introduced in the late 1950's and has become a Goebel tradition. Each employee of W. Goebel Porzellanfabrik, regardless of his/her position or the department he/she is working in receives such a special plaque on the occasion of his/her 25th, 40th or 50th anniversary with Goebel. These special plaques normally sell for $1000–2000 depending on the age, style, and condition of the plaque.

Special personalized plaques were made available to Goebel Collectors' Club *local chapter* members in 1984 for a limited time. It was necessary to belong to an officially authorized "local chapter" of the GCC. The plaque sold for $50. HUM 187 was also used for many other special occasions, such as Festivals, Expos, shows, conventions, etc. This 20th Anniversary plaque, to the right, sold for $125 in 1997.

*188/I (TM 2)*          *188/0 (TM 6)*          *188 4/0 (TM 1)*

## HUM 188
### Celestial Musician

Originally molded by master sculptor Reinhold Unger in 1948, this figurine has never had a major restyling. Older models are slightly larger, have a bluish-green gown and an open quartered base. Newer models are slightly smaller, have a green gown and a closed flat base, and some have 1948 incised copyright date. According to factory information, this figurine was also sold in white overglaze finish at one time, but would now be considered extremely rare in that finish. A new smaller size was first released in 1983. Designed by master sculptor Gerhard Skrobek and Maria Mueller in 1982, this new size measures 5½" and is incised 188/0 on the bottom. Original issue price was $80 in 1983. The older large size has been renumbered 188/I. A new miniature size figurine, 188 4/0 in a matte finish was put on the market in 1993 with suggested retail price of $90. It has an incised 1991 copyright date and a "First Issue 1993" decal. Large size (188/I) was (TW) "Temporarily Withdrawn" in January 1999.

| | | | | |
|---|---|---|---|---|
| ☐ 188 4/0 | 3⅛" | (CE) | ❼ | $124–130 |
| ☐ 188 4/0 | 3⅛" | (OE) | ❽ | $124 |
| ☐ 188 | 7" | (CE) | ❶ | $1500–2000 |
| ☐ 188 | 7" | (CE) | ❷ | $850–1100 |
| ☐ 188 | 7" | (CE) | ❸ | $425–475 |
| ☐ 188 | 7" | (CE) | ❹ | $375–425 |
| ☐ 188 | 7" | (CE) | ❺ | $330–350 |
| ☐ 188 | 7" | (CE) | ❻ | $320–330 |
| ☐ 188/I | 7" | (CE) | ❻ | $310–320 |
| ☐ 188/I | 7" | (TW) | ❼ | $300–310 |
| ☐ 188/0 | 5½" | (CE) | ❻ | $260–270 |
| ☐ 188/0 | 5½" | (CE) | ❼ | $255–260 |
| ☐ 188/0 | 5½" | (OE) | ❽ | $255 |

*Incised "M.I. Hummel"*

### HUM 189
### Old Woman Knitting (CN)
This unusual piece was made as a sample only in 1948 by master sculptor Arthur Moeller and was not approved by the Siessen Convent for production. It was not considered typical of Sister M.I. Hummel's work, although it is an exact replica of one of her early sketches. This early sample does have the familiar "M.I. Hummel" signature and is part of the Robert L. Miller collection. Listed as a Closed Number on 18 February 1948 and will not be produced again. Often referred to as one of the "Mamas" and the "Papas." Several other examples have been found in recent years.

☐ 189 . . . . . 6¾" . . . . . . . . . . (CN) . . . . . . . . $15,000–20,000

*Incised "M.I. Hummel"*

### HUM 190
### Old Woman Walking to Market (CN)
This unusual piece was made as a sample only in 1948 by master sculptor Arthur Moeller and was not approved by the Siessen Convent for production. It was not considered typical of Sister M.I. Hummel's work, although it is an exact replica of one of her early sketches. This early sample *does* have the familiar "M.I. Hummel" signature and is part of the Robert L. Miller collection. Listed as a Closed Number on 18 February 1948 and will not be produced again. Often referred to as one of the "Mamas" and the "Papas." Several other examples have been found in recent years.

☐ 190 . . . . . 6¾" . . . . . . . . . . (CN) . . . . . . . . $15,000–20,000

*Old Postcard Drawing*

*Incised "M.I. Hummel"*

## HUM 191
### Old Man Walking to Market (CN)

This unusual piece was made as a sample only in 1948 by master sculptor Arthur Moeller and was not approved by the Siessen Convent for production. It was not considered typical of Sister M.I. Hummel's work, although it is an exact replica of one of her early sketches. This early sample *does* have the familiar "M.I. Hummel" signature and is part of the Robert L. Miller collection. Listed as a Closed Number on 18 February 1948 and will not be produced again. Often referred to as one of the "Mamas" and the "Papas." Several other examples have been found in recent years. The original drawing appeared on old German post card.

☐ 191 . . . . . 6¾" . . . . . . . . . . (CN) . . . . . . . $15,000–20,000

---

**HUM TERM**

**DECIMAL POINT:** This incised "period" or dot was used in a somewhat random fashion by the W. Goebel Porzellanfabrik over the years. The decimal point is and was primarily used to reduce confusion in reading the incised numbers on the underside of the figurines. Example: 66. helps one realize that the designation is sixty-six and not ninety-nine.

---

*Old style (TM 2)*          *New style (TM 3)*

## HUM 192
### Candlelight, Candleholder

Originally modeled by master sculptor Reinhold Unger in 1948 with a long red ceramic candle. Later restyled by master sculptor Theo R. Menzenbach in 1958 with a short candleholder ending in angels hands. Both models have a receptical for holding a wax candle. Older models are slightly larger. Old name: "Carrier of Light." The incised copyright date on both models is 1948. Both *long* and *short* candle variations can be found with (TM 3) "stylized" trademarks. Listed as (TW) "Temporarily Withdrawn" in January 1999, but may be reinstated at some future date.

☐ 192 . . . . . 6¾ to 7″ . . . . . . (CE). . . ❶ . . . $1350–1800
☐ 192 . . . . . 6¾ to 7″ . . . . . . (CE). . . ❷ . . . $800–1000
☐ 192 . . . . . 6¾ to 7″ . . . . . . (CE). . . ❸ . . . $600–700 (Long candle)
☐ 192 . . . . . 6¾ to 7″ . . . . . . (CE). . . ❸ . . . $350–375 (Short candle)
☐ 192 . . . . . 6¾ to 7″ . . . . . . (CE). . . ❹ . . . $315–350
☐ 192 . . . . . 6¾ to 7″ . . . . . . (CE). . . ❺ . . . $290–315
☐ 192 . . . . . 6¾ to 7″ . . . . . . (CE). . . ❻ . . . $275–290
☐ 192 . . . . . 6¾ to 7″ . . . . . . (TW) . . ❼ . . . $270–275

**HUM 193**
**Angel Duet, Candleholder**
First modeled by master sculptor Reinhold Unger in 1948 and later restyled by master sculptor Theo R. Menzenbach in 1958. Notice the position of angel's arm in rear view—this was changed by Menzenbach because he thought it would be easier for artists to paint—looks better and is a more natural position. Menzenbach began working at the Goebel factory in October 1948, at the age of 18. He left the factory in October 1961 to start his own business as a commercial artist. He is still living and resides in Germany, near Coburg. According to factory information, this figurine was also sold in white overglaze finish at one time—extremely rare. Also produced without holder for candle—see HUM 261. Listed as (TW) "Temporarily Withdrawn" in January 1999, but may be reinstated at some future date.

☐ 193 . . . . . 5" . . . . . . . . . . . (CE). . . ❶ . . . $1350–1800
☐ 193 . . . . . 5" . . . . . . . . . . . (CE). . . ❷ . . . $600–700
☐ 193 . . . . . 5" . . . . . . . . . . . (CE). . . ❸ . . . $325–400
☐ 193 . . . . . 5" . . . . . . . . . . . (CE). . . ❹ . . . $290–325
☐ 193 . . . . . 5" . . . . . . . . . . . (CE). . . ❺ . . . $265–290
☐ 193 . . . . . 5" . . . . . . . . . . . (CE). . . ❻ . . . $255–265
☐ 193 . . . . . 5" . . . . . . . . . . . (TW) . . ❼ . . . $250–255

*New*          *Old*

**HUM 194**
**Watchful Angel**
Originally modeled by master sculptor Reinhold Unger in 1948 and later restyled by master sculptor Gerhard Skrobek in 1959. Older models are usually larger. Most models have an incised 1948 copyright date. Old name: "Angelic Care" or "Guardian Angel."

| | | | | | |
|---|---|---|---|---|---|
| ☐ 194 | . . . . 6¼ to 6¾″ | . . . . . (CE) | . . . ❶ | . . . | $1600–2100 |
| ☐ 194 | . . . . 6¼ to 6¾″ | . . . . . (CE) | . . . ❷ | . . . | $650–800 |
| ☐ 194 | . . . . 6¼ to 6¾″ | . . . . . (CE) | . . . ❸ | . . . | $475–575 |
| ☐ 194 | . . . . 6¼″ | . . . . . . . . . (CE) | . . . ❹ | . . . | $400–475 |
| ☐ 194 | . . . . 6¼″ | . . . . . . . . . (CE) | . . . ❺ | . . . | $370–400 |
| ☐ 194 | . . . . 6¼″ | . . . . . . . . . (CE) | . . . ❻ | . . . | $365–370 |
| ☐ 194 | . . . . 6¼″ | . . . . . . . . . (CE) | . . . ❼ | . . . | $360–365 |
| ☐ 194 | . . . . 6¼″ | . . . . . . . . . (OE) | . . . ❽ | . . . | $360 |

195/I (TM 2)                                195 2/0 (TM 4)

## HUM 195
### Barnyard Hero
First modeled by master sculptor Reinhold Unger in 1948. Originally made in one size only with the incised number 195. A smaller size was produced in the mid-1950's with the incised number 195 2/0. Both sizes have been restyled in recent years. Many size variations as well as variation in position of boy's hands in small size only: old model has one hand on each side of fence; new model, one hand on top of the other one. Most models have an incised 1948 copyright date. Large size (195/I) was listed as (TW) "Temporarily Withdrawn" in January 1999, but may be reinstated at some future date.

| | | | | | |
|---|---|---|---|---|---|
| ☐ 195 2/0 | 3¾ to 4″ | (CE) | ❷ | $350–425 |
| ☐ 195 2/0 | 3¾ to 4″ | (CE) | ❸ | $275–300 |
| ☐ 195 2/0 | 3¾ to 4″ | (CE) | ❹ | $225–275 |
| ☐ 195 2/0 | 3¾ to 4″ | (CE) | ❺ | $200–220 |
| ☐ 195 2/0 | 3¾ to 4″ | (CE) | ❻ | $195–200 |
| ☐ 195 2/0 | 3¾ to 4″ | (CE) | ❼ | $190–195 |
| ☐ 195 2/0 | 3¾ to 4″ | (OE) | ❽ | $195 |
| ☐ 195/I | 5½″ | (CE) | ❷ | $600–700 |
| ☐ 195/I | 5½″ | (CE) | ❸ | $475–525 |
| ☐ 195/I | 5½″ | (CE) | ❹ | $420–475 |
| ☐ 195/I | 5½″ | (CE) | ❺ | $375–420 |
| ☐ 195/I | 5½″ | (CE) | ❻ | $360–375 |
| ☐ 195/I | 5½″ | (TW) | ❼ | $350–360 |
| ☐ 195 | 5¾ to 6″ | (CE) | ❶ | $1000–1200 |
| ☐ 195 | 5¾ to 6″ | (CE) | ❷ | $650–750 |

*196/I (TM 3)*          *196/0 (TM 2)*

**HUM 196**
**Telling Her Secret**
When first modeled in 1948 by master sculptor Reinhold Unger this figurine was produced in one size only with the incised number 196. A smaller size was issued in the
mid-1950's with the incised number 196/0. Some older models have "0" size designator
directly under the 196 rather than 196/0. At the same time, the large size was changed
to 196/I. Slightly restyled in recent years. Most models have an incised 1948 copyright
date. Old name: "The Secret." The girl on the right is the same as HUM 258. "Which
Hand?" HUM 196/I (large size only) was (TW) "Temporarily Withdrawn" from production
on 31 December 1984, but may be reinstated at some future date.

| | | | | |
|---|---|---|---|---|
| ☐ 196/0 | 5 to 5½" | (CE) | ❷ | $600–725 |
| ☐ 196/0 | 5 to 5½" | (CE) | ❸ | $450–500 |
| ☐ 196/0 | 5 to 5½" | (CE) | ❹ | $390–450 |
| ☐ 196/0 | 5 to 5½" | (CE) | ❺ | $360–390 |
| ☐ 196/0 | 5 to 5½" | (CE) | ❻ | $355–360 |
| ☐ 196/0 | 5 to 5½" | (CE) | ❼ | $350–355 |
| ☐ 196/0 | 5 to 5½" | (OE) | ❽ | $350 |
| ☐ 196/I | 6½ to 6¾" | (CE) | ❷ | $750–950 |
| ☐ 196/I | 6½ to 6¾" | (CE) | ❸ | $500–550 |
| ☐ 196/I | 6½ to 6¾" | (CE) | ❹ | $450–500 |
| ☐ 196/I | 6½ to 6¾" | (CE) | ❺ | $425–450 |
| ☐ 196/I | 6½ to 6¾" | (TW) | ❻ | $400–425 |
| ☐ 196 | 6¾" | (CE) | ❶ | $1200–1500 |
| ☐ 196 | 6¾" | (CE) | ❷ | $800–1000 |

*197/I (TM 4)*         *197 2/0 (TM 6)*

## HUM 197
## Be Patient

When first modeled in 1948 by master sculptor Reinhold Unger this figurine was produced in one size only with the incised number 197. A smaller size was issued in the
mid-1950's with the incised number 197 2/0. At the same time, the large size was
changed to 197/I. Both sizes have been restyled with the new textured finish and usually have an incised 1948 copyright date. Old name: "Mother of Ducks." The large size
197/I was (TW) "Temporarily Withdrawn" from production in January 1999.

☐ 197 2/0 . . . 4¼ to 4½" . . . . . (CE). . . ❷ . . . $400–500
☐ 197 2/0 . . . 4¼ to 4½" . . . . . (CE). . . ❸ . . . $300–350
☐ 197 2/0 . . . 4¼ to 4½" . . . . . (CE). . . ❹ . . . $260–300
☐ 197 2/0 . . . 4¼ to 4½" . . . . . (CE). . . ❺ . . . $240–260
☐ 197 2/0 . . . 4¼ to 4½" . . . . . (CE). . . ❻ . . . $235–240
☐ 197 2/0 . . . 4¼ to 4½" . . . . . (CE). . . ❼ . . . $230–235
☐ 197 2/0 . . . 4¼ to 4½" . . . . . (**OE**). . . ❽ . . . $235
☐ 197/I. . . . . 6 to 6¼" . . . . . . . (CE). . . ❷ . . . $500–650
☐ 197/I. . . . . 6 to 6¼" . . . . . . . (CE). . . ❸ . . . $425–475
☐ 197/I. . . . . 6 to 6¼" . . . . . . . (CE). . . ❹ . . . $360–425
☐ 197/I. . . . . 6 to 6¼" . . . . . . . (CE). . . ❺ . . . $350–360
☐ 197/I. . . . . 6 to 6¼" . . . . . . . (CE). . . ❻ . . . $340–350
☐ 197/I. . . . . 6 to 6¼" . . . . . . . (TW). . . ❼ . . . $330–340
☐ 197 . . . . . 6¼" . . . . . . . . . . . (CE). . . ❶ . . . $800–1000
☐ 197 . . . . . 6¼" . . . . . . . . . . . (CE). . . ❷ . . . $550–700

**HUM 198**
**Home From Market**
When first modeled in 1948 by master sculptor Arthur Moeller this figurine was produced in one size only with the incised number 198. A smaller size was issued in the mid-1950's with the incised number 198 2/0. At the same time, the large size was changed to 198/I. Many size variations with older models slightly larger than new. Both sizes have been restyled and now have an incised 1948 copyright date. The small size 198 2/0 has been slightly restyled in recent years, with new hair style and smaller tie. A small size 4½" has also been found with incised number 198 only (no size designator). The large size (198/I) was listed as (TW) "Temporarily Withdrawn" in January 1999, but may be reinstated at some future date.

| | | | | |
|---|---|---|---|---|
| ☐ 198 | 4½" | (CE) | ❷ | $325–375 |
| ☐ 198 2/0 | 4½ to 4¾" | (CE) | ❷ | $300–350 |
| ☐ 198 2/0 | 4½ to 4¾" | (CE) | ❸ | $225–250 |
| ☐ 198 2/0 | 4½ to 4¾" | (CE) | ❹ | $200–225 |
| ☐ 198 2/0 | 4½ to 4¾" | (CE) | ❺ | $190–200 |
| ☐ 198 2/0 | 4½ to 4¾" | (CE) | ❻ | $185–190 |
| ☐ 198 2/0 | 4½ to 4¾" | (CE) | ❼ | $180–185 |
| ☐ 198 2/0 | 4½ to 4¾" | (OE) | ❽ | $180 |
| ☐ 198/I | 5½" | (CE) | ❷ | $400–500 |
| ☐ 198/I | 5½" | (CE) | ❸ | $325–375 |
| ☐ 198/I | 5½" | (CE) | ❹ | $275–325 |
| ☐ 198/I | 5½" | (CE) | ❺ | $260–275 |
| ☐ 198/I | 5½" | (CE) | ❻ | $250–260 |
| ☐ 198/I | 5½" | (TW) | ❼ | $240–245 |
| ☐ 198 | 5¾ to 6" | (CE) | ❶ | $650–800 |
| ☐ 198 | 5¾ to 6" | (CE) | ❷ | $450–550 |

*199 (TM 1)   Old style   (TM 3)*          *199/I (TM 4)   New style   (TM 4)*

## HUM 199
### Feeding Time

When first modeled in 1948 by master sculptor Arthur Moeller this figurine was produced in one size only with the incised number 199. A smaller size was issued in the mid-1950's with the incised number 199/0. At the same time, the large size was changed to 199/I. Both sizes were restyled in the mid-1960's by master sculptor Gerhard Skrobek. The girl is blonde on older figurines—changed to dark hair and new facial features on newer ones. Note position of girl's hand under bowl in new style figurines. All small size and the new large size figurines have an incised 1948 copyright date. Small size (199/0) sometimes found with old style head and new style hand under bowl. Large size (199/I) was listed as (TW) "Temporarily Withdrawn" in January 1999, but may be reinstated at some future date.

| | | | | |
|---|---|---|---|---|
| ☐ 199/0 | 4¼ to 4½″ | (CE) | ❷ | $400–475 |
| ☐ 199/0 | 4¼ to 4½″ | (CE) | ❸ | $300–350 |
| ☐ 199/0 | 4¼ to 4½″ | (CE) | ❹ | $265–300 |
| ☐ 199/0 | 4¼ to 4½″ | (CE) | ❺ | $245–265 |
| ☐ 199/0 | 4¼ to 4½″ | (CE) | ❻ | $240–245 |
| ☐ 199/0 | 4¼ to 4½″ | (CE) | ❼ | $235–240 |
| ☐ 199/0 | 4¼ to 4½″ | (OE) | ❽ | $235 |
| ☐ 199/I | 5½ to 5¾″ | (CE) | ❷ | $475–575 |
| ☐ 199/I | 5½ to 5¾″ | (CE) | ❸ | $425–475 |
| ☐ 199/I | 5½ to 5¾″ | (CE) | ❹ | $375–425 |
| ☐ 199/I | 5½ to 5¾″ | (CE) | ❺ | $340–375 |
| ☐ 199/I | 5½ to 5¾″ | (CE) | ❻ | $325–340 |
| ☐ 199/I | 5½ to 5¾″ | (TW) | ❼ | $315–325 |
| ☐ 199 | 5¾″ | (CE) | ❶ | $800–1000 |
| ☐ 199 | 5¾″ | (CE) | ❷ | $525–625 |

---
**HUM TERM**

**FULL BEE:** The term "Full Bee" refers to the trademark used by the Goebel Co. from 1950 to 1957. Early usage of this trademark was incised into the material. Later versions of the "full bee" were stamped into the material.

---

*200/I (TM 2)*          *200/0 (TM 2)*

## HUM 200
### Little Goat Herder

When first modeled in 1948 by master sculptor Arthur Moeller this figurine was made in one size only with the incised number 200. A smaller size was issued in the mid-1950's with the incised number 200/0. At the same time, the large size was changed to 200/I. Both sizes have been restyled with only minor changes. Older models have a blade of grass between hind legs of the small goat. Newer models do not. Newer models have an incised 1948 copyright date. Older pieces slightly larger. Old name: "Goat Boy." Some "full bee" (TM 2) trademark examples in the small size (200/0) version have been found with a slight variation in the signature—the initials "M.I." are directly above the "Hummel."

| | | | | |
|---|---|---|---|---|
| ☐ 200/0 | 4½ to 4¾" | (CE) | ❷ | $400–500 |
| ☐ 200/0 | 4½ to 4¾" | (CE) | ❸ | $300–325 |
| ☐ 200/0 | 4½ to 4¾" | (CE) | ❹ | $270–300 |
| ☐ 200/0 | 4½ to 4¾" | (CE) | ❺ | $245–270 |
| ☐ 200/0 | 4½ to 4¾" | (CE) | ❻ | $240–245 |
| ☐ 200/0 | 4½ to 4¾" | (CE) | ❼ | $235–240 |
| ☐ 200/0 | 4½ to 4¾" | (OE) | ❽ | $235 |
| ☐ 200/I | 5 to 5½" | (CE) | ❷ | $450–550 |
| ☐ 200/I | 5 to 5½" | (CE) | ❸ | $350–400 |
| ☐ 200/I | 5 to 5½" | (CE) | ❹ | $300–350 |
| ☐ 200/I | 5 to 5½" | (CE) | ❺ | $280–300 |
| ☐ 200/I | 5 to 5½" | (CE) | ❻ | $275–280 |
| ☐ 200/I | 5 to 5½" | (CE) | ❼ | $270–275 |
| ☐ 200/I | 5 to 5½" | (OE) | ❽ | $270 |
| ☐ 200 | 5½ to 5¾" | (CE) | ❶ | $650–850 |
| ☐ 200 | 5½ to 5¾" | (CE) | ❷ | $500–600 |

*201/I (TM 3)*     *201 2/0 (TM 4)*

## HUM 201
### Retreat To Safety

When first modeled in 1948 by master sculptor Reinhold Unger this figurine was produced in one size only with the incised number 201. A smaller size was issued in the mid-1950's with the incised number 201 2/0. At the same time, the large size was changed to 201/I. Both sizes have been restyled in recent years. Many size variations as well as variation in the position of boy's hands in small size only: old model has one hand on each side of fence; new model, one hand on top of the other one. Most models have an incised 1948 copyright date. Old name: "Afraid." Large size (201/I) was listed as (TW) "Temporarily Withdrawn" in January 1999, but may be reinstated at some future date.

| | | | | |
|---|---|---|---|---|
| ☐ 201 2/0 | 3¾ to 4″ | (CE) | ❷ | $350–425 |
| ☐ 201 2/0 | 3¾ to 4″ | (CE) | ❸ | $275–300 |
| ☐ 201 2/0 | 3¾ to 4″ | (CE) | ❹ | $225–275 |
| ☐ 201 2/0 | 3¾ to 4″ | (CE) | ❺ | $200–220 |
| ☐ 201 2/0 | 3¾ to 4″ | (CE) | ❻ | $195–200 |
| ☐ 201 2/0 | 3¾ to 4″ | (CE) | ❼ | $190–195 |
| ☐ 201 2/0 | 3¾ to 4″ | (OE) | ❽ | $190 |
| ☐ 201/I | 5½ to 5¾″ | (CE) | ❷ | $600–700 |
| ☐ 201/I | 5½ to 5¾″ | (CE) | ❸ | $475–525 |
| ☐ 201/I | 5½ to 5¾″ | (CE) | ❹ | $420–475 |
| ☐ 201/I | 5½ to 5¾″ | (CE) | ❺ | $375–420 |
| ☐ 201/I | 5½ to 5¾″ | (CE) | ❻ | $360–375 |
| ☐ 201/I | 5½ to 5¾″ | (TW) | ❼ | $350–360 |
| ☐ 201 | 5¾ to 6″ | (CE) | ❶ | $1000–1200 |
| ☐ 201 | 5¾ to 6″ | (CE) | ❷ | $650–750 |

*Factory sample*                    *Miller collection*

## HUM 202
## Old Man Reading Newspaper,
## Table Lamp (CN)

This unusual piece was made as a sample only in 1948 by master sculptor Arthur Moeller and was not approved by the Siessen Convent for production. It was not considered typical of Sister M.I. Hummel's work, although it is an exact replica of one of her early sketches. Same figure as HUM 181 except on lamp base. Listed as a Closed Number on 18 August 1948. The sample model is from Goebel factory archives.

☐ 202 . . . . . 8¼" . . . . . . . . . . (CN) . . . . . . . $15,000–20,000

---

**HUM TERM**

**DOUGHNUT BASE**: A term used to describe the raised circular support on the underside of a figurine. Many figurine bases with a circle inside the regular circular base gave rise to the term, but has now been used to describe many bases with the circular support on the underside.

---

*203/I (TM 3)*  *203 2/0 (One bare foot)*  *203 2/0 (Two shoes)*

## HUM 203
### Signs of Spring (CE)

When first modeled in 1948 by master sculptor Arthur Moeller this figurine was produced in one size only with the incised number 203. A smaller size was issued in the mid-1950's with the incised number 203 2/0. At the same time, the large size was changed to 203/I. Many size variations. At one time, small size only, was made with the girl wearing both shoes. Full bee trademark pieces found both with or without shoe. Newer models have an incised 1948 copyright date. Old name: "Scandal." "Two shoe" variety considered rare. Both sizes of "Signs of Spring" were permanently retired by Goebel in the fall of 1990 and will not be produced again. The 1990 retail list price was $120 for the small size and $155 for the large.

☐ 203 2/0. . . 4" . . . . . . . . . . . (CE). . . ❷ . . . $1200–1500 (with two shoes)
☐ 203 2/0. . . 4" . . . . . . . . . . . (CE). . . ❷ . . . $425–500
☐ 203 2/0. . . 4" . . . . . . . . . . . (CE). . . ❸ . . . $350–400
☐ 203 2/0. . . 4" . . . . . . . . . . . (CE). . . ❹ . . . $275–350
☐ 203 2/0. . . 4" . . . . . . . . . . . (CE). . . ❺ . . . $250–275
☐ 203 2/0. . . 4" . . . . . . . . . . . (CE). . . ❻ . . . $225–250
☐ 203/I . . . . 5 to 5½" . . . . . . (CE). . . ❷ . . . $500–600
☐ 203/I . . . . 5 to 5½" . . . . . . (CE). . . ❸ . . . $400–450
☐ 203/I . . . . 5 to 5½" . . . . . . (CE). . . ❹ . . . $350–400
☐ 203/I . . . . 5 to 5½" . . . . . . (CE). . . ❺ . . . $300–325
☐ 203/I . . . . 5 to 5½" . . . . . . (CE). . . ❻ . . . $275–300
☐ 203 . . . . . 5¼" . . . . . . . . . . . (CE). . . ❶ . . . $750–1000
☐ 203 . . . . . 5¼" . . . . . . . . . . . (CE). . . ❷ . . . $550–650

FINAL ISSUE
1990

**NOTE:** See page 488 RARE VARIATIONS in the back of book for an unusual variation of this figurine.

187

*Old style (TM 2)*                    *New style (TM 5)*

## HUM 204
### Weary Wanderer
Many size variations. Most models have 1949 as the incised copyright date. Old name: "Tired Little Traveler." Has been restyled with the new textured finish. The word "Lauterbach" on the back of figurine is the name of a village used in an old German song. The first model was made by master sculptor Reinhold Unger in 1949. Occasionally found with blue eyes. This variation would command a premium of $2000 to $3000, if authenticated. "Weary Wanderer" was (TW) "Temporarily Withdrawn" from production in January 1999, but may be reinstated at some future date.

☐ 204 . . . . . 5½ to 6″ . . . . . . (CE). . . ❶ . . . $700–900
☐ 204 . . . . . 5½ to 6″ . . . . . . (CE). . . ❷ . . . $500–600
☐ 204 . . . . . 5½ to 6″ . . . . . . (CE). . . ❸ . . . $375–425
☐ 204 . . . . . 5½ to 6″ . . . . . . (CE). . . ❹ . . . $325–375
☐ 204 . . . . . 5½ to 6″ . . . . . . (CE). . . ❺ . . . $300–325
☐ 204 . . . . . 5½ to 6″ . . . . . . (CE). . . ❻ . . . $295–300
☐ 204 . . . . . 5½ to 6″ . . . . . . (TW) . . ❼ . . . $280–290

*Rear view*

**HUM 205**
**M.I. Hummel Dealer's Plaque**
**(in German) (CE)**
This German dealer's plaque was first modeled by master sculptor Reinhold Unger in 1949. There are three color variations of lettering: all black lettering, black and red combination, and all black except the capital letters O, H and F in red lettering. Usually has an incised crown mark in addition to other trademarks. The all-black variety usually has a "Made in U.S. Zone, Germany" stamped on bottom. Listed in factory records as a Closed Edition on 18 June 1949 although it is found with the stylized trademark (in addition to the crown), indicating they were painted at a later date.

- [ ] 205 . . . . . 5½ × 4¼" . . . . . (CE) . . . ❶ . . . $1400–1700
- [ ] 205 . . . . . 5½ × 4¼" . . . . . (CE) . . . ❷ . . . $1000–1200
- [ ] 205 . . . . . 5½ × 4¼" . . . . . (CE) . . . ❸ . . . $850–1000

---

**HUM TERM**

**DUBLER**: A "Dubler" figurine is one produced during the W.W.II time period by the Herbert Dubler Co. Inc. of New York City. These pieces were substitutes for genuine Goebel "M.I. Hummel" figurines when Goebel "Hummels" were not coming into the U.S. The Dubler figurines were made of plaster of paris and were distributed by the Crestwick Co. of New York which later became Hummelwerk and ultimately the present Goebel United States firm.

---

**HUM TERM**

**STYLIZED TRADEMARK**: The symbol used by the Goebel Company from 1957 until 1964. It is recognized by the V with a bumblebee that has triangular or "stylized" wings.

| Crown (TM 1) | Full Bee (TM 2) | Current (TM 6) |

## HUM 206
### Holy Water Font, Angel Cloud

This holy water font was originally modeled by master sculptor Reinhold Unger in 1949 but has been restyled several times. At least three different variations. Early models do not have rim on back side of bowl. Also color variations on lip of water bowl. Has been considered rare in the older trademarks but was put back into current production in 1978 and can now be found with 5, 6 and 7 trademarks at more reasonable prices. Newer models have an incised 1949 copyright date. Listed as (TW) "Temporarily Withdrawn" in January 1999.

☐ 206 . . . . . 3¼ × 4¾" . . . . . (CE). . . **❶** . . . $350–500
☐ 206 . . . . . 3¼ × 4¾" . . . . . (CE). . . **❷** . . . $250–350
☐ 206 . . . . . 3¼ × 4¾" . . . . . (CE). . . **❸** . . . $200–250
☐ 206 . . . . . 3¼ × 4¾" . . . . . (CE). . . **❹** . . . $70–90
☐ 206 . . . . . 3¼ × 4¾" . . . . . (CE). . . **❺** . . . $65–70
☐ 206 . . . . . 3¼ × 4¾" . . . . . (CE). . . **❻** . . . $62–65
☐ 206 . . . . . 3¼ × 4¾" . . . . . (TW) . . **❼** . . . $60–62

| Newer style | Old style |

## HUM 207
### Holy Water Font, Heavenly Angel

This holy water font was originally modeled by master sculptor Reinhold Unger in 1949 and is the highest numbered piece with the crown trademark. Older models have a hole on the back for hanging while the newer models have a visible hole on the front. Early models do not have rim on the back side of bowl. Newer models have an incised 1949 copyright date. The "Heavenly Angel" motif was used on the First Annual Plate HUM 264 in 1971.

☐ 207 . . . . . 3 × 5". . . . . . . . (CE). . . **❶** . . . $350–500
☐ 207 . . . . . 3 × 5". . . . . . . . (CE). . . **❷** . . . $150–175
☐ 207 . . . . . 3 × 5". . . . . . . . (CE). . . **❸** . . . $100–125
☐ 207 . . . . . 3 × 5". . . . . . . . (CE). . . **❹** . . . $75–90

*(prices continued on next page)*

| 207 | 3 × 5″ | (CE) | ❺ | $70–75 |
| 207 | 3 × 5″ | (CE) | ❻ | $65–70 |
| 207 | 3 × 5″ | (CE) | ❼ | $62–65 |
| 207 | 3 × 5″ | (OE) | ❽ | $62 |

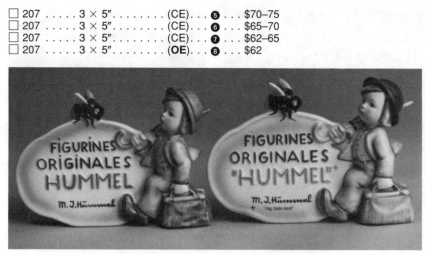

*Old style (TM 2)*              *Newer style (TM 3)*

## HUM 208
### M.I. Hummel Dealer's Plaque
### (In French)(CE)
Originally modeled in 1949 by master sculptor Reinhold Unger. Two known variations. Made with dotted "i" and without quotation marks on Hummel. Newer model has quotation marks: "HUMMEL" + "Reg. trademark."

| 208 | 5½ × 4″ | (CE) | ❷ | $4,000–6,000 |
| 208 | 5½ × 4″ | (CE) | ❸ | $3,000–4,000 |

## HUM 209
### M.I. Hummel Dealer's Plaque
### (In Swedish) (CE)
This extremely rare plaque was first modeled in 1949 by master sculptor Reinhold Unger and was apparently issued in extremely limited quantities. Some have sold for over $7,000.

| 209 | 5½ × 4″ | (CE) | ❷ | $4,000–6,000 |

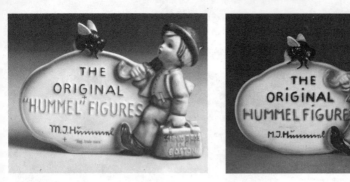

## HUM 210
### M.I. Hummel Dealer's Plaque
### (Schmid Bros.) (CE)

Normal dealers's plaque in English with "SCHMID BROS. INC. BOSTON" embossed on side of satchel of "Merry Wanderer." This extremely rare plaque was first modeled in 1950 by master sculptor Reinhold Unger. Also made with dotted "i" and without quotation marks. Very few are known to exist. Schmid Bros. was one of the early importers of "M.I. Hummel" figurines in 1935.

☐ 210 . . . . . 5½ × 4″ . . . . . . (CE). . . ❷ . . . $20,000–25,000

*Unpainted sample*

## HUM 211
### M.I. Hummel Dealer's Plaque (in English) (CE)

This is probably the most rare of all "M.I. Hummel" dealer's plaques. The only known painted example was located in 1975 by Major Larry Spohn and his wife Anne while they were living in Germany, and is now in the Robert L. Miller collection. All the lettering on this plaque is in lower case and the word "Oeslau" is used as the location of W. Goebel Porzellanfabrik. Modeled in 1950 by master sculptor Reinhold Unger. The exact purpose or reason for designing this plaque still remains a mystery today. Note quotation marks (",") around "Hummel" on white unpainted sample.

☐ 211 . . . . . 5½ × 4″ . . . . . . (CE). . . ❷ . . . $20,000–25,000

**HUM 212**
**Orchestra (CN)**
Most notes from the Goebel factory state: "No information available" on this number. However, one old list indicates "Orchestra A-F" and the date "13 May 51." This is possibly a number assigned to a Hummel orchestra as a set, such as Hummel Nativity Set HUM 214. Another note states: "Modeled by Arthur Moeller in 1951."

☐ 212 . . . . . (CN) . . . . . . . .

**HUM 213**
**M.I. Hummel Dealer's Plaque**
**(in Spanish) (CE)**
This Spanish dealer's plaque was first modeled in 1951 by master sculptor Reinhold Unger and apparently only a very limited number were produced. Considered extremely rare.

☐ 213 . . . . . 5¾ × 4¼" . . . . . (CE). . . ❷ . . . $8,000–10,000

```
┌──────────────── HUM TERM ────────────────┐
│                                           │
│    TEMPORARILY WITHDRAWN: A designa-      │
│    tion assigned by the W. Goebel Porzellan-│
│    fabrik to indicate that a particular item is │
│    being withdrawn from production for some │
│    time, but may be reinstated at a future date. │
│                                           │
└───────────────────────────────────────────┘
```

**HUM 214**
**Nativity Set with Wooden Stable**
This set was modeled by master sculptor Reinhold Unger in 1951. First produced and sold in 1952. Normally sold as a set but is also available in individual pieces. At one time this set was produced and sold in white overglaze finish but is no longer sold this way. The white overglaze finish is considered rare and usually brings a premium. Early production of HUM 214 A (Virgin Mary and Infant Jesus) was made in one piece. Because of production problems, it was later produced as two separate pieces, both with the same number (214 A) incised on the bottom of each piece. The one-piece unit was sold in white overglaze finish as well as full color finish and both are considered rare today. Two different styles of lambs (HUM 214/O) have been used with the Nativity sets—note variations in photo. Some Nativity set pieces have an incised 1951 copyright date. HUM 214/C, 214/D, 214/E and 214/H are not always included in sets and are considered "optional" pieces. The wooden stable is usually sold separately. The sixteenth piece, "Flying Angel" HUM 366, was added to the set in 1963. Goebel also produces three different camels to match this set which do not have the "M.I. Hummel" signature since they were not designed by Sister Hummel. In 1985 the "Infant Jesus" (214/A) was renumbered to *214 A/K* which is now incised on the bottom of this piece only. The "K" refers to the German word "Kinder" which means child in English. New production of the HUM 214 nativity set are now being numbered with (/1) size designator: Example: *214/A* now *214/A/1*. This nativity set was also produced in terra cotta finish—probably experimentally only.

| | | |
|---|---|---|
| 214/A . . . . . . . . . | 214/A/1 | Virgin Mary and Infant Jesus (one piece-CE) |
| 214/A . . . . . . . . . | 214/A/1 | Virgin Mary |
| 214/A (or 214 A/K) . | 214/A/K/1 | Infant Jesus |
| 214/B . . . . . . . . . | 214/B/1 | Joseph |
| 214/C . . . . . . . . . | 214/C/1 | Angel standing, "Good Night" |
| 214/D . . . . . . . . . | 214/D/1 | Angel kneeling, "Angel Serenade" |
| 214/E . . . . . . . . . | 214/E/1 | We Congratulate |
| 214/F. . . . . . . . . . | 214/F/1 | Shepherd standing with sheep |
| 214/G . . . . . . . . . | 214/G/1 | Shepherd kneeling |
| 214/H . . . . . . . . . | 214/H/1 | Shepherd Boy, kneeling with flute "Little Tooter" |
| 214/J. . . . . . . . . . | 214/J/1 | Donkey |
| 214/K . . . . . . . . . | 214/K/1 | Ox (cow) |
| 214/L. . . . . . . . . . | 214/L/1 | Moorish king, standing |
| 214/M . . . . . . . . . | 214/M/1 | King, kneeling on one knee |
| 214/N . . . . . . . . . | 214/N/1 | King, kneeling with cash-box |
| 214/O . . . . . . . . . | 214/O/1 | Lamb |
| 366 . . . . . . . . . . . | 366/1 | Flying Angel |

*New Style*          *Rare Old Style*

*Nativity set in color*

*Discontinued white nativity set*

195

|  |  |  |  |  | COLOR | WHITE |
|---|---|---|---|---|---|---|
| ☐ 214A | 1 PIECE 6½" | (CE) | ❷ | | ☐ $2000–2500 | ☐ $2500–3000 |
| ☐ 214A | 6¼" to 6½" | (CE) | ❷ | | ☐ $300–400 | ☐ $395–495 |
| ☐ 214A | 6¼" to 6½" | (CE) | ❸ | | ☐ $250–285 | ☐ $320–395 |
| ☐ 214A | 6¼" to 6½" | (CE) | ❹ | | ☐ $220–250 | ☐ $245–320 |
| ☐ 214A | 6¼" to 6½" | (CE) | ❺ | | ☐ $210–220 | ☐ $195–220 |
| ☐ 214A | 6¼" to 6½" | (CE) | ❻ | | ☐ $205–210 | ☐ $195–220 |
| ☐ 214A/1 | 6¼" to 6½" | (CE) | ❼ | | ☐ $200–205 | — |
| ☐ 214A/M/1 | 6¼" to 6½" | (OE) | ❽ | | ☐ $200 | — |
| ☐ 214A | 1½ × 3½" | (CE) | ❷ | | ☐ $110–135 | ☐ $210–260 |
| ☐ 214A | 1½ × 3½" | (CE) | ❸ | | ☐ $95–100 | ☐ $160–210 |
| ☐ 214A | 1½ × 3½" | (CE) | ❹ | | ☐ $90–95 | ☐ $85–110 |
| ☐ 214A | 1½ × 3½" | (CE) | ❺ | | ☐ $85–90 | ☐ $60–70 |
| ☐ 214A/K | 1½ × 3½" | (CE) | ❻ | | ☐ $80–85 | ☐ $60–70 |
| ☐ 214A/K/1 | 1½ × 3½" | (CE) | ❼ | | ☐ $75–80 | — |
| ☐ 214A/K/1 | 1½ × 3½" | (OE) | ❽ | | ☐ $75 | — |
| ☐ 214B | 7½" | (CE) | ❷ | | ☐ $300–400 | ☐ $345–420 |
| ☐ 214B | 7½" | (CE) | ❸ | | ☐ $250–285 | ☐ $270–345 |
| ☐ 214B | 7½" | (CE) | ❹ | | ☐ $220–250 | ☐ $220–270 |
| ☐ 214B | 7½" | (CE) | ❺ | | ☐ $210–220 | ☐ $170–195 |
| ☐ 214B | 7½" | (CE) | ❻ | | ☐ $205–210 | ☐ $145–170 |
| ☐ 214B/1 | 7½" | (CE) | ❼ | | ☐ $200–205 | — |
| ☐ 214B/1 | 7½" | (OE) | ❽ | | ☐ $200 | — |
| ☐ 214C | 3½" | (CE) | ❷ | | ☐ $160–200 | ☐ $365–415 |
| ☐ 214C | 3½" | (CE) | ❸ | | ☐ $125–145 | ☐ $315–365 |
| ☐ 214C | 3½" | (CE) | ❹ | | ☐ $115–125 | ☐ $265–315 |
| ☐ 214C | 3½" | (CE) | ❺ | | ☐ $110–115 | — — |
| ☐ 214C | 3½" | (CE) | ❻ | | ☐ $105–110 | — — |
| ☐ 214C/1 | 3½" | (CE) | ❼ | | ☐ $100–105 | — |
| ☐ 214C/1 | 3½" | (OE) | ❽ | | ☐ $100 | — |
| ☐ 214D | 3" | (CE) | ❷ | | ☐ $160–200 | ☐ $240–290 |
| ☐ 214D | 3" | (CE) | ❸ | | ☐ $125–145 | ☐ $215–240 |
| ☐ 214D | 3" | (CE) | ❹ | | ☐ $115–125 | ☐ $165–215 |
| ☐ 214D | 3" | (CE) | ❺ | | ☐ $110–115 | — — |
| ☐ 214D | 3" | (CE) | ❻ | | ☐ $105–110 | — — |
| ☐ 214D/1 | 3" | (CE) | ❼ | | ☐ $100–105 | — |
| ☐ 214D/1 | 3" | (OE) | ❽ | | ☐ $100 | — |
| ☐ 214E | 3¾" | (CE) | ❷ | | ☐ $320–390 | ☐ $395–470 |
| ☐ 214E | 3¾" | (CE) | ❸ | | ☐ $250–285 | ☐ $320–395 |
| ☐ 214E | 3¾" | (CE) | ❹ | | ☐ $215–250 | ☐ $270–320 |
| ☐ 214E | 3¾" | (CE) | ❺ | | ☐ $195–200 | — — |
| ☐ 214E | 3¾" | (CE) | ❻ | | ☐ $190–195 | — — |
| ☐ 214E/1 | 3¾" | (CE) | ❼ | | ☐ $185–190 | — |
| ☐ 214E/1 | 3¾" | (OE) | ❽ | | ☐ $185 | — |
| ☐ 214F | 7" | (CE) | ❷ | | ☐ $340–415 | ☐ $370–470 |
| ☐ 214F | 7" | (CE) | ❸ | | ☐ $270–310 | ☐ $270–370 |
| ☐ 214F | 7" | (CE) | ❹ | | ☐ $230–270 | ☐ $220–270 |
| ☐ 214F | 7" | (CE) | ❺ | | ☐ $210–215 | — — |
| ☐ 214F | 7" | (CE) | ❻ | | ☐ $205–210 | — — |
| ☐ 214F/1 | 7" | (CE) | ❼ | | ☐ $200–205 | — |
| ☐ 214F/1 | 7" | (OE) | ❽ | | ☐ $200 | — |
| ☐ 214G | 5" | (CE) | ❷ | | ☐ $255–310 | ☐ $270–320 |
| ☐ 214G | 5" | (CE) | ❸ | | ☐ $200–225 | ☐ $220–270 |
| ☐ 214G | 5" | (CE) | ❹ | | ☐ $170–200 | ☐ $170–220 |
| ☐ 214G | 5" | (CE) | ❺ | | ☐ $165–170 | — — |
| ☐ 214G | 5" | (CE) | ❻ | | ☐ $160–165 | — — |

*(prices continued on next page)*

| | | | | COLOR | WHITE |
|---|---|---|---|---|---|
| ☐ 214G/1 | 5″ | (CE) | ❼ | ☐ $155–160 | — |
| ☐ 214G/1 | 5″ | (OE) | ❽ | ☐ $155 | — |
| ☐ 214H | 3¾″ to 4″ | (CE) | ❷ | ☐ $230–280 | ☐ $270–320 |
| ☐ 214H | 3¾″ to 4″ | (CE) | ❸ | ☐ $180–205 | ☐ $220–270 |
| ☐ 214H | 3¾″ to 4″ | (CE) | ❹ | ☐ $160–180 | ☐ $170–220 |
| ☐ 214H | 3¾″ to 4″ | (CE) | ❺ | ☐ $155–160 | — — |
| ☐ 214H | 3¾″ to 4″ | (CE) | ❻ | ☐ $150–155 | — — |
| ☐ 214H/1 | 3¾″ to 4″ | (CE) | ❼ | ☐ $145–150 | — |
| ☐ 214H/1 | 3¾″ to 4″ | (OE) | ❽ | ☐ $145 | — |
| ☐ 214J | 5″ | (CE) | ❷ | ☐ $130–160 | ☐ $180–255 |
| ☐ 214J | 5″ | (CE) | ❸ | ☐ $100–115 | ☐ $155–180 |
| ☐ 214J | 5″ | (CE) | ❹ | ☐ $95–100 | ☐ $130–155 |
| ☐ 214J | 5″ | (CE) | ❺ | ☐ $90–95 | — — |
| ☐ 214J | 5″ | (CE) | ❻ | ☐ $85–90 | — — |
| ☐ 214J/1 | 5″ | (CE) | ❼ | ☐ $84–85 | — |
| ☐ 214J/1 | 5″ | (OE) | ❽ | ☐ $84 | — |
| ☐ 214K | 3½″ to 6¼″ | (CE) | ❷ | ☐ $130–160 | ☐ $180–255 |
| ☐ 214K | 3½″ to 6¼″ | (CE) | ❸ | ☐ $100–115 | ☐ $155–180 |
| ☐ 214K | 3½″ to 6¼″ | (CE) | ❹ | ☐ $95–100 | ☐ $130–155 |
| ☐ 214K | 3½″ to 6¼″ | (CE) | ❺ | ☐ $90–95 | — — |
| ☐ 214K | 3½″ to 6¼″ | (CE) | ❻ | ☐ $85–90 | — — |
| ☐ 214K/1 | 3½″ to 6¼″ | (CE) | ❼ | ☐ $84–85 | — |
| ☐ 214K/1 | 3½″ to 6¼″ | (OE) | ❽ | ☐ $84 | — |
| ☐ 214L | 8 to 8¼″ | (CE) | ❷ | ☐ $340–415 | ☐ $375–475 |
| ☐ 214L | 8 to 8¼″ | (CE) | ❸ | ☐ $270–310 | ☐ $275–375 |
| ☐ 214L | 8 to 8¼″ | (CE) | ❹ | ☐ $230–270 | ☐ $225–275 |
| ☐ 214L | 8 to 8¼″ | (CE) | ❺ | ☐ $215–220 | — — |
| ☐ 214L | 8 to 8¼″ | (CE) | ❻ | ☐ $210–215 | — — |
| ☐ 214L/1 | 8 to 8¼″ | (CE) | ❼ | ☐ $205–210 | — |
| ☐ 214L/1 | 8 to 8¼″ | (OE) | ❽ | ☐ $205 | — |
| ☐ 214M | 5½″ | (CE) | ❷ | ☐ $315–415 | ☐ $375–475 |
| ☐ 214M | 5½″ | (CE) | ❸ | ☐ $265–300 | ☐ $275–375 |
| ☐ 214M | 5½″ | (CE) | ❹ | ☐ $225–265 | ☐ $225–275 |
| ☐ 214M | 5½″ | (CE) | ❺ | ☐ $210–215 | — — |
| ☐ 214M | 5½″ | (CE) | ❻ | ☐ $205–210 | — — |
| ☐ 214M/1 | 5½″ | (CE) | ❼ | ☐ $200–205 | — |
| ☐ 214M/1 | 5½″ | (OE) | ❽ | ☐ $200 | — |
| ☐ 214N | 5½″ | (CE) | ❷ | ☐ $315–385 | ☐ $375–475 |
| ☐ 214N | 5½″ | (CE) | ❸ | ☐ $245–280 | ☐ $275–375 |
| ☐ 214N | 5½″ | (CE) | ❹ | ☐ $210–245 | ☐ $225–275 |
| ☐ 214N | 5½″ | (CE) | ❺ | ☐ $195–200 | — — |
| ☐ 214N | 5½″ | (CE) | ❻ | ☐ $190–195 | — — |
| ☐ 214N/1 | 5½″ | (CE) | ❼ | ☐ $185–190 | — |
| ☐ 214N/1 | 5½″ | (OE) | ❽ | ☐ $185 | — |
| ☐ 214O | 1¾″ × 2½″ | (CE) | ❷ | ☐ $42–52 | ☐ $105–130 |
| ☐ 214O | 1¾″ × 2½″ | (CE) | ❸ | ☐ $35–38 | ☐ $80–105 |
| ☐ 214O | 1¾″ × 2½″ | (CE) | ❹ | ☐ $32–35 | ☐ $55–70 |
| ☐ 214O | 1¾″ × 2½″ | (CE) | ❺ | ☐ $30–32 | — — |
| ☐ 214O | 1¾″ × 2½″ | (CE) | ❻ | ☐ $28–30 | — — |
| ☐ 214O/1 | 1¾″ × 2½″ | (CE) | ❼ | ☐ $25–28 | — |
| ☐ 214O/1 | 1¾″ × 2½″ | (OE) | ❽ | ☐ $25 | — |
| ☐ 366 | 3½″ | (CE) | ❹ | ☐ $215–265 | ☐ $225–275 |
| ☐ 366 | 3½″ | (CE) | ❺ | ☐ $160–165 | ☐ $150–175 |
| ☐ 366 | 3½″ | (CE) | ❻ | ☐ $155–160 | ☐ $150–175 |

*(prices continued on next page)*

197

☐ 366/1 . . . . 3½″ . . . . . . . . . (CE) . . **❼** . . . ☐ $150–155 . . . . . . —
☐ 366/1 . . . . 3½″ . . . . . . . . . (**OE**) . . **❽** . . . ☐ $150 . . . . . . . . . —

☐ Wooden stable, to fit 12–16 piece sets . . . . . . . Current retail $115
☐ Wooden stable, to fit 3 piece sets . . . . . . . . . . Current retail $50

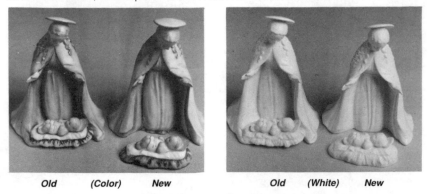

*Old* *(Color)* *New*       *Old* *(White)* *New*

A new small size Nativity set was first announced in 1988. Three pieces only were released—Mary, Infant Jesus and Joseph—and sold as a set for $185. In 1989 four other pieces were released—the donkey, ox, lamb and Flying Angel. In 1990 the three Kings were released. In 1991 the two Shepherds and Little Tooter were released with the possibility of others to follow in future years.

| | | | | | |
|---|---|---|---|---|---|
| ☐ 214 A/M/0 . . | Mary . . . . . . . . . . . . | 5¼″ . . . . | (CE) . . . . . . | **❻** . . . . . | $160–165 |
| ☐ 214 A/M/0 . . | Mary . . . . . . . . . . . . | 5¼″ . . . . | (CE) . . . . . . | **❼** . . . . . | $155–160 |
| ☐ 214 A/M/0 . . | Mary . . . . . . . . . . . . | 5¼″ . . . . | (**OE**) . . . . . . | **❽** . . . . . | $155 |
| ☐ 214 A/K/0 . . | Infant Jesus . . . . . . . | 2⅞″ . . . . | (CE) . . . . . . | **❻** . . . . . | $55–60 |
| ☐ 214 A/K/0 . . | Infant Jesus . . . . . . . | 2⅞″ . . . . | (CE) . . . . . . | **❼** . . . . . | $52–55 |
| ☐ 214 A/K/0 . . | Infant Jesus . . . . . . . | 2⅞″ . . . . | (**OE**) . . . . . . | **❽** . . . . . | $52 |
| ☐ 214 B/0 . . . . | Joseph . . . . . . . . . | 6⅛″ . . . . | (CE) . . . . . . | **❻** . . . . . | $160–165 |
| ☐ 214 B/0 . . . . | Joseph . . . . . . . . . | 6⅛″ . . . . | (CE) . . . . . . | **❼** . . . . . | $155–160 |
| ☐ 214 B/0 . . . . | Joseph . . . . . . . . . | 6⅛″ . . . . | (**OE**) . . . . . . | **❽** . . . . . | $155 |
| ☐ 214 D/0 . . . . | Angel Serenade . . . . | 2⅞″ . . . . | (**OE**) . . . . . | **❼–❽** . . . . | $90 |
| ☐ 366/0 . . . . . . | Flying Angel . . . . . . . | 2¾″ . . . . | (CE) . . . . . . | **❻** . . . . . | $130–135 |
| ☐ 366/0 . . . . . . | Flying Angel . . . . . . . | 2¾″ . . . . | (CE) . . . . . . | **❼** . . . . . | $124–130 |
| ☐ 366/0 . . . . . . | Flying Angel . . . . . . . | | (**OE**) . . . . . . | **❽** . . . . . | $124 |
| ☐ 214 J/0 . . . . | Donkey . . . . . . . . . | 3⅞″ . . . . | (CE) . . . . . . | **❻** . . . . . | $60–65 |
| ☐ 214 J/0 . . . . | Donkey . . . . . . . . . | 3⅞″ . . . . | (CE) . . . . . . | **❼** . . . . . | $58–60 |
| ☐ 214 J/0 . . . . | Donkey . . . . . . . . . | | (**OE**) . . . . . . | **❽** . . . . . | $58 |
| ☐ 214 K/0 . . . . | Ox . . . . . . . . . . . . . | 2¾″ . . . . | (CE) . . . . . . | **❻** . . . . . | $60–65 |
| ☐ 214 K/0 . . . . | Ox . . . . . . . . . . . . . | 2¾″ . . . . | (CE) . . . . . . | **❼** . . . . . | $58–60 |
| ☐ 214 K/0 . . . . | Ox . . . . . . . . . . . . . | | (**OE**) . . . . . . | **❽** . . . . . | $58 |
| ☐ 214 O/0 . . . . | Lamb . . . . . . . . . . | 1½″ . . . . | (CE) . . . . . . | **❻** . . . . . | $28–30 |
| ☐ 214 O/0 . . . . | Lamb . . . . . . . . . . | 1½″ . . . . | (CE) . . . . . . | **❼** . . . . . | $25–28 |
| ☐ 214 O/0 . . . . | Lamb . . . . . . . . . . | | (**OE**) . . . . . . | **❽** . . . . . | $25 |
| ☐ 214 L/0 . . . . | King Standing . . . . . | 6¼″ . . . . | (CE) . . . . . . | **❻** . . . . . | $180–185 |
| ☐ 214 L/0 . . . . | King Standing . . . . . | 6¼″ . . . . | (CE) . . . . . . | **❼** . . . . . | $175–180 |
| ☐ 214 L/0 . . . . | King Standing . . . . . | | (**OE**) . . . . . . | **❽** . . . . . | $175 |
| ☐ 214 M/0 . . . . | King on one knee . . | 4¼″ . . . . | (CE) . . . . . . | **❻** . . . . . | $170–175 |
| ☐ 214 M/0 . . . . | King on one knee . . | 4¼″ . . . . | (CE) . . . . . . | **❼** . . . . . | $165–170 |
| ☐ 214 M/0 . . . . | King on one knee . . . . . . . . . | | (**OE**) . . . . . . | **❽** . . . . . | $165 |
| ☐ 214 N/0 . . . . | King on two knees . . | 4½″ . . . . | (CE) . . . . . . | **❻** . . . . . | $165–170 |

*(prices continued on next page)*

198

| ☐ 214 N/0 | .... King on two knees .. 4½".... | (CE)...... ❼ ..... | $160–165 |
| ☐ 214 N/0 | .... King on two knees ........ | (**OE**)...... ❽ ..... | $160 |
| ☐ 214 F/0 | .... Shepherd Standing .. 5¾".... | (CE)...... ❻ ..... | $180–185 |
| ☐ 214 F/0 | .... Shepherd Standing .. 5¾".... | (CE)...... ❼ ..... | $175–180 |
| ☐ 214 F/0 | .... Shepherd Standing........ | (**OE**)...... ❽ ..... | $175 |
| ☐ 214 G/0 | .... Shepherd Kneeling .. 4" ..... | (CE)...... ❻ ..... | $145–150 |
| ☐ 214 G/0 | .... Shepherd Kneeling .. 4" ..... | (CE)...... ❼ ..... | $140–145 |
| ☐ 214 G/0 | .... Shepherd Kneeling ........ | (**OE**)...... ❽ ..... | $140 |
| ☐ 214 H/0 | .... Little Tooter ....... 3¼".... | (CE)...... ❻ ..... | $120–125 |
| ☐ 214 H/0 | .... Little Tooter ....... 3¼".... | (CE)...... ❼ ..... | $118–120 |
| ☐ 214 H/0 | .... Little Tooter............. | (**OE**)...... ❽ ..... | $118 |

## HUM 215 (CN)
Factory records indicate: A child Jesus standing with lamb in arms. Listed as a Closed Number on 16 August 1951. No known examples.

☐ 215 ................. (CN).......

## HUM 216 (CN)
Factory records indicate: Joyful, ashtray without rest for cigarette. Listed as a Closed Number on 10 September 1951. No known examples.

☐ 216 ................. (CN).......

**TM 2**          **TM 4**

### HUM 217
### Boy With Toothache
First modeled by master sculptor Arthur Moeller in 1951. Older figurines are slightly larger. Older models have " © WG" after the "M.I. Hummel" signature."Old name: "At the Dentist" or "Toothache." Newer models have an incised 1951 copyright date. Some slight variations in color are found, but would not affect value.

| ☐ 217 | ..... 5¼ to 5½" ..... | (CE)... ❷ ... | $425–525 |
| ☐ 217 | ..... 5¼ to 5½" ..... | (CE)... ❸ ... | $320–370 |
| ☐ 217 | ..... 5¼ to 5½" ..... | (CE)... ❹ ... | $270–320 |
| ☐ 217 | ..... 5¼ to 5½" ..... | (CE)... ❺ ... | $250–270 |
| ☐ 217 | ..... 5¼ to 5½" ..... | (CE)... ❻ ... | $245–250 |
| ☐ 217 | ..... 5¼ to 5½" ..... | (CE)... ❼ ... | $240–245 |
| ☐ 217 | ..... 5¼ to 5½" ..... | (**OE**)... ❽ ... | $240 |

*New style (OE)*          *Old style (CE)*

## HUM 218
### Birthday Serenade

First modeled by master sculptor Reinhold Unger in 1952. Early models bearing an incised 1952 copyright date have boy playing horn, girl playing accordion. Remodeled in 1964 by master sculptor Gerhard Skrobek. Newer models bearing an incised 1965 copyright date have boy playing accordion, girl playing horn. This change was made at the request of the convent. The large size (HUM 218/0) had been considered rare but is again back in production with current trademark with boy playing accordion and girl playing horn with an incised 1952 copyright date. This was an error as it should have been 1965. Note that a tie has been added to the boy when he plays the accordion. Both styles can be found with TM 3 or TM 4 trademark. Large size (218/0) was listed as (TW) "Temporarily Withdrawn" in January 1999, but may be reinstated at some future date.

- [ ] 218 2/0. . . 4¼ to 4½" . . . . . (CE). . . ❷ . . . $600–650
- [ ] 218 2/0. . . 4¼ to 4½" . . . . . (CE). . . ❸ . . . $550–600 (Old style)
- [ ] 218 2/0. . . 4¼ to 4½" . . . . . (CE). . . ❸ . . . $260–290 (New Style)
- [ ] 218 2/0. . . 4¼ to 4½" . . . . . (CE). . . ❹ . . . $450–550 (Old Style)
- [ ] 218 2/0. . . 4¼ to 4½" . . . . . (CE). . . ❹ . . . $225–260 (New Style)
- [ ] 218 2/0. . . 4¼ to 4½" . . . . . (CE). . . ❺ . . . $210–225
- [ ] 218 2/0. . . 4¼ to 4½" . . . . . (CE). . . ❻ . . . $205–210
- [ ] 218 2/0. . . 4¼ to 4½" . . . . . (CE). . . ❼ . . . $200–205
- [ ] 218 2/0. . . 4¼ to 4½" . . . . . (OE). . . ❽ . . . $200
- [ ] 218/0 . . . . 5¼". . . . . . . . . . (CE). . . ❷ . . . $875–975
- [ ] 218/0 . . . . 5¼". . . . . . . . . . (CE). . . ❸ . . . $775–875 (Old Style)
- [ ] 218/0 . . . . 5¼". . . . . . . . . . (CE). . . ❸ . . . $450–500 (New Style)
- [ ] 218/0 . . . . 5¼". . . . . . . . . . (CE). . . ❹ . . . $725–825 (Old Style)
- [ ] 218/0 . . . . 5¼". . . . . . . . . . (CE). . . ❹ . . . $370–450 (New Style)
- [ ] 218/0 . . . . 5¼". . . . . . . . . . (CE). . . ❺ . . . $350–370
- [ ] 218/0 . . . . 5¼". . . . . . . . . . (CE). . . ❻ . . . $340–350
- [ ] 218/0 . . . . 5¼". . . . . . . . . . (TW). . . ❼ . . . $330–340
- [ ] 218 . . . . . 5¼". . . . . . . . . . (CE). . . ❷ . . . $900–1000
- [ ] 218/1 . . . . 5¼". . . . . . . . . . (CE). . . ❷ . . . $1000–1500

(218/1 possible factory error)

*"Little Velma"*

**HUM 219**
**Little Velma (CE)**
This figurine was designed in 1952 by master sculptor Reinhold Unger. According to factory records this figurine was produced in very limited numbers (possibly less than 100 pieces) because of its similarity to other models. The name "Little Velma" was affectionately assigned to this piece in honor of the lady who first brought it to the attention of, and sold it to, this author. Most of these figurines must have been shipped to Canada as most known examples can be traced to that country.

☐ 219 2/0. . . 4″ . . . . . . . . . . . (CN). . . ❷ . . . $4,000–6,000

---

**HUM TERM**

**HOLLOW MOLD**: The term used by "M. I. Hummel" collectors to describe a figurine that is open on the underside of the base. With these particular bases the collector can visually see into the cavity of the figurine.

---

201

*220 2/0 (TM 2)*          *260F (TM 4)*          *214E (TM 2)*

**HUM 220**

**We Congratulate (with base)**

First modeled by master sculptor Arthur Moeller in 1952. Early production pieces have the incised number 220 2/0. Later production dropped the 2/0 size designator and added the 1952 incised copyright date. This figurine is the same as HUM 214/E and HUM 260/F in the Nativity Sets, except with base and no flowers in girl's hair. Also note lederhosen strap added to boy.

☐ 220 . . . . . 3¾ to 4″ . . . . . . (CE). . . ❷ . . . $325–400
☐ 220 . . . . . 3¾ to 4″ . . . . . . (CE). . . ❸ . . . $240–275
☐ 220 . . . . . 3¾ to 4″ . . . . . . (CE). . . ❹ . . . $210–240
☐ 220 . . . . . 3¾ to 4″ . . . . . . (CE). . . ❺ . . . $200–210
☐ 220 . . . . . 3¾ to 4″ . . . . . . (CE). . . ❻ . . . $195–200
☐ 220 . . . . . 3¾ to 4″ . . . . . . (CE). . . ❼ . . . $190–195
☐ 220 . . . . . 3¾ to 4″ . . . . . . (**OE**). . ❽ . . . $190
☐ 220 2/0. . . 4″ . . . . . . . . . . . (CE). . . ❷ . . . $475–575

*Incised signature (HUM 214 E)*          *Painted signature*

202

*(Factory sample)*

### HUM 221
### Happy Pastime, Candy Jar (CN)
This candy jar was made as a sample only and was never produced for sale. First modeled by master sculptor Arthur Moeller in 1952. To my knowledge, there are no examples in private collections.

☐ 221 . . . . . . . . . . . . . . . . . (CN). . . . . . . $5,000–10,000

*Two variations*

### HUM 222
### Madonna Plaque (with metal frame) (CE)
Originally modeled by master sculptor Reinhold Unger in 1952. There are basically two different styles of metal frames—both pictured here. Found without frame with full bee trademark but unconfirmed if actually sold that way. Similar in design to HUM 48 "Madonna Plaque." Usually found with gray or tan felt backing, which would have to be removed to see the incised number. The number 222 is normally found upside down!

☐ 222 . . . . . 4 × 5″. . . . . . . . (CE). . . . ❷ . . . $750–1250
☐ 222 . . . . . 4 × 5″. . . . . . . . (CE). . . . ❸ . . . $750–1000

*223 (TM 2)*       *101 (TM 3)*

## HUM 223
### To Market, Table Lamp

This lamp was originally modeled by master sculptor Arthur Moeller in 1937 as HUM 101 and later restyled by him in 1952. It is similar to the original model with the exception of the size and a flower added to branch of tree trunk. Measures 5¼ across the base. Called "Surprise" in old catalogue and sold for $25 in 1955. "To Market" table lamp was "Temporarily Withdrawn" from production on 31 December 1989, but may be reinstated at some future date. For a limited time, it was sold through Danbury Mint at $495 (10 monthly payments of $49.50 each. Plus sales tax.)—but is *no longer available* from them. We list as (OE) "Open Edition" since they are available in Germany and other markets, but are *NOT* currently available in the U.S. market.

| | | | | |
|---|---|---|---|---|
| ☐ 223 | 9½" | (CE) | ❷ | $700–850 |
| ☐ 223 | 9½" | (CE) | ❸ | $650–700 |
| ☐ 223 | 9½" | (CE) | ❹ | $575–650 |
| ☐ 223 | 9½" | (CE) | ❺ | $540–575 |
| ☐ 223 | 9½" | (CE) | ❻ | $525–540 |
| ☐ 223 | 9½" | (CE) | ❼ | $495–500 |
| ☐ 223 | 9½" | **(OE)** | ❽ | $495–500 (Estimated Price) |

*224/II (TM 2)*         *224/I (TM 2)*

**HUM 224**
**Wayside Harmony, Table Lamp**
This lamp was modeled by master sculptor Reinhold Unger in 1952 and is actually a restyling of HUM II/111 "Wayside Harmony" lamp made in 1938. Large size same as small with the exception of a flower on branch of tree trunk. Small size measures 4¼" across base. Large size measures 6¼" across base. Early examples of the large (9½") size usually found without size designator, incised 224 only and usually have a switch on the base. Both sizes of "Wayside Harmony" table lamps were (TW) "Temporarily Withdrawn" from production on 31 December 1989, but may be reinstated at some future date. We list as (OE) "Open Edition" since they are available in Germany and other markets, but are *NOT* currently available in the U.S. market. They were produced with (TM 7) trademark and will bear (TM 8) in future production.

☐ 224/I . . . . 7½" . . . . . . . . . (CE). . . ❷ . . . $550–600
☐ 224/I . . . . 7½" . . . . . . . . . (CE). . . ❸ . . . $450–475
☐ 224/I . . . . 7½" . . . . . . . . . (CE). . . ❹ . . . $425–450
☐ 224/I . . . . 7½" . . . . . . . . . (CE). . . ❺ . . . $400–425
☐ 224/I . . . . 7½" . . . . . . . . . (CE). . . ❻ . . . $350–400
☐ 224/I . . . . 7½" . . . . . . . . . (CE). . . ❼ . . . $350–400 (Estimated Price)
☐ 224/I . . . . 7½" . . . . . . . . . **(OE)**. . ❽ . . . $350–400 (Estimated Price)
☐ 224/II . . . 9½" . . . . . . . . . (CE). . . ❷ . . . $650–800
☐ 224/II . . . 9½" . . . . . . . . . (CE). . . ❸ . . . $500–600
☐ 224/II . . . 9½" . . . . . . . . . (CE). . . ❹ . . . $475–500
☐ 224/II . . . 9½" . . . . . . . . . (CE). . . ❺ . . . $450–475
☐ 224/II . . . 9½" . . . . . . . . . (CE). . . ❻ . . . $400–450
☐ 224/II . . . 9½" . . . . . . . . . (CE). . . ❼ . . . $400–450 (Estimated Price)
☐ 224/II . . . 9½" . . . . . . . . . **(OE)**. . ❽ . . . $400–450 (Estimated Price)
☐ 224 . . . . . 9½ " . . . . . . . . . (CE). . . ❷ . . . $650–800
☐ 224 . . . . . 9½ " . . . . . . . . . (CE). . . ❸ . . . $500–600

225/II (TM 2)       225/I (TM 5)

**HUM 225**
**Just Resting, Table Lamp**
This lamp was modeled by master sculptor Reinhold Unger in 1952 and is actually a restyling of HUM II/112 "Just Resting" lamp made in 1938. Large size same as small with the exception of a flower on branch of tree trunk. Small size measures 4¼″ across base. Large size measures 6¼″ across base. Early examples of the large (9½″) size usually found without size designator, incised 225 only and usually have a switch on the base. Both sizes of "Just Resting" table lamps were (TW) "Temporarily Withdrawn" from production on 31 December 1989, but may be reinstated at some future date. See: "Just Resting, Table Lamp" HUM 11/112. We list as (OE) "Open Edition" since they are available in Germany and other markets, but are *NOT* currently available in the U.S. market. They were produced with (TM 7) trademark and will bear (TM 8) in future production.

| | | | | |
|---|---|---|---|---|
| ☐ 225/I | 7½″ | (CE) | ❷ | $550–600 |
| ☐ 225/I | 7½″ | (CE) | ❸ | $450–475 |
| ☐ 225/I | 7½″ | (CE) | ❹ | $425–450 |
| ☐ 225/I | 7½″ | (CE) | ❺ | $400–425 |
| ☐ 225/I | 7½″ | (CE) | ❻ | $350–400 |
| ☐ 225/I | 7½″ | (CE) | ❼ | $350–400 (Estimated Price) |
| ☐ 225/I | 7½″ | (OE) | ❽ | $350–400 (Estimated Price) |
| ☐ 225/II | 9½″ | (CE) | ❷ | $650–800 |
| ☐ 225/II | 9½″ | (CE) | ❸ | $500–600 |
| ☐ 225/II | 9½″ | (CE) | ❹ | $475–500 |
| ☐ 225/II | 9½″ | (CE) | ❺ | $450–475 |
| ☐ 225/II | 9½″ | (CE) | ❻ | $400–450 |
| ☐ 225/II | 9½″ | (CE) | ❼ | $400–450 (Estimated Price) |
| ☐ 225/II | 9½″ | (OE) | ❽ | $400–450 (Estimated Price) |
| ☐ 225 | 9½″ | (CE) | ❷ | $650–800 |
| ☐ 225 | 9½″ | (CE) | ❸ | $500–600 |

## HUM 226
## Mail Is Here, The
Originally modeled by master sculptor Arthur Moeller in 1952. Older pieces are slightly larger in size. Also called "Mail Coach." Usually has an incised 1952 copyright date. Some older examples have a very faint "M. I. Hummel" signature while others have the signature painted on because of this light impression. Refer to HUM 140 "Mail is Here" plaque for another version of this same motif.

| | | | | | |
|---|---|---|---|---|---|
| ☐ 226 | . . . . . 4½ × 6¼" | . ./ . . | (CE) | . . . ❷ | . . . $1100–1350 |
| ☐ 226 | . . . . . 4¼ × 6" | . ./ . . . | (CE) | . . . ❸ | . . . $850–1000 |
| ☐ 226 | . . . . . 4¼ × 6" | . ./ . . . | (CE) | . . . ❹ | . . . $700–800 |
| ☐ 226 | . . . . . 4¼ × 6" | . . . . . . | (CE) | . . . ❺ | . . . $650–700 |
| ☐ 226 | . . . . . 4¼ × 6" | . . . . . . | (CE) | . . . ❻ | . . . $625–650 |
| ☐ 226 | . . . . . 4¼ × 6" | . . . . . . | (CE) | . . . ❼ | . . . $615–625 |
| ☐ 226 | . . . . . 4¼ × 6" | . . . . . . | (OE) | . . . ❽ | . . . $615 |

---

### HUM TERM

**MEL**: A Goebel-produced figurine with the letters "MEL" incised somewhere on the base of the piece. These pieces were designed from original drawings by Sister M.I. Hummel, but for some undetermined reasons were not approved by the Siessen Convent for inclusion in the "M.I. Hummel" line of figurines.

HUM 227 (TM 4)          HUM 228 (TM 4)

**HUM 227**
**She Loves Me, She Loves Me Not Table Lamp**
This lamp was first modeled in 1953 by master sculptor Arthur Moeller and has been restyled several times. On the older lamps the figure is much larger and the boy's eyes are open. On the newer models the eyes are looking down. Same motif as HUM 174 of the same name. Measures 4″ across the base. Refer to HUM 251 for matching bookends. "She Loves Me, She Loves Me Not" table lamp was (TW) "Temporarily Withdrawn" from production on 31 December 1989, but may be reinstated at some future date.

☐ 227 . . . . . 7½″ . . . . . . . . . . (CE) . . . ❷ . . . $650–850
☐ 227 . . . . . 7½″ . . . . . . . . . . (CE) . . . ❸ . . . $475–525
☐ 227 . . . . . 7½″ . . . . . . . . . . (CE) . . . ❹ . . . $425–475
☐ 227 . . . . . 7½″ . . . . . . . . . . (CE) . . . ❺ . . . $400–425
☐ 227 . . . . . 7½″ . . . . . . . . . . (TW) . . ❻ . . . $375–400

**HUM 228**
**Good Friends, Table Lamp**
This lamp was first modeled in 1953 by master sculptor Arthur Moeller and had been restyled several times. On the older lamps the figure is much larger and the tree trunk post has a smoother finish. Same motif as HUM 182 of the same name. Measures 4¼″ across the base. Refer to HUM 251 for matching bookends. "Good Friends" table lamp was (TW) "Temporarily Withdrawn" from production on 31 December 1989, but may be reinstated at some future date.

☐ 228 . . . . . 7½″ . . . . . . . . . . (CE) . . . ❷ . . . $650–850
☐ 228 . . . . . 7½″ . . . . . . . . . . (CE) . . . ❸ . . . $475–525
☐ 228 . . . . . 7½″ . . . . . . . . . . (CE) . . . ❹ . . . $425–475
☐ 228 . . . . . 7½″ . . . . . . . . . . (CE) . . . ❺ . . . $400–425
☐ 228 . . . . . 7½″ . . . . . . . . . . (TW) . . ❻ . . . $375–400

HUM 229 (TM 5)          HUM 230 (TM 5)

## HUM 229
### Apple Tree Girl, Table Lamp
This lamp was first modeled in 1953 by master sculptor Arthur Moeller and has been restyled several times. On the older lamps the figure is much larger but the post still measures only 7½ inches. Measures 4¼″ across base. Old name: "Spring" or "Springtime." Refer to HUM 252 for matching bookends. "Apple Tree Girl" table lamp was (TW) "Temporarily Withdrawn" from production on 31 December 1989, but may be reinstated at some future date.

☐ 229 . . . . . 7½″ . . . . . . . . . . (CE) . . . ❷ . . . $900–1000
☐ 229 . . . . . 7½″ . . . . . . . . . . (CE) . . . ❸ . . . $475–525
☐ 229 . . . . . 7½″ . . . . . . . . . . (CE) . . . ❹ . . . $425–475
☐ 229 . . . . . 7½″ . . . . . . . . . . (CE) . . . ❺ . . . $400–425
☐ 229 . . . . . 7½″ . . . . . . . . . . (TW) . . ❻ . . . $375–400

## HUM 230
### Apple Tree Boy, Table Lamp
This lamp was first modeled in 1953 by master sculptor Arthur Moeller and has been restyled several times. On the older lamps the figure is much larger but the post still measures only 7½ inches. Measures 4¼″ across base. Old name: "Autumn" or "Fall" table lamp. Refer to HUM 252 for matching bookends. "Apple Tree Boy" table lamp was (TW) "Temporarily Withdrawn" from production on 31 December 1989, but may be reinstated at some future date.

☐ 230 . . . . . 7½″ . . . . . . . . . . (CE) . . . ❷ . . . $900–1000
☐ 230 . . . . . 7½″ . . . . . . . . . . (CE) . . . ❸ . . . $475–525
☐ 230 . . . . . 7½″ . . . . . . . . . . (CE) . . . ❹ . . . $425–475
☐ 230 . . . . . 7½″ . . . . . . . . . . (CE) . . . ❺ . . . $400–425
☐ 230 . . . . . 7½″ . . . . . . . . . . (TW) . . ❻ . . . $375–400

| 231 | *New style* | 234 | | 231 | *Old style* | 234 |

## HUM 231
### Birthday Serenade, Table Lamp

This lamp was first modeled by master sculptor Reinhold Unger and was restyled in 1976 by master sculptor Rudolf Wittman. The early model measures 6″ across the base and has a hole for electrical switch on top of the base. Had been considered rare but was put back into production with 5 and 6 trademarks. Early models have an incised 1954 copyright date. The musical instruments have been reversed on the current production models. Refer to HUM 218 "Birthday Serenade" figurine for more details. Both sizes of "Birthday Serenade" table lamps were (TW) "Temporarily Withdrawn" from production on 31 December 1989, but may be reinstated at some future date.

☐ 231 . . . . . 9¾″. . . . . . . . . . (CE). . . ❷ . . . $2000–3000
☐ 231 . . . . . 9¾″. . . . . . . . . . (CE). . . ❺ . . . $550–600
☐ 231 . . . . . 9¾″. . . . . . . . . . (TW) . . ❻ . . . $500–550

## HUM 234
### Birthday Serenade, Table Lamp

This smaller size lamp was also modeled in 1954 by master sculptor Reinhold Unger and the first sample was painted in October 1954 by artist Georg Mechtold (initials "GM"). Similar to HUM 231 with the exception of having no flower on branch of tree trunk. Older models have an incised 1954 copyright date. Restyled in 1976 by master sculptor Rudolf Wittmann with the musical instruments in the reverse position. Had been considered rare but was put back into production with 5 and 6 trademarks. Trademark 4 examples can be found in either style. Both sizes of "Birthday Serenade" table lamps were (TW) "Temporarily Withdrawn" from production on 31 December 1989, but may be reinstated at some future date.

☐ 234 . . . . . 7¾″. . . . . . . . . . (CE). . . ❷ . . . $1600–2100
☐ 234 . . . . . 7¾″. . . . . . . . . . (CE). . . ❸ . . . $1100–1600
☐ 234 . . . . . 7¾″. . . . . . . . . . (CE). . . ❹ . . . $500–1100
☐ 234 . . . . . 7¾″. . . . . . . . . . (CE). . . ❺ . . . $450–500
☐ 234 . . . . . 7¾″. . . . . . . . . . (TW) . . ❻ . . . $425–450

*Hum 232 (Old style)*            *HUM 235 (Old style)*

## HUM 232
### Happy Days, Table Lamp
This lamp was first modeled in 1954 by master sculptor Reinhold Unger and was restyled in 1976. The early model measures 6″ across the base and has a hole for electrical switch at top of base. Had been considered rare but was again put back into production with 5 and 6 trademarks. Early models have an incised 1954 copyright date. Both sizes of "Happy Days" table lamps were (TW) "Temporarily Withdrawn" from production on 31 December 1989, but may be reinstated at some future date.

| ☐ 232 | 9¾″ | (CE) | ❷ | $1200–1700 |
| ☐ 232 | 9¾″ | (CE) | ❺ | $525–550 |
| ☐ 232 | 9¾″ | (TW) | ❻ | $500–525 |

## HUM 233 (CN)
Factory records indicate a sample of a "boy feeding birds." Listed as a Closed Number on 7 September 1954. No known examples. Gerhard Skrobek, master modeler at the factory, stated that this was the first figure he modeled after starting to work at W. Goebel Porzellanfabrik in 1954. Skrobek later restyled this figurine which now appears as HUM 300 "Bird Watcher," issued in 1979.

## HUM 235
### Happy Days, Table Lamp
This smaller size lamp was also modeled in 1954 by master sculptor Reinhold Unger and the first sample was painted in October 1954 by artist Georg Mechtold (initials "GM"). Similar to HUM 232 with the exception of having no flower on branch of tree trunk. Older models have an incised 1954 copyright date. Restyled in 1976 and again put back into production until 1989 when both sizes of "Happy Days" table lamps were (TW) "Temporarily Withdrawn" from production on 31 December 1989, but may be reinstated at some future date.

| ☐ 235 | 7¾″ | (CE) | ❷ | $900–1100 |
| ☐ 235 | 7¾″ | (CE) | ❸ | $625–850 |
| ☐ 235 | 7¾″ | (CE) | ❹ | $500–625 |
| ☐ 235 | 7¾″ | (CE) | ❺ | $475–500 |
| ☐ 235 | 7¾″ | (TW) | ❻ | $450–475 |

*236 A*                    *236 B*

## HUM 236 A & B (CN)

Original research revealed no information about this number, so it was listed as an open number (ON) in our previous price guide. Sample models were located at the Goebel factory in 1984 and were put on display at the Goebel Collectors' Club in Tarrytown, N.Y. Designed in 1954 by master sculptor Arthur Moeller but for some unknown reason they were not approved by the Siessen Convent for production. Pictured here are the only known examples.—Goebel factory archives.

☐ 236 A. . . . 6½″. . . . . . . . . . (CN). . . ❷ . . . $10,000–15,000
☐ 236 B. . . . 6½″. . . . . . . . . . (CN). . . ❷ . . . $10,000–15,000

**HUM 237**
**Star Gazer, Wall Plaque (CN)**
This plaque was made as a sample only and not produced for sale as an open edition. This white overglaze (unpainted) example was recently located at the Goebel factory and is pictured here for the first time in any book, price guide, or catalogue regarding the subject of "M.I. Hummel" figurines. Was designed in 1954 and apparently rejected by Siessen Convent for production. Note the "M.I. Hummel" signature in the left hand corner. I have not been able to confirm the name of the original modeler of this rare item. Now part of the Robert L. Miller collection.

☐ 237 . . . . . 4¾ × 5″ . . . . . . (CN). . . ❷ . . . $10,000–15,000

+-------------------------------------------+
|                 HUM TERM                  |
|  **WHITE OVERGLAZE**: The term used to    |
|  designate an item that has not been      |
|  painted, but has been glazed and fired.  |
|  These pices are completely white. All "M.I. |
|  Hummel" items are produced in this finish |
|  before being individually hand painted.  |
+-------------------------------------------+

| 238 A | 238 B | 238 C |

## HUM 238 A
### Angel With Lute
One of a set of three small angel figures known as the "Angel Trio." Similar to HUM 38 except without holder for candle. Modeled by master sculptor Gerhard Skrobek in 1967. Has a 1967 incised copyright date. Occasionally found in TM 3.

☐ 238 A.... 2 to 2½" ...... (CE)... ❸ ... $100–125
☐ 238 A.... 2 to 2½" ...... (CE)... ❹ ... $80–100
☐ 238 A.... 2 to 2½" ...... (CE)... ❺ ... $75–80
☐ 238 A.... 2 to 2½" ...... (CE)... ❻ ... $70–75
☐ 238 A.... 2 to 2½" ...... (CE)... ❼ ... $68–70
☐ 238 A.... 2 to 2½" ...... (OE)... ❽ ... $68

## HUM 238 B
### Angel With Accordion
One of a set of three small angel figures known as the "Angel Trio." Similar to HUM 39 except without holder for candle. Modeled by master sculptor Gerhard Skrobek in 1967. Has a 1967 incised copyright date. Occasionally found in TM 3.

☐ 238 B.... 2 to 2½" ...... (CE)... ❸ ... $100–125
☐ 238 B.... 2 to 2½" ...... (CE)... ❹ ... $80–100
☐ 238 B.... 2 to 2½" ...... (CE)... ❺ ... $75–80
☐ 238 B.... 2 to 2½" ...... (CE)... ❻ ... $70–75
☐ 238 B.... 2 to 2½" ...... (CE)... ❼ ... $68–70
☐ 238 B.... 2 to 2½" ...... (OE)... ❽ ... $68

## HUM 238 C
### Angel With Trumpet
One of a set of three small angel figures known as the "Angel Trio." Similar to HUM 40 except without holder for candle. Modeled by master sculptor Gerhard Skrobek in 1967. Has a 1967 incised copyright date. Occasionally found in TM 3.

☐ 238 C.... 2 to 2½" ...... (CE)... ❸ ... $100–125
☐ 238 C.... 2 to 2½" ...... (CE)... ❹ ... $80–100
☐ 238 C.... 2 to 2½" ...... (CE)... ❺ ... $75–80
☐ 238 C.... 2 to 2½" ...... (CE)... ❻ ... $70–75
☐ 238 C.... 2 to 2½" ...... (CE)... ❼ ... $68–70
☐ 238 C.... 2 to 2½" ...... (OE)... ❽ ... $68

*239 A*          *239 B*          *239 C*          *239 D*

## HUM 239 A
### Girl With Nosegay
This set of three small children figurines is known as the "Children Trio." Similar to HUM 115, 116 and 117 but without holder for candle. Modeled by master sculptor Gerhard Skrobek in 1967. Has a 1967 incised copyright date. Occasionally found in TM 3.

☐ 239 A. . . . 3½″. . . . . . . . . . (CE). . . ❸ . . . $150–200
☐ 239 A. . . . 3½″. . . . . . . . . . (CE). . . ❹ . . . $80–100
☐ 239 A. . . . 3½″. . . . . . . . . . (CE). . . ❺ . . . $75–80
☐ 239 A. . . . 3½″. . . . . . . . . . (CE). . . ❻ . . . $70–75
☐ 239 A. . . . 3½″. . . . . . . . . . (CE). . . ❼ . . . $68–70
☐ 239 A. . . . 3½″. . . . . . . . . . (OE). . . ❽ . . . $68

## HUM 239 B
### Girl With Doll

☐ 239 B. . . . 3½″. . . . . . . . . . (CE). . . ❸ . . . $150–200
☐ 239 B. . . . 3½″. . . . . . . . . . (CE). . . ❹ . . . $80–100
☐ 239 B. . . . 3½″. . . . . . . . . . (CE). . . ❺ . . . $75–80
☐ 239 B. . . . 3½″. . . . . . . . . . (CE). . . ❻ . . . $70–75
☐ 239 B. . . . 3½″. . . . . . . . . . (CE). . . ❼ . . . $68–70
☐ 239 B. . . . 3½″. . . . . . . . . . (OE). . . ❽ . . . $68

## HUM 239 C
### Boy With Horse

☐ 239 C. . . . 3½″. . . . . . . . . . (CE). . . ❸ . . . $150–200
☐ 239 C. . . . 3½″. . . . . . . . . . (CE). . . ❹ . . . $80–100
☐ 239 C. . . . 3½″. . . . . . . . . . (CE). . . ❺ . . . $75–80
☐ 239 C. . . . 3½″. . . . . . . . . . (CE). . . ❻ . . . $70–75
☐ 239 C. . . . 3½″. . . . . . . . . . (CE). . . ❼ . . . $68–70
☐ 239 C. . . . 3½″. . . . . . . . . . (OE). . . ❽ . . . $68

## HUM 239 D
### Girl With Fir Tree
In the fall of 1997, a 4th figurine was added to this set; HUM 239 D "Girl with Fir Tree," similar to HUM 116 candleholder.

☐ 239 D. . . . 3½″. . . . . . . . . . (CE). . . ❼ . . . $68–70
☐ 239 D. . . . 3½″. . . . . . . . . . (OE). . . ❽ . . . $68

239 A/0          239 B/0          239 C/0          239 D/0

## HUM 239 Ornaments

This set of four small children ornaments were issued in the fall of 1997. They are the same as HUM 239 A, B, C, and D figurines, but are without bases; are made as hanging ornaments, with a brass ring in each head. The model number and trademark are stamped on the feet of each ornament. Also sold in European market without brass ring in head and no base.

(with ring)          (without ring)

☐ 239 A/0 . . . . . ☐ 239 A/X . . . . . . 3″ . . . . . (OE) . . . . ❼–❽ . . . $68
☐ 239 B/0 . . . . . ☐ 239 B/X . . . . . . 3″ . . . . . (OE) . . . . ❼–❽ . . . $68
☐ 239 C/0 . . . . . ☐ 239 C/X . . . . . 3″ . . . . . (OE) . . . . ❼–❽ . . . $68
☐ 239 D/0 . . . . . ☐ 239 D/X . . . . . 3″ . . . . . (OE) . . . . ❼–❽ . . . $68

**TM 2**               **TM 4**

## HUM 240
## Little Drummer

First modeled by master sculptor Reinhold Unger in 1955. Older pieces are usually slightly larger. Has an incised 1955 copyright date. Sometimes listed as "Drummer" even in recent price lists and catalogues. Similar to boy in HUM 50 "Volunteers."

☐ 240 . . . . . 4 to 4¼″ . . . . . . (CE) . . . ❷ . . . $300–375
☐ 240 . . . . . 4 to 4¼″ . . . . . . (CE) . . . ❸ . . . $240–260
☐ 240 . . . . . 4 to 4¼″ . . . . . . (CE) . . ❹ . . . $195–240
☐ 240 . . . . . 4 to 4¼″ . . . . . . (CE) . . ❺ . . . $185–195
☐ 240 . . . . . 4 to 4¼″ . . . . . . (CE) . . ❻ . . . $180–185
☐ 240 . . . . . 4 to 4¼″ . . . . . . (CE) . . ❼ . . . $175–180
☐ 240 . . . . . 4 to 4¼″ . . . . . . (OE) . . ❽ . . . $175

**HUM 241**
**Angel Lights, Candleholder**
First released in the U.S. market in 1978 with a suggested retail price of $100. This number was assigned to this newly designed piece in error. Sometimes referred to as "Angel Bridge." Originally modeled by master sculptor Gerhard Skrobek in 1976, this is an adaptation of HUM 21 "Heavenly Angel." Usually sold with a round plate which this piece is designed to fit. Found with trademarks 5 and 6 only. Sometimes listed as "241 B" but only the number 241 is incised on this item. "Angel Lights" candleholder was "Temporarily Withdrawn" (TW) from production on 31 December 1989, but may be reinstated at some future date.

☐ 241 ..... 10⅓ × 8⅓″ .... (CE)... ❺ ... $400–500
☐ 241 ..... 10⅓ × 8⅓″ .... (TW) .. ❻ ... $300–350

*HUM 241 (CN)*

**HUM 241**
**Holy Water Font, Angel Joyous News With Lute (CN)**
This font was first modeled by master sculptor Reinhold Unger in 1955. Has a stamped 1955 copyright date. Made as a sample only and not produced for sale as an open edition. Listed as a Closed Number on 6 April 1955. Several examples of this font are now in private collections including the Robert L. Miller collection.

☐ 241 ..... 3 × 4½″ ...... (CN)... ❷ ... $1,500–2,000

217

**HUM 242
Holy Water Font, Angel Joyous News With Trumpet (CN)**
This font was first modeled by master sculptor Reinhold Unger in 1955. Has a stamped 1955 copyright date. Made as a sample only and not produced for sale as an open edition. Listed as a Closed Number on 6 April 1955. Several examples of this font are now in private collections including the Robert L. Miller collection.

*HUM 242 (CN)*

☐ 242 . . . . . 3 × 4½″ . . . . . . (CN). . . ❷ . . . $1,500–2,000

**HUM 243
Holy Water Font, Madonna And Child**
This font was first modeled by master sculptor Reinhold Unger in 1955. Has an incised 1955 copyright date. Apparently not put on the market until the mid-1960's. Earliest catalogue listing found is 1967. No known variations have been recorded.

☐ 243 . . . . . 3⅛ × 4″ . . . . . . (CE). . . ❷ . . . $250–300
☐ 243 . . . . . 3⅛ × 4″ . . . . . . (CE). . . ❸ . . . $100–125
☐ 243 . . . . . 3⅛ × 4″ . . . . . . (CE). . . ❹ . . . $75–100
☐ 243 . . . . . 3⅛ × 4″ . . . . . . (CE). . . ❺ . . . $70–75
☐ 243 . . . . . 3⅛ × 4″ . . . . . . (CE). . . ❻ . . . $65–70
☐ 243 . . . . . 3⅛ × 4″ . . . . . . (CE). . . ❼ . . . $62–65
☐ 243 . . . . . 3⅛ × 4″ . . . . . . (**OE**). . . ❽ . . . $62

**HUM 244 (ON)**
Factory records contain no information at all regarding this number. It has therefore been listed as an Open Number and may be assigned to a future item.

**HUM 245 (ON)**
Factory records contain no information at all regarding this number. It has therefore been listed as an Open Number and may be assigned to a future item.

### HUM 246
### Holy Water Font, Holy Family
Master sculptor Theo R. Menzenbach modeled this font in 1955. Earliest catalogue listing is in 1955 Second Edition Schmid Brothers. Has an incised 1955 copyright date. No known variations have been recorded.

| | | | | |
|---|---|---|---|---|
| ☐ 246 | 3⅛ × 4½″ | (CE) | ❷ | $250–300 |
| ☐ 246 | 3⅛ × 4½″ | (CE) | ❸ | $100–150 |
| ☐ 246 | 3⅛ × 4½″ | (CE) | ❹ | $75–100 |
| ☐ 246 | 3⅛ × 4½″ | (CE) | ❺ | $70–75 |
| ☐ 246 | 3⅛ × 4½″ | (CE) | ❻ | $65–70 |
| ☐ 246 | 3⅛ × 4½″ | (CE) | ❼ | $62–65 |
| ☐ 246 | 3⅛ × 4½″ | (OE) | ❽ | $62 |

### HUM 247
### Standing Madonna With Child (CN)
This beautiful Madonna with Child was originally modeled by master sculptor Reinhold Unger in 1955. Restyled in a slightly smaller version by master sculptor Theo R. Menzenbach in 1961. Both versions were rejected by the Siessen Convent for some unknown reason and were never produced as an open edition. Factory samples only, none known to be in private collections.

| | | | |
|---|---|---|---|
| ☐ 247 | 11½″ | (CN) | $10,000–15,000 |
| ☐ 247 | 13″ | (CN) | $10,000–15,000 |

248/0          248/I

## HUM 248
### Holy Water Font, Guardian Angel
This font was first modeled by master sculptor Gerhard Skrobek in 1958. Most models have an incised 1959 copyright date. This is a restyled version of HUM 29 which was discontinued at the time HUM 248 was introduced. This font was originally modeled in two sizes (248/0 and 248/I) but to my knowledge the large size was never put on the market. Factory information reveals that in the future it will be made in only the smaller size and "0" size designator will eventually disappear—so far this has not happened. Small size (248/0) was listed as (TW) "Temporarily Withdrawn" in January 1999.

☐ 248/0 . . . . 2⅜ × 5⅜" . . . . . (CE). . . ❸ . . . $200–250
☐ 248/0 . . . . 2⅜ × 5⅜" . . . . . (CE). . . ❹ . . . $75–100
☐ 248/0 . . . . 2⅜ × 5⅜" . . . . . (CE). . . ❺ . . . $70–75
☐ 248/0 . . . . 2¼ × 5½" . . . . . (CE). . . ❻ . . . $65–70
☐ 248/0 . . . . 2¼ × 5½" . . . . . (TW) . . ❼ . . . $62–65
☐ 248/I . . . . 2¾ × 6¼" . . . . . (CE). . . ❸ . . . $1,000–1,500

## HUM 249
### Madonna and Child (in relief)
### Wall Plaque (CN)
This wall plaque was made as a sample only and not produced for sale as an open edition. Similar to HUM 48/V except without background or frame. Actually, the piece that I saw and is pictured here was simply a cut-out of HUM 48/V in an unfinished state, with no number or signature on the back—apparently an idea that was rejected or stopped before it was even completed. Possibly the work of master sculptor Reinhold Unger who modeled the first HUM 48 in 1936.

☐ 249 . . . . . 6¾ × 8¾" . . . . . (CN). . . . . . . . $10,000–15,000

*250 A & B (priced as set)*     *251 A & B (priced as set)*

**HUM 250 A**
**Little Goat Herder, Bookend**
**HUM 250 B**
**Feeding Time, Bookend**
Factory records indicate these bookends were designed by a team of modelers in 1960. First sold in the U.S in 1964. The bookends are simply normal figurines affixed to a wooden base. Refer to HUM 199 and HUM 200 for more information. Current models have current figurines. This pair of bookends was (TW) "Temporarily Withdrawn" from production on 31 December 1989, but may be reinstated at some future date.

☐ 250 A&B. . 5½″. . . . . . . . . . (CE). . . ❷ . . . $550–750
☐ 250 A&B. . 5½″. . . . . . . . . . (CE). . . ❸ . . . $375–425
☐ 250 A&B. . 5½″. . . . . . . . . . (CE). . . ❺ . . . $325–350
☐ 250 A&B. . 5½″. . . . . . . . . . (TW) . . ❻ . . . $300–325


**HUM 251 A**
**Good Friends, Bookend**
**HUM 251 B**
**She Loves Me, She Loves Me Not! Bookend**
Factory records indicate these bookends were designed by a team of modelers in 1960. First sold in the U.S. in 1964. The bookends are simply normal figurines affixed to a wooden base. Refer to HUM 174 and HUM 182 for more information. Current models have current figurines. This pair of bookends was (TW) "Temporarily Withdrawn" from production on 31 December 1989, but may be reinstated at some future date.

☐ 251 A&B. . 5″ . . . . . . . . . . . (CE). . . ❷ . . . $550–750
☐ 251 A&B. . 5″ . . . . . . . . . . . (CE). . . ❸ . . . $375–425
☐ 251 A&B. . 5″ . . . . . . . . . . . (CE). . . ❺ . . . $325–350
☐ 251 A&B. . 5″ . . . . . . . . . . . (TW) . . ❻ . . . $300–325

---

**PRICES IN THIS GUIDE**

We are in a period of DISCOUNTING of many items in our society."M.I. Hummel" figurines are no exception. The prices in this guide give the relative values in relationship to new or current prices of (TM 8) trademark items. If the new figurines are discounted, the older models will likely be discounted, too, but possibly in a lesser degree. This guide reduces all items to one common denominator.

*252 A & B (priced as set)*

**HUM 252 A**
**Apple Tree Girl, Bookend**
**HUM 252 B**
**Apple Tree Boy, Bookend**
Factory records indicate these bookends were designed by a team of modelers in 1962. First sold in the U.S. in 1964. The bookends are simply normal figurines affixed to a wooden base. Refer to HUM 141 and HUM 142 for more information. Current models have current figurine. "Apple Tree Girl and Boy" bookends were (TW) "Temporarily Withdrawn" from production on 31 December 1989, but may be reinstated at some future date.

☐ 252 A&B. . 5″ . . . . . . . . . . . (CE). . . ❸ . . . $375–425
☐ 252 A&B. . 5″ . . . . . . . . . . . (CE). . . ❺ . . . $325–350
☐ 252 A&B. . 5″ . . . . . . . . . . . (TW) . . ❻ . . . $300–325

**HUM 253 (CN)**
Factory records indicate a girl with basket similar to the one in HUM 52 "Going to Grandma's." No known examples.

☐ 253 . . . . . 4½″ . . . . . . . . . . (CN). . .

**HUM 254 (CN)**
Factory records indicate a girl playing a mandolin similar to the one in HUM 150 "Happy Days." Factory archives sample only. Refer to HUM 557 "Strum Along" for possible small version of this figurine issued in 1995.

☐ 254 . . . . . 4¼″ . . . . . . . . . . (CN). . .

### HUM 255
### Stitch in Time

First modeled by a combination of sculptors in 1962. Has an incised 1963 copyright date. First sold in the U.S. in 1964. Similar to one of the girls used in HUM 256 "Knitting Lesson" and HUM 177 "School Girls." No unusual variations have been recorded. A new miniature size figurine was issued in 1990 with a suggested retail price of $65 to match a new miniature plate series called the "Little Homemakers"—one each year for four years. This is the third in the series. The normal size will be renumbered 255/I and the old number 255 is now classified as a closed edition because of this change. The miniature size HUM 255 4/0 was (TW) "Temporarily Withdrawn" from production on 31 December 1997 and the large size (255/I) in January 1999.

| | | | | | |
|---|---|---|---|---|---|
| ☐ 255 4/0 | 3″ | (CE) | ❻ | $125–140 |
| ☐ 255 4/0 | 3″ | (CE) | ❼ | $115–120 |
| ☐ 255 | 6½ to 6¾″ | (CE) | ❸ | $550–800 |
| ☐ 255 | 6½ to 6¾″ | (CE) | ❹ | $375–425 |
| ☐ 255 | 6½ to 6¾″ | (CE) | ❺ | $350–375 |
| ☐ 255 | 6½ to 6¾″ | (CE) | ❻ | $340–350 |
| ☐ 255/I | 6½ to 6¾″ | (TW) | ❼ | $325–335 |

### HUM 256
### Knitting Lesson

First modeled by a combination of sculptors in 1962. Has an incised 1963 copyright date. First sold in the U.S. in 1964. Similar to two girls used in HUM 177 "School Girls." No unusual variations have been recorded. Listed as (TW) "Temporarily Withdrawn" in January 1999.

| | | | | | |
|---|---|---|---|---|---|
| ☐ 256 | 7½″ | (CE) | ❸ | $875–1150 |
| ☐ 256 | 7½″ | (CE) | ❹ | $625–750 |
| ☐ 256 | 7½″ | (CE) | ❺ | $550–575 |
| ☐ 256 | 7½″ | (CE) | ❻ | $540–550 |
| ☐ 256 | 7½″ | (TW) | ❼ | $525–535 |

*257 (TM 5)*       *257 2/0 (TM 6)*       *With HummelScape*

## HUM 257
### For Mother

First modeled by a combination of sculptors in 1962. Has an incised 1963 copyright date. First sold in the U.S. in 1964. No unusual variations have been recorded. A new small size HUM 257 2/0 was issued in 1985 at a suggested retail price of $50. This new small size figurine has an incised 1984 copyright date. The large size has now been renumbered 257/0. In 1996 a 2¾″ size (3¼″ with base) with incised model number 257 5/0 was produced as part of the "Pen Pals" series of personalized name card table decorations. The original issue price was $55. The small size HUM 257 2/0 was released with a musical HummelScape combination price of $165 in 1999.

☐ 257 5/0. . . 2¾″. . . . . . . . . . (**OE**). . . ❼ . . . $55
☐ 257 2/0. . . 4″ . . . . . . . . . . . (**CE**). . . ❻ . . . $150–155
☐ 257 2/0. . . 4″ . . . . . . . . . . . (**CE**). . . ❼ . . . $145–150
☐ 257 2/0. . . 4″ . . . . . . . . . . . (**OE**). . . ❽ . . . $145
☐ 257 . . . . . 5 to 5¼″ . . . . . . (**CE**). . . ❸ . . . $625–825
☐ 257 . . . . . 5 to 5¼″ . . . . . . (**CE**). . . ❹ . . . $265–300
☐ 257 . . . . . 5 to 5¼″ . . . . . . (**CE**). . . ❺ . . . $250–265
☐ 257 . . . . . 5 to 5¼″ . . . . . . (**CE**). . . ❻ . . . $245–250
☐ 257/0 . . . . 5 to 5¼″ . . . . . . (**CE**). . . ❻ . . . $240–245
☐ 257/0 . . . . 5 to 5¼″ . . . . . . (**CE**). . . ❼ . . . $235–240
☐ 257/0 . . . . 5 to 5¼″ . . . . . . (**OE**). . . ❽ . . . $235

### HUM 258
### Which Hand?

First modeled by a combination of sculptors in 1962. Has an incised 1963 copyright date. First sold in the U.S. in 1964. Similar to girl used in HUM 196 "Telling Her Secret." No unusual variations have been recorded.

| | | | | | |
|---|---|---|---|---|---|
| ☐ 258 | 5¼ to 5½″ | (CE) | ❸ | $625–825 |
| ☐ 258 | 5¼ to 5½″ | (CE) | ❹ | $265–300 |
| ☐ 258 | 5¼ to 5½″ | (CE) | ❺ | $245–265 |
| ☐ 258 | 5¼ to 5½″ | (CE) | ❻ | $240–245 |
| ☐ 258 | 5¼ to 5½″ | (CE) | ❼ | $235–240 |
| ☐ 258 | 5¼ to 5½″ | (OE) | ❽ | $235 |

*(Factory sample)*

### HUM 259
### Girl With Accordion (CN)

Modeled by a combination of sculptors in 1962, this figurine depicts a girl playing an accordion as in HUM 218 "Birthday Serenade." This piece was made as a sample only and not produced for sale as an open edition. Listed as a Closed Number on factory records of 8 November 1962.

☐ 259 . . . . . 4″ . . . . . . . . . . . (CN). . . ❸ . . . $5,000–10,000

225

*Large size nativity set*

## HUM 260
### Large Nativity Set (with wooden stable)
This large size Nativity Set was first modeled in 1968 by current master sculptor Gerhard Skrobek. First sold in the U.S. in the early 1970's. Various styles of wooden stables have been produced through the years. The stable is priced at $440 currently, although it is usually included in the price of the set. This set consists of sixteen pieces, larger and more detailed than the small Nativity set HUM 214. Individual pieces can be purchased separately but are normally sold as a set. This large size Nativity Set was "temporarily withdrawn" (TW) from production on 31 December 1989, but may be reinstated at some future date.

260 A Madonna
260 B Saint Joseph
260 C Infant Jesus
260 D Good Night
260 E Angel Serenade
260 F We Congratulate
260 G Shepherd, standing
260 H Sheep, standing with lamb
260 J Shepherd Boy, kneeling
260 K Little Tooter
260 L Donkey, standing
260 M Cow, lying
260 N Moorish King, standing
260 O King, standing
260 P King, kneeling
260 R One Sheep, lying

*(prices on next page)*

| □ | 260 | . . . . . SET 16 PIECES. (CE) | . . . ❹ | . . . $6050–6305 (Includes Stable) |
|---|---|---|---|---|
| □ | 260 | . . . . . SET 16 PIECES. (CE) | . . . ❺ | . . . $5890–6050 (Includes Stable) |
| □ | 260 | . . . . . SET 16 PIECES. (TW) | . . ❻ | . . . $5745–5890 (Includes Stable) |
| □ | 260A | . . . 9¾". . . . . . . . . . (CE) | . . . ❹ | . . $625–650 |
| □ | 260A | . . . 9¾". . . . . . . . . . (CE) | . . . ❺ | . . $600–625 |
| □ | 260A | . . . 9¾". . . . . . . . . . (TW) | . . ❻ | . . $575–600 |
| □ | 260B | . . . 11¾". . . . . . . . . (CE) | . . . ❹ | . . $625–650 |
| □ | 260B | . . . 11¾". . . . . . . . . (CE) | . . . ❺ | . . $600–625 |
| □ | 260B | . . . 11¾". . . . . . . . . (TW) | . . ❻ | . . $575–600 |
| □ | 260C | . . . 5¾". . . . . . . . . . (CE) | . . . ❹ | . . $140–150 |
| □ | 260C | . . . 5¾". . . . . . . . . . (CE) | . . . ❺ | . . $135–140 |
| □ | 260C | . . . 5¾". . . . . . . . . . (TW) | . . ❻ | . . $130–135 |
| □ | 260D | . . . 5¼". . . . . . . . . . (CE) | . . . ❹ | . . $170–180 |
| □ | 260D | . . . 5¼". . . . . . . . . . (CE) | . . . ❺ | . . $165–170 |
| □ | 260D | . . . 5¼". . . . . . . . . . (TW) | . . ❻ | . . $160–165 |
| □ | 260E | . . . 4¼". . . . . . . . . . (CE) | . . . ❹ | . . $165–170 |
| □ | 260E | . . . 4¼". . . . . . . . . . (CE) | . . . ❺ | . . $160–165 |
| □ | 260E | . . . 4¼". . . . . . . . . . (TW) | . . ❻ | . . $155–160 |
| □ | 260F | . . . 6¼". . . . . . . . . . (CE) | . . . ❹ | . . $435–460 |
| □ | 260F | . . . 6¼". . . . . . . . . . (CE) | . . . ❺ | . . $425–435 |
| □ | 260F | . . . 6¼". . . . . . . . . . (TW) | . . ❻ | . . $415–425 |
| □ | 260G | . . . 11¾". . . . . . . . . (CE) | . . . ❹ | . . $620–650 |
| □ | 260G | . . . 11¾". . . . . . . . . (CE) | . . . ❺ | . . $600–620 |
| □ | 260G | . . . 11¾". . . . . . . . . (TW) | . . ❻ | . . $590–600 |
| □ | 260H | . . . 3¾". . . . . . . . . . (CE) | . . . ❹ | . . $120–125 |
| □ | 260H | . . . 3¾". . . . . . . . . . (CE) | . . . ❺ | . . $115–120 |
| □ | 260H | . . . 3¾". . . . . . . . . . (TW) | . . ❻ | . . $110–115 |
| □ | 260J. | . . . . 7". . . . . . . . . . . (CE) | . . . ❹ | . . $355–370 |
| □ | 260J. | . . . . 7". . . . . . . . . . . (CE) | . . . ❺ | . . $345–355 |
| □ | 260J. | . . . . 7". . . . . . . . . . . (TW) | . . ❻ | . . $340–345 |
| □ | 260K | . . . 5⅛". . . . . . . . . . (CE) | . . . ❹ | . . $205–220 |
| □ | 260K | . . . 5⅛". . . . . . . . . . (CE) | . . . ❺ | . . $200–205 |
| □ | 260K | . . . 5⅛". . . . . . . . . . (TW) | . . ❻ | . . $195–200 |
| □ | 260L | . . . 7½". . . . . . . . . . (CE) | . . . ❹ | . . $165–170 |
| □ | 260L | . . . 7½". . . . . . . . . . (CE) | . . . ❺ | . . $160–165 |
| □ | 260L | . . . 7½". . . . . . . . . . (TW) | . . ❻ | . . $155–160 |
| □ | 260M | . . . 6 x 11". . . . . . . (CE) | . . . ❹ | . . $180–190 |
| □ | 260M | . . . 6 x 11". . . . . . . (CE) | . . . ❺ | . . $175–180 |
| □ | 260M | . . . 6 x 11". . . . . . . (TW) | . . ❻ | . . $170–175 |
| □ | 260N | . . . 12¾". . . . . . . . . (CE) | . . . ❹ | . . $585–615 |
| □ | 260N | . . . 12¾". . . . . . . . . (CE) | . . . ❺ | . . $575–585 |
| □ | 260N | . . . 12¾". . . . . . . . . (TW) | . . ❻ | . . $565–575 |
| □ | 260O | . . . 12". . . . . . . . . . (CE) | . . . ❹ | . . $585–615 |
| □ | 260O | . . . 12". . . . . . . . . . (CE) | . . . ❺ | . . $575–585 |
| □ | 260O | . . . 12". . . . . . . . . . (TW) | . . ❻ | . . $565–575 |
| □ | 260P | . . . 9". . . . . . . . . . . (CE) | . . . ❹ | . . $560–570 |
| □ | 260P | . . . 9". . . . . . . . . . . (CE) | . . . ❺ | . . $550–560 |
| □ | 260P | . . . 9". . . . . . . . . . . (TW) | . . ❻ | . . $540–550 |
| □ | 260R | . . . 3¼ × 4". . . . . . . (CE) | . . . ❹ | . . $75–80 |
| □ | 260R | . . . 3¼ × 4". . . . . . . (CE) | . . . ❺ | . . $70–75 |
| □ | 260R | . . . 3¼ × 4". . . . . . . (TW) | . . ❻ | . . $65–70 |
| □ | 260S | . . . . STABLE . . . . . . (OE) | . . . – | . . $450 |

### HUM 261
### Angel Duet
Same name and same design as HUM 193 but without holder for candle. Modeled by master sculptor Gerhard Skrobek in 1968. Has an incised copyright date of 1968 on the bottom of each piece. Notice position of angel's arm in rear view. HUM 193 candle-holder can be found with arms in either position while HUM 261 is found with arm in lower position only. Difficult to find with "three line" (TM 4) trademark.

| □ 261 | 5″ | (CE) | ❹ | $650–850 |
| □ 261 | 5″ | (CE) | ❺ | $265–290 |
| □ 261 | 5″ | (CE) | ❻ | $260–265 |
| □ 261 | 5″ | (CE) | ❼ | $255–260 |
| □ 261 | 5″ | (OE) | ❽ | $255 |

*261 (TM 4)*          *193 (TM 2)*

---

**HUM TERM**

**LIMITED EDITION:** A figurine that is produced for a specific time period or in a limited quantity.

**HUM 262**
**Heavenly Lullaby**
This is the same design as HUM 24/I "Lullaby" without the hole for candle. Modeled by master sculptor Gerhard Skrobek in 1968. Has an incised copyright date of 1968 on the bottom of each piece. Difficult to find with "three line" (TM 4) trademark. Listed as (TW) "Temporarily Withdrawn" in January 1999.

☐ 262 . . . . . 3½ × 5″ . . . . . . (CE). . . **④** . . . $650–850
☐ 262 . . . . . 3½ × 5″ . . . . . . (CE). . . **⑤** . . . $230–250
☐ 262 . . . . . 3½ × 5″ . . . . . . (CE). . . **⑥** . . . $220–230
☐ 262 . . . . . 3½ × 5″ . . . . . . (TW) . . **⑦** . . . $210–215

**HUM 263 (CN)**
**Merry Wanderer, Wall Plaque (in relief)**
This unique wall plaque, modeled by master sculptor Gerhard Skrobek in 1968, was made as a sample model only and not produced for sale as an open edition. It is simply a "Merry Wanderer" figurine made without a base, slightly flattened on the back side with a hole provided for hanging. The example in our collection has the incised number 263 and the "three line" (TM4) trademark as well as the incised "M.I. Hummel" signature. The front view photo does not give the appearance of depth that can be shown in the rear view. It looks like it would be possible for a collector to make such a plaque by taking HUM 7/0, "Merry Wanderer," removing the base and grinding the back so that it would hang flat against the wall. But then, of course, you would *not* have the incised number or signature, nor the "three line" trademark!

☐ 263 . . . . . 4 × 5⅜″ . . . . . . (CN). . . **④** . . . $10,000–15,000

*Special Worker's Plate Inscription*

**HUM 264**
**Annual Plate, 1971**
**Heavenly Angel (CE)**
1971 was the 100th anniversary of W. Goebel Porzellanfabrik. The annual plate was issued in commemoration of that occasion. Each employee of the company was presented with a 1971 Annual Plate bearing a special inscription on the back. These plates with the special inscription have become a highly sought-after collector's item because of the very limited production. Produced with the "three line" (TM 4) trademark only. The original issue price was $25.

☐ 264 . . . . . 7½" . . . . . . . . . . (CE) . . . ❹ . . . $500–750
☐ 264 . . . . . 7½" . . . . . . . . . . (CE) . . . ❹ . . . $1,200–1,500 (Worker's Plate)

*Rate factory sample of 1948 Christmas plate.*
*Never issued or sold on the market.*

Note: There were some 1971 Hummel plates made without the two holes on the back, which were normally placed there so that cord or wire could be put through them for hanging purposes. These plates were purposely made without the holes and were shipped to the British Isles in order to qualify for a lower rate of duty. With the hanging holes made in the plates, British Customs Department would charge a higher rate of duty since the plate would be classified as a decorative or luxury item rather than the more practical dinner plate classification. In my opinion, the missing holes will not affect the value of your plate one way or the other. In fact, some collectors may prefer the more rare one without the holes!

**HUM 265**
**Annual Plate, 1972**
**Hear Ye, Hear Ye (CE)**
Produced with TM 4 and TM 5 trademarks. Change was made in mid-production year. The original issue price was $30.

☐ 265 . . . . . 7½" . . . . . . . . . . (CE). . . ❹ . . . $50–75
☐ 265 . . . . . 7½" . . . . . . . . . . (CE). . . ❺ . . . $50–75

**HUM 266**
**Annual Plate,1973**
**Globe Trotter(CE)**
The original issue price was $32.50. "Hummel" *trivia*: This is the only plate in this series that has only 32 stars around the border—all the rest have 33!

☐ 266 . . . . . 7½" . . . . . . . . . . (CE). . . ❺ . . . $150–200

**HUM 267**
**Annual Plate, 1974**
**Goose Girl (CE)**
The original issue price was $40.

☐ 267 . . . . . 7½" . . . . . . . . . . (CE). . . ❺ . . . $50–75

"Winner"                          "Loser"

**HUM 268**
**Annual Plate, 1975**
**Ride Into Christmas (CE)**
Two different samples were produced for the 1975 plate. The winning design was "Ride Into Christmas." The losing design was the "Little Fiddler" plate pictured here. There were only two or three of these samples produced—so actually it is a "winner" as far as value is concerned! Value: $5,000 +. The original issue price was $50.

☐ 268 . . . . . 7½" . . . . . . . . . . (CE) . . . ❺ . . . $50–75

**HUM 269**
**Annual Plate, 1976**
**Apple Tree Girl (CE)**
The original issue price was $50.

☐ 269 . . . . . 7½" . . . . . . . . . . (CE) . . . ❺ . . . $50–75

Enrich your knowledge and enjoyment of *M.I. Hummel* figurines with membership in the M.I. Hummel Club. Make new friends and share your love for *M.I. Hummel* with other *Hummel* enthusiasts.

Membership in the Club brings a world of benefits, including:

- An authentic *M.I. Hummel* figurine as a free gift of welcome, valued at $90 ($150 CDN)

- The members-only quarterly magazine, INSIGHTS

- The opportunity to purchase figurines made exclusively for Club members

- Entrance to the Club House, exclusive members-only section of the *M.I. Hummel* web site

- Official *M.I. Hummel* membership card

- An attractive binder and collector's log

- Club travel opportunities

- Club services, such as the Research Department and Collector's Market

- Local Chapters to share information with collectors near you

- Inside information on *M.I. Hummel* figurines

- Free gifts when you give Gift Memberships

For more information, contact Membership Services at 1-800-666-CLUB (2582) or log onto our web site at www.mihummel.com.

# NEW MEMBER APPLICATION

Goebel Plaza, P.O. Box 11, Pennington, New Jersey 08534-0011

**Please enroll me as a new member.**

My check ❑    Money order ❑    For U.S. $50 or CDN $75* for one year is enclosed.

We honor:    AMEX ❑    MC ❑    VISA ❑    DISCOVER (U.S. only) ❑

___

CREDIT CARD NUMBER                                    EXPIRATION DATE

___

CREDIT CARD BILLING ADDRESS

___

NAME AS IT APPEARS ON CARD

✔

___

SIGNATURE                                            DATE

(PLEASE PRINT)

| NAME, FIRST | | | | | | | | | | | | | | MIDDLE INITIAL | |

| NAME, LAST | | | | | | | | | | | | | | | | |

← FOLD HERE (right)

FOLD HERE (left)

| STREET ADDRESS | | | | | | | | | | | | | | | | |

| U.S. CITY | | | | | | | | | | | | | APT. NUMBER | | |

| STATE | | ZIP + 4 | | | | | | | | | | | | | |

| CANADA CITY | | | | | | | | | | | | | APT. NUMBER | | |

| PROVINCE | | | | POSTAL CODE | | | | | | | | | | |

| AREA CODE | | PHONE NUMBER | | | | | | | | | | | | | |

| E-MAIL ADDRESS | | | | | | | | | | | | | | | | |

Within 6 to 8 weeks you will send me my membership card, redemption forms, and membership package with an authentic *M.I. Hummel* figurine and binder.

\* For credit card purchases, use U.S. price. Credit card company will establish and apply the exchange rate.

MEMBERSHIP FEE IS SUBJECT TO CHANGE WITHOUT NOTICE. CURRENT FEE VALID UNTIL MAY 31, 2001.          MG8E00

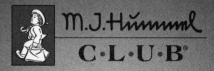

## M.J. Hummel
### C·L·U·B®

# Join Now!

To experience the benefits of belonging, simply fill out the
attached registration form and send it along with your personal
check or money order payable to the M.I. Hummel Club in the
envelope provided. One year's membership fee is $50 ($75 CDN*).
Price is subject to change. Credit card orders are also welcome.
To enroll over the phone call the Club at 1-800-666-CLUB (2582),
or you can join immediately on our web site at
www.mihummel.com.

FOLD
HERE

FROM:

Please
Place
Stamp
Here

M.I. HUMMEL CLUB
GOEBEL PLAZA
P.O. BOX 11
PENNINGTON   NJ   08534-0011

*Early sample*                              *Restyled version*

### HUM 270
### Annual Plate, 1977 Apple Tree Boy (CE)
Note the picture on the 1977 plate. The one shown here on the left is an early sample piece. Before production commenced, the boy's shoes were changed to a slightly different angle and the boy's stockings were reversed (his right one is higher than the left in most known examples). If your plate is exactly like this picture, you have a rare plate! The original issue price was $52.50.

☐ 270 . . . . . 7½" . . . . . . . . . . (CE). . . **❺** . . . $5000 + (Early Sample)
☐ 270 . . . . . 7½" . . . . . . . . . . (CE). . . **❺** . . . $50–75

### HUM 271
### Annual Plate, 1978
### Happy Pastime (CE)
The original issue price was $65.

### HUM 272
### Annual Plate, 1979
### Singing Lesson (CE)
The original issue price was $90.

☐ 271 . . . . . 7½" . . . . . . . . . . (CE). . . **❺** . . . $50–75
☐ 272 . . . . . 7½" . . . . . . . . . . (CE). . . **❺** . . . $40–60

233

**HUM 273**
**Annual Plate, 1980**
**School Girl (CE)**
The original issue price was $100.

**HUM 274**
**Annual Plate, 1981**
**Umbrella Boy (CE)**
The original issue price was $100.

☐ 273 . . . . . 7½" . . . . . . . . . . (CE). . . ❻ . . . $40–60
☐ 274 . . . . . 7½" . . . . . . . . . . (CE). . . ❻ . . . $50–75

**HUM 275**
**Annual Plate, 1982**
**Umbrella Girl (CE)**
The original issue price was $100.

**HUM 276**
**Annual Plate, 1983**
**Postman (CE)**
The original issue price was $108.

☐ 275 . . . . . 7½" . . . . . . . . . . (CE). . . ❻ . . . $125–150
☐ 276 . . . . . 7½" . . . . . . . . . . (CE). . . ❻ . . . $200–250

**HUM 277**
**Annual Plate, 1984**
**Little Helper (CE)**
The original issue price was $108.

☐ 277 . . . . . 7½″. . . . . . . . . . (CE). . . ❻ . . . $50–75

**HUM 278**
**Annual Plate, 1985**
**Chick Girl (CE)**
The original issue price was $110.

☐ 278 . . . . . 7½″. . . . . . . . . . (CE). . . ❻ . . . $50–75

**HUM 279**
**Annual Plate, 1986**
**Playmates (CE)**
The original issue price was $125.

☐ 279 . . . . . 7½″. . . . . . . . . . (CE). . . ❻ . . . $125–200

### HUM 280
### Anniversary Plate, 1975
### Stormy Weather (CE)

First edition of a series of plates issued at five year intervals. The inscription on the back applied by blue decal reads: "First edition M.I. Hummel Anniversary Plate 'Stormy Weather' 1975 hand painted." The original issue price was $100.

☐ 280 . . . . . 10″ . . . . . . . . . (CE). . . ❺ . . . $100–150

### HUM 281
### Anniversary Plate, 1980
### Ring Around The Rosie (two girls only) (CE)

Second edition of a series of plates issued at five year intervals. The inscription on the back reads: "Second edition M.I. Hummel Anniversary Plate 1980 'Spring Dance' hand painted." Trademark: (TM 6) 1978. Labeled "Spring Dance in error. See HUM 353 "Spring Dance" and HUM 348 "Ring Around the Rosie." The original issue price was $225.

☐ 281 . . . . . 10″ . . . . . . . . . (CE). . . ❻ . . . $100–150

### HUM 282
### Anniversary Plate, 1985
### Auf Wiedersehen (CE)

Third and last of a series of plates issued at five year intervals. The inscription on the back reads: "Third and final edition M.I. Hummel Anniversary Plate 1985 hand painted." A small round decal reads: "50 Jahre 1935–1985 M.I. Hummel Figuren." Trademark (TM 6) 1980. The original issue price was $225.

☐ 282 . . . . . 10″ . . . . . . . . . (CE). . . ❻ . . . $150–200

**HUM 283**
**Annual Plate, 1987**
**Feeding Time (CE)**
Designed by master sculptor Gerhard Skrobek in 1983. The original issue price was $135.

☐ 283 . . . . . 7½" . . . . . . . . . . (CE). . . ❻ . . . $250–300

**HUM 284**
**Annual Plate, 1988**
**Little Goat Herder (CE)**
Designed by master sculptor Gerhard Skrobek in 1983. The original issue price was $145.

☐ 284 . . . . . 7½" . . . . . . . . . . (CE). . . ❻ . . . $125–150

**HUM 285**
**Annual Plate, 1989**
**Farm Boy (CE)**
Designed by master sculptor Gerhard Skrobek in 1983. The original issue price was $160.

☐ 285 . . . . . 7½" . . . . . . . . . . (CE). . . ❻ . . . $100–125

**HUM 286**
**Annual Plate, 1990**
**Shepherd's Boy (CE)**
Designed by master sculptor Gerhard Skrobek in 1983. The original issue price was $170.

☐ 286 . . . . . 7½" . . . . . . . . . . (CE). . . ❻ . . . $150–200

**HUM 287**
**Annual Plate, 1991**
**Just Resting (CE)**
Designed by master sculptor Gerhard Skrobek in 1983. The original issue price was $196.

**HUM 288**
**Annual Plate, 1992**
**Wayside Harmony (CE)**
Designed by master sculptor Gerhard Skrobek in 1983. 22nd in a series of 25. The original issue price was $210.

☐ 287 . . . . . 7½″ . . . . . . . . . . (CE). . . **❻** . . . $150–200
☐ 287 . . . . . 7½″ . . . . . . . . . . (CE). . . **❼** . . . $150–200
☐ 288 . . . . . 7½″ . . . . . . . . . . (CE). . . **❼** . . . $150–200

**HUM 289**
**Annual Plate, 1993**
**Doll Bath (CE)**
Designed by master sculptor Gerhard Skrobek in 1983. 23rd in a series of 25. The original issue price was $210.

**HUM 290**
**Annual Plate, 1994**
**Doctor (CE)**
Designed by master sculptor Gerhard Skrobek in 1983. 24th in a series of 25. The original issue price was $210.

☐ 289 . . . . . 7½″ . . . . . . . . . . (CE). . . **❼** . . . $150–200
☐ 290 . . . . . 7½″ . . . . . . . . . . (CE). . . **❼** . . . $150–200

**HUM 291**
**Annual Plate, 1995**
**Come Back Soon**
Designed by master sculptor Gerhard Skrobek in 1983. 25th and final plate in a series of 25. The original issue price was $250.

☐ 291 ..... 7½".......... (CE)... ❼ ... $175–250

**HUM 292**
**Meditation Plate**
First released in the U.S. market in 1992, the first in the Annual Series of four plates called "Friends Forever". Modeled by master sculptor Gerhard Skrobek in 1991. It has the 1989 copyright date along with the (TM 7) trademark applied by blue decal on the back of plate. The original issue price was $180 in 1992.

☐ 292 ..... 7⅛".......... (CE)... ❼ ... $100–150

**HUM 293**
**For Father Plate**
First released in the U.S. market in 1993, the second in the Annual Series of four plates called "Friends Forever". Modeled by master sculptor Gerhard Skrobek in 1991. It has the 1991 copyright date along with the (TM 7) trademark applied by blue decal on the back of the plate. The original issue price was $195 in 1993.

☐ 293 ..... 7⅛".......... (CE)... ❼ ... $100–150

### HUM 294
### Sweet Greetings Plate

First released in the U.S. market in 1994, the third in the Annual Series of four plates called "Friends Forever". Modeled by master sculptor Gerhard Skrobek in 1991. It has the 1991 copyright date along with the (TM 7) trademark applied by blue decal on the back of the plate. The original issue price was $205 in 1994.

☐ 294 . . . . . 7⅛" . . . . . . . . . . (CE) . . . ❼ . . . $100–150

### HUM 295
### Surprise Plate

First released in the U.S. market in 1995, the fourth and final edition plate in the Annual Series called "Friends Forever". Modeled by master sculptor Gerhard Skrobek in 1991. It has the 1991 copyright date along with the (TM 7) trademark applied by blue decal on the back of plate. The original issue price was $210 in 1995.

☐ 295 . . . . . 7⅛" . . . . . . . . . . (CE) . . . ❼ . . . $100–150

### HUM 296
### Winter Melody Plate

First released in the U.S. market in 1996, the first in an Annual Series of four plates entitled "Four Seasons". "WINTER" modeled by master sculptor Helmut Fischer in 1995. It has the 1995 copyright date along with the (TM 7) trademark applied by blue decal on the back of the plate. It features original artwork by Sister Maria Innocentia Hummel, combined with a three dimensional, sculptural relief of HUM 457 "Sound the Trumpet". The original issue price was $195 in 1996.

☐ 296 . . . . . 7½" . . . . . . . . . . (CE) . . . ❼ . . . $195–200

### HUM 297
### Springtime Serenade Plate

First released in the U.S. market in 1997, the second in an Annual Series of four plates entitled "Four Seasons". "SPRING" modeled by master sculptor Helmut Fischer in 1995. It has the 1995 copyright date along with the (TM 7) trademark applied by blue decal on the back of the plate. It features original artwork by Sister Maria Innocentia Hummel, combined with a three dimensional, sculptural relief of HUM 414 "In Tune". The original issue price was $195 in 1997.

☐ 297 . . . . . 7½" . . . . . . . . . (CE). . . ❼ . . . $195–200

### HUM 298
### Summertime Stroll Plate

Scheduled for release in the U.S. market in 1998, the third in an Annual Series of four plates entitled "Four Seasons". "SUMMER" modeled by master sculptor Helmut Fischer in 1995. It has the 1995 copyright date along with the (TM 7) trademark applied by blue decal on the back of the plate. It features original artwork by Sister Maria Innocentia Hummel, combined with a three dimensional, sculptural relief of HUM 327 "The Run-A-Way". The original issue price was $195 in 1998.

☐ 298 . . . . . 7½" . . . . . . . . . (CE). . . ❼ . . . $195–200

### HUM 299
### Autumn Glory Plate

Scheduled for release in the U.S. market in 1999, the fourth in an Annual Series of four plates entitled "Four Seasons". "FALL" modeled by master sculptor Helmut Fischer in 1995. It has the 1995 copyright date along with the (TM 7) trademark applied by blue decal on the back of the plate. It features original artwork by Sister Maria Innocentia Hummel, combined with a three dimensional, sculptural relief of HUM 426 "Pay Attention." The original issue price was $195 in 1999.

☐ 299 . . . . . 7½" . . . . . . . . . (CE). . . ❼ . . . $195–200

*(TM 2)*  *(TM 5)*

**HUM 300**
**Bird Watcher**
First sold in the U.S. in 1979. The original issue price was $80. At one time called "Tenderness." Has an incised 1956 copyright date. An early sample of this figure was modeled in 1954 by Gerhard Skrobek and was assigned the number HUM 233 (CN). Skrobek stated that this was the first figure he modeled after starting to work at the Goebel factory in 1954. An early sample model with the full bee trademark, incised 1954 date, is in the Robert L. Miller collection.

☐ 300 . . . . . 5″ . . . . . . . . . . . (CE). . . ❷ . . . $4000–5000 (Early Sample)
☐ 300 . . . . . 5″ . . . . . . . . . . . (CE). . . ❸ . . . $2000–2500 (Early Sample)
☐ 300 . . . . . 5″ . . . . . . . . . . . (CE). . . ❹ . . . $1500–2000 (Early Sample)
☐ 300 . . . . . 5″ . . . . . . . . . . . (CE). . . ❺ . . . $260–280
☐ 300 . . . . . 5″ . . . . . . . . . . . (CE). . . ❻ . . . $255–260
☐ 300 . . . . . 5″ . . . . . . . . . . . (CE). . . ❼ . . . $250–255
☐ 300 . . . . . 5″ . . . . . . . . . . . (**OE**). . . ❽ . . . $250

---

**HUM TERM**

**DECIMAL POINT:** This incised "period" or dot was used in a somewhat random fashion by the W. Goebel Porzellanfabrik over the years. The decimal point is and was primarily used to reduce confusion in reading the incised numbers on the underside of the figurines. Example: 66. helps one realize that the designation is sixty-six and not ninety-nine.

*Early sample (TM 3)*       *New style (TM 6)*

**HUM 301**
**Christmas Angel**
First released in the U.S. market in 1989. Originally called: "Delivery Angel." An early sample model of this figure was modeled by Theo R. Menzenbach in 1957. Menzenbach stated that it was not approved by the Siessen Convent for production. The sample model in our collection has an early stylized (TM 3) trademark and 1957 incised copyright date. Original issue price was $160 in 1989. Was restyled by master sculptor Gerhard Skrobek in the late 1980's but still has the 1957 copyright date.

☐ 301 . . . . . 6¼" . . . . . . . . . . (CE). . . ❸ . . . $4,000–5,000 (Early Sample)
☐ 301 . . . . . 6" . . . . . . . . . . (CE). . . ❻ . . . $295–300
☐ 301 . . . . . 6" . . . . . . . . . . (CE). . . ❼ . . . $290–295
☐ 301 . . . . . 6" . . . . . . . . . . (OE). . . ❽ . . . $290

**HUM 302**
**Concentration (PFE)**
First modeled by master sculptor Arthur Moeller in 1955. Originally called "Knit One, Purl Two." Girl is similar to HUM 255 "Stitch in Time." Listed on factory records as a Possible Future Edition (PFE) and may be released at some future date, subject to possible minor changes.

☐ 302 . . . . . 5" . . . . . . . . . . (CE). . . ❷ . . . $4,000–5,000 (Early Sample)
☐ 302 . . . . . 5" . . . . . . . . . . (PFE) . . . . . . .

### HUM 303
### Arithmetic Lesson (PFE)
Originally called "School Lesson." Modeled by master sculptor Arthur Moeller in 1955. Notice similarity to middle boy in HUM 170 "School Boys" and girl from HUM 177 "School Girls." Listed on factory records as a Possible Future Edition (PFE) and may be released at some future date, subject to possible minor changes.

☐ 303 . . . . . 5¼" . . . . . . . . . . (CE). . . ❷ . . . $4,000–5,000 (Early Sample)
☐ 303 . . . . . 5¼" . . . . . . . . . . (PFE) . . . . .

### HUM 304
### Artist, The
Originally modeled by master sculptor Karl Wagner in 1955 and later restyled by master sculptor Gerhard Skrobek in 1970. First introduced in the U.S. market in 1971. Has an incised 1955 copyright date. Could possibly be found in (TM 2) and (TM 3) trademarks, but would be considered extremely rare. Had (TM 4) trademark when first issued in quantity in 1971. Note: artist Karl Wagner is no longer living. The original issue price in 1971 was $18. Known variation on (TM 2) "full bee" example has a small drop of paint shown on base. The Artist motif was used for a new plaque issued in 1993 for the grand opening of the M.I. Hummel Museum in New Braunfels, Texas. See HUM 756 for photo.

☐ 304 . . . . . 5½" . . . . . . . . . . (CE). . . ❷ . . . $4,000–5,000 (Early Sample)
☐ 304 . . . . . 5½" . . . . . . . . . . (CE). . . ❸ . . . $2000–3000 (Early Sample)
☐ 304 . . . . . 5½" . . . . . . . . . . (CE). . . ❹ . . . $1000–1200
☐ 304 . . . . . 5½" . . . . . . . . . . (CE). . . ❺ . . . $300–330
☐ 304 . . . . . 5½" . . . . . . . . . . (CE). . . ❻ . . . $290–300
☐ 304 . . . . . 5½" . . . . . . . . . . (CE). . . ❼ . . . $285–290
☐ 304 . . . . . 5½" . . . . . . . . . . (OE). . . ❽ . . . $285

### HUM 305
### Builder, The

First introduced in the U.S. market in 1963, this figurine was originally modeled in 1955 by master sculptor Gerhard Skrobek. Has an incised 1955 copyright date. An example with (TM 2) trademark would be considered rare.

| | | | | | |
|---|---|---|---|---|---|
| ☐ 305 | 5½" | (CE) | ❷ | $4000–5000 (Early Sample) |
| ☐ 305 | 5½" | (CE) | ❸ | $1000–1500 |
| ☐ 305 | 5½" | (CE) | ❹ | $325–375 |
| ☐ 305 | 5½" | (CE) | ❺ | $300–325 |
| ☐ 305 | 5½" | (CE) | ❻ | $290–300 |
| ☐ 305 | 5½" | (CE) | ❼ | $285–290 |
| ☐ 305 | 5½" | (**OE**) | ❽ | $285 |

### HUM 306
### Little Bookkeeper

First introduced in the U.S. market in 1962, this figurine was originally modeled in 1955 by master sculptor Arthur Moeller. Has an incised 1955 copyright date. A "Little Bookkeeper" with a full bee, trademark 2, was recently purchased at auction in New York at a fraction of the true value. An example with (TM 2) trademark would be considered rare.

| | | | | | |
|---|---|---|---|---|---|
| ☐ 306 | 4¾" | (CE) | ❷ | $4000–5000 (Early Sample) |
| ☐ 306 | 4¾" | (CE) | ❸ | $1000–1500 |
| ☐ 306 | 4¾" | (CE) | ❹ | $370–450 |
| ☐ 306 | 4¾" | (CE) | ❺ | $345–370 |
| ☐ 306 | 4¾" | (CE) | ❻ | $340–345 |
| ☐ 306 | 4¾" | (CE) | ❼ | $335–340 |
| ☐ 306 | 4¾" | (**OE**) | ❽ | $335 |

*New style (TM 4)*          *Old style (TM 2)*

**HUM 307**
**Good Hunting**
First introduced in the U.S. market in 1962, this figurine was originally modeled by master sculptor Reinhold Unger and sculptor Helmut Wehlte in 1955. Has an incised 1955 copyright date. Hat, brush, collar, hair and position of binoculars have some variations. An example with (TM 2) trademark would be considered rare. The word "musterzimmer" means "painter's sample" and should not have been removed from factory. Possibly shipped out by accident.

☐ 307 . . . . . 5″ . . . . . . . . . . . . . (CE). . . ❷ . . . $4000–5000 (Early Sample)
☐ 307 . . . . . 5″ . . . . . . . . . . . . . (CE). . . ❸ . . . $1000–1500
☐ 307 . . . . . 5″ . . . . . . . . . . . . . (CE). . . ❹ . . . $375–425
☐ 307 . . . . . 5″ . . . . . . . . . . . . . (CE). . . ❺ . . . $290–320
☐ 307 . . . . . 5″ . . . . . . . . . . . . . (CE). . . ❻ . . . $285–290
☐ 307 . . . . . 5″ . . . . . . . . . . . . . (CE). . . ❼ . . . $280–285
☐ 307 . . . . . 5″ . . . . . . . . . . . . . (**OE**). . . ❽ . . . $280

---
**HUM TERM**

**MUSTERZIMMER**: The German word meaning sample model designating that this piece is to be held at the W. Goebel Porzellanfabrik in the "sample room" to be used for future reference by production artists.

---

*New (TM 5)*            *Old (TM 2)*

**HUM 308**
**Little Tailor**
First introduced in the U.S. market in 1972. Originally modeled by master sculptor Horst Ashermann in 1955. Later restyled by current master sculptor Gerhard Skrobek in 1972. Early model on the right has an incised 1955 copyright date while the restyled version on the left has an incised 1972 copyright date. Both styles can be found in (TM 5) trademark. The original issue price was $24 in 1972.

☐ 308 . . . . . 5¼ to 5¾″ . . . . . (CE). . . ❷ . . . $4000–5000 (Early Sample)
☐ 308 . . . . . 5¼ to 5¾″ . . . . . (CE). . . ❸ . . . $2000–3000 (Early Sample)
☐ 308 . . . . . 5¼ to 5¾″ . . . . . (CE). . . ❹ . . . $1000–1500 (Difficult to find)
☐ 308 . . . . . 5¼ to 5¾″ . . . . . (CE). . . ❺ . . . $750–900 (Old Style)
☐ 308 . . . . . 5¼ to 5¾″ . . . . . (CE). . . ❺ . . . $300–330 (New Style)
☐ 308 . . . . . 5¼ to 5¾″ . . . . . (CE). . . ❻ . . . $290–300
☐ 308 . . . . . 5¼ to 5¾″ . . . . . (CE). . . ❼ . . . $285–290
☐ 308 . . . . . 5¼ to 5¾″ . . . . . (**OE**). . . ❽ . . . $285

---
**HUM TERM**

**THREE LINE TRADEMARK:** The symbol used by the W. Goebel Porzellanfabrik from 1964 until 1972 as their factory trademark. The name for this trademark was adopted to recognize that the V and bee was accompanied by three lines of print to the right of the V. Also known as TM 4.

---

| Early sample | Current production |

## HUM 309
### With Loving Greetings
First released in the U.S. market in 1983. Modeled in 1955 by master sculptor Karl Wagner. Originally called "Greetings From" on old factory records, but later changed to "With Loving Greetings." The original issue price was $80 in 1983. Notice the ink stopper beside the ink bottle and an extra paint brush under the boy's left arm. This is an early sample model and these two items were eliminated for production reasons. When originally introduced in 1983, the ink bottle was blue and the message was a deep turquoise. In 1987 this was changed to a brown ink bottle and the message to a periwinkle blue. Listed as (TW) "Temporarily Withdrawn" in January 1999.

☐ 309 . . . . . 3½" . . . . . . . . . . . . . . (CE). . . ❷ . . . $4000–5000 (Early Sample)
☐ 309 . . . . . 3¼ to 3½" . . . . . (CE). . . ❸ . . . $3000–4000 (Early Sample)
☐ 309 . . . . . 3¼ to 3½" . . . . . (CE). . . ❹ . . . $2000–3000 (Early Sample)
☐ 309 . . . . . 3¼ to 3½" . . . . . (CE). . . ❺ . . . $1000–2000 (Early Sample)
☐ 309 . . . . . 3¼ to 3½" . . . . . (CE). . . ❻ . . . $250–300 (Blue)
☐ 309 . . . . . 3¼ to 3½" . . . . . (CE). . . ❻ . . . $230–240 (Brown)
☐ 309 . . . . . 3¼ to 3½" . . . . . (TW) . . ❼ . . . $220–225

### HUM 310
### Searching Angel, Wall Plaque
First introduced in the U.S. market in 1979 along with two other "M.I. Hummel" items. This plaque was originally called "Angelic Concern" on factory records, but later changed to above name. Has an incised 1955 copyright date and was modeled by master sculptor Gerhard Skrobek in 1955. Very limited production in "Goebel Bee" (TM 5) trademark. Some catalogues list this piece as number 310 A in error; the incised number is 310 only. The original issue price was $55 in 1979. Listed as (TW) "Temporarily Withdrawn" in January 1999.

☐ 310 . . . . . 4¼ to 3¼" . . . . . (CE). . . ❷ . . . $2000–3000 (Early Sample)
☐ 310 . . . . . 4¼ to 3¼" . . . . (CE). . . ❸ . . . $1200–1700 (Early Sample)
☐ 310 . . . . . 4¼ to 3¼" . . . . . (CE). . . ❹ . . . $1000–1500 (Early Sample)
☐ 310 . . . . . 4¼ to 3¼" . . . . . (CE). . . ❺ . . . $300–500
☐ 310 . . . . . 4¼ to 3¼" . . . . . (CE). . . ❻ . . . $135–140
☐ 310 . . . . . 4¼ to 3¼" . . . . . (TW) . . ❼ . . . $135–140

**New style (TM 4)**            **Old style (TM 2)**

## HUM 311
### Kiss Me
First introduced in the U.S. market in 1961. Originally modeled by master sculptor Reinhold Unger in 1955. Later restyled in 1963 by master sculptor Gerhard Skrobek at the request of the Convent. The doll was redesigned to look more like a doll instead of a child. Has an incised 1955 copyright date. Both styles can be found with (TM 3) and (TM 4) trademarks. An example with a "full bee" (TM 2) trademark would be considered rare.

☐ 311 . . . . . 6 to 6¼″ . . . . . . (CE). . . ❷ . . . $4000–5000 (Early Sample)
☐ 311 . . . . . 6 to 6¼″ . . . . . . (CE). . . ❸ . . . $800–1100 (Old Style)
☐ 311 . . . . . 6 to 6¼″ . . . . . . (CE). . . ❸ . . . $450–500 (New Style)
☐ 311 . . . . . 6 to 6¼″ . . . . . . (CE). . . ❹ . . . $650–950 (Old Style)
☐ 311 . . . . . 6 to 6¼″ . . . . . . (CE). . . ❹ . . . $375–450 (New Style)
☐ 311 . . . . . 6 to 6¼″ . . . . . . (CE). . . ❺ . . . $345–375
☐ 311 . . . . . 6 to 6¼″ . . . . . . (CE). . . ❻ . . . $340–345
☐ 311 . . . . . 6 to 6¼″ . . . . . . (CE). . . ❼ . . . $335–340
☐ 311 . . . . . 6 to 6¼″ . . . . . . (OE). . . ❽ . . . $335

*Early sample (TM 2)*          *(TM 7)*

## HUM 312
### Honey Lover (EE)
First modeled by master sculptor Helmut Wehlte in 1955. This figurine was originally called "In the Jam Pot" on factory records, but later changed to the above name. This early sample model pictured here has a "full bee" (TM 2) trademark and is part of the Robert L. Miller collection. Announced in 1991, "Honey Lover" will be an EXCLUSIVE EDITION available to "M.I. Hummel Club" members only, who have belonged to the Club continuously for 15 years. Issued by means of a redemption card to those who are eligible. The original issue price was $190. This figurine now brings $400–500 on the secondary market.

☐ 312 . . . . . 4″ . . . . . . . . . . . (CE) . . . ❷ . . . $4,000–5,000 (Early Sample)
☐ 312/1 . . . . 3¾″ . . . . . . . . . . (CE) . . . ❻ . . . $400–500
☐ 312/1 . . . . 3¾″ . . . . . . . . . . (CE) . . . ❼ . . . $230–235
☐ 312/1 . . . . 3¾″ . . . . . . . . . . (EE) . . . ❽ . . . $235
(M.I.H. Club Members only)

## HUM 313
### Sunny Morning (PFE)
This figurine was originally called "Slumber Serenade" on factory records, but later changed to "Sunny Morning." Modeled in 1955 by master sculptor Arthur Moeller. This early sample model pictured here has a "full bee" (TM 2) trademark and is part of the Robert L. Miller collection. Listed on factory records as a Possible Future Edition (PFE) and may be released at some future date, subject to possible minor changes.

☐ 313 . . . . . 3¾″ . . . . . . . . . . (CE) . . . ❷ . . . $4,000–5,000 (Early Sample)
☐ 313 . . . . . 3¾″ . . . . . . . . . . (PFE) . . . . . . .

*Old style (TM 2)*    *Early sample (TM 2)*    *New style (TM 5)*

## HUM 314
### Confidentially

First introduced in the U.S. market in 1972. Originally modeled by master sculptor Horst Ashermann in 1955. Later restyled by master sculptor Gerhard Skrobek in 1972. Skrobek completely restyled it by changing the stand, adding a tie to the boy and giving it the new textured finish. The early models have an incised 1955 copyright date while the restyled version has an incised 1972 copyright date. When first put on the market in 1972 it was in the old style and had the (TM 4) trademark. Older trademarks such as (TM 2) and (TM 3) would be considered rare. The original issue price in 1972 was $22.50. Listed as (TW) "Temporarily Withdrawn" in January 1999, but may be reinstated at some future date.

☐ 314 . . . . . 5¼ to 5¾" . . . . . (CE). . . ❷ . . . $4000–5000 (Early Sample)
☐ 314 . . . . . 5¼ to 5¾" . . . . . (CE). . . ❸ . . . $2000–3000 (Early Sample)
☐ 314 . . . . . 5¼ to 5¾" . . . . . (CE). . . ❹ . . . $1000–1200
☐ 314 . . . . . 5¼ to 5¾" . . . . . (CE). . . ❺ . . . $800–950 (Old Style)
☐ 314 . . . . . 5¼ to 5¾" . . . . . (CE). . . ❺ . . . $350–390 (New Style)
☐ 314 . . . . . 5¼ to 5¾" . . . . . (CE). . . ❻ . . . $340–350
☐ 314 . . . . . 5¼ to 5¾" . . . . . (TW) . . ❼ . . . $325–335

---

### HUM TERM

**UNDERGLAZE:** The term used to describe especially the number 5 trademark that appears actually underneath the glaze as opposed to the later version of the number 5 trademark that appears on the top of the glaze.

### HUM 315
### Mountaineer

First introduced in the U.S. market at the N.Y. World's Fair in 1964. Has an incised 1955 copyright date. Originally modeled by master sculptor Gerhard Skrobek in 1955. Older models are slightly smaller and have a green stick rather than the dark gray stick found on the newer models. If found with (TM 2) trademark would be considered rare.

☐ 315 . . . . . 5″ . . . . . . . . . . . (CE). . . ❷ . . . $4000–5000 (Early Sample)
☐ 315 . . . . . 5″ . . . . . . . . . . . (CE). . . ❸ . . . $750–1000
☐ 315 . . . . . 5″ . . . . . . . . . . . (CE). . . ❹ . . . $280–400
☐ 315 . . . . . 5″ . . . . . . . . . . . (CE). . . ❺ . . . $260–280
☐ 315 . . . . . 5″ . . . . . . . . . . . (CE). . . ❻ . . . $255–260
☐ 315 . . . . . 5″ . . . . . . . . . . . (CE). . . ❼ . . . $250–255
☐ 315 . . . . . 5″ . . . . . . . . . . . (OE). . . ❽ . . . $250

### HUM 316
### Relaxation (PFE)

This figurine was originally called "Nightly Ritual" on factory records, but later changed to "Relaxation." Modeled by master sculptor Karl Wagner in 1955. Listed on factory records as a Possible Future Edition (PFE) and may be released at some future date, subject to possible minor changes. Several examples of "Relaxation" are now in private collections including the Robert L. Miller collection.

☐ 316 . . . . . 4″ . . . . . . . . . . . (CE). . . ❷ . . . $4,000–5,000 (Early Sample)
☐ 316 . . . . . 4″ . . . . . . . . . . . (PFE). . . . . . .

## HUM 317
## Not For You!

First introduced in the U.S. market in 1961. Has an incised 1955 copyright date. Originally modeled by master sculptor Arthur Moeller in 1955. Some catalogues and price lists incorrectly show size as 6″. The collector should not rely on the measurements in price lists and catalogues as being absolutely accurate, as there have been many typographical errors in them throughout the years. In this book, we used the "bracket" system and show the smallest to the largest size known, verified by actual measurement. If found with (TM 2) trademark would be considered rare.

☐ 317 . . . . . 5½″ . . . . . . . . . (CE). . . ❷ . . . $4,000–5,000 (Early Sample)
☐ 317 . . . . . 5½″ . . . . . . . . . (CE). . . ❸ . . . $750–1000
☐ 317 . . . . . 5½″ . . . . . . . . . (CE). . . ❹ . . . $330–430
☐ 317 . . . . . 5½″ . . . . . . . . . (CE). . . ❺ . . . $290–320
☐ 317 . . . . . 5½″ . . . . . . . . . (CE). . . ❻ . . . $285–290
☐ 317 . . . . . 5½″ . . . . . . . . . (CE). . . ❼ . . . $280–285
☐ 317 . . . . . 5½″ . . . . . . . . . (OE). . . ❽ . . . $280

*Early sample (TM 2)*                    *(TM 7)*

## HUM 318
## Art Critic

First modeled by master sculptor Horst Ashermann in 1955. Has an incised 1955 copyright date. First released in the U.S. Market in 1991. It has a "FIRST ISSUE 1991" backstamp. The original issue price was $230. Listed as (TW) "Temporarily Withdrawn" in January 1999.

☐ 318 . . . . . 5¾″ . . . . . . . . . (CE). . . ❷ . . . $4,000–5,000 (Early Sample)
☐ 318 . . . . . 5⅜″ . . . . . . . . . (CE). . . ❻ . . . $330–340
☐ 318 . . . . . 5⅜″ . . . . . . . . . (TW) . . ❼ . . . $315–325

### HUM 319
### Doll Bath
First introduced in the U.S. market in 1962. Has an incised 1956 copyright date. Originally modeled by master sculptor Gerhard Skrobek in 1956 and was restyled with the new textured finish in the early 1970's. If found with (TM 2) trademark would be considered rare.

☐ 319 . . . . . 5″ . . . . . . . . . . . (CE). . . ❷ . . . $4000–5000 (Early Sample)
☐ 319 . . . . . 5″ . . . . . . . . . . . (CE). . . ❸ . . . $750–1000
☐ 319 . . . . . 5″ . . . . . . . . . . . (CE). . . ❹ . . . $375–430
☐ 319 . . . . . 5″ . . . . . . . . . . . (CE). . . ❺ . . . $345–370
☐ 319 . . . . . 5″ . . . . . . . . . . . (CE). . . ❻ . . . $340–345
☐ 319 . . . . . 5″ . . . . . . . . . . . (CE). . . ❼ . . . $335–340
☐ 319 . . . . . 5″ . . . . . . . . . . . (OE). . . ❽ . . . $335

*Early sample (TM 2)*    *Current production (TM 7)*

### HUM 320
### Professor, The
Originally modeled in 1955 by master sculptor Gerhard Skrobek. First released in the U.S. market in the fall of 1991. 320/0 has an incised 1989 copyright date, and "FIRST ISSUE 1992" backstamp. The original issue price was $180 in 1991.

☐ 320 . . . . . 5½ to 5¾″ . . . . . (CE). . . ❷ . . . $4000–5000 (Early Sample)
☐ 320/0 . . . . 4⅞″ . . . . . . . . . . (CE). . . ❼ . . . $240–250
☐ 320/0 . . . . 4⅞″ . . . . . . . . . . (OE). . . ❽ . . . $240

*Early sample (TM 2)*

*Current style (TM 5)*

**HUM 321**
**Wash Day**

First introduced in the U.S. market in 1963. Has an incised 1957 copyright date. Originally modeled in 1955 by master sculptor Reinhold Unger and Helmut Wehlte. Notice early sample model pictured here. Older pieces are usually slightly larger in size. If found with trademark 2 would be considered rare. A new miniature size figurine was issued in 1989 with a suggested retail price of $60 to match a new miniature plate series called the "Little Homemakers"—one each year for four years. This is the second in the series. The miniature size figurine has an incised 1987 copyright date. The original size will be renumbered 321/1 and the old number 321 is now classified as a closed edition (CE) because of this change. The miniature size (321 4/0) was "Temporarily Withdrawn" (TW) from production on 31 December 1997.

☐ 321 4/0. . . 3″ . . . . . . . . . . . (CE). . . ❻ . . . $125–140
☐ 321 4/0. . . 3″ . . . . . . . . . . . (TW) . . ❼ . . . $120–125
☐ 321 . . . . . 5½ to 6″ . . . . . . (CE). . . ❷ . . . $4000–5000 (Early Sample)
☐ 321 . . . . . 5½ to 6″ . . . . . . (CE). . . ❸ . . . $750–1000
☐ 321 . . . . . 5½ to 6″ . . . . . . (CE). . . ❹ . . . $400–450
☐ 321 . . . . . 5½ to 6″ . . . . . . (CE). . . ❺ . . . $360–390
☐ 321 . . . . . 5½ to 6″ . . . . . . (CE). . . ❻ . . . $355–360
☐ 321/1 . . . . 5½ to 6″ . . . . . . (CE). . . ❻ . . . $350–355
☐ 321/1 . . . . 5½ to 6″ . . . . . . (CE). . . ❼ . . . $345–350
☐ 321/1 . . . . 5½ to 6″ . . . . . . (**OE**). . . ❽ . . . $345

*321 4/0   (TM 6)*

*German*       *Spanish*       *English*

## HUM 322
### Little Pharmacist

First introduced in the U.S. market in 1962. Originally modeled by master sculptor Karl Wagner in 1955. Most examples have an incised 1955 copyright date. Older models are slightly larger in size. Several variations on label of bottle; "Rizinusol" (German for Castor Oil) and "Vitamins" are most common. Also found with "Castor bil" (Spanish for Castor Oil). If found with (TM 2) trademark would be considered rare. On 31 December 1984 the German language variation was temporarily withdrawn (TW) from production but may be reinstated at some future date. This variation now commands a premium of $100–200 more than "Vitamins" when found. "Little Pharmacist" was restyled in the fall of 1987. The figurine has a new base with a smoother surface and rounded corners and edges. It is slightly smaller in size, the eyeglass stems disappear into the hair and his bowtie has been straightened. On his coat the button tape now runs along a curve rather than straight up and down, and a breast pocket has been added. Also, on the back there is a wider coat strap with two buttons instead of one. In 1990 a few pieces of the "Little Pharmacist" were accidentally produced in the new style with the German "Rizinusol" decal on the bottle and the English "Recipe" on the paper boy is holding. Only a few of these rare pieces have been found and would have a value of $1000–1500.

| | | | | | |
|---|---|---|---|---|---|
| ☐ 322 | 5¾ to 6″ | (CE) | ❷ | $4000–5000 | (Early Sample) |
| ☐ 322 | 5¾ to 6″ | (CE) | ❸ | $750–1000 | |
| ☐ 322 | 5¾ to 6″ | (CE) | ❹ | $320–380 | |
| ☐ 322 | 5¾ to 6″ | (CE) | ❹ | $2000–3000 | (Castor Bil) |
| ☐ 322 | 5¾ to 6″ | (CE) | ❺ | $290–320 | |
| ☐ 322 | 5¾ to 6″ | (CE) | ❻ | $285–290 | |
| ☐ 322 | 5¾ to 6″ | (CE) | ❼ | $280–285 | |
| ☐ 322 | 5¾ to 6″ | (OE) | ❽ | $280 | |

*Back view*    *Old style*       *Old style*       *New style*

### HUM 323
### Merry Christmas, Wall Plaque
First introduced in the U.S. market in 1979 along with two other "M.I. Hummel" items, HUM 310 "Searching Angel" plaque and HUM 300 "Bird Watcher." Has an incised 1955 copyright date. Originally modeled by master sculptor Gerhard Skrobek in 1955. The original issue price in 1979 was $55. Very limited production in "Goebel bee" (TM 5) trademark. Listed as (TW) "Temporarily Withdrawn" in January 1999.

| | | | | | |
|---|---|---|---|---|---|
| ☐ 323 | 5¼ × 3½" | (CE) | ❷ | $2,000–3,000 | (Early Sample) |
| ☐ 323 | 5¼ × 3½" | (CE) | ❸ | $1,200–1,700 | (Early Sample) |
| ☐ 323 | 5¼ × 3½" | (CE) | ❹ | $1,000–1,500 | (Early Sample) |
| ☐ 323 | 5¼ × 3½" | (CE) | ❺ | $300–500 | |
| ☐ 323 | 5¼ × 3½" | (CE) | ❻ | $140–145 | |
| ☐ 323 | 5¼ × 3½" | (TW) | ❼ | $135–140 | |

*Early sample (TM 2)*

### HUM 324
### At The Fence (PFE)
Originally called "The Other Side of the Fence" on factory records, but later changed to "At The Fence." Modeled in 1955 by master sculptor Arthur Moeller. This early sample model pictured here has a "full bee" (TM 2) trademark and is part of the Robert L. Miller collection. Listed on factory records as a Possible Future Edition (PFE) and may be released at some future date, subject to possible minor changes.

| | | | | | |
|---|---|---|---|---|---|
| ☐ 324 | 4¾" | (CE) | ❷ | $4,000–5,000 | (Early Sample) |
| ☐ 324 | 4¾" | (PFE) | | | |

### HUM 325
### Helping Mother (PFE)

This figurine was originally modeled by master sculptor Arthur Moeller in August 1955 and the first sample was painted in July 1956 by artist "F/K"—the initials used by Franz Kirchner. Originally called "Mother's Aid" on old factory records but later changed to "Helping Mother." Similar in design to HUM 133 "Mother's Helper" and when released will only be the second "M.I. Hummel" figurine designed with a cat. This early sample model pictured here has the "full bee" (TM 2) trademark and is in the Robert L. Miller collection.

☐ 325 . . . . . 5″ . . . . . . . . . . . . (CE). . . ❷ . . . $4,000–5,000 (Early Sample)
☐ 325 . . . . . 5″ . . . . . . . . . . . . (PFE). . . . . . .

**HUM 326   (TM 2)**          **HUM 794   (PFE)**

### HUM 326
### Being Punished, Wall Plaque (PFE)

This figurine was originally modeled by master sculptor Gerhard Skrobek in July 1957 and the first sample was painted by artist Franz Kirchner in August 1957. Originally called "Naughty Boy" on old factory records but later changed to "Being Punished." This piece has a hole on the back for hanging as a plaque or will sit upright on base. Has an incised 1955 copyright date on back. This early sample model pictured here has the "full bee" (TM 2) trademark and is part of the Robert L. Miller collection. See HUM 794 "Best Buddies" (PFE) for "Possible Future Edition".

☐ 326 . . . . . 4 × 5″ . . . . . . . . (CE). . . ❷ . . . $4,000–5,000 (Early Sample)
☐ 326 . . . . . 4 × 5″ . . . . . . . . (PFE). . . . . . .

*New style (TM 5)*          *Old style (TM 5)*

**HUM 327**
**Run-A-Way, The**
First introduced in the U.S. market in 1972. Originally modeled by master sculptor Helmut Wehlte in 1955 and later restyled by master sculptor Gerhard Skrobek in 1972. Skrobek completely restyled this figure with the new textured finish and variations in the location of basket, hat and shoes. Slight color variations also. The early models have an incised 1955 copyright date while the restyled version has an incised 1972 copyright date. When first put on the market in 1972 it was in the old style and had the "three line" (TM 4) trademark. Older trademarks such as (TM 2) and (TM 3) would be considered rare. The original issue price in 1972 was $28.50. This motif was used for HUM 298 "Summertime Stroll" plate issued in 1998.

☐ 327. . . . . . 5¼" . . . . . . . . . . (CE). . . ❷ . . . $4000–5000 (Early Sample)
☐ 327. . . . . . 5¼" . . . . . . . . . . (CE). . . ❸ . . . $2000–3000 (Early Sample)
☐ 327. . . . . . 5¼" . . . . . . . . . . (CE). . . ❹ . . . $1100–1300
☐ 327. . . . . . 5¼" . . . . . . . . . . (CE). . . ❺ . . . $900–1000 (Old Style)
☐ 327. . . . . . 5¼" . . . . . . . . . . (CE). . . ❺ . . . $300–330 (New Style)
☐ 327. . . . . . 5¼" . . . . . . . . . . (CE). . . ❻ . . . $295–300
☐ 327. . . . . . 5¼" . . . . . . . . . . (CE). . . ❼ . . . $290–295
☐ 327. . . . . . 5¼" . . . . . . . . . . (OE). . . ❽ . . . $290

---

**HUM TERM**

**RARE**: (Webster) marked by unusual quality, merit, or appeal. Distinctive, superlative or extreme of its kind, seldom occuring or found, uncommon.

---

*Early sample (TM 2)*          *(TM 4)*

## HUM 328
### Carnival

First introduced in the U.S. market in 1963. Originally modeled by master sculptors Reinhold Unger and Helmut Wehlte in 1955. Early sample model with "full bee" (TM 2) trademark has a 1955 incised copyright date. Later models have a 1957 incised copyright date. Older examples are slightly larger with only minor variations. The object under the child's arm is a noise maker or "slapstick," a device generally made of wood and paper or cloth—popular with stage comedians. Note difference in size and position of pom-poms on early sample model. This early sample model was purchased from a German lady in New York and is now part of the Robert L. Miller collection. Confirmed as (TW) "Temporarily Withdrawn" in November 1999, but may be reinstated at some future date.

| | | | | | |
|---|---|---|---|---|---|
| ☐ 328 | 5¾ to 6″ | (CE) | ❷ | $4,000–5,000 | (Early Sample) |
| ☐ 328 | 5¾ to 6″ | (CE) | ❸ | $750–1000 | |
| ☐ 328 | 5¾ to 6″ | (CE) | ❹ | $280–325 | |
| ☐ 328 | 5¾ to 6″ | (CE) | ❺ | $260–280 | |
| ☐ 328 | 5¾ to 6″ | (CE) | ❻ | $250–260 | |
| ☐ 328 | 5¾ to 6″ | (TW) | ❼ | $240–245 | |

---

### HUM TERM

**STYLIZED TRADEMARK:** The symbol used by the Goebel Company from 1957 until 1964. It is recognized by the V with a bumblebee that has triangular or "stylized" wings.

**HUM 329**
**Off To School (PFE)**
Originally called "Kindergarten Romance" on factory records, but later changed to "Off To School." Modeled by master sculptor Arthur Moeller in 1955. It has an incised 1955 copyright date. The boy is quite similar to HUM 82 "School Boy" while the girl is completely new. Listed on factory records as a Possible Future Edition (PFE) and may be released at some future date, subject to possible minor changes.

☐ 329 . . . . . 5″ . . . . . . . . . . . (CE). . . ❷ . . . $4,000–5,000 (Early Sample)
☐ 329 . . . . . 5″ . . . . . . . . . . . (PFE). . . . . . .

*Early sample (TM 2)*       *(TM 6)*

**HUM 330**
**Baking Day**
First introduced to the U.S. market in 1985. Originally called "Kneading Dough" on old factory records, but later changed to "Baking Day." Modeled by master sculptor Gerhard Skrobek in 1955. It has an incised 1955 copyright date. The original issue price in 1985 was $95. Listed as (TW) "Temporarily Withdrawn" in January 1999.

☐ 330 . . . . . 5¼″. . . . . . . . . . . (CE). . . ❷ . . . $4,000–5,000 (Early Sample)
☐ 330 . . . . . 5¼″. . . . . . . . . . . (CE). . . ❸ . . . $2,500–3,000 (Early Sample)
☐ 330 . . . . . 5¼″. . . . . . . . . . . (CE). . . ❹ . . . $2,000–2,500 (Early Sample)
☐ 330 . . . . . 5¼″. . . . . . . . . . . (CE). . . ❺ . . . $1,500–2,000 (Early Sample)
☐ 330 . . . . . 5¼″. . . . . . . . . . . (CE). . . ❻ . . . $330–340
☐ 330 . . . . . 5¼″. . . . . . . . . . . (TW) . . ❼ . . . $310–320

*Original Style (TM 2)*                    *Commemorative Issue (TM 6)*

## HUM 331
### Crossroads

First introduced in the U.S. market in 1972. Modeled by master sculptor Arthur Moeller in 1955. It has an incised 1955 copyright date. The original issue price in 1972 was $45.00. In the summer of 1990, Goebel announced a worldwide limited edition of 20,000 pieces in a uniquely altered form, to commemorate the first anniversary of the opening of the Berlin Wall. The difference between the original 1972 version and the new limited edition version is significant and symbolic. Originally, midway up the signpost was a small sign which read "HALT". Now, like so many similar signs along the East/West border, the sign lies on the ground. Original issue price of commemorative issue was $360. During the production of this special figurine, the factory changed trademarks. Consequently, approximately 15,000 pieces bear the (TM 6) trademark and the remaining 5,000 bear the (TM 7) trademark. The numbers were not consistant, so it is possible to have a piece numbered 17,000 with a (TM 6) trademark. Naturally the (TM 7) trademark pieces will usually bring a higher price on the secondary market because of the fewer number of pieces bearing this trademark. A third variation was released in 1992 and was sold only through U.S. Military base exchange stores. This edition consists of three pieces—the regular Crossroads figurine with the "HALT" sign up in the original position, but with a special colored decal of the American and the German flags on the bottom of the figurine. The second piece is a ceramic replica of the crumbled Berlin Wall. A special inscription reads: "With esteem and grateful appreciation to the United States Military Forces for the preservation of Peace and Freedom". The same inscription is on the brass plate attached to the third piece in the set, a black hardwood display base. This limited edition consists of 20,000 sets worldwide and are hand numbered on the bottom of the Berlin Wall piece. Originally *military* issue price was $265 in 1992.

*(prices on next page)*

| | | | | | |
|---|---|---|---|---|---|
| ☐ 331 | 6¾" | (CE) | ❷ | $4,000–5,000 (Early Sample) |
| ☐ 331 | 6¾" | (CE) | ❸ | $2,000–3,000 (Early Sample) |
| ☐ 331 | 6¾" | (CE) | ❹ | $750–1000 |
| ☐ 331 | 6¾" | (CE) | ❺ | $490–540 |
| ☐ 331 | 6¾" | (CE) | ❻ | $480–490 (Original Style) |
| ☐ 331 | 6¾" | (CE) | ❻ | $750–900 (Commemorative) |
| ☐ 331 | 6¾" | (CE) | ❼ | $950–1200 (Commemorative) |
| ☐ 331 | 6¾" | (CE) | ❼ | $475–480 (Original Style) |
| ☐ 331 | 6¾" | (Military Only) | ❼ | $500–750 (Three Piece Set) |
| ☐ 331 | 6¾" | (OE) | ❽ | $475 (Original Style) |

**Rare old sample**　　**Normal position**

This early sample model has the trombone reversed. Research at the factory indicated this was probably an accident in assembling the separate clay molds and possibly this is the only one made that way. We are unaware of any others having been found. The "full bee" example in our collection has the trombone in the normal position.

This three piece set originally sold only through U.S. Military base exchange stores, but can now be purchased on the secondary market. Original military price was $260.

## HUM TERM

**RATTLE:** All "M.I. Hummel" figurines are hollow on the inside. Occasionally, when the figurine is fired, a small piece of clay will drop off on the inside. This little bit of clay when dry will cause a slight rattle. Actually, it does not hurt the figurine or affect the value one way or the other. I would not even call it a flaw, as it does not detract from the appearance. Actually, it is one means of identification that might come in handy sometime!

**Red (TM 2)**      **Blue (TM 3)**

### HUM 332
### Soldier Boy

First introduced in the U.S. market in 1963. Modeled by master sculptor Gerhard Skrobek in 1955. The early prototype model in our collection has a full bee trademark and a 1955 incised copyright date. Later models have a 1957 incised copyright date. Older pieces are slightly larger and usually have a red ornament on hat while the newer pieces have a blue one. Trademark 4 can be found with either red or blue. On older models the "M.I. Hummel" signature is located on the side of the base while newer models have signature on top of the base. A special commemorative edition was issued in 1994. See back of book for information. Listed as (TW) "Temporarily Withdrawn" in January 1999.

| | | | | |
|---|---|---|---|---|
| ☐ 332 | 5¾ to 6" | (CE) | ❷ | $4000–5000 (Early Sample) |
| ☐ 332 | 5¾ to 6" | (CE) | ❸ | $1000–1500 |
| ☐ 332 | 5¾ to 6" | (CE) | ❹ | $280–650 (Red Ornament) |
| ☐ 332 | 5¾ to 6" | (CE) | ❺ | $260–280 |
| ☐ 332 | 5¾ to 6" | (CE) | ❻ | $250–260 |
| ☐ 332 | 5¾ to 6" | (TW) | ❼ | $240–245 |

**HUM 726 (TM 7)**

### HUM 333
### Blessed Event

First introduced in the U.S. market at the N.Y. World's Fair in 1964. Originally modeled by master sculptor Arthur Moeller in 1955. Found with either 1955, 1956 or 1957 incised copyright dates.

| | | | | |
|---|---|---|---|---|
| ☐ 333 | 5¼ to 5½" | (CE) | ❷ | $4000–5000 (Early Sample) |
| ☐ 333 | 5¼ to 5½" | (CE) | ❸ | $750–1000 |
| ☐ 333 | 5¼ to 5½" | (CE) | ❹ | $420–600 |
| ☐ 333 | 5¼ to 5½" | (CE) | ❺ | $390–420 |
| ☐ 333 | 5¼ to 5½" | (CE) | ❻ | $385–390 |
| ☐ 333 | 5¼ to 5½" | (CE) | ❼ | $380–385 |
| ☐ 333 | 5¼ to 5½" | (OE) | ❽ | $380 |

*Old style (TM 4)*          *New style (TM 5)*

## HUM 334
### Homeward Bound

First introduced in the U.S. market in 1971 along with three other new releases: HUM 304 "Artist," HUM 340 "Letter to Santa Claus" and HUM 347 "Adventure Bound." "Homeward Bound" was originally modeled by master sculptor Arthur Moeller in 1956 and later restyled by master sculptor Gerhard Skrobek in 1974. Found with either 1955 or 1956 incised copyright dates in early models. The restyled version has the new textured finish and no support pedestal under the goat. Current model has an incised 1975 copyright date. "Homeward Bound" can be found in both "Old style" as well as "New style" in both (TM 4) and (TM 5) trademarks. The original issue price in 1971 was $35. Listed as (TW) "Temporarily Withdrawn" in January 1999.

☐ 334 . . . . . 5¼" . . . . . . . . . . (CE). . . ❷ . . . $4,000–5,000 (Early Sample)
☐ 334 . . . . . 5¼" . . . . . . . . . . (CE). . . ❸ . . . $1,000–1,500
☐ 334 . . . . . 5¼" . . . . . . . . . . (CE). . . ❹ . . . $700–850 (Old style)
☐ 334 . . . . . 5¼" . . . . . . . . . . (CE). . . ❹ . . . $475–500 (New style)
☐ 334 . . . . . 5¼" . . . . . . . . . . (CE). . . ❺ . . . $425–475 (Old style)
☐ 334 . . . . . 5¼" . . . . . . . . . . (CE). . . ❺ . . . $390–430 (New style)
☐ 334 . . . . . 5¼" . . . . . . . . . . (CE). . . ❻ . . . $380–390
☐ 334 . . . . . 5¼" . . . . . . . . . . (TW) . . ❼ . . . $360–370

---

**HUM TERM**

**ASSEMBLERS NUMBER**: The small incised number (usually two digits) on the bottom of the figurine identifies the person who assembled the individual soft clay parts of the figurine. Smaller than the incised model number or the copyright date. Has no real meaning to the collector, only for Goebel production control.

*335 (TM 2)        335/0 (TM 7)*

**HUM 335**
**Lucky Boy**
Modeled by master sculptor Arthur Moeller in 1956. Originally called "Fair Prizes" on old factory records, but later changed to "Lucky Boy." First put on the market in 1995 in a limited edition of 25,000 pieces,—15,000 for the U.S. market with a "60th Anniversary Goebel" commemorative backstamp. The remaining 10,000 were available for the rest of the world in 1996 with a "Goebel 125th Anniversary" backstamp. Restyled by master sculptor Helmut Fischer in 1989 in a smaller 4½" size with incised model number 335/0. It has an incised 1989 copyright date along with the current (TM 7) trademark. The official issue price was $190 in the U.S. when released in 1995. (Was not available in Canada.) "Lucky Boy" (335/0) was permanently retired by Goebel in 1996 and will never be produced again in that size.

☐ 335 . . . . . 5¾" . . . . . . . . . . (CE). . . ❷ . . . $4,000–5,000 (Early Sample)
☐ 335 . . . . . 5¾" . . . . . . . . . . (CE). . . ❸ . . . $3,000–4,000 (Early Sample)
☐ 335/0 . . . . 4½" . . . . . . . . . . (CE). . . ❼ . . . $190–200

*New (TM 4)        Old (TM 4)*

**HUM 336**
**Close Harmony**
First introduced in the U.S. market in 1963. Found with either 1955, 1956 or 1957 copyright dates. Originally modeled in 1956 by master modeler Gerhard Skrobek and in 1962 he also restyled it. The current production has been restyled but bears the 1955 incised copyright date. Older models have variations in girl's hairstyle and position of stockings.

☐ 336 . . . . . 5¼ to 5½" . . . . . (CE). . . ❷ . . . $4000–5000 (Early Sample)
☐ 336 . . . . . 5¼ to 5½" . . . . . (CE). . . ❸ . . . $1000–1500
☐ 336 . . . . . 5¼ to 5½" . . . . . (CE). . . ❹ . . . $390–525
☐ 336 . . . . . 5¼ to 5½" . . . . . (CE). . . ❺ . . . $360–390
☐ 336 . . . . . 5¼ to 5½" . . . . . (CE). . . ❻ . . . $355–360
☐ 336 . . . . . 5¼ to 5½" . . . . . (CE). . . ❼ . . . $350–355
☐ 336 . . . . . 5¼ to 5½" . . . . . (**OE**). . . ❽ . . . $350

*New (TM 5)*          *Old (TM 4)*

**HUM 337**
**Cinderella**
First introduced in the U.S. market in 1972. First modeled by master sculptor Arthur Moeller in March 1956. First sample painted by artist Franz Kirchner in July 1956. Later restyled by master sculptor Gerhard Skrobek in 1972. Early models have a 1958 or 1960 incised copyright date while the restyled version has a 1972 copyright date. Completely restyled with Skrobek's new textured finish and girl's eyes looking down. The older models have eyes open. When first put on the market in 1972 it was in the old style and had the (TM 4) trademark. Older trademarks such as (TM 2) and (TM 3) would be considered rare. The original issue price in 1972 was $26.50. Also found with a fourth bird on girl's left shoulder.

| | | | | | |
|---|---|---|---|---|---|
| ☐ 337 | 4½″ | (CE) | ❷ | $4000–5000 (Early Sample) |
| ☐ 337 | 4½″ | (CE) | ❸ | $3000–4000 (Early Sample) |
| ☐ 337 | 4½″ | (CE) | ❹ | $1500–1700 (Old style) |
| ☐ 337 | 4½″ | (CE) | ❺ | $1200–1500 (Old style) |
| ☐ 337 | 4½″ | (CE) | ❺ | $345–375 (New style) |
| ☐ 337 | 4½″ | (CE) | ❻ | $340–345 |
| ☐ 337 | 4½″ | (CE) | ❼ | $335–340 |
| ☐ 337 | 4½″ | (OE) | ❽ | $335 |

**HUM 338**
**Birthday Cake, Candleholder**
First released in the U.S. market in 1989. Has an incised 1956 copyright date. The original issue price was $95 in 1989. Originally called "A Birthday Wish" on old factory records, but later changed to "Birthday Cake." Modeled by master sculptor Gerhard Skrobek in March 1956. First sample painted by Harald Sommer in July 1956. This early sample model pictured here has the "full bee" trademark and is part of the Robert L. Miller collection. Listed as (TW) "Temporarily Withdrawn" in January 1999.

| | | | | | |
|---|---|---|---|---|---|
| ☐ 338 | 3¾″ | (CE) | ❷ | $4000–5000 (Early Sample) |
| ☐ 338 | 3¾″ | (CE) | ❸ | $3000–4000 |
| ☐ 338 | 3½″ | (CE) | ❻ | $170–175 |
| ☐ 338 | 3½″ | (TW) | ❼ | $165–170 |

267

*New restyled model (TM 7)*       *Early sample model (TM 3)*

## HUM 339
### Behave (EE)

First modeled by master sculptor Helmut Wehlte in 1956. Originally called "Walking Her Dog" on old factory records, but later changed to "Behave!" The early (TM 3) "stylized" trademark sample model was found in a home in New York City. It had originally been on display at the New York World's Fair in 1964. It has an incised 1956 copyright date and a painting date of 5/60 with O.S. artist initials. It is now part of the Robert L. Miller collection. "Behave!" was formerly listed as a (PFE) Possible Future Edition. Restyled by master sculptor Gerhard Skrobek in 1974. Changes were made in the base, girls hair style, color and style of rag doll, no leash for dog, position of dog's ears and dog's tail attached firmly to girl's dress. Announced in 1996, "Behave" will be an EXCLUSIVE EDITION available to "M.I. Hummel Club" members only, who have belonged to the Club continuously for 20 years. Issued by means of a redemption card to those who are eligible. The restyled figurine still has an incised 1956 copyright date along with the (TM 7) trademark. The original issue price was $350 in 1996. This figurine now sells for $450–500 on the secondary market.

| | | | | | |
|---|---|---|---|---|---|
| ☐ 339 | 5¾" | (CE) | ❷ | $5,000–10,000 | (Early Sample) |
| ☐ 339 | 5¾" | (CE) | ❸ | $4,000–5,000 | (Early Sample) |
| ☐ 339 | 5½" | (CE) | ❼ | $450–500 | (Secondary Market) |
| ☐ 339 | 5½" | (EE) | ❽ | $360 | (with Redemption card) |

(M.I.H. Club Members Only)

---

**HUM TERM**

**DOUBLE FULL BEE:** This term is used to describe the Goebel Company trademark found on some "M.I. Hummel" figurines. On "double full bee" pieces the full bee trademark is found both incised and stamped.

---

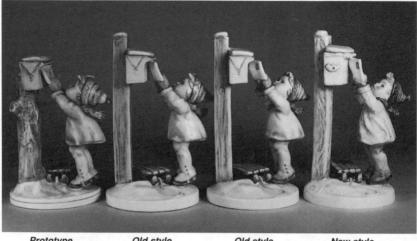

| Prototype | Old style | Old style | New style |
|-----------|-----------|-----------|-----------|
| (TM 2) | (TM 2) | (TM 3) | (TM 4) |

## HUM 340
### Letter to Santa Claus

First introduced in the U.S. market in 1971. Originally modeled by master sculptor Helmut Wehlte in April 1956. Early sample was painted in September 1957 by artist Guenther Neubauer (former Chief Sample Painter at Goebel). Completely restyled by current master sculptor Gerhard Skrobek in 1970. The prototype mailbox on a tree trunk apparently was rejected in favor of the wooden post style. This piece has a full bee trademark, stamped 1956 copyright date and artist initials "HS" (probably Harald Sommer) along with a June 1956 date. The current production has new textured finish and color variations on girl's hats and leggings. (TM 4), (TM 5), (TM 6) and (TM 7) trademark models have an incised 1957 copyright date. The original issue price in 1971 was $30.

☐ 340 . . . . . 6¼" . . . . . . . . . . . (CE). . . ❷ . . . $15,000–20,000 (Prototype)
☐ 340 . . . . . 7¼" . . . . . . . . . . . (CE). . . ❷ . . . $4,000–5,000 (Early Sample)
☐ 340 . . . . . 7¼" . . . . . . . . . . . (CE). . . ❸ . . . $3,000–4,000 (Early Sample)
☐ 340 . . . . . 7¼" . . . . . . . . . . . (CE). . . ❹ . . . $750–1000
☐ 340 . . . . . 7¼" . . . . . . . . . . . (CE). . . ❺ . . . $390–430
☐ 340 . . . . . 7¼" . . . . . . . . . . . (CE). . . ❻ . . . $385–390
☐ 340 . . . . . 7¼" . . . . . . . . . . . (CE). . . ❼ . . . $380–385
☐ 340 . . . . . 7¼" . . . . . . . . . . . (OE). . . ❽ . . . $380

---

### HUM TERM

**OUT OF PRODUCTION:** A term used by the Goebel Company to designate items that are not currently in production, yet have not been given an official classification as to their eventual fate. Some items listed as out of production may become closed editions, remain temporarily withdrawn, or ultimately return to current production status.

### HUM 341
### Birthday Present

Originally named "The Birthday Present" on old factory records, but later changed to just "Birthday Present". First modeled by master sculptor Gerhard Skrobek in 1956. The smaller version, 341 3/0, modeled by master sculptor Helmut Fischer in 1989. It has an incised 1989 copyright date along with the (TM 7) trademark. Also bears the "First Issue 1994" oval decal and "Special Event" backstamp. This figurine was available at District Manager Promotions and in-store events in 1994. The figurine may be re-introduced without the special backstamp. The original issue price was $140 in 1994.

| | | | | | |
|---|---|---|---|---|---|
| ☐ 341 | 5 to 5⅓" | (CE) | ❷ | $4000–5000 (Early Sample) |
| ☐ 341 | 5 to 5⅓" | (CE) | ❸ | $3000–4000 (Early Sample) |
| ☐ 341 | 5 to 5⅓" | (CE) | ❹ | $2000–3000 (Early Sample) |
| ☐ 341 3/0 | 3¾" | (CE) | ❼ | $170–175 |
| ☐ 341 3/0 | 3¾" | (OE) | ❽ | $170 |

### HUM 342
### Mischief Maker

First introduced in the U. S. market in 1972. Originally modeled by master sculptor Arthur Moeller in 1956. Found with either 1958 or 1960 copyright dates. No major variations have been recorded in size or design. Older models have a dark green hat on boy while newer models have a blue hat. The original issue price in 1972 was $26.50. Listed as (TW) "Temporarily Withdrawn" in January 1999.

| | | | | | |
|---|---|---|---|---|---|
| ☐ 342 | 5" | (CE) | ❷ | $4000–5000 (Early Sample) |
| ☐ 342 | 5" | (CE) | ❸ | $2000–3000 (Early Sample) |
| ☐ 342 | 5" | (CE) | ❹ | $750–1000 |
| ☐ 342 | 5" | (CE) | ❺ | $340–370 |
| ☐ 342 | 5" | (CE) | ❻ | $330–340 |
| ☐ 342 | 5" | (TW) | ❼ | $310–320 |

---

**HUM TERM**

**BACKSTAMP OR TRADEMARK:** The official legal mark that Goebel places on the bottom of all "M.I. Hummel" products.

## HUM 343
### Christmas Song

First introduced in the U.S. market in 1981. Originally called "Singing Angel" on old factory records, but later changed to "Christmas Song." Modeled by master sculptor Gerhard Skrobek in 1956. The original issue price in 1981 was $85. An early stylized (TM 3) sample model was recently located in the Philadelphia area. It has a 1957 incised copyright date and a painting date of 6/60 with O.S. artist initials. It is now part of the Robert L. Miller collection. A new miniature size figurine, HUM 343 4/0 with a matte finish was released in the U.S. market in 1996. It has an incised 1991 copyright date in addition to (TM 7) trademark, a combination "First Issue 1996" and "125th Anniversary Goebel" backstamp. The official issue price was $115 in 1996.

| | | | | | |
|---|---|---|---|---|---|
| ☐ 343 4/0 | 3½" | (CE) | ❼ | $115–120 |
| ☐ 343 4/0 | 3½" | (OE) | ❽ | $124 |
| ☐ 343 | 6½" | (CE) | ❷ | $4,000–5,000 (Early Sample) |
| ☐ 343 | 6½" | (CE) | ❸ | $2,000–3,000 (Early Sample) |
| ☐ 343 | 6½" | (CE) | ❹ | $1,000–2,000 (Early Sample) |
| ☐ 343 | 6½" | (CE) | ❺ | $750–1000 |
| ☐ 343 | 6½" | (CE) | ❻ | $260–265 |
| ☐ 343 | 6½" | (CE) | ❼ | $255–260 |
| ☐ 343/I | 6½" | (OE) | ❽ | $255 |

## HUM 344
### Feathered Friends

First introduced in the U.S. market in 1972. Modeled by master sculptor Gerhard Skrobek in 1956. Has an incised 1956 copyright date on the base. "Full bee" (TM 2) and "early stylized" (TM 3) examples have appeared on the market. The original issue price in 1972 was $27.50.

| | | | | | |
|---|---|---|---|---|---|
| ☐ 344 | 4¾" | (CE) | ❷ | $4,000–5,000 (Early Sample) |
| ☐ 344 | 4¾" | (CE) | ❸ | $2,000–3,000 (Early Sample) |
| ☐ 344 | 4¾" | (CE) | ❹ | $750–1000 |
| ☐ 344 | 4¾" | (CE) | ❺ | $350–370 |
| ☐ 344 | 4¾" | (CE) | ❻ | $340–350 |
| ☐ 344 | 4¾" | (CE) | ❼ | $330–340 |
| ☐ 344 | 4¾" | (OE) | ❽ | $330 |

**New (TM 2)**　　**Old (TM 5)**

## HUM 345
### A Fair Measure
First introduced in the U.S. market in 1972. Originally modeled by master sculptor Helmut Wehlte in August 1956. First sample was painted by artist "W/Ha" Werner Hausschild in August 1957. Later restyled by master sculptor Gerhard Skrobek in 1972. Early "full bee" sample (TM 2) has a stamped 1957 copyright date. Early production models have 1956 incised copyright date. Completely restyled with new textured finish, boy's eyes looking down and weights on scale reversed. Current model has a 1972 incised copyright date. Original issue price in 1972 was $27.50. Listed as (TW) "Temporarily Withdrawn" in January 1999.

| | | | | |
|---|---|---|---|---|
| ☐ 345 | 5½ to 5¾" | (CE) | ❷ | $4,000–5,000 (Early Sample) |
| ☐ 345 | 5½ to 5¾" | (CE) | ❸ | $2,000–3,000 (Early Sample) |
| ☐ 345 | 5½ to 5¾" | (CE) | ❹ | $1,000–1,200 |
| ☐ 345 | 5½ to 5¾" | (CE) | ❺ | $800–1000 (Old Style) |
| ☐ 345 | 5½ to 5¾" | (CE) | ❺ | $350–390 (New Style) |
| ☐ 345 | 5½ to 5¾" | (CE) | ❻ | $340–350 |
| ☐ 345 | 5½ to 5¾" | (TW) | ❼ | $325–335 |

## HUM 346
### Smart Little Sister, The
First introduced in the U. S. market in 1962. Originally modeled by master sculptor Gerhard Skrobek in 1956. Has an incised 1956 copyright date on the bottom. No unusual variations have been recorded. Girl is similar to HUM 367, "Busy Student."

| | | | | |
|---|---|---|---|---|
| ☐ 346 | 4¾" | (CE) | ❷ | $4,000–5,000 (Early Sample) |
| ☐ 346 | 4¾" | (CE) | ❸ | $1,000–1,500 |
| ☐ 346 | 4¾" | (CE) | ❹ | $330–375 |
| ☐ 346 | 4¾" | (CE) | ❺ | $300–330 |
| ☐ 346 | 4¾" | (CE) | ❻ | $290–300 |
| ☐ 346 | 4¾" | (CE) | ❼ | $285–290 |
| ☐ 346 | 4¾" | (OE) | ❽ | $285 |

*"Full Bee" (TM 2)*

**HUM 347**
**Adventure Bound**
First introduced in the U.S. market in 1971. The original issue price in 1971 was $400. Sometimes known as the "Seven Swabians." Has an incised 1957 copyright date. The original clay model was sculpted by Theo R. Menzenbach. Menzenbach began working at the Goebel factory in October 1948, at the age of 18. He left the factory in October 1961 to start his own business as a commercial artist. He is still living and resides in Germany, near Coburg. An early prototype with "full bee" (TM 2) trademark was painted in October 1957 and is now part of the Robert L. Miller collection.

- ☐ 347 . . . . . 7½ × 8¼″ . . . . . (CE). . . ❷ . . . $10,000–15,000 (Early Sample)
- ☐ 347 . . . . . 7½ × 8¼″ . . . . . (CE). . . ❸ . . . $6,000–7,000 (Early Sample)
- ☐ 347 . . . . . 7½ × 8¼″ . . . . . (CE). . . ❹ . . . $4,500–5,500
- ☐ 347 . . . . . 7½ × 8¼″ . . . . . (CE). . . ❺ . . . $4,100–4,200
- ☐ 347 . . . . . 7½ × 8¼″ . . . . . (CE). . . ❻ . . . $4,000–4,100
- ☐ 347 . . . . . 7½ × 8¼″ . . . . . (CE). . . ❼ . . . $3,980–4,000
- ☐ 347 . . . . . 7½ × 8¼″ . . . . . (**OE**). . . ❽ . . . $4,000

> **NOTE**: Sister Hummel's original drawing was based upon an old Swabian fairy tale about seven children out in the woods, thought they saw a *big* lion but only turned out to be a *little* bunny rabbit!

*"Early Stylized" (TM 3)*

## HUM 348
### Ring Around The Rosie

The original clay model was sculpted by Gerhard Skrobek, master modeler at the factory, in 1957. First introduced in the U.S. market in 1960 for the 25th anniversary of the introduction of "M.I. Hummel" figurines. Incised on the bottom: "© by W. Goebel, Oeslau 1957." Older models are usually slightly larger. Originally sold for less than $70 when first introduced for sale.

| | | | | | |
|---|---|---|---|---|---|
| ☐ 348 | 6¾ to 7″ | (CE) | ❷ | $10,000–15,000 (Early Sample) |
| ☐ 348 | 6¾ to 7″ | (CE) | ❸ | $4,000–5,000 |
| ☐ 348 | 6¾″ | (CE) | ❹ | $3,500–4,000 |
| ☐ 348 | 6¾″ | (CE) | ❺ | $3,100–3,200 |
| ☐ 348 | 6¾″ | (CE) | ❻ | $3,000–3,100 |
| ☐ 348 | 6¾″ | (CE) | ❼ | $2,860–3,000 |
| ☐ 348 | 6¾″ | (OE) | ❽ | $3,000 |

---
### HUM TERM
---

> **OESLAU:** Name for the village where the W. Goebel Porzellanfabrik is located. Oeslau is now a part of the City of Rödental, Germany.

### HUM 349
### Florist (PFE)

Originally called "Flower Lover" on old factory records, but later changed to "The Florist" and finally just "Florist." First modeled by master sculptor Gerhard Skrobek in 1957. Now listed on factory records as a Possible Future Edition (PFE) and may be released at some future date, subject to possible minor changes. Recently found in (TM 4) trademark with a 4/62 painting date.

| | | | | |
|---|---|---|---|---|
| ☐ 349 | 6¾" | (CE) | ❷ | $4,000–5,000 (Early Sample) |
| ☐ 349 | 6¾" | (CE) | ❸ | $3,000–4,000 (Early Sample) |
| ☐ 349 | 6¾" | (CE) | ❹ | $2,000–3,000 (Early Sample) |
| ☐ 349 | 6¾" | (PFE) | | |

### HUM 350
### On Holiday

First introduced in the U.S. market in 1981. Originally called "Holiday Shopper" on old factory records, but later changed to "On Holiday." Modeled by master sculptor Gerhard Skrobek in 1964. The original sample model was 5½" in height and had a bottle in the basket, but later reduced in size, by Gerhard Skrobek in 1980. Original issue price was $85 in 1981. Has an incised 1965 copyright date. This figurine was recently found with (TM 4) trademark, a painting date of 12/80, and artist's initials "Bo" in the 4¼" size.

| | | | | |
|---|---|---|---|---|
| ☐ 350 | 5½" | (CE) | ❸ | $4,000–5,000 (Early Sample) |
| ☐ 350 | 4¼" | (CE) | ❹ | $2,000–3,000 (Early Sample) |
| ☐ 350 | 4¼" | (CE) | ❺ | $1,500–2,000 |
| ☐ 350 | 4¼" | (CE) | ❻ | $185–190 |
| ☐ 350 | 4¼" | (CE) | ❼ | $180–185 |
| ☐ 350 | 4¼" | (OE) | ❽ | $180 |

### HUM 351
### Botanist, The
First introduced in the U.S. market in the fall of 1982. Originally called "Remembering" on old factory records, but later changed to "The Botanist" and finally just "Botanist." First modeled by master sculptor Gerhard Skrobek in 1965. Has an incised 1972 copyright date on the bottom. The original issue price was $84 in 1982. Recently found with 1965 copyright date.

| | | | | |
|---|---|---|---|---|
| ☐ 351 . . . . . 4 to 4¼" . . . . . . (CE). . . ❹ . . . $2,000–3,000 (Early Sample) |
| ☐ 351 . . . . . 4 to 4¼" . . . . . . (CE). . . ❺ . . . $1,500–2,000 |
| ☐ 351 . . . . . 4 to 4¼" . . . . . . (CE). . . ❻ . . . $210–220 |
| ☐ 351 . . . . . 4 to 4¼" . . . . . . (CE). . . ❼ . . . $205–210 |
| ☐ 351 . . . . . 4 to 4¼" . . . . . . (OE). . . ❽ . . . $205 |

### HUM 352
### Sweet Greetings
First released in the U.S. market in 1981. Originally called "Musical Morning" on old factory records, but later changed to "Sweet Greetings." Modeled by master sculptor Gerhard Skrobek in 1964. Has an incised 1964 copyright date on the bottom of the base. The original issue price was $85 in 1981. The "Early Sample" figurine on the left is in a private collection in Florida.

| | | | | |
|---|---|---|---|---|
| ☐ 352 . . . . . 6¼". . . . . . . . . . (CE). . . ❹ . . . $4,000–5,000 (Early Sample) |
| ☐ 352 . . . . . 4¼". . . . . . . . . . (CE). . . ❺ . . . $1,500–2,000 |
| ☐ 352 . . . . . 4¼". . . . . . . . . . (CE). . . ❻ . . . $210–220 |
| ☐ 352 . . . . . 4¼". . . . . . . . . . (CE). . . ❼ . . . $205–210 |
| ☐ 352 . . . . . 4¼". . . . . . . . . . (OE). . . ❽ . . . $205 |

*353/I (TM 4)*                          *353/0 (TM 4)*

## HUM 353
### Spring Dance
First introduced in the U.S. market in 1964. According to factory records, this was first modeled in1962 by a combination of modelers. Until recently, "Spring Dance" was the highest numbered figurine made in two sizes; HUM 396 "Ride Into Christmas" now has that distinction. Note: HUM 408/0 "Smiling Through" (CE)—the /0 indicates that more than one size was produced, but so far a larger size has not been put on the market. (See HUM 408). The small size 353/0 has been considered rare, having been produced in very limited quantities in 1964 and then not produced again until 1978. Some of the early pieces have sold for as high as $3,000. It is again in current production with the (TM 5), (TM 6) and (TM 7) trademarks. Both sizes have an incised 1963 copyright date. In 1982 the large size 353/I was listed as (TW) "Temporarily Withdrawn" on company records, to be possibly reinstated at a future date. The "Spring Dance" design consists of two of the four girls from HUM 348 "Ring Around The Rosie."

☐ 353/0 . . . . 5¼″ . . . . . . . . . (CE) . . . ❸ . . . $3000–5000 (Early Sample)
☐ 353/0 . . . . 5¼″ . . . . . . . . . (CE) . . . ❹ . . . $2000–3000
☐ 353/0 . . . . 5¼″ . . . . . . . . . (CE) . . . ❺ . . . $390–420
☐ 353/0 . . . . 5¼″ . . . . . . . . . (CE) . . . ❻ . . . $380–390
☐ 353/0 . . . . 5¼″ . . . . . . . . . (CE) . . . ❼ . . . $370–380
☐ 353/0 . . . . 5¼″ . . . . . . . . . (OE) . . . ❽ . . . $370
☐ 353 . . . . 6¾″ . . . . . . . . . (CE) . . . ❸ . . . $3000–5000 (Early Sample)
☐ 353/I . . . . 6¾″ . . . . . . . . . (CE) . . . ❸ . . . $1000–2000
☐ 353/I . . . . 6¾″ . . . . . . . . . (CE) . . . ❹ . . . $650–750
☐ 353/I . . . . 6¾″ . . . . . . . . . (CE) . . . ❺ . . . $575–600
☐ 353/I . . . . 6¾″ . . . . . . . . . (TW) . . ❻ . . . $550–575

| 354 A | 354 B | 354 C |

## HUM 354 A
### Holy Water Font, Angel With Lantern (CN)
This early prototype font has the incised number 354 only, on the back. According to factory information, this design was not approved by the Siessen Convent as a font. It was then restyled into a figurine and approved as HUM 357 "Guiding Angel." Now listed on factory records as a Closed Number.

☐ 354 A. . . . 3¼ × 5″ . . . . . . (CN). . . . . . . .

## HUM 354 B
### Holy Water Font, Angel With Trumpet (CN)
This early prototype font has the incised number 355 only, on the back. According to factory information, this design was not approved by the Siessen Convent as a font. It was then restyled into a figurine and approved as HUM 359 "Tuneful Angel." Now listed on factory records as a Closed Number.

☐ 354 B. . . . 3¼ × 5″ . . . . . . (CN). . . . . . . .

## HUM 354 C
### Holy Water Font, Angel With Bird (CN)
This early prototype font has the incised number 356 only, on the back. According to factory information, this design was not approved by the Siessen Convent as a font. It was then restyled into a figurine and approved as HUM 358 "Shining Light." Now listed on factory records as a Closed Number.

☐ 354 C. . . . 3¼ × 5″ . . . . . . (CN). . . . . . . .

---

**PRICES IN THIS GUIDE**

We are in a period of DISCOUNTING of many items in our society."M.I. Hummel" figurines are no exception. The prices in this guide give the relative values in relationship to new or current prices of (TM 8) trademark items. If the new figurines are discounted, the older models will likely be discounted, too, but possibly in a lesser degree. This guide reduces all items to one common denominator.

**HUM 355**
**Autumn Harvest**
First introduced in the U.S. market in 1972. Originally modeled by master sculptor Gerhard Skrobek in 1963. Has an incised 1963 or 1964 copyright date on the bottom. No major variations have been recorded in size, color or design. The original issue price in 1972 was $22.50.

| | | | | | |
|---|---|---|---|---|---|
| ☐ 355 | 5″ | (CE) | ❸ | $2,000–3,000 (Early Sample) |
| ☐ 355 | 5″ | (CE) | ❹ | $1,000–1,500 |
| ☐ 355 | 5″ | (CE) | ❺ | $245–270 |
| ☐ 355 | 5″ | (CE) | ❻ | $240–245 |
| ☐ 355 | 5″ | (CE) | ❼ | $235–240 |
| ☐ 355 | 5″ | (OE) | ❽ | $235 |

**HUM 356**
**Gay Adventure**
Was originally called "Joyful Adventure" when first released in the U.S. market in 1972. Originally modeled by master sculptor Gerhard Skrobek in 1963. It has an incised 1971 copyright date on the bottom. Slightly restyled with the new textured finish on current models. Early models have slightly different construction on the underside of base. The original issue price in 1972 was $22.50.

| | | | | | |
|---|---|---|---|---|---|
| ☐ 356 | 4¾″ | (CE) | ❸ | $2,000–3,000 (Early Sample) |
| ☐ 356 | 4¾″ | (CE) | ❹ | $1,000–1,500 |
| ☐ 356 | 4¾″ | (CE) | ❺ | $240–260 |
| ☐ 356 | 4¾″ | (CE) | ❻ | $235–240 |
| ☐ 356 | 4¾″ | (CE) | ❼ | $230–235 |
| ☐ 356 | 4¾″ | (OE) | ❽ | $230 |

*357 (TM 4)*          *358 (TM 4)*          *359 (TM 4)*

## HUM 357
### Guiding Angel
First released in the U.S. market in 1972. Originally modeled by master sculptor Reinhold Unger in 1958. Has an incised 1960 copyright date. The original issue price in 1972 was $11. Usually offered, along with HUM 358 and HUM 359, as a set of three angels, although priced separately.

☐ 357 . . . . . 2¾" . . . . . . . . . (CE) . . . ❹ . . . $175–225
☐ 357 . . . . . 2¾" . . . . . . . . . (CE) . . . ❺ . . . $110–120
☐ 357 . . . . . 2¾" . . . . . . . . . (CE) . . . ❻ . . . $105–110
☐ 357 . . . . . 2¾" . . . . . . . . . (CE) . . . ❼ . . . $100–105
☐ 357 . . . . . 2¾" . . . . . . . . . (OE) . . . ❽ . . . $100

## HUM 358
### Shining Light
First released in the U.S. market in 1972. Originally modeled by master sculptor Reinhold Unger in 1958. Has an incised 1960 copyright date. The original issue price in 1972 was $11. Usually offered, along with HUM 357 and HUM 359, as a set of three angels, although priced separately.

☐ 358 . . . . . 2¾" . . . . . . . . . (CE) . . . ❹ . . . $175–225
☐ 358 . . . . . 2¾" . . . . . . . . . (CE) . . . ❺ . . . $110–120
☐ 358 . . . . . 2¾" . . . . . . . . . (CE) . . . ❻ . . . $105–110
☐ 358 . . . . . 2¾" . . . . . . . . . (CE) . . . ❼ . . . $100–105
☐ 358 . . . . . 2¾" . . . . . . . . . (OE) . . . ❽ . . . $100

## HUM 359
### Tuneful Angel
First released in the U.S. market in 1972. Originally modeled by master sculptor Reinhold Unger in 1958. Has an incised 1960 copyright date. Usually offered, along with HUM 357 and HUM 358, as a set of three angels, although priced separately. The original issue price in 1972 was $11.

☐ 359 . . . . . 2¾" . . . . . . . . . (CE) . . . ❹ . . . $175–225
☐ 359 . . . . . 2¾" . . . . . . . . . (CE) . . . ❺ . . . $110–120
☐ 359 . . . . . 2¾" . . . . . . . . . (CE) . . . ❻ . . . $105–110
☐ 359 . . . . . 2¾" . . . . . . . . . (CE) . . . ❼ . . . $100–105
☐ 359 . . . . . 2¾" . . . . . . . . . (OE) . . . ❽ . . . $100

*360 B (TM 3)*  *360 A (TM 3)*  *360 C (TM 3)*

### HUM 360/A
### Wall Vase, Boy and Girl

One of a set of three wall vases that had been considered rare but is again in current production with the 5 and 6 trademarks. According to factory records, this vase was modeled by master sculptor Gerhard Skrobek in 1959. Early models incised on back: "© by W. Goebel 1958." The new model reissued in 1979 has been slightly restyled and has copyright date 1958 only incised on back. "Temporarily withdrawn" (TW) from production on 31 December 1989, but may be reinstated at some future date.

☐ 360A .... 4½ × 6″ ...... (CE)... ❸ ... $525–675
☐ 360A .... 4½ × 6″ ...... (CE)... ❺ ... $170–180
☐ 360A .... 4½ × 6″ ...... (TW) .. ❻ ... $160–170

### HUM 360/B
### Wall Vase, Boy

One of a set of three wall vases that had been considered rare but is again in current production with the 5 and 6 trademarks. According to factory records, this vase was modeled by master sculptor Gerhard Skrobek in 1959. Early models incised on back: "© by W. Goebel 1958." The new model reissued in 1979 has been slightly restyled and has copyright date 1958 only incised on back. "Temporarily withdrawn" (TW) from production on 31 December 1989, but may be reinstated at some future date.

☐ 360B .... 4½ × 6″ ...... (CE)... ❸ ... $500–650
☐ 360B .... 4½ × 6″ ...... (CE)... ❺ ... $150–160
☐ 360B .... 4½ × 6″ ...... (TW) .. ❻ ... $140–150

### HUM 360/C
### Wall Vase, Girl

One of a set of three wall vases that had been considered rare but is again in current production with the 5 and 6 trademarks. According to factory records, this vase was modeled by master sculptor Gerhard Skrobek in 1959. Early models incised on back: "© by W. Goebel 1958." The new model reissued in 1979 has the trunk of the tree slightly restyled and has copyright date 1958 only incised on back. "Temporarily withdrawn" (TW) from production on 31 December 1989, but may be reinstated at some future date.

☐ 360C .... 4½ × 6″ ...... (CE)... ❸ ... $500–650
☐ 360C .... 4½ × 6″ ...... (CE)... ❺ ... $150–160
☐ 360C .... 4½ × 6″ ...... (TW) .. ❻ ... $140–150

**HUM 361**
**Favorite Pet**
First released in the U.S. market at the N.Y. World's Fair in 1964. Originally modeled by master sculptor Theo R. Menzenbach in 1959. Has an incised 1960 copyright date. No unusual variations have been recorded.

☐ 361 . . . . . 4½″ . . . . . . . . . . (CE). . . ❷ . . . $4,000–5,000 (Early Sample)
☐ 361 . . . . . 4½″ . . . . . . . . . . (CE). . . ❸ . . . $1,200–1,700
☐ 361 . . . . . 4½″ . . . . . . . . . . (CE). . . ❹ . . . $375–450
☐ 361 . . . . . 4½″ . . . . . . . . . . (CE). . . ❺ . . . $345–375
☐ 361 . . . . . 4½″ . . . . . . . . . . (CE). . . ❻ . . . $340–345
☐ 361 . . . . . 4½″ . . . . . . . . . . (CE). . . ❼ . . . $335–340
☐ 361 . . . . . 4½″ . . . . . . . . . . (**OE**). . . ❽ . . . $335

**HUM 362**
**I Forgot (PFE)**
Originally called "Thoughtful" on old factory records, but later changed to "I Forgot." First modeled by master sculptor Theo R. Menzenbach in 1959. Now listed on factory records as a Possible Future Edition (PFE) and may be released at some future date, subject to possible minor changes. Recently found in (TM 5) trademark with a 9/73 painting date, now in the Robert L. Miller collection.

☐ 362 . . . . . 5½″ . . . . . . . . . . (CE). . . ❷ . . . $4,000–5,000 (Early Sample)
☐ 362 . . . . . 5½″ . . . . . . . . . . (CE). . . ❸ . . . $3,000–4,000 (Early Sample)
☐ 362 . . . . . 5½″ . . . . . . . . . . (CE). . . ❹ . . . $2,000–3,000 (Early Sample)
☐ 362 . . . . . 5½″ . . . . . . . . . . (CE). . . ❺ . . . $1,000–2,000
☐ 362 . . . . . 5½ . . . . . . . . . . (PFE). . . . . . .

**HUM 363**
**Big Housecleaning**
First introduced in the U.S. market in 1972. Originally modeled by master sculptor Gerhard Skrobek in 1959. Has as incised 1960 copyright date on the bottom. No major variations have been recorded in size, color or design. The original issue price in 1972 was $28.50. Listed as (TW) "Temporarily Withdrawn" in January 1999, but may be reinstated at some future date.

☐ 363 . . . . . 4″ . . . . . . . . . . . . (CE) . . . **2** . . . $4,000–5,000 (Early Sample)
☐ 363 . . . . . 4″ . . . . . . . . . . . . (CE) . . . **3** . . . $2,000–3,000
☐ 363 . . . . . 4″ . . . . . . . . . . . . (CE) . . . **4** . . . $1,000–1,500
☐ 363 . . . . . 4″ . . . . . . . . . . . . (CE) . . . **5** . . . $345–375
☐ 363 . . . . . 4″ . . . . . . . . . . . . (CE) . . . **6** . . . $335–345
☐ 363 . . . . . 4″ . . . . . . . . . . . . (TW) . . **7** . . . $315–325

---

**HUM TERM**

**CURRENT TRADEMARK**: Designates the symbol presently being used by the W. Goebel Porzellanfabrik to represent the company's trademark.

---

**HUM TERM**

**SECONDARY MARKET**: The buying and selling of items after the initial retail purchase has been transacted. Often times this post-retail trading is also referred to as the "after market." This very publication is intended to serve as a guide for the secondary market values of "M. I. Hummel" items.

(TM 6)                *Unpainted sample (TM 5)*

## HUM 364
### Supreme Protection (CE)

Modeled by master sculptor Gerhard Skrobek in 1963. Originally called "Blessed Madonna and Child" on old factory records but later changed to "Supreme Protection." First put on the market in 1984 and was limited to the total of that year's production and will not be produced in future years. It has an incised 1964 copyright date. The inscription on the bottom of the figurine applied by blue decal reads: "1909–1984 IN CELEBRATION OF THE 75th ANNIVERSARY OF THE BIRTH OF SISTER M.I. HUMMEL" plus the current TM 6 Goebel trademark. Early production of this figurine had an error in the decal that read "M.*J.* Hummel" rather that "M.*I.* Hummel." This was first corrected by cutting off the hook of the "J" on the decal, but still did not completely look like an "I." Ultimately corrected to read "M.I. Hummel." Of the three versions, the most difficult variation to find is the "altered J" variety. The original issue price in 1984 was $150. Originally came in a dark brown, specially designed, padded presentation case with brass fasteners. The box was inscribed: "M.I. Hummel-IN CELEBRATION OF THE 75th ANNIVERSARY OF THE BIRTH OF SISTER MARIA INNOCENTIA HUMMEL" in gold lettering. "Supreme Protection" is now listed as a Closed Edition (CE) and will not be produced again.

☐ 364 . . . . . 9 to 9¼" . . . . . . (CE). . . ❹ . . . $3,000–4,000 (Early Sample)
☐ 364 . . . . . 9 to 9¼" . . . . . . (CE). . . ❺ . . . $2,000–3,000 (Early Sample)
☐ 364 . . . . . 9 to 9¼" . . . . . . (CE). . . ❻ . . . $350–400
☐ 364 . . . . . 9 to 9¼" . . . . . . (CE). . . ❻ . . . $400–600 ("M.J." variation)
☐ 364 . . . . . 9 to 9¼" . . . . . . (CE). . . ❻ . . . $600–850 (Altered "J" variation)

*(TM 4)*

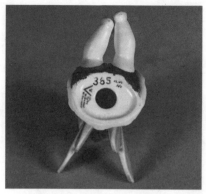

*(TM 4) bottom view*

**HUM 365**
**Hummele (EE)**
First released in 1999 to honor the 90th Anniversary of the birth of Sister M. I. Hummel, as a special Exclusive Edition (EE) for "M. I Hummel Club" members only (with Club redemption form) for this one year only. (Retires as of 31 May 2000.) It is the first Club figurine to bear the new "Year 2000 Backstamp" and (TM 8) trademark. It has an incised 1964 copyright date. Originally called "The Wee Angel" on old factory records, but later changed to "Littlest Angel" and finally to "Hummele". Modelled by master sculptor Gerhard Skrobek in 1963. Recently found in (TM 4) trademark with a 12/64 painting date. It has blue eyes. This piece is now in the Robert L. Miller collection.

☐ 365 . . . . . 2¾" . . . . . . . . . . (CE). . . ❹ . . . $2000–3000 (Early Sample)
☐ 365 . . . . . 2¾" . . . . . . . . . . (EE). . . ❽ . . . . $145

**HUM 366**
**Flying Angel**
First modeled by master sculptor Gerhard Skrobek in 1963, this piece was designed as an addition to the small Nativity Set, HUM 214. Makes an excellent decoration or ornament for hanging on the Christmas tree. See photo of HUM 214 Nativity Set for application. At one time was produced and sold in white overglaze finish. It is presently limited to full color finish only. In 1989 a new smaller size "Flying Angel" was released in the U.S. market. It has an incised 366/0 model number and a 1987 copyright date. The issue price was $65 in 1989. The large size 366 has been renumbered 366/I.

☐ 366/0 . . . . 3" . . . . . . . . . . . (CE). . . ❻ . . . $130–135
☐ 366/0 . . . . 3" . . . . . . . . . . . (CE). . . ❼ . . . $124–130
☐ 366/0 . . . . 3" . . . . . . . . . . . (OE). . . ❽ . . . $124
☐ 366 . . . . . 3½" . . . . . . . . . . (CE). . . ❹ . . . $225–275
☐ 366 . . . . . 3½" . . . . . . . . . . (CE). . . ❺ . . . $160–165
☐ 366 . . . . . 3½" . . . . . . . . . . (CE). . . ❻ . . . $155–160
☐ 366 . . . . . 3½" . . . . . . . . . . (CE). . . ❼ . . . $150–155
☐ 366/I . . . . 3½" . . . . . . . . . . (OE). . . ❽ . . . $150

285

### HUM 367
### Busy Student

First released in the U.S. market in 1964. Originally modeled in 1962 by a combination of modelers. Has an incised 1963 copyright date. Similar to the little girl in HUM 346 "Smart Little Sister." No major variations have been reported in size, color or design.

| ☐ 367 | 4¼" | (CE) | ❸ | $850–1100 |
| ☐ 367 | 4¼" | (CE) | ❹ | $225–275 |
| ☐ 367 | 4¼" | (CE) | ❺ | $200–215 |
| ☐ 367 | 4¼" | (CE) | ❻ | $195–200 |
| ☐ 367 | 4¼" | (CE) | ❼ | $190–195 |
| ☐ 367 | 4¼" | (OE) | ❽ | $190 |

### HUM 368
### Lute Song (PFE)

Originally called "Lute Player" on old factory records, but later changed to "Lute Song." First modeled by master sculptor Gerhard Skrobek in July 1964. Notice the similarity between this figure and the girl in HUM 336 "Close Harmony." Now listed on factory records as a Possible Future Edition (PFE) and may be released at some future date, subject to possible minor changes. Recently found in (TM 4) trademark with a 12/65 painting date. Now in the Robert L. Miller collection.

| ☐ 368 | 5" | (CE) | ❹ | $2,000–3,000 (Early Sample) |
| ☐ 368 | 5" | (PFE) | | |

286

**HUM 369**
**Follow The Leader**
First introduced in the U.S. market in 1972. This figurine was first modeled by master sculptor Gerhard Skrobek in February 1964. It has an incised 1964 copyright date on the bottom. The original issue price in 1972 was $110. No major variations have been recorded in size, color or design.

☐ 369 . . . . . 7" . . . . . . . . . . . . (CE). . . ❸ . . . $4000–5000 (Early Sample)
☐ 369 . . . . . 7" . . . . . . . . . . . . (CE). . . ❹ . . . $1700–2200
☐ 369 . . . . . 7" . . . . . . . . . . . . (CE). . . ❺ . . . $1400–1500
☐ 369 . . . . . 7" . . . . . . . . . . . . (CE). . . ❻ . . . $1375–1400
☐ 369 . . . . . 7" . . . . . . . . . . . . (CE). . . ❼ . . . $1350–1375
☐ 369 . . . . . 7" . . . . . . . . . . . . (OE). . . ❽ . . . $1350

---

**HUM TERM**

**MODEL**: This term most often refers to a particular "M.I. Hummel" figurine, plate, bell, or other item in the line. When not used in reference to a specific motif, the word model also can refer to the sculptor's working model from which the figurines are made.

### HUM 370
### Companions (PFE)

Originally called "Brotherly Love" on old factory records, but later changed to "Companions." Originally modeled by master sculptor Gerhard Skrobek in May 1964. Now listed on factory records as a Possible Future Edition (PFE) and may be released at some future date, subject to possible minor changes. Recently found in (TM 5) trademark in a 9/73 painting date. Now in the Robert L. Miller collection.

| ☐ 370 | 5" | (CE) | ❹ | $3,000–4,000 (Early Eample) |
| ☐ 370 | 5" | (CE) | ❺ | $2,000–3,000 (Early Sample) |
| ☐ 370 | 5" | (PFE) | | |

### HUM 371
### Daddy's Girls

First introduced in the U.S. market in 1989. Originally called "Sisterly Love" on old factory records, but later changed to "Daddy's Girls". Modeled by master sculptor Gerhard Skrobek in May 1964. The original issue price was $130 in 1989. It has an incised 1964 copyright date.

| ☐ 371 | 4¾" | (CE) | ❹ | $3,000–4,000 (Early Sample) |
| ☐ 371 | 4¾" | (CE) | ❺ | $2,000–3,000 (Early Sample) |
| ☐ 371 | 4¾" | (CE) | ❻ | $265–275 |
| ☐ 371 | 4¾" | (CE) | ❼ | $260–265 |
| ☐ 371 | 4¾" | (OE) | ❽ | $260 |

### HUM 372
### Blessed Mother (PFE)

Originally called "Virgin Mother and Child" on old factory records, but later changed to "Blessed Mother." Modeled by master sculptor Gerhard Skrobek in May 1964. Now listed on factory records as a Possible Future Edition (PFE) and may be released at some future date, subject to possible minor changes. Recently found in (TM 4) with a 11/73 painting date. Now in the Robert L. Miller collection.

☐ 372 . . . . . 10¼" . . . . . . . . . (CE). . . ❹ . . . $3,000–4,000 (Early Sample)
☐ 372 . . . . . 10¼" . . . . . . . . . (PFE). . . . . . .

### HUM 373
### Just Fishing

This figurine was first released in the U.S. market in 1985. Originally called "The Fisherman" on old factory records, but later changed to "Just Fishing." Modeled by master sculptor Gerhard Skrobek in 1964. It has an incised 1965 copyright date on the bottom. The original issue price was $85 in 1985. Was first listed as an *ashtray* on Goebel price lists but later changed to a figurine listing. Found with either an old shoe or a fish on end of pole. Listed as (TW) "Temporarily Withdrawn" in January 1999, but may be reinstated at some future date.

☐ 373 . . . . . 4¼ to 4½" . . . . . (CE). . . ❹ . . . $3,000–4,000 (Early Sample)
☐ 373 . . . . . 4¼ to 4½" . . . . . (CE). . . ❺ . . . $1,000–1,500
☐ 373 . . . . . 4¼ to 4½" . . . . . (CE). . . ❻ . . . $265–275
☐ 373 . . . . . 4¼ to 4½" . . . . . (TW) . . ❼ . . . $250–260

**HUM 374**
**Lost Stocking**
This figurine was one of twenty-four new motifs first released in the U.S. market in 1972. Originally modeled by master sculptor Gerhard Skrobek in 1965. It has an incised 1965 copyright date. No major variations have been recorded in size, color or design. The original issue price in 1972 was $17.50.

☐ 374 . . . . . 4½" . . . . . . . . . . (CE) . . . ❸ . . . $3,000–4,000 (Early Sample)
☐ 374 . . . . . 4½" . . . . . . . . . . (CE) . . . ❹ . . . $1,000–1,500
☐ 374 . . . . . 4½" . . . . . . . . . . (CE) . . . ❺ . . . $185–200
☐ 374 . . . . . 4½" . . . . . . . . . . (CE) . . . ❻ . . . $180–185
☐ 374 . . . . . 4½" . . . . . . . . . . (CE) . . . ❼ . . . $175–180
☐ 374 . . . . . 4½" . . . . . . . . . . (**OE**) . . . ❽ . . . $175

*Early Sample (TM 4)*          *Current Production (TM 7)*

**HUM 375**
**Morning Stroll**
Originally called "Walking the Baby" on old factory records, but later changed to "Morning Stroll". First modeled by master sculptor Gerhard Skrobek in 1964 with an incised 1964 copyright date. The small size, HUM 375 3/0 was released in the U.S. market in 1994, modeled by master sculptor Helmut Fischer in 1991. It has an incised 1991 copyright date and the "First Issue 1994" oval decal on the bottom. The official issue price was $170 in 1994.

☐ 375 . . . . . 4¾" . . . . . . . . . . (CE) . . . ❹ . . . $3,000–4,000 (Early Sample)
☐ 375 3/0 . . . 3¾" . . . . . . . . . . (CE) . . . ❼ . . . $205–210
☐ 375 3/0 . . . 3¾" . . . . . . . . . . (**OE**) . . . ❽ . . . $205

### HUM 376
### Little Nurse

This figurine was first released in the U.S. market in the fall of 1982. Originally called "First Aid" on old factory records, but later changed to "Little Nurse." Modeled by master sculptor Gerhard Skrobek in April 1965. It has an incised 1972 copyright date on the bottom. The original issue price was $95 in 1982. Recently found with (TM 5) trademark and incised 1965 copyright date.

☐ 376 . . . . . 4″ . . . . . . . . . . . . (CE). . . ❹ . . . $3,000–4,000 (Early Sample)
☐ 376 . . . . . 4″ . . . . . . . . . . . . (CE). . . ❺ . . . $2,000–3,000
☐ 376 . . . . . 4″ . . . . . . . . . . . . (CE). . . ❻ . . . $290–295
☐ 376 . . . . . 4″ . . . . . . . . . . . . (CE). . . ❼ . . . $280–285
☐ 376 . . . . . 4″ . . . . . . . . . . . . (OE). . . ❽ . . . $280

### HUM 377
### Bashful!

First released in the U.S. market in 1972. Originally modeled by master sculptor Gerhard Skrobek in January 1966. It usually was found with an incised 1966 copyright date, but occasionally found with a 1971 incised date. Models in current production have no incised date at all. No major variations have been recorded in size, color or design. The original issue price was $17.50 in 1972. Recently found with (TM 4) trademark and a 11/69 painting date. Now in the Robert L. Miller collection.

☐ 377 . . . . . 4¾″ . . . . . . . . . . (CE). . . ❹ . . . $3,000–4,000 (Early Sample)
☐ 377 . . . . . 4¾″ . . . . . . . . . . (CE). . . ❹ . . . $1,000–1,500 (Production Model)
☐ 377 . . . . . 4¾″ . . . . . . . . . . (CE). . . ❺ . . . $245–270
☐ 377 . . . . . 4¾″ . . . . . . . . . . (CE). . . ❻ . . . $240–245
☐ 377 . . . . . 4¾″ . . . . . . . . . . (CE). . . ❼ . . . $235–240
☐ 377 . . . . . 4¾″ . . . . . . . . . . (OE). . . ❽ . . . $235

### HUM 378
### Easter Greetings!
First released in the U.S. market in 1972 as one of twenty-four new motifs released that year. Originally modeled by master sculptor Gerhard Skrobek in January 1966. It has an incised 1966 or 1971 copyright date on the bottom. No major variations have been found in size, color or design. The original issue price was $24 in 1972. Listed as (TW) "Temporarily Withdrawn" in January 1999, but may be reinstated at some future date.

☐ 378 . . . . . 5 to 5¼″ . . . . . . (CE). . . ❹ . . . $3,000–4,000 (Early Sample)
☐ 378 . . . . . 5 to 5¼″ . . . . . . (CE). . . ❹ . . . $1,000–1,500
☐ 378 . . . . . 5 to 5¼″ . . . . . . (CE). . . ❺ . . . $245–270
☐ 378 . . . . . 5 to 5¼″ . . . . . . (CE). . . ❻ . . . $240–245
☐ 378 . . . . . 5 to 5¼″ . . . . . . (TW) . . ❼ . . . $225–235

### HUM 379
### Don't Be Shy (PFE)
Originally called "One For You—One For Me" on old factory records, but later changed to "Don't Be Shy." This figurine was first modeled by master sculptor Gerhard Skrobek in February 1966. It is now listed on factory records as a Possible Future Edition (PFE) and may be released at some future date, subject to possible minor changes. Recently found with (TM 3) trademark.

☐ 379 . . . . . 4¼ to 4½″ . . . . . (CE). . . ❸ . . . $4,000–5,000 (Early Sample)
☐ 379 . . . . . 4¼ to 4½″ . . . . . (CE). . . ❹ . . . $3,000–4,000 (Early Sample)
☐ 379 . . . . . 4¼ to 4½″ . . . . . (PFE). . . . . . .

### HUM 380
### Daisies Don't Tell (CE)
First introduced in 1981 for members of the Goebel Collector's Club only as "Special Edition No. 5." Was not sold as an open edition but can be purchased on the secondary market at premium prices. The original issue price was $80 in the U.S. and $95 in Canada. It has an incised 1972 copyright date and the (TM 6) trademark. The original name was "Does He?" on old factory records. Modeled by master sculptor Gerhard Skrobek in February 1966. Also found with incised 1966 copyright date.

☐ 380 . . . . . 5" . . . . . . . . . . . . (CE). . . ❹ . . . $3,000–4,000 (Early Sample)
☐ 380 . . . . . 5" . . . . . . . . . . . . (CE). . . ❺ . . . $1,000–2,000
☐ 380 . . . . . 5" . . . . . . . . . . . . (CE). . . ❻ . . . $275–300

### HUM 381
### Flower Vendor
First introduced in the U.S. market in 1972. Originally modeled by master sculptor Gerhard Skrobek in October 1966. It has an incised 1971 copyright date on the underside of the base. No major variations have been found in size, color or design. The original issue price was $24 in 1972. Also found with incised 1967 copyright date.

☐ 381 . . . . . 5¼" . . . . . . . . . . . (CE). . . ❹ . . . $3,000–4,000 (Early Sample)
☐ 381 . . . . . 5¼" . . . . . . . . . . . (CE). . . ❺ . . . $300–330
☐ 381 . . . . . 5¼" . . . . . . . . . . . (CE). . . ❻ . . . $290–300
☐ 381 . . . . . 5¼" . . . . . . . . . . . (CE). . . ❼ . . . $285–290
☐ 381 . . . . . 5¼" . . . . . . . . . . . (OE). . . ❽ . . . $285

### HUM 382
### Visiting An Invalid

First released in the U.S. market in 1972. Originally modeled by master sculptor Gerhard Skrobek in October 1966. It has an incised 1971 copyright date on the underside of the base. No major variations have been noticed in size, color or design. The original issue price was $26.50 in 1972. Also found with incised 1967 copyright date. Listed as (TW) "Temporarily Withdrawn" in January 1999, but may be reinstated at some future date.

| ☐ 382 | 5″ | (CE) | ❹ | $1,000–1,500 |
| ☐ 382 | 5″ | (CE) | ❺ | $245–270 |
| ☐ 382 | 5″ | (CE) | ❻ | $240–245 |
| ☐ 382 | 5″ | (TW) | ❼ | $225–230 |

### HUM 383
### Going Home

This figurine was first released in the U.S. market in the spring of 1985. Originally called "Fancy Free" on old factory records, but later changed to "Going Home." Modeled by master sculptor Gerhard Skrobek in November 1966. It has an incised 1967 or 1972 copyright date on the bottom. The original issue price in 1985 was $125. "Going Home" has now been made into two separate figurines. See HUM 561 "Grandma's Girl" and HUM 562 "Grandpa's Boy".

| ☐ 383 | 5″ | (CE) | ❹ | $3,000–4,000 (Early Sample) |
| ☐ 383 | 5″ | (CE) | ❺ | $2,000–3,000 |
| ☐ 383 | 5″ | (CE) | ❻ | $380–390 |
| ☐ 383 | 5″ | (CE) | ❼ | $370–380 |
| ☐ 383 | 5″ | (OE) | ❽ | $370 |

**HUM 384**
**Easter Time**

First introduced in the U.S. market in 1972. Originally modeled by master sculptor Gerhard Skrobek in January 1967. It has an incised 1971 copyright date on the underside of the base. No major variations have been recorded in size, color or design. The original issue price was $27.50 in 1972. Also called "Easter Playmates" in some catalogues.

| | | | | | |
|---|---|---|---|---|---|
| ☐ 384 | 4" | (CE) | ❹ | $1,000–1,500 |
| ☐ 384 | 4" | (CE) | ❺ | $300–330 |
| ☐ 384 | 4" | (CE) | ❻ | $290–300 |
| ☐ 384 | 4" | (CE) | ❼ | $285–290 |
| ☐ 384 | 4" | (OE) | ❽ | $285 |

**HUM 385**
**Chicken-Licken**

First introduced in the U.S. market in 1972 as one of twenty-four new motifs released that year. Originally modeled by master sculptor Gerhard Skrobek in June 1967. It has an incised 1971 copyright date on the bottom of the base. The original issue price was $28.50 in 1972. A new miniature size figurine, without the fence, was issued in 1991 with a suggested retail price of $80 to match a new miniature plate series called the "Little Homemakers"–one each year for four years. This is the fourth and last in this series. It has an incised 1987 copyright date. The miniature size (385 4/0) was (TW) "Temporarily Withdrawn" from production on 31 December 1997, and then listed as a (CE) Closed Edition in January 1999.

| | | | | | |
|---|---|---|---|---|---|
| ☐ 385 4/0 | 3¼" | (CE) | ❻ | $125–140 |
| ☐ 385 4/0 | 3¼" | (CE) | ❼ | $115–120   (CE) Jan '99 |
| ☐ 385 | 4¾" | (CE) | ❹ | $1,000–1,500 |
| ☐ 385 | 4¾" | (CE) | ❺ | $350–370 |
| ☐ 385 | 4¾" | (CE) | ❻ | $340–350 |
| ☐ 385 | 4¾" | (CE) | ❼ | $330–340 |
| ☐ 385 | 4¾" | (OE) | ❽ | $330 |

### HUM 386
### On Secret Path
First introduced in the U.S. market 1972. Originally modeled by master sculptor Gerhard Skrobek in July 1967. It has an incised 1971 copyright date on the bottom of the base. No major variations have been found in size, color or design. The original issue price was $26.50 in 1972.

| | | | | | | |
|---|---|---|---|---|---|---|
| ☐ 386 | . . . . . 5¼" | . . . . . . . . . | . . . (CE) | . . . | ❹ | . . . $1,000–1,500 |
| ☐ 386 | . . . . . 5¼" | . . . . . . . . . | . . . (CE) | . . . | ❺ | . . . $300–330 |
| ☐ 386 | . . . . . 5¼" | . . . . . . . . . | . . . (CE) | . . . | ❻ | . . . $290–300 |
| ☐ 386 | . . . . . 5¼" | . . . . . . . . . | . . . (CE) | . . . | ❼ | . . . $285–290 |
| ☐ 386 | . . . . . 5¼" | . . . . . . . . . | . . . (OE) | . . . | ❽ | . . . $285 |

*(Note bird on early sample)*        *(TM 4)*

### HUM 387
### Valentine Gift (CE)
This figurine was first introduced in 1977 for members of the Goebel Collectors' Club only and not sold in Open Edition. Originally modeled by master sculptor Gerhard Skrobek in July 1967. It has an incised 1972 copyright date along with the (TM 5)

*(continued on next page)*

trademark. Also bears the inscription "EXCLUSIVE SPECIAL EDITION No. 1 FOR MEMBERS OF THE GOEBEL COLLECTORS' CLUB" applied by blue decal. The original issue price was $45 in addition to the member's redemption card. Translation of message on heart: "I Love You Very Much" or "I Like You." Several examples without the special inscription but with (TM 4) trademark only have appeared on the market. Some have 1968 or 1971 copyright date and usually sell for $2000–3000.

☐ 387 . . . . . 5¾ . . . . . . . . . . (CE). . . ❹ . . . $5000–7500 (with bird)
☐ 387 . . . . . 5¾ . . . . . . . . . . (CE). . . ❹ . . . $2000–3000
☐ 387 . . . . . 5¾ . . . . . . . . . . (CE). . . ❺ . . . $450–600

388                                    388 M

## HUM 388
### Little Band, Candleholder
This piece is a candleholder with three figurines, HUM 389, HUM 390 and HUM 391, attached to a round ceramic base. Modeled by master sculptor Gerhard Skrobek in December 1967. It has an incised 1968 copyright date. Little Band, Candleholder was "Temporarily Withdrawn" (TW) from production on 31 December 1990, but may be reinstated at some future date.

☐ 388 . . . . . 3 x 4¾ . . . . . . . (CE). . . ❹ . . . $350–450
☐ 388 . . . . . 3 x 4¾ . . . . . . . (CE). . . ❺ . . . $300–350
☐ 388 . . . . . 3 x 4¾ . . . . . . . (TW) . . ❻ . . . $275–300

## HUM 388 M
### Little Band, Candleholder on Music Box
Same as HUM 388 but fastened on a music box. There are variations in type of music box as well as tunes played. The music box is usually Swiss-made and not produced by Goebel. This Music Box was "Temporarily Withdrawn" (TW) from production on 31 December 1990, but may be reinstated at some future date.

☐ 388M . . . . 3 x 4¾ . . . . . . . (CE). . . ❹ . . . $475–500
☐ 388M . . . . 3 x 4¾ . . . . . . . (CE). . . ❺ . . . $450–475
☐ 388M . . . . 3 x 4¾ . . . . . . . (TW) . . ❻ . . . $400–425

389            390            391

**HUM 389**
**Girl With Sheet of Music**
One of a set of three sometimes referred to as the "Little Band." Originally modeled by master sculptor Gerhard Skrobek in May 1968. It has an incised 1968 copyright date and only found in trademarks 4, 5, 6 and 7.

☐ 389 . . . . . 2½" . . . . . . . . . . (CE). . . ❹ . . . $175–225
☐ 389 . . . . . 2½" . . . . . . . . . . (CE). . . ❺ . . . $110–120
☐ 389 . . . . . 2½" . . . . . . . . . . (CE). . . ❻ . . . $105–110
☐ 389 . . . . . 2½" . . . . . . . . . . (CE). . . ❼ . . . $100–105
☐ 389 . . . . . 2½" . . . . . . . . . . (OE). . . ❽ . . . $100

**HUM 390**
**Boy With Accordion**
One of a set of three sometimes referred to as the "Little Band." Originally modeled by master sculptor Gerhard Skrobek in May 1968. It has an incised 1968 copyright date and only found in trademarks 4, 5, 6 and 7.

☐ 390 . . . . . 2½" . . . . . . . . . . (CE). . . ❹ . . . $175–225
☐ 390 . . . . . 2½" . . . . . . . . . . (CE). . . ❺ . . . $110–120
☐ 390 . . . . . 2½" . . . . . . . . . . (CE). . . ❻ . . . $105–110
☐ 390 . . . . . 2½" . . . . . . . . . . (CE). . . ❼ . . . $100
☐ 390 . . . . . 2½" . . . . . . . . . . (OE). . . ❽ . . . $100

**HUM 391**
**Girl With Trumpet**
One of a set of three sometimes referred to as the "Little Band." Originally modeled by master sculptor Gerhard Skrobek in May 1968. It has an incised 1968 copyright date and only found in trademarks 4, 5, 6 and 7.

☐ 391 . . . . . 2½" . . . . . . . . . . (CE). . . ❹ . . . $175–225
☐ 391 . . . . . 2½" . . . . . . . . . . (CE). . . ❺ . . . $110–120
☐ 391 . . . . . 2½" . . . . . . . . . . (CE). . . ❻ . . . $105–110
☐ 391 . . . . . 2½" . . . . . . . . . . (CE). . . ❼ . . . $100–105
☐ 391 . . . . . 2½" . . . . . . . . . . (OE). . . ❽ . . . $100

*392*

**HUM 392**
**Little Band (on base)**
Same as HUM 388 but without socket for candle. Modeled by master sculptor Gerhard Skrobek in May 1968. It has an incised 1968 copyright date. On 31 December 1984 this figurine was listed as "Temporarily Withdrawn" (TW) from production by Goebel but could possibly be reinstated at some future date.

| | | | | | |
|---|---|---|---|---|---|
| ☐ 392 | 3 × 4¾″ | (CE) | ❹ | $350–450 |
| ☐ 392 | 3 × 4¾″ | (CE) | ❺ | $300–350 |
| ☐ 392 | 3 × 4¾″ | (TW) | ❻ | $275–300 |

*392 M*

**HUM 392 M**
**Little Band on Music Box**
Same as HUM 392 but fastened on a music box. There are variations in type of music box as well as in tunes played. The music box is usually Swiss-made and not produced by Goebel. This Music Box was "Temporarily Withdrawn" (TW) from production on 31 December 1990, but may be reinstated at some future date.

| | | | | | |
|---|---|---|---|---|---|
| ☐ 392 M | 3 × 4¾″ | (CE) | ❹ | $475–500 |
| ☐ 392 M | 3 × 4¾″ | (CE) | ❺ | $450–475 |
| ☐ 392 M | 3 × 4¾″ | (TW) | ❻ | $400–425 |

---
**HUM TERM**

**SAMPLE MODEL**: Generally a figurine that was made as a sample only and not approved by the Siessen Convent for production. Sample models (in the true sense of the term) are extremely rare items and command a premium price on the secondary market.

---

### HUM 393
### Holy Water Font, Dove (PFE)

This holy water font was modeled by master sculptor Gerhard Skrobek in June 1968. The inscription reads: "Come Holy Spirit." Now listed on factory records as a Possible Future Edition (PFE) and may be released at some future date, subject to possible minor changes. Recently found with (TM 4) and a 8/69 painting date, now part of the Robert L. Miller collection.

☐ 393 . . . . . 2¾ × 4¼" . . . . . (CE). . . ❹ . . . $2,000–3,000 (Early Sample)
☐ 393 . . . . . 2¾ × 4¼" . . . . . (PFE). . . . . . .

### HUM 394
### Timid Little Sister

First released in the U.S. market in 1981 along with five other figurines. Originally modeled by master sculptor Gerhard Skrobek in February 1972. It has an incised 1972 copyright date on the underside of the base. The original issue price was $190 in 1981. The girl normally does *not* have eyelashes.

☐ 394 . . . . . 7" . . . . . . . . . . . (CE). . . ❺ . . . $3,000–4,000 (Early Sample)
☐ 394 . . . . . 7" . . . . . . . . . . . (CE). . . ❻ . . . $500–525
☐ 394 . . . . . 7" . . . . . . . . . . . (CE). . . ❼ . . . $495–500
☐ 394 . . . . . 7" . . . . . . . . . . . (OE). . . ❽ . . . $495

*395 Early sample (TM 5)*          *395/0 (TM 7)*

## HUM 395
### Shepherd Boy

Originally named "Young Shepherd" on old factory records, but later changed to "Shepherd Boy." This figurine was modeled by master sculptor Gerhard Skrobek in February 1971, with an incised 1972 copyright date. A smaller version, without the fence was released in 1996 with a combination "First Issue 1996" and "125th Anniversary Goebel" backstamp. The smaller 395/0 version was modeled by master sculptor Helmut Fischer in 1989 with an incised 1989 copyright date in addition to the (TM 7) trademark. The original issue price was $295 in 1996. The Early Sample model was recently found with (TM 5) trademark and a 11/73 painting date, and is now in the Robert L. Miller collection.

☐ 395 . . . . . 6¾″ . . . . . . . . . . (CE). . . ❺ . . . $3,000–4,000 (Early Sample)
☐ 395/0 . . . . 4⅞″ . . . . . . . . . . (CE). . . ❼ . . . $310–315
☐ 395/0 . . . . 4⅞″ . . . . . . . . . . (OE). . . ❽ . . . $310

---

### HUM TERM

**SECONDARY MARKET**: The buying and selling of items after the initial retail purchase has been transacted. Often times this post-retail trading is also referred to as the "after market." This very publication is intended to serve as a guide for the secondary market values of "M. I. Hummel" items.

301

*396 2/0 (TM 6)*          *396/I (TM 6)*                    *396 /III (TM 7)*

## HUM 396
### Ride Into Christmas
This design was first introduced in the U.S. market in 1972. First modeled by master sculptor Gerhard Skrobek in December 1970. It has an incised 1971 copyright date. The original issue price was $48.50 on the 1972 price list. A smaller model was released in 1982 with the incised number 396 2/0 and incised 1981 copyright date. The small version was also modeled by Gerhard Skrobek but in 1980. The original issue price was $95 in 1982. The large size has been renumbered 396/I and the old number 396 is now classified as a closed edition because of this change. This same motif is used on the 1975 Annual Plate, HUM 268. The new large size (396/III) was modeled by Gerhard Skrobek in 1991. It has an incised 1991 copyright date, and may be released at some future date.

| | | | | | |
|---|---|---|---|---|---|
| ☐ 396 2/0 | 4¼″ | (CE) | ❻ | $275–285 |
| ☐ 396 2/0 | 4¼″ | (CE) | ❼ | $260–265 |
| ☐ 396 2/0 | 4¼″ | (**OE**) | ❽ | $275 |
| ☐ 396 | 5¾″ | (CE) | ❹ | $2000–2500 |
| ☐ 396 | 5¾″ | (CE) | ❺ | $550–575 |
| ☐ 396 | 5¾″ | (CE) | ❻ | $525–550 |
| ☐ 396/I | 5¾″ | (CE) | ❻ | $500–525 |
| ☐ 396/I | 5¾″ | (CE) | ❼ | $495–500 |
| ☐ 396/I | 5¾″ | (**OE**) | ❽ | $495 |
| ☐ 396/III | 8⅝″ | (PFE) | ❼ | |

*"Christmas Delivery"*
*HUM 2014*
*Released in 1997*

### HUM 397
### Poet, The
First released in the U.S. market in 1994. Modeled by master sculptor Gerhard Skrobek in 1973. It has an incised 1974 copyright date and the "First Issue 1994" oval decal on the bottom along with (TM 7) trademark. The issue price was $220 in 1994. Now listed as (TW) "Temporarily Withdrawn" in January 1999. A new 4" size (397 3/0) called "Poet at the Podium" was released in 1998 as a Member's Exclusive (PE) *Preview Edition* for Club year 22. Modeled by master sculptor Helmut Fischer in 1988. It has an incised 1988 copyright date along with the (TM 7) trademark. Also bears the "Club Exclusive 1998/99" backstamp. The official issue price was $150 in the U.S., in addition to member's redemption card. To be retired 31 May 2000.

☐ 397 . . . . . 6" . . . . . . . . . . . (CE). . . ❹ . . . $3,000–4,000 (Early Sample)
☐ 397 3/0. . . 4" . . . . . . . . . . . (PE). . . ❼ . . . $150–175 (Club Exclusive)
☐ 397/I . . . . 6¼" . . . . . . . . . . (TW) . . ❼ . . . $250–260

*Poet at the Podium*

### HUM 398
### Spring Bouquet (PFE)
This figurine was first modeled by master sculptor Gerhard Skrobek in 1973. Presently listed on factory records as a Possible Future Edition (PFE) and may be released at some future date, subject to possible minor changes.

☐ 398 . . . . . 6¼" . . . . . . . . . . (CE). . . ❺ . . . $3,000–4,000 (Early Sample)
☐ 398 . . . . . 6¼" . . . . . . . . . . (PFE). . . . . . .

## HUM 399
### Valentine Joy (CE)

This figurine was first introduced in 1980 for members of the Goebel Collectors' Club only and not sold as an Open Edition. Originally modeled by master sculptor Gerhard Skrobek. It has an incised 1979 copyright date along with the (TM 6) trademark. Also bears the inscription "EXCLUSIVE SPECIAL EDITION No. 4 FOR MEMBERS OF THE GOEBEL COLLECTORS' CLUB" applied by blue decal. The original issue price was $95 in the U.S. and $105 in Canada, in addition to the member's redemption card. Translation of message on heart: "I Like You." The early sample of this piece is larger in size, has a rounded base showing grass and a bird at boy's feet. It has an incised 1973 copyright date along with the (TM 5) trademark.

*Early sample (TM 5)*      *(TM 6)*

☐ 399 . . . . . 6¼" . . . . . . . . . . (CE). . . ❺ . . . $5,000–7,500 (Early Sample)
☐ 399 . . . . . 5¾" . . . . . . . . . . (CE). . . ❻ . . . $250–300

## HUM 400
### Well Done! (PFE)

This figurine was first modeled by master sculptor Gerhard Skrobek in 1973. Presently listed on factory records as a Possible Future Edition (PFE) and may be released at some future date, subject to possible minor changes.

☐ 400 . . . . . 6¼" . . . . . . . . . . (CE). . . ❺ . . . $3,000–4,000 (Early Sample)
☐ 400 . . . . . 6¼" . . . . . . . . . . (PFE). . . . . . .

### HUM 401
### Forty Winks (PFE)
This figurine was first modeled by master sculptor Gerhard Skrobek in 1973. Presently listed on factory records as a Possible Future Edition (PFE) and may be released at some future date, subject to possible minor changes.

☐ 401 . . . . . 5¼" . . . . . . . . . . (CE). . . **❺** . . . $3,000–4,000 (Early Sample)
☐ 401 . . . . . 5¼" . . . . . . . . . . (PFE) . . . . . . .

### HUM 402
### True Friendship (PFE)
This figurine was first modeled by master sculptor Gerhard Skrobek in 1973. Presently listed on factory records as a Possible Future Edition (PFE) and may be released at some future date, subject to possible minor changes.

☐ 402 . . . . . 4¾" . . . . . . . . . . (CE). . . **❺** . . . $3,000–4,000 (Early Sample)
☐ 402 . . . . . 4¾" . . . . . . . . . . (PFE) . . . . . . .

### HUM 403
### An Apple A Day
This figurine was first modeled by master sculptor Gerhard Skrobek in 1973. First released in the U.S. Market in 1989. It has an incised 1974 copyright date. The original issue price was $195 in 1989.

☐ 403 . . . . . 6½" . . . . . . . . . (CE). . . ❺ . . . $3,000–4,000 (Early Sample)
☐ 403 . . . . . 6½" . . . . . . . . . (CE). . . ❻ . . . $340–350
☐ 403 . . . . . 6½" . . . . . . . . . (CE). . . ❼ . . . $330–340
☐ 403 . . . . . 6½" . . . . . . . . . (OE). . . ❽ . . . $330

### HUM 404
### Sad Song (PFE)
This figurine was first modeled by master sculptor Gerhard Skrobek in 1973. Presently listed on factory records as a Possible Future Edition (PFE) and may be released at some future date, subject to possible minor changes.

☐ 404 . . . . . 6¼" . . . . . . . . . (CE). . . ❺ . . . $3,000–4,000 (Early Sample)
☐ 404 . . . . . 6¼" . . . . . . . . . (PFE). . . . . . .

### HUM 405
### Sing With Me
This figurine was first released in the U.S. market in 1985 along with three other new models formerly listed as Possible Future Editions (PFE). Modeled by master sculptor Gerhard Skrobek in 1973. It has an incised 1973 or 1974 copyright date on the bottom. The original issue price was $125 in the U.S. and $158 in Canada. Listed as (TW) "Temporarily Withdrawn" in January 1999, but may be reinstated at some future date.

☐ 405 . . . . . 5″ . . . . . . . . . . . (CE). . . **5** . . . $3,000–4,000 (Early Sample)
☐ 405 . . . . . 5″ . . . . . . . . . . . (CE). . . **6** . . . $375–385
☐ 405 . . . . . 5″ . . . . . . . . . . . (TW) . . **7** . . . $350–360

### HUM 406
### Pleasant Journey (CE)
This figurine was first released in the U.S. market in 1987 along with four other new figurines. This is the second figurine in the Century Collection and was produced for this one year only in the twentieth century. It was modeled by master sculptor Gerhard Skrobek in 1974 but has an incised 1976 copyright date. A circular inscription applied by blue decal reads: "M.I. HUMMEL CENTURY COLLECTION 1987 XX" and the name "PLEASANT JOURNEY" along with the (TM 6) trademark. The issue price was $500 in the U.S. and $695 in Canada.

☐ 406 . . . . . 7⅛ × 6½″ . . . . . (CE). . . **5** . . . $5,000–6,000 (Early Sample)
☐ 406 . . . . . 7⅛ × 6½″ . . . . . (CE). . . **6** . . . $2,750–3,000

**HUM 407**
**Flute Song (PFE)**
This figurine was first modeled by master sculptor Gerhard Skrobek in 1974. Presently listed on factory records as a Possible Future Edition (PFE) and may be released at some future date, subject to possible minor changes.

☐ 407 . . . . . 6″ . . . . . . . . . . . (CE) . . . ❺ . . . $3,000–4,000 (Early Sample)
☐ 407 . . . . . 6″ . . . . . . . . . . . (PFE) . . . . . . .

*Early sample (TM 5)*      *408/0 (TM 6)*

**HUM 408**
**Smiling Through (CE)**
This figurine was first introduced in 1985 for members of the Goebel Collector's Club only and not sold as an Open Edition. Originally modeled by master sculptor Gerhard Skrobek from an original drawing by sister M.I. Hummel. It has an incised 1983 copyright date along with the (TM 6) trademark. Also bears the inscription "EXCLUSIVE SPECIAL EDITION No. 9 FOR MEMBERS OF THE GOEBEL COLLECTORS' CLUB" applied by blue decal. The original issue price was $125 in the U.S. and $165 in Canada, in addition to the member's redemption card. It is interesting to note the incised model number of 408/0, which indicates that more than one size was produced. The club piece was designed to be smaller, more uniform in size to the other club figurines. See HUM 690 for more information.

☐ 408 . . . . . 5½″ . . . . . . . . . . . (CE) . . . ❺ . . . $4,000–5,000 (Early Sample)
☐ 408/0 . . . . 4¾″ . . . . . . . . . . . (CE) . . . ❻ . . . $350–375

### HUM 409
### Coffee Break (CE)

This figurine was first introduced in 1984 for members of the Goebel Collector's Club only and not sold as an Open Edition. Originally modeled by master sculptor Gerhard Skrobek from an original drawing by Sister M.I. Hummel. It has an incised 1976 copyright date along with the (TM 6) trademark. Also bears the inscription "EXCLUSIVE SPECIAL EDITION No. 8 FOR MEMBERS OF THE GOEBEL COLLECTORS' CLUB" applied by blue decal. The original issue price was $90 in the U.S. and $110 in Canada, in addition to the member's redemption card. "Coffee Break" can now be purchased on the secondary market at premium prices.

☐ 409 . . . . . 4" . . . . . . . . . . . (CE). . . ❺ . . . $3,000–4,000 (Early Sample)
☐ 409 . . . . . 4" . . . . . . . . . . . (CE). . . ❻ . . . $300–325

### HUM 410
### Little Architect, The

First released in the U.S. market in 1993. Originally called "Truant" on old factory records, but later changed to "The Little Architect". Modeled by master sculptor Gerhard Skrobek in 1978. It has an incised 1978 copyright date and the "First Issue 1993" oval decal on the bottom along with the current (TM 7) trademark. The official issue price was $290 in 1993.

☐ 410 . . . . . 6" . . . . . . . . . . . (CE). . . ❺ . . . $3,000–4,000 (Early Sample)
☐ 410/I . . . . 6" . . . . . . . . . . . (CE). . . ❼ . . . $345–350
☐ 410/I . . . . 6" . . . . . . . . . . . (OE). . . ❽ . . . $345

**HUM 411**
**Do I Dare? (PFE)**
This figurine was first modeled by master sculptor Gerhard Skrobek in 1978. Presently listed on factory records as a Possible Future Edition (PFE) and may be released at some future date, subject to possible minor changes.

☐ 411 . . . . . 6″ . . . . . . . . . . . . (CE). . . ❺ . . . $3,000–4,000 (Early Sample)
☐ 411 . . . . . 6″ . . . . . . . . . . . . (PFE). . . . . . .

**HUM 412**
**Bath Time**
This figurine was first modeled by master sculptor Gerhard Skrobek in 1978. First introduced in the U.S. market in 1990. It has an incised 1978 copyright date. Original issue price was $300 in 1990.

☐ 412 . . . . . 6¼″. . . . . . . . . . . (CE). . . ❺ . . . $3,000–4,000 (Early Sample)
☐ 412 . . . . . 6¼″. . . . . . . . . . . (CE). . . ❻ . . . $520–530
☐ 412 . . . . . 6¼″. . . . . . . . . . . (CE). . . ❼ . . . $500–510
☐ 412 . . . . . 6¼″. . . . . . . . . . . (**OE**). . . ❽ . . . $500

### HUM 413
### Whistler's Duet
This figurine was first modeled by master sculptor Gerhard Skrobek in 1979. First released in the U.S. market in the fall of 1991, the original issue price was $235. Now listed as (TW) "Temporarily Withdrawn" in January 1999, but may be reinstated at some future date.

☐ 413 ..... 4 to 4½″ ...... (CE)... **⑤** ... $3,000–4,000 (Early Sample)
☐ 413 ..... 4 to 4½″ ...... (CE)... **⑥** ... $500–1000
☐ 413 ..... 4 to 4½″ ...... (TW) .. **⑦** ... $320–330

### HUM 414
### In Tune
First released in the U.S. market in 1981. Modeled by Gerhard Skrobek in 1979. This figurine was designed to match the fourth edition of the annual bell series, HUM 703 "In Tune" 1981 Annual. The figurine has an incised 1979 copyright date on the bottom of the base and is found only in 6 trademark. The original issue price was $115 in 1981. This same motif was used on HUM 297 "Springtime Serenade" plate in 1997. Now listed as (TW) "Temporarily Withdrawn" in January 1999, but may be reinstated at some future date.

☐ 414 ..... 4″ ........... (CE)... **⑤** ... $3,000–4,000 (Early Sample)
☐ 414 ..... 4″ ........... (CE)... **⑥** ... $330–340
☐ 414 ..... 4″ ........... (TW) .. **⑦** ... $310–320

**HUM 415**
**Thoughtful**
First released in the U.S. market in 1981. Modeled by Gerhard Skrobek in 1979. This figurine was designed to match the third edition of the annual bell series, HUM 702 "Thoughtful" 1980 Annual. The figurine has an incised 1980 copyright date on the bottom of the base. The original issue price was $105 in 1981. A Special Commemorative Edition of 2,000 pieces was issued in the fall of 1996 with master sculptor Gerhard Skrobek's signature, to co-inside with the release of his autobiography, "Hummel & Me, Life Stories," by Gerhard Skrobek.

☐ 415 . . . . . 4½" . . . . . . . . . (CE) . . . ❻ . . . $270–280
☐ 415 . . . . . 4½" . . . . . . . . . (LE) . . . ❼ . . . $260–300 (Special Edition)
☐ 415 . . . . . 4½" . . . . . . . . . (CE) . . . ❼ . . . $255–260
☐ 415 . . . . . 4½" . . . . . . . . . (**OE**) . . . ❽ . . . $255

**HUM 416**
**Jubilee (CE)**
This special limited edition figurine was issued in 1985 in celebration of the Golden Anniversary of the introduction of the first "M.I. Hummel" figurines in 1935. It was modeled by master sculptor Gerhard Skrobek in 1979 and has an incised 1980 copyright date. This figurine was limited to the total of the 1985 production and will not be produced in future years. On the bottom is the special inscription which reads: "50 YEARS M.I. HUMMEL FIGURINES 1935–1985" in a circular design. Directly below is "THE LOVE LIVES ON" in addition to the current (TM 6) trademark, all applied by blue decal. Originally sold in a special white padded presentation case. The original issue price was $200 in the U.S. and $270 in Canada.

☐ 416 . . . . . 6¼" . . . . . . . . . (CE) . . . ❻ . . . $500–600

## HUM 417
### Where Did You Get That? (PFE)
This figurine was first modeled by master sculptor Gerhard Skrobek in 1982 and has an incised 1982 copyright date. Presently listed on factory records as a Possible Future Edition (PFE) and may be released at some future date, subject to possible minor changes. This figurine has now been made into two separate figurines. See HUM 485 "Gift From A Friend" and HUM 486 "I Wonder."

☐ 417 . . . . . 5¼" . . . . . . . . . . (PFE) . . . . . . .

## HUM 418
### What's New?
First introduced in the U.S. market in 1990. This figurine was modeled by master sculptor Gerhard Skrobek in 1980. It has an incised 1980 copyright date. Original issue price was $200 in 1990. In 1996, A Special Edition of "What's New?" was issued with special "INSIGHTS" logo and Dutch flag on outside of newspaper.

☐ 418 . . . . . 5¼" . . . . . . . . . . (CE) . . . ❻ . . . $340–350
☐ 418 . . . . . 5¼" . . . . . . . . . . (LE) . . . ❼ . . . $330–340 (Special Edition)
☐ 418 . . . . . 5¼" . . . . . . . . . . (CE) . . . ❼ . . . $330–340
☐ 418 . . . . . 5¼" . . . . . . . . . . (**OE**) . . . ❽ . . . $330

313

### HUM 419
### Good Luck! (PFE)
This figurine was first modeled by master sculptor Gerhard Skrobek in 1981. Presently listed on factory records as a Possible Future Edition (PFE) and may be released at some future date, subject to possible minor changes.

☐ 419 . . . . . 6¼" . . . . . . . . . . (PFE). . . . . . .

### HUM 420
### Is It Raining?
First introduced in the U.S. market in 1989. This figurine was modeled by master sculptor Gerhard Skrobek in 1981. It has an incised 1981 copyright date. Original issue price was $175 in 1989.

☐ 420 . . . . . 6" . . . . . . . . . . . (CE). . . ❻ . . . $330–340
☐ 420 . . . . . 6" . . . . . . . . . . . (CE). . . ❼ . . . $320–330
☐ 420 . . . . . 6" . . . . . . . . . . . (OE). . . ❽ . . . $320

314

**HUM 421**
**It's Cold (CE)**

This figurine was first introduced in 1982 for members of the Goebel Collectors' Club only and not sold as an Open Edition. Originally modeled by master sculptor Gerhard Skrobek from an original drawing by Sister M.I. Hummel. It has an incised 1981 copyright date along with the 6 trademark. Also bears the inscription "EXCLUSIVE SPECIAL EDITION No. 6 FOR MEMBERS OF THE GOEBEL COLLECTORS' CLUB" applied by blue decal. The official issue price was $80 in the U.S. and $95 in Canada, in addition to the member's redemption card. This figurine can be purchased on the secondary market at premium prices.

☐ 421 . . . . . 5 to 5¼" . . . . . . (CE). . . ❻ . . . $350–400

**HUM 422**
**What Now? (CE)**

This figurine was first introduced in 1983 for members of the Goebel Collectors' Club only and not sold as an Open Edition. Originally modeled by master sculptor Gerhard Skrobek from an original drawing by Sister M.I. Hummel. It has an incised 1981 copyright date along with the (TM 6) trademark. Also bears the inscription "EXCLUSIVE SPECIAL EDITION No. 7 FOR MEMBERS OF THE GOEBEL COLLECTORS' CLUB" applied by blue decal. The official issue price was $80 in the U.S. and $95 in Canada, in addition to the member's redemption card. This figurine can be purchased on the secondary market at premium prices.

☐ 422 . . . . . 5¼" . . . . . . . . . . (CE). . . ❻ . . . $350–400

**HUM 423**
**Horse Trainer**
First introduced in the U.S. market in 1990. This figurine was modeled by master sculptor Gerhard Skrobek in 1980. It has an incised 1981 copyright date. The original issue price was $155 in 1990.

☐ 423 . . . . . 4½″ . . . . . . . . . . (CE). . . ❻ . . . $260–265
☐ 423 . . . . . 4½″ . . . . . . . . . . (CE). . . ❼ . . . $255–260
☐ 423 . . . . . 4½″ . . . . . . . . . . (**OE**). . . ❽ . . . $255

**HUM 424**
**Sleep Tight**
First released in the U.S. market in 1990. This figurine was modeled by master sculptor Gerhard Skrobek in 1980. It has an incised 1981 copyright date. The original issue price was $155 in 1990.

☐ 424 . . . . . 4½″ . . . . . . . . . . (CE). . . ❻ . . . $260–265
☐ 424 . . . . . 4½″ . . . . . . . . . . (CE). . . ❼ . . . $255–260
☐ 424 . . . . . 4½″ . . . . . . . . . . (**OE**). . . ❽ . . . $255

## HUM 425
### Pleasant Moment (PFE)
This figurine was first modeled by master sculptor Gerhard Skrobek in 1980. It has an incised 1981 copyright date. Presently listed on factory records as a Possible Future Edition (PFE) and may be released at some future date, subject to possible minor changes.

☐ 425 . . . . . 4½" . . . . . . . . . (PFE) . . . . . . .

*426 (Factory Sample)*

*426 3/0 (TM7)*

## HUM 426
### Pay Attention
This figurine was first modeled by master sculptor Gerhard Skrobek in 1980. It has an incised 1981 copyright date. This same motif was used on HUM 299 1999 "Autumn Glory" plate. A new smaller size (426 3/0) was released in 1999 with a "First Issue 1999" decal, (TM 7) trademark and 1997 copyright date. Modeled by master sculptor Helmut Fischer in 1997. The original issue price was $175 in 1999.

☐ 426 . . . . . 5¾" . . . . . . . . . (PFE) . . ❻ . . . $1,500–2,000 (Early Sample)
☐ 426 3/0 . . . 4¼" . . . . . . . . . (CE) . . . ❼ . . . $180–185
☐ 426 3/0 . . . 4¼" . . . . . . . . . (**OE**) . . ❽ . . . $180

*427 3/0 (TM 7)*

## HUM 427
### Where Are You?

This figurine was first modeled by master sculptor Gerhard Skrobek in 1980. It has an incised 1981 copyright date. A new smaller size (427 3/0) was released in 1999 with a "First Issue 1999" decal, (TM 7) trademark and 1997 copyright date. Modeled by master sculptor Helmut Fischer in 1997. The original issue price was $175 in 1999.

*427 (Factory Sample)*

☐ 427 . . . . . 5¾" . . . . . . . . . . (PFE). . . ❻ . . . $1,500–2,000 (Early Sample)
☐ 427 3/0. . . 4¼" . . . . . . . . . . (CE). . . ❼ . . . $180–185
☐ 427 3/0. . . 4¼" . . . . . . . . . . (**OE**). . . ❽ . . . $180

## HUM 428
### Summertime Surprise

This figurine was first modeled by master sculptor Gerhard Skrobek in 1980 in the 5¾" size with an incised 1981 copyright date. It was listed as a (PFE) Possible Future Edition under the name of "I Won't Hurt You" until 1989 when master sculptor Helmut Fischer modeled it in the 3½" size with model number 428 3/0, under the name of "Summertime Surprise." The small size was first released in the U. S. market in the fall of 1997 with a "First Issue 1998" backstamp. It has an incised 1989 copyright date and the (TM 7) trademark. The original issue price was $140 in 1997.

☐ 428 . . . . . 5¾" . . . . . . . . . . (CE). . . ❻ . . . $2,000–3,000 (Early Sample)
☐ 428 3/0. . . 3½" . . . . . . . . . . (CE). . . ❼ . . . $150–155
☐ 428 3/0. . . 3½" . . . . . . . . . . (**OE**). . . ❽ . . . $150

## HUM 429
## Hello World (CE)

This was first introduced in 1989 for members of the M.I. Hummel Club only and not sold as an Open Edition. Originally modeled by master sculptor Gerhard Skrobek in 1980. It has an incised 1983 copyright date along with either the (TM6) or (TM7) trademark. Also bears the inscription: "EXCLUSIVE EDITION 1989/90 M.I. HUMMEL CLUB" applied by blue decal. A large black flying bumble bee is located on the bottom. The official issue price was $130 in the U.S., in addition to the member's redemption card. This figurine can now be purchased on the secondary market at premium prices. Early production pieces are labeled "Goebel Collectors' Club" while later pieces have "M.I. Hummel Club" decal.

☐ 429 . . . . . 5½". . . . . . . . . . (CE). . . ❻ . . . $350–400
☐ 429 . . . . . 5½". . . . . . . . . . (CE). . . ❼ . . . $300–350

## HUM 430
## In "D" Major

First released in the U.S. market in 1989. This figurine was modeled by master sculptor Gerhard Skrobek in 1980. It has an incised 1981 copyright date. The original issue price was $135 in 1989. In the rear view—the "K B" on the boundry stone the little boy is sitting on means: "Koenigreich Bayern". English: "Kingdom of Bavaria".

☐ 430 . . . . . 4¼". . . . . . . . . . (CE). . . ❻ . . . $240–245
☐ 430 . . . . . 4¼". . . . . . . . . . (CE). . . ❼ . . . $235–240
☐ 430 . . . . . 4¼". . . . . . . . . . (OE). . . ❽ . . . $235

*(Factory Sample)*

## HUM 431
### The Surprise (CE)
This figurine was first introduced in 1988 for members of the Goebel Collectors' Club only and not sold as an Open Edition. Originally modeled by master sculptor Gerhard Skrobek in 1980. It has an incised 1981 copyright date along with the current (TM6) trademark. Also bears the inscription: "EXCLUSIVE SPECIAL EDITION No. 12 FOR MEMBERS OF THE GOEBEL COLLECTORS' CLUB" applied by blue decal. A large black flying bumble bee is located on the bottom of the base. The original price was $125 in the U.S., in addition to the member's redemption card. "The Surprise" can now be purchased on the secondary market at premium prices. There is *no* club inscription on Factory Sample.

☐ 431 . . . . . 4¼ to 5½" . . . . . (CE) . . . ❻ . . . $2000–3000 (Early Sample)
☐ 431 . . . . . 5½" . . . . . . . . . . (CE) . . . ❻ . . . $300–350

## HUM 432
### Knit One, Purl One
First released in the U.S. market in 1983. Modeled by master sculptor Gerhard Skrobek in 1982. This figurine was designed especially to match the sixth edition of the annual bell series, HUM 705 "Knit One" 1983 annual. The figurine has an incised 1982 copyright date. The original issue price was $52 in the U.S. and $74 in Canada.

☐ 432 . . . . . 3" . . . . . . . . . . . (CE) . . . ❻ . . . $150–155
☐ 432 . . . . . 3" . . . . . . . . . . . (CE) . . . ❼ . . . $145–150
☐ 432 . . . . . 3" . . . . . . . . . . . (OE) . . . ❽ . . . $145

### HUM 433
### Sing Along
First released in the U.S. market in 1987. Modeled by master sculptor Gerhard Skrobek in 1981. This figurine was designed especially to match the ninth edition of the annual bell series, HUM 708 "Sing Along" 1986 annual. The figurine has an incised 1982 copyright date on the bottom of the base. The original issue price was $145 in the U.S. and $200 in Canada. Listed as (TW) "Temporarily Withdrawn" in January 1999, but may be reinstated at some future date.

☐ 433 . . . . . 4½″ . . . . . . . . . . (CE). . . ❻ . . . $330–340
☐ 433 . . . . . 4½″ . . . . . . . . . . (TW) . . ❼ . . . $310–320

### HUM 434
### Friend or Foe?
First released in the U.S. market in 1991. Has "FIRST ISSUE 1991" decal. Modeled by master sculptor Gerhard Skrobek in 1981. It has an incised 1983 copyright date. The original issue price was $190.

☐ 434 . . . . . 4″ . . . . . . . . . . . (CE). . . ❻ . . . $260–265
☐ 434 . . . . . 4″ . . . . . . . . . . . (CE). . . ❼ . . . $255–260
☐ 434 . . . . . 4″ . . . . . . . . . . . (OE). . . ❽ . . . $255

321

**HUM 435 (Early Sample)**

### HUM 435
### Delicious
This figurine was first modeled by master sculptor Gerhard Skrobek in 1981 in the 6″ size with an incised 1982 copyright date. It was listed as a (PFE) Possible Future Edition until 1986 when master sculptor Helmut Fischer modeled it in the 3⅞″ size with model number 435 3/0. This small size was first released in the U. S. market in 1996 with a combination "First Issue 1996" and the "125th Anniversary Goebel" backstamp. It has an incised 1988 copyright date and the (TM 7) trademark. The original issue price was $155 in 1996.

☐ 435 . . . . . 6″ . . . . . . . . . . . (CE). . . ❻ . . . $2,000–3,000 (Early Sample)
☐ 435 3/0. . . 3⅞″. . . . . . . . . . (CE). . . ❼ . . . $165–170
☐ 435 3/0. . . 3⅞″. . . . . . . . . . (OE). . . ❽ . . . $165

### HUM 436
### An Emergency (PFE)
This figurine was first modeled by master sculptor Gerhard Skrobek in 1981. It has an incised 1983 copyright date. Presently listed on factory records as a Possible Future Edition (PFE) and may be released at some future date, subject to possible minor changes.

☐ 436 . . . . . 5½″. . . . . . . . . . (PFE). . . . . . .

### HUM 437
### Tuba Player
First released in the U.S. market in 1989. This figurine was modeled by master sculptor Gerhard Skrobek in 1982. It has an incised 1983 copyright date. The original issue price was $160 in 1989.

☐ 437 . . . . . 6¼" . . . . . . . . . (CE) . . . ❻ . . . $330–340
☐ 437 . . . . . 6¼" . . . . . . . . . (CE) . . . ❼ . . . $320–330
☐ 437 . . . . . 6¼" . . . . . . . . . (OE) . . . ❽ . . . $320

### HUM 438
### Sounds of the Mandolin
First released in the U.S. market in 1988. This figurine was modeled by master sculptor Gerhard Skrobek in 1982. It has an incised 1984 copyright date. It was originally called "Mandolin Serenade" but later changed to "Sounds of the Mandolin" at time of release. The original issue price was $65 in 1988.

☐ 438 . . . . . 3¾" . . . . . . . . . (CE) . . . ❻ . . . $155–160
☐ 438 . . . . . 3¾" . . . . . . . . . (CE) . . . ❼ . . . $150–155
☐ 438 . . . . . 3¾" . . . . . . . . . (OE) . . . ❽ . . . $150

### HUM 439
### A Gentle Glow, Candleholder
First released in the U.S. market in 1987. Modeled by master sculptor Gerhard Skrobek in 1982. The figurine has an incised 1983 copyright date on the bottom of the base and is found only in the current (TM 6) trademark. The original issue price was $110 in the U.S. and $160 in Canada. Listed as (TW) "Temporarily Withdrawn" in January 1999, but may be reinstated at some future date.

☐ 439 . . . . . 5¼ to 5½" . . . . . (CE). . . ❻ . . . $240–250
☐ 439 . . . . . 5¼ to 5½" . . . . . (TW) . . ❼ . . . $230–240

### HUM 440
### Birthday Candle, Candleholder (CE)
This figurine was first introduced in 1986 for members of the Goebel Collectors' Club only and not sold as an Open Edition. Originally modeled by master sculptor Gerhard Skrobek from an original drawing by Sister M.I. Hummel. It has an incised 1983 copyright date along with the current (TM 6) trademark. Also bears the inscription "EXCLUSIVE SPECIAL EDITION No. 10 FOR MEMBERS OF THE GOEBEL COLLECTORS' CLUB" applied by blue decal. Also a circular "CELE-BRATING 10 YEARS OF THE GOEBEL COLLECTORS' CLUB." The original issue price was $95 in the U.S. and $140 in Canada, in addition to the member's redemption card. "Birthday Candle" can now be purchased on the secondary market at premium prices.

☐ 440 . . . . . 5½" . . . . . . . . . . (CE). . . ❻ . . . $350–400

**HUM 441**
**Call To Worship, Clock (CE)**
First released in the U.S. market in 1988. This figurine, an actual working clock, battery operated, with chimes. It was modeled by master sculptor Gerhard Skrobek in 1982. This is the third figurine in the Century Collection and was produced for only this one year in the twentieth century. It has an incised 1983 copyright date. A circular inscription applied by blue decal reads: "M.I. HUMMEL CENTURY COLLECTION 1988 XX" and the current (TM 6) trademark. The issue price was $600 in 1988.

☐ 441 . . . . . 13″ . . . . . . . . . (CE) . . . ❻ . . . $1,400–1,500

**HUM 442**
**Chapel Time, Clock (CE)**
This figurine, an actual working clock, was first modeled by master sculptor Gerhard Skrobek in 1982. It has an incised 1983 copyright date. Released in 1986, it was produced for one year only as a limited edition and will be not produced again in the twentieth century. Hand lettered XX to signify the twentieth century. The suggested retail price was $500 in the U.S. and $650 in Canada. Several variations are noted: Early production of "Chapel Time" had a closed bell tower with only painted windows. In later production, the bell tower windows were opened to allow air to escape more easily during the firing process. A third variation is in the small round window directly beneath the bell tower but above the clock. Slight variations have been noted in the base construction and color variations on the face of the clock. The clock is battery operated, using one "C" cell battery and keeps accurate time.

☐ 442 . . . . . . 11½″ . . . . . (CE) . . . ❻ . . . . $1,750–2,000 (Open windows/closed hole)
☐ 442 . . . . . . 11½″ . . . . . (CE) . . . ❻ . . . . $2,000–2,500 (Painted windows variation)
☐ 442 . . . . . 11½″ . . . . . . (CE) . . . ❻ . . . $2,500–3,000 (Open windows/open hole)

*(Factory Sample)*                              *Rear view*

## HUM 443
### Country Song, Clock (PFE)
This figurine, an actual working clock, was first modeled by master sculptor Gerhard Skrobek in 1982. It has an incised 1983 copyright date. Presently listed on factory records as a Possible Future Edition (PFE) and may be released at some future date, subject to possible minor changes.

☐ 443 . . . . . 8″ . . . . . . . . . . . (PFE). . . . . . .

## HUM 444 — (PFE) Still under development
## HUM 445 — (PFE) Still under development

## HUM 446
### A Personal Message (PFE)
This figurine was first modeled by master sculptor Gerhard Skrobek in 1983. Presently listed on factory records as a Possible Future Edition (PFE) and may be released at some future date, subject to possible minor changes.

☐ 446 . . . . . 3¾″ . . . . . . . . . . (PFE). . . . . . .

327

### HUM 447
### Morning Concert (CE)

This figurine was first introduced in 1987 for members of the Goebel Collectors' Club only and not sold as an Open Edition. Originally modeled by master sculptor Gerhard Skrobek from an original drawing by Sister M. I. Hummel. It has an incised 1984 copyright date along with the current (TM6) trademark. Also bears the inscription: "EXCLUSIVE SPECIAL EDITION No. 11 FOR MEMBERS OF THE GOEBEL COLLECTORS' CLUB" applied by blue decal. The original issue price was $98 in the U. S., in addition to the member's redemption card. "Morning Concert" can now be purchased on the secondary market at premium prices.

☐ 447 . . . . . 5¼" . . . . . . . . . (CE) . . . ❻ . . . $250–300

**HUM: 448 Rear view**

**HUM 448 Side view**

328

*(Factory Sample)*

**HUM 448**
**Children's Prayer (PFE)**
This beautiful figurine was modeled by master sculptor Gerhard Skrobek in 1983. It has an incised 1984 copyright date. Presently listed on factory records as a Possible Future Edition (PFE) and may be released at some future date, subject to possible minor changes.

☐ 448 . . . . . 8¼" . . . . . . (PFE). . . . . . . .

**HUM 449**
**The Little Pair (EE)**
This figurine was first modeled by master sculptor Gerhard Skrobek in 1984. It has an incised 1985 copyright date. Announced in 1990, "The Little Pair" will be an EXCLUSIVE EDITION available to "M.I. Hummel Club" members only, who have belonged to the Club continuously for 10 years. Issued by means of a redemption card to those who are eligible. The original issue price was $170. Scheduled to retire on 31 May 2000.

☐ 449 . . . . . 5 to 5¼" . . . . . . (CE). . . ❻ . . . $350–400
☐ 449 . . . . . 5 to 5¼" . . . . . . (CE). . . ❼ . . . $220–225
☐ 449 . . . . . 5 to 5¼" . . . . . . (EE). . . ❽ . . . $225
(M.I.H. Club Members Only)

*450/0*

**HUM 450**
**Will It Sting? (EE)**
Members' Exclusive Edition (EE) for Club year 24. This figurine was first released in 2000 for members of the M.I. Hummel Club only and <u>not</u> sold as an (OE) "Open Edition" to the general public. First modeled by master sculptor Gerhard Skrobek in 1984. Size 450/0 was modeled by master sculptor Helmut Fischer in 1990. It has an incised 1990 copyright date along with the (TM 8) trademark. Also bears the inscription: "EXCLUSIVE EDITION 2000/01 M.I. HUMMEL CLUB" applied by blue decal. A large black flying bumblebee is located on the bottom. The official issue price was $260 in 2000, in addition to the members' redemption card.

☐ 450 . . . . . 5¾" . . . . . . . . . . (CE). . . ❻ . . . $2000–3000 (Early Sample)
☐ 450/0 . . . . 5" . . . . . . . . . . . (EE). . . ❽ . . . $260
(M.I.H. Club Members Only)

**HUM 451**
**Just Dozing**
First released in the U. S. market in 1995. Modeled by master sculptor Gerhard Skrobek in 1984. It has an incised 1984 copyright date along with (TM7) trademark. Also bears the "First Issue 1995" oval decal on the bottom. The official issue price was $220 in 1995.

☐ 451 . . . . . 4¼″ . . . . . . . . . (CE) . . . ❼ . . . $250–255
☐ 451 . . . . . 4¼″ . . . . . . . . . (OE) . . . ❽ . . . $250

**HUM 452**
**Flying High (CE)**
First released in the U. S. market in 1988 as a hanging ornament. Modeled by master sculptor Gerhard Skrobek in 1984. It has an incised 1984 copyright date. The original issue price was $75 in 1988. Early releases were not dated. Later pieces dated 1988 with "First Edition" decal. Third variation was dated but without "First Edition" decal. Undated pieces bring a premium.

☐ 452 . . . . . 4½ × 2¾″ . . . . . (CE) . . . ❻ . . . $250–300 (undated)
☐ 452 . . . . . 4½ × 2¾″ . . . . . (CE) . . . ❻ . . . $175–200 (dated with "First Edition")
☐ 452 . . . . . . 4½ × 2¾″ . . . . . . (CE) . . . ❻ . . . . $175–200 (dated without "First Edition")

331

**HUM 453**
**Accompanist, The**
First released in the U. S. market in 1988. Modeled by master sculptor Gerhard Skrobek in 1984. It has an incised 1984 copyright date. The original issue price was $39 in 1988.

☐ 453 . . . . . 3¼" . . . . . . . . . . (CE). . . ❻ . . . $120–125
☐ 453 . . . . . 3¼" . . . . . . . . . . (CE). . . ❼ . . . $124–125
☐ 453 . . . . . 3¼" . . . . . . . . . . (**OE**). . . ❽ . . . $124

**HUM 454**
**Song Of Praise**
First released in the U. S. market in 1988. Modeled by master sculptor Gerhard Skrobek in 1984. It has an incised 1984 copyright date. The original issue price was $39 in 1988.

☐ 454 . . . . . 3" . . . . . . . . . . . (CE). . . ❻ . . . $125–130
☐ 454 . . . . . 3" . . . . . . . . . . . (CE). . . ❼ . . . $124–125
☐ 454 . . . . . 3" . . . . . . . . . . . (**OE**). . . ❽ . . . $124

## HUM 455
### Guardian, The

First released in the U. S. market in 1991. Modeled by master sculptor Gerhard Skrobek in 1984. It has an incised 1985 copyright date. The original issue price was $140. It has been noted that there are two different base constructions on this figurine. Also produced without the bird as part of the "Personal Touch Personalization" program. This figurine, minus the bird, can be personalized with a name or date by a Goebel artist for a $20 fee.

☐ 455 . . . . . 2¾ × 3½″ . . . . . (CE). . . ❻ . . . $190–200
☐ 455 . . . . . 2¾ × 3½″ . . . . . (CE). . . ❼ . . . $190–195
☐ 455 . . . . . 2¾ × 3½″ . . . . . (OE). . . ❽ . . . $190

## HUM 456
### Sleep, Little One, Sleep (PFE)

This figurine was first modeled by master sculptor Gerhard Skrobek in 1984. Presently listed on factory records as a Possible Future Edition (PFE) and may be released at some future date, subject to possible minor changes.

☐ 456 . . . . . 4¼″ . . . . . . . . . (PFE) . . . . . . .

**HUM 457**
**Sound The Trumpet**
First released in the U. S. market in 1988. Modeled by master sculptor Gerhard Skrobek in 1984. It has an incised 1984 copyright date. The original issue price was $45 in 1988.

☐ 457 . . . . . 3″ . . . . . . . . . . . (CE). . . **❻** . . . $130–135
☐ 457 . . . . . 3″ . . . . . . . . . . . (CE). . . **❼** . . . $128–130
☐ 457 . . . . . 3″ . . . . . . . . . . . (**OE**). . . **❽** . . . $128

**HUM 458**
**Storybook Time**
First released in the U.S. market in the fall of 1991. Modeled by master sculptor Gerhard Skrobek in 1984. It has an incised 1985 copyright date. The original issue price was $330.

☐ 458 . . . . . 5¼″ . . . . . . . . . . (CE). . . **❼** . . . $460–470
☐ 458 . . . . . 5¼″ . . . . . . . . . . (**OE**). . . **❽** . . . $460

**HUM 459**
**In The Meadow**
First released in the U. S. market in 1987. Modeled by master sculptor Gerhard Skrobek in 1984. The figurine has an incised 1985 copyright date. The original issue price was $110 in the U. S. and $160 in Canada.

☐ 459 . . . . . 4″ . . . . . . . . . . . (CE) . . . ❻ . . . $240–245
☐ 459 . . . . . 4″ . . . . . . . . . . . (CE) . . . ❼ . . . $235–240
☐ 459 . . . . . 4″ . . . . . . . . . . . (**OE**) . . . ❽ . . . $235

**HUM 460**
**Goebel Authorized Retailer Plaque**
This authorized retailer plaque was issued to all authorized "M. I. Hummel" retailers in 1986 and became the official identification for distributors of Hummel figurines. It replaced the older HUM 187 dealers plaque with "Merry Wanderer" that has been in use, with many variations, since the late 1940's. You will notice the boy is similar to the middle boy on HUM 170 "School Boys." The new plaque has an incised "M. I. Hummel" signature on the back as well as the decal signature on the front. It has an incised 1984 copyright date along with the current (TM6) trademark on the bottom. It is also known as "The Tally." This plaque was issued in nine decal variations for use in other countries (languages). Only the U.S. version was discontinued in December 1989, to be replaced by HUM 187A with new graphics. (See HUM 187)

☐ 460 . . . 5 × 6″ U.S. VERSION. (CE) . . ❻ . . $200–225
☐ 460 . . . 5 × 6″ BRITISH . . . . . (CE) . . ❻ . . $500–750   (**OE**) . . ❼ . . $300–500
☐ 460 . . . 5 × 6″ GERMAN . . . . (CE) . . ❻ . . $750–1000   (**OE**) . . ❼ . . $300–500
☐ 460 . . . 5 × 6″ DUTCH . . . . . (CE) . . ❻ . . $900–1500   (**OE**) . . ❼ . . $300–500
☐ 460 . . . 5 × 6″ ITALIAN . . . . . (CE) . . ❻ . . $900–1500   (**OE**) . . ❼ . . $300–500
☐ 460 . . . 5 × 6″ FRENCH . . . . . (CE) . . ❻ . . $750–1000   (**OE**) . . ❼ . . $300–500
☐ 460 . . . 5 × 6″ SWEDISH . . . . (CE) . . ❻ . . $750–1000   (**OE**) . . ❼ . . $300–500
☐ 460 . . . 5 × 6″ SPANISH . . . . (CE) . . ❻ . . $900–1500   (**OE**) . . ❼ . . $300–500
☐ 460 . . . 5 × 6″ JAPANESE . . . (Issued in 1996) . . . . . . . (**OE**) . . ❼ . . $500–750

☐ UNITED STATES

☐ BRITISH

☐ GERMAN

☐ DUTCH

☐ ITALIAN

☐ FRENCH

☐ SWEDISH

☐ SPANISH

☐ JAPANESE

HUM 460 AS SERVICE AWARD

336

**HUM 461**
**In The Orchard (PFE)**
This figurine was first modeled by master sculptor Gerhard Skrobek in 1984. Presently listed on factory records as a Possible Future Edition (PFE) and may be released at some future date, subject to possible minor changes. See HUM 727 "Garden Treasures" for smaller variation of this figurine.

☐ 461 . . . . . 5½" . . . . . . . . . (PFE). . . . . . .

*(Factory Sample)*

**HUM 462**
**Tit For Tat (PFE)**
This figurine was first modeled by master sculptor Gerhard Skrobek in 1984. Presently listed on factory records as a Possible Future Edition (PFE) and may be released at some future date, subject to possible minor changes.

☐ 462 . . . . . 3¾" . . . . . . . . . (PFE). . . . . . .

**Early sample (TM 6)**          **(TM 7)**

## HUM 463
### My Wish Is Small (CE)

Members' Exclusive Edition for Club Year 16. This figurine was first introduced in 1992 for members of the M.I. HUMMEL CLUB only and not sold as an open edition. Modeled by master sculptor Gerhard Skrobek in 1985. It has an incised 1985 copyright date along with the (TM7) trademark. Also bears the inscription: "EXCLUSIVE EDITION 1992/93 M.I. HUMMEL CLUB" applied by blue decal. A large black flying bumble bee is located on the bottom. The original issue price was $170 in the U.S., in addition to the member's redemption card. Note: The Early Sample model has a square base, while the normal production figuring has a round base.

☐ 463 . . . . . 5½" . . . . . . . . . . (CE) . . . ❻ . . . $2000–2500 (Early Sample)
☐ 463/0 . . . . 5½ to 5¾" . . . . . (CE) . . . ❼ . . . $250–300

## HUM 464
### Young Scholar (PFE)

This figurine was first modeled by master sculptor Gerhard Skrobek in 1985. Presently listed on factory records as a Possible Future Edition (PFE) and may be released at some future date, subject to possible minor changes.

☐ 464 . . . . . 5⅛" . . . . . . . . . . (PFE) . . . . . . .

338

## HUM 465
### Where Shall I Go? (PFE)
This figurine was first modeled by master sculptor Gerhard Skrobek in 1985 and has an incised 1985 copyright date. It is based on a portrait sketched by Sister Hummel in 1938. His name was Jochen Edinger, just recently deceased after a short illness. This figurine is presently listed on factory records as a Possible Future Edition (PFE) and may be released at some future date, subject to possible changes. The original drawing and this Early Sample model are owned by Mr. & Mrs. Robert L. Miller.

☐ 465 . . . . . 4¼" . . . . . . . . . . (CE) . . . ❻ . . . $4,000–5,000 (Early Sample)
☐ 465 . . . . . 4¼" . . . . . . . . . . (PFE) . . . . . . .

## HUM 466
### DoReMi (PFE)
This figurine was first modeled by master sculptor Gerhard Shrobek in 1985. Presently listed on factory records as a Possible Future Edition (PFE) and may be released at some future date, subject to possible minor changes.

☐ 466 . . . . . 5½" . . . . . . . . . . (PFE) . . . . . . .

**HUM 467**
**Kindergartner, The**
First released in the U. S. market in 1987.
Modeled by master sculptor Gerhard
Skrobek in 1985. The figurine has an
incised 1985 copyright date. The original
issue price was $100 in 1987.

☐ 467 . . . . . 5¼″. . . . . . . . . . (CE). . . ❻ . . . $240–245
☐ 467 . . . . . 5¼″. . . . . . . . . . (CE). . . ❼ . . . $235–240
☐ 467 . . . . . 5¼″. . . . . . . . . . **(OE)**. . . ❽ . . . $235

**HUM 468**
**Come On (PFE)**
This figurine was first modeled by mas-
ter sculptor Gerhard Skrobek in 1986.
Presently listed on factory records as a
Possible Future Edition (PFE) and may be
released at some future date, subject to
possible minor changes.

☐ 468 . . . . . 5¼″. . . . . . . . . . (PFE). . . . . . .

**HUM 469**
**Starting Young (PFE)**
This figurine was first modeled by master sculptor Gerhard Skrobek in 1986. Presently listed on factory records as a Possible Future Edition (PFE) and may be released at some future date, subject to possible minor changes.

☐ 469 . . . . . 4¾" . . . . . . . . . . (PFE) . . . . . . .

**HUM 470**
**Time Out (PFE)**
This figurine was first modeled by master sculptor Gerhard Skrobek in 1986. Presently listed on factory records as a Possible Future Edition (PFE) and may be released at some future date, subject to possible minor changes.

☐ 470 . . . . . 4½" . . . . . . . . . . (PFE) . . . . . . .

**HUM 471**
**Harmony In Four Parts (CE)**
This figurine was first released in the U.S. market in 1989 along with seven other new figurines. This is the fourth figurine in the Century Collection and was produced for only this one year in the twentieth century. It was modeled by master sculptor Gerhard Skrobek in 1986. It has an incised 1987 copyright date. A circular inscription applied by blue decal reads: "M.I. HUMMEL CENTURY COLLECTION 1989 XX" and the name "HARMONY IN FOUR PARTS" along with the (TM6) trademark. The issue price was $850 in 1989.

☐ 471 . . . . . 9¾" . . . . . . . . . . (CE). . . ❻ . . . $2,000–2,500

────────── **HUM TERM** ──────────

**COPYRIGHT DATE:** This is the date that is often times incised into the bottom of an M.I. Hummel figurine. This date represents the year in which the figurine design was registered with the United States copyright office. Many M.I. Hummel figurines are registered and then do not go into general production for several years after the initial copyright is registered. The incised date is NOT the date that the figurine was necessarily produced or painted.

## HUM 472
### On Our Way (CE)
This figurine was first released in the U.S. market in 1992 along with five other new figurines. This is the seventh figurine in the Century Collection and will be produced for this one year only in the twentieth century. It was modeled by master sculptor Gerhard Skrobek in 1986 but has an incised 1987 copyright date. A circular inscription applied by blue decal reads: "M.I. HUMMEL CENTURY COLLECTION 1992 XX" and the name "ON OUR WAY" along with the current (TM 7) trademark. The issue price was $950 in 1992.

☐ 472 . . . . . 8 to 8¼″ . . . . . . (CE). . . ❻ . . . $2,000–3,000 (Early Sample)
☐ 472 . . . . . 8 to 8¼″ . . . . . . (CE). . . ❼ . . . $1,200–1,500

## HUM 473
### Reprecht (Knecht Ruprecht) (LE)
This figurine was first modeled by master sculptor Gerhard Skrobek in 1986 under the name of "Father Christmas." It has an incised 1987 copyright date. Released in the spring of 1997 in a (LE) Limited Edition of 20,000 sequentially-numbered pieces. A companion figurine of "St. Nicholas' Day," (HUM 2012) was released at the same time with matching edition numbers at a specially-reduced price of $1,000 (per set) for members of the "M.I. Hummel Club."

*(St. Nicholas' Day)*

☐ 473 . . . . . 6″ . . . . . . . . . . . (CE). . . ❻ . . . $2,000–3,000 (Early Sample)
☐ 473 . . . . . 6 to 6¼″ . . . . . . (LE). . . ❼ . . . $460

343

### HUM 474
### Gentle Care (PFE)
This figurine was first modeled by master sculptor Gerhard Skrobek in 1986. Presently listed on factory records as a Possible Future Edition (PFE) and may be released at some future date, subject to possible minor changes.

☐ 474 . . . . . 6″ . . . . . . . . . . . (PFE) . . . . . . .

### HUM 475
### Make A Wish
First released in the U.S. market in 1989. This figurine was modeled by master sculptor Gerhard Skrobek in 1986. It has an incised 1987 copyright date. Original issue price was $135 in 1989. This figurine was (TW) "Temporarily Withdrawn" from the U.S. market only at the end of 1997. Once again listed as (TW) "Temporarily Withdrawn" in January 1999, but may be reinstated at some future date.

☐ 475 . . . . . 4½″ . . . . . . . . . . (CE) . . . **❻** . . . $240–250
☐ 475 . . . . . 4½″ . . . . . . . . . . (TW) . . **❼** . . . $225–230

**HUM 476**
**A Winter Song**
First released in the U.S. market in 1988. Modeled by master sculptor Gerhard Skrobek in 1987. It has an incised 1987 copyright date. The original issue price was $45 in 1988.

☐ 476 . . . . . 4″ . . . . . . . . . . . . (CE). . . ❻ . . . $140–145
☐ 476 . . . . . 4″ . . . . . . . . . . . . (CE). . . ❼ . . . $135–140
☐ 476 . . . . . 4″ . . . . . . . . . . . . **(OE)**. . . ❽ . . . $135

**HUM 477**
**A Budding Maestro**
First released in the U.S. market in 1988. Modeled by master sculptor Gerhard Skrobek in 1987. It has an incised 1987 copyright date. The original issue price was $45 in 1988. This figurine was (TW) "Temporarily Withdrawn" from the U.S. market only at the end of 1997. Once again listed as (TW) "Temporarily Withdrawn" in January 1999, but may be reinstated at some future date.

☐ 477 . . . . . 4″ . . . . . . . . . . . . (CE). . . ❻ . . . $130–135
☐ 477 . . . . . 4″ . . . . . . . . . . . . (TW) . . ❼ . . . $120–125

### HUM 478
### I'm Here
First released in the U.S. market in 1989. Modeled by master sculptor Gerhard Skrobek in 1987. It has an incised 1987 copyright date. The original issue price was $50 in 1989.

☐ 478 . . . . . 3″ . . . . . . . . . . . . (CE). . . ❻ . . . $135–140
☐ 478 . . . . . 3″ . . . . . . . . . . . . (CE). . . ❼ . . . $130–135
☐ 478 . . . . . 3″ . . . . . . . . . . . . (**OE**). . . ❽ . . . $130

*(TM 7)*          *(TM 6)*

### HUM 479
### I Brought You A Gift (CE)
First released in the U.S. market in 1989 as a *free* gift for joining the M.I. HUMMEL CLUB (formerly Goebel Collectors' Club). Modeled by master sculptor Gerhard Skrobek in 1987. It has an incised 1987 copyright date. Early models have a special blue decal: "Goebel Collectors' Club" in addition to a black flying bumble bee, in a half circle. Later models have: "M.I. Hummel Club". Some examples have eye lashes, some do not. This figurine can now be purchased on the secondary market at premium prices. This figurine was permanently retired on 31 May 1996.

☐ 479 . . . . . 4″ . . . . . . . . . . . . (CE). . . ❻ . . . $150–175
☐ 479 . . . . . 4″ . . . . . . . . . . . . (CE). . . ❼ . . . $125–150

**HUM 480**
**Hosanna**
First released in the U.S. market in 1989. Modeled by master sculptor Gerhard Skrobek in 1987. It has an incised 1987 copyright date. The original issue price was $68 in 1989.

☐ 480 . . . . . 4" . . . . . . . . . . (CE). . . ❻ . . . $130–135
☐ 480 . . . . . 4" . . . . . . . . . . (CE). . . ❼ . . . $128–130
☐ 480 . . . . . 4" . . . . . . . . . . (**OE**). . . ❽ . . . $128

**HUM 481**
**Love From Above (CE)**
First released in the U.S. market in 1989, the second in the annual series of ornaments. Modeled by master sculptor Gerhard Skrobek in 1987. It has an incised 1987 copyright date. The original issue price was $75 in 1989.

☐ 481 . . . . . 3¼" . . . . . . . . . (CE). . . ❻ . . . $125–150

### HUM 482
### One For You, One For Me
First released in the U.S. market in 1989. Modeled by master sculptor Gerhard Skrobek in 1987. It has an incised 1987 copyright date. The original issue price was $50 in 1989. In 1996 a 2¼" size (2¾" with base) with model number 482 5/0 was produced as part of the "Pen Pals" series of personalized name card table decorations. The original issue price was $55.

| | | | | |
|---|---|---|---|---|
| ☐ 482 5/0 | 2¾" | (OE) | ❼ | $55 |
| ☐ 482 | 3" | (CE) | ❻ | $130–135 |
| ☐ 482 | 3" | (CE) | ❼ | $128–130 |
| ☐ 482 | 3" | (OE) | ❽ | $128 |

### HUM 483
### I'll Protect Him
First released in the U.S. market in 1989. Modeled by master sculptor Gerhard Skrobek in 1987. It has an incised 1987 copyright date. The original issue price was $55 in 1989.

| | | | | |
|---|---|---|---|---|
| ☐ 483 | 3¾" | (CE) | ❻ | $105–110 |
| ☐ 483 | 3¾" | (CE) | ❼ | $100–105 |
| ☐ 483 | 3¾" | (OE) | ❽ | $100 |

**HUM 484**
**Peace On Earth (CE)**
First released in the U.S. market in 1990,
the third in the Annual Series of Ornaments. Modeled by master sculptor Gerhard Skrobek in 1987. It has an incised
1987 copyright date. The original issue
price was $80.

☐ 484 . . . . . 3¼" . . . . . . . . . . (CE). . . ❻ . . . $125–150

**HUM 485**
**Gift From A Friend (CE)**
This figurine was first introduced in 1991
for members of the M.I. Hummel Club
only and not sold as an open edition.
Modeled by master sculptor Gerhard
Skrobek in 1988. It has an incised 1988
copyright date. Also bears the inscription:
"EXCLUSIVE EDITION 1991/92 M.I.
HUMMEL CLUB" applied by blue decal. A
large black flying bumble bee is located
on the bottom. The official issue price was
$160 in 1991, in addition to the member's
redemption card. Can now be purchased
on the secondary market at premium
prices.

☐ 485 . . . . . 5" . . . . . . . . . . . (CE). . . ❻ . . . $300–350
☐ 485 . . . . . 5" . . . . . . . . . . . (CE). . . ❼ . . . $250–300

---

**━━━━━━ HUM TERM ━━━━━━**

**OPEN EDITION:** Pieces currently in W.
Goebel's production program.

## HUM 486
### I Wonder (CE)

This figurine was first introduced in 1990 for members of the M.I. Hummel Club only and not sold as an open edition. Modeled by master sculptor Helmut Fischer in 1988. It has an incised 1988 copyright date. Also bears the inscription: "EXCLUSIVE EDITION 1990/91 M.I. HUMMEL CLUB" applied by blue decal. A large black flying bumble bee is located on the bottom. The official issue price was $140 in the U.S., in addition to the member's redemption card. Can now be purchased on the secondary market at premium prices.

☐ 486 . . . . . 5¼" . . . . . . . . . (CE). . . ❻ . . . $300–350
☐ 486 . . . . . 5¼" . . . . . . . . . (CE). . . ❼ . . . $250–300

## HUM 487
### Let's Tell The World (CE)

This figurine was first released in the U.S. market in 1990. This is the fifth figurine in the Century Collection and will be produced for only this one year in the twentieth century. It was modeled by master sculptor Gerhard Skrobek in 1987. It has an incised 1988 copyright date. A circular inscription applied by blue decal reads: "M.I. HUMMEL CENTURY COLLECTION 1990 XX" and "1935-1990-55 Years of M.I. Hummel Figurines" in a straight line through the circle, along with the (TM 6) trademark. The official issue price was $875 in 1990.

☐ 487 . . . . . 10½ × 7" . . . . . . (CE). . . ❻ . . . $1,500–1,800

## HUM 488
### What's That? (PE)
Members' Exclusive *Preview* Edition for Club year 21. This figurine was first introduced in 1997 for members of the M. I. Hummel Club only and not sold as an open edition. Modeled by master sculptor Helmut Fischer in 1988. It has an incised 1988 copyright date along with (TM 7) trademark. Also bears the inscription: "EXCLUSIVE EDITION 1997/98 M. I. HUMMEL CLUB" applied by blue decal. A large black flying bumble bee is located on the bottom. The original issue price was $150 in 1997, in addition to the member's redemption card. Designed as a companion piece to HUM 555 "One, Two, Three." Goebel reserves the right to reintroduce this figurine as an open edition, minus the special backstamp.

☐ 488 . . . . . 4" . . . . . . . . . . . (PE) . . . ❼ . . . $150

## HUM 489
### Pretty Please
First released in the U. S. market in 1996. Modeled by master sculptor Helmut Fischer in 1988 It has an incised 1988 copyright date along with (TM 7) trademark. Also bears the "First Issue 1996" and "Goebel 125th Anniversary" backstamp. Designed as a companion piece to HUM 535 "No Thank You" as part of the "Cozy Companions" series. "Pretty Please" is similar to girl from HUM 47 "Goose Girl." The official issue price was $120 in 1996.

☐ 489 . . . . . 3½" . . . . . . . . . . (CE) . . . ❼ . . . $128–130
☐ 489 . . . . . 3½" . . . . . . . . . . (OE) . . . ❽ . . . $128

### HUM 490
### Carefree
First released in the U.S. market in the fall of 1996. Modeled by master sculptor Helmut Fischer in 1988. It has an incised 1988 copyright date along with (TM 7) trademark. Also bears the "First Issue 1997" oval decal on the bottom. Designed as a companion piece to HUM 564 "Free Spirit" as part of the "Cozy Companions" series. The official price was $120 in 1996.

☐ 490 . . . . . 3½" . . . . . . . . . . . (CE). . . **❼** . . . $128–130
☐ 490 . . . . . 3½" . . . . . . . . . . . (**OE**). . . **❽** . . . $128

### HUM 491–492   (PFE) STILL UNDER DEVELOPMENT

### HUM 493
### Two Hands, One Treat (CE)
First released in the U.S. market in 1991 as a *free* gift for renewing membership in the M.I. HUMMEL CLUB for the 1991/92 Club year. Modeled by master sculptor Helmut Fischer in 1988. It has an incised 1988 copyright date, in addition to a special blue decal: "M.I. HUMMEL CLUB" along with a black flying bumble bee, in a half circle. Can now be purchased on the secondary market at premium prices.

☐ 493 . . . . . 4" . . . . . . . . . . . (CE). . . **❼** . . . $125–150

## HUM 494 (PFE) STILL UNDER DEVELOPMENT

**HUM 495**
**Evening Prayer**
First released in the U.S. market in the fall of 1991. Modeled by master sculptor Helmut Fischer in 1988. It has an incised 1988 copyright date. The original issue price was $95 in 1991. Similar to girl on HUM 67 "Doll Mother," but with different colors.

☐ 495 . . . . . 3¾". . . . . . . . . . (CE). . . ❼ . . . $128–130
☐ 495 . . . . . 3¾". . . . . . . . . . (OE). . . ❽ . . . $128

## HUM 496–497 (PFE) STILL UNDER DEVELOPMENT

**HUM 498**
**All Smiles (LE)**
First released in the U.S. market in the spring of 1997. Modeled by master sculptor Helmut Fischer in 1988. It has an incised 1988 copyright date. Released as a Limited Edition (LE) of 25,000 sequentially-numbered pieces. (Only 15,000 will be released in the U.S.) Similar to girl from HUM 196 "Telling Her Secret" but with a longer dress and no pigtails. Original issue price was $175 in 1997.

☐ 498 . . . . . 4". . . . . . . . . . . (LE). . . ❼ . . . $175–200

353

**HUM 499   (PFE) STILL UNDER DEVELOPMENT**

**HUM 500**
This number was assigned to a Mother's Day plate that was never issued.

**HUM 501–508   DOLL HEADS**

**HUM 509   DOLL PARTS (arms & legs)**
**HUM 510   Carnival Doll**
**HUM 511   DOLL PARTS (arms & legs)**
**DANBURY MINT DOLLS**
The following numbers were assigned to dolls produced for Danbury Mint starting in 1988.

**HUM 512   Umbrella Girl Doll**
**HUM 513   Little Fiddler Doll**
**HUM 514   Friend or Foe Doll**
**HUM 515   Kiss Me Doll**
**HUM 516   Merry Wanderer Doll**
**HUM 517   Goose Girl Doll**
**HUM 518   Umbrella Boy Doll**
**HUM 519   Ride Into Christmas Doll**
**HUM 520   (ON) STILL UNDER DEVELOPMENT**
**HUM 521   School Girl Doll (By Goebel Retailers)**
**HUM 522   Little Scholar Doll (By Goebel Retailers)**
**HUM 523   (ON) STILL UNDER DEVELOPMENT**
**HUM 524   Valentine Gift Doll**
**HUM 525–529   (ON) STILL UNDER DEVELOPMENT**

**HUM 530**
**Land in Sight (CE)**
First released in the U.S. market in the fall of 1991. Modeled by master sculptor Gerhard Skrobek in 1988. Issued as a limited production of 30,000 pieces, individually numbered, to commemorate the 500th anniversary of Columbus's discovery of America. The inscription reads: "1492-1992—The Quincentennial of America's Discovery" applied by blue decal. It has an incised 1988 copyright date. The "M.I. Hummel" signature is located on the back side of the boat. The original issue price was $1600.

☐ 530 . . . . . 9 × 9½″ . . . . . . (CE). . . ❼ . . . $1,800–2,250

### HUM 533
### Ooh, My Tooth
First released in the U.S. market in 1995. Modeled by master sculptor Gerhard Skrobek in 1988. It has an incised 1988 copyright date along with the (TM7) trademark. Also bears the "First Issue 1995" oval decal and "SPECIAL EVENT" backstamp. This figurine will be available at District Manager Promotions and in-store events, but may be re-introduced as part of the regular line, but minus the special backstamp. The original issue price was $110.

☐ 533 . . . . . 3″ . . . . . . . . . . . (CE). . . ❼ . . . $135–140
☐ 533 . . . . . 3″ . . . . . . . . . . . (**OE**). . . ❽ . . . $135

### HUM 534
### A Nap
First released in the U.S. market in 1991. Modeled by master sculptor Gerhard Skrobek in 1988. It has an incised 1988 copyright date. The original issue price was $95 in 1991.

☐ 534 . . . . . 2¼″ . . . . . . . . . . (CE). . . ❻ . . . $145–150
☐ 534 . . . . . 2¼″ . . . . . . . . . . (CE). . . ❼ . . . $140–145
☐ 534 . . . . . 2¼″ . . . . . . . . . . (**OE**). . . ❽ . . . $140

*(Backs are interesting, too!)*

**HUM 535**
**No Thank You**
First released in the U.S. market in 1996. Modeled by master sculptor Helmut Fischer in 1988. It has an incised 1988 copyright date along with (TM 7) trademark. Also bears the "First Issue 1996" and "Goebel 125th Anniversary" backstamp. Designed as a companion piece to HUM 489 "Pretty Please" as part of the "Cozy Companions" series. The official issue price was $120 in 1996.

☐ 535 . . . . . 3½" . . . . . . . . . . (CE). . . ❼ . . . $128–130
☐ 535 . . . . . 3½" . . . . . . . . . . (OE). . . ❽ . . . $128

**HUM 536**
**Christmas Surprise (CE)**
First released in the U.S. market in 1998. Modeled by master sculptor Helmut Fischer in 1988. It has an incised 1988 copyright date along with the (TM 7) trademark. Limited Edition of 15,000 pieces were sold exclusively on QVC starting at 12:00 AM EST on 19 November 1998 and sold out the complete edition in one day! Came with a HummelScape "Musikfest" display Collector's Set. This figurine was introduced and retired and mold-breaking ceremony was held all on the same day! The issue price was $139.50 (plus shipping) in 1998.

☐ 536 3/0. . . 4" . . . . . . . . . . . (CE). . . ❼ . . . $150–175

## HUM 538
### School's Out
First released in the U.S. market in 1997. Modeled by master sculptor Helmut Fischer in 1988. It has an incised 1988 copyright date along with (TM 7) trademark. Also bears the "First Issue 1997" oval decal on the bottom. The girl is similar to girl from HUM 329 (PFE) "Off to School." The official issue price was $170 in 1997.

☐ 538 . . . . . 4" . . . . . . . . . . . . (CE). . . ❼ . . . $180–185
☐ 538 . . . . . 4" . . . . . . . . . . . . (OE). . . ❽ . . . $180

## HUM 539
### Good News
First released in 1996 at the "M.I. Hummel Club" convention in Coburg, Germany for those members attending. First released in the U.S. market in 1997. Modeled by master sculptor Helmut Fischer in 1988 and has an incised 1988 copyright date. Part of the "Personal Touch" program; two initials or two numbers can be permanently applied by a Goebel artist for a personalization fee of $20. The original issue price was $180 in 1997.

☐ 539 . . . . . 4½" . . . . . . . . . . (CE). . . ❼ . . . $200–205
☐ 539 . . . . . 4½" . . . . . . . . . . (OE). . . ❽ . . . $200

## HUM 540
### Best Wishes

First released in 1996 at the "M.I. Hummel Club" convention in Coburg, Germany for those members attending. First released in the U.S. market in 1997. Modeled by master sculptor Helmut Fischer in 1988 and has an incised 1988 copyright date. Part of the "Personal Touch" program; two initials or two numbers can be permanently applied by a Goebel artist for a $20 personalization fee. Also used as a 1997 "SPECIAL EVENT" figurine with a flying bumble bee decal on one of the flowers. The original issue price was $180 in 1997.

| | | | | | |
|---|---|---|---|---|---|
| ☐ 540 | 4⅝" | (CE) | **7** | $190–195 |
| ☐ 540 | 4⅝" | (OE) | **8** | $190 |

## HUM 541
### Sweet As Can Be

Members' Exclusive *Preview* Edition for Club year 17. This figurine was first introduced in 1993 for members of the M.I. Hummel Club only and not sold as an open edition. Modeled by master sculptor Helmut Fischer in 1988. It had an incised 1988 copyright date along with the (TM 7) trademark. Also bears the inscription: "EXCLUSIVE EDITION 1993/94 M.I. HUMMEL CLUB" applied by blue decal. A large black flying bumble bee is located on the bottom. The official issue price was $125 in the U.S., in addition to the member's redemption card. Goebel reintroduced this figurine as an open edition in 1998 minus the special Club backstamp as part of a "Happy Birthday" HummelScape (Mark # 925-D) gift set at $160. Similar to one girl from HUM 176 "Happy Birthday."

| | | | | | |
|---|---|---|---|---|---|
| ☐ 541 | 4⅛" | (CE) | **7** | $125–135 |
| ☐ 541 | 4⅛" | (OE) | **8** | $135 |

**HUM 542 — (PFE) STILL UNDER DEVELOPMENT**

### HUM 543 (PFE)
### I'm Sorry
This figurine was first modeled by master sculptor Gerhard Skrobek in 1988. It has an incised 1988 copyright date. Presently listed on factory records as a (PFE) Possible Future Edition and may be released at some future date, subject to possible minor changes.

☐ 543 . . . . . 4⅛″ . . . . . . (PFE). . . . . . . . . . .

## HUM 544 — (PFE) STILL UNDER DEVELOPMENT

### HUM 545
### Come Back Soon
First released in the U.S. market in 1995. Modeled by master sculptor Helmut Fischer in 1989. Designed as a matching figurine for the 25th and final issue of the annual plate series. It has an incised 1989 copyright date and the "First Issue 1995" oval decal on the bottom. The official issue price was $135 in 1995.

☐ 545 . . . . . 4¼″ . . . . . . . . . . (CE). . . ❼ . . . $170–175
☐ 545 . . . . . 4¼″ . . . . . . . . . . (OE). . . ❽ . . . $170

**HUM 548**
**Flower Girl (EE)**
Announced in 1990, "Flower Girl" will be an EXCLUSIVE EDITION available to "M.I. Hummel Club" members only, who have belonged to the Club continuously for 5 years. Issued by means of a redemption card to those who are eligible. Modeled by master sculptor Helmut Fischer in 1989. It has an incised 1989 copyright date. The original issue price was $105. Now scheduled to retire on 31 May 2000.

☐ 548 . . . . . 4½" . . . . . . . . . . (CE) . . . ❻ . . . $150–200
☐ 548 . . . . . 4½" . . . . . . . . . . (CE) . . . ❼ . . . $145–150
☐ 548 . . . . . 4½" . . . . . . . . . . (EE) . . . ❽ . . . $145
(M.I.H. club members only)

**HUM 549**
**A Sweet Offering (CE)**
First released in the U.S. market in 1993 as a FREE gift for renewing membership in the M.I. HUMMEL CLUB for the 1993/94 Club year. Modeled by master sculptor Helmut Fischer in 1992. It has an incised 1992 copyright date. It bears the inscription: "M.I. HUMMEL CLUB Membership Year 1993/94" in addition to be black flying bumble bee, in a half circle. It is similar to the girl from HUM 52 "Going To Grandma's". Can be purchased on the secondary market at premium prices.

☐ 549 3/0 . . . 3½" . . . . . . . . . . (CE) . . . ❼ . . . $80–100

### HUM 553
### Scamp

First released in the U.S. market in the fall of 1991. Modeled by master sculptor Helmut Fischer in 1989. It has an incised 1989 copyright date. The boy is similar to "Max" on HUM 123 "Max and Moritz". The original issue price was $95 in 1991. Designed as a companion figurine to HUM 768 "Pixie" in the "Cozy Companion" series.

☐ 553 . . . . . 3½″ . . . . . . . . . (CE). . . ❼ . . . $128–130
☐ 553 . . . . . 3½″ . . . . . . . . . (**OE**). . . ❽ . . . $128

### HUM 554
### Cheeky Fellow

Members' first Exclusive *Preview* Edition for Club year 16. This figurine was first introduced in 1992 for members of the M.I. Hummel Club only and not sold as an open edition. Modeled by master sculptor Helmut Fischer in 1989. It has an incised 1989 copyright date along with the (TM7) trademark. Also bears the inscription: "EXCLUSIVE EDITION 1992/93 M.I. HUMMEL CLUB" applied by blue decal. A large black flying bumble bee is located on the bottom. The original issue price was $120 in the U.S., in addition to the member's redemption card. Goebel reserves the right to re-introduce this figurine as an open edition, minus the special backstamp. The boy is similar to "Moritz" on HUM 123 "Max & Moritz."

☐ 554 . . . . . 4⅛″ . . . . . . (CE) . . . . . . ❼ . . . $135–150
☐ 554 . . . . . 4⅛″ . . . . . . (**OE**) . . . . . . ❽ . . . $135

### HUM 555
### One, Two, Three
Members' Exclusive *Preview* Edition for Club year 20. First released in the U.S. market in 1996 for members of the M.I. Hummel Club only and not sold as an open edition. Modeled by master sculptor Helmut Fischer in 1989. It has an incised 1989 copyright date along with the (TM 7) trademark. Also bears the inscription: "EXCLUSIVE EDITION 1996/97 M. I. HUMMEL CLUB" applied by blue decal. A large black flying bumble bee is located on the bottom. The official issue price was $145 in the U.S., in addition to the member's redemption card. Goebel reserves the right to reintroduce this figurine as an open edition, minus the special backstamp.

☐ 555 . . . . . 3⅞" . . . . . . . . . . (CE). . . ❼ . . . $145–175

### HUM 556
### One Plus One
First released in the U.S. market in 1993. Modeled by master sculptor Helmut Fischer in 1989. It has an incised 1989 copyright date along with the (TM7) trademark. Also bears the "First Issue 1993" oval decal and "SPECIAL EVENT" backstamp. This figurine was available at District Manager Promotions and in-store events, but was re-introduced as part of the regular line, but minus the special backstamp. The original issue price was $115.

☐ 556 . . . . . 4" . . . . (Special Event) . . ❼ . . . $160–200
☐ 556 . . . . . 4" . . . . . . . . . . . . (CE). . . ❼ . . . $155–160
☐ 556 . . . . . 4" . . . . . . . . . . . . (OE). . . ❽ . . . $155

### HUM 557
### Strum Along

Members' Exclusive *Preview* Edition for Club year 19. This figurine was first introduced in 1995 for members of the M.I. Hummel Club only and not sold as an open edition. Modeled by master sculptor Helmut Fischer in 1989. It has an incised 1989 copyright date along with the (TM 7) trademark. Also bears the inscription: "EXCLUSIVE EDITION 1995/96 M.I. HUMMEL CLUB" applied by blue decal. A large black flying bumble bee is located on the bottom. The official issue price was $135 in the U.S., in addition to the member's redemption card, Goebel reserves the right to re-introduce this figurine as an open edition, minus the special backstamp. Girl similar to girl from HUM 150 "Happy Days."

☐ 557 . . . . . 3⅞" . . . . . . . . . (CE) . . . ❼ . . . $145–150
☐ 557 . . . . . 3⅞" . . . . . . . . . (OE) . . . ❽ . . . $145

### HUM 558
### Little Troubadour

Members' Exclusive *Preview* Edition for Club year 18. This figurine was first introduced in 1994 for members of the M.I. Hummel Club only and not sold as an open edition. Modeled by master sculptor Helmut Fischer in 1989. It has an incised 1989 copyright date along with the (TM 7) trademark. Also bears the inscription: "EXCLUSIVE EDITION 1994/95 M.I. HUMMEL CLUB" applied by blue decal. A large black flying bumble bee is located on the bottom. The official issue price was $130 in the U.S., in addition to the member's redemption card. Goebel reserves the right to re-introduce this figurine as an open edition, minus the special backstamp. Boy similar to boy from HUM 150 "Happy Days".

☐ 558 . . . . . 4 to 4⅛" . . . . . . (CE) . . . ❼ . . . $135–140
☐ 558 . . . . . 4 to 4⅛" . . . . . . (OE) . . . ❽ . . . $135

---

**HUM TERM**

**Exclusive Edition (EE):** Pieces that are originally sold only to members of the M.I. Hummel Club.

---

### HUM 559
### Heart and Soul
First released in the U.S. market in 1996. Modeled by master sculptor Helmut Fischer in 1988. It has an incised 1989 copyright date along with the (TM 7) trademark. Also bears "First Issue 1996" and "Goebel 125th Anniversary" backstamp. Designed as a companion piece to HUM 761 "From the Heart" as part of the "Cozy Companions" series. The official issue price was $120 in 1996.

☐ 559 . . . . . 3½" . . . . . . . . . . (CE). . . ❼ . . . $128–130
☐ 559 . . . . . 3½" . . . . . . . . . . (OE). . . ❽ . . . $128

### HUM 560
### Lucky Fellow (CE)
First released in the U.S. market in 1992 as a FREE gift for renewing membership in the M.I. HUMMEL CLUB for the 1992/93 Club year. Modeled by master sculptor Helmut Fischer in 1989. It has an incised 1989 copyright date. It bears the inscription: "M.I. HUMMEL CLUB" in addition to a black flying bumble bee, in a half circle, along with (TM7) trademark. Not sold as an (OE) Open Edition, but can be purchased on the secondary market.

☐ 560 . . . . . 3⅝" . . . . . . . . . . (CE). . . ❼ . . . $75–100

### HUM 561
### Grandma's Girl
First released in the U.S. market in the summer of 1990. Modeled by master sculptor Helmut Fischer in 1989. It has an incised 1989 copyright date. The girl is a smaller verison of the same girl on HUM 383 "Going Home". The original issue price was $100 in 1990.

☐ 561 . . . . . 4" . . . . . . . . . . . (CE). . . ⑥ . . . $175–180
☐ 561 . . . . 4" . . . . . . . . . . . (CE). . . ⑦ . . . $170–175
☐ 561 . . . . . 4" . . . . . . . . . . . **(OE)**. . . ⑧ . . . $170

### HUM 562
### Grandpa's Boy
First released in the U.S. market in the summer of 1990. Modeled by master sculptor Helmut Fischer in 1989. It has an incised 1989 copyright date. The boy is a smaller version of the same boy on HUM 383 "Going Home". The original issue price was $100 in 1990.

☐ 562 . . . . . 4¼" . . . . . . . . . (CE). . . ⑥ . . . $175–180
☐ 562 . . . . . 4¼" . . . . . . . . . (CE). . . ⑦ . . . $170–175
☐ 562 . . . . . 4¼" . . . . . . . . . **(OE)**. . . ⑧ . . . $170

### HUM 563
### Little Visitor (CE)
Members' Exclusive Edition for Club year 18. This figurine was first introduced in 1994 for members of the M.I. Hummel Club only and not sold as an open edition. Modeled by master sculptor Helmut Fischer in 1991. It has an incised 1991 copyright date along with the (TM7) trademark. Also bears the inscription: "EXCLUSIVE EDITION 1994/95 M.I. HUMMEL CLUB" applied by blue decal. A large black flying bumble bee is located on the bottom. The official issue price was $180 in the U.S., in addition to the member's redemption card.

☐ 563/0 . . . . 5⅛″ . . . . . . . . . . (CE) . . . ❼ . . . $200–225

### HUM 564
### Free Spirit
First released in the U.S. market in the fall of 1996. Modeled by master sculptor Helmut Fischer in 1988. It has an incised 1989 copyright date along with the (TM 7) trademark. Also bears the "First Issue 1997" oval decal on the bottom. Designed as a companion piece to HUM 490 "Carefree" as part of the "Cozy Companions" series. The official issue price was $120 in 1996.

☐ 564 . . . . . 3½″ . . . . . . . . . . (CE) . . . ❼ . . . $128–130
☐ 564 . . . . . 3½″ . . . . . . . . . . (OE) . . . ❽ . . . $128

─────────── HUM TERM ───────────

**OPEN EDITION:** Pieces currently in W. Goebel's production program.

366

## HUM 565   (PFE) STILL UNDER DEVELOPMENT

### HUM 566
### The Angler
First released in the U.S. market in 1995. Modeled by master sculptor Gerhard Skrobek in 1989. It has an incised 1989 copyright date along with (TM 7) trademark. Also bears the "First Issue 1995" oval decal on the bottom. The official issue price was $320 in 1995.

☐ 566 . . . . . 5⅞" . . . . . . . . . . (CE). . . ❼ . . . $370–380
☐ 566 . . . . . 5⅞" . . . . . . . . . . (**OE**). . . ❽ . . . $370

## HUM 567–568   (PFE) STILL UNDER DEVELOPMENT

"O Canada"

### HUM 569
### A Free Flight
First released in the U.S. market in 1993. Modeled by master sculptor Gerhard Skrobek in 1989. It has an incised 1989 copyright date and the "First Issue 1993" oval decal on the bottom. The official issue price was $185 in 1993. A special figurine sold only in Canada was released in 1997, with special decals and backstamp. The retail price was approximately $200 (in U.S. funds).

☐ 569 . . . . . 4¾" . . . . . . . . . . (CE). . . ❼ . . . $205–210
☐ 569 . . . . . 4¾" . . . . . . . . . . (**OE**). . . ❽ . . . $205

### HUM 571
**Angelic Guide (CE)**
First released in the U.S. market in 1991, the fourth in the Annual Series of ornaments. Modeled by master sculptor Gerhard Skrobek in 1989. It has an incised 1989 copyright date. The original issue price was $95 in 1991.

☐ 571 . . . . . 4″ . . . . . . . . . . . (CE). . . ❻ . . . $150–200
☐ 571 . . . . . 4″ . . . . . . . . . . . (CE). . . ❼ . . . $125–150

### HUM 572
**COUNTRY DEVOTION (PFE)**
This figurine was first modeled by master sculptor Gerhard Skrobek in 1989. It has an incised 1989 copyright date. Presently listed on factory records as a (PFE) Possible Future Edition and may be released at some future date, subject to possible minor changes.

☐ 572 . . . . . 11″ . . . . . . . . . (PFE). . .

**HUM 574**
**Rock-A-Bye (CE)**
This figurine was first introduced in the U.S. market in 1994. This is the ninth figurine in the Century Collection and was produced for only this one year in the twentieth century. It was modeled by master sculptor Helmut Fischer in 1991. It has an incised 1991 copyright date. A circular inscription applied by blue decal reads: "M.I. HUMMEL CENTURY COLLECTION 1994 XX" and the name "Rock-A-Bye" along with the (TM7) trademark. The original issue price was $1150 in 1994.

☐ 574 . . . . . 7½″ . . . . . . . . . (CE). . . ❼ . . . $1200–1500

**M.I. Hummel**
**ANGEL OF CHRISTMAS**
**ORNAMENT SERIES**
First released in the U.S. market in 1990 and were sold exclusively by mail order through the Danbury Mint of Norwalk, Connecticut, at the rate of one every other month. Modeled by master sculptor Helmut Fischer in 1988. They have an incised "M.I. Hummel" signature and the Goebel (TM6) trademark, but do *NOT* have an incised model number. The original issue price was $39.50 each (plus sales tax and $2.50 shipping and handling).

*HUM 575*
*Heavenly Angel*

*HUM 576*
*Festival Harmony*
*w/mandolin*

*HUM 577*
*Festival Harmony*
*w/flute*

**HUM 578**
*Celestial Musician*

**HUM 581**
*Prayer of Thanks*

**HUM 582**
*Gentle Song*

## ANGELS OF CHRISTMAS
## ORNAMENT SERIES

Also produced in white overglaze with painted facial features only and gold tipped wings. Can be purchased from your local "M.I. Hummel" dealer. List price: $38.

**HUM 579**
*Song of Praise*

**HUM 580**
*Angel with Lute*

**HUM 585**
*Angel in Cloud*

**HUM 586**
*Angel with Trumpet*

|  |  |  | (in color) |  |  | (in white) |  |
|---|---|---|---|---|---|---|---|
| ☐ 575 | 3" | **(CE)** | ❻ | $45–50 | (OE) | ❼ | $38 |
| ☐ 576 | 3" | **(CE)** | ❻ | $45–50 | (OE) | ❼ | $38 |
| ☐ 577 | 3" | **(CE)** | ❻ | $45–50 | (OE) | ❼ | $38 |
| ☐ 578 | 3" | **(CE)** | ❻ | $45–50 | (OE) | ❼ | $38 |
| ☐ 579 | 2½" | **(CE)** | ❻ | $45–50 | (OE) | ❼ | $38 |
| ☐ 580 | 2½" | **(CE)** | ❻ | $45–50 | (OE) | ❼ | $38 |
| ☐ 581 | 3" | **(CE)** | ❻ | $45–50 | (OE) | ❼ | $38 |
| ☐ 582 | 3" | **(CE)** | ❻ | $45–50 | (OE) | ❼ | $38 |
| ☐ 583 | OPEN NUMBER | **(ON)** | | | | | |
| ☐ 584 | OPEN NUMBER | **(ON)** | | | | | |
| ☐ 585 | 2½" | **(CE)** | ❻ | $45–50 | (OE) | ❼ | $38 |
| ☐ 586 | 2½" | **(CE)** | ❻ | $45–50 | (OE) | ❼ | $38 |

**HUM 587–595   (ON) OPEN NUMBERS**

**HUM 596**
**Thanksgiving Prayer**
**Annual Ornament (CE)**
First released in the U.S. market in 1997. Modeled by master sculptor Helmut Fischer in 1995. It has *NO* incised copyright date that I can find, but does have a "First Issue 1997" oval cello sticker on the lower gown of the angel. "Hummel" only is incised on the back. Incised model number 596 and (TM 7) trademark, plus 1995 applied by blue decal on the bottom of this very small area. A brass ring is attached to top of head for hanging as an ornament. Original issue price was $120 in 1997. Similar to HUM 641 "Thanksgiving Prayer" but without base.

☐ 596 . . . . . 2¾ to 3″ . . . . . . (CE). . . ❼ . . . $120–125

**HUM 597**
**Echoes of Joy**
**Annual Ornament (CE)**
First released in the U.S. market in the fall of 1997. Modeled by master sculptor Helmut Fischer in 1996. It has *NO* incised copyright date that I can find, but does have a "First Issue 1998" oval cello sticker on the lower gown of the angel. "Hummel" only is incised on the back. Incised model number 597 and (TM 7) trademark, plus 1996 applied by blue decal on the bottom of this very small area. A brass ring is attached to top of head for hanging as an ornament. Original issue price was $120 in 1997. Similar to HUM 642 "Echoes of Joy" figurine but without base.

☐ 597 . . . . . 2¾ to 3″ . . . . . . (CE). . . ❼ . . . $120–125

**HUM 598**
**Joyful Noise**
**Annual Ornament (CE)**
First released in the U.S. market in the fall of 1998. Modeled by master sculptor Helmut Fischer in 1995. It has NO incised copyright date that I can find, but does have a "First Issue 1999" oval cello sticker on the lower gown of angel. "Hummel" only is incised on the back. Incised model number 598 and (TM 7) trademark, plus 1996 applied by blue decal on the bottom of this very small area. A brass ring is attached to top of head for hanging as an ornament. Original issue price was $120 in 1998. Similar to HUM 643 "Joyful Noise" figurine but without base.

□ 598 . . . . . 2¾ to 3″ . . . . . . (CE). . . **❼** . . . $120–125

**HUM 599**
**Light The Way**
**Annual Ornament**
First released in the U.S. maket in the fall of 1999. Modeled by master sculptor Helmut Fischer in 1995. It has an incised 1995 copyright date in addition to a "First Issue 2000" oval cello sticker on the lower gown of angel. Incised "Hummel" only on back, incised model number 599 and (TM 8) trademark on the bottom. A brass ring is attached to top of head for hanging as an ornament. Original issue price was $120 in 1999. Similar to HUM 715 "Light The Way" figurine but without base.

□ 599 . . . . . 2¾ to 3″ . . . . . . (**OE**). . . **❽** . . . $120

*"The Four Hummel Sisters"*

Katarina     Vicktoria     Berta     Centa

## HUM 600
### We Wish You The Best (CE)

This figurine was first released in the U.S. market in 1991. This is sixth figurine in the Century Collection and was produced for only this one year in the twentieth century. Modeled by master sculptor Helmut Fischer in 1989. It has an incised 1989 copyright date. A circular inscription applied by blue decal reads: "M.I. HUMMEL CENTURY COLLECTION 1991 XX" and the name "We Wish You The Best". The original issue price was $1300 in 1991.

☐ 600 . . . . . 8¼" × 9½" . . . . . (CE). . . ❻ . . . $1,800–2,000
☐ 600 . . . . . 8¼" × 9½" . . . . . (CE). . . ❼ . . . $1,600–1,800

## HUM 601–607    (ON) OPEN NUMBERS

## HUM 608
### Blossom Time

First released in the U.S. market in 1996. Modeled by master sculptor Helmut Fischer in 1989. It has an incised 1989 copyright date along with the (TM 7) trademark. Also bears a combination "First Issue 1996" and "Goebel 125th Anniversary" backstamp on the bottom. The official issue price was $155 in 1996.

☐ 608 . . . . . 3⅛" . . . . . . . . . . (CE). . . ❼ . . . $165–175
☐ 608 . . . . . 3⅛" . . . . . . . . . . (OE). . . ❽ . . . $165

**HUM IV/608 (LE)**
**Blossom Time, Music Box**
In 1999 a new music box was produced with model number IV/608 in a Limited Edition (LE) of only 500 pieces and sold exclusively through The Hummel Museum and Art Gallery in New Braunfels, Texas. Melody played "Edelweiss". The original issue price was $250 in 1999. It has a (TM 7) trademark and an incised 1999 copyright date.

☐ IV/608 . . . 5½″ . . . . . . . . . . (LE) . . . ❼ . . . $250–300

**HUM 609 (ON) OPEN NUMBER**

**HUM 610 (PFE)**
**April Shower**
This figurine was first modeled by master sculptor Helmut Fischer in 1989. It has an incised 1990 copyright date. Presently listed on factory records as a (PFE) Possible Future Edition and may be released at some future date, subject to possible minor changes.

☐ 610 . . . . . 9⅜″ . . . . . . . . . . (PFE) . . .

**HUM 611 (PFE)**
**Sunny Song**
This figurine was first modeled by master sculptor Helmut Fischer in 1989. It has an incised 1990 copyright date. Presently listed on factory records as a (PFE) Possible Future Edition and may be released at some future date, subject to possible minor changes.

☐ 611 . . . . . 5⅛″ . . . . . . . . . (PFE) . . .

**HUM 612 (PFE)**
**Lazybones**
This figurine was first modeled by master sculptor Helmut Fischer in 1989. It has an incised 1990 copyright date. Presently listed on factory records as a (PFE) Possible Future Edition and may be released at some future date, subject to possible minor changes.

☐ 612 . . . . . 3⅞″ . . . . . . . . . (PFE) . . .

### HUM 613 (PFE)
### What's Up

This figurine was first modeled by master sculptor Helmut Fischer in 1989. It has an incised 1990 copyright date. Presently listed on factory records as a (PFE) Possible Future Edition and may be released at some future date, subject to possible minor changes. John Riedl was the model for this figurine in 1939, when he became the first American child to sit for Sister M. I. Hummel. He still lives in Central Ohio.

☐ 613 . . . . . 5½" . . . . . . . . . . (PFE) . . . (Emil Fink postcard Nr. 798)

### HUM 614 (PFE)
### Harmonica Player

This figurine was first modeled by master sculptor Helmut Fischer in 1989. It has an incised 1990 copyright date. Presently listed on factory records as a (PFE) Possible Future Edition and may be released at some future date, subject to possible minor changes. John Riedl was the model for this figurine in 1939, when he became the first American child to sit for Sister M. I. Hummel. He still lives in Central Ohio.

☐ 614 . . . . . 5½" . . . . . . . . . . (PFE) . . . (Emil Fink postcard Nr. 799)

*Factory Sample*

*Normal Production*

**Note: Base Construction**

## HUM 615
### Private Conversation

Members' Exclusive Edition (EE) for Club year 23. This figurine was first introduced in 1999 for members of the M. I. Hummel Club only and <u>not</u> sold as an Open Edition (OE). Modeled by master sculptor Helmut Fischer in 1989. It has an incised 1990 copyright date along with the (TM 7) trademark. Also bears: "EXCLUSIVE EDITION 1999/2000 M.I. HUMMEL CLUB" club decal, plus a black flying bumble bee on the bottom. The official issue price was $260 in addition to member's redemption card. Figure will be available until 31 May 2000.

☐ 615 . . . . . 4½″ . . . . . . . . . . (EE) . . . . . . . . $260

## HUM 616
### Parade of Lights

First released in the U.S. market in 1993. Modeled by master sculptor Helmut Fischer in 1990. It has an incised 1990 copyright date and the "First Issue 1993" oval decal on the bottom. The little clown is holding a "paper" lantern, but made out of ceramics. It is a companion piece for HUM 328 "Carnival" which was released in 1963. The official issue price was $235 in 1993.

☐ 616 . . . . . 6″ . . . . . . . . . . . (CE) . . . **❼** . . . $285–290
☐ 616 . . . . . 6″ . . . . . . . . . . . (OE) . . . **❽** . . . $285

**HUM 620**
**A Story from Grandma (CE)**
This figurine was released in the U.S. market in 1995. It was an (EE) Exclusive Edition for M.I. Hummel Club members only and was not made available to the general public. Sequentially numbered limited edition of 10,000 pieces worldwide. It bears a Club Exclusive backstamp, and comes with a Certificate of Authenticity. It was offered for one year only, from 1 June 1995 through 31 May 1996. Modeled by a team of artists in 1993 and has an incised 1993 copyright date. The official issue price was $1,300 in 1995. Available on the secondary market only.

☐ 620 . . . . 8″ . . . . . . . (CE) . . . . . . . ❼ . . . . $1,500–1,600

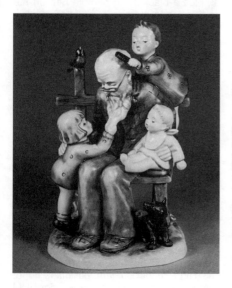

**HUM 621**
**At Grandpa's (CE)**
First released in the U.S. market in the fall of 1994. It was an (EE) Exclusive Edition for M.I. Hummel Club members only and was not made available to the general public. Sequentially numbered limited edition of 10,000 pieces world-wide. It bears a Club Exclusive back-stamp, and comes with a Certificate of Authenticity. It was offered for one year only, from 1 June 1994 through 31 May 1995. Modeled by a team of artists in 1993 and has an incised 1993 copyright date. The official issue price was $1,300 in 1994. Available on the secondary market only.

☐ 621 . . . . . 9″ . . . . . . . . . . . (CE) . . . ❼ . . . $1,500–1,600

### HUM 622
### Light Up The Night (CE)
First released in the U.S. market in 1992, the fifth in the Annual Series of Ornaments. Modeled by master sculptor Gerhard Skrobek in 1990. It has an incised 1990 copyright date. The original issue price was $95.

☐ 622 . . . . . 3¼" . . . . . . . . . . (CE) . . . ❼ . . . $125–150

### HUM 623
### Herlad on High (CE)
First released in the U.S. market in 1993. The sixth and final issue in the Annual Series of Ornaments. Modeled by master sculptor Gerhard Skrobek in 1990. It has *no* incised copyright date that I can find, but does have 1993 fired on the lower end of angel's gown. "FINAL ISSUE" and (TM 7) trademark are fired on the underside of gown. The original issue price was $155 in 1993.

☐ 623 . . . . . 2¾ x 4½" . . . . . . (CE) . . . ❼ . . . $175–200

### HUM 624   (ON) OPEN NUMBER

**HUM 625**
**Goose Girl Vase**

This special combination "Sampler" offer was released in 1997. Contained the small size HUM 47 3/0 "Goose Girl" figurine in combination with a bisque porcelain vase with "Goose Girl" in bas relief on the front. This combination retailed for $200. The retail value of the figurine was $185 plus only $15 for the vase. The vase is a first for Goebel—it has the (TM 7) trademark with 1989 copyright date applied by blue decal on the bottom, in addition to the "M.I. Hummel" signature incised on the vase.

☐ 625 . . . . . 4 × 3½" . . . . . . . (CE) . . . ❼ . . . $50–75

*(Backs are interesting, too!)*

**HUM 626**
**I Didn't Do It (CE)**

Members' Exclusive Edition for Club year 17. This figurine was first introduced in 1993 for members of the M.I. HUMMEL CLUB only and not sold as an open edition. Modeled by master sculptor Helmut Fischer in 1992. It has an incised 1992 copyright date, along with the inscription: "EXCLUSIVE EDITION 1993/94 M.I. HUMMEL CLUB" applied by blue decal. A large black flying bumble bee is located on the bottom. The official issue price was $175 in the U.S., in addition to the member's redemption card. This figurine can be purchased on the secondary market at premium prices.

☐ 626 . . . . . 5½" . . . . . . . . . . (CE) . . . ❼ . . . $200–225

**HUM 628**
**Gentle Fellowship (LE)**
First released in the U.S. market in 1995, the third and final figurine in the UNICEF series. HUM 662 "Friends Together" in 1993 and HUM 754 "We Come In Peace" in 1994. It bears a special UNICEF Commemorative "Limited Edition No. ____ of 25,000" backstamp in addition to the (TM 7) trademark. Modeled by master sculptor Helmut Fischer in 1992. It has an incised 1992 copyright date. The original issue price was $550 in 1995. A $25 contribution was made to the U.S. Committee for UNICEF as part of a co-operative fund raising effort.

☐ 628 . . . . . 5¾" . . . . . . . . . . (LE) . . . ❼ . . . $550

**HUM 629**
**From Me To You (CE)**
First released in the U.S. market in 1995 as a FREE gift for renewing membership in the M.I. HUMMEL CLUB for the 1995/96 Club year. Modeled by master sculptor Helmut Fischer in 1992. It has an incised 1992 copyright date. It bears the inscription: "M.I. HUMMEL CLUB Membership Year 1995/96" in addition to a black flying bumble bee, in a half circle. It is similar to girl from HUM 199 "Feeding Time". Can now be purchased on the secondary market at premium prices.

☐ 629 . . . . . 3½" . . . . . . . . . (CE) . . . ❼ . . . $100–125

### HUM 630
### For Keeps (CE)

First released in the U.S. market in 1994 as a FREE gift for renewing membership in the M.I. HUMMEL CLUB for the 1994/95 Club year. Modeled by master sculptor Helmut Fischer in 1992. It has an incised 1992 copyright date. It bears the inscription: "M.I. HUMMEL CLUB Membership Year 1994/95" in addition to a black flying bumble bee, in a half circle. It is similar to the boy from HUM 200 "Little Goat Herder". Can now be purchased on the secondary market at premium prices.

☐ 630 . . . . . 3½" . . . . . . . . . (CE) . . . ❼ . . . $100–125

**HUM 631   (ON) OPEN NUMBER**

### HUM 632
### At Play (CE)

Members' Exclusive Edition (EE) for Club year 22. This figurine was first introduced in 1998 for members of the M. I. Hummel Club only and not sold as an Open Edition (OE). Modeled by master sculptor Helmut Fischer in 1990. It has an incised 1990 copyright date along with the (TM 7) trademark. Also bears: "EXCLUSIVE EDITION 1998/99 M.I. HUMMEL CLUB" applied by blue decal, plus a black flying bumble bee located on the bottom. The official issue price was $260 in 1998, in addition to member's redemption card.

☐ 632 . . . . . 3½" . . . . . . . . . (CE) . . . ❼ . . . $260–300

**HUM 633**
**I'm Carefree**
First released in the U.S. market in 1994. Modeled by master sculptor Helmut Fischer in 1990. It has an incised 1990 copyright date and the "First Issue 1994" oval decal on the bottom. The official issue price was $365. The incised "M.I. HUMMEL" signature is located on the rear of the wagon on early production figurines, but later changed to the left side of wagon (left side as boy is facing front) because of production problems. Possibly fewer than 1000 pieces have signature on rear.

☐ 633 . . . . . 4¾ × 4¼″ . . . . . (CE). . . **7** . . . $750–900 (signature on back)
☐ 633 . . . . . 4¾ × 4¼″ . . . . . (CE). . . **7** . . . $420–430 (signature on side)
☐ 633 . . . . . 4¾ × 4¼″ . . . . . (**OE**). . . **8** . . . $420 (signature on side)

*Rear view*

*Left side view*

### HUM 634
### Sunshower (LE)
First released in the U.S. market in the fall of 1997. Modeled by master sculptor Helmut Fischer in 1990. It has an incised 1990 copyright date. Created as a Limited Edition (LE) of 10,000 pieces to celebrate the 60th anniversary of HUM 71 "Stormy Weather" which was first issued in 1937. Designed as a companion piece to "Stormy Weather" with some minor changes. It has a "First Issue 1997" backstamp. The original issue price was $360 in 1997.

☐ 634 2/0 . . . . . . . . . . . . . . (LE) . . . ❼ . . . $360–375

### HUM 635
### Welcome Spring (CE)
This figurine was first released in the U.S. market in 1993. This is the eighth figurine in the Century Collection and was produced for only this one year in the twentieth century. Modeled by master sculptor Helmut Fischer in 1990. It has an incised 1990 copyright date. A circular inscription applied by blue decal reads: "M.I. HUMMEL CENTURY COLLECTION 1993 XX" and the name "Welcome Spring" along with the (TM 7) trademark. The original issue price was $1085 in 1993.

☐ 635 . . . . . 12¼" . . . . . . . . (CE) . . . ❼ . . . $1500–1800

---

**HUM TERM**

**MUSTERZIMMER**: The German word meaning sample model designating that this piece is to be held at the W. Goebel Porzellanfabrik in the "sample room" to be used for future reference by production artists.

---

## HUM 638
### The Botanist Vase

This special combination "Sampler" offer was released in 1998. Contained HUM 351 "The Botanist" figurine in combination with a bisque porcelain vase with bas relief figurine on the front and the Hummel Museum, Inc. logo on the back. This combination set was released for $210. It has (TM 7) trademark with a 1997 copyright date applied by blue decal on the bottom, in addition to the "M.I. Hummel" signature incised on the vase.

☐ 638 . . . . . 4 x 3½″ . . . . . . . (CE). . . ❼ . . . $50–75

---

**HUM-INFO**

An authentic Goebel "M.I. Hummel" Figurine will always have a plain incised model number. It will *never* have an alphabetical prefix in front of the number (such as: HM, FE, HX etc). *If* it *has* an alphabetical pre-fix—it is a *Goebel* item and not "M.I. Hummel." Alphabetical letters may appear after a HUM number (such as: A, B, C etc)—this indicates that it is part of a set. Example: HUM 239 A, 239 B, or 239 C. This is a good "rule of thumb" guide to remember when looking at a figurine with a *Goebel* trademark.

*641/0*          *641 4/0*

### HUM 641
### Thanksgiving Prayer

Both sizes were released in the U.S. market in 1997. Modeled by master sculptor Helmut Fischer in 1991 and 1995. Both have the "First Issue 1997" oval decal. The large size has an incised 1991 copyright date, while the small size has an incised 1995 copyright date. The small size has a matte finish while the large size has the normal glazed finish. The original issue price was $180 for the large (641/0) while the small (641 4/0) was $120 in 1997.

| | | | | |
|---|---|---|---|---|
| ☐ 641 4/0. . . 3¼" . . . . . . . . . . | (CE). . . | ❼ | . . . | $125–130 |
| ☐ 641 4/0. . . 3¼" . . . . . . . . . . | (OE). . . | ❽ | . . . | $125 |
| ☐ 641/0 . . . . 5" . . . . . . . . . . . | (CE). . . | ❼ | . . . | $190–195 |
| ☐ 641/0 . . . . 5" . . . . . . . . . . . | (OE). . . | ❽ | . . . | $190 |

*642/0*          *642 4/0*

### HUM 642
### Echoes of Joy

Both sizes were released in the U.S. market in 1997. Modeled by master sculptor Helmut Fischer in 1991 and 1995. Both have the "First Issue 1998" oval decal. The large size has an incised 1991 copyright date, while the small size has an incised 1995 copyright date. The small size has a matte finish while the large size has the normal glazed finish. The original issue price was $180 for the large (642/0) while the small (642 4/0) was $120 in 1997.

| | | | | |
|---|---|---|---|---|
| ☐ 642 4/0. . . 3⅛" . . . . . . . . . . | (CE). . . | ❼ | . . . | $125–130 |
| ☐ 642 4/0. . . 3⅛" . . . . . . . . . . | (OE). . . | ❽ | . . . | $125 |
| ☐ 642/0 . . . . 5⅛" . . . . . . . . . . | (CE). . . | ❼ | . . . | $190–195 |
| ☐ 642/0 . . . . 5⅛" . . . . . . . . . . | (OE). . . | ❽ | . . . | $190 |

*643/0*      *643 4/0*

### HUM 643
### Joyful Noise

Both sizes were released in the U.S. market in 1999. Modeled by master sculptor Helmut Fischer in 1991 and 1996. Both have the "First Issue 1999" oval decal. The large size has an incised 1991 copyright date, while the small size has an incised 1996 copyright date. The small size has a matte finish while the large size has the normal glazed finish. The original issue price was $180 for the large (643/0) while the small (643 4/0) was $120 in 1999.

| | | | | | |
|---|---|---|---|---|---|
| ☐ 643 4/0 . . . 3" . . . . . . . . . . . (CE) . . . ❼ . . . $125–130 |
| ☐ 643 4/0 . . . 3" . . . . . . . . . . . (**OE**) . . . ❽ . . . $124 |
| ☐ 643/0 . . . . 5" . . . . . . . . . . . (CE) . . . ❼ . . . $185–190 |
| ☐ 643/0 . . . . 5" . . . . . . . . . . . (**OE**) . . . ❽ . . . $185 |

### HUM 644    (ON) OPEN NUMBER

### HUM 645
### Christmas Song
### Annual Ornament (CE)

First released in the U.S. market in 1996. Modeled by master sculptor Helmet Fischer in 1991. It has *no* incised copyright date that I can find, but does have a "First Issue 1996" round cello sticker, with "125th Anniversary Goebel" on the lower gown of the angel. "Hummel" only is incised on the back. The incised model number 645 and (TM 7) trademark, plus 1991 copyright date applied by blue decal on the bottom of this very small area. A brass ring is attached to top of head for hanging as an ornament. Original issue price was $115 in 1996. Similar to HUM 343 4/0 "Christmas Song" but without base.

☐ 645 . . . . . 3¼" . . . . . . . . . . (CE) . . . ❼ . . . $120–130

### HUM 646
### Celestial Musician
### Annual Ornament (CE)

First released in the U.S. market in 1993. Modeled by master sculptor Gerhard Skrobek in 1991. It has *no* incised copyright date that I can find, but does have a "First Issue 1993" oval cello sticker on the lower gown of the angel. "Hummel" only incised on the back. Incised model number 646 and (TM 7) trademark, plus 1991 applied by blue decal on the bottom of this very small area. A brass ring is attached to top of head for hanging as an ornament. Original issue price was $90 in 1993. Similar to HUM 188 "Celestial Musician" but without base.

□ 646 . . . . . 2⅞" . . . . . . . . . . (CE) . . . ➐ . . . $120–130

### HUM 647
### Festival Harmony with Mandolin
### Annual Ornament (CE)

First released in the U.S. market in 1994. Modeled by master sculptor Helmut Fischer in 1991. It has *no* incised copyright date that I can find, but does have a "First Issue 1994" oval cello sticker on the lower gown of the angel. "Hummel" only incised on the back. Incised model number 647 and (TM 7) trademark, plus 1991 applied by blue decal on the bottom of this very small area. A brass ring is attached to top of head for hanging as an ornament. Original issue price was $95 in 1994. Similar to HUM 172 "Festival Harmony (mandolin)" but without base.

□ 647 . . . . . 2¾" . . . . . . . . . . (CE) . . . ➐ . . . $120–130

### HUM 648
### Festival Harmony with Flute
### Annual Ornament (CE)

First released in the U.S. market in 1995. Modeled by master sculptor Gerhard Skrobek in 1991. It has *no* incised copyright date that I can find, but does have a "First Issue 1995" oval cello sticker on the lower gown of the angel. "Hummel" only incised on the back. Incised model number 648 and (TM 7) trademark, plus 1991 applied by blue decal on the bottom of this very small area. A brass ring is attached to top of head for hanging as an ornament. Original issue price was $100 in 1995. Similar to HUM 173 "Festival Harmony (flute)" but without base.

☐ 648 . . . . . 2¾″ . . . . . . . . . . (CE) . . . ❼ . . . $120–130

### HUM 649
### Fascination (LE)

First released in the U.S. market on October 5, 1996 at Goebel's National Open House promotions by participating retailers honoring Goebel's 125th Anniversary. Modeled by master sculptor Helmut Fischer in 1990. It has an incised 1991 copyright date along with (TM 7) trademark. Produced in a worldwide Limited Edition (LE) of 25,000 sequentially-numbered pieces with only 15,000 available in the U.S. The original issue price was $190 in 1996.

☐ 649/0 . . . . 4¾″ . . . . . . . . . (LE) . . . ❼ . . . $190

**HUM 650–657   (ON) OPEN NUMBERS**

**HUM 658**
**Playful Blessing (CE)**
Members' Exclusive Edition (EE) for Club year 21. This figurine was first introduced in 1997 for members of the M.I. Hummel Club only and *not* sold as an open edition (OE). Modeled by master sculptor Helmut Fischer in 1992. It has an incised 1992 copyright date along with the (TM 7) trademark. Also bears the inscription: "EXCLUSIVE EDITION 1997/98 M.I. HUMMEL CLUB" applied by blue decal. A large black flying bumble bee is located on the bottom. The official issue price was $260 in 1997, in addition to the member's redemption card.

☐ 658 . . . . . 3½″ . . . . . . . . . . (CE). . . **7** . . . $260–300

**HUM 659 (ON) OPEN NUMBER**

**HUM 660**
**Fond Goodbye (CE)**
This figurine was first released in the U.S. market in 1997. This is the 12th figurine on the Century Collection and was produced for only this one year in the twentieth century. It was modeled by master sculptor Helmut Fischer in 1991. It has an incised 1992 copyright date. A circular inscription applied by blue decal reads: "M.I. Hummel CENTURY COLLECTION 1997 XX" and the name "Fond Goodbye" along with the (TM 7) trademark. The original issue price was $1450 in 1997.

☐ 660 . . . . . 6⅞ × 11″ . . . . . . (CE). . . **7** . . . $1,500–1,600

**HUM 661 (ON) OPEN NUMBER**

## HUM 662
### Friends Together

First released in the U.S. market in 1993 in both sizes. The small size, HUM 662/0 as an Open Edition (OE) and will become part of the regular line. It bears a special Commemorative UNICEF backstamp along with (TM 7) trademark. The large size, HUM 662/I is the first in a series in co-operation with the United Nations UNICEF Commit-

tee. It is a limited edition of 25,000 pieces, each sequentially numbered, and bears a special UNICEF Limited Edition backstamp, in addition to No. ____ of 25,000 along with the (TM 7) trademark. Both sizes were modeled by master sculptor Helmut Fischer in 1990 and both have an incised 1992 copyright date. The original issue price was $260 and $475 respectively. A $25 contribution was made to the U.S. Committee for UNICEF as part of a co-operative fund raising effort.

☐ 662/0 . . . . 4¼" . . . . . . . . . . (**OE**). . . ❼ . . . $300 (Commemorative Edition)
☐ 662/I . . . . 6" . . . . . . . . . . . (LE) . . . ❼ . . . $550 (limited to 25,000)

## HUM 663–666   (ON) OPEN NUMBERS

## HUM 667
### Pretty As A Picture (PFE)

This figurine was first modeled by master sculptor Gerhard Skrobek in 1992. It has an incised 1992 copyright date. Presently listed on factory records as a (PFE) Possible Future Edition and may be released at some future date, subject to possible minor changes.

☐ 667 . . . . . 7⅛" . . . . . . . . . . (PFE) . . .

---

**HUM TERM**

**BACKSTAMP OR TRADEMARK:** The official legal mark that Goebel places on the bottom of all "M.I. Hummel" products.

---

**HUM 668**
**Strike Up the Band (CE)**
This figurine was first released in the U.S. market in 1995. This is the tenth figurine in the Century Collection and was produced for only this one year in the twentieth century. It was modeled by master sculptor Helmut Fischer in 1993. It has an incised 1993 copyright date. A circular inscription applied by blue decal reads: "M.I. HUMMEL CENTURY COLLECTION 1995 XX" and the name "Strike Up the Band" along with the (TM 7) trademark. The original issue price was $1200 in 1995.

☐ 668 . . . . . 7⅜" . . . . . . . . . . (CE) . . . ❼ . . . $1,400–1,500

---

**PRICES IN THIS GUIDE**

We are in a period of DISCOUNTING of many items in our society. "M.I. Hummel" figurines are no exception. The prices in this guide give the relative values in relationship to new or current prices of (TM 8) trademark items. If the new figurines are discounted, the older models will likely be discounted, too, but possibly in a lesser degree. This guide reduces all items to one common denominator.

M.I. Hummel
## KITCHEN MOULD COLLECTION (CE)
First released in the U.S. market in 1991 and were sold exclusively by mail order through The Danbury Mint of Norwalk, Connecticut, at the rate of one every three months. They have an incised "M.I. Hummel" signature and the Goebel (TM 6 or TM 7) trademark, but do *NOT* have an incised model number. Modeled by master sculptor Helmut Fischer in 1989. The original issue price was $99 each (plus sales tax and $4.50 shipping and handling).

*HUM 669*

*HUM 670*

*HUM 671*

*HUM 672*

*HUM 673*

*HUM 674*

| | | | | |
|---|---|---|---|---|
| ☐ 669 | 7½" | (CE) | ❻ – ❼ | $150–175 |
| ☐ 670 | 7½" | (CE) | ❻ – ❼ | $150–175 |
| ☐ 671 | 7½" | (CE) | ❻ – ❼ | $150–175 |
| ☐ 672 | 8" | (CE) | ❻ – ❼ | $150–175 |
| ☐ 673 | 8" | (CE) | ❻ – ❼ | $150–175 |
| ☐ 674 | 8" | (CE) | ❻ – ❼ | $150–175 |

Found with either trademark ❻ or ❼.

**(CE) CLOSED EDITION – NO LONGER AVAILABLE**

**HUM 675   (ON) OPEN NUMBER**

**THE DANBURY MINT**
**47 Richards Avenue**
**Norwalk, Connecticut 06857**

**Call toll free: 800-243-4664**

HUM 676                                    HUM 677

## HUM 676–677
### Apple Tree Girl/Apple Tree Boy, Candle Stick Holders (CE)
First released in the U.S. market in 1989 and were sold exclusively by mail order through The Danbury Mint of Norwalk, Connecticut, at the rate of one every three months. Modeled by master sculptor Helmut Fischer in 1989. They have an incised 1988 copyright date. The original issue price was $142.50 each (plus sales tax and $3.00 shipping and handling).

☐ 676 . . . . . 6½″ . . . . . . . . (CE) . . ❻ or ❼ . $200–250
☐ 677 . . . . . 6½″ . . . . . . . . (CE) . . . . ❻ . . . $200–250

HUM 678                                    HUM 679

## HUM 678–679
### She Loves Me, She Loves Me Not/Good Friends Candle Stick Holders (CE)
First released in the U.S. market in 1990 and were sold exclusively by mail order through The Danbury Mint of Norwalk, Connecticut, at the rate of one every three months. Modeled by master sculptor Helmut Fischer in 1989. They have an incised 1989 copyright date. The original issue price was $142.50 each (plus sales tax and $3.00 shipping and handling).

☐ 678 . . . . . 6½″ . . . . . . . . (CE) . . ❻ or ❼ . $200–250
☐ 679 . . . . . 6½″ . . . . . . . . (CE) . . . . ❻ . . . $200–250

## HUM 690
### Smiling Through, Plaque (CE)

This round plaque was first issued in 1978 for members of the Goebel Collector's Club only and not sold as an Open Edition. Originally modeled by master sculptor Gerhard Skrobek from an original drawing by Sister M.I. Hummel. There is nothing incised on the back but the inscription "EXCLUSIVE SPECIAL EDITION No. 2 HUM 690 FOR MEMBERS OF THE GOEBEL COLLECTORS' CLUB" is applied by blue decal. Also has (TM 5) trademark and W. Germany 1978. No holes are provided for hanging. The original issue price was $50 in the U.S. and $55 in Canada, in addition to the member's redemption card. This plaque can be purchased on the secondary market at premium prices. This same motif of "Smiling Through" was made into a figurine and released in 1985 as "EXCLUSIVE SPECIAL EDITION No. 9" for members of the Goebel Collectors' Club. See HUM 408.

☐ 690 . . . . . 5¾" . . . . . . . . . . (CE). . . **❺** . . . $75–100

## HUM 691   (ON) OPEN NUMBER

## HUM 692
### Christmas Song
### Christmas Plate 1996 (CE)

Second issue in the Annual Christmas Plate series. Modeled by master sculptor Helmut Fischer in 1994. It bears a special "125th Anniversary Goebel" backstamp, plus (TM 7) trademark and 1994 copyright date applied by blue decal. Also has an incised "M.I. Hummel" signature on the front plus a decal signature on the back. The original issue price was $130 in 1996.

☐ 692 . . . . . 5⅞" . . . . . . . . . . (CE). . . **❼** . . . $50–75

### HUM 693
### Festival Harmony with Flute
### Christmas Plate 1995 (CE)
First issue in new series of Annual Christmas plates. Modeled by master sculptor Helmut Fischer in 1994. It bears a special backstamp which reads: "M.I. Hummel Annual Christmas Plate, W. Goebel Porzellanfabrik, Rödental". Also has an incised "M.I. Hummel" signature in addition to: "HUM 693 (TM 7) trademark and 1994 copyright date applied by blue decal. The original issue price was $125 in 1995.

☐ 693 . . . . . 5⅞″ . . . . . . . . . . (CE). . . ❼ . . . $50–75

### HUM 694
### Thanksgiving Prayer
### Christmas Plate 1997 (CE)
Third issue in the Annual Christmas plate series. Modeled by master sculptor Helmut Fischer in 1994. It bears an "M.I. Hummel Annual Christmas Plate 1997 Rödental, Germany" backstamp, plus (TM 7) trademark and 1995 copyright date applied by blue decal. Also has an incised "M.I. Hummel" signature on the front. The original issue price was $140 in 1997.

☐ 694 . . . . . 5⅞″ . . . . . . . . . . (CE). . . ❼ . . . $50–75

### HUM 695
### Echoes of Joy
### Christmas Plate 1998 (CE)
Fourth issue in the Annual Christmas plate series. Modeled by master sculptor Helmut Fischer in 1996. It bears an "M.I. Hummel Annual Christmas Plate 1998 Rödental, Germany" backstamp, plus (TM 7) trademark and 1996 copyright date applied by blue decal. Also has an incised "M.I. Hummel" signature on the front. The original issue price was $145 in 1997.

☐ 695 . . . . . 5⅞″ . . . . . . . . . . (CE). . . ❼ . . . $100–145

**HUM 696**
**Joyful Noise**
**Christmas Plate 1999 (CE)**
Fifth issue in the Annual Christmas plate series. Modeled by master sculptor Helmut Fischer in 1995. It bears an "M.I. Hummel Annual Christmas Plate 1999 Rödental, Germany" backstamp, plus (TM 7) trademark and 1996 copyright date applied by blue decal. Also has an incised "M.I. Hummel" signature on the front. The original issue price was $145 in 1998.

☐ 696 ..... 5⅞" ......... (CE)... **❼** ... $145–150

**HUM 697**
**Light The Way**
**Christmas Plate 2000**
Sixth issue in the Annual Christmas plate series. Modeled by master sculptor Helmut Fischer in 1995. It bears an "M.I. Hummel Annual Christmas Plate 2000 Rödental, Germany" backstamp, plus (TM 8) trademark and 1996 copyright date applied by blue decal. Also has an incised "M.I. Hummel" signature on the front. The original issue price was $145 in 1999.

☐ 697 ..... 5⅞" ......... (**OE**)... **❽** ... $145

Hundreds and hundreds of hours have gone into this 8th edition of the "No. 1 Price Guide to M.I. Hummel Figurines". We have checked, rechecked and even double checked all information, prices etc. We sincerely want this to be the most accurate, complete and up to date guide to "M.I. Hummel" figurine collecting on the market today. We want it to be *your* "bible"! — as some of you have said. We apologize if we have omitted any pertinent information, missed any typographical errors, or "goofed" in any way. We have tried our best! If you have any questions, suggestions, opinions or criticisms — please call or write. Our address and phone number is in the front of this book.

Sincerely,

*Robert L. Miller*

### HUM 698
### Heart's Delight

First released in the U.S. market in the fall of 1997. Modeled by master sculptor Helmut Fischer in 1996. It has an incised 1996 copyright date along with (TM 7) trademark. Also bears the "First Issue 1998" oval decal on the bottom. It comes with a separate *red* wooden chair. The official issue price was $220 in 1997 with chair included.

☐ 698 . . . . . 4″ (5″ w/chair) . . (CE). . . ❼ . . . $230–235
☐ 698 . . . . . 4″ (5″ w/chair) . . (**OE**). . . ❽ . . . $230

### HUM 699
### Love In Bloom

First released in the U.S. market in the fall of 1997. Modeled by master sculptor Helmut Fischer in 1996. It has an incised 1996 copyright date along with (TM 7) trademark. Also bears the "First Issue 1998" oval decal on the bottom. Incised "Hummel" only on back of figurine. It comes with a natural finish wooden wagon. The official issue price was $220 in 1997 with wagon included.

☐ 699 . . . . . 4¼″ (5″ w/wagon) (CE). . . ❼ . . . $230–235
☐ 699 . . . . . 4¼″ (5″ w/wagon) (**OE**). . . ❽ . . . $230

### HUM 700
### Annual Bell 1978, Let's Sing (CE)
First edition in a series of annual bells. The motif of HUM 110 "Let's Sing" is in bas-relief on the front, and 1978 is embossed in red on the reverse side along with the "M.I. Hummel" signature. "HUM 700" is affixed by blue decal along with the (TM5) trademark on the inside of the bell. The original issue price was $50 in 1978.

□ 700 . . . . . 6" . . . . . . . . . . . (CE). . . ❺ . . . $30–50

### HUM 701
### Annual Bell 1979, Farewell (CE)
Second edition in a series of annual bells. The motif of HUM 65 "Farewell" is in bas-relief on the front, and 1979 is embossed in red on the reverse side along with the "M.I. Hummel" signature. "HUM 701" is affixed by blue decal along with the (TM5) trademark on the inside of bell. The original issue price was $70 in 1979.

□ 701 . . . . . 6" . . . . . . . . . . . (CE). . . ❺ . . . $25–35

### HUM 702
### Annual Bell 1980, Thoughtful (CE)
Third edition in a series of annual bells. The motif of HUM 415 "Thoughtful" is in bas-relief on the front, and 1980 is embossed in red on the reverse side along with the "M.I. Hummel" signature. "HUM 702" is affixed by blue decal along with the (TM6) trademark on the inside of bell. The original issue price was $85 in 1980.

□ 702 . . . . . 6" . . . . . . . . . . . (CE). . . ❻ . . . $25–35

399

### HUM 703
### Annual Bell 1981, In Tune (CE)
Fourth edition of the annual bell series. The motif of HUM 414 "In Tune" is in bas-relief on the front, and 1981 is embossed in red on the reverse side along with the "M.I. Hummel" signature. "HUM 703" is affixed by blue decal along with the (TM6) trademark on the inside of bell. The original issue price was $85 in 1981.

☐ 703 . . . . . 6″ . . . . . . . . . . (CE). . . ❻ . . . $30–50

### HUM 704
### Annual Bell 1982, She Loves Me (CE)
Fifth edition of the annual bell series. The motif of HUM 174 "She Loves Me, She Loves Me Not!" is in bas-relief on the front, and 1982 is embossed in red on the reverse side along with the "M.I. Hummel" signature. "HUM 704" is affixed by blue decal along with the (TM6) trademark on the inside of bell. The original issue price was $85 in 1982.

☐ 704 . . . . . 6″ . . . . . . . . . . (CE). . . ❻ . . . $50–75

### HUM 705
### Annual Bell 1983, Knit One (CE)
Sixth edition of the annual bell series. The motif of HUM 432 "Knit One, Purl One" is in bas-relief on the front, and 1983 is embossed in red on the reverse side along with the "M.I. Hummel" signature. "HUM 705" is affixed by blue decal along with the (TM6) trademark on the inside of bell. The original issue price was $90 in 1983.

☐ 705 . . . . . 6″ . . . . . . . . . . (CE). . . ❻ . . . $50–75

### HUM 706
### Annual Bell 1984, Mountaineer (CE)
Seventh edition of the annual bell series. The motif of HUM 315 "Mountaineer" is in bas-relief on the front, and 1984 is embossed in red on the reverse side along with the "M.I. Hummel" signature. "HUM 706" is affixed by blue decal along with the (TM6) trademark on the inside of bell. The original issue price was $90 in 1984.

☐ 706 . . . . . 6″ . . . . . . . . . . . (CE). . . ❻ . . . $50–75

### HUM 707
### Annual Bell 1985, Sweet Song (CE)
Eighth edition of the annual bell series. The motif of HUM 389 "Girl with Sheet of Music" is in bas-relief on the front, and 1985 is embossed in red on the reverse side along with the "M.I. Hummel" signature. "HUM 707" is affixed by blue decal along with the (TM6) trademark on the inside of bell. The original issue price was $90 in 1985. Also has small round decal "1935–1985 50 Years M.I. Hummel."

☐ 707 . . . . . 6″ . . . . . . . . . . . (CE). . . ❻ . . . $50–75

### HUM 708
### Annual Bell 1986, Sing Along (CE)
Ninth edition of the annual bell series. The motif of HUM 433 "Sing Along" was released in 1987, is in bas-relief on the front, and 1986 is embossed in red on the reverse side along with the "M.I. Hummel" signature. "HUM 708" is affixed by blue decal along with the (TM6 ) trademark on the inside of bell. The original issue price was $100 in 1986.

☐ 708 . . . . . 6″ . . . . . . . . . . . (CE). . . ❻ . . . $75–100

### HUM 709
### Annual Bell 1987, With Loving Greetings (CE)
Tenth edition of the annual bell series. The motif of HUM 309 "With Loving Greetings" is in bas-relief on the front, and 1987 is embossed in red on the reverse side along with the "M.I. Hummel" signature. "HUM 709" is affixed by blue decal along with the (TM6) trademark on the inside of bell. The original issue price was $110 in 1987.

☐ 709 . . . . . 6″ . . . . . . . . . . . (CE). . . ❻ . . . $75–150

### HUM 710
### Annual Bell 1988, Busy Student (CE)
Eleventh edition of the annual bell series. The motif of HUM 367 "Busy Student" is in bas-relief on the front, and 1988 in red on the reverse side along with the "M.I. Hummel" signature. "HUM 710" is affixed by blue decal along with the (TM6) trademark on the inside of bell. The original issue price was $120 in 1988.

☐ 710 . . . . . 6″ . . . . . . . . . . . (CE). . . ❻ . . . $75–150

### HUM 711
### Annual Bell 1989, Latest News (CE)
Twelfth edition of the annual bell series. The motif of HUM 184 "Latest News" is in bas-relief on the front, and 1989 in red on the reverse side along with the "M.I. Hummel" signature. "HUM 711" is affixed by blue decal along with the (TM6) trademark on the inside of bell. The original issue price was $135 in 1989.

☐ 711 . . . . . 6″ . . . . . . . . . . . (CE). . . ❻ . . . $75–150

### HUM 712
### Annual Bell 1990, What's New? (CE)
Thirteenth edition of the annual bell series. The motif of HUM 418 "What's New?" is in bas-relief on the front, and 1990 in red on the reverse side along with the "M.I. Hummel" signature. "HUM 712" is affixed by blue decal along with the (TM6) trademark on the inside of bell. The original issue price was $140 in 1990.

☐ 712 . . . . . 6" . . . . . . . . . . . (CE). . . ❻ . . . $75–150

### HUM 713
### Annual Bell 1991, Favorite Pet (CE)
Fourteenth edition of the annual bell series. The motif of HUM 361 "Favorite Pet" is in bas-relief on the front, and 1991 in red on the reverse side along with the "M.I. Hummel" signature. "HUM 713" is affixed by blue decal along with the (TM 6) or (TM 7) trademark on the inside of the bell. The original issue price was $150 in 1991.

☐ 713 . . . . . 6" . . . . . . . . . . . (CE). . . ❻ . . . $75–150
☐ 713 . . . . . 6" . . . . . . . . . . . (CE). . . ❼ . . . $75–150

FINAL ISSUE
1992

### HUM 714
### Annual Bell 1992, Whistler's Duet (CE)
Fifteenth and *final* edition of the annual bell series. The motif of HUM 413 "Whistler's Duet" is in bas-relief on the front, and 1992 in red on the reverse side along with the "M.I. Hummel" signature. "HUM 714" is affixed by blue decal along with the (TM7) trademark on the inside of the bell. The original issue price was $160 in 1992.

☐ 714 . . . . . 6" . . . . . . . . . . . (CE). . . ❼ . . . $80–150

**HUM 715**
**Light The Way**
Both sizes were released in the U.S. market in the fall of 1999. Modeled by master sculptor Helmut Fischer in 1995. Both have the "First Issue 2000" backstamp. The large size has an incised 1995 copyright date, while the small size has an incised 1996 copyright date. The small size has a matte finish, while the large size has the normal glazed finish. The original issue price was $180 for the large (715/0) while the small (715 4/0) was $120 in 1999.

☐ 715 4/0. . . . 3″ . . . . . . . . . . . **(OE)**. . . **❽** . . . $120
☐ 715/0 . . . . 5″ . . . . . . . . . . . . **(OE)**. . . **❽** . . . $180

**HUM 716   (ON) OPEN NUMBER**

**HUM 717**
**Valentine Gift Plaque (CE)**
To celebrate the 20th anniversary of the M.I. HUMMEL CLUB, this special plaque was issued in 1996 for Club members only. It was available to all Club members from 1 March 1996 through 31 December 1996 with special redemption form. It has an incised 1995 copyright date along with (TM 7) trademark. It has an incised "M.I. Hummel" signature diagonally on the back. The issue price was $250 plus $20 personalization fee in 1996.

☐ 717 . . . . . 5¼ × 6½″ . . . . . **(CE)**. . . **❼** . . . $270–300

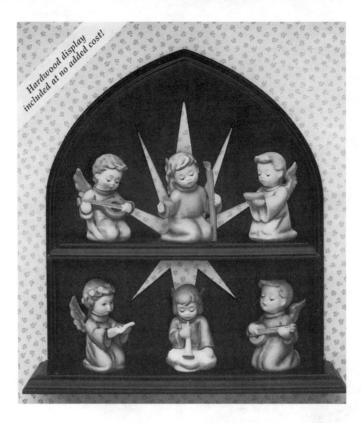

Hardwood display included at no added cost!

**HUM 718**
M. I. Hummel
**Heavenly Angels**
First released in the U.S. market in 1999 and were sold exclusively by mail order through the Danbury Mint in Norwalk, Connecticut at the rate of one every three months. Modeled by master sculptor Helmut Fischer in 1996. They have an incised "M.I. Hummel" signature and the (TM 7) trademark. The original issue price was $90 each (plus tax and $7.50 shipping and handling). A hardwood display included at a no added cost.

☐ 718/A . . . . Let It Shine . . . . **(OE)**. . . ❼ . . . $90
☐ 718/B . . . . Hush-A-Bye . . . **(OE)**. . . ❼ . . . $90
☐ 718/C . . . . Holy Offering . . . **(OE)**. . . ❼ . . . $90
☐ 718/D . . . . Join In Song . . . **(OE)**. . . ❼ . . . $90
☐ 718/E . . . . Peaceful Sounds **(OE)**. . . ❼ . . . $90
☐ 214/D/0 . . Angel Serenade **(OE)**. . . ❼ . . . $90

**HUM 720**
**On Parade**
First released for sale to Military Post Exchanges in January 1998 and to local U.S. retailers in mid-1998. Modeled by master sculptor Helmut Fischer in 1994. It has an incised 1995 copyright date along with the (TM 7) trademark. Also bears "First Issue 1998" oval decal backstamp. The original issue price was $165 in 1998. Boy is similar to boy from HUM 50 "Volunteers."

☐ 720 . . . . . 4¾" . . . . . . . . . . (CE) . . . ❼ . . . $170–175
☐ 720 . . . . . 4¾" . . . . . . . . . . (**OE**) . . . ❽ . . . $170

**HUM 721**
**Trio of Wishes (LE)**
First released in the U.S. market in 1997, the second in the series called the "Trio Collection." Produced in a worldwide limited edition of 20,000 sequentially-numbered pieces. It comes with an oval hard wood base for display. It was modeled by master sculptor Helmut Fischer in 1995 and has an incised 1995 copyright date along with (TM 7) trademark. The official issue price was $475 in 1997.

☐ 721 . . . . . 4½" . . . . . . . . . . (LE) . . . ❼ . . . $500–600

**HUM 722**
**Little Visitor Plaque**
Beginning in January 1996, Goebel designed this special plaque for those visiting the factory in Rödental, Germany. Modeled by master sculptor Helmut Fischer in 1995. It has an incised 1995 copyright date along with the (TM 7) trademark. It can be purchased at the Information Center for DM 185 (U.S. $115) approximate. The plaque can be personalized while you wait, but you must take the plaque with you, as the factory will not ship.

☐ 722 . . . . . 4¾ × 5″ . . . . . . (CE). . . ❼ . . . DM 185
☐ 722 . . . . . 4¾ × 5″ . . . . . . (**OE**). . . ❽ . . . DM 185

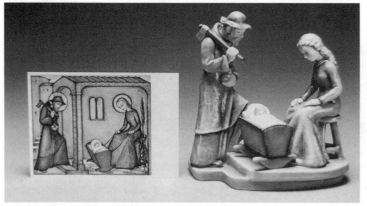

*Postcard Drawing*

**HUM 723 (PFE)**
**Silent Vigil**
This figurine was first modeled by master sculptor Helmut Fischer in 1995. It has an incised 1995 copyright date. Presently listed on factory records as a (PFE) Possible Future Edition and may be released at some future date, subject to possible minor changes.

☐ 723 . . . . . 6¾ . . . . . . . . . . (PFE). . .

### HUM 726
### Soldier Boy Plaque
### (LE)

First released in 1996, this special plaque was sold exclusively by the U.S. Military post exchanges at a cost of $140 plus shipping charges. It is a Limited Edition (LE) of 7500 pieces. It bears the (TM 7) trademark and has an incised "M.I. Hummel" signature diagonally on the back. Modeled by master sculptor Helmut Fischer in 1996. It has an incised 1996 copyright date.

☐ 726 . . . . . 5½ × 6¾" . . . . . (LE) . . . ❼ . . . $150–250

### HUM 727
### Garden Treasures (EE)

First released in the U.S. market in 1998 as a FREE gift for renewing membership in M.I. HUMMEL CLUB for the 1998/99 club year (year 22). Modeled by master sculptor Helmut Fischer in 1996. It bears the inscription: "M.I. HUMMEL CLUB Membership Year 1998/99" in addition to a black flying bumble bee, in a half circle. It is similar to HUM 461 "In The Orchard" (PFE).

☐ 727 . . . . . 3½" . . . . . . . . . . (EE) . . . ❼ . . . $80–100
(M.I.H. Club Members Only)

**HUM 728   (ON) OPEN NUMBER**

**HUM 729**
**Nature's Gift**
First released in the U.S. market in 1997 as a FREE gift for renewing membership in the M.I. HUMMEL CLUB for the 1997/98 club year. Modeled by master sculptor Helmut Fischer in 1996. It has an incised 1996 copyright date. It bears the inscription: "M.I. HUMMEL CLUB Membership Year 1997–1998" in addition to a black flying bumble bee, in a half circle. It is similar to HUM 74 "Little Gardener."

□ 729 . . . . . 3¾". . . . . . . . . . (CE). . . ❼ . . . $80–100

**HUM 730**
**Anniversary Bell 1985, Just Resting (CN)**
This bell was designed by master sculptor Gerhard Skrobek in 1978 for release in 1985 but for some unknown reason it was NEVER ISSUED. Several examples are known to exist in private collections—both in color and white overglaze (unpainted).

□ 730 . . . . . 7⅛ × 4" . . . . . . (CN). . . ❻ . . . $1500–2000

409

### HUM 731 (PFE)
### Best Friends
This figurine was first modeled by master sculptor Helmut Fischer in 1992. It has an incised 1992 copyright date. Presently listed on factory records as a (PFE) Possible Future Edition and may be released at some future date, subject to possible minor changes.

☐ 731 . . . . . 5½″ . . . . . . . . . (PFE) . . .

### HUM 732 (PFE)
### For My Sweetheart
This figurine was first modeled by master sculptor Helmut Fischer in 1992. It has an incised 1993 copyright date. Presently listed on factory records as a (PFE) Possible Future Edition and may be released at some future date, subject to possible minor changes.

☐ 732/I . . . . 5¾″ . . . . . . . . . (PFE) . . .

*HUM 735 (1989)*

*HUM 736 (1988)*

*HUM 737 (1987)*

*HUM 738 (1986)*

## HUM 735–738
### Celebration Plate Series (CE)

To celebrate the tenth anniversary of The Goebel Collectors' Club, a special series of four plates was issued for members of the Goebel Collectors' Club only. Each plate features a former club figurine in bas-relief. Issued one per year starting in 1986. Not sold as an Open Edition, but available with a redemption card only. The first edition in the series is "Valentine Gift" HUM 738. In the subsequent three years, the motif was "Valentine Joy" HUM 737, "Daisies Don't Tell" HUM 736 and "It's Cold" HUM 735. This series was designed by master sculptor Gerhard Skrobek in 1985. Each plate measures 6¼ inches in diameter, has the incised "M.I. Hummel" signature, and has the special inscription on the back: "EXCLUSIVELY FOR MEMBERS OF THE GOEBEL COLLECTORS' CLUB" affixed by blue decal.

☐ 735 . . . . . 6¼" . . . . . . . . . . (CE). . . ❻ . . . $50–60
☐ 736 . . . . . 6¼" . . . . . . . . . . (CE). . . ❻ . . . $50–60
☐ 737 . . . . . 6¼" . . . . . . . . . . (CE). . . ❻ . . . $50–60
☐ 738 . . . . . 6¼" . . . . . . . . . . (CE). . . ❻ . . . $50–60

### HUM 739
### Call To Glory

First released in the U.S. market in 1994. Modeled by master sculptor Helmut Fischer in 1992. It has an incised 1992 copyright date and the "First Issue 1994" oval decal on the bottom. This figurine comes with three authentic flags of the U.S., Germany, and Europe. (Only one flag at a time can be displayed). I made a small plastic base with two holes to display the other flags. The issue price was $250.

☐ 739/I .... 5¾"......... (CE)... ❼ ... $285–290
☐ 739/I .... 5¾"......... (OE)... ❽ ... $285

### HUM 740  (ON) OPEN NUMBER

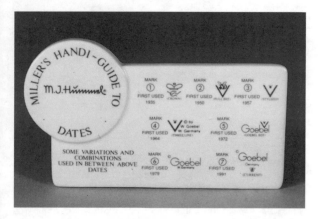

### GOEBEL WZ4 or 004 Plaque

This is a universal porcelain standard stock plaque made in blank, that can be used for various advertising purposes simply by adding a message by decal, then fired. It measures 3 × 5⅛", has an incised 1966 copyright date, an incised WZ 4 or 004 model number, and the GOEBEL trademark (NOT to be confused with "M.I. Hummel" TM 7 trademark). Normally sell for approximately $25–30.

*HUM 741 (1985)*

*HUM 742 (1987)*

*HUM 743 (1986)*

*HUM 744 (1984)*

## HUM 741–744
### Little Music Maker Series (CE)

This series was first issued in 1984 as a four part bisque-porcelain "M.I. Hummel" miniature plate series called the "Little Music Makers." Each was a limited production plate which was produced for one year only. Modeled by master sculptor Gerhard Skrobek in 1982. A matching miniature figurine was released each year as an open edition to coincide with each plate. The original plate issue price was $30 in 1984, $30 in 1985, $35 in 1986 and $40 in 1987.

☐ 741 . . . . . 4" . . . . . . . . . . . . (CE). . . ❻ . . . $25–30
☐ 742 . . . . . 4" . . . . . . . . . . . . (CE). . . ❻ . . . $25–30
☐ 743 . . . . . 4" . . . . . . . . . . . . (CE). . . ❻ . . . $25–30
☐ 744 . . . . . 4" . . . . . . . . . . . . (CE). . . ❻ . . . $25–30

*HUM 745 (1988)*

*HUM 746 (1989)*

*HUM 747 (1990)*

*HUM 748 (1991)*

## HUM 745–748
### Little Homemakers (CE)

This series was first issued in 1988 as a four part bisque-porcelain "M.I. Hummel" miniature plate series called the "Little Homemakers." Each is a limited production plate being produced for one year only. Modeled by master sculptor Gerhard Skrobek in 1986. A matching figurine is released each year as an open edition to coincide with each plate. The original issue price was $45 in 1988, $50 in 1989, $50 in 1990, $70 in 1991.

☐ 745 . . . . . 4" . . . . . . . . . . . . (CE). . . ❻ . . . $25–30
☐ 746 . . . . . 4" . . . . . . . . . . . . (CE). . . ❻ . . . $25–30
☐ 747 . . . . . 4" . . . . . . . . . . . . (CE). . . ❻ . . . $25–30
☐ 748 . . . . . 4" . . . . . . . . . . . . (CE). . . ❻ . . . $25–30
☐ 748 . . . . . 4" . . . . . . . . . . . . (CE). . . ❼ . . . $25–30

## HUM 749 (ON) OPEN NUMBER

### HUM 750
### M.I. Hummel Anniversary Clock
### Goose Girl

First released in the U.S. market in 1995. The ceramic clock face modeled by master sculptor Helmut Fischer in 1993. It has an incised "M.I. Hummel" signature on the clock face in the lower right-hand corner. (TM7) trademark is on back of the ceramic face. The entire clock is made in Germany. The official issue price was $200 in 1995.

☐ 750 . . . . . 12″ . . . . . . . . (OE) . . . . ❼–❽ . . $225

### HUM 751
### Love's Bounty (CE)

First released in the U.S. market in 1996. This is the 11th figurine in the Century Collection and was produced for only this one year in the twentieth century. It was modeled by master sculptor Helmut Fischer in 1993. It has an incised 1993 copyright date, a combination circular "First Issue 1996" and "125th Anniversary Goebel" backstamp. Inscription reads: "M.I. Hummel CENTURY COLLECTION 1996 XX" plus "1871 W. Goebel Porzellanfabrik 1996" and the name "Love's Bounty" along with the (TM 7) trademark. It comes with an oval wood base with anniversary information on the bottom in addition to a brass plate inscribed: 1871–1996–125 W. Goebel Porzellanfabrik. Early production has an incised "125" in the bouquet of flowers the boy is holding, while on later production, the "125" is applied by decal. The official issue price was $1200 in 1996.

☐ 751 . . . . . 6½ × 8½″ . . . . . (CE) . . . ❼ . . . $1500–1600

415

## HUM 752 (ON) OPEN NUMBER

### HUM 753 (PFE)
### Togetherness

This figuring was first modeled by master sculptor Helmut Fischer in 1993. It has an incised 1994 copyright date. Presently listed on factory records as a (PFE) Possible Future Edition and may be released at some future date, subject to possible minor changes. See: HUM 325 "Helping Mother" and HUM 306 "Little Bookkeeper" for comparison.

☐ 753 . . . . . 5⅞" . . . . . . . . . (PFE) . . .

### HUM 754
### We Come In Peace

First released in the U.S. market in the fall of 1994. Similar to HUM 31 "Silent Night Candleholder" which was originally modeled in 1935 by Arthur Moeller. It is the second in a series in co-operation with the United Nations UNICEF Committee. It bears a special UNICEF Commemorative Edition backstamp. Restyled and resculpted by master sculptor Helmut Fischer in 1993 and subsequently renamed. It has an incised 1993 copyright date. The original issue price was $350 in 1994. A $25 contribution will be made to the U.S. Committee for UNICEF as part of a co-operative fund raising effort.

☐ 754 . . . . . 3½ × 5" . . . . . . (OE) . . . ❼ . . . $385

416

### HUM 755
### Heavenly Angel Tree Topper
First released in the U.S. market in 1994. This is the first "M.I. Hummel" tree topper ever created. Modeled by master sculptor Helmut Fischer in 1992. It has an incised 1992 copyright date and the "First Issue 1994" oval decal on the bottom along with the (TM7) trademark. Same basic design as HUM 21 "Heavenly Angel", except it has no feet or ceramic base. The color is a rose/salmon rather than the green of HUM 21. A wooden display stand is provided for normal display. The official issue price was $450 in 1994. Listed as (TW) "Temporarily Withdrawn" in January 1999, but may be reinstated at some future date.

☐ 755 . . . . . 7¾" . . . . . . . . . (TW). . . ❼ . . . . $495–500

### HUM 756
### The Artist Plaque
First released in the U.S. market in 1993 for the Grand Opening of the M.I. Hummel Museum in New Braunfels, Texas. Modeled by master sculptor Helmut Fischer in 1993. It has an incised 1993 copyright date along with (TM7) trademark. The M.I. Hummel signature is also incised diagonally on the back as well as the decal signature on the front. This plaque was reissued without the Grand Opening designation. The original issue price was $260 in 1993.

☐ 756 . . . . . 5 × 6¾" . . . . . . (CE). . . ❼ . . . $350–500

### HUM 757
### A Tuneful Trio (LE)
First released in the U.S. market in 1996, the first in a new series called the "Trio Collection." Produced in a worldwide limited edition of 20,000 sequentially-numbered pieces. It comes with a hard wood base for display. Modeled by master sculptor Helmut Fischer in 1993 and has an incised 1993 copyright date, special "First Issue 1996" decal in combination with the Goebel 125th Anniversary backstamp. To avoid breakage, the lamp post is made of wood, not ceramic. The official issue price was $450 in 1996.

☐ 757 . . . . . 4⅞" . . . . . . . . . . (LE) . . . ❼ . . . $475–485

### HUM 758
### Nimble Fingers
First released in the U.S. market in 1996. Modeled by master sculptor Helmut Fischer in 1993. It has an incised 1993 copyright date along with (TM 7) trademark. It has a special round "First Issue 1996" decal in combination with "Goebel 125th Anniversary" backstamp. Designed as a companion piece to HUM 759 "To Keep You Warm". Accompanied by a wooden bench large enough to hold both pieces. The original issue price was $225 in 1996.

☐ 758 . . . . . 4½" . . . . . . . . . . (CE) . . . ❼ . . . $240–245
☐ 758 . . . . . 4½" . . . . . . . . . . (OE) . . . ❽ . . . $240

### HUM 759
### To Keep You Warm
First released in the U.S. market in 1995. Modeled by master sculptor Helmut Fischer in 1993. It has an incised 1993 copyright date along with (TM7) trademark. Also bears the "First Issue 1995" oval decal on the bottom. The official issue price was $195 in 1995. It comes with a separate wooden chair.

☐ 759 . . . . . 5" . . . . . . . . . . . (CE). . . ❼ . . . $240–245
☐ 759 . . . . . 5" . . . . . . . . . . . (**OE**). . . ❽ . . . $240

### HUM 760
### Country Suitor (CE)
Members' Exclusive Edition for Club year 19. This figurine was first introduced in 1995 for members of the M.I. HUMMEL CLUB only and not sold as an open edition. Modeled by master sculptor Helmut Fischer in 1993. It has an incised 1993 copyright date along with the (TM 7) trademark. Also bears the inscription: EXCLUSIVE EDITION 1995/96 M.I. HUMMEL CLUB" applied by blue decal. A large black flying bumble bee is located on the bottom. The official issue price was $195 in the U.S., in addition to the member's redemption card. This figurine can be purchased on the secondary market at premium prices.

☐ 760 . . . . . 5½" . . . . . . . . . . (CE). . . ❼ . . . $195–225

### HUM 761
### From the Heart

First released in the U.S. market in 1996. Modeled by master sculptor Helmut Fischer in 1993. It has an incised 1993 copyright date along with the (TM7) trademark. Also bears "First Issue 1996" and "Goebel 125th Anniversary" backstamp. Designed as a companion piece to HUM 559 "Heart and Soul" as part of the "Cozy Companions" series. The official issue price was $120 in 1996.

☐ 761 . . . . . 3½" . . . . . . . . . . (CE). . . ❼ . . . $128–130
☐ 761 . . . . . 3½" . . . . . . . . . . (OE). . . ❽ . . . $128

### HUM 762
### Roses Are Red

First released in the U.S. market in the fall of 1997. Modeled by master sculptor Helmut Fischer in 1993. It has an incised 1993 copyright date along with the (TM7) trademark. Also bears the "First Issue 1998" oval decal backstamp on the bottom. The official issue price was $120 in 1997.

☐ 762 . . . . . 3⅞" . . . . . . . . . . (CE). . . ❼ . . . $128–130
☐ 762 . . . . . 3⅞" . . . . . . . . . . (OE). . . ❽ . . . $128

### HUM 763 (PFE)
### Happy Returns

This figurine was first modeled by master sculptor Gerhard Skrobek in 1993. It has an incised 1994 copyright date. Presently listed on factory records as a (PFE) Possible Future Edition and may be released at some future date, subject to possible minor changes. It is a combination similar to HUM 17 "Congratulations" and HUM 9 "Begging His Share", but with a different dog!

☐ 763 . . . . . 7⅛" . . . . . . . . . . (PFE) . . .

### HUM 764
### Mission Madonna (PFE)

Modeled by master sculptor Helmut Fischer in 1993. The first example of this figurine was presented to His Eminence John Cardinal O'Connor of New York in 1996. Presently listed on factory records as a Possible Future Edition (PFE) and may be released at some future date, subject to possible minor changes.

☐ 764 . . . . . 10½" . . . . . . . . . (PFE) . . . ❼ . . . .

---

**HUM TERM**

**BACKSTAMP OR TRADEMARK:** The official legal mark that Goebel places on the bottom of all "M.I. Hummel" products.

### HUM 765 (PFE)
### First Love

This figurine was first modeled by master sculptor Helmut Fischer in 1993. It has an incised 1994 copyright date. Presently listed on factory records as a (PFE) Possible Future Edition and may be released at some future date, subject to possible minor changes. The boy is similar to HUM 174 "She Loves Me, She Loves Me Not!" and (Hummel drawing ARS H 126 "She Loves Me?"). The girl is from Hummel drawing ARS H 127 "He Loves Me?", but has not been made into a figurine so far.

☐ 765 . . . . . 6⅜" . . . . . . . . . (PFE) . . .

### HUM 766
### Here's My Heart

First released in the U.S. market in the fall of 1997. This is the 13th figurine in the Century Collection and will be produced for this one year only of 1998 in the twentieth century. It was modeled by master sculptor Helmut Fischer in 1994. It has an incised 1994 copyright date. A circular inscription applied by blue decal reads: "M.I. HUMMEL CENTURY COLLECTION 1998 XX" and the name "Here's My Heart" along with the (TM 7) trademark. The original issue price was $1375 in 1997.

☐ 766 . . . . . 10¾" . . . . . . . . . (CE) . . . ❼ . . . $1450–1600

## HUM 767
### Puppy Love, Display Plaque

First released in the U.S. market in 1995. Modeled by master sculptor Helmut Fischer in 1993. It has an incised 1993 copyright date along with the (TM7) trademark. Also bears a special backstamp: "Special Edition 1995" in German and English. The official issue price was $240 in 1995.

☐ 767 . . . . . 4½ × 7¼" . . . . . (CE). . . ❼ . . . $300–350

## HUM 768
### Pixie

First released in the U.S. market in 1995. Modeled by master sculptor Helmut Fischer in 1994. It has an incised 1994 copyright date along with (TM7) trademark. Also bears the "First Issue 1995" oval decal on the bottom. Designed as a companion piece to HUM 553 "Scamp" as part of the "Cozy Companions" series. The official issue price was $105 in 1995.

☐ 768 . . . . . 3½" . . . . . . . . . . (CE). . . ❼ . . . $130–135
☐ 768 . . . . . 3½" . . . . . . . . . . **(OE)**. . . ❽ . . . $130

**HUM 771**
**Practice Makes Perfect**
First released in the U.S. market in the fall of 1996. Modeled by master sculptor Helmut Fischer in 1994. It has an incised 1994 copyright date and the "First Issue 1997" oval decal backstamp. Incised "Hummel" only on back of boy. It comes with a separate wooden rocking chair. The official issue price was $250 in 1997.

☐ 771 . . . . . 4¾" . . . . . . . . . . (CE). . . ❼ . . . $260–265
☐ 771 . . . . . 4¾" . . . . . . . . . . (OE). . . ❽ . . . $260

**PRACTICE <u>DOES</u> MAKE PERFECT!**

**A <u>HAPPY</u> PAINTER IN THE FACTORY!**

*HUM 775*
*1989 (Ride into Christmas)*

*HUM 776*
*1990 (Letter to Santa Claus)*

*HUM 777*
*1991 (Hear Ye, Hear Ye)*

*HUM 778*
*1992 (Harmony in Four Parts)*

## HUM 775–778
### Christmas Bells (CE)

This series was first issued in 1989 as a four part bisque-porcelain bell series. Each is a limited production item being produced for one year only. Modeled by master sculptor Helmut Fischer in 1987–88. The original issue price was $35 in 1989, $37.50 in 1990, $39.50 in 1991 and $45 in 1992.

☐ 775 . . . . . 3¼″ . . . . . . . . . . (CE). . . ❻ . . . $30–40
☐ 776 . . . . . 3¼″ . . . . . . . . . . (CE). . . ❻ . . . $30–40
☐ 777 . . . . . 3¼″ . . . . . . . . . . (CE). . . ❼ . . . $30–40
☐ 778 . . . . . 3¼″ . . . . . . . . . . (CE). . . ❼ . . . $30–40

**HUM 779**
*1993 (Celestial Musician)*

**HUM 780**
*1994 (Festival Harmony, Mandolin)*

**HUM 781**
*1995 (Festival Harmony, Flute)*

**HUM 782**
*1996 (Christmas Song)*

**HUM 779–782**
**Christmas Bells (CE)**
This series of Christmas Bells was first issued in 1993 as a four part bisque-porcelain bell series. Each is a limited production item being produced for one year only. Modeled by master sculptor Helmut Fischer in 1991-92. The original issue price was $50 in 1993, $50 in 1994, $55 in 1995, and $65 in 1996.

☐ 779 . . . . . 3¼" . . . . . . . . . . (CE). . . ❼ . . . $25–35
☐ 780 . . . . . 3¼" . . . . . . . . . . (CE). . . ❼ . . . $25–35
☐ 781 . . . . . 3¼" . . . . . . . . . . (CE). . . ❼ . . . $25–35
☐ 782 . . . . . 3¼" . . . . . . . . . . (CE). . . ❼ . . . $25–35

**HUM 783**
*1997 (Thanksgiving Prayer)*

**HUM 784**
*1998 (Echoes of Joy)*

**HUM 785**
*1999 (Joyful Noise)*

**HUM 786**
*2000 (Light the Way)*

### HUM 783–786
### Christmas Bells

This series of Christmas Bells was first issued in 1997 as a four part bisque-porcelain bell series III. Each is a limited production item being produced for one year only. Modeled by master sculptor Helmut Fischer in 1995-96. The original issue price was $68 in 1997, and $70 in 1998.

☐ 783 . . . . . 3¼″ . . . . . . . . . . (CE). . . ❼ . . . $70–75
☐ 784 . . . . . 3¼″ . . . . . . . . . . (CE). . . ❼ . . . $70–75
☐ 785 . . . . . 3¼″ . . . . . . . . . . (CE). . . ❼ . . . $70–75
☐ 786 . . . . . 3¼″ . . . . . . . . . . (**OE**). . . ❽ . . . $70

## HUM 787
### Traveling Trio (LE)

First released in the U.S. market in the fall of 1997, the third and final figurine in the "Trio Collection" series. Produced in a worldwide limited edition of 20,000 sequentially-numbered pieces. Modeled by master sculptor Helmut Fischer in 1995 and has an incised 1995 copyright date along with (TM 7) trademark. It comes with a hard wood base for display. The official issue price was $490 in 1997. Similar to HUM 331 "Crossroads."

☐ 787 . . . . . 5¼" . . . . . . . . . (LE) . . . ❼ . . . $490–500

## HUM 788
### Perpetual Calendar (Hello)

First released in the U.S. market in the fall of 1995. Modeled by master sculptor Helmut Fischer in 1995. It has an incised 1995 copyright date along with (TM 7) trademark. Has wood holder for calendar cards—months are both in English and German—dates are perpetual. Has an incised "M.I. Hummel" signature on the base just behind the figurine. The original issue price was $295 in 1995. HUM 124 "Hello" was originally modeled by master sculptor Arthur Moeller in 1939 but has been restyled several times through the years. Listed as (TW) "Temporarily Withdrawn" in January 1999.

☐ 788/A (Hello) . . . . . 7½ × 6⅛" . . . . (TW) . . . . ❼ . . . . $295–300

**HUM 788**
**Perpetual Calendar (Sister)**
First released in the U.S. market in the fall of 1995. Modeled by master sculptor Helmut Fischer in 1995. It has an incised 1995 copyright date along with (TM 7) trademark. Has wood holder for calendar cards—months are both in English and German—dates are perpetual. Has an incised "M.I. Hummel" signature on the base just behind the figurine. The original issue price was $295 in 1995. HUM 98 "Sister" was originally modeled by master sculptor Arthur Moeller in 1938 and has changed very little through the years. Listed as (TW) "Temporarily Withdrawn" in January 1999.

☐ 788/B (Sister). . . . . 7½ × 5⅝″ . . . . (TW) . . . . ❼ . . . . $295–300

**HUM 789   (ON) OPEN NUMBER**

**HUM 790**
**Celebrate With Song (CE)**
Members' Exclusive Edition for Club year 20. This figurine was first introduced in 1996 for members of the M.I. Hummel Club only and not sold as an open edition. Modeled by master sculptor Helmut Fischer in 1994. It has an incised 1994 copyright date along with the (TM 7) trademark. Also bears the inscription: "EXCLUSIVE EDITION 1996/97 M.I. HUMMEL CLUB 1977 (20) 1997" applied by blue decal. A black flying bumble bee is located within a semi-circle on the bottom. The official issue price was $295 in the U.S., in addition to the member's redemption card, valid until 31 May 1998.

☐ 790 . . . . . 5⅞″ . . . . . . . . . . (CE) . . . ❼ . . . $295–325

### HUM 791
### May Dance
First released in the U.S. market in the spring of 2000 as a "Special Event" figurine, available in North America this one year only at "Mai Fest" Celebrations, M.I. Hummel Artist and Goebel Sales Representative Events occurring from 1 April through 31 December 2000. Modeled by master sculptor Helmut Fischer in 1996. It has the (TM 8) trademark and a "Special Event" decal on the bottom. The official issue price was $199 in 2000.

☐ 791 . . . . . 7" . . . . . . . . . . (OE). . . ❽ . . . $199

### HUM 792   (ON) OPEN NUMBER

### HUM 793
### Forever Yours
First released in the U.S. market in 1996 as a FREE gift for renewing membership in the M.I. HUMMEL CLUB for the 1996/97 Club year. Modeled by master sculptor Helmut Fischer in 1994. It has an incised 1994 copyright date. It bears the inscription: "M.I. HUMMEL CLUB" in addition to a black flying bumble bee, in a half circle, plus the (TM 7) trademark. It comes with a gold medallion that reads "First Issue 1996/97." Can now be purchased on the secondary market at premium prices.

☐ 793 . . . . . 4⅛" . . . . . . . . . . (CE). . . ❼ . . . $75–100

---
**HUM TERM**

**CLOSED EDITION (CE):** Pieces formerly in W. Goebel production program but no longer produced. Also, <u>models</u> that are still being produced, but have a <u>trademark</u> that is no longer used, are shown as (CE) "Closed Editions."

---

HUM 794 "Best Buddies"           HUM 326

## HUM 794 (PFE)
**Best Buddies**
This figurine was first modeled by master sculptor Helmut Fischer in 1995. It has an incised 1996 copyright date. Presently listed on factory records as a (PFE) Possible Future Edition and may be released at some future date, subject to possible minor changes. See HUM 326 "Being Punished, Wall Plaque" (PFE), for comparison.

☐ 794 . . . . . 3½″ . . . . . . . . . . (PFE) . . .

### HUM 795
**From My Garden**
First released in the U.S. market in 1997. Modeled by master sculptor Helmut Fischer in 1994. It has an incised 1994 copyright date along with the (TM 7) trademark. Also bears the "First Issue 1997" oval decal on the bottom. The official issue price was $180 in 1997.

☐ 795/0 . . . . 4⅞″ . . . . . . . . . . (CE) . . . ❼ . . . $190–195
☐ 795/0 . . . . 4⅞″ . . . . . . . . . . (OE) . . . ❽ . . . $190

**Postcard Drawing**

### HUM 796 (PFE)
### Brave Voyager
This figurine was first modeled by master sculptor Helmut Fischer in 1994. It has an incised 1994 copyright date. Presently listed on factory records as a (PFE) Possible Future Edition and may be released at some future date, subject to possible minor changes.

☐ 796 . . . . . 3⅞" . . . . . . . . . . (PFE) . . .

### HUM 797 (PFE)
### Rainy Day Bouquet
This figurine was first modeled by master sculptor Helmut Fischer in 1994. It has an incised 1995 copyright date. Presently listed on factory records as a (PFE) Possible Future Edition and may be released at some future date, subject to possible minor changes.

☐ 797 . . . . . 5⅛" . . . . . . . . . . (PFE) . . .

☐ 799 . . . . . 5⅞″ . . . . . . . (PFE) . . .

**HUM 799 (PFE)**
**Vagabond**
This figurine was first modeled by master sculptor Helmut Fischer in 1994. It has an incised 1995 copyright date. Presently listed on factory records as a (PFE) Possible Future Edition and may be released at some future date, subject to possible minor changes.

☐ 800 . . . . . . 3⅝″ . . . . . (OE) . . . . ❽ . . . $300

**HUM 800**
**Proud Moments**
First released in the U.S. market in the fall of 1999. Modeled by master sculptor Helmut Fischer in 1998. It has an incised 1998 copyright date in addition to a "First Issue 2000 MILLENNIUM" oval decal and the (TM 8) trademark. The original issue price was $300 in 1999.

## HUM 801 (ON) OPEN NUMBER

### HUM 802 (PFE)
### Brave Soldier

This figurine was first modeled by master sculptor Helmut Fischer in 1996. It has an incised 1997 copyright date. Presently listed on factory records as a (PFE) Possible Future Edition and may be released at some future date, subject to possible minor changes.

☐ 802 . . . . . 5⅛″. . . . . . . . . (PFE). . .

## HUM 803–804 (ON) OPEN NUMBERS

### HUM 805 (PFE)
### Little Toddler

This figurine was first modeled by master sculptor Helmut Fischer in 1996. It has an incised 1997 copyright date. Presently listed on factory records as a (PFE) Possible Future Edition and may be released at some future date, subject to possible minor changes.

☐ 805 . . . . . 2¾″. . . . . . . . . (PFE). . .

434

### HUM 814
### Peaceful Blessing
First released in the U.S. market in the fall of 1998. Modeled by master sculptor Helmut Fischer in 1997. It has an incised 1997 copyright date along with the (TM 7) trademark and the "First Issue 1999" oval decal backstamp. The official issue price was $180 in 1999.

☐ 814 . . . . . 4½" . . . . . . . . . . (CE). . . ❼ . . . $185–190
☐ 814 . . . . . 4½" . . . . . . . . . . (OE). . . ❽ . . . $185

### HUM 815
### Heavenly Prayer
First released in the U.S. market in the fall of 1998. Modeled by master sculptor Helmut Fischer in 1997. It has an incised 1997 copyright date along with the (TM 7) trademark and the "First Issue 1999" oval decal backstamp. The official issue price was $180 in 1999.

☐ 815 . . . . . 4⅞ to 5" . . . . . . (CE). . . ❼ . . . $185–190
☐ 815 . . . . . 4⅞ to 5" . . . . . . (OE). . . ❽ . . . $185

### HUM 820
**Caribbean Collection Plaque (LE)**
Modeled by master sculptor Helmut Fischer in 1997. It has an incised 1997 copyright date. First released in the Cayman Islands B.W.I., (British West Indies) in 1999 and sold exclusively by Kirk Freeport Plaza, Ltd. along with 10 other models of M.I. Hummel figurines with a special floral backstamp and the words "CARIBBEAN COLLECTION". The original issue price was $127 plus shipping and handling. (My total was $157.70 which included next day air charges.) Limited to approximately 300 pieces, but could be reissued.

☐ 820 . . . . . 3¾ to 6″ . . . . . . (LE) . . . ❼ . . . $160–200

### HUM 821   (ON) OPEN NUMBER

*(Back View)*

### HUM 822
**Hummelnest**
First released in Rödental, Germany in the fall of 1997 as a new Visitors Plaque for those visiting the Goebel Factory. It can be personalized while you wait. Modeled by master sculptor Helmut Fischer in 1997. It has an incised 1997 copyright date along with the (TM 7) trademark and measures 5¼″ W × 4⅜″ H. The original issue price was DM 195 (approximately U.S. $100) in 1999.

**HUM 823   (ON) OPEN NUMBER**
**HUM 824–825   SEE: INTERNATIONAL SECTION**

**HUM 826**
**Little Maestro (LE)**
First released in the U.S. market in the fall of 1999. Modeled by master sculptor Helmut Fischer in 1997. It has an incised 1997 copyright date along with the (TM 8) trademark and the "First Issue 2000 MILLENNIUM" oval decal backstamp. Produced in a Limited Edition of 20,000 pieces worldwide. Came with a FREE jointed, mohair, Steiff Teddy Bear and a porcelain medallion. The official issue price was $425 in 1999.

☐ 826/I . . . . 5½″ . . . . . . (LE) . . . . . ❽ . . . . $425

**HUM 827**
**Daydreamer Plaque**
First released in Rödental, Germany in the fall of 1999 as a new Visitors plaque for those visiting the Goebel Factory. It can be personalized while you wait. Modeled by master sculptor Helmut Fischer in 1998 and has an incised 1998 copyright date along with the (TM 7) trademark. It has the "First Issue 2000 MILLENNIUM" oval decal backstamp. The official issue price was $140 in 1999. Similar to girl from HUM 196 "Telling Her Secret".

☐ 827 . . . . . 3½″ × 4⅜″ . . . (CE) . . . . ❼ . . . . $140–145
☐ 827 . . . . . 3½″ × 4⅜″ . . . (**OE**) . . . . ❽ . . . . $140

**HUM 828**
**Over The Horizon**
A plaque similar to "Daydreamer" HUM 827 with boy on right side, is scheculed for release in the U.S. market in mid-2000. Has (TM 8) and will retail for $140.

**HUM 829–834   (ON) OPEN NUMBERS**

**HUM 835**
**Garden Splendor**
A figurine scheduled to be released in the European market only in 2000. Measures 3.25″ (8cm) and retails for DM 249.

**HUM 860–874 Miniature Bells**
Fifteen (15) miniature bells to be released in the European market only in January 2000, with the remaining 10 bells to be available in July 2000 and January 2001. They measure 3.75″ (9.5cm) and retail for DM 49. A Wooden Board rack will retail for DM 95 according to recent information just received.

**HUM 876**
**Heavenly Angel Ornament**
This bell shaped ornament was released in the European market in 1999. At the present time it is NOT scheduled for release in the U.S. market. It measures 3⅜ inches (8.5 cm). Does have an incised M.I. Hummel signature on the front, but I am not sure of the trademark or copyright date as I have <u>not</u> seen the reverse side of this ornament. The issue price in Germany was DM 39 in 1999.

**HUM 877**
**Ride Into Christmas Ornament**
This Christmas Tree shaped ornament was released in the European market in 1999. At the present time it is NOT scheduled for release in the U.S. market. It measures 4⅛ inches (10.5 cm). Does have an incised M.I. Hummel signature on the front, but I am not sure of the trademark or copyright date as I have <u>not</u> seen the reverse side of this ornament. The issue price in Germany was DM 39 in 1999.

---

Two other ornaments were released in the European market as part of this set. They were:

HUM 2110 A star shaped ornament with HUM 2014 "Christmas Delivery" on the front.

HUM 2111 A snowflake shaped ornament with HUM 2002 "Making New Friends" on the front.

---

**HUM 878–885 (ON) OPEN NUMBERS**

# Century Collection Mini Plates

## A New Series of Mini-Plates to Match the Acclaimed *M.I. Hummel* Century Collection

During the final 14 years of the 20th Century, we have all been enjoying an exquisite series of limited edition M.I. Hummel figurines available for one year only. The Century Collection showcases each piece in ample size, rich in detail, and among the finest work ever produced by Goebel.

Now that the century has ended, the Century Collection has, too. Last year's "Fanfare" figurine (HUM 1999) is the final edition in this series.

To honor this collection, Goebel has introduced the Century Collection Mini Plate Series. Fourteen small plates feature the Century Collection motifs in miniature, using a special decal-on-relief technique. Each plate is 4 inches in diameter and affordably priced at just $30 each.

An attractive wall display has been specially designed, making it easy to exhibit your mini-plate collection. Crafted in fine walnut, the display retails for $100.

| | | | | |
|---|---|---|---|---|
| ☐ 886 | Chapel Time . . . . . . . 1986 | | ☐ 893 | Welcome Spring. . . . . . 1993 |
| ☐ 887 | Pleasant Journey . . . . . 1987 | | ☐ 894 | Rock-A-Bye . . . . . . . . 1994 |
| ☐ 888 | Call to Worship . . . . . . 1988 | | ☐ 895 | Strike Up the Band . . . 1995 |
| ☐ 889 | Harmony in Four Parts. 1989 | | ☐ 896 | Love's Bounty. . . . . . . 1996 |
| ☐ 890 | Let's Tell the World . . . 1990 | | ☐ 897 | Fond Goodbye . . . . . . 1997 |
| ☐ 891 | We Wish You the Best . 1991 | | ☐ 898 | Here's My Heart . . . . . 1998 |
| ☐ 892 | On Our Way . . . . . . . . 1992 | | ☐ 899 | Fanfare . . . . . . . . . . . 1999 |

## HUM 900
### Merry Wanderer Plaque (with bumblebee) (EE)
First released in the U.S. market in the fall of 1999, as a special Exclusive Edition for M.I. Hummel Club members only. Modeled by master sculptor Helmut Fischer in 1998. It has an incised 1998 copyright date along with the (TM 8) trademark. Incised on the back of the Collectors Club plaque only: "Original Goebel archival plaque ca. 1947". The official issue price was $195 in 1999, with the members redemption card. Both the Collectors plaque and the Authorized Retailer plaque have "Goebel Rödental Germany" embossed on the satchel.

☐ 900 . . . . . 4 × 5¾″ . . . . . (OE) . . . . ❽ . . . . $195 (Retailers)
☐ 900 . . . . . 4 × 5¾″ . . . . . (OE) . . . . ❽ . . . . $195 (Collectors)
(M.I.H. Club Members Only)

## HUM 920
### Star Gazer Plate
This Special MILLENNIUM Edition plate bears a special 60th Anniversary back-stamp honoring HUM 132 "Star Gazer" figurine which was first created in 1939 by master sculptor Arthur Moeller and restyled in 1980 by master sculptor Gerhard Skrobek. "Star Gazer" plate was modeled by master sculptor Helmut Fischer in 1999. It has an incised 1999 copyright date along with the (TM 8) trademark. The official issue price was $198 in 2000.

☐ 920 . . . . . 7½″ . . . . . . . . (OE) . . . . ❽ . . . . $198

## HUM 921
### Garden Splendor, Plate
A year 2000 Millennium plate scheduled for release in the European market only. Measures 7.25″ (18cm) and retails for DM 275.

# "M.I. Hummel"
# MINIATURE PLATE SERIES
## HUM 971–995

**P**roduced in 1995 for sale in the European market only. They were originally released for sale at the rate of four plates at a time, but are now all readily available in Europe. So far, they have NOT been sold by Goebel of North America in the U.S. market. They are individually boxed and priced at approximately $20 each in U.S. dollars. They <u>DO</u> have HUM numbers 971 through 995, and have a 1995 copyright date as part of the (TM 7) trademark applied by blue decal on the back of each 3¼ inch plate. Two hardwood panels can be purchased for displaying all 25 plates in the series.

These miniature plates may now be ordered in the United States from Danbury Mint, Norwalk, CT. Priced at $19.95 each (plus any applicable tax and $2.50 shipping and handling). The first plate is shipped separately. Thereafter, you will receive the remaining 24 plates in shipments of two every other month, yet you need pay for only one plate per month. A custom-designed hardwood display is also available for $19.95 (plus any applicable sales tax and $2.50 shipping and handling).

# HUM 806–968
# International "M.I. Hummel" Figurines

The following eight "M.I. Hummel" figurines are the original "Hungarian" figurines discovered in 1976 by a man in Vienna, Austria. He had acquired them from a lady in Budapest, who had purchased them at the weekly flea market—one at a time, over a six-month period. He in turn sold them to (this author) collector Robert L. Miller, a supermarket owner in Eaton, Ohio, as a gift for his wife, Ruth.

"M.I. Hummel" figurines have always been typically German, with German-style dress or costumes; in 1940 the W. Goebel company decided to produced a line of "M.I. Hummel" figurines in the national dress of other countries. Sister M.I. Hummel made many sketches of children in their native costumes. Master modelers Reinhold Unger and Arthur Moeller then turned the sketches into the adorable figurines you see on the following pages. Due to the events of World War II, production of the International Figurines series was not started. After the discovery in 1976 of the "Hungarian" figurines, a thorough search of the factory was conducted, including the checking and rechecking of old records. Twenty-four prototypes were found and are pictured here. Most of the people involved in the original project are no longer living; therefore the information contained here may not be absolutely accurate or complete. Since 1976, several duplicates of some models and new variations of others have been found, usually selling in the $10,000 to $15,000 price range, depending on condition. Several models have also been found *without* the "M.I. Hummel" signature; these would have much less value to most collectors. Author/collector Miller says, "I feel certain that there are still more rare finds to be made in the future, maybe even some Russian models! Happy Hunting!"

*The following eight "M.I. Hummel" figurines were purchased by Robert L. Miller for a little less than $500 total (not each) in 1976.*

HUM 809          HUM 807          HUM 832(A)          HUM 854

| HUM 904 | HUM 806 | HUM 841 | HUM 851 |

Note: All International figurines were modeled by master sculptors Arthur Moeller or Reinhold Unger in 1940.

The following thirty International "M.I. Hummel" figurines are a combination of the Robert L. Miller Collection as well as the Goebel Archives Collection.

☐ *HUM 806 Bulgarian A. Moeller*

☐ *HUM 807 Bulgarian A. Moeller*

☐ *HUM 808 Bulgarian A. Moeller*

☐ *HUM 809 Bulgarian A. Moeller*

☐ *HUM 810(A) Bulgarian R. Unger*

☐ *HUM 810(B) Bulgarian R. Unger*

☐ *HUM 811 Bulgarian R. Unger*

☐ *HUM 812(A) Serbian R. Unger*

☐ *HUM 812(B) Serbian R. Unger*

☐ *HUM 813 Serbian R. Unger*

☐ *HUM 824(A) Swedish A. Moeller*

☐ *HUM 824(B) Swedish A. Moeller*

444

☐ HUM 825(A) Swedish A. Moeller    ☐ HUM 825(B) Swedish A. Moeller    ☐ HUM 831 Slovak   R. Unger

☐ HUM 832(B) Slovak   R. Unger    ☐ HUM 833 Slovak   R. Unger    ☐ HUM 841   Czech   R. Unger

☐ HUM 842(A)   Czech   R. Unger    ☐ HUM 842(B)   Czech   R. Unger    ☐ HUM 851 Hungarian A. Moeller

☐ *HUM 852(A) Hungarian A. Moeller*

☐ *HUM 852(B) Hungarian A. Moeller*

☐ *HUM 853(A) Hungarian A. Moeller*

☐ *HUM 853(B) Hungarian A. Moeller*

☐ *HUM 854 Hungarian A. Moeller*

☐ *HUM 904   Serbian   R. Unger*

☐ *HUM 913   Serbian   R. Unger*

☐ *HUM 947 Serbian A. Moeller*

☐ *HUM 968   Serbian   R. Unger*

# HUM 834 ????
# Little Fiddler "Slovak International"????

HUM 834 "Slovak" ???

HUM 904 Serbian R. Unger, 1940

A figurine was found in Eastern Europe several years ago, in a badly damaged condition. It had NO Goebel trademark, NO incised model number (only a paper sticker with 834 written in pencil), NO incised "M. I. Hummel" signature, but it *did* have the "appearance" of being genuine! Could this figurine possibly be an "International" design? It is now in a private collection in the United States; sorry, not mine!

A *second* figurine (photo above, left) fitting this same description has reportedly been found in Hungary, also with some damage. I have *not* examined this figurine in person, but according to Goebel factory records, they did indeed produce a "Little Fiddler" figurine with "Slovak" costume in 1940, but are *not* sure who the sculptor was! According to their product-book, the sculptor was Arthur Moeller. According to their sculpting diary, the sculptor was Reinhold Unger. Whether Moeller or Unger, it would seem safe to conclude that Goebel may have produced these two "Little Fiddler" figurines. The design is quite similar to HUM 904 Serbian "Little Fiddler" also pictured above for comparison.

Possibly, as time goes by, we may find some better examples; with the "M. I. Hummel" signature, with the Goebel "crown" trademark, and the incised model number 834. Until then—the search goes on!

---

**HUM TERM**

**"INTERNATIONAL":** This name is given to the group of M.I. Hummel figurines that were produced in 1940 with the national dress of other countries. Master sculptors Reinhold Unger and Arthur Moeller translated Sister Hummel's sketches into Goebel M.I. Hummel figurines. The "Internationals" are highly sought-after by collectors.

---

**HUM 1999**
**Fanfare (CE)**

First released in the U.S. market in the fall of 1998. This is the 14th and final figurine in the Century Collection and was produced for only this one year (1999) in the twentieth century. It was modeled by master sculptors Helmut Fischer and Marion Huschka in 1993. It has an incised 1993 copyright date. A circular inscription applied by blue decal reads: "M.I. Hummel 1999 XX FINAL EDITION–CENTURY COLLECTION" and the name "Fanfare" along with the (TM 7) trademark. Came with a hardwood base with brass plaque: "CENTURY COLLECTION 1999/LETZTE AUSGABE - FINAL EDITION". The official issue price was $1275 in 1999. The incised "M.I. Hummel" signature is perpendicular on the back of the figurine.

☐ 1999 . . . . 11″ . . . . . . . . . . (CE) . . . ❼ . . . $1275–1300

## HUM 2000
### Worldwide Wanderers (LE)

First released in the U.S. market in the fall of 1999 in a sequentially-numbered Limited Edition (LE) of 2000 pieces worldwide (plus 200 Artist Proofs). Modeled by master sculptors Helmut Fischer and Tamara Fuchs in 1998. It has an incised 1998 copyright date, a special "Year 2000 Millennium" backstamp along with the (TM 8) trademark. It comes with a black hardwood, velvet-covered base and a porcelain Certificate of Authenticity. The official issue price was $4,500 in 1999.

☐ 2000 .... 9½″ × 17¼″ × 8½″ ....... (LE)..... ❽ ... $4,500

(8½″ H × 10¾″ L × 9½″ W)

### The Wanderers (LE)

Released in the fall of 1999, this set includes five figurines representing the continents on a tiered wooden display surrounding a German, full-lead crystal globe. Limited Edition (LE) of 2,000 sets created exclusively for North America. The official issue price was $1,250 in 1999.

**HUM 2002**
**Making New Friends**
First released in the U.S. market in the fall of 1996. Modeled by master sculptor Helmut Fischer in 1996. It has an incised 1996 copyright date along with the (TM 7) trademark. It has a combination "First Issue 1996" and "125th Anniversary 1871–1996 Goebel" backstamp applied by a round blue decal on the bottom. The boy with sled is an "interpretation" of HUM 396 "Ride Into Christmas" figurine. The official issue price was $595 in 1996.

☐ 2002 .... 6½" ........ (CE)... ❼ ... $595–600
☐ 2002 .... 6½" ........ (**OE**)... ❽ ... $595

**HUM 2003**
**Dearly Beloved**
First released in the U.S. market in 1998. Modeled by master sculptor Helmut Fischer in 1997. It has an incised 1997 copyright date along with the (TM 7) trademark. It comes with a black hardwood base and a brass plate for engraving name or message. A new work of art, approved by the Convent of Siessen, based upon an interpretation of Sister M.I. Hummel's original art. The official issue price was $450 in 1998.

☐ 2003 .... 6⅝" ........ (CE)... ❼ ... $475–500
☐ 2003 .... 6⅝" ........ (**OE**)... ❽ ... $475

This unique figurine was presented to Robert L. and Ruth A. Miller on the occasion of their 50th wedding anniversary from the Goebel Company in Germany. A replica of HUM 2003 "Dearly Beloved" with Bob and Ruth's faces from their wedding picture taken 50 years ago. Bob is holding a "spiral-bound" version of his M.I. Hummel Price Guide and there is a bumblebee on his top hat. Ruth is holding a bouquet of roses, which were the same flowers in her wedding bouquet of 50 years ago. A special congratulatory letter from Dieter E. Schneider and Kenneth G. Le Fevre topped off the presentation. The letter relates "It is a one-of-a-kind piece, which—like their marriage—has no duplicate (not even in our archives)." This special figurine was modeled by master sculptor Helmut Fischer in 1999. It does NOT have an "M.I. Hummel" signature. Estimated value—PRICELESS!

Dieter E. Schneider, Chief Executive W. Goebel Porzellanfabrik
Kenneth G. Le Fevre, President Goebel of North America

**HUM 2004**
**Pretzel Girl**
First released in the U.S. market in the fall of 1998. Modeled by master sculptor Helmut Fischer in 1996. It has an incised 1996 copyright date along with the (TM 7) trademark and the "First Issue 1999" oval decal backstamp. Listed as a Special Event Collector's Set with a FREE Oktoberfest HummelScape (Mark # 1000–D) at participating retailers. Pretzel Girl is now listed as a (CE) "Closed Edition" in the U.S. market, but is still available in other markets worldwide. The official issue price was $185 for the set in 1998.

☐ 2004 . . . . 4″ . . . . . . . (CE) . . . . . ❼ . . . . $185–200

**HUM 2005–2006   (ON) OPEN NUMBERS**

**HUM 2007**
**Tender Love (LE)**
First released in the U.S. market in the spring of 1998 for the Spring Open House event at participating retailers in the U.S. Modeled by master sculptor Helmut Fischer in 1996. It has an incised 1996 copyright date along with the (TM 7) trademark. Produced in a sequentially-numbered limited edition of 25,000 pieces worldwide (15,000 in the U.S.) The official issue price was $198 in 1998.

☐ 2007 . . . . 4¼″ . . . . . (LE) . . . . . . ❼ . . . . $198

### HUM 2008
### Frisky Friends (LE)
First released in the U.S. market in the fall of 1997 for the Fall Open House event on 25 October 1997 at participating retailers. Modeled by master sculptor Helmut Fischer in 1996. It has an incised 1996 copyright date along with the (TM 7) trademark. Produced in a sequentially-numbered limited edition of 25,000 pieces worldwide (15,000 in the U.S.) The official issue price was $198 in 1997.

☐ 2008 .... 4¼" ..... (LE)...... ❼ .... $198

**HUM 2009–2011   (ON) OPEN NUMBERS)**

### HUM 2012
### St. Nicholas' Day (LE)
First released in the U.S. market in the fall of 1997. Modeled by master sculptor Helmut Fischer in 1996. It has an incised 1996 copyright date along with the (TM 7) trademark. Produced in a sequentially-numbered limited edition of 20,000 pieces worldwide (only 10,000 for the U.S.). A companion piece to HUM 473 "Ruprecht" (formerly "Father Christmas") also a limited edition of 20,000 pieces. The little child is based on HUM 476 "Winter Song." The official issue price was $650 in 1997, but was sold as a matching-numbered set with "Ruprecht" ($450 official issue price) for the combination price of $1000. The January 1, 2000 price list shows $1,100 for the pair.

☐ 2012 .... 6¾" ..... (LE)...... ❼ .... $650–700

**HUM 2013   (ON) OPEN NUMBER**

### HUM 2014
### Christmas Delivery

First released in the U.S. market in 1997. Modeled by master sculptor Helmut Fischer in 1997. It has an incised 1997 copyright date along with the (TM 7) trademark. A new work of art, approved by the Convent of Siessen based on an interpretation of HUM 424 "Sleep Tight" and HUM 396 "Ride Into Christmas." The official issue price was $485 in 1997.

☐ 2014/I. . . . 5¾" . . . . . . . . . . (CE). . . ❼ . . . $495–500
☐ 2014/I. . . . 5¾" . . . . . . . . . . (**OE**). . . ❽ . . . $495

### HUM 2015
### Wonder of Christmas (LE)

First released in the U.S. market in the fall of 1998. Modeled by master sculptor Helmut Fischer in 1997. It has an incised 1997 copyright date along with the (TM 7) trademark. Sold in a Limited Edition (20,000 pieces) Collectors Set with a FREE Limited Edition Steiff Teddy Bear and a matching Porcelain Medallion. The official issue price was $575 for the two piece set in 1998.

☐ 2015 . . . . 7" . . . . . . . . . . (LE) . . . ❼ . . . $575

### HUM 2016–2024    (ON) OPEN NUMBERS

### HUM 2025/A
### Wishes Come True (EE)

First released in the U.S. market in the spring of 2000 as an Exclusive Edition for members of the M.I. HUMMEL CLUB only and not sold as an open edition to the general public. Modeled by master sculptor Helmut Fischer in 1997. It has an incised 1997 copyright date along with the (TM 8) trademark and bears the Club exclusive backstamp. The official issue price was $695 in 2000, plus the members redemption card.

☐ 2025/A . . . . . . . . . . . . **(EE)** . . . . ❽ . . . . . . $695
(M.I.H. Club Members Only)

### HUM 2026–2029   (ON) OPEN NUMBERS

### HUM 2030
### Fire Fighter

First released in the U.S. market in the fall of 1999. Modeled by master sculptor Helmut Fischer in 1997. It has an incised 1997 copyright date along with the (TM 8) trademark and the "First Issue 2000 MIL-LENNIUM" oval decal backstamp. Comes with FREE "To the Rescue" Hummel-Scape, (Mark # 1020–D) a $75 value. The official issue price was $250 in 1999.

☐ 2030 . . . . 4¼" . . . . . . **(OE)** . . . . ❽ . . . . . . $250

**HUM 2035**
**First Snow (LE)**

**HUM 2036**
**Let It Snow (LE)**

These two figurines were first released in the U.S. market in the fall of 1999. Both were modeled by master sculptor Helmut Fischer in 1997. They both have an incised 1997 copyright date along with the (TM 7) trademark and the "First Issue 1999" oval decal backstamp. They were issued as part of a Collector's Set called "Frosty Friends" in combination with a white Steiff mohair snowman bear, in a Limited Edition (LE) of 20,000 sets worldwide. The official issue price was $598 in 1999.

☐ 2035 .... 5½"........... (LE)... ❼ ... $318 (Estimated Price)
☐ 2036 .... 5"............ (LE)... ❼ ... $280 (Estimated Price)

——————— **HUM TERM** ———————

**BLACK LIGHT**: A black light is simply an ultraviolet light. (According to Webster's Dictionary: situated beyond the visible spectrum at its violet end—use of radiation having a wavelength shorter than those of X-rays.) We have a small hand-held unit that plugs into a 110-volt outlet. When used in a dark room (with no other light source) it will show if a figurine has been repainted, but will not show breaks, cracks, or other repairs. When held close to a perfect undamaged figurine, the figurine will appear violet in color. If a portion has been repainted, it will be noticably lighter in color. However, if a figurine has been professionally restored and re-fired, the black light will be unable to detect this repair. It is my personal opinion that a black light is of little real value to a collector since most repaired pieces also can be detected just as well with the naked eye or with the help of a good magnifying glass.

**HUM 2037    (ON) OPEN NUMBER**

**HUM 2038**
**In The Kitchen**
First released in the U.S. market in the fall of 1999. Modeled by master sculptor Helmut Fischer in 1998. It has an incised 1998 copyright date along with the (TM 8) trademark and the "First Issue 2000 MILLENNIUM" oval decal bookstamp. It comes with a FREE "Kozy Kitchen" HummelScape, (Mark # 1009–D) a $75 value. The official issue price was $250 in 1999.

☐ 2038 . . . . . . 4½″ . . . . . (OE) . . . . . ❽ . . . . $250

**HUM 2039    (ON) OPEN NUMBER**

**HUM 2040**
**One Coat or Two?**
First released in the U.S. market in the fall of 1999. Modeled by master sculptor Helmut Fischer in 1998. It has an incised 1998 copyright date along with the (TM 8) trademark and the "First Issue 2000 MILLENNIUM" oval decal backstamp. It comes with a FREE "Painting Pals" HummelScape, (Mark # 1019–D) a $75 value. The official issue price was $250 in 1999.

☐ 2040 . . . . . . 4½″ . . . . . (OE) . . . . . ❽ . . . . $250

### HUM 2049/A
### Cuddles
First released in the U.S. market in the fall of 1998. Modeled by master sculptor Helmut Fischer in 1997. It has an incised 1997 copyright date along with the (TM 7) trademark and the "First Issue 1998" oval decal backstamp. The official issue price was $80 in 1998.

☐ 2049/A . . . . 3½" . . . . . (CE) . . . . . ❼. . . . $88–90
☐ 2049/A . . . . 3½" . . . . . (**OE**) . . . . . ❽. . . . $88

### HUM 2049/B
### My Best Friend
First released in the U.S. market in the fall of 1998. Modeled by master sculptor Helmut Fischer in 1997. It has an incised 1997 copyright date along with the (TM 7) trademark and the "First Issue 1998" oval decal backstamp. The official issue price was $80 in 1998.

☐ 2049/B . . . . 3½" . . . . . (CE) . . . . . ❼. . . . $88–90
☐ 2049/B . . . . 3½" . . . . . (**OE**) . . . . . ❽. . . . $88

**HUM 2050/A**
**Messages of Love**

First released in the U.S. market in the spring of 1999. Modeled by master sculptor Helmut Fischer in 1997. It has an incised 1997 copyright date along with the (TM 7) trademark and the "First Issue 1999" oval decal backstamp. This figurine was used as a promotional piece for "Miller's EXPO '99" with a black bumblebee on the letter. The official issue price was $85 in 1999.

| | | | | | |
|---|---|---|---|---|---|
| ☐ 2050/A | 3½" | (CE) | ❼ | $88–90 |
| ☐ 2050/A | 3½" | **(OE)** | ❽ | $88 |

**HUM 2050/B**
**Be Mine**

First released in the U.S. market in the spring of 1999. Modeled by master sculptor Helmut Fischer in 1997. It has an incised 1997 copyright date along with the (TM 7) trademark and "First Issue 1999" oval decal backstamp. The official issue price was $85 in 1999.

| | | | | | |
|---|---|---|---|---|---|
| ☐ 2050/B | 3½" | (CE) | ❼ | $88–90 |
| ☐ 2050/B | 3½" | **(OE)** | ❽ | $88 |

### HUM 2051/A
### Once Upon A Time

First released in the U.S. market in June of 1998. Modeled by master sculptor Helmut Fischer in 1997. It has an incised 1997 copyright date along with the (TM 7) trademark and the "First Issue 1998" oval decal backstamp. This figurine was used as a promotional piece for "Miller's EXPO '98" with a black bumblebee on the book (200 pieces only). The official issue price was $80 in 1998.

☐ 2051/A .... 3½" ..... (CE) ..... ❼.... $88–90
☐ 2051/A .... 3½" ..... **(OE)** ..... ❽.... $88

### HUM 2051/B
### Let's Play

First released in the U.S. market in the fall of 1998. Modeled by master sculptor Helmut Fischer in 1997. It has an incised 1997 copyright date along with the (TM 7) trademark and the "First Issue 1998" oval decal backstamp. The official issue price was $80 in 1998.

☐ 2051/B .... 3⅜" ..... (CE) ..... ❼.... $88–90
☐ 2051/B .... 3⅜" ..... **(OE)** ..... ❽.... $88

### HUM 2052
### Pigtails (EE)

First released in the U.S. market in 1999 as a FREE gift for renewing membership in the M.I. HUMMEL CLUB for 1999/00 club year. Modeled by master sculptor Helmut Fischer in 1998. It has an incised 1998 copyright date. It bears the inscription: "M.I. HUMMEL CLUB Membership Year 1999/2000" in addition to a black bumblebee in a half circle. It is a companion piece to HUM 2071 "Lucky Charmer."

☐ 2052 . . . . . . 3¼" . . . . . (EE) . . . . . ❼ . . . . $90–100
(M.I.H. Club Members Only)

### HUM 2053
### Playful Pals (LE)

First released in the U.S. market in the fall of 1998. Modeled by master sculptor Helmut Fischer in 1997. It has an incised 1997 copyright date along with the (TM 7) trademark. It has <u>NO</u> "First Issue" backstamp. Produced in a sequentially-numbered Limited Edtion of 25,000 pieces worldwide. Comes with FREE HummelScape: "Autumn Frolic" (Mark # 1001–D).

☐ 2053 . . . . . . 3½" . . . . . (LE). . . . . . ❼ . . . . $198

**HUM 2060**
**European Wanderer**
This three piece set was first released in the U.S. market in 1999. Modeled by master sculptors Helmut Fischer and Tamara Fuchs in 1998. It has an incised 1998 copyright date along with the (TM 8) trademark and the "First Issue 2000 MILLENNIUM" oval decal backstamp. Comes with a ceramic globe and a hardwood base. The official issue price was $250 in 1999.

☐ 2060 . . . . . . 4¼" . . . . . **(OE)** . . . . . ❽ . . . . $250

**HUM 2061**
**American Wanderer**
This three piece set was first released in the U.S. market in 1999. Modeled by master sculptors Helmut Fischer and Tamara Fuchs in 1998. It has an incised 1998 copyright date along with the (TM 8) trademark and "First Issue 2000 MILLENNIUM" oval decal backstamp. Comes with a ceramic globe and a hardwood base. The official issue price was $250 in 1999.

☐ 2061 . . . . . . 5" . . . . . . . **(OE)** . . . . . ❽ . . . . $250

**HUM 2062**
**African Wanderer**
This three piece set was first released in the U.S. market in 1999. Modeled by master sculptors Helmut Fischer and Tamara Fuchs in 1998. It has an incised 1998 copyright date along with the (TM 8) trademark and "First Issue 2000 MILLENNIUM" oval decal backstamp. Comes with a ceramic globe and a hardwood base. The official issue price was $250 in 1999.

☐ 2062 . . . . . . 4¼" . . . . . (**OE**) . . . . . **8** . . . . $250

**HUM 2063**
**Asian Wanderer**

This three piece set was first released in the U.S. market in 1999. Modeled by master sculptors Helmut Fischer and Tamara Fuchs in 1998. It has an incised 1998 copyright date along with the (TM 8) trademark and "First Issue 2000 MILLENNIUM" oval decal backstamp. Comes with a ceramic globe and a hardwood base. The official issue price was $250 in 1999.

☐ 2063 . . . . . . 4½" . . . . . (**OE**) . . . . . **8** . . . . $250

---

**————— HUM TERM —————**

**CURRENT PRODUCTION:** The term used to describe those items currently being produced by the W. Goebel Porzellanfabrik of Rödental, West Germany.

463

### HUM 2064
### Australian Wanderer
This three piece set was first released in the U.S. market in 1999. Modeled by master sculptors Helmut Fischer and Tamara Fuchs in 1998. It has an incised 1998 copyright date along with the (TM 8) trademark and "First Issue 2000 MILLENNIUM" oval decal backstamp. Comes with a ceramic globe and a hardwood base. The official issue price was $250 in 1999.

☐ 2064 . . . . . . 4¼" . . . . . (OE) . . . . . **8** . . . . $250

### HUM 2065   (ON) OPEN NUMBER

### HUM 2066
### Peaceful Offering (LE)
First released in the U.S. market in the spring of 1999. Modeled by master sculptor Helmut Fischer in 1998. It has an incised 1998 copyright date along with the (TM 7) trademark. It has <u>NO</u> "First Issue" backstamp. Produced in a sequentially-numbered Limited Edition of 25,000 pieces worldwide. Came with FREE Collector's Set HummelScape: "Friendship in Bloom" (Mark # 1004–D).

☐ 2066 . . . . . . 6" . . . . . . . (LE) . . . . . . **7** . . . . $198

---
#### ——— HUM TERM ———

**TEMPORARILY WITHDRAWN:** A designation assigned by the W. Goebel Porzellanfabrik to indicate that a particular item is being withdrawn from production for some time, but may be reinstated at a future date.

---

## HUM 2067
### Sweet Treats
First released in the U.S. market in the fall of 1999. Modeled by master sculptor Helmut Fischer in 1998. It has a stamped (TM 7) trademark and 1998 copyright date stamped on the feet and a small brass hook on the head for hanging as an ornament. The official issue price was $75 or FREE with $150 purchase of M.I. Hummel products by members of the "M.I. Hummel Club" with redemption card.

☐ 2067/A/0 . . . 3⅛″ . . . . . (OE) . . . . . ❼ . . . . $75

**HUM 2068–2070 (ON) OPEN NUMBERS**

## HUM 2071
### Lucky Charmer (EE)
First released in the U.S. market in 1999 as a companion piece to HUM 2052 "Pigtails". Formerly called a "Preview Edition" but now called an "Exclusive Edition" for Club members only and not available from Goebel to the general public. Modeled by master sculptor Helmut Fischer in 1999. It has an incised 1998 copyright date. It bears the inscription: "M.I. HUMMEL CLUB Membership Year 1999/2000" in addition to a black bumblebee in a half circle. The official issue price was $90 in 1999 with redemption card. It will be retired as of 31 May 2000.

☐ 2071 . . . . . . 3½″ . . . . . (EE) . . . . . ❼ . . . . $90
(M.I.H. Club Members Only)

*2074/A*          *2074/A/0*

### HUM 2074
### Christmas Gift
First released in the U.S. market in 1998 as a FREE ornament with the purchase of $150 or more of M.I. Hummel merchandise between 1 November and 31 December 1998 at participating retailers or while supplies last. Released as a figurine with normal base in early 1999. Modeled by master sculptor Helmut Fischer in 1998. It has an incised 1998 copyright date along with the (TM 7) trademark. It has <u>NO</u> "FIrst Issue" backstamp. The official issue price was $90 in 1999.

☐ 2074/A/0 . . . 3¼" . . . . . (CE) . . . . . ❼ . . . . $80–90
☐ 2074/A . . . . 3½" . . . . . (CE) . . . . . ❼ . . . . $90–95
☐ 2074/A . . . . 3½" . . . . . (OE) . . . . . ❽ . . . . $90

### HUM 2077
### First Bloom        (2077/A)
### A Flower For You    (2077/B)
First released in the U.S. market in the fall of 1999 at participating retailer or in early 2000 for others. Modeled by master sculptor Helmut Fischer in 1999. Both figurines have an incised 1999 copyright date along with the (TM 8) trademark. They have the "FIrst Issue 2000" backstamp. The official issue price was $85 each in 1999.

☐ 2077/A . . . . 3¼" . . . . . (OE) . . . . . ❽ . . . . $85
☐ 2077/B . . . . 3¼" . . . . . (OE) . . . . . ❽ . . . . $85

### HUM 2085
### Little Farm Hand (LE)
First released in the U.S. market in the fall of 1999. Modeled by master sculptor Helmut Fischer in 1999. It has an incised 1999 copyright date along with the (TM 8) trademark. It has <u>NO</u> "First Issue" back-stamp. Produced in a sequentially-numbered Limited Edition of 25,000 pieces worldwide. Comes with a FREE "Millennium Harvest" HummelScape (Mark # 1013–D) a $75 value. The official issue price was $198 in 1999.

☐ 2085 . . . . . . 4½″ . . . . . (LE) . . . . . . ❽ . . . . $198

### HUM 2086
### Spring Sowing (LE)
First released in the U.S. market in the spring of 2000. Modeled by master sculptor Helmut Fischer in 1999. It has an incised 1999 copyright date along with the (TM 8) trademark. Produced in a sequentially-numbered Limited Edition of 25,000 pieces worldwide. Comes with a FREE "Seeds of Friendship" HummelScape Collectors Set, (Mark # 1014–D) a $75 value. The official issue price was $198 in 2000. Companion piece to HUM 2085 "Millennium Harvest" (Little Farm Hand).

☐ 2086 . . . . . . 3½″ . . . . . (LE) . . . . . . ❽ . . . . $198

### HUM 2087/A
### Sharpest Student (EE)

First released in the U.S. market in the spring of 2000 as an Exclusive Edition for members of the M.I. Hummel Club only and not sold as an open edition to the general public. Modeled by master sculptor Helmut Fischer in 1999. It has as incised 1999 copyright date along with the (TM 8) trademark and bears the Club exclusive backstamp. The official issue price was $95 in 2000, plus the members redemption card.

□ 2087/A .... 4"....... (EE) ..... ❽.... $95

### HUM 2087/B
### Honor Student (EE)

First released in the U.S. market in the spring of 2000 as a FREE gift for renewing membership in the M.I. HUMMEL Club for the 2000/01 club year. Modeled by master sculptor Helmut Fischer in 1999. It has an incised 1999 copyright date along with the (TM 8) trademark and bears the Club exclusive backstamp.

□ 2087/B .... 3¾" ..... (EE) ..... ❽.... $85–100

## HUM 2093
### Pretzel Boy

First released in the U.S. market in the fall of 1999 as a companion piece to HUM 2004 "Pretzel Girl." Modeled by master sculptor Helmut Fischer in 1999. It has an incised 1999 copyright date along with the (TM 8) trademark and the "First Issue 2000 Millennium" backstamp. Listed as a Special Event Collector's Set with a FREE "Bavarian Bier Garten" HummelScape, (Mark # 1016–D) a $75 value at participating retailers. The official issue price was $185 in 1999.

☐ 2093 . . . . . . 4″ . . . . . . . (OE) . . . . . ❽ . . . . $185

## HUM 2094
### Christmas Wish (CE)

First released in the U.S. market in 1999. Modeled by master sculptor Helmut Fischer in 1999. It has an incised 1999 copyright date along with the (TM 8) trademark and an "Exclusive Edition" backstamp on the bottom. A Limited Edition of 20,000 pieces were sold exclusively on QVC starting at 12 AM EST on 17 November 1999 and sold out the complete edition in only one day! Came with a "Christmas Wish" Collector's Set (Musikfest Display) HummelScape: (Mark # 1017–D). The issue price was $139.50 (plus shipping) in 1999.

☐ 2094 . . . . . . 4″ . . . . . . . (CE) . . . . . ❽ . . . . $150–200

**HUM 2095–2109   (ON) OPEN NUMBERS**
**HUM 2110   Ornament, "Christmas Delivery" (European Market only)**
**HUM 2111   Ornament, "Making New Friends" (European Market only)**

# Other Hummel Related Items

## Unnumbered
## "M.I. Hummel" Figurine
### "Madonna With Wings"

This very rare, unusual, signed "M.I. Hummel" figurine is truly a collector's item. Found several years ago in Munich, Germany, this beautiful "Madonna with Wings" figurine had been in the possession of a German family for many years, but they could not remember its background or from where it came. The figurine is not numbered nor does it have a trademark—only an incised "X" on the bottom, in addition to the "M.I. Hummel" signature on the back. Research reveals that this piece was in all probability modeled by master sculptor Reinhold Unger in the late 1930's or early 1940's. For some unknown reason it was not approved for production by the Siessen Convent or possibly by Sister Hummel herself. This piece, however, is found pictured in an old 1950 Goebel catalogue listed has "Mel 08" and priced at 11 DM. It is not known whether it was actually produced and marketed at that time. If they were produced, they would not have the "M.I. Hummel" signature. It is the signature that makes this figurine unique, rare and fascinating.

# Bust of Sister M.I. Hummel

This white bisque bust in the likeness of Sister Maria Innocentia Hummel was created by master sculptor Gerhard Skrobek in 1965. It was originally used as a display piece for showrooms or dealer displays featuring Hummel items. It has the signature of "Skrobek 1965" in addition to "HU1" incised on the back. In recent years it has become a collector's item and is sought after by many avid "M.I. Hummel" lovers. They were originally given to dealers at no cost; but we did, however, purchase two of these large busts in the early 1970's from a store in New York at a cost of $30 each. A smaller version of the same bust with the "M.I. Hummel" signature incised on the front of the base was put on the market in 1967 with the incised number "HU2" and the (TM 4) trademark. These originally sold for $6 each. This same small-size bust was again put on the market in 1977 for a brief time, retailing for $15 to $17 each, but has once again been discontinued from current production. A third variation of the Sister Hummel bust was issued in 1979 as: "EXCLUSIVE SPECIAL EDITION No. 3 FOR MEMBERS OF THE GOEBEL COLLECTORS' CLUB" only. This piece has an incised "HU 3" as well as 1978 incised copyright date on the bottom. It is in full color with the "M.I. Hummel" signature painted in white on the front. While these busts are not officially classified as true Hummel figurines, they do make a nice addition to any Hummel collection.

*HU 1*        *HU 2*        *HU 3*

☐ HU1 . . . . . 13″ . . . . . . . . . . (CE) . . . ❹ . . . $2500–2750
☐ HU2 . . . . . 5½″ . . . . . . . . . . (CE) . . . ❹ . . . $175–200
☐ HU2 . . . . . 5½″ . . . . . . . . . . (CE) . . . ❺ . . . $150–175
☐ HU3 . . . . . 5½″ . . . . . . . . . . (CE) . . . ❺ . . . $350–400

# Factory Workers Plate

This anniversary plate was produced by W. Goebel Porzellanfabrik, by and for the workers at the factory where the Goebel annual plates are manufactured. Probably as few as 100 were produced and were not made available to the general public. The "M.I. Hummel" signature is on each of the ten individual plates.

☐ Factory Workers Plate . . . . . . . . . . . . $1500–2000   (uncolored)
☐ Factory Workers Plate . . . . . . . . . . . . $2000–2500   (colored variation)

# Early Goebel Plaque

*Early* Goebel *plaque (front view)*          *Early* Goebel *plaque (back view)*

Produced in hard porcelain, both in light blue background and a chocolate brown color. Measures 2½ × 4¾" on a beveled base. The embossed inscription on the back reads:

W. GOEBEL
Porzellanfabrik Oeslau
und Wilhelmsfeld
Oeslau b. Coburg

☐ Goebel Plaque (Blue) . . . . . . . . . 2½" × 4¾" . . . . . . . . . . . . . . $750–1000
☐ Goebel Plaque (Brown) . . . . . . . . 2½" × 4¾" . . . . . . . . . . . . . . $750–1000

# Goebel Camels:
## Traditionally Used With "M.I. Hummel" Nativity Sets

These three Goebel camels were designed to be used with the "M.I. Hummel" Nativity Sets, either HUM 214 or HUM 260. The standing camel HX306/0 has an incised 1960 copyright date and has been on the market since the early 1960's. The kneeling camel (Dromedary) and the lying camel (Bactrian) were both released in 1980 for the first time. All three have been produced both in full color and white overglaze (unpainted) finishes. All models are in current production and are usually found wherever the "M.I. Hummel" figurines are sold. Currently being produced in color only. In 1991 three smaller versions of the same camels were added to the line to go with the new smaller size nativity sets, HUM 214/0.

☐ HX 306/0 . . . . . . 8½″ . . . . . (**OE**) . . . . . Standing . . . . . (color) . . . . $285
☐ HX 306/0 . . . . . . 8½″ . . . . . (**TW**) . . . . . Standing . . . . . (white) . . . . $275–300
☐ 46 820–12 . . . . . 5½″ . . . . . (**OE**) . . . . . Kneeling . . . . . (color) . . . . $285
☐ 46 820–12 . . . . . 5½″ . . . . . (**TW**) . . . . Kneeling . . . . . (white) . . . . $275–300
☐ 46 821–11 . . . . . 4½″ . . . . . (**OE**) . . . . . Lying . . . . . . . (color) . . . . $285
☐ 46 821–11 . . . . . 4½″ . . . . . (**TW**) . . . . . Lying . . . . . . . (white) . . . . $275–300
☐ 46 837 . . . . . . . 6½″ . . . . . (**OE**) . . . . . Standing . . . . . (color) . . . . $230
☐ 46 838 . . . . . . . 4″ . . . . . (**OE**) . . . . . Kneeling . . . . . (color) . . . . $230
☐ 46 839–09 . . . . . 3¼″ . . . . . (**OE**) . . . . . Lying . . . . . . . (color) . . . . $230

# The "Mel" Signature Hum"mel"

**A** collector will occasionally happen on to a "Hummel"-like figurine that does not have the usual "M.I. Hummel" signature on it. The figurine will have all of the general appearances of an older genuine "M.I. Hummel" figurine, including the Goebel factory trademark, in addition to the letters "Mel" (the last part of "Hummel") incised on it.

To the best of my knowledge, these items have been designed from original drawings by Sister M.I. Hummel, but for some undetermined reasons were not approved by the Siessen Convent for inclusion in the "M.I. Hummel" line of figurines.

Notice the photo of the "Child in Bed" candy dish. Goebel master sculptor Arthur Moeller modeled this piece in 1945. Since it did not win convent approval, it was later marketed with "Mel 6" incised on the bottom of it. Several other "Mel" items have appeared through the years. The most common of these are the Mel 1, Mel 2 and Mel 3 candlestick holders, modeled by former master sculptor Reinhold Unger in 1939. In the mid-1950's, these items were remodeled by master sculptor Gerhard Skrobek and assigned the model numbers Hum 115 "Girl with Nosegay," Hum 116 "Girl with Fir Tree" and Hum 117 "Boy with Horse" candlesticks with the "M.I. Hummel" signature.

Also modeled by master sculptor Arthur Moeller were Mel 4 "Box with Boy on Top" in 1942, Mel 5 "Box with Girl on Top" in 1942, Mel 6 "Box with Child in Bed on Top" in 1945 and Mel 7 "Box with Sitting Child on Top" in 1946. All "Mel" items were discontinued in 1962, according to Goebel factory information.

Apparently, the "Mel" designation must have been a "catch-all" label intended as a way of marketing these rejected items. I am of the opinion, however, that it was also used to designate *experimental* items. In our years of research, we have

accidentally "stumbled" on two other figurine models with the "Mel" label. Both of them were "International" designs. How many more "Mel" designs will show up in the future is anyone's guess.

*Mel 6*

*Mel 7*

# Listing of "Mel" Items

The following is a listing of "Mel" items recently found in old factory records (sculpting diaries) at W. Goebel Porzellanfabrik in Roedental, Germany—thanks to the efforts of Veronika Schmidt, research specialist at the factory. Please note that Mel 6, Mel 7, and Mel 8 were used twice: in 1940 and then again in 1945 and 1946.

| | | | | Sculptor | Year | Value |
|---|---|---|---|---|---|---|
| ☐ Mel 1 | = | Hum 115 | girl w/nosegay | R. Unger | 1939 | $300–500 |
| ☐ Mel 2 | = | Hum 116 | girl w/fir tree | R. Unger | 1939 | $300–500 |
| ☐ Mel 3 | = | Hum 117 | boy with horse | R. Unger | 1939 | $300–500 |
| ☐ Mel 4 | | box with boy on lid | | A. Moeller | 1942 | no known examples |
| ☐ Mel 5 | | box with girl on lid | | A. Moeller | 1942 | no known examples |
| ☐ Mel 6 | | box w/ child in bed on top | | A. Moeller | 1945 | $2000–3000 |
| ☐ Mel 7 | | box w/ sitting child on top | | A. Moeller | 1946 | $2000–3000 |
| ☐ Mel 8 | | angel bust/madonna w/wings | | R. Unger | 1945 | $5000–7000 |
| | | | | | | |
| ☐ Mel 6 | = | Hum 806 | Bulgarian | A. Moeller | 1940 | $10000–15000 |
| ☐ Mel 7 | = | Hum 807 | Bulgarian | A. Moeller | 1940 | $10000–15000 |
| ☐ Mel 8 | = | Hum 808 | Bulgarian | A. Moeller | 1940 | $10000–15000 |
| | | | | | | |
| ☐ Mel 9 | = | Hum 809 | Bulgarian | A. Moeller | 1940 | $10000–15000 |
| ☐ Mel 10 | = | Hum 810 | Bulgarian | R. Unger | 1940 | $10000–15000 |
| ☐ Mel 11 | = | Hum 811 | Bulgarian | R. Unger | 1940 | $10000–15000 |
| ☐ Mel 12 | = | Hum 812 | Serbian | R. Unger | 1940 | $10000–15000 |
| ☐ Mel 13 | = | Hum 813 | Serbian | R. Unger | 1940 | $10000–15000 |
| | | | | | | |
| ☐ Mel 14 | = | Hum 137/B | Plaque | A. Moeller | 1940 | $2000–3000 |
| ☐ Mel 15 | = | Hum 138 | Plaque | A. Moeller | 1940 | $2000–3000 |
| ☐ Mel 16 | = | Hum 139 | Plaque | A. Moeller | 1940 | $2000–3000 |
| | | | | | | |
| ☐ Mel 24 | = | Hum 824 | Swedish | A. Moeller | 1940 | $10000–15000 |
| ☐ Mel 25 | = | Hum 825 | Swedish | A. Moeller | 1940 | $10000–15000 |
| ☐ Mel 31 | = | Hum 831 | Slovak | R. Unger | 1940 | $10000–15000 |
| ☐ Mel 32 | = | Hum 832 | Slovak | R. Unger | 1940 | $10000–15000 |
| ☐ Mel 41 | = | Hum 841 | Czech | R. Unger | 1940 | $10000–15000 |
| ☐ Mel 42 | = | Hum 842 | Czech | R. Unger | 1940 | $10000–15000 |
| ☐ Mel 51 | = | Hum 851 | Hungarian | A. Moeller | 1940 | $10000–15000 |
| ☐ Mel 52 | = | Hum 852 | Hungarian | A. Moeller | 1940 | $10000–15000 |
| ☐ Mel 53 | = | Hum 853 | Hungarian | A. Moeller | 1940 | $10000–15000 |
| ☐ Mel 54 | = | Hum 854 | Hungarian | A. Moeller | 1940 | $10000–15000 |

---

## HUM TERM

**HUM NO.:** Mold number or model number incised on the bottom of each "M.I. Hummel" figurine at the factory. This number is used for identification purposes.

# Copies from Around the World

I t has been said that one of the most sincere compliments that can be given to an artist is to have his work copied. I think this holds true when it comes to the "M.I. Hummel" figurines. W. Goebel Porzellanfabrik of Rödental, Germany, has had the exclusive right to produce Hummel figurines, based upon the artwork of Sister Maria Innocentia Hummel, since 1935. The figurines have become so popular over the years that many countries around the world have tried to copy these designs. Korea, Taiwan, Japan, Germany, England and even the United States have all made copies. Most of these are quite inferior in quality when compared to the originals made by Goebel. But a few of the copies are better than others—namely, the Japanese and the English—and we've chosen to show you some of these better copies.

The Japanese have probably succeeded in making the best copies, with the English running a close second. The Japanese finish and colors are more like the originals and sometimes, at first glance, they may fool even an experienced collector. The Japanese have copied the designs but, to my knowledge, have never gone so far as to copy the familiar "M.I. Hummel" signature. On the other hand the English finish is quite shiny and they did copy the signature on their early production models. The English figurines were made by "Beswick" during the war years of 1940 and 1941.

It is, of course, most unethical, if not always illegal, to make copies of Hummel figurines. The question of copies, look-alikes, fakes and their legality is a lengthy and complicated subject and it is not our intention here to delve into that issue. We want only to show readers a few of the better examples of copies that have been done, so as to show how closely they may resemble the originals.

*Top photo: HUM 97 (far left) beside English copy #903; HUM 5 (far right) beside English copy #906. Middle photo at left, HUM 71 (far left) with English copy #908; photo at right, HUM 184 (far right) with Japanese copy. HUM 201 with Japanese copy at left.*

*Bottom view typical Beswick markings*

*This English "Beswick" figurine was recently found in England. A copy of HUM 86 "Happiness". It does have an incised "M.I. Hummel" signature as well as the incised number 990.*

# RARE/UNIQUE SAMPLE VARIATIONS OF "M.I. HUMMEL" FIGURINES

*HUM 13/0 with attached pot*

*HUM 13/0 with attached bowl*

**P**ictured here are six very rare early sample pieces—four having been located in Germany and two found in the United States.

Webster's definitions—RARE: marked by unusual quality, merit, or appeal. Distinctive, superlative or extreme of its kind, seldom occurring or found, uncommon. UNIQUE: being the only one, sole, being without a like or equal.

I truly believe that four of these six examples fit Webster's definitions of both *rare* and *unique* at this point in time! "Little Hiker" and "Joyful" have been found in duplicates, so they would only be considered rare.

For some unknown reason, the Sisters at Siessen Convent, who must approve for production all figurines based upon Sister M.I. Hummel's artwork, did not approve these variations. Possibly they felt it would lessen the value of the original artwork when using it in a utilitarian item. This is only speculation on my part because they did approve useful items such as ashtrays, candy bowls, lamp bases, book ends, candleholders and wall vases. Possibly only a whim, impulse, or passing fancy prevented these unique pieces from being produced and sold on the open market.

Whatever the reason, I, for one, am extremely pleased that these four pieces are in our collection and the other two are in a very good friend's collection in the mid west.

*HUM 16/1 with pot*

*HUM 17/0 with attached pot*

478

**HUM 47/0 with attached bowl**          **HUM 53 with attached pot**

According to the Goebel factory product book, the following "M.I. Hummel" figurines with attached pots/bowls were produced as samples only in 1935 and 1936. Unfortunately, Goebel did not retain any of these samples for their archives.

| | | | |
|---|---|---|---|
| ☐ HUM II/1 | Puppy Love | w/pot from ZF 9 | A. Moeller 1935 |
| ☐ HUM II/4 | Little Fiddler | w/pot from ZF 9 | A. Moeller 1935 |
| ☐ HUM II/5 | Strolling Along | w/pot from ZF 9 | A. Moeller 1935 |
| ☐ HUM II/11/0 | Merry Wanderer | w/pot from ZF 9 | A. Moeller 1935 |
| ☐ HUM II/13/0 | Meditation | w/pot from ZF 9 | R. Unger 1935 |
| ☐ HUM II/13/0 | Meditation | w/bowl from KZ 27/I | R. Unger 1935 |
| ☐ HUM II/16/I | Little Hiker | w/pot from ZF 9 | A. Moeller 1935 |
| ☐ HUM II/17/0 | Congratulations | w/pot from ZF 9 | R. Unger 1935 |
| ☐ HUM II/47/0 | Goose Girl | w/pot from ZF 9 | A. Moeller 1936 |
| ☐ HUM III/47/0 | Goose Girl | w/bowl from KZ 27/I | A. Moeller 1936 |
| ☐ HUM II/49 | To Market | w/bowl from KZ 27/I | A. Moeller 1936 |
| ☐ HUM II/53 | Joyful | w/pot from ZF 9 | R. Unger 1936 |
| ☐ HUM II/57 | Chick Girl | w/pot from ZF 9 | A. Moeller 1936 |
| ☐ HUM II/58 | Playmates | w/pot from ZF 9 | R. Unger 1936 |

The above chart has a complete listing of the 14 items that the factory has recorded. Six of the 14 we know about, have examples of, and pictures of. We know now that there can be duplicates of these extremely rare pieces, since two of the HUM 16/0 "Little Hiker" figurines with attached pots are now in private collections. We have no photos of the other missing pieces, so just what they look like is not known at this time. Whether they have a normal figurine base like "Meditation," or whether they are without the bases, such as "Little Hiker" or "Congratulations," is unknown. They might not necessarily have a model number or a signature, but will probably have the Goebel "crown" trademark.

Now that you have this exciting new information, go out there and scour the countryside, visit garage sales, flea markets and antique shops for the eight remaining "M.I. Hummel" figurines with attached pots or bowls. If you find one, give me a call—maybe we can make a deal! Good luck!

# "M.I. HUMMEL" FAIENCE

## A BRIEF HISTORY OF GLAZES

Colored glazes have been used on ceramics since 3,000 B.C. (Glazes applied to pottery not only serve as a form of decoration, but also make the objects watertight.) The Chinese developed lead glazes in the third century B.C. Tin glazes are believed to have originated in Mesopotamia in the ninth century A.D.; they were used in the Near East, China and India to cover tiles and handcrafted art objects. The Moors brought the tin-glazing tech-

nique with them to Spain, where Valencia became famous for it.

In the 15th century, Italian potters at Faenza began using the technique to make majolica. Their majolica was highly popular, and the term *faience* was named for the town. Soon, this method for decorating ceramics was used in Florence, Urbino and Venice. France and, later, The Netherlands also produced tin-glazed wares in such famous places as Nevers, Rouen and Delft.

HUM 4 (TM 1)    HUM 7/1 (TM 1)    HUM 9 (TM 1+1)

As you may know, Franz Goebel of W. Goebel Porzellanfabrik first conceived the idea of producing porcelain figurines based on the drawings of Sister M.I. Hummel in 1934. Upon being granted the right to create such figurines, the Rödental, Germany, porcelain company began experimenting with various materials (including porcelain and terra

cotta) and decorative techniques for making these new pieces. The goal of these experimentations was to find the best way for Goebel artists to create and finish pieces in colors that would most closely match those found in Sister M.I. Hummel's original art.

Aware of this brief trial-and-error period, Sister M.I. Hummel requested that samples of the various materials and finishes be made and exhibited at international trade fairs, such as the one held in Leipzig, Germany, to test the public's reaction to them. For this reason, we have very early M.I. Hummel figurines in porcelain and terra cotta (such as the HUM 136/V "Friends"), as well as pieces decorated in the faience technique (such as the HUM 33 "Joyful" ash tray and HUM 113 "Heavenly Song" candleholder). Public acceptance of these pieces was very limited, so their production never advanced beyond the sample stage.

Faience (pronounced *fay-ontz* or *fi-ons*) is a term for earthenware decorated with opaque colored glazes. (While now used for all kinds of glazed pottery, faience is the French word for the *porzellana di Faenza*— fine tin-glazed and painted earthenware made in Faenza, Italy.) Faience pieces, made of white earthenware or colored clays, were either shaped on a potter's wheel or formed in molds and assembled by hand. After open-air drying, these pieces were kiln-fired at temperatures of 900 to 1,100 degrees Centigrade. Still porous after firing, they were then dipped into a liquid tin glaze, which gave the pieces an overall white covering.

Colored glazes were then applied, and the pieces were refired at a lower temperature. (In some factories, firing methods were reversed; the first firing was at a temperature about 100 degrees lower than the second firing.) To prevent the pieces from sticking to the capsule in the round kilns, which were fired with coal, the tin glaze was wiped off the bottom of the bases before firing.

Goebel's faience pieces based on Sister M.I. Hummel's artwork were fired in small muffles that the company used exclusively for samples. The colors of these pieces are soft and flow into one another; some have a more or less messy appearance. Also, the solid tin glaze may have left the "M.I. Hummel" signature partly illegible. The faience technique permitted only a narrow range of colors and the surface was glossier than desired. The company felt that it detracted from the unique character of the original art, so only a very small quantity of these items was produced.

*This "Hear Ye, Hear Ye" faience figurine is 7¼ inches high was recently found in Germany*

Very few of these early faience pieces are known to exist in private collections. Their prices have varied greatly, due to public ignorance about just what they are. The uninformed sold them for a mere fraction of their true value. Items this rare, in my opinion, should be valued from $5,000 to $10,000 each, depending on the size and condition of the example. So, here's a new game for lovers of M.I. Hummel figurines: now that you are informed, look for these rare faience pieces—and hope that you find one being offered by a seller who has no idea of what he or she possesses.

# GOEBEL
# CRYSTAL "M.I. HUMMEL" FIGURINES

**F**irst released in Europe as a test market item early in 1991 and then in the U.S. market in the summer of 1991. These twelve models, rendered in 24% lead crystal with a silky matte finish, are replicas of the original ceramic "M.I. Hummel" figurines. They have an incised "M.I. Hummel" signature and the Goebel (TM6) trademark with a 1990 date. They do not have an incised model number. Now listed as (CE) Closed Editions:

☐ Apple Tree Girl . . . . . . . . . 3¾″ . . . . . . . . . . (CE) . . . . . . . ❻ . . . . . $50–60
☐ Botanist . . . . . . . . . . . . . . 3⅛″ . . . . . . . . . . (CE) . . . . . . . ❻ . . . . . $50–60
☐ Visiting An Invalid . . . . . . . . 3¾″ . . . . . . . . . . (CE) . . . . . . . ❻ . . . . . $50–60
☐ Meditation . . . . . . . . . . . . . 3½″ . . . . . . . . . . (CE) . . . . . . . ❻ . . . . . $50–60
☐ Merry Wanderer . . . . . . . . . 3½″ . . . . . . . . . . (CE) . . . . . . . ❻ . . . . . $50–60
☐ Postman . . . . . . . . . . . . . . 3⅞″ . . . . . . . . . . (CE) . . . . . . . ❻ . . . . . $50–60
☐ Soloist . . . . . . . . . . . . . . . 3″ . . . . . . . . . . . (CE) . . . . . . . ❻ . . . . . $30–40
☐ Little Sweeper . . . . . . . . . . 2⅞″ . . . . . . . . . . (CE) . . . . . . . ❻ . . . . . $30–40
☐ Village Boy . . . . . . . . . . . . 3″ . . . . . . . . . . . (CE) . . . . . . . ❻ . . . . . $30–40
☐ For Mother . . . . . . . . . . . . 2⅞″ . . . . . . . . . . (CE) . . . . . . . ❻ . . . . . $30–40
☐ Sister . . . . . . . . . . . . . . . . 2⅞″ . . . . . . . . . . (CE) . . . . . . . ❻ . . . . . $30–40
☐ March Winds . . . . . . . . . . . 2⅞″ . . . . . . . . . . (CE) . . . . . . . ❻ . . . . . $30–40

The following *six* items were originally sold only in Europe, but were available in the U.S. also. Now listed as (CE) Closed Editions:

☐ Apple Tree Boy . . . . . . . . . 3¾″ . . . . . . . . . . (CE) . . . . . . . ❻ . . . . . $75–100
☐ For Father . . . . . . . . . . . . . 3¾″ . . . . . . . . . . (CE) . . . . . . . ❻ . . . . . $75–100
☐ Kindergartener . . . . . . . . . . 3½″ . . . . . . . . . . (CE) . . . . . . . ❻ . . . . . $75–100
☐ School Boy . . . . . . . . . . . . 3½″ . . . . . . . . . . (CE) . . . . . . . ❻ . . . . . $75–100
☐ Grandma's Girl . . . . . . . . . . 3½″ . . . . . . . . . . (CE) . . . . . . . ❻ . . . . . $75–100
☐ Grandpa's Boy . . . . . . . . . . 3½″ . . . . . . . . . . (CE) . . . . . . . ❻ . . . . . $75–100

Several crystal pieces were produced exclusively for the Avon Company as promotional items. They all have the "M.I. Hummel" signature and year of issue:

☐ For Mother (trinket box) . . . . . . . . . . . . . . 4¼″ . . . . . . . . 1993 . . . . . $50–75
☐ Soloist (crystal bell) . . . . . . . . . . . . . . . . 5½″ . . . . . . . . 1994 . . . . . $50–75
☐ Song of Praise (candleholder) . . . . . . . . . 3¾″ . . . . . . . . 1995 . . . . . $50–75
☐ Watchful Angel (plate) . . . . . . . . . . . . . . . 8½″ . . . . . . . . 1996 . . . . . $50–75

# BERLIN AIRLIFT MEMORIAL EDITION WITH AUF WIEDERSEHEN

In 1993 a special limited edition (25,000 sets worldwide) was produced as a memorial to the Berlin Airlift. The three piece set includes the M.I. Hummel figurine "Auf Wiedersehen" HUM 153, with a special backstamp featuring the flags of the U.S., Germany, Britain and France. It stands beside a porcelain replica of the Airlift Memorial that is located at Templehof Airport in Berlin. The 7⅜" high memorial replica bears a special commemorative backstamp and sets on a wooden base with an engraved brass plaque which reads: "In commemoration of the Berlin Airlift—a heroic effort to keep a city free, June 26, 1948 to September 30, 1949", in both English and German. The original issue price was $330 in 1993.

☐ 153/0 . . . . 3 piece set Berlin Airlift . . . . . (LE) . . . ❼ . . . $350–400

## CHECKPOINT CHARLIE
## LIMITED COMMEMORATIVE EDITION

In 1994 a special limited edition of 20,000 individually numbered sets worldwide was produced and sold only through U.S. military base exchange stores, as a tribute to military personnel, a symbol of the cold war, and a guarantee of freedom for West Berlin. The three piece set includes the M.I. Hummel figurine "Soldier Boy" HUM 332, with special backstamp, a 4" high Checkpoint Charlie replica with wooden base and 8⅝" wide plaque with wood posts. The brass plaque on the base reads: "We are defending the freedom of Paris, London and New York when standing up for liberty in Berlin" (John F. Kennedy). Original *military* issue price was $195 in 1994.

☐ 332 . . . . . 3 piece set Checkpoint Charlie . . . (LE) . . . . ❼ . . . $350–400

# WOODEN DEALER PLAQUE

☐ Wooden Dealer Plaque . . . . . . . 33″ × 22½″ × 2½″ . . . . . . . . $5,000–10,000

These large wooden dealer plaques were made by a woodworking shop in the Goebel factory area of Rödental, Germany in the mid 1950's. According to factory records, about 100 plaques were made and given to good customers for display purposes. They were hand decorated with artist's oil paints by Messrs. Gunther Neubauer and Harald Sommer. The plaques weigh approximately twenty pounds and measure 33 inches long by 22½ inches high. They vary in thickness from ⅞ inch to 2½ inches at the thickest part. Most of plaques have been found in Germany, but many years ago we purchased one in the Boston area. There is no Goebel trademark, only a large "**A**" within a circle and a bolt of lightning running through the "**A**" incised on the back.

## FLYING "FULL BEE" DISPLAY

This blue three-dimensional ceramic and plastic version of the Goebel 1950 trademark (TM 2) was used for display purposes. It has the incised number "WZ 1" and the (TM 2) "full bee" trademark on the bottom.

☐ "Full Bee" Display . . . . . . . . . . . . 4¾ × 5″ . . . . . . . ❷ . . . . . . $2000–2500

# "M.I. Hummel"
# FOUR SEASONS MUSIC BOX SERIES

*1987 Winter*

*1988 Spring*

*1989 Summer*

*1998 Fall*

This series of four limited edition music boxes was first released in 1987, then one each succeeding year. Called the "Four Season Music Box" series with a world wide limited production of 10,000 pieces individually numbered. Originally sculpted by master sculptor Gerhard Skrobek and chief master sample painter Gunther Neubauer, who created the model, which was then carried out in the woodcarving by Anri of Italy. Inside the box is a goldplated 36-note Swiss movement by Reuge. Each piece carries the M.I. Hummel signature carved in wood on the top.

|  |  | Issue Price |  |  |
|---|---|---|---|---|
| ☐ 1987 Ride into Christmas | $390 | (CE) | $800–1000 |
| ☐ 1988 Chick Girl | $400 | (CE) | $600–750 |
| ☐ 1989 In Tune | $425 | (CE) | $600–750 |
| ☐ 1990 Umbrella Girl | $450 | (CE) | $800–1000 |

# ARS AG—CHRISTMAS PLATES 1987–1990

*Celestial Musician*

*Angel Duet*

*Guiding Light*

*Tender Watch*

This series was first issued in 1987 as a four part, decal produced, Christmas plate. Each plate was limited to 20,000 consecutively numbered pieces. Produced in the Goebel factory depicting original drawings of Sister M.I. Hummel under license of ARS AG, Switzerland, owner of the copyrights of the original paintings.

| ☐ 1987 | 7½" | (CE) | ❻ | $60–75 |
| ☐ 1988 | 7½" | (CE) | ❻ | $50–60 |
| ☐ 1989 | 7½" | (CE) | ❻ | $50–60 |
| ☐ 1990 | 7½" | (CE) | ❻ | $50–60 |

# M.I. HUMMEL "PEN PALS"

First released in the U.S. market in 1996, this set of six "name card table decorations" is actually made of "mini-mini" M.I. Hummel figurines cemented to a small porcelain base. They come with a special wipe-off pen for personalizing each with a name, date, or special greeting. Each figurine has it's own incised model number on the bottom of the figurine's base, but cannot be seen since it has been securely cemented to a separate base. This base has only the (TM 7) trademark applied by blue decal; nothing else. The only way to see the model number is to separate the two pieces. This is extremely difficult to do and is really not necessary since I have already done this for you (and me); curiosity got the better of me! Goebel found a strong, hard cement (not rubber base) for joining these two pieces. The company did not intend for them to come apart! The original issue price was $55 each in 1996.

*View of the base and figurine when separated.*

*View of the bottoms of base and figurine.*

| | | | |
|---|---|---|---|
| ☐ 43 5/0 | March Winds | 3" | 3¼" with base |
| ☐ 51 5/0 | Village Boy | 3" | 3¼" with base |
| ☐ 98 5/0 | Sister | 2⅞" | 2⅞" with base |
| ☐ 135 5/0 | Soloist. | 3" | 3¼" with base |
| ☐ 257 5/0 | For Mother | 3" | 3¼" with base |
| ☐ 482 5/0 | One For You, One For Me | 2¼" | 2½" with base |

# A RARE VARIATION
# YOU BE THE JUDGE!
# UNSIGNED "M.I. HUMMEL" FIGURINE

"Sunny Days" signed "Ugr"          "Stormy Weather" HUM 71 (TM 1)

This figurine was recently located in the City of Coburg, Germany, approximately five miles from Rödental where the Goebel factory is located. It does *not* have the usual "M.I. Hummel" signature nor the Goebel trademark. The only markings is the incised "Ugr." on the bottom, which undoubtedly stands for Reinhold Unger, one of the first Goebel master sculptors to translate Sister M.I. Hummel's artwork into three dimentional form. Unger also created "Stormy Weather" based upon another Hummel drawing. This figurine, based upon the drawing of "Sunny Days", apparently was rejected by the sisters at Siessen Convent. It is now part of the Robert L. Miller collection.

---

### HUM TERM

**RÖDENTAL**: The town in Germany where the W. Goebel Porzellanfabrik is situated. Rödental is located near Coburg and lies only a few miles from the former East German border. In 1981 Rödental became the official Sister City of Eaton, Ohio due to the longtime "Hummel" relationship with Robert L. Miller.

# A RARE VARIATION

**Rare Variation HUM 203**                    **HUM 203 (TM 1)**

A s I have always said, you can never tell when or where a *rare* "M.I. Hummel" figurine will turn up. This is a good example. This rare prototype (four post version) of HUM 203 "Signs of Spring" was recently found in Arizona. Sold by a retired military man who had served in Europe during WW II. He was stationed close to the area of Germany where the Goebel factory was located—that a young German girl would visit the Army quarters each week and would sell "M.I. Hummel" figurines as souvenirs. He had purchased a number of figurines and had kept them all through the years until recently, when he decided to dispose of some of his old items. He sold 39 figurines to a local antique shop. An alert "Hummel" dealer spotted them and purchased all 39 items. Noticing the difference between this old "Signs of Spring" and the current model, he gave me a call for my opinion. I stated that I had never seen or heard of a major variation of this figurine and requested a photograph for comparison. After receiving the photos and several phone calls later, this rare prototype "Signs of Spring" is now part of the Robert L. Miller collection. I would be remiss if I did not commend the alert dealer, Ron Brixey for his professional, business-like and ethical handling of the sale of this figurine.

---

**HUM TERM**

**PROTOTYPE**: This term as used by Goebel means the "one and only sample" (first out of the mother mold) that is presented to the Siessen Convent of any newly developed "M.I. Hummel" figurine.

---

# "M.I. Hummel" Calendars/Kalenders

**M**.I. Hummel Kalenders (German) were first published by Goebel in 1951 in the German version only. Each kalender contained thirteen color photographs of M.I. Hummel figurines with varying backgrounds. The first English version calendar was published for the 1954 year using the same photographs that were used in the 1953 German version. This continued on with few exceptions, (note 1964 German/1965 English and 1975 German/1976 English) until the 1988/1989 years when the size, style and format were drastically changed. These older Calendar/Kalenders are now highly collectible and bring from $50 to $2,000 on the secondary market.

☐      *1951 German*      ☐      *1952 German*

☐      *1953 German*      ☐      *1954 English*      ☐      *1954 German*

☐ *1955 English*  ☐ *1955 German*  ☐ *1956 English*

☐ *1956 German*  ☐ *1957 English*  ☐ *1957 German*

☐ *1958 English*  ☐ *1958 German*  ☐ *1959 English*

490

☐ *1959 German*

☐ *1960 English*

☐ *1960 German*

☐ *1961 English*

☐ *1961 German*

☐ *1962 English*

☐ *1962 German*

☐ *1963 English*

☐ *1963 German*

☐ *1964 English*  ☐ *1964 German*  ☐ *1965 English*

☐ *1965 German*  ☐ *1966 English*  ☐ *1966 German*

☐ *1967 English*  ☐ *1967 German*  ☐ *1968 English*

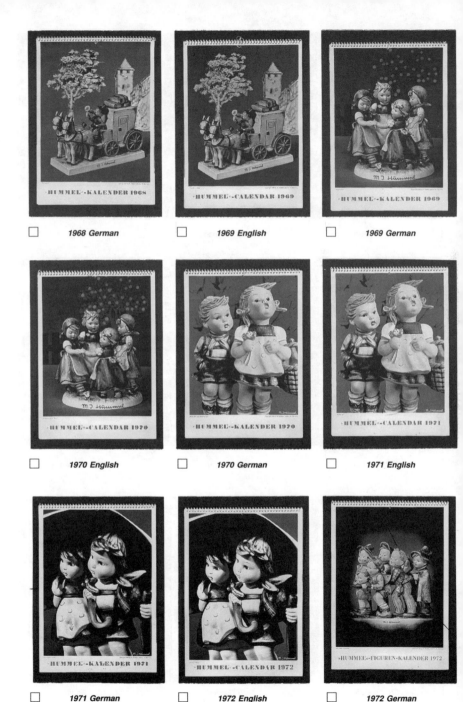

□ 1968 German □ 1969 English □ 1969 German

□ 1970 English □ 1970 German □ 1971 English

□ 1971 German □ 1972 English □ 1972 German

493

☐ **1973 English**

☐ **1973 German**

☐ **1974 English**

☐ **1974 German**

☐ **1975 English**

☐ **1975 German**

☐ **1976 English**

☐ **1976 German**

☐ **1977 English**

☐ *1977 German*

☐ *1978 English*

☐ *1978 German*

☐ *1979 English*

☐ *1979 German*

☐ *1980 English*

☐ *1980 German*

☐ *1981 English*

☐ *1981 German*

☐ **1982 English**

☐ **1982 German**

☐ **1983 English**

☐ **1983 German**

☐ **1984 English**

☐ **1984 German**

☐ **1985 English**

☐ **1985 German**

☐ **1986 English**

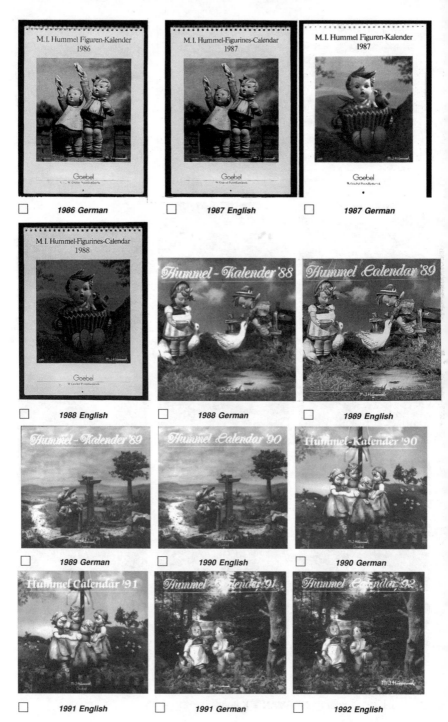

☐ **1986 German**          ☐ **1987 English**          ☐ **1987 German**

☐ **1988 English**         ☐ **1988 German**          ☐ **1989 English**

☐ **1989 German**          ☐ **1990 English**         ☐ **1990 German**

☐ **1991 English**         ☐ **1991 German**          ☐ **1992 English**

497

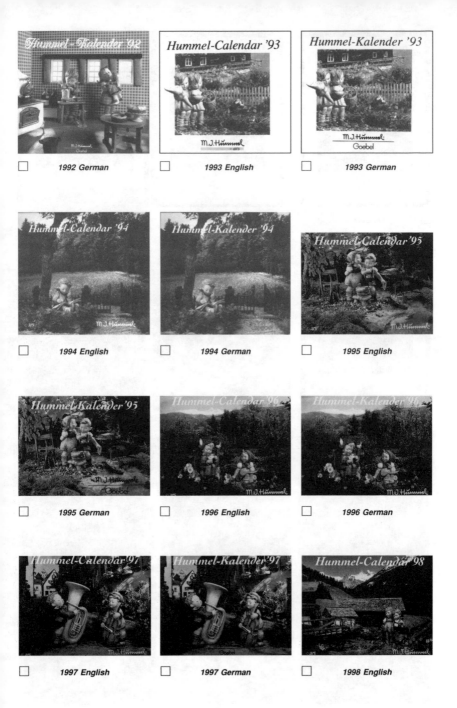

1992 German

1993 English

1993 German

1994 English

1994 German

1995 English

1995 German

1996 English

1996 German

1997 English

1997 German

1998 English

ENGLISH = **C**alendar    GERMAN = **K**alender

498

☐ **1998 German** ☐ **1999 English** ☐ **1999 German**

☐ **2000 English** ☐ **2000 German**

---

## EXPRESSIONS OF YOUTH

**M**any collectors have been fascinated and intrigued by the unfinished "white-ware" figurines. These are simply unfinished figurines about half way through the normal production process. This is the condition of each M.I. Hummel figurine as it reaches the painting department. In order to satisfy this urge to own a figurine in "white-ware", in 1992 Goebel issued seven popular items in this finish with only the facial features painted in addition to a little shadow on the base. All items bear the (TM7) trademark and the 1991 copyright date applied by blue decal, and the words: Expressions of Youth in red letters. Now listed as (CE) "Closed Editions".

|  |  |  |  |  | Issue Price | Current Price |
|---|---|---|---|---|---|---|
| ☐ HUM 2/1 | Little Fiddler | 7½" | (CE) | $230 | $200–250 |
| ☐ HUM 7/1 | Merry Wanderer | 7" | (CE) | $230 | $200–250 |
| ☐ HUM 13/V | Meditation | 13¾" | (CE) | $720 | $720–750 |
| ☐ HUM 15/II | Hear Ye, Hear Ye | 7½" | (CE) | $230 | $200–250 |
| ☐ HUM 21/II | Heavenly Angel | 8¾" | (CE) | $230 | $200–250 |
| ☐ HUM 47/II | Goose Girl | 7½" | (CE) | $230 | $200–250 |
| ☐ HUM 89/II | Little Cellist | 7½" | (CE) | $230 | $200–250 |

# "Made in China"

I never thought I would see the day that any M.I. Hummel figurine would be labeled "China." But, I guess we really **do** live in a changing world!

Back in Sept. 1998 I responded to an advertisement from Danbury Mint of Norwalk, Conn., and ordered two sets of M.I. Hummel angel candlesticks at $111 per set.

The first set to arrive was comprised of two beige-colored candlesticks that were identical in shape, measuring 5¾ inches tall, with a different "Hummel" angel on each of the two sides (front and back). By facing them side by side (front of one and back of the other) I had a pair!

The second set was designed the same way: two angels, one on each side. Thus, my four candlesticks, lined up side by side, do have four different M.I. Hummel motifs.

They are well made and have the incised M.I. Hummel signature on the front and back of each candlestick. However, they do **not** have the usual incised HUM model number on the bottom. The only marks are the "Goebel" blue decal name with the copyright sign, "1996" directly underneath, and "China" applied with a cello sticker in a reddish-brown color. Two of the four candlesticks have the number "3014" in a blue decal directly above Goebel—nothing else.

The candlesticks measure 5¾ inches high, having a 3½-inch wide round base with a ⅝-inch round hole in the center. They appear to be formed from the usual "ceramic" material as used in their German-made counterparts.

The Danbury advertisement states: "fine glazed porcelain." The artwork seems to be hand painted, and is in bas-relief (like other M.I. Hummel plates, bells, vases, etc.), rather than flat decals.

The fact that the candlesticks were produced in China rather than Germany, and that they do not have the incised HUM model numbers on the bottom was disappointing to me. But, all in all, I am satisfied with my purchase and the price I paid.

I re-read the Danbury advertisement and could find no mention of just where the candlesticks were manufactured. I guess I just assumed they were made in Germany.

I am glad that I now have some of the "first?" M.I. Hummel items produced in China. And according to the Danbury Mint (Dec. 1, 1999), they are still available for purchase.

# Plaques Honoring U.S. Military

☐ *U.S. Navy*

☐ *U.S. Marines*

☐ *U.S. Air Force*

☐ *U.S. Coast Guard*

☐ *U.S. Army*

Five new military plaques honoring the U.S. Military have been released and sold exclusively through the U.S. Military Post Exchanges. The five represent the separate branches of service. Each plaque is actually a three piece set. It consists of the 4¾ inch figurine HUM 720 "On Parade" (one half of HUM 50 "Volunteers"), a round stand-up plaque with either U.S. Army, Navy, Air Force, Marines, or Coast Guard emblem in brilliant colors, and a wooden base with a brass plate reading: "Tribute To A Proud Heritage". The 4-inch round plaque has the incised number "030" along with the Goebel (NOT HUMMEL) trademark. The retail price through the military for each three-piece set was only $119 plus $3 shipping. HUM 720 "On Parade" retails for $170 on year 2000 Suggested Retail price list.

501

# GOEBEL M.I. HUMMEL DOLLS
## by Dean A. Genth

## GOEBEL DOLL HISTORY

1867     William Goebel purchased estate at Oeslau. Business was slate-boards, slate pencils and marbles.

1876     Detleff Goebel, father, employed by porcelain factory of Hermann Hertschenreuther moved to join son in Oeslau and together they built a small porcelain factory, which they called "Wilhelmsfeld."

1879     Production started with porcelain kilns and used the firm name of F & W Goebel. They produced household pottery.

1887     The first 12″ porcelain socket head dolls were produced bearing Numbers 34/2/0, 34/0, 34/1 & 34/10.

1893     Franz Detleff sold his interest to his son and the firm now bears the name of William Goebel.

1911     William Goebel died. Max Louis Goebel, his son purchased a porcelain factory of his own at Kronach and continued his father's business. The porcelain factory at Oeslau employed 400 workers and had 4 kilns.

1913     The factory now had 13 kilns.

1921     Moller, Unger and Simon sculptured new porcelain doll heads.

Prior to 1900 F & W Goebel doll heads appeared with a two digit number. Their mark was a triangle with a half moon.

From 1900 the "Crown" with the letters W. G. appeared. The exception being the doll heads produced for Max Handwerck of Waltershausen which had "half moon" mark, although the mold was produced after 1910. Those dolls were known as Bebe Elite.

## WELCOME TO THE WORLD OF GOEBEL DOLLS

With this extensive doll making history, it was no wonder that Goebel decided to transform the work of Sister Hummel into dolls. Recognizing the success of her paintings and figurines, the first Hummel dolls were produced in the early 1950's.

Hummel dolls can be identified in a number of ways:
1. M.I. Hummel signature is found incised or molded on the back of doll's head along the neckline.
2. A Goebel trademark is also molded in the head and/or the body.
3. Older dolls may have an oval sticker on the shoe.
4. Dolls were sold with a wrist tag which identified the doll and the manufacturer.
5. The clothing has M.I. Hummel signature sewn in the seams.
6. All Hummel dolls have movable heads, arms, and legs.
7. Size of doll varies with the series and can range from 8″ to 16″.
8. All Hummel dolls are similar in looks to M.I. Hummel figurines.

## MATERIALS GOEBEL DOLLS WERE MADE FROM

*Composition:*

There are four categories of Hummel dolls. The first is composition. Composition material was used to produce the head, arms and legs. The body was manufactured from a different type materal.

Karl Wagner is credited for designing the original "Hummel Doll." The head, arms and legs were produced by an affiliate of W. Goebel out of a material composed of rubber and earthenware and dried rather than fired. This material was developed by technical director Max Pechtold. The bodies were produced by another factory in Neustadt.

There were only two sizes documented. There were six (6) in the 1500 Series, which stood 16″ and twenty-five (25) in the 1700 Series which stood 11″ tall.

These dolls have hand painted eyes, molded hair, movable legs and arms and were sold completely dressed. The production of composition dolls was phased out around 1953 when Goebel produced these parts out of a rubber material.

*Rubber:*

The rubber material was used to produce the head, arms, legs and any accessories. Karl Wagner again is given credit for the design. The trademark found on the rubber dolls was generally the "Vee Bee" mark. The doll has hand painted eyes, movable legs, head and arms and was sold completely dressed. Due to the material used in production, there are few dolls around in "mint" condition. The rubber shrinks and becomes sticky which destroys the doll and the value. There are three sizes of dolls in this material. Six (6) dolls are 16″ tall and the series number in unknown. The 1700 Series dolls stand 12″ tall and there are known examples of these dolls. There also was a 10″ tall baby doll which had glass eyes instead of painted ones in this era. Production ceased prior to 1960 when the next category of Hummel Dolls were released.

*Vinyl:*

Vinyl has been defined by one of the categories as being made from rubber and vinyl. Karl Wagner again is credited for designs and styles of dolls in this period. These dolls were being manufactured officially by Eingetragin Warenzeicher for W. Goebel as part of the toy division known as Hummerwerk Spielwaren. The vinyl dolls were available as early as 1960 and would have stylized Bee trademarks. There are more styles and sizes in the vinyl period than any other category.

There are 5 basic divisions of vinyl doll:
1. 12 inch – Hummel – 1700 Series
   In 1960 Hummel dolls were offered in 19 different motifs and were priced at $13.50.
   In 1976 Hummel dolls began to re-appear and some had been restyled. In 1981 there were four (4) new releases. They were "Weary Wanderer," "Lost Stocking," "Visiting an Invalid" and "On Secret Path" as well as the new Baby dolls. They all sold for $50.00 at that time. They were also renumbered to the 1900 Series. The 12″ vinyl dolls were discontinued on December 31, 1984.
2. In 1967 a new series was introduced. There were six (6) styles and they stood 8″ tall and were the 1800 Series. This size is found only in a stylized bee. Each doll has hand painted eyes and molded hair. Arms, legs and head are movable. Two different types of wrist tags can be found on this series, one is triangular and the other is rectangular. This series ended in the mid 1970's.
3. The 1960 Series has little information available. They were created by Karl Wagner in 1958 and were 13¾″ doll. These dolls had rooted hair and hand painted eyes.
4. 2960 Series has little information. They were created by Karl Wagner in 1964 as a 13¾″ doll. These dolls had rooted hair and glass eyes.
5. Hummel Baby Dolls came in two sizes, 10″ and 16″. The dolls are the same except they have different colored glass eyes and are dressed according to sex. The 10″ doll can be found with three different styles of clothing.

*Porcelain:*

The porcelain dolls are actually earthenware and have a cloth body. Originally referred to as the 2100 Series, until 1985 with the second release. The dolls were designed by Helmut Fischer and produced at Goebel. There are 8 dolls in this series. The four released in 1983 sold for $175.00 and were "Postman," "Birthday Serenade

Boy and Girl" and "On Holiday." Four more were released in 1985 and sold for $175,00 and were entitled "Lost Sheep," "Easter Greeting," "Signs of Spring" and "Carnival." The dolls stand 15¾" tall and have Goebel (TM 6) trademark. The Siessen Convent had final approval on the designs. These dolls were discontinued December 31, 1988.

In closing Goebel also did many other dolls. Redheads were modeled by Karl Wagner and were based on the art work of Charolette Byj. There is also example of a blonde doll known to exist.

Goebel Friar Tuck and ERBS dolls were also manufactured by Goebel. We also know Goebel made toys as evidenced by the Tanz Baby and the Mainzelmannchen. Les Petis, has two dolls known as "Beat Fan" and "Hitch Hiker." Pumuck was created in 1971 also by Karl Wagner. Ernie dolls were introduced in the late 1950's and were based on the work of Erna Reiber better known as NASHA.

## HUMMEL DOLL LIST

### 1101 Series

☐ 1101 A–H Baby (with dress variations) . . . . . . . . 13" . . . . (CE) . . . . $100–200

Description: Handpainted face, modelled hair, moveable head, arms and legs. Two variations produced: 1) with glass eyes, 2) with "sleeping" eyes. Hair sewn in. Sold with cradle

### 1102 Series

☐ 1102 A–H Baby (with dress variations) . . . . . . . . . 10" . . . . (CE) . . . . $100–200

Description: Handpainted face, modelled hair, moveable head, arms and legs. Two variations produced: 1) with glass eyes, 2) with "sleeping" eyes. Sold with cradle

### 1500 Series

☐ 1501–Gretl (Sister) . . . . . . . . . . . . . . . . . . . . . . . . . 16" . . . . (CE) . . . . $150–250
☐ 1502–Seppl (Brother) . . . . . . . . . . . . . . . . . . . . . . . 16" . . . . (CE) . . . . $150–250
☐ 1503–Bertl (Little Shopper) . . . . . . . . . . . . . . . . . . 16" . . . . (CE) . . . . $150–250
☐ 1504–Hansl (Little Hiker) . . . . . . . . . . . . . . . . . . . . 16" . . . . (CE) . . . . $150–250
☐ 1505–Liesl (Happy Pastime) . . . . . . . . . . . . . . . . . 16" . . . . (CE) . . . . $150–250
☐ 1506–Max (Brother) . . . . . . . . . . . . . . . . . . . . . . . . 16" . . . . (CE) . . . . $150–250
☐ 1507–Wanderbub (Merry Wanderer) . . . . . . . . . . . 16" . . . . (CE) . . . . $150–250

Description: Hand painted faces, modelled hair, moveable legs.

### 1600 Series

☐ 1601–Gretl (Sister) . . . . . . . . . . . . . . . . . . . . . . . . . 11" . . . . (CE) . . . . $150–200
☐ 1602–Seppl (Brother) . . . . . . . . . . . . . . . . . . . . . . . 11" . . . . (CE) . . . . $150–200
☐ 1603–Bertl (Little Shopper) . . . . . . . . . . . . . . . . . . 11" . . . . (CE) . . . . $150–200
☐ 1604–Hansel (Little Hiker) . . . . . . . . . . . . . . . . . . . 11" . . . . (CE) . . . . $150–200
☐ 1605–Liesl (Happy Pastime) . . . . . . . . . . . . . . . . . 11" . . . . (CE) . . . . $150–200
☐ 1606–Maxl (Brother) . . . . . . . . . . . . . . . . . . . . . . . . 11" . . . . (CE) . . . . $150–200
☐ 1607–Wanderbub (Merry Wanderer) . . . . . . . . . . . 11" . . . . (CE) . . . . $150–200
☐ 1608–Felix (Chimney Sweep) . . . . . . . . . . . . . . . . . 11" . . . . (CE) . . . . $150–200

Description: Handpainted faces, modelled hair, immoveable legs.

### 1700 Series

☐ 1701–Gretl (Sister) . . . . . . . . . . . . . . . . . . . . . . . 11"/12" . . . . (CE) . . . . $150–200
☐ 1702–Seppl (Brother) . . . . . . . . . . . . . . . . . . . . . . 11"/12" . . . . (CE) . . . . $150–200
☐ 1703–Bertl (Little Shopper) . . . . . . . . . . . . . . . . . 11"/12" . . . . (CE) . . . . $150–200

☐ 1704–Hansl (Little Hiker) . . . . . . . . . . . . . . . 11″/12″ . . . . (CE) . . . . $150–200
☐ 1705–Liesl (Happy Pastime). . . . . . . . . . . . . . 11″/12″ . . . . (CE) . . . . $150–200
☐ 1706–Maxl (Brother) . . . . . . . . . . . . . . . . . . . 11″/12″ . . . . (CE) . . . . $150–200
☐ 1707–Wanderbub (Merry Wanderer) . . . . . . . . 11″/12″ . . . . (CE) . . . . $150–200
☐ 1708–Felix (Chimney Sweep). . . . . . . . . . . . . . 11″/12″ . . . . (CE) . . . . $150–200
☐ 1709–Rosl (School Girl). . . . . . . . . . . . . . . . . . 11″/12″ . . . . (CE) . . . . $100–200
☐ 1710–Peterle (School Boy). . . . . . . . . . . . . . . . 11″/12″ . . . . (CE) . . . . $100–200
☐ 1711–Mirel (Girl Baby Doll) . . . . . . . . . . . . . . . 11″/12″ . . . . (CE) . . . . $100–200
☐ 1712–Franel (Boy Baby Doll) . . . . . . . . . . . . . . 11″/12″ . . . . (CE) . . . . $100–200
☐ 1713–Miriandl (Favorite Pet). . . . . . . . . . . . . . . 11″/12″ . . . . (CE) . . . . $100–200
☐ 1714–Jackl (Little Goatherder) . . . . . . . . . . . . . 11″/12″ . . . . (CE) . . . . $100–200
☐ 1715–Christl (Weary Wanderer) . . . . . . . . . . . . 11″/12″ . . . . (CE) . . . . $100–200
☐ 1716–Schorschl (Farm Boy) . . . . . . . . . . . . . . . 11″/12″ . . . . (CE) . . . . $100–200
☐ 1717–Ganseliesl (Goose Girl) . . . . . . . . . . . . . 11″/12″ . . . . (CE) . . . . $150–200
☐ 1718–Anderl (Accordian Boy) . . . . . . . . . . . . . 11″/12″ . . . . (CE) . . . . $100–200
☐ 1719–Nachwachter (Hear Ye, Hear Ye) . . . 11″/12″ . . . . (CE) . . . . $150–200
☐ 1720–Brieftrager (Postman) . . . . . . . . . . . . . . . 11″/12″ . . . . (CE) . . . . $150–200
☐ 1721–Schusterjunge (Boots). . . . . . . . . . . . . . . 11″/12″ . . . . (CE) . . . . $150–200
☐ 1722–Skihaserl (Skier). . . . . . . . . . . . . . . . . . . 11″/12″ . . . . (CE) . . . . $150–200
☐ 1723–Konditor (Baker). . . . . . . . . . . . . . . . . . . 11″/12″ . . . . (CE) . . . . $150–200
☐ 1724–Radibub (For Father) . . . . . . . . . . . . . . . 11″/12″ . . . . (CE) . . . . $150–200
☐ 1725–Puppenmetterchen (Doll Mother) . . . . . . 11″/12″ . . . . (CE) . . . . $150–200

Description:   Handpainted faces, modelled hair, moveable head, arms, and legs.

1800 Series

☐ 1801–Rosl (Little Sweeper) . . . . . . . . . . . . . . . 8″ . . . . . (CE) . . . . $100–200
☐ 1802–Rudi (Home From Market). . . . . . . . . . . . 8″ . . . . . (CE) . . . . $100–200
☐ 1803–Vroni. . . . . . . . . . . . . . . . . . . . . . . . . . . . 8″ . . . . . (CE) . . . . $100–200
☐ 1804–Seppl (Boy with Toothache). . . . . . . . . . . 8″ . . . . . (CE) . . . . $100–200
☐ 1805–Mariandl (Favorite Pet) . . . . . . . . . . . . . . 8″ . . . . . (CE) . . . . $100–200
☐ 1806–Jackl. . . . . . . . . . . . . . . . . . . . . . . . . . . . 8″ . . . . . (CE) . . . . $100–200
☐ 1809–Rosl (School Girl). . . . . . . . . . . . . . . . . . 14″ . . . . . (CE) . . . . $125–250
☐ 1810–Peterle (School Boy). . . . . . . . . . . . . . . . 14″ . . . . . (CE) . . . . $125–250
☐ 1811–Mirel (Little Gardener). . . . . . . . . . . . . . . 14″ . . . . . (CE) . . . . $125–250
☐ 1811–Franel (School Girl) . . . . . . . . . . . . . . . . 14″ . . . . . (CE) . . . . $125–250

Description:   Handpainted faces, modelled hair, moveable head, arms and legs. Two
               variations produced: 1) with glass eyes and hair sewn in, 2) with "sleep-
               ing" eyes and hair sewn in.

1900 Series

☐ 1901–Gretel (Sister) . . . . . . . . . . . . . . . . . . . . 12″ . . . . . (CE) . . . . $100–150
☐ 1902–Seppl (Brother) . . . . . . . . . . . . . . . . . . . 12″ . . . . . (CE) . . . . $100–150
☐ 1905–Liesl (Happy Pastime). . . . . . . . . . . . . . . 12″ . . . . . (CE) . . . . $100–150
☐ 1906–Wanderbub (Merry Wanderer) . . . . . . . . 12″ . . . . . (CE) . . . . $100–150
☐ 1908–Felix (Chimney Sweep). . . . . . . . . . . . . . 12″ . . . . . (CE) . . . . $100–150
☐ 1909–Rosl (School Girl). . . . . . . . . . . . . . . . . . 12″ . . . . . (CE) . . . . $100–150
☐ 1910–Peterle (School Boy). . . . . . . . . . . . . . . . 12″ . . . . . (CE) . . . . $100–150
☐ 1914–Ganseliesl (Goose Girl) . . . . . . . . . . . . . 12″ . . . . . (CE) . . . . $100–150
☐ 1917–Radibub (For Father) . . . . . . . . . . . . . . . 12″ . . . . . (CE) . . . . $100–150
☐ 1925–Krankenbesuch (Merry Wanderer) . . . . . 12″ . . . . . (CE) . . . . $100–150
☐ 1926–              (Lost Stocking) . . . . . . . . . 12″ . . . . . (CE) . . . . $100–150
☐ 1927–              (Visiting An Invalid) . . . . . . 12″ . . . . . (CE) . . . . $100–150
☐ 1928–              (On Secret Path). . . . . . . . 12″ . . . . . (CE) . . . . $100–150

Description:   Handpainted faces, vinyl heads and bodies. Moveable head, arms, and
               legs.

### 1960 Series

☐ 1960/A–Sonny . . . . . . . . . . . . . . . . . . . . . . . . 14″ . . . . (CE) . . . . $150–200
☐ 1960/C–Gabi . . . . . . . . . . . . . . . . . . . . . . . . . 14″ . . . . (CE) . . . . $150–200
☐ 1960/E–Reni . . . . . . . . . . . . . . . . . . . . . . . . . 14″ . . . . (CE) . . . . $150–200

Description:   Have glass eyes and rooted hair.

### 1961 Series

☐ 1961/A–Helga . . . . . . . . . . . . . . . . . . . . . . . . 14″ . . . . (CE) . . . . $150–200
☐ 1961/C–Rotkappchen . . . . . . . . . . . . . . . . . . . 14″ . . . . (CE) . . . . $150–200
☐ 1961/D–Angelika . . . . . . . . . . . . . . . . . . . . . . 14″ . . . . (CE) . . . . $150–200
☐ 1961/E–Astrid. . . . . . . . . . . . . . . . . . . . . . . . . 14″ . . . . (CE) . . . . $150–200
☐ 1961/F–Fred . . . . . . . . . . . . . . . . . . . . . . . . . . 14″ . . . . (CE) . . . . $150–200
☐ 1961/G–Anke. . . . . . . . . . . . . . . . . . . . . . . . . . 14″ . . . . (CE) . . . . $150–200

Description:   Have sleeping eyes and rooted hair.

## PORCELAIN DOLLS

☐ Postman . . . . . . . . . . . . . 15¾″ . . . . . . (CE) . . . . 1983 . .**6** . . . $250–300
☐ Birthday Serenade/Boy . . . 15¾″ . . . . . . (CE) . . . . 1983 . .**6** . . . $250–300
☐ Birthday Serenade/Girl . . . 15¾″ . . . . . . (CE) . . . . 1983 . .**6** . . . $250–300
☐ On Holiday . . . . . . . . . . . 15¾″ . . . . . . (CE) . . . . 1983 . .**6** . . . $250–300
☐ Lost Sheep . . . . . . . . . . . 15¾″ . . . . . . (CE) . . . . 1985 . .**6** . . . $250–300
☐ Signs of Spring . . . . . . . . 15¾″ . . . . . . (CE) . . . . 1985 . .**6** . . . $250–300
☐ Carnival . . . . . . . . . . . . . 15¾″ . . . . . . (CE) . . . . 1985 . .**6** . . . $250–300
☐ Easter Greetings . . . . . . . 15¾″ . . . . . . (CE) . . . . 1985 . .**6** . . . $250–300

## M.I. HUMMEL DOLLS
### (Current Models)

☐ HUM 515   Kiss Me . . . . . . . . . . . . . . . . . . . . . . 14″ . . . . (OE). . . . . . . $200
☐ HUM 524   Valentine Gift . . . . . . . . . . . . . . . . . . 16″ . . . . (OE). . . . . . . $200
☐ HUM 950   Apple Tree Girl . . . . . . . . . . . . . . . . . 14″ . . . . (OE). . . . . . . $250
☐ HUM 951   Apple Tree Boy. . . . . . . . . . . . . . . . . . 14″ . . . . (OE). . . . . . . $250
☐ HUM 960   Ride Into Christmas. . . . . . . . . . . . . . 11″ . . . . (OE). . . . . . . $200
☐ HUM 1066  School Girl. . . . . . . . . . . . . . . . . . . . 14″ . . . . (OE). . . . . . . $200
☐ HUM 1067  Little Scholar. . . . . . . . . . . . . . . . . . . 14″ . . . . (OE). . . . . . . $200

# M.I. HUMMEL MINIATURES
## by Dean A. Genth

Founded in 1978, Goebel Miniatures were produced in Camarillo, CA and were sculpted by artist Robert Olszewski. Miniature M.I. Hummel figurines were some of the most popular miniatures produced between 1978–1994.

### "PRE-GOEBEL" M.I. HUMMEL MINIATURES
### by OLSZEWSKI

In 1977, master artist Robert Olszewski began production of miniature M.I. Hummel figurines. These pieces were not authorized at that time by the W. Goebel Porzellanfabrik in Rödental, Germany. Mr. Olszewski had naively begun production of these pieces without giving any thought to any infringement of the Goebel copyright. When this matter was brought to Mr. Olszewski's attention in July of 1978, he immediately sent a letter to Mr. Goebel explaining what had happened. Word soon came from the Goebel company that Mr. Dieter Schneider from Goebel would visit and tour the Olszewski miniature studio. Soon after Mr. Schneider's visit, Mr. Olszewski accepted a contract to begin work for the W. GOEBEL PORZELLANFABRIK. In order to observe the provisions of this contract, Mr. Olszewski could not produce any of the 14 miniatures he had previously made. Of those fourteen miniatures, five were miniature M.I. Hummel figurines. These Olszewski pre-Goebel M.I. Hummel Miniatures have become quite valuable to both Hummel collectors and miniature collectors. Original Olszewski handcrafted boxes for the "pre-Goebels" are valued at $100 each.

- [ ] Kiss Me . . . . . . . . . . . . . (CE) . . . . . $1000–2000
- [ ] Stormy Weather . . . . . . . (CE) . . . . . $1000–2000
- [ ] Barnyard Hero . . . . . . . . (CE) . . . . . $1000–2000
- [ ] Ring Around the Rosie . . (CE) . . . . . $1000–2000
- [ ] Ride Into Christmas . . . . (CE) . . . . . $1000–2000

| HUMMELSCAPES | | |
|---|---|---|
| A Wish for Mother | 980027 | $50.00 |
| Castle on a Hill | 818134 | $75.00 |
| Christmas Frolic | 818141 | $75.00 |
| Going to Church | 818136 | $75.00 |
| Heavenly Harmonies | 818013 | $100.00 |
| Strolling Through the Park | 818135 | $75.00 |
| Winter Wonderland | 818140 | $75.00 |

## GOEBEL M.I. HUMMEL MINIATURES—

- ☐ GMS No. 247-P . . . . . 1⅛″ . . . . Honey Lover . . . . . . . . . . (CE) . . $200–250
- ☐ GMS No. 248-P . . . . . . ⅞″ . . . . Valentine Gift . . . . . . . . . (CE) . . $300–400
- ☐ GMS No. 249-P . . . . . . ⅞″ . . . . What Now. . . . . . . . . . . . (CE) . . $250–300
- ☐ GMS No. 250-P . . . . . . ⅞″ . . . . Little Fiddler . . . . . . . . . . (CE) . . $110–155
- ☐ GMS No. 251-P . . . . . . ⅞″ . . . . Stormy Weather . . . . . . . (CE) . . $130–175
- ☐ GMS No. 252-P . . . . . . ⅞″ . . . . Doll Bath . . . . . . . . . . . (CE) . . $105–150
- ☐ GMS No. 253-P . . . . . . ⅞″ . . . . Little Sweeper . . . . . . . . . (CE) . . $105–150
- ☐ GMS No. 254-P . . . . . . ⅞″ . . . . Merry Wanderer . . . . . . . (CE) . . $105–195
- ☐ GMS No. 255-P . . . . . . ⅞″ . . . . Postman. . . . . . . . . . . . (CE) . . $105–115
- ☐ GMS No. 256-P . . . . . . ⅞″ . . . . Visiting An Invalid . . . . . . (CE) . . $115–125
- ☐ GMS No. 257-P . . . . . . ⅞″ . . . . Apple Tree Boy . . . . . . . . (CE) . . $130–155
- ☐ GMS No. 262-P . . . . . . 1″ . . . . Baker. . . . . . . . . . . . . (CE) . . $105–115
- ☐ GMS No. 263-P . . . . . . 1″ . . . . Waiter . . . . . . . . . . . . . (CE) . . $115–125
- ☐ GMS No. 264-P . . . . . . ¾″ . . . . Cinderella . . . . . . . . . . . . (CE) . . $115–125
- ☐ GMS No. 265-P . . . . . . ⅞″ . . . . Serenade . . . . . . . . . . (CE) . . $105–115
- ☐ GMS No. 266-P . . . . . . ⅞″ . . . . Accordian Boy. . . . . . . . . (CE) . . $105–115
- ☐ GMS No. 267-P . . . . . . ⅞″ . . . . We Congratulate . . . . . . . (CE) . . $130–140
- ☐ GMS No. 268-P . . . . . . ¾″ . . . . Busy Student . . . . . . . . . (CE) . . $105–115
- ☐ GMS No. 269-P . . . . . . ⅞″ . . . . Morning Concert . . . . . . . (CE) . . $200–250
- ☐ GMS No. 279-P . . . . . . ¹³⁄₁₆″ . . . . Ride Into Christmas . . . . (CE) . . $200–250
- ☐ GMS No. 280-P . . 1″ × ¾″ . . . . Merry Wanderer Plaque . . (CE) . . $135–175
- ☐ GMS No. 281-P . . . . . . ⅞″ . . . . School Boy . . . . . . . . . . (CE) . . $150–200
- ☐ GMS No. 282-P . . . . . . ⅞″ . . . . Wayside Harmony . . . . . . (CE) . . $180–200
- ☐ GMS No. 283-P . . . . . . ⅞″ . . . . Goose Girl . . . . . . . . . . . (CE) . . $150–200

## FIGURINE MINIATURES—

- ☐ Mail Is Here Clock Tower . . . . . 7¾″ . . . . . . . . . . . . . . . . (**OE**) . . . . . . $575
  826504   931-D   Olszewski 1992
  Made in Thailand
- ☐ Ring Around The Rosie . . . . . . 9½″ . . . . . . . . . . . . . . . . . (LE) . . . . . . $675
  826101   932-D (186-P)   Goebel 1994/5
  Made in China   (Limited Edition 10,000 pieces)

508

# The M.I. Hummel Club®
## (Formerly: Goebel Collectors' Club)

**F**ounded in 1977 as the Goebel Collectors' Club, the first of its kind, this important organization continues its early established tradition as a collector's information service.

The services it imparts are many. By having constant access to its members through its quarterly magazine, INSIGHTS, personal correspondence between members and Club staff, and one-on-one discussions at various collectors' shows and in-store promotions, the Club is constantly aware of the needs of its members and seeks to respond in as much depth as possible.

There are a variety of aspects to Club membership, enough to satisfy collectors at all levels. Whether one owns one *M.I. Hummel* figurine, or 100, or any number in between, the pages of *INSIGHTS* can open doors of knowledge.

The special articles focus on the history of the figurines, the life of Sister Maria Innocentia Hummel, the intricacies of production, and helpful hints on how to decorate with your figurines. Its pages are filled with pleasurable reading and full-color photographs.

For the intermediate and advanced collector there is the knowledge that any question, no matter how obscure, will be thoroughly researched by the Club, calling on the available records at the factory as well as its own files developed over the years.

All members can share in the Club's expanded opportunities by joining a Local Chapter, comprised of members in any given regional area who meet on a regular basis for the purpose of sharing and imparting knowledge, and having a great deal of fun while doing it. The Club publishes a quarterly Chapter newsletter called Chapter & Verse.

There are exclusive purchase opportunities for Club members as well. In each year of membership, *M.I. Hummel* treasures are produced for members only, with the Club's own backstamp attesting to that exclusivity. Through a redemption card issued for each, these handcrafted motifs are available for purchase by members at select stores throughout North America or direct from the Club.

A winsome *M.I. Hummel* figurine gift is presented from the Club to each new member; through this unique welcome gift, members can already feel the specialness of the organization they have just joined.

A custom designed fact-filled binder, each member's introduction to knowledge, is another exciting benefit. The Club also holds a funfilled biennial convention for members only.

The Club offers an extensive travel program as well. Thousands have traveled on these trips designed for lovers of *M.I. Hummel* figurines, and their guests. Each trip to Europe includes a behind-the-scenes tour of the Goebel factory in Bavaria, Germany (the home of the figurines), available *only* to members on these trips. (Members who travel on their own know to carry their membership cards with them; the card, their "passport" to many pleasures, is their free ticket to lunch when visiting the factory.)

The European M.I. Hummel Club was introduced and the International M.I. Hummel Club was launched. Members have the opportunity to make fascinating contacts with members from around the world.

The M.I. Hummel Club—your open door to enjoyment, fascination and a fulfilling experience.

For more information, please call or write the M.I. Hummel Club, Goebel Plaza, P.O. Box 11, Pennington NJ 08534-0011. 1-800-666-CLUB (2582). You can also e-mail the Club at memsrv@mihummel.com or visit the Club @ www.mihummel.com.

**PREVIEW EDITIONS (PE)** (Ended with Club Year No. 22)

| | | | | |
|---|---|---|---|---|
| ☐ Cheeky Fellow | HUM 554 | 16 | 1992/93 | $120 |
| ☐ Sweet As Can Be | HUM 541 | 17 | 1993/94 | $125 |
| ☐ Little Troubadour | HUM 558 | 18 | 1994/95 | $130 |
| ☐ Strum Along | HUM 557 | 19 | 1995/96 | $135 |
| ☐ One, Two, Three | HUM 555 | 20 | 1996/97 | $145 |
| ☐ What's That? | HUM 488 | 21 | 1997/98 | $150 |
| ☐ The Poet at the Podium | HUM 397/3/0 | 22 | 1998/99 | $150 |

# Figurines Issued Exclusively for Members of The M.I. Hummel Club
## (Formerly: The Goebel Collectors' Club)

| | | | | Issue Price |
|---|---|---|---|---|
| ☐ Valentine Gift | HUM 387 | No. 1 | 1977 | $45 |
| ☐ Smiling Through, Plaque | HUM 690 | No. 2 | 1978 | $50 |
| ☐ Sister M.I. Hummel Bust | HU 3 | No. 3 | 1979 | $75 |
| ☐ Valentine Joy | HUM 399 | No. 4 | 1980 | $95 |
| ☐ Daisies Don't Tell | HUM 380 | No. 5 | 1981 | $80 |
| ☐ It's Cold | HUM 421 | No. 6 | 1982 | $80 |
| ☐ What Now? | HUM 422 | No. 7 | 1983 | $90 |
| ☐ Coffee Break | HUM 409 | No. 8 | 1984 | $90 |
| ☐ Smiling Through | HUM 408 | No. 9 | 1985 | $125 |
| ☐ Birthday Candle | HUM 440 | No. 10 | 1986 | $95 |
| ☐ Morning Concert | HUM 447 | No. 11 | 1987 | $98 |
| ☐ The Surprise | HUM 431 | No. 12 | 1988 | $125 |
| ☐ Hello World | HUM 429 | No. 13 | 1989/90 | $130 |
| ☐ I Wonder | HUM 486 | No. 14 | 1990/91 | $140 |
| ☐ Gift from a Friend | HUM 485 | No. 15 | 1991/92 | $160 |
| ☐ My Wish Is Small | HUM 463/0 | No. 16 | 1992/93 | $170 |
| ☐ I Didn't Do It | HUM 626 | No. 17 | 1993/94 | $175 |
| ☐ Little Visitor | HUM 563/0 | No. 18 | 1994/95 | $180 |
| ☐ Country Suitor | HUM 760 | No. 19 | 1995/96 | $195 |
| ☐ Celebrate With Song | HUM 790 | No. 20 | 1996/97 | $295 |
| ☐ Playful Blessing | HUM 658 | No. 21 | 1997/98 | $260 |
| ☐ At Play | HUM 632 | No. 22 | 1998/99 | $260 |
| ☐ Private Conversation | HUM 615 | No. 23 | 1999/00 | $260 |
| ☐ Will It Sting? | HUM 450/0 | No. 24 | 2000/01 | $260 |
| ☐ Miniature Valentine Gift Necklace | | | 1983 | $85 |
| ☐ Miniature What Now? Necklace | | | 1986 | $125 |
| ☐ Miniature Honey Lover Pendant | | | 1994 | $165 |
| ☐ At Grandpa's | HUM 621 | | 1994 | $1300 |
| ☐ A Story from Grandma | HUM 620 | | 1995 | $1300 |
| ☐ Sharpest Student | HUM 2087/A | | 2000/01 | $95 |
| ☐ Wishes Come True | HUM 2025/A | | 2000/01 | $625 |
| ☐ I Brought You a Gift | HUM 479 | | 1989–90 | FREE GIFT |
| ☐ Merry Wanderer Pendant | Sterling Silver | | 1990–91 | FREE GIFT |
| ☐ Two Hands, One Treat | HUM 493 | | 1991–92 | FREE GIFT |
| ☐ Lucky Fellow | HUM 560 | | 1992–93 | FREE GIFT |
| ☐ A Sweet Offering | HUM 549/3/0 | | 1993–94 | FREE GIFT |
| ☐ For Keeps | HUM 630 | | 1994–95 | FREE GIFT |
| ☐ From Me To You | HUM 629 | | 1995–96 | FREE GIFT |
| ☐ Forever Yours | HUM 793 | | 1996–97 | FREE GIFT |
| ☐ Nature's Gift | HUM 729 | | 1997–98 | FREE GIFT |
| ☐ Garden Treasures | HUM 727 | | 1998–99 | FREE GIFT |
| ☐ Pigtails | HUM 2052 | | 1999–00 | FREE GIFT |
| ☐ Honor Student | HUM 2087/B | | 2000–01 | FREE GIFT |

**CELEBRATION PLATE SERIES**

| | | | |
|---|---|---|---|
| ☐ Valentine Gift | HUM 738 | 1986 | $90 |
| ☐ Valentine Joy | HUM 737 | 1987 | $98 |
| ☐ Daisies Don't Tell | HUM 736 | 1988 | $115 |
| ☐ It's Cold | HUM 735 | 1989 | $120 |

**ANNIVERSARY FIGURINES**

| | | | |
|---|---|---|---|
| ☐ Flower Girl (5 years) RETIRED | HUM 548 | 1990 | $105 |
| ☐ Sunflower Friends (5 years) | HUM 2104 | 2000 | $195 |
| ☐ Little Pair (10 years) RETIRED | HUM 449 | 1990 | $170 |
| ☐ Miss Beehaving (10 years) | HUM 2105 | 2000 | $240 |
| ☐ Honey Lover (15 years) | HUM 312/I | 1991 | $190 |
| ☐ Behave! (20 years) | HUM 339 | 1996 | $350 |

# Glossary of Terms

**AIR HOLES:** Air holes are tiny holes intentionally made in the figurines during production to prevent the pieces from exploding during the firing process. These air holes are usually placed so carefully in the figurines that often times they go unnoticed by the casual observer.

**ANNIVERSARY EXCLUSIVES:** Figurines offered exclusively to M.I. Hummel Club members of 5, 10, 15 or 20 years of membership.

**ANNIVERSARY PINS:** In the Club year in which you celebrate your 5th, 10th, 15th or 20th anniversary, you will receive a special pin to mark the occasion.

**ARS:** The shortened form of ARS EDITION GmbH of Munich, West Germany. Ars Edition was formerly known as Ars Sacra Josef Müeller Verlag, a German publishing house, selling postcards, postcard-calendars and prints of M.I. Hummel, which first published the Hummel Art. Today Ars Edition GmbH is licensee for Hummel books, calendars, cards and stationery. Owner: Mr. Marcel Nauer (grandson of Dr. Herbert Dubler).

**AUTHORIZED M.I. HUMMEL CLUB RETAILER:** A merchant granted the authority by an official "M.I. Hummel" distributor to redeem M.I. Hummel Club exclusive editions and promote the Club.

**ARS AG:** A corporation based in Zug, Switzerland holding the two-dimensional rights of original M.I. Hummel drawings as well as the two-dimensional rights for reproductions of M.I. Hummel products made by Goebel. "Ars" is the Latin word for art.

**ARTIST'S MARK:** The artist's mark is the signature of the face painter, the artist who paints the face of the figurine. This signature is usually in the form of a set of initials accompanied by the date. These artist's marks almost always appear in black on the underside of the figurine's base.

**ASSEMBLERS NUMBER:** The small incised number (usually two digits) on the bottom of the figurine identifies the person who assembled the individual soft clay parts of the figurine. Smaller than the incised model number or the copyright date. Has no real meaning to the collector, only for Goebel production control.

**BACKSTAMP or TRADEMARK:** The official legal mark that Goebel places on the bottom of all "M.I. Hummel" products.

**BAS RELIEF:** Sculptural relief in which the projection from the surrounding surface is slight. This type of raised work is found on the annual and anniversary "M.I. Hummel" plates.

**BESWICK:** The Beswick Company of England produced some copies of "M.I. Hummel" figurines around the W.W. II time period. There are approximately eleven known models of "Beswick Hummels." The Beswick pieces usually have a very shiny appearance and are marked on the underside with a model number incised into the base and the Beswick trademark which reads "Beswick England" set in a circle. A facsimile of the "M.I. Hummel" signature was used along with the term "Original Hummel Studios." The Beswick Company was acquired by the Royal Doulton Company of England. No records are known to exist of any agreement or contracts which might have given the Beswick Company the right to produce "M.I. Hummel" figurines.

**BISQUE:** This is a term used to describe ceramic pieces which have not been glazed, but are hard-fired and vitreous.

**CHIP:** The term used to describe a flaw in a ceramic figurine which reaches beyond the painted surface and the glazing. A chip in a ceramic figurine is usually rough to the touch and greatly affects the value of the item.

**CLOSED EDITION:** Pieces formerly in W. Goebel production program but no longer produced.

**CLOSED NUMBER:** An identification number in W. Goebel's numerical identification system that was used to identify a design or sample models for possible production, but then for various reasons never authorized for release.

**CLUB YEAR:** The M.I. Hummel Club year spans from 1 June to 31 May. Membership year dates from the time you first joined the Club.

**COPYRIGHT DATE:** This is the date that is often times incised into the bottom of an M.I. Hummel figurine. This date represents the year in which the figurine design was registered with the United States copyright office. Many M.I. Hummel figurines are registered and then do not go into general production for several years after the initial copyright is registered. The incised date is NOT the date that the figurine was necessarily produced or painted.

**CRAZING:** This is the term used to describe the existence of several minute cracks in the glaze of a figurine. This is a natural condition that develops as the ceramic material ages. Some pieces will become "crazed" at a faster rate than others. Many factors of production as well as the humidity of the environment where the figurine is displayed can play a part in this process.

**CURRENT PRODUCTION:** The term used to describe those items currently being produced by the W. Goebel Porzellanfabrik Rödental, Germany.

**CURRENT TRADEMARK:** Designates the symbol presently being used by the W. Goebel Porzellanfabrik to represent the company's trademark.

**DECIMAL POINT:** This incised "period" or dot was used in a somewhat random fashion by the W. Goebel Porzellanfabrik over the years. The decimal point is and was primarily used to reduce confusion in reading the incised numbers on the underside of the figurines. Example: 66. helps one realize that the designation is sixty-six and not ninety-nine.

**DOUBLE CROWN:** This term is used to describe the Goebel Company trademark found on some "M.I. Hummel" figurines. On "double crown" pieces the crown trademark is usually found incised and stamped.

**DOUGHNUT BASE:** A term used to describe the raised circular support on the underside of a figurine. Many figurine bases with a circle inside the regular circular base gave rise to the term, but has now been used to describe many bases with the circular support on the underside.

**DUBLER:** A "Dubler" figurine is one produced during the W.W. II time period by the Herbert Dubler Co. Inc. of New York City. These pieces were substitutes for genuine Goebel "M.I. Hummel" figurines when Goebel "Hummels" were not coming into the U.S. The Dubler figurines were made of plaster of paris and were distributed by the Crestwick Co. of New York which later became Hummelwerk and ultimately the present Goebel United States firm.

**EXCLUSIVE EDITION:** (EE) Figurines created only for M.I. Hummel Club members. This edition bears a special Club backstamp and will never be released to the general public, but can usually be purchased on the secondary market.

**FAIENCE:** (pronounced *fay-ontz* or *fi-ons*) is a term for earthenware decorated with opaque colored glazes. A few early samples were produced experimentally by Goebel on "M.I. Hummel" figurines using this technic.

**FINAL ISSUE:** A term used by Goebel to refer to a figurine that has been permanently retired from production and will not be produced again.

**FIRST ISSUE:** A term used by Goebel since 1990 on all newly released figurines during the first year of production.

**FULL BEE:** The term "Full Bee" refers to the trademark used by the Goebel Co.

from 1950 to 1957. Early usage of this trademark was incised into the material. Later versions of the "full bee" were stamped into the material.

**GOEBEL BEE:** A name used to describe the trademark used by the Goebel Company from 1972 until 1979. This trademark incorporates the GOEBEL name with the V and bee.

**GOEBEL COLLECTORS' CLUB:** The name given to the organization formerly located in Tarrytown, New York for collectors of items produced by the W. Goebel Porzellanfabrik of West Germany. In 1989 the name was officially changed to the "M.I. Hummel Club."

**HERBERT DUBLER, INC:** Founded in 1934 in New York, importing products from the publishing house "Ars Sacra Joseph Mueller Munich", named after Dr. Herbert Dubler, son in law of Mr. Joseph Mueller. During WW II and thereafter this company distributed Hummel products such as cards, calendars and books. During that time the "Dubler Figurines" were put on the market. Herbert Dubler, Inc. was renamed "CHRESTWICK, INC." honoring the president, Mr. Alfred E. Wick. In 1956 the company was sold to W. Goebel Porzellanfabrik and became known as "Hummelwerk, Inc." and later changed to "Goebel United States".

**HOLLOW MOLD:** The term used by "M.I. Hummel" collectors to describe a figurine that is open on the underside of the base. With these particular bases the collector can visually see into the cavity of the figurine.

**HUM NO.:** Mold number or model number incised on the bottom of each "M.I. Hummel" figurine at the factory. This number is used for identification purposes.

**"INTERNATIONAL":** This name is given to the group of M.I. Hummel figurines that were produced in 1940 with the national dress of other countries. Master sculptors Reinhold Unger and Arthur Moeller translated Sister Hummel's sketches into Goebel M.I. Hummel figurines. The "Internationals" are highly sought-after by collectors.

**LIMITED EDITION (LE):** A figurine that is produced for a specific time period or in a limited quantity.

**LOCAL CHAPTERS:** Groups of M.I. Hummel Club members who meet locally to study "M.I. Hummel" figurines.

**MEL:** A Goebel-produced figurine with the letters "MEL" incised somewhere on the base of the piece. These pieces were designed from original drawings by Sister M.I. Hummel, but for some undetermined reasons were not approved by the Siessen Convent for inclusion in the "M.I. Hummel" line of figurines.

**MODEL:** This term most often refers to a particular "M.I. Hummel" figurine, plate, bell, or other item in the line. When not used in reference to a specific motif, the word model also can refer to the sculptor's working model from which the figurines are made.

**MOLD GROWTH:** In the earlier days of figurine production the working molds were made of plaster of paris. As these molds were used, the various molded parts became larger due to the repeated usage. With modern technology at the Goebel factory and the use of acrylic resin molds, this problem has been eliminated and today the collector finds very few size differences within a given size designation.

**MOLD INDUCTION DATE (MID):** A coined or invented term used by the uninformed—never used by Goebel. The correct term is "copyright date" (CRD). The incised date on the bottom of your figurine is the year of *creation* date. This creation date is used for the U.S. copyright recordation. The copyright law says that the year of creation date has to be part of the product and incised with the respective year. It can vary between two and three years from the completion of the clay model by the Goebel master sculptor to the final creation respective copyright year. In some instances the creation date and the copyright application are in the same year, in others not. EXAMPLE: HUM 559 "Heart and Soul" was modeled by master sculptor Helmut Fischer in 1988, but has the incised

1989 *copyright date* on the bottom of the figurine, and was released in the U.S. market in 1996.

**MOTHER MOLD SAMPLE:** This term used by Goebel refers to the original samples out of the mother mold. The very FIRST piece out of the mother mold is what Goebel refers to as a "prototype"— the <u>one</u> and <u>only</u> sample that is presented to the Siessen Convent of any newly developed "M.I. Hummel" figurine. All others are "mother mold samples".

**MUSTERZIMMER:** The German word meaning sample model designating that this piece is to be held at the W. Goebel Prozellanfabrik in the "sample room" to be used for future reference by production artists.

**OESLAU:** Name for the village where the W. Goebel Porzellanfabrik is located. Oeslau is now a part of the City of Rödental, Germany. The name Oeslau appears on Hum 348 "Ring Around The Rosie".

**OPEN EDITION:** Pieces currently in W. Goebel's production program.

**OUT OF PRODUCTION:** A term used by the Goebel Company to designate items that are not currently in production, yet have not been given an official classification as to their eventual fate. Some items listed as out of production may become closed editions, remain temporarily withdrawn, or ultimately return to current production status.

**OVERSIZE (OE):** This description refers to a piece that has experienced "mold growth" size expansion. A figurine that measures larger than the standard size is said to be "oversized."

**PAINT FLAKE:** The term used to designate a flaw in a ceramic figurine whereby the paint has been chipped. This type flaw does not go beyond the glazed surface.

**PAINT RUB:** A general wearing away of the paint surface of a figurine in a particular spot. This condition is usually caused by excessive handling of a figurine, thin paint in a given area of the figurine, or the excessive use of abrasive cleaners.

**PAINTER'S SAMPLE:** A figurine used by the painters at the Goebel factory which serves as a reference figurine for the painting of subsequent pieces. The painters of "M.I. Hummel" figurines attempt to paint their individual pieces to match the painter's sample as precisely as possible. Painter's Samples are sometimes marked with a red line around the side of the base.

**POSSIBLE FUTURE EDITIONS (PFE):** Figurines that have been modeled but not yet released for sale to the public.

**PREVIEW EDITION (PE):** Figurines with an M.I. Hummel Club backstamp offered exclusively to members for a special preview period. After its first two years of production, it may become an open edition (OE) available to the general public, bearing a regular Goebel backstamp only.

**PROTOTYPE:** This term used by Goebel means the "one and only sample" (first out of the mother mold) that is presented to the Siessen Convent of any newly developed "M.I. Hummel" figurine.

**RATTLE:** All "M.I. Hummel" figurines are hollow on the inside. Occasionally, when the figurine is fired, a small piece of clay will drop off on the inside. This little bit of clay when dry will cause a slight rattle. Actually, it does not hurt the figurine or affect the value one way or the other. I would not even call it a flaw, as it does not detract from the appearance. Actually, it is one means of identification that might come in handy sometime!

**REINSTATED:** The term used to indicate that a figurine has been placed back into production by the W. Goebel Porzellanfabrik after some prior classification of non-production.

**RETIRED:** A term used by Goebel to refer to a figurine that has been permanently removed from production. The molds are broken and the figurine will never be produced again.

**RÖDENTAL:** The town in Germany where the W. Goebel Porzellanfabrik is situated. Rödental is located near Coburg and lies only a few miles from the former East German border. In 1981 Rödental became the official Sister City of Eaton, Ohio due to the longtime "Hummel" relationship with Robert L. Miller and the International "Hummel" Festival held annually at Eaton, Ohio. (Now held in Dayton, Ohio).

**SAMPLE MODEL:** Generally a figurine that was made as a sample only and not approved by the Siessen Convent for production. Sample models (in the true sense of the term) are extremely rare items and command a premium price on the secondary market.

**SECONDARY MARKET:** The buying and selling of items after the initial retail purchase has been transacted. Often times this post-retail trading is also referred to as the "after market." This very publication is intended to serve as a guide for the secondary market values of "M.I. Hummel" items.

**SIESSEN CONVENT:** Located in Wuerttemberg region of Germany near Saulgau. This facility is where Sister M.I. Hummel resided after taking her vows. She continued to sketch in a studio inside the convent until her untimely death at the age of 37 in 1946. The Siessen Convent houses the Sisters of the Third Order of St. Francis. Sister Hummel is buried in the cemetery located on the Convent grounds.

**"SLASH" MARK:** At one time, an imperfect or flawed figurine produced by Goebel and found during final inspection was marked by grinding a small groove or "slash" through the trademark. These pieces were then sold to factory employees as "seconds." Some of these "slash" marked pieces eventually found their way on to the secondary market and sold to uninformed collectors.

**STYLIZED TRADEMARK:** The symbol used by the Goebel Company from 1957 until 1964. It is recognized by the V with a bumblebee that has triangular or "stylized" wings.

**TEMPORARILY WITHDRAWN (TW):** A designation assigned by the W. Goebel Porzellanfabrik to indicate that a particular item is being withdrawn from production for some time, but may be reinstated at a future date.

**TERRA COTTA:** A reddish clay used in an experimental fashion by artisans at the W. Goebel Porzellanfabrik. There are a few sample pieces of "M.I. Hummel" figurines that were produced with the terra cotta material. These terra cotta pieces have the look of the reddish-brown clay and were not painted.

**THREE LINE TRADEMARK:** The symbol used by the W. Goebel Porzellanfabrik from 1964 until 1972 as their factory trademark. The name for this trademark was adopted to recognize that the V and bee was accompanied by three lines of print to the right of the V. also known as TM4.

**TM:** Abbreviation for trademark.

**TW:** Abbreviation for temporarily withdrawn.

**UNDERGLAZE:** The term used to describe especially the number 5 trademark that appears actually underneath the glaze as opposed to the later version of the number 5 trademark that appears on the top of the glaze.

**U.S. ZONE:** The words "U.S. ZONE—GERMANY" were used on figurines produced by the W. Goebel Porzellanfabrik after W.W. II when the country of Germany was yet undivided and the Goebel factory was part of the U.S. Zone. The U.S. ZONE marking was used either alone or with the Crown trademark from 1946 until 1948. Once the country was divided into East and West, the W. Goebel Porzellanfabrik used the Western or West designation.

**WAFFLE BASE:** Another term to describe the quartered or divided bases.

**WHITE OVERGLAZE:** The term used to designate an item that has not been painted, but has been glazed and fired. These pieces are completely white. All "M.I. Hummel" items are produced in this finish before being individually hand painted.

# About the Artists

**H**andmade in the W. Goebel Porzellanfabrik studios in Rödental, Germany, "M.I. Hummel" figurines enjoy a unique advantage. This art form has been developed in close cooperation with and through the personal assistance and advice of the artist herself, **Sister Maria Innocentia Hummel**, both at the factory and at the Convent of Siessen. Though gentle and gifted with a fine sense of humor, she was very demanding when it came to her art. Master sculptors Arthur Moeller and Reinhold Unger had many discussions with her, and she commented in detail in her bold, clear handwriting when she looked at samples. She did not hesitate to take up the modeler's stick or the painter's fine brush to make her intentions understood. Millions of collectors and friends all over the world have loved and revered the outcome of this artistic collaboration which continues today, long after the death of Sister Maria Innocentia, through the art authorities at the convent.

The sculptors, known for so masterfully transforming two-dimensional art into this new dimension, brought varied experience and training to their work. **Arthur Moeller** was born in 1885 at Rudolstadt in Thuringia. After completing basic studies of modeling at a fine arts studio, he left home to work with a number of porcelain factories. He developed his talents at the Arts and Crafts Academy in Dresden and afterwards at the Academy for Applied Arts in Munich, the same school where Sister M.I. Hummel was to enroll one generation later. From his artistic hands and imagination came works that were shown in Paris and Munich. In 1911, Max Louis Goebel, third-generation head of the company, became aware of this talented young artist and invited him to work with the company. When Moeller died in 1972 in the 86th year of his life, he had been with the company for nearly 50 years. Besides his demanding tasks at the Goebel atelier, Moeller found time to exhibit at fine art shows in Munich, Coburg and Kulmbach. He was a master of the small form. This very special gift enabled him to contribute an immense wealth to the Goebel range. When the

*Arthur Moeller*

time came to create charming figurines from Sister M.I. Hummel's artwork, he and his equally gifted colleague, Reinhold Unger, were the right men for the task.

**Reinhold Unger** also came from Thuringia where he was born in 1880, near where the Goebel factory owned its ancestral porcelain factory. Unger studied at the Fine Art School of Professor Hutschenreuther in Lichte and worked afterwards with the Kunstanstalt Gaigl in Munich.

His works were shown at fine art exhibitions in Munich and he came to work in the Goebel atelier upon the invitation of Max Louis Goebel in 1915. After a fine and fruitful collaboration of 50 years, Unger died in 1974 in the 94th year of his life. His work was highly praised by the press and fine art authorities. On special trips into Upper Bavaria he had absorbed impressions of both the folk art and the deep religious feelings of the area, all of which were incorporated into his artwork. This ability enabled him to develop, through close collaboration with Arthur Moeller and Sister M.I. Hummel, those lovely figurines which were to conquer the hearts of millions. In general, it can be said that most of the religious items incised "M.I. Hummel" and made before 1958 were sculpted by Unger.

*Reinhold Unger*

*Gerhard Skrobek*

Third in this prestigious line of "M.I. Hummel" sculptors is **Gerhard Skrobek**, who joined Goebel in 1951. After his birth in Silesia in 1922, his parents, who thrived in an environment of music and painting, soon moved to Berlin where young Gerhard was exposed to a wealth of museums. He would go to the zoological gardens and sit for hours observing and sketching the animals. His decision to turn to sculpture led him to the renowned Reimannschule where he studied under the prestigious Melzer. In 1946, Skrobek went to Coburg to continue his art studies with the well-known sculptor Poertzel, who created many porcelain pieces for W. Goebel Porzellanfabrik. Skrobek travelled extensively at this time and exhibited in Coburg and Munich. In 1951 he joined Goebel and soon became one of its leading sculptors. He was entrusted to continue the tradition of sculpting the "M.I. Hummel" figurines, and under his talented and guiding hands much of the original artwork was turned into figurines. He also contributed the "M.I. Hummel" plates and bells to the line and created the eight-foot "Merry Wanderer," the famous landmark in front of the Goebel Collectors' Club Gallery and Museum in Tarrytown, New York. "Today's Children" and "Co-Boy" figurines are his creations, and many Goebel series such as Charlot Byj and the Wildlife Collection attest to his talents.

Traditions of quality continue, and the closeness between the Convent of Siessen and the sculptor's atelier at Goebel is strongly maintained.

**Karl Wagner** was born on March 30, 1900 in Holenbrunn/Oberfranken. At the age of 16, he entered the Nuernberg School of Arts where his work won one award and six commendations. From 1920 to 1922 he studied at the Art Academy of Stuttgart. After completing his studies, he entered the ceramics industry as an artist and sculptor. In 1936 he joined W. Goebel Porzellanfabrik.

From 1936 until 1972, when the sculptor retired, he created many figurines for Goebel including several in the **M.I. Hummel** and **Disney** lines. In 1949, Wagner was named master sculptor for Goebel's new toy division, **Hummelwerk-Spielwaren KG**. He was responsible for the modelling and technical preparations of all of the products, including animals and the **M.I. Hummel** dolls. Two years after his retirement, Karl Wagner died on December 4, 1974.

**Guenthur Neubauer** was born on February 3, 1932 in Noerdbohmen, in what is today Czechoslavakia. When he was a schoolboy the war brought him to Coburg, Bavaria, where he began his apprenticeship with W. Goebel Porzellanfabrik in March 1948.

**Karl Wagner**                    **Gunther Neubauer**

Mr. Neubauer's tremendous creative talent, especially evident in his drawings, was recognized and encouraged by his teacher, master sculptor Arthur Moeller. After three years of schooling in the factory, Neubauer passed the arduous ceramic and porcelain tests. The most artistically talented graduate of his class, he was immediately brought into production to decorate the more difficult figurines. During this time, he accomplished the rare feat of becoming an expert in both under and overglaze decorating.

The following years were marked by Neubauer's rapid advancement through the artistic ranks at Goebel. In 1953 he became the sample painter for a group of approximately 30 artists. Two years later he assumed the responsibility for the design development of new products and of new production methods. After passing the state exams in 1961, he was certified as a master of ceramics.

Since 1960 Neubauer has participated in both the teaching of apprentices and the development of production methods. As department manager and chief master sample painter, he is responsible for the decoration of all underglazed and overglazed collectibles. As a teacher, he instructed all of the apprentices in the fine ceramic division from 1966 through 1974, and today he is the prime instructor for the underglaze painting education of all apprentices.

In 1956 Neubauer married another talented sample painter with Goebel, who died after a long illness in 1985. Their only daughter, Heike, has inherited her parents' artistic aptitude, and is an interior decorator.

In addition to being an active sportsman, participating in swimming, walking and skiing, Mr. Neubauer enjoys painting in both watercolors and oils, and he is an accomplished photographer. He has recently retired from Goebel after almost 50 years.

**Franz Kirchner** was born on September 12, 1935 in Neersof, a town not far from W. Goebel Porzellanfabrik in Rödental, Bavaria. Upon graduation from junior high school, he decided to pursue a career as an artist and, on August 8, 1949, entered the three-year apprentice program at Goebel.

After the successful completion of the program in 1952, he began work in Goebel's decorating department. Through continued schooling and expanded artistic experience, he became a qualified master of under and overglaze painting.

Due to his artistic talent and conscientiousness, Mr. Kirchner was made a master sample painter in 1955. Today as assistant manager of the decorating department, he is responsible for the sample decoration of new pieces.

Mr. Kirchner has travelled throughout Germany and in the U.S. demonstrating

*Franz Kirchner*

*Helmut Fischer*

his craft. On a recent trip to the U.S. he appeared at the Hunter Mt., NY German Alps Festival and at the International Plate and Collectibles Exposition in South Bend, IN.

In his spare time, he develops his talents as a fine artist, specializing in landscapes. He is also a musician, and is an active member of a band focusing on traditional German music, in which he plays both the clarinet and saxophone. He also enjoys walking and working in his garden.

**Helmut Fischer** As a master sculptor at W. Goebel Porzellanfabrik (WGP), Germany, Helmut Fischer is entrusted with the difficult task of transforming the two-dimensional art of Sister M.I. Hummel into the world-famous figurines that bear her name.

Highly imaginative and talented, Helmut combines his creativity and sculpting expertise to create a wide range of *M.I. Hummel*® figurine motifs. Fourth in a prestigious line of *M.I. Hummel* sculptors, Helmut continues the Goebel tradition of quality and handcraftsmanship.

Born in Coburg in 1950, Helmut comes from a family of skilled craftsmen who recognized his talent and encouraged his development. At the age of 14, Fischer followed his father's suggestion and enrolled in the Goebel apprenticeship program as a sculptor. Three years later,

he passed the difficult exam given by the Chamber of Commerce and Industry in Coburg. After joining Goebel, he utilized his talent and skills to create numerous models of porcelain, fine earthenware and glass.

In the 1980's, Helmut created several series including Serengeti, a true-to-nature collection of animal sculptures, the DeGrazia collection, based on the artwork of Ted DeGrazia, as well as Goebel's line of Walt Disney figurines, based on the artwork of the Disney Company. His works have been exhibited in the *Museum der Deutschen Porzellanindustrie* in Hohenberg an der Eger, Germany, and he was recognized as a "Works-of-Art" artist in the United States in 1986.

Since 1988, Helmut has been entrusted with the development and sculpting responsibilities of M.I. Hummel figurines including the Century Collection figurine "We Wish You the Best." With his unique artistic talents and over 20 years of experience with the company, Helmut has also assumed the reins of M.I. Hummel Master Sculptor position at WGP.

Helmut lives in Neustadt, Germany, and enjoys drawing, photographing nature, kayaking and riding his mountain bike. He speaks English, though not fluently, and is looking forward to his next trip to the U.S.

*Marion (Müller) Huschka*

**Marion (Müller) Huschka** was born on October 15, 1959 in Rödental, Germany. She is the fourth generation in her family to be employed with W. Goebel Porzellanfabrik. Her father is presently supervisor in the whiteware department, her mother works in the office and her sister is in the painting department. Marion started her employment in 1976 with her apprenticeship and examination in 1979 as a sculptor (WGP and occupational training centre for ceramic art in Selb, Germany) was complete. In 1982 she participated in a Study Trip to Italy. She was also a student of Master Sculptor Gerhard Skrobek whose guidance and artistic instructions prepared her for sculpting M.I. Hummel figurines. Since 1981 she has been a "Sculptor-Trainer" of new students at Goebel. Due to the support she is giving the young trainee sculptors, she was called into the board of examiners for sculptors at the Chamber of Commerce and Trade in Coburg for ceramic vocations in 1982. In 1984, Marion participated in the Goebel Facsimle Factory Promotion Tour in California. She has been responsible for most of the Disney/Hummel look-alike figurines, including the large seven figure Disney "Adventure Bound" figurine. This was the most complicated Disney figurine ever produced by W. Goebel Porzellanfabrik which was limited to 25 pieces. Along with Mr. Skrobek and Mr. Fischer, Ms. Huschka has recently achieved "Works of Art" status. Marion has a good knowledge of the English language and speaks fluent English. She lives in Rödental with her husband and daughter. Her hobbies include landscape drawing, riding, gardening, and hiking with her family. Marion Elke Huschka is a very talented, personable lady.